FROM WORLD WAR TO COLD WAR

Also by David Reynolds

From World War to Cold War

Churchill, Roosevelt, and the International History of the 1940s

DAVID REYNOLDS

OXFORD
UNIVERSITY PRESS

OXFORD
UNIVERSITY PRESS

ML   Great Clarendon Street, Oxford OX2 6DP

Oxford University Press is a department of the University of Oxford.
It furthers the University's objective of excellence in research, scholarship,
and education by publishing worldwide in

Oxford New York

Auckland Cape Town Dar es Salaam Hong Kong Karachi
Kuala Lumpur Madrid Melbourne Mexico City Nairobi
New Delhi Shanghai Taipei Toronto

With offices in

Argentina Austria Brazil Chile Czech Republic France Greece
Guatemala Hungary Italy Japan Poland Portugal Singapore
South Korea Switzerland Thailand Turkey Ukraine Vietnam

Oxford is a registered trade mark of Oxford University Press
in the UK and in certain other countries

Published in the United States
by Oxford University Press Inc., New York

British Library Cataloguing in Publication Data

Data available

Library of Congress Cataloging in Publication Data

Data available

Typeset by Newgen Imaging Systems (P) Ltd., Chennai, India
Printed in Great Britain
on acid-free paper by
Biddles Ltd., King's Lynn, Norfolk

ISBN 0–19–928411–3   978–0–19–928411–5

1 3 5 7 9 10 8 6 4 2

Harry Hinsley
Zara Steiner
Christopher Thorne
Donald Cameron Watt

With respect and affection

Contents

V COLD WAR

VI PERSPECTIVES

Abbreviations

ABCA	Army Bureau of Current Affairs
ADM	Admiralty papers (TNA)
AG	Adjutant General
CA	Confidential Annex
CAB	Cabinet Office papers (TNA)
CAC	Churchill Archives Centre, Churchill College, Cambridge
CHAR	Chartwell Papers (CAC)
CHUR	Churchill Papers (CAC)
CIGS	Chief of the Imperial General Staff
CO	Colonial Office papers (TNA)
COS	Chiefs of Staff (UK)
DDEL	Dwight D. Eisenhower Library, Abilene, Kansas
ED	Board of Education papers (TNA)
ETO	European Theater of Operations, US Army
FDRL	Franklin D. Roosevelt Library, Hyde Park, New York
FO	Foreign Office papers (TNA)
FRUS	US Department of State, *Foreign Relations of the United States* (Washington, DC: Government Printing Office, various years)
HLRO	House of Lords Record Office, London
HSTL	Harry S. Truman Library, Independence, Missouri
INF	Ministry of Information papers (TNA)
JCS	Joint Chiefs of Staff (USA)
KCL	Liddell Hart Centre for Military Archives, King's College, London
LC	Library of Congress, Washington, DC
NA	US National Archives, College Park, Maryland
NC	Neville Chamberlain papers, Birmingham University Library
OF	Official File (FDRL or HSTL)
PPF	President's Personal File (FDRL or HSTL)
PREM	Prime Minister's Papers (TNA)
PSF	President's Secretary's File (FDRL or HSTL)
RG	Record Group (NA)
TNA	The National Archives of the UK: Public Record Office, Kew, Surrey
WM	War Cabinet minutes (TNA)
WO	War Office papers (TNA)
WP	War Cabinet papers (TNA)

Introduction

The 'special relationship' seems inescapable. True believer or iconoclastic sceptic, no one writing about contemporary British foreign policy can avoid referring to this clichéd concept. In the 1970s, after Britain entered the European Community, many predicted that it would be consigned to the dustbin of history. But then came the Falklands War. Another round of obituaries was written in the early 1990s, after the collapse of the Soviet empire. But that was before two Gulf Wars against Iraq. Like it or loathe it, the term 'special relationship' is still central to the lexicon of British diplomacy, trotted out every time a Prime Minister flies to Washington or a President deigns to visit London. To understand why, we need to go back to the 1940s. The phrase and the idea were born in the Second World War and nurtured by the onset of the Cold War. We still live in the shadow of this, the most dramatic and decisive decade of the twentieth century.

Although global in scope, the 'World War' was, in many ways, a series of connected regional conflicts. Germany and Japan, though part of the Axis, fought entirely separate wars; on the Allied side, Britain and the United States left the bulk of the land war in Europe to the Red Army. The Soviets, for their part, did not enter the Asian War until its final days, while the Americans tried to minimize involvement in Britain's Mediterranean operations and to keep the British at arm's length from the Pacific War. The opening chapter shows how the label 'World War' was stamped on these conflicts *at the time* by Adolf Hitler and particularly Franklin Roosevelt as part of their 'ideologizing' of events. But the regional nature of the conflict must be borne in mind if we wish to understand the strengths and limitations of the wartime Anglo-American alliance.

Although we normally date the Second World War from September 1939, the catalytic moment came in May–June 1940, with the fall of France in only six weeks. The surprise collapse of what still seemed the strongest power in Europe transformed the Continental balance of power. It also had global repercussions, forcing Britain into reliance on the United States, spurring Hitler into a hubristic attack on the Soviet Union, and emboldening Italy and Japan to make their own bids for regional hegemony, which culminated in the attack on Pearl Harbor in December 1941. The revolution of 1940 is the theme of Chapter 2.

Next I explore the broad character of the wartime Anglo-American alliance. Looking in turn at different areas of the war effort—military, economic, and diplomatic—Chapter 3 underlines the degree to which pre-war rivalries continued, particularly over commerce and empire. But I also stress that the wartime alliance, when measured against other bilateral relations between two major powers, was characterized by a remarkable degree of cooperation in the strategy for victory and in designs for a new post-war order. As historical fact, the wartime Anglo-American relationship was truly 'special'.

The term 'special relationship' was popularized by Winston Churchill—'half-American but all British', as the obituaries liked to say. It was central to his foreign policy as Prime Minister from May 1940 to July 1945, and Part II of this book explores the evolution of that policy as Churchill picked up the pieces after the French collapse and sought to draw America into a long-term relationship. Chapter 4 underlines his remarkable achievement in reorienting British policy in the crisis of 1940, when Britain's prospects were bleak, as Churchill privately acknowledged. To justify continuing the struggle, Churchill needed to offer more than pugnacious rhetoric, important though that was. The reiterated assertion that America was just about to enter the war was central to his reasons (or rationalizations) for not seeking a compromise peace in 1940.

Some revisionist historians have argued that, by fighting on, Churchill sold out British power in a credulous search for transatlantic amity. Chapter 5 offers a detailed rebuttal, showing that the British could not have secured an acceptable peace from Nazi Germany in 1940–1 but also that they never had a credible strategy for winning the war single-handedly. Even Churchill's long-term goal was probably a negotiated peace with a non-Nazi German government. Total victory depended on the might of America and Russia and, as Chapter 6 shows, the price for that was a grand strategy that violated Churchill's deepest preferences. Although this chapter emphasizes his waning influence in the last year of the war, when America was fully mobilized, the three essays in Part II, taken as a whole, suggest how much Churchill the diplomatist managed to achieve given the appallingly weak hand he inherited in 1940.

Yet the wartime alliance was only possible because Churchill was met halfway by Franklin Roosevelt, who in 1940–1 circuitously drew his country into full belligerency and then on to a new global hegemony. Roosevelt's style, very different from Churchill's, is examined in two contrasting case studies documenting his acute sensitivity to the larger forces of cultural values and public opinion that set the parameters for official diplomacy. Chapter 7 shows how he tried to use the British royal visit of 1939—on the face of it a prime symbol of the ideological gulf between the Old World and the New—to mobilize popular support for Britain. In Chapter 8, we find him selecting a new American Ambassador to London in 1941 who could reach out to the British left and the forces of reform that, FDR believed, were about to transform wartime Britain. These vignettes illustrate Roosevelt's almost feline fascination with the details of diplomacy, in contrast with Churchill's love of sweeping statements of policy. In writing about Roosevelt, however, it is easy to forget that he was virtually paralysed from the waist down and unable to move unaided for the whole of his twelve-year presidency. The effect of this handicap on FDR's style as a leader is the theme of Chapter 9. It looks at the way the wheelchair president relied on others to be his eyes and ears, and sketches some consequences for his diplomacy.

We must not, however, dwell exclusively on Churchill, Roosevelt, and their inner circles. The war saw a remarkable and unprecedented intermingling of the two populations, not least because nearly three million American soldiers passed through the United Kingdom during the Second World War. The cultural and social dimensions of the wartime alliance provide the theme of Part IV. In 1941–2 Whitehall sought to counter the Hollywood image of America as a land of violence and corruption by a vigorous campaign to develop American studies in British schools and universities (Chapter 10). In 1942–3 Churchill's Cabinet debated whether to establish a covert colour bar to discourage British people from fraternizing with black American soldiers (Chapter 11). And in 1943–4, the two armies ran a series of exchanges between American and British army units, to improve relations between GIs and Tommies in the build-up to D-Day (Chapter 12). In all these cases, the British had an eye not just to wartime exigencies but also to their larger goal of a close post-war transatlantic relationship.

There was, however, a third partner in what Churchill liked to call 'the Grand Alliance'. After the titanic victory at Stalingrad in 1942–3, Roosevelt was determined to forge a relationship with Stalin. Although Churchill was more sceptical, his subsequent image as a Cold Warrior should not obscure the way that, during the war, he as much as Roosevelt invested remarkable faith in Stalin as a 'moderate' surrounded by sinister and shadowy hardliners, for reasons examined in Chapter 13. And when Churchill spoke out about Soviet expansion at Fulton in March 1946, popularizing another famous slogan, the 'iron curtain', close examination of his speech (Chapter 14) suggests he deliberately played up the Soviet threat to justify his main argument, the need for a post-war special relationship. The break-up of the Big Three in 1945–8 and the ensuing division of Europe are traced in Chapter 15, which stresses the impact of the war in shaping the Cold War. This is especially evident in the centrality of the intractable 'German question' and in the way that wartime images, such as the concept of 'totalitarianism' and the 'lessons' of appeasement, constituted the ideological lenses through which the events of the late 1940s were perceived.

The final section of the book offers some broader perspectives on the era of the Second World War. Chapter 16 considers how it helped turn America into a superpower—another neologism of the 1940s. This development owed much to the country's industrial strength, but there was no necessary connection between economic power and military power. To account for the timing and direction of America's entry on the global stage, I explore four explanatory frameworks—environment, interests, intentions, and institutions.

If 'superpower' was the defining idea for post-war diplomacy in America, Britain's was the 'special relationship'. Chapter 17 looks at the word and the reality, at how far Anglo-American relations might be termed 'special' in the decades since 1945. Using a political slogan as an analytical term is, of course, problematic but, developing the argument of Chapter 3, I suggest two uses for the phrase: special in *importance* to each country and to the world, and special in *quality* compared with other bilateral diplomatic relationships. Although Britain's unusual importance for America waned after the first post-war decade, the relationship has remained unusual in quality particularly in intelligence and nuclear weaponry. And ministers and officials in London and Washington still instinctively talk immediately and naturally about the issues of the day with their opposite numbers. This larger 'consultative' relationship is another continuity between the era of Roosevelt and Churchill and that of Bush and Blair, and it rests on a deeper shared tradition of political and economic liberalism.

The essays in this book have been written over two decades. Most started life as papers delivered to a variety of international audiences, from Moscow to Washington, from the Netherlands to New Jersey. During the process, my views and approach have developed and, I hope, matured. That said, I believe these essays hang together as a sustained argument, outlined above, and also that they reflect a distinct methodology.

My approach to the history of Anglo-American relations has been termed 'functionalist'. At a colloquial level, this word implies an interest in how the relationship actually operated behind the surface forms. More technically, it refers to the theory of 'functional cooperation', which examines how states interact positively but short of formal union in various areas of international life. The subtitle of my first book, about Anglo-American relations in the period 1937 to 1941—'a study in competitive cooperation'—has been dubbed 'the epitome of Functionalism'.[1]

Functionalism is not, however, a label that I would use. My work has undoubtedly been influenced by the realist approach to international relations. In other words, I take seriously the centrality of the state and the concepts of power and national interest. But, as many have noted, realism is at best a crude tool, at worst positively unhelpful.[2] The 'state' is not a unitary actor: we need to understand the dynamics of policy-making and the complexities of bureaucratic politics. As critics of realism have also noted and as I explored in *Britannia Overruled*, 'power' takes many forms—tangible and intangible, hard and soft.[3] The 'special relationship' as idea and practice constitutes a classic case study in

---

[1] David Reynolds, *The Creation of the Anglo-American Alliance: A Study in Competitive Cooperation, 1937–1941* (London, 1981); cf. Alex Danchev, *On Specialness: Essays in Anglo-American Relations* (London, 1998), 3.

[2] e.g. John A. Vasquez, *The Power of Power Politics: From Classical Realism to Neotraditionalism* (Cambridge, 1998), and Jack Donnelly, *Realism and International Relations* (Cambridge, 2000).

[3] David Reynolds, *Britannia Overruled: British Policy and World Power in the Twentieth Century* (London, 1991), ch. 1.

what can (and cannot) be done with soft power. Nor is 'national interest' an objective category: much depends on the ideological and cultural framework in which the state is conceived. That is evidently true of a self-styled revolutionary power such as Bolshevik Russia, but during the 1940s US foreign policy-makers adopted the position that their country could not be secure except within a world conforming to American values.

While indeed interested in the functions behind the forms—believing it essential to get behind Churchillian rhetoric about the unity of the 'English-speaking peoples' by probing where British and American interests overlapped and conflicted—I therefore also believe that form matters. Many of the chapters here—and on a larger scale my book *Rich Relations*, on the American 'occupation' of wartime Britain[4]—emphasize the need to understand Anglo-American relations within the framework of 'culture' as well as 'power'. Policy-makers viewed the challenges of Anglo-American relations in the fast-changing world of the 1940s through lenses formed by their background, education, and heritage. They also tried to shape social and cultural trends, such as the influx of American GIs, for diplomatic ends. And all the time they manipulated (and were manipulated by) language, a prime vehicle of culture. Thus, this book pays particular attention to terms such as 'world war', 'special relationship', or 'iron curtain', seeking to understand how they arose historically and how their usage has influenced our understanding of the 1940s. The essays that follow are about function and form; they deal with power and policy, culture and discourse. I shall reflect in more detail on their methodological implications in my final chapter.

[4] David Reynolds, *Rich Relations: The American Occupation of Britain, 1942–1945* (London, 1995).

I

WORLD WAR

1

The Origins of 'The Second World War'

Historical Discourse and International Politics

It is now impossible to imagine the twentieth century without the terms 'First World War' and 'Second World War'. Together they define the first half of the century, with the 'pre-war' and 'inter-war' eras as punctuation marks. They also conjure up the ultimate horror, World War III, lurid imaginings of which helped prevent the Cold War from turning hot. Yet use of the phrase 'world war' for these conflicts was by no means axiomatic. While some countries applied this label to the war of 1914–18, others did not, and a firm consensus developed only during the 1940s. As concepts, therefore, it took the 'Second World War' to create the First. Even after 1945, however, the terminology was not adopted automatically. Only in 1948 did the British government conclude as a matter of policy that the country had just been fighting the 'Second World War'; other major belligerents, notably Russia, China, and Japan, continue to use quite different language. To a large extent, the discourse of world war was a German and American construction—foreshadowed in their conflict of 1917–18 and then confirmed in the ideological struggle between Roosevelt and Hitler in 1939–41.

Although as historians we now live in an Age of Discourse, these terminological issues have attracted surprisingly little attention from scholars. Most volumes about the two great conflicts take their titles for granted.[1] Here I can only be suggestive, raising questions rather than resolving them: much more work can profitably be done in journals, books, and archives. In this chapter I look at the way the conflict of 1914–18 was labelled, at signs of a rethink in the 1930s, and then, in greater detail, at how the war of 1939–45 was conceptualized. My main focus is on Britain, France, Germany, and the United States. The result is a striking example of how historical language is politically

A slightly longer version of this chapter, ending with some observations on the concept of globalization, was originally published in the *Journal of Contemporary History*, 38 (2003), 29–44. For helpful comments on a draft, I am grateful to Cambridge colleagues Christopher Clark, Richard J. Evans, Emma Rothschild, John A. Thompson, and Robert Tombs.

[1] For a rare exception see the brief but suggestive comments about 1914–18 in Hew Strachan, *The First World War, i: To Arms* (Oxford, 2001), 694–5.

generated. It offers a case study worthy of closer attention by practitioners of the new 'conceptual history'.[2]

The nature of the historical problem may be quickly grasped by anyone seeking to follow up references to the two conflicts in those putative newspapers of record, *The Times* of London and the *New York Times*. Each publishes an annual index. From August 1914 *The Times* indexed the conflict under the heading of 'War, European', before shifting from April 1917 (the month of American entry) to 'War, The Great'. It retained the latter terminology in its quarterly indexes right through the 1920s and 1930s, but dropped it from April 1940 in favour of 'War (1914–1918)'. The new conflict of 1939–45 was indexed from the start as 'War, 1939–'. After the Axis powers were defeated *The Times* adopted the parallel categories of 'War (1914–18)' and 'War (1939–1945)', and these it retains to the present day. Strictly speaking, the two World Wars did not happen as far as *The Times* is concerned.

Yet they do figure in the indexes of its transatlantic counterpart. From August 1914 the *New York Times* half-yearly index adopted the term 'European War', and this remained its main heading into the 1930s. From July 1919, however, it started offering a cross-reference to the main entry under the heading 'World War'. In January 1935 'World War' itself became the main entry, and 'European War' the subsidiary cross-reference. September 1939 saw 'European War' revived as a functional heading for the current conflict. In the index for July–December 1941 Soviet participation was absorbed into this, now massive, entry under the subheading 'Eastern Front'. But 'World War' had now been amended to 'World War I (1914–18)' and there was a new cross-reference 'World War II (December 7, 1941)' directing readers to the entries listed under 'European War, Far East'. From January 1942 'European War' disappeared and the main headings were simply 'World War I' and 'World War II'. This has been the practice of the *New York Times* ever since.

This simple comparison hints at a broad pattern. We find Britain and generally France on one side of the conceptual divide, and the United States and Germany on the other.

In the 1920s and 1930s British writing about the conflict of 1914–18 usually adopted the titles 'the War' or 'the Great War'—the latter with its echoes of the twenty-years war against France in the era of the Revolution and Napoleon. Thus the collection of official documents edited by G. P. Gooch and Harold Temperley was entitled *British Documents on the Origins of the War 1898–1914*. C. R. M. F. Cruttwell's standard overview, first published by Oxford University Press in 1934, was called *A History of the Great War, 1914–1918*. A very rare exception in the immediate post-war years was the two-volume study by Charles

---

[2] On this genre see Melvin Richter, *The History of Political and Social Concepts: A Critical Introduction* (New York, 1995).

Repington, published in 1920. This was entitled *The First World War (1914–1918)*. But Repington did little to exploit that theme in the book itself, which was largely an edited version of his diary as a war correspondent. The term 'World War' is used in the third volume (1927) of Winston Churchill's memoir-cum-history, *The World Crisis*, but is not evident in the first two (1923) or the last two (1929 and 1931).[3]

In France 'la Guerre' or 'la Grande Guerre' were the most widely used titles for memoirs and studies. Examples are Victor Giraud's *Histoire de la Grande Guerre* (1920), and Marshal Foch's *Mémoires pour servir à l'histoire de la Guerre de 1914–1918*, which appeared in 1931. Again there were some exceptions. The Paris-based 'Société de l'Histoire de la Guerre', founded in 1918, began publishing its own quarterly academic journal from April 1923, under the title *Revue d'histoire de la Guerre Mondiale*. Its principal editor was the diplomatic historian and war veteran Pierre Renouvin whose teaching responsibilities at the Sorbonne included a course on 'l'étude critique des sources de l'histoire de la guerre mondiale'. Funded by the Society, this was offered from December 1922 and was billed as the first of its kind in Europe. From it came Renouvin's study of the immediate origins of the war, published in French in 1925 and in English translation three years later.[4] But 'la Guerre' or 'la Grande Guerre' remained the most common French labels.

What, then, of Germany and America? It is instructive to see the fate of book titles in the process of translation. The Gooch and Temperley volumes of *British Documents on the Origins of the War 1898–1914* became *Die britischen amtlichen Dokumente über den Ursprung des Weltkriegs 1898–1914*. The memoirs of the American commander in Europe, General John J. Pershing, were published in France in 1931 under the title *Mes souvenirs de la Guerre*, whereas the original American edition had appeared as *My Experiences in the World War*. It is to Germany and America, in different ways, that we must look for the origins of 'the World War'.

In Germany the term 'Weltkrieg' was used from the start to define the conflict, and it was also overwhelmingly the preferred title for memoirs. This is understandable when we recall that Germany's lack of status as a world power (*Weltmacht*) had become an obsession in the Wilhelmine era. The concept of

---

[3] Winston S. Churchill, *The World Crisis, 1916–1918* (London, 1927), e.g. 9, 96, 252. I have also found one reference in *The Eastern Front* (London, 1931), 222. According to Churchill's official biographer, the title *The World Crisis* was forced on him by his American publisher, Scribners—Martin Gilbert, *Winston S. Churchill*, vol. iv (London, 1975), 754. In 1916, when out of office, Churchill had written four articles on aspects of the conflict for the *New York Tribune*, which that paper unilaterally entitled 'Four Great Chapters of the World War'—see Chartwell papers CHAR 8/34 (Churchill Archives Centre, Churchill College, Cambridge, henceforth CAC).

[4] *Revue d'histoire de la Guerre Mondiale*, 1 (1923), esp. 94, 288–95; cf. Pierre Renouvin, *The Immediate Origins of the War (28th June–4th August 1914)*, trans. Theodore Carswell Hume (New Haven, 1928), pp. viii–ix. The title La Grande Guerre was used from 1915 for the serial publication of official communiqués from the various belligerents: *La Grande Guerre: recueil des communiqués officiels* (Paris, 1915–17).

Weltmacht has been traced right back to 1809. Although by the end of the nineteenth century it was almost a synonym for *Grossmacht* (Great Power), the word did have distinctive referrents, notably the idea that a large navy and numerous colonies were the marks of a true world power. Supremely Britain fell into this category: as early as 1833 Leopold von Ranke had spoken of it as 'eine kolossale Weltmacht'.[5]

Anglo-German rivalry in the decade or so before 1914 turned on Britain's imperial and naval hegemony and Germany's bid for world power. Logically, then, for Germans the ensuing war was a world war. This was the line taken in the post-war memoirs of the Kaiserreich's 1914 elite. Thus the former Chancellor, Theobold von Bethmann Hollweg, in his *Reflections on the World War* (completed just as the Treaty of Versailles was being signed), blamed Russia for turning the Pan-Slav issue in the Balkans into a European crisis. But, he argued, this European conflict only developed into 'World Revolution' because of the participation of Britain, which, in turn, drew in her colonies from India to Canada, and also the United States. None of these countries was deeply concerned about the Dardanelles or the Balkans, but all had an interest in ensuring that Britain's world empire (*Weltimperium* or *Weltreich*) was not weakened by the struggle. With Britain's ally, Japan, also an active participant in the early stages, claimed Bethmann, 'under pressure from England the war became a campaign of annihilation (*Vernichtungskampf*) by the entire world against Germany'.[6] The same line may be found in the 1919 memoirs of the pre-war Foreign Minister, Gottlieb von Jagow: 'through England's entry the conflict became truly a world war.'[7] And the former Austrian Foreign Minister, Count Czernin, while more critical of aggressive 'Prussian tendencies', offered a similar analysis of how the conflict became globalized. 'Belgium and Luxembourg were treated on the Bismarckian principle of "Might before Right" and the world rose against Germany. I say world, because England's power extended over the world.'[8]

From this perspective, the term 'World War' therefore seemed entirely apt. Germany felt itself to be a 'middle power', encircled in Europe and denied 'world power' across the seas. The term *Mittelmacht* connoted both geography and size.[9] Even the socialist Karl Kautsky employed the vocabulary of 'world war' and 'world revolution' for his post-war polemic against the Wilhelmine regime.[10]

[5] Otto Brunner et al., *Geschichtliche Grundbegriffe: Historische Lexikon zur politisch-sozialen Sprache in Deutschland*, vol. iii (Stuttgart, 1978), esp. 932–3.

[6] Theobold von Bethmann Hollweg, *Betrachtungen zum Weltkriege* (Berlin, 1919), i. 189–90.

[7] Gottlieb von Jagow, *Ursachen und Ausbruch des Weltkrieges* (Berlin, 1919), 194.

[8] Count Ottokar Czernin, *In the World War* (London, 1919), 15.

[9] Cf. Dr Kurt Jagow, *Daten des Weltkrieges: Vorgeschichte und Verlauf bis Ende 1921* (Leipzig, 1922), 49–50.

[10] Karl Kautsky, *Wie der Weltkrieg entstand* (Berlin, 1919). Note that the translation into English was entitled *The Guilt of William Hohenzollern* (London, 1920).

'World War' was also the preferred term in the United States, albeit for very different reasons. As we have seen, the *New York Times* adopted it once the United States entered the conflict in April 1917, and it became the standard terminology for popular and official accounts of the conflict in the United States.[11] The reason was partly geographical. In 1914–16 the term 'European War' seemed entirely appropriate since the major belligerents were all European. Japan's active involvement occurred only in the opening weeks of the conflict. By contrast 1917 saw the entry of America (April), China (August), and Brazil (October) and this gave the war new global dimensions.[12]

But ideology also played a part. For nearly three years President Woodrow Wilson had sought to keep out of the European conflict, despite his country's deepening economic ties to Britain which German U-boat warfare was intended to sever. He had been at pains to distance America morally from the warring parties, speaking of 'Peace without Victory' and outlining principles of disarmament, anti-imperialism, and freedom of the seas which were a critique of the Entente as much as the Central Powers. In many ways April 1917 was therefore a humiliating defeat for the President, so he took pains to insist that he was not simply being dragged into the European war but was becoming a belligerent to implement his own vision. This was nothing less than 'to make the world safe for democracy'. Not just Europe but 'the world', because the European conflict, in Wilson's eyes, was symptomatic of the interconnected global problems of modernity to which he had frequently alluded in statements on both foreign and domestic policy.[13]

Wilson envisaged the League of Nations as an instrument of world peace. This implied that the preceding conflict was nothing less than a world war. In America as in Germany, therefore, the normative prompted the descriptive, with the conceptual terminology growing out of national war aims. For the Kaiserreich this was a world war because the root issue was world power; for Wilsonians the conflict was defined as a world war because the goal was world peace. Germany and America were both second-rank players seeking international influence, albeit in very different forms. In both cases ideology, as much as geography, shaped their vocabulary. The story would be similar a quarter-century later.

By the 1930s, 'world war' was becoming more popular in France. The Paris publisher Jules Tallandier issued a series of popular paperbacks under the series title 'La Guerre Mondiale: pages vécues'. In 1933 Camille Bloch, one of Renouvin's colleagues at the Sorbonne and in the Société de la Grande Guerre, published a short book entitled *Les Causes de la Guerre Mondiale: précis historiques*.

---

[11] Again there were exceptions, e.g. Charles G. Dawes, *A Journal of the Great War* (2 vols., Boston, 1921).   [12] Cf. Marc Ferro, *The Great War* (London, 1973), 205.
[13] Lloyd E. Ambrosius, *Woodrow Wilson and the American Diplomatic Tradition: The Treaty Fight in Perspective* (Cambridge, 1987), ch. 1; cf. Patrick Devlin, *Too Proud to Fight: Woodrow Wilson's Neutrality* (London, 1974), esp. 670–88.

And in Britain in 1930 the military journalist Basil Liddell Hart brought out a study of wartime strategy, rather misleadingly called *The Real War*. The revised edition, four years later, appeared under the new title *A History of the World War 1914–1918*. Although Liddell Hart did not explain the reason for his second choice, it seems to have reflected the flood of twentieth-anniversary reflections in 1934 on the war and its significance.[14] This may also account for the parallel shift in *New York Times* indexing, mentioned above, whereby the main heading from 1935 became 'World War' rather than 'European War'.

Intimations of a future conflict played a part, as well as anniversaries from the past. In 1931–2 Japan occupied Manchuria, in 1933–4 Hitler's Germany was rearming. In autumn 1934 the journalist 'Johannes Steel' (pseudonym for Herbert Steel) published *The Second World War*, his 'bird's-eye view of the political situation in Europe'. He forecast a second world war by the middle of 1935, sparked in Europe by Franco-German conflict over the Saarland, Austria, and hegemony in Eastern Europe. This, he predicted, would prompt Japan to conquer the Soviet Far East while Russia was still weak and the world distracted. Although his prophecy was not fulfilled, such talk was now in the air. In China both communist and nationalist writers spoke frequently from 1931 about an impending 'second world war'. 'How many years do we have to prepare for the Second World War?' the Nationalist leader Chiang Kai-shek asked in 1932 in a speech to the Army Staff College. Like many, he forecast that it would start in 1936. Even though that proved premature, the renewal of Sino-Japanese war on a far larger scale from July 1937 revived such predictions. The communist theorist Zhou En-lai wrote in February 1938 that the fascist 'aggressor nations' were so ambitious that they would 'start the second world war without thinking'.[15]

Despite such prophecies, however, it was by no means axiomatic that the conflict of 1939–45 should be termed 'the Second World War'. That term has never been officially adopted by several of the major belligerent countries.

Throughout the history of the Soviet Union, for instance, the conflict was always known as 'The Great Patriotic War'—the title coined by *Pravda*, the party newspaper, on 23 June 1941, the day after Hitler's invasion began. This phrase linked the conflict with the struggle against Napoleon ('The Patriotic War') and established from the start the prevailing theme of Soviet wartime domestic propaganda, namely to play down the ideological aspects of the struggle and highlight national history and culture. For the Soviet regime the war of 1914–17 was, by contrast, a tsarist and capitalist war, to be marginalized in history and memory. *The Unknown War*, the American title of Churchill's 1931

---

[14] On the original title see Hew Strachan, ' "The Real War": Liddell Hart, Cruttwell, and Falls', in Brian Bond (ed.), *The First World War and British Military History* (Oxford, 1991), 46–7.

[15] Johannes Steel, *The Second World War* (New York, 1934), esp. pp. xv, 150–1, 156–7, 214–16; Youli Sun, *China and the Origins of the Pacific War, 1931–1941* (New York, 1993), 15–17, 99.

study of the Eastern Front, was equally apt within the Soviet Union, despite the country's two million dead. Here was an ironic contrast with the intense memorialization of the Great War in the West.[16]

In China, too, the discourse of war has been circumscribed. The preferred term for 1937–45 is The War of Resistance against Japan (*Kang-Ri Zhan-zheng*). This also reflects both geography and ideology. Japan was China's only direct enemy, occupying vast tracts of the country from 1937, and assistance from Britain and America was of limited significance—political symbolism more than substantial aid. Moreover, the communist regime that came to power in 1949 chose to celebrate its own victory rather than the inter-capitalist conflict that had made victory possible. Like Soviet Russia it also focused on the October Revolution rather than the war of 1914–17. Not until the waning of communist ideology in the 1980s did Beijing start encouraging a new interest in the war of 1937–45, though still under the label 'War of Resistance against Japan'.[17]

Nor was the concept of world war employed in Japan. Its brutal and massive invasion of China remained an undeclared war and was therefore dubbed, in a characteristic Japanese euphemism, as 'The China Incident'. After the conflict expanded in December 1941 to include the United States and the European colonial powers, it was described as the 'Greater East Asian War' (*Dai Tōa sensō*). Under the American occupation after 1945 the 'Pacific War' (*Taiheyō sensō*) became the official title, but nationalist revisionist writers revived the earlier term in the 1960s.[18]

Of course, none of these belligerents was involved globally. Japan and China did not join in the European conflict, and Stalin did not break the Soviet–Japanese neutrality pact of 1941 until a few days before Japan's surrender in August 1945. France was in a different category from 1914–18, having been knocked out of the war after nine months in June 1940. From London, Charles de Gaulle tried to rally the French by declaring that the battle of France was not the end because this was 'une guerre mondiale' involving the British Empire and the industrial might of the United States.[19] But de Gaulle's 'Free French' were now bit players in the conflict, marginal to both events and discourse. Great Britain, a full participant for whom this was truly a world war, did not readily adopt the term.

---

[16] Nina Tumarkin, *The Living and the Dead: The Rise and Fall of the Cult of World War II in Russia* (New York, 1994), 61; Catherine Merridale, *Night of Stone: Death and Memory in Russia* (London, 2000), 122–7.

[17] Arthur Waldron, 'China's New Remembering of World War II: The Case of Zhang Zizhong', *Modern Asian Studies*, 30 (1996), 869–96.

[18] Saburō Ienaga, *The Pacific War, 1931–45* (New York, 1978), 247–56.

[19] Address of 18 June 1940 in Charles de Gaulle, *Mémoires de guerre: l'appel, 1940–1942* (Paris, 1954), 267. In the English translation of Jean Lacouture's biography, 'une guerre mondiale' has been rendered 'a worldwide war', which is true to de Gaulle's emphasis but obscures his exact use of words. See Lacouture, *De Gaulle: The Rebel, 1890–1944*, trans. Patrick O'Brien (New York, 1990), 225.

A few weeks after war broke out, the British politician Duff Cooper, who had resigned from Chamberlain's Cabinet after Munich, published his speeches for the period October 1938 to August 1939 under the title *The Second World War: First Phase*. He claimed that the invasion of Poland and the Anglo-French declaration of war brought to an end 'the period of unopposed aggression and bloodless victory', and 'the second World War entered upon a new phase'.[20] But official statements usually referred simply to 'the War'. Certainly most people saw it as a continuation of the former struggle against Germany. From October 1939 the Amalgamated Press in London started publishing an illustrated fortnightly magazine on the conflict entitled *The Second Great War*. And in August 1940 Churchill, by then Prime Minister, spoke of 'this second war against German aggression'.[21] On 12 June 1941 he referred more specifically to 'the war against Nazism'. It was not until 14 July, after the invasion of Russia, that he used the term 'a great world war'. And on 26 December 1941, nearly three weeks after Pearl Harbor, he told the US Congress: 'Twice in a single generation the catastrophe of world war has fallen upon us.'[22]

The predominant British label, however, was still 'the War'. In June 1944 the publishers Macmillan asked for an official government ruling, noting that a good many American publications were already using the terms 'First World War' and 'Second World War'. The Cabinet Secretary, Sir Edward Bridges, commented:

'Great War' certainly seems pretty inappropriate now. The alternatives which first occur to one are:

'War of 1914–18' and 'War of 1939–?'
'First World War' and 'Second World War'
'Four Years' War' and 'Five (or six, or seven) Years' War'

Asked for his opinion, Churchill circled 'First World War' and 'Second World War' but Bridges eventually decided not to make any official statement. 'After all, this is a matter which is going to be decided by popular judgment. This is not really one for a Government decision and I do not think it would be right to go beyond informal guidance when occasion offers.'[23] And Churchill himself equivocated. When embarking on his war memoirs in April 1946 he used the working title 'The Second Great War'. It was not until September 1947, little more than seven months before serialization was to begin in America and Britain, that he committed himself to the title 'The Second World War'.[24]

---

[20] Duff Cooper, *The Second World War: First Phase* (London, 1939), quoting p. 339.

[21] *Into Battle: War Speeches by the Rt. Hon. Winston S. Churchill*, compiled by Charles Eade (London, 1941), 252.

[22] *The Unrelenting Struggle: War Speeches by the Rt. Hon. Winston S. Churchill*, compiled by Charles Eade (London, 1942), 169, 187, 339.

[23] Bridges to Martin, 24 June 1944, and to Laithwaite, 10 July 1944, Cabinet Office papers, CAB 103/286 (The National Archives: Public Record Office, Kew—henceforth TNA).

[24] See Churchill papers CHUR 4/41A, esp. fo. 52, 84, 127, 130 (CAC).

Norman Brook, Bridges' successor as Cabinet Secretary, favoured a firmer official nod toward the term 'Second World War'. When the issue was raised again in a Commons question in October 1946, Prime Minister Clement Attlee, following Brook's advice, replied: 'I rather doubt whether it is necessary to prescribe an official designation for use on all occasions. On the whole, I think that the phrase "Second World War" is likely to be generally adopted. But there may be occasions, as for example for inscriptions, when the addition of the years will be regarded as appropriate.'[25] The issue was not decided unequivocally until the turn of 1947–8 when the first volumes of the British official histories of the war were ready for publication and it became urgent to agree on a formal title for the series. Llewellyn Woodward, the Oxford historian, told Brook bluntly: 'I think "Second World War" is much the best term. There is the important point that this term or more briefly "World War II" is already used, universally, in the United States. It would be convenient for us to use the same term (and very inconvenient to use a different one).' Many Commonwealth countries were writing their own official war histories and it was necessary to consult them. Canada, New Zealand, South Africa, India, and Pakistan all agreed with the term 'Second World War' but Australia dissented, on the grounds that 'there have been more than two wars that spread as widely as the war of 1914–18'.[26] This is, of course, an argument advanced by many historians of the eighteenth century[27] and Churchill himself had used the term 'The First World War' repeatedly in *Marlborough*—his account of the 'Grand Alliance' against Louis XIV published in the 1930s.[28]

In January 1948, the Cabinet's 'Committee for the Control of the Official Histories' was formally asked to adjudicate. Rejecting alternatives such as 'the Six Years War', it agreed to the title 'History of the Second World War'. In discussion the point was made that Churchill intended to use that phrase as the title of his war memoirs. The Committee's decision was endorsed by the Prime Minister on 27 January 1948.[29] British publication of the first volume of Churchill's memoirs in October 1948 served to consecrate the phrase, but two other surveys of the conflict published earlier that year in London also used the

[25] House of Commons, *Debates*, 30 Oct. 1946, 5th series, vol. 428, col. 608; cf. Brook to Bridges, 26 Oct. 1946 and Bridges to Attlee, 28 Oct. 1946, CAB 103/286.

[26] See CAB 103/286, esp. Woodward to Brook, 20 Oct. 1947, and Govt. of Australia to Cab. Office, 26 Nov. 1947. The Australian official series is entitled 'History of the War of 1939–45', following the pattern of its predecessor series 'History of the War of 1914–18'.

[27] 'One vanity of the twentieth century', writes historian Geoffrey Blainey, 'is the belief that it experienced the first world wars, but at least five wars in the eighteenth century involved so many nations and spanned so much of the globe that they could also be called world wars.' Geoffrey Blainey, *The Causes of War*, 3rd ed. (London, 1988), 228; cf. Jack S. Levy, *War in the Great Power System, 1495–1975* (Lexington, Ky., 1983), esp. 75 and 189 (nn. 33 and 35).

[28] Winston S. Churchill, *Marlborough: His Life and Times* (4 vols., London, 1991), e.g. i. 2, 212, 298, 404.

[29] See CAB 134/105, esp. meeting of 21 Jan. 1948, minute 7, and Attlee endorsement of 27 Jan. 1948.

same title.[30] And in France the Société d'Histoire de la Guerre resumed operations in November 1950 with the first issue of what it called *Revue d'histoire de la Deuxième Guerre Mondiale*.[31]

As Woodward implied, the 'Second World War' was another American victory. This was the preferred term in the United States, and most of the Western world followed suit. It might seem in retrospect that for Americans its adoption was a natural response to Pearl Harbor: after Japan attacked the United States the conflict was truly a world war, as the *New York Times* index suggested. But, as in 1914–18, geography alone was not decisive. In fact, the shift in American terminology had begun months before Pearl Harbor. Once again, the crucial actors were Germany and the United States or, more precisely, Adolf Hitler and Franklin Roosevelt.

Hitler, a veteran of the Kaiser's army, shared the German propensity to describe 1914–18 as a world war. In *Mein Kampf*, published in two volumes in 1925–6, the fifth chapter of volume i is entitled 'Der Weltkrieg'. In the foreign policy chapters at the end of volume ii, Hitler asserted that 'Germany will either be a world power or there will be no Germany' but he gave the conventional Welt-vocabulary his own racist twist. Behind British policy and that of Bolshevik Russia he discerned the ubiquitous, malevolent power of world Jewry. He even wrote contortedly of 'the Marxist shock troops of international Jewish stock exchange capital'. During the war, he insisted, it was the Jews who 'systematically stirred up hatred against Germany until state after state abandoned neutrality and, renouncing the true interests of the peoples, entered the services of the World War coalition'. He spoke of 'the leaders of the projected Jewish world empire' committed to 'the annihilation of Germany'. The original German version of the book referred to the Jews as 'the world enemy' (*Weltfeind*).[32]

It is a commonplace that *Mein Kampf* is in no way a 'blueprint' for the war that eventually followed. But the book was the seedbed of some of Hitler's most virulent ideas. After the *Kristallnacht* pogroms of November 1938 had revived in his mind the supposed linkage between Jewish conspiracy and international war, he delivered his notorious 'prophecy' on 30 January 1939, the sixth anniversary of his 'seizure' of power. He told the Reichstag: 'if the international finance Jewry (*Finanzjudentum*), both inside and outside Europe, should succeed in plunging the nations once again into a world war, the result will be not the bolshevization

---

[30] Cyril Falls, *The Second World War* (London, 1948) and J. F. C. Fuller, *The Second World War 1939–45: A Strategical and Tactical History* (London, 1948).

[31] The final issue of *Revue d'histoire de la Guerre Mondiale* was published in October 1939. A slip was inserted informing readers that publication was being temporarily suspended, 'en raison de circonstances', but promising that it would resume as soon as possible. *Revue d'histoire de la Guerre Mondiale*, 17/4 (Oct. 1939), opposite p. 305.

[32] Adolf Hitler, *Mein Kampf*, trans. Ralph Mannheim (London, 1972), quoting 597, 568, 583; cf. the single-volume German edition (Munich, 1933), 725.

of the earth and thereby the victory of Jewry, but the annihilation (*Vernichtung*) of the Jewish race in Europe!'[33]

Among Hitler's many reasons for the speech may well have been Franklin Roosevelt. The American President was engaged in a long battle to persuade his countrymen that isolationism was no longer a credible policy. He pitched his argument on two levels. One was geopolitical: the claim that, because in the age of airpower America's oceanic barriers were no longer insuperable, events in Europe could therefore impinge on American security. FDR's other theme was ideological. As he put in his annual message on 4 January 1939: 'God-fearing democracies of the world...cannot safely be indifferent to international lawlessness anywhere.' In late 1938 Roosevelt had been involved in efforts to promote Jewish emigration from Europe; Hitler mentioned this issue on 30 January just before uttering his lurid prophecy. Next day FDR told Senators that for the last three years there had been 'in the making a policy of world domination between Germany, Italy and Japan' which, he claimed, now amounted to 'an offensive and defensive alliance'.[34]

By January 1939, therefore, the ideological battlelines had been drawn between Roosevelt and Hitler. The Führer was prophesying a new world war unleashed by Jewish money power; the President was globalizing events to prod his countrymen out of their regional cocoon. For the moment, Hitler's gaze was concentrated on Europe: Poland in 1939, France in 1940, the Balkans and Russia in 1941. *Weltkrieg* was usually absent from his speeches, except at moments of stress.[35] But as the struggle over American neutrality reached its climax in the spring of 1941, it was Roosevelt who introduced the term 'second world war' into the lexicon of American politics.

On 31 May 1940, the President had warned of the danger of 'a world-wide war', and, on 3 January 1941, he spoke of the reality of 'a world at war'. But he took a huge stride further on 8 March 1941, the day on which the Lend-Lease bill finally passed the Senate. In a radio address he spoke of 'the first World War' and then started a sentence with this phrase: 'When the second World War began a year and a half ago.' A week later, to press correspondents, he referred to 'the first World War' and 'the present war'. And in another radio speech on 27 May 1941, he also made reference to 'the first World War' and 'this second World War',

---

[33] Max Domarus (ed.), *Hitler: Reden und Proklamationen 1932–1945* (4 vols., Munich, 1965), 1058. The passage remains controversial. Ian Kershaw attaches great importance to it in his recent biography *Hitler, 1936–1945: Nemesis* (London, 2000), 152–3. For an alternative interpretation, depicting it as more propaganda than substance, see Hans Mommsen, 'Hitler's Reichstag Speech of 30 January 1939', *History and Memory*, 9 (1997), 147–61.

[34] *The Public Papers and Addresses of Franklin D. Roosevelt, 1939* (London, 1940), 3; Donald B. Schewe (ed.), *Franklin D. Roosevelt and Foreign Affairs, 1937–1939* (14 vols., New York, 1979–83), xiii. 200.

[35] For instance in his anti-British tirade on 8 November 1939—the annual celebration of the 1923 putsch: 'In the first World War England was not the victor, but rather others were the victors. And in the second—of this I can assure you—England will be even less the victor!' (Domarus, *Hitler: Reden und Proklamationen*, 1412).

arguing that 'what started as a European war has developed, just as the Nazis always intended it should develop, into a world war for world domination'.[36]

Why did Roosevelt begin using the term 'second World War' in public from the spring of 1941? Firm evidence is lacking but at least three reasons may be inferred. In part, it was probably a response to signs of growing Axis collaboration. The assertions in his 30 January 1939 speech about a virtual alliance had been given credibility by their Tripartite Pact of September 1940. Second, the President may now have judged that it was no longer politically necessary to shy away from analogies with 1917. The 1930s had been dominated by a 'never again' mentality, but the fall of France and the Battle of Britain aroused a growing popular conviction that America's security and values were bound up with British survival. Passage of Lend-Lease had given Congressional endorsement to that new mood. Third, FDR's public talk of a 'second World War' may have reflected the mounting intelligence evidence during the spring that Hitler was about to invade the Soviet Union. Operation Barbarossa on 22 June opened up a massive new front across Eastern Europe and Eurasia. From then on 'world war' became a recurrent theme in Roosevelt's speeches.[37]

While redefining international events as part of a world war, Roosevelt was already anticipating the world peace that he believed must follow. In January 1941 he had set out his vision of 'a world founded on four essential human freedoms'. This, he claimed, was 'no vision of a distant millennium' but of a 'world order' that was 'attainable in our own time and generation'.[38] In August 1941, meeting with Churchill off Newfoundland, he developed the Four Freedoms in the eight-point Atlantic Charter. For Churchill the meeting was something of a disappointment. Fervently hoping for an American declaration of war, he had to be content with a declaration of war aims.[39] But the Axis powers, uncertain of what secret agreements lay behind the rhetorical façade, were convinced that this was a huge forward step towards American belligerency. To claim that the Atlantic meeting was the trigger for Hitler's decision to embark on *Endlösung*, the final solution to the Jewish problem, may well be an exaggeration, but in August 1941 the Führer told Josef Goebbels that his January 1939 prophecy of world war was coming true with 'a certainty to be thought almost

---

[36] Roosevelt, *Public Papers, 1940* (1941), 250, 651, and *Public Papers, 1941* (1942), 45, 61, 181, 187. On drafts of the 27 May speech FDR personally amended 'during the World War' to 'during the first World War' and replaced 'today' with 'in this second World War'—see Master Speech file, box 60, speech 1368, 3rd draft, p. 10, and 5th draft, p. 9 (Franklin D. Roosevelt Library, Hyde Park, New York—henceforth FDRL).

[37] For instance, his press statement of 24 July on oil exports to Japan: 'There is a world war going on, and has been for some time—nearly two years' (*Public Papers, 1941*, 280). For fuller discussion on FDR's possible reasons see David Reynolds, *From Munich to Pearl Harbor: Roosevelt's America and the Origins of the Second World War* (Chicago, 2001), 131–2, 182–3.

[38] Roosevelt, *Public Papers, 1940*, 672, speech of 6 Jan. 1941.

[39] David Reynolds, 'The Atlantic "Flop": British Foreign Policy and the Churchill–Roosevelt Meeting of August 1941', in Douglas Brinkley and David Facey-Crowther (eds.), *The Atlantic Charter* (New York, 1994), 129–50.

uncanny'. And it was in this mood, in September, that he sanctioned the deportation of German and Austrian Jews to the east—in Ian Kershaw's words, 'a massive step' towards the Final Solution.[40]

Of course, Japan's attack on Pearl Harbor in December 1941 transformed international affairs. With the declarations of war on America by Japan, Germany, and Italy, this had become truly a world war. But, as in 1914–18, ideology played a significant role in establishing the terminology. For Hitler, as for the apologists of the Kaiserreich, the goal was world power—now with the novel twist that this time the real obstacle was not the British Empire but the underlying global Jewish conspiracy. For Roosevelt, like Wilson, the goal was a new world order. But whereas Americans had defined the conflict of 1914–18 as a world war *after* they entered it, Roosevelt was already using that terminology *before* Pearl Harbor in order to prod Americans from isolationism to belligerency. Hitler and Roosevelt were both waging 'world war', in fact and in name, for their own ends. Hitler lost, Roosevelt won. In doing so he established America as the dominant superpower for the remainder of the twentieth century. Moreover, he also created the dominant international paradigm for conceptualizing the century's two greatest conflicts.

It should also be noted, however, that FDR seems not to have intended this as a permanent label. Asked by the War Department to designate an official title for the conflict, he remarked at a press conference on 3 April 1942: 'I don't think the Second World War is particularly effective.' The President said he wanted 'a very short name' conveying the idea that 'this is a war for the preservation of smaller peoples and the Democracies of the world'. He even asked the public for suggestions and over the next two weeks the War Department received more than 15,000 letters and cards. Suggestions included 'The War for Civilization', 'The War against Enslavement', 'The People's War', and 'The Free-World War'.[41]

In a speech on 14 April 1942, FDR used the term 'The Survival War' but the Office of War Information noted that it did not translate well into French, German, or Italian. As Sam Rosenman, one of FDR's speechwriters, observed, the phrase also sounded 'somewhat defeatist in tone' and Axis propaganda gleefully claimed that it was the Americans and British who were desperately fighting for survival and that the Axis would triumph in a Darwinian struggle of the fittest. In June, Roosevelt thought the suggestion of 'Everyman's War' was 'an excellent one. Let us start using the words.' But nothing was made official

---

[40] Tobias Jersak, 'Die Interaktion von Kriegsverlauf und Judenvernichtung: Ein Blick auf Hitlers Strategie im Spätsommer 1941', *Historische Zeitschrift*, 268 (1999), 311–74; cf. Kershaw, *Hitler 1936–1945*, 472–81, 960–1, quoting from 474 and 479.

[41] McNarney to Watson, 26 Mar. 1942, and War Dept. daily tabulations of correspondence, 7–20 Apr. 1942, in President's Official File OF 4675-D (FDRL); *Complete Presidential Press Conferences of Franklin D. Roosevelt* (25 vol., New York, 1972), xix. 252–3, 3 Apr. 1942.

and the hunt went cold.[42] Two years later, on 30 May 1944, when asked by the press whether he had ever found a better name for the war, FDR said he thought 'rather well' of a phrase he had recently heard, 'The Tyrant's War'. Again this got nowhere.[43]

As often, therefore, *c'est le provisoire qui dure*. The slogan FDR had used to help draw Americans into the conflict in 1941 became the label that made history. In the process, the Second World War begat the First. But to talk in the same breath of 'the two world wars' may blur our awareness of differences between those conflicts. The Second was more truly global than the First. This was because of what happened in 1940.

[42] Roosevelt, *Public Papers, 1942*, 193–4, speech of 14 Apr. 1942; cf. Pflaum to Early, 8 Apr., Early to FDR, 20 Apr., Rosenman to FDR, 24 Apr., Office of Emergency Management report, 17 Apr., and FDR to King, 17 June 1942—all OF 4675-D.
[43] *Complete Presidential Press Conferences*, xxiii. 197, 30 May 1944.

2

1940

Fulcrum of the Twentieth Century?

In the early morning of Friday 10 May 1940, German troops invaded Holland and Belgium. The next six weeks have become some of the most celebrated in the history of the twentieth century.[1] By 15 May the German armour had punched a 50-mile-wide hole through the weakest part of the French front around Sedan, and the French premier, Paul Reynaud, was already telling his British counterpart, Winston Churchill, 'we are beaten; we have lost the battle'.[2] On the night of the 20th the Germans reached Abbeville, at the mouth of the Somme, cutting off the British and Belgian forces, together with many of the French. Although a third of a million men were eventually evacuated from the beaches around Dunkirk between 27 May and 4 June, the German advance resumed on the following day and Paris fell on the 14th. Three days later a new French government requested an armistice, and this was duly signed on 21 June, in the same railway carriage in the forest of Compiègne in which Germany had capitulated 22 years before. The Anglo-French alliance was finished. An unprepared Britain was left to fight on alone.

The story is so familiar as to be almost a cliché. Viewed with hindsight, 1940 has cast a long shadow back over the preceding decade. In Britain, interpretations were shaped for a generation by the brilliant political polemic, *Guilty Men*, written by three Beaverbrook journalists, among them Michael Foot, in four days during the Dunkirk evacuation. This bestseller (over 200,000 copies) started with the 'defenceless' troops on the beaches of Dunkirk—'an Army doomed *before* they took the field'—and then reviewed the events of the 1930s so as to indict a generation of politicians who 'took over a great empire, supreme in arms and secure in liberty' and 'conducted it to the edge of national

Apart from minor corrections and a slightly revised ending, this chapter takes the form in which it was originally published in *International Affairs*, 66 (1990), 325–50. It was given as a conference paper at the Institute of General History, Academy of Sciences of the USSR, Moscow, in Nov. 1989.

[1] For recent discussions see Ernest R. May, *Strange Victory: Hitler's Conquest of France* (New York, 2000), and Julian Jackson, *The Fall of France: The Nazi Invasion of 1940* (Oxford, 2003).   [2] Winston S. Churchill, *The Second World War* (6 vols., London, 1948–54), ii. 38.

annihilation'.[3] This picture of June 1940 as the almost inevitable outcome of 1930s appeasement and complacency remains dominant to this day. The French equivalent of *Guilty Men* (also written in the white heat of disaster, though not published in France until 1946) was Marc Bloch's *Strange Defeat*. Bloch believed that 'the immediate occasion' for the debacle was 'the utter incompetence of the High Command', but, as befits an inspirer of the *Annales* school of historical sociology and a student of *mentalités*, he found its roots 'at a much deeper level' in the values, politics, education, and social structure of a whole generation. Behind the guilty men, in short, was a guilty society. This *longue durée* interpretation of 1940, dwelling on the political and ideological weaknesses of the Third Republic, remains a dominant view of the fall of France, embodied in such classics as William Shirer's *Collapse of the Third Republic*.[4]

Common to such interpretations is the assumption that the French collapse in 1940 was inevitable, or at least highly predictable. Indeed many standard texts on international relations summarize the events briefly, almost without comment.[5] Or, to put it another way, it is assumed that events of great consequence must have equally great causes, reaching back deep into the past—be they socio-political developments within the defeated nations, or perhaps broad shifts in the balance of international economic power.[6]

Yet this sense of inevitability is questionable. Germany went to war in 1939 seriously short of essential raw materials and economically unable to sustain a long conflict. Its fuel supplies in May 1940 were a third *less* than they had been in September 1939, despite the loopholes in the Allied blockade through Italy and Russia and the limited nature of the fighting in Poland and Norway. 'The great western offensive was a one-shot affair: success, and Germany would acquire the economic base to fight a long war; failure, and the war would be over.'[7] Likewise, much recent work in France has eschewed determinism and emphasized the contingency of events in 1940. 'France collapsed in battle for military reasons, and military explanations can sufficiently—if not completely—account for its defeat.'[8] The French *were* prepared for mobile warfare and for defence in depth.

[3] 'Cato', *Guilty Men* (London, 1940), 16, 19; Paul Addison, *The Road to 1945: British Politics and the Second World War* (London, 1975), 110.

[4] Marc Bloch, *Strange Defeat: a Statement of Evidence Written in 1940*, trans. by Gerard Hopkins (Oxford, 1949), 25, 125; William L. Shirer, *The Collapse of the Third Republic: an Inquiry into the Fall of France in 1940* (London, 1970), esp. pp. xvii–xviii.

[5] e.g. Graham Ross, *The Great Powers and the Decline of the European States System, 1914–1945* (London, 1983), 128–9; P. M. H. Bell, *The origins of the Second World War in Europe* (London, 1986), 270.

[6] Paul Kennedy, *The Rise and Fall of the Great Powers: Economic Change and Military Conflict from 1500 to 2000* (London, 1988), 310–20, 340.

[7] Williamson Murray, *The Change in the European Balance of Power, 1938–1939: the Path to Ruin* (Princeton, 1984), 361; see also pp. 326–32.

[8] Robert A. Doughty, 'The French armed forces, 1918–40', in Allan R. Millett and Williamson Murray, eds., *Military Effectiveness*, ii: *The Interwar Period* (Boston, Mass., 1988), 66. Cf. Jean Doise and Maurice Vaisse, *Diplomatie et outil militaire, 1871–1969* (Paris, 1987), 334: 'la défaite de 1940 a été d'abord militaire'. For what follows see also R. H. S. Stolfi, 'Equipment for victory in France

In equipment (except aircraft) they were not notably deficient—overall they had more tanks than the Germans, of equal or even better quality, and their army led the world in motorized units. There were inadequacies in key areas, particularly anti-aircraft and anti-tank weapons and modern fighters, but none of these was decisive by itself.

What mattered was the strategic use to which the equipment was put. The French were unprepared for the Germans' concentrated use of armour, in close coordination with tactical airpower, at a weak point on their front where they believed, incorrectly, that the Ardennes made rapid German advance unlikely. Had the German crossing of the Meuse been slowed by even 48 hours, much more effective reinforcement would have been possible. Failure here was compounded, indeed partly caused, by the French strategy of concentrating on a rapid advance into Belgium to hold not merely the Dyle but, as agreed the previous winter, the Breda line, which left most of their best motorized and armoured units far from the crucial Meuse battle as it unfolded.

These strategic failings in turn reveal a larger problem—'the defeat of 1940 was an *Allied* collapse'.[9] The Belgian operation was necessary because in 1936 Belgium reversed its postwar policy of alliance with France and opted for its pre-1914 expedient of neutrality. The Belgians hoped to avoid German attack, yet they knew full well that, if this came, French help would be essential. Likewise, the British were hardly a major asset. On 10 May the RAF had only 450 aircraft in France, about a third of its serviceable total, whereas the French had 1,400. In the crucial area of fighters, the British had only six squadrons in France on 10 May. By the 16th another 14 had been despatched, but then all except three squadrons were withdrawn from France following a Cabinet decision on 18 May to concentrate on home defence. On land the British contribution was even less impressive. The line-up on the Western Front on 10 May was 141 German divisions against 144 Allied. Of the latter, 104 were French, 22 Belgian, 8 Dutch and only 10 British.[10]

These are, of course, only the crudest of indicators. Nor should they be taken as denigration of the courage of British servicemen involved—the RAF, for instance, sustained higher losses in the seven weeks of the Battle of France than in the whole of the Battle of Britain.[11] The point is simply this: Britain had a larger population than France and produced more than twice its manufacturing output, yet this was not translated into military power at what proved to be the crucial moment in 1940. French strategic errors and the lack of Allied support, as

in 1940', *History*, 1–20; Robert Young, *In Command of France: French Foreign Policy and Military Planning 1933–1940* (Cambridge, Mass., 1978).

[9] Jeffery A. Gunsburg, *Divided and Conquered: the French High Command and the Defeat of the West, 1940* (London, 1979), p. xxii.

[10] P. M. H. Bell, *A Certain Eventuality: Britain and the Fall of France* (Farnborough, Hants, 1974), 18–20; William Carr, *From Poland to Pearl Harbor: the Making of the Second World War* (London, 1985), 93.   [11] R. J. Overy, *The Air War, 1939–1945* (London, 1980), 34.

much as social decay or long-term economic trends, explain the strange defeat of 1940.

Yet similar deficiencies had also been apparent in August 1914, when the Germans attacked on the Western Front. Belgium started the First War as a neutral, Britain was unready and under-represented, and the French advanced in the wrong place (Lorraine) while the Germans drove through Flanders towards Paris. In 1914, crucially, the pace of war was slower than in 1940, but it was still a close-run thing. The second time, however, there was no miracle on the Marne—only at Dunkirk, and that helped save Britain, not France.

The point of this comparison is not merely to underline the chanciness of Hitler's victory, but also to introduce the central theme of this essay, namely that, because 1940 did not go the same way as 1914, the two wars were very different. The Churchillian preoccupation of many historians with 1914–45 as another 'thirty years' war' over German hegemony can blind us to this. It is deeply misleading, for instance, to say that 'the second World War was, in large part, a repeat performance of the first'.[12] In less than 40 days a jumped-up Austrian corporal had done what the Kaiser's best generals had failed to achieve in four years. With Norway, Denmark, and much of East–Central Europe in Nazi hands, with Spain, Sweden, and the Balkans sliding under German influence, Hitler was the dominant force in Europe from the Bay of Biscay to the Black Sea.

This introduction has sought to show that the events of May/June 1940 were not a foregone conclusion, and that they fundamentally changed the balance of power in Europe in a way that four years of fighting in 1914–18 failed to do. If we can grasp the magnitude of 1940, then we are in a better position to understand its consequences. For, more than anything else, it was the fall of France which turned a European conflict into a world war and helped reshape international politics in patterns that endured for nearly half a century, until the momentous events of 1989. Arguably 1940 was the fulcrum of the twentieth century.

The following sections examine the impact of the German victories on the great powers—first on Britain, then on America and Russia, and finally on the Rome/Berlin/Tokyo axis—before looking at the long-term consequences of 1940 for the post-war world.

For the British government, the French collapse came as a devastating shock. Neville Chamberlain, recently displaced by Churchill as Prime Minister, described Paul Reynaud's despairing phone call on 15 May as 'incredible news'.[13] It was only on the 17th that the government began serious contingency planning

---

[12] A. J. P. Taylor, *The Origins of the Second World War* (Harmondsworth, 1964), 41.
[13] Neville Chamberlain, diary, 15 May 1940, Chamberlain papers, NC 2/24A (Birmingham University Library).

for a French collapse. Britain had gone to war in 1939 in the expectation that it and its allies had superior staying power in a long conflict, drawing on Britain's naval, financial, and imperial strength. It was accepted that the crucial point would be the first few weeks of serious fighting, when the Germans were likely to launch land attacks on France and air attacks on Britain, but it was assumed that these could be countered and that 'once we had been able to develop the full fighting strength of the Empire, we should regard the outcome of the war with confidence'.[14] There were of course those, including Churchill, who questioned the wisdom of a passive 'long war' strategy, particularly during the deliberate inertia of the winter of 1939–40. But Sir John Colville, Private Secretary to both Chamberlain and Churchill, recalled later that Colonel Hastings Ismay, Military Secretary to the War Cabinet, was the only man he ever heard predicting prior to 10 May 1940 that the French armies would collapse before the German onslaught. The consensus view was expressed by Lord Halifax, the Foreign Secretary, when he wrote in his diary on 25 May: 'the mystery of what looks like the French failure is as great as ever. The one firm rock on which everybody had been willing to build for the last two years was the French Army, and the Germans walked through it like they did through the Poles.'[15]

By 'the last two years' Halifax was referring to the policy adopted from early 1939 of close military ties with France. After Munich there was a growing recognition that, to quote Sir Orme Sargent of the Foreign Office, 'we have used France as a shield, behind which we have maintained ourselves in Europe since our disarmament [after 1919]'.[16] Anglo-French staff talks, the imposition of conscription, and the commitment of a British Expeditionary Force were all products of this new mood—in marked contrast with the determination to avoid continental commitments to France that had characterized most of the period since the war.[17] We have seen that in 1939–40 the British contribution to the French effort was hardly impressive, but the two countries were now allies, Britain was mobilizing its strength for war and, most portentous, behind the scenes senior policy-makers were talking in radical terms about the need to put Anglo-French cooperation on a permanent footing.

I am not primarily thinking here of the celebrated declaration of Anglo-French Union on 16 June, with its offer of common citizenship and joint organs of government. That, in reality, was a last-ditch effort to keep France in the war or else gain control of the French fleet.[18] More significant were the ideas per-colating in the Foreign Office in the early months of 1940, under pressure from

[14] Chiefs of Staff, 'European appreciation', 20 Feb. 1939, para. 268, CAB 16/183A, DP(P) 44 (TNA).

[15] John Colville, *Footprints in Time* (London, 1976), 92; Halifax diary, 25 May 1940, Hickleton papers, A 7.8.4 (Borthwick Institute, York).

[16] Minute of 17 Oct. 1938 in Young, *In Command of France*, 214.

[17] Cf. Anne Orde, *Great Britain and International Security, 1920–1926* (London, 1978).

[18] Avi Shlaim, 'Prelude to downfall: The British offer of union to France, June 1940', *Journal of Contemporary History*, 9 (1947), 27–63.

France for punitive war aims against Germany, including French control of the Rhineland. The British believed, as in 1919, that this would be disastrous, but the history of the interwar years made it clear that French security fears were well founded. Chastened, the British government revived another idea advanced in 1919, that of a British guarantee of French security, but this time they extended it in far-reaching ways. On 28 February 1940 Sargent advised that the only alternative to a punitive peace would be to reassure the French that after the war they could 'count on such a system of close and permanent cooperation between France and Great Britain—political, military and economic—as will for all international purposes make of the two countries a single unit in post-war Europe. Such a unit would constitute an effective—perhaps the only effective counter-weight to the unit of 80 million Germans in the middle of Europe...' This, he argued, was the only way of achieving a stable peace. Yet, he continued, 'the British public is quite unprepared for such a development'. It 'would at first sight appear to most as an alarming and dangerous surrender of Great Britain's liberty of action or maybe of sovereignty... and it will need a considerable amount of education before the British public will get accustomed to the notion of their having to make this unpalatable and unprecedented sacrifice on the altar of European peace'. Sargent therefore urged that a major campaign of public education be mounted. His ideas were taken up enthusiastically by Halifax and by the Prime Minister, Neville Chamberlain. The latter noted: 'I entirely agree with this memorandum & shall be glad if the M[inistry] of Information can do something to draw attention to the importance of the subject.' Over the next few months the theme was elaborated in ministerial speeches, and plans were drawn up by the Ministry and by the government's Board of Education for a campaign reaching down to British schools as well as out to the adult public.[19]

The significance of these moves should not, of course, be exaggerated. In private, policy-makers lamented the chaotic state of French politics, public enthusiasm for France remained lukewarm, and progress on institutional planning for permanent Anglo-French cooperation was slow.[20] But Sargent's proposals and the top-level support they secured indicate what would probably have been the trend of British policy had the Anglo-French alliance continued. Faced with the bankruptcy of their diplomacy since 1919, British policy-makers were seriously contemplating a radical shift towards an institutionalized *entente cordiale* as the basis of a lasting peace.

But the Anglo-French alliance did not continue. It collapsed in the summer of 1940 amid bitter mutual recrimination about French ineptitude and British treachery, and after the Royal Navy's attack on the French fleet early in July, the

[19] Minutes by Sargent, 28 Feb. 1940, Halifax, 29 Feb. and Chamberlain, 1 Mar., FO 371/24298, C4444/9/17; Board of Education memo 18, 'The French and ourselves', Apr. 1940, ED 138/27 (TNA). See also Peter Ludlow, 'The unwinding of appeasement', in Lothar Kettenacker, ed., *Das 'Andere Deutschland' im Zweiten Weltkrieg: Emigration and Widerstand in internationaler Perspektive* (Stuttgart, 1977), esp. pp. 28–46.   [20] Bell, *Certain Eventuality*, 7–10.

two ex-Allies seemed for a time close to war with each other. Unable now to cling to the 'rock' of the French army, the British had two options open—compromise peace, or transatlantic salvation.

Contrary to British patriotic mythology, it was not a foregone conclusion that the country did fight on in 1940.[21] The War Cabinet debated the issue on 26–8 May, early in the Dunkirk crisis when it seemed that no more than 50,000 troops could be evacuated. Even Churchill had private doubts at times that summer. Certainly the prospects were bleak if Britain had to carry on alone. For survival, let alone victory, US assistance on an unprecedented scale was clearly vital.

For most of the period since 1919, Anglo-American relations had been cool and often suspicious. America's 'betrayal' of the League of Nations was only the first of a series of US actions—over war debts, naval rivalry, the 1931–2 Manchurian crisis, and the Depression—that convinced British leaders that the United States could not be relied on. 'I am afraid that, taught by experience, I have little faith in America', noted the Permanent Under-Secretary at the Foreign Office, Sir Alexander Cadogan, in February 1939. Wearily he dismissed speculation about how the United States might 'act' in the event of a European war: 'I am only too afraid that the word is intended in its histrionic sense.' Such scepticism was strengthened by the US neutrality legislation of the 1930s, which restricted trade with belligerent countries in an effort to avoid repetition of the financial ties and naval incidents that had helped draw America into the First World War. Added to this doubt about the United States was an element of fear. In the latter stages of the previous war, American financial power had given President Woodrow Wilson leverage over Allied diplomacy and peace aims. Many British leaders had no desire for that to be repeated, if Britain and France could defeat Germany largely on their own. 'Heaven knows', wrote Chamberlain in January 1940, 'I don't want the Americans to fight for us—we should have to pay too dearly for that if they had a right to be in on the peace terms...' Of course, he and his colleagues recognized that some US diplomatic and economic assistance was essential, and in the long term they hoped that, as in 1914–18, Americans would be 'educated' by events into a sounder attitude to the war and the British cause. But in early 1940 most neither expected nor even desired a close Anglo-American alliance.[22]

The events of May/June 1940 ended this equivocation. Winston Churchill, the new Prime Minister, had always been a more ardent wooer of America than most British politicians, and his elevation undoubtedly accelerated the change of policy. But even the suspicious Chamberlain acknowledged by 19 May 1940 that 'our only hope, it seems to me, lies in Roosevelt & the U.S.A.'[23] When the

---

[21] See the discussion in Chapter 4.

[22] For this paragraph see David Reynolds, *The Creation of the Anglo-American Alliance, 1937–1941: A Study in Competitive Cooperation* (London, 1981), chs. 1–3, quotations from pp. 45 (Cadogan), 78 (Chamberlain).   [23] Chamberlain diary, 19 May 1940, NC 2/24A.

Chiefs of Staff started to plan for the prospect of fighting on alone, they stressed on 25 May that their central assumption was that the United States 'is willing to give us full economic and financial support, *without which we do not think we could continue the war with any chance of success*'.[24] By the middle of June, as France fell, Churchill was appealing openly to Roosevelt for a US declaration of war. His pleas were unavailing but, from now on, the creation of an Anglo-American alliance was the central object of British foreign policy. And, looking ahead, even in the dark days of mid-1940 the British were now projecting such an alliance as the basis of a post-war order. In July 1940 Halifax wrote to Sir Maurice Hankey, who had been chairing the committee to examine plans for post-war Anglo-French collaboration, to say that this committee was now dissolved. In his letter, drafted by Sargent, previously the leading apostle of Anglo-French cooperation, Halifax commented: 'It may well be that instead of studying closer union with France, we shall find ourselves contemplating the possibility of some sort of special association with the U.S.A.' He warned that 'this is a matter which cannot be rushed'. Nevertheless, 'this does not mean we ought not to bear it always in mind. Indeed henceforth it ought, I think, to replace the idea of Anglo-French Union among the various plans which we may make for the future.'[25]

That reorientation was of course culturally more natural for the British: the Americans spoke the same language, they were regarded by many Britons as being essentially of the same stock, and the idea of a special relationship with the United States had been a recurrent feature of British thought in the early part of the century.[26] Hankey spoke for many in mid-1940 when he observed: 'it is almost a relief to be thrown back on the resources of the Empire and of America'. He also noted that 'if we are successful we shall expose the fallacy of the glib statement that Great Britain is no longer an island . . . we shall have disproved the strategical theories on which our policy has been based in recent years. There will be no strategical object in seeking alliance with France and other continental States that have proved so unreliable.'[27] Having moved away from isolationism only recently—in 1938–9—most British policy-makers now felt that the events of 1940 had confirmed their underlying prejudices about the French and the continent after all. There followed an outpouring of retrospective 'wisdom' about the supposed decadence and cowardice of the French.

[24] Memo of 25 May 1940, para. I, CAB 66/7, WP (40) 168 (TNA). Italics in the original.

[25] Halifax to Hankey, 15 July 1940, FO 371/25206, W8602/8602/49 (TNA).

[26] For background see David Reynolds,'Rethinking Anglo-American relations', *International Affairs*, 65 (1988–9), esp. pp. 94–9, and more generally, David Dimbleby and David Reynolds, *An Ocean Apart: the Relationship between Britain and America in the Twentieth Century* (London, 1988).

[27] Hankey to Sir Samuel Hoare, 19 July 1940, Templewood papers, T/XIII/17 (Cambridge University Library); Eleanor M. Gates, *End of the Affair: the Collapse of the Anglo-French Alliance, 1939–40* (London, 1981), 381. See also John C. Cairns, 'A nation of shopkeepers in search of a suitable France, 1919–40', *American Historical Review*, 79 (1974), esp. pp. 742–3.

In the summer of 1940, as Lord Beaverbrook put it triumphantly, 'we are all splendid Isolationists now'.[28] In so far as British leaders looked beyond the next few months, the idea of a peacetime alliance with France had been replaced by that of a 'special association' with the United States. Although the latter was more innately congenial to most Britons, it would not, as we have seen, have become conceivable but for the fall of France. Indeed, if that debacle had not occurred, the trend of British policy would probably have been towards closer association with France and greater involvement in continental Europe. The post-war import of this will be considered at the end of this chapter.

In Britain at least, it is customary to say that the Second World War began in September 1939. Yet what actually began then was a limited European war, confined to Britain, France, Germany and, briefly, Poland. Since the mid-1930s British military planners had worked with the nightmare worst-case assumption of a three-enemy war—against Germany, Italy, and Japan—but the latter two powers remained neutral, albeit malevolent, in September 1939. On the sidelines too were the Soviet Union, which signed a non-aggression pact with Germany in August, and the United States, whose stance was one of neutrality tilted benevolently towards the Allies. What all these powers would have done had the Western Front held in 1940 is difficult to say. What can be shown, however, is how the European revolution of 1940 opened up new problems and/or opportunities for each of them which, cumulatively, paved the way to a truly global conflict.

To take the United States first. American strategy, no less than Britain's, had assumed that France would hold the Western Front. Despite expressions of unease at Allied lethargy in the winter of 1939–40, US rearmament was slow and ineffective. Although the leading world economy, America stood only twentieth in the ranking of world military powers. The Dutch were nineteenth.[29] In May 1940 the United States could field only five army divisions totalling 80,000 men, backed by 160 pursuit planes and 52 heavy bombers, while its one-ocean navy was largely based at Hawaii as a deterrent against Japan, leaving the Atlantic coast virtually defenceless.[30] The fall of France therefore caused near-panic in Washington. Massive military appropriations were rushed through Congress but, as Bernard Baruch, 'czar' of First World War mobilization, observed, 'you cannot just order a Navy as you would a pound of coffee, or vegetables and meat, and say, we will have that for dinner. It takes time. It takes organization.'[31] In the meantime, the United States had to make do as best it could.

[28] A. J. P. Taylor, *Beaverbrook* (Harmondsworth, 1974), 566.

[29] Christopher Thorne, *The Far Eastern War: States and Societies, 1941–45* (London: 1986), 211–12.

[30] Robert Dallek, *Franklin D. Roosevelt and American Foreign Policy, 1932–1945* (New York, 1979), 221–2.

[31] Bernard Baruch to Walter Lippmann, 30 Apr. 1940, Lippmann papers, 55/178 (Sterling Library, Yale University).

Essentially there were two options available in 1940. One—widely canvassed within the Roosevelt administration and urged publicly by newspapers such as the *Chicago Tribune*—was to concentrate on the defence of the American hemisphere. That meant, for instance, pulling the fleet back from Pearl Harbor to the Californian and Atlantic coasts, leaving Japan free to control the Pacific, and not provoking the Axis by quixotic gestures of support for beleaguered Britain. But Roosevelt believed that traditional ideas about a self-contained Western hemisphere were outmoded. He and others feared that if Hitler gained control of the French and British fleets Germany would be in a position to isolate and menace the United States, assisted perhaps by bases in fascist countries of Latin America. Consequently the belated US rearmament drive from May 1940 was complemented by a growing commitment to the British cause, on grounds both of ideological sympathy with a fellow democracy and of national interest in maintaining a 'front line' in Europe behind which America could rearm.

The next twelve months saw a series of American moves that brought the country closer to Britain and to eventual war with Germany. First came the barter of 50 old destroyers in September 1940 in return for leases to build bases on eight British Atlantic islands and a pledge that the British fleet would never be surrendered. Then, in early 1941, with Britain running out of gold and dollars, Roosevelt persuaded Congress to couple a new rearmament drive with the option of loaning *matériel* to countries whose survival was deemed to benefit the United States. Following this measure—known to history as Lend-Lease— the President employed the US navy ever more extensively and intensively in the Atlantic, until something close to an undeclared naval war with Germany existed by the autumn of 1941. Even though Roosevelt still held back from the brink, his démarches of 1940–41 unrolled inexorably from the basic decision he made after the fall of France: to back Britain as America's front line.[32]

Both these developments—America as 'the arsenal of democracy' and as the ally of Britain—would probably have happened anyway, albeit more slowly. Even if France had not fallen, America would, as in 1914–18, probably have been drawn into a growing logistic and diplomatic involvement in the Allied cause. But in 1918, despite the extent of America's economic and manpower commitment, the British and French were still influential actors. And because the Central Powers collapsed so suddenly and unexpectedly in the autumn of 1918, the war ended before America reached the point of maximum potential leverage over the Western Allies. What some perceptive British policy-makers, such as General Jan Smuts, particularly feared in 1918 was that if the conflict continued into 1919 or 1920 Britain would be reduced to virtual dependence on

[32] See Reynolds, *Creation of the Anglo-American Alliance*, chs. 4–8; Dallek, *Roosevelt and American Foreign Policy*, chs. 10–11; also Warren F. Kimball, *The Most Unsordid Act: Lend-Lease, 1939–1941* (Baltimore, 1969); Waldo Heinrichs, *Threshold of War: Franklin D. Roosevelt and American Entry into World War II* (New York, 1988).

America. 'If peace comes now,' Smuts wrote in October 1918, 'it will be a British peace . . . given to the world by the same Empire that settled the Napoleonic wars a century ago.' But, Smuts warned, in 1919 or 1920 the peace which would then be imposed 'on an utterly exhausted Europe will be an American peace' because 'in another year of war the United States will have taken our place as the first military, diplomatic and financial power of the world'.[33]

What Smuts feared for 1920 came true in 1940. Hitler's devastating victories left Britain heavily dependent on American help. It still took time for America to mobilize its resources, of course. In his war memoirs Churchill was at pains to note that 'until July 1944 Britain and her Empire had a substantially larger number of divisions in *contact with the enemy* than the United States', taking account not only of the European and African theatres but also the war against Japan.[34] But the fall of France made America's *ultimate* dominance in the Anglo-American alliance and in the affairs of Europe much more likely. Britain needed US machine tools, raw materials, and weapons to keep its armies supplied. By 1944, about 60 per cent of all the combat munitions of the Allies were being produced in the United States.[35] Britain needed US credits, Lend-Lease, to free itself from the need to maintain normal exports to pay for essential imports and thus enable itself to concentrate on war production. By 1944 British exports were about 30 per cent of their 1938 volume, and over half Britain's total balance of payments deficit during the war was funded by the United States.[36] Above all, because Britain now had no major continental ally, it desperately needed the vast population resources of the United States to help it establish a foothold across the Channel, let alone push a Western Front towards Berlin. In short, with the Europeans this time so hopelessly unable to contain Germany themselves, the United States was likely to play a much larger part than it did in 1917–19 in both the victory and the peace-making.

The position of the Soviet Union was also transformed by the fall of France. From the early 1930s, faced by threats on two sides from the growing bellicosity of Germany and Japan, Soviet policy had inclined towards the concept of collective security, with Stalin allowing foreign minister Maxim Litvinov to try to improve relations with the anti-fascist western democracies. In the winter following Munich, that orientation changed. After the sacrifice of Czechoslovakia, the Soviet government inferred that the British and French were unlikely to offer serious impediment to German control of Eastern Europe. In this they were basically right.

Of course, British policy did change in the spring of 1939, after Hitler broke the Munich agreement and took over the rest of the Czech lands. This prompted

---

[33] Smuts, memo, 24 Oct. 1918, CAB 24/67, GT 6091(TNA).
[34] Churchill, *Second World War*, ii. 5.
[35] Alan S. Milward, *War, Economy and Society, 1939–1945* (Berkeley, 1977), 70.
[36] W. K. Hancock and M. M. Gowing, *British War Economy* (London, 1975), 521; R. S. Sayers, *British Financial Policy, 1939–1945* (London, 1956), 498.

guarantees to key East European states, including Poland and Romania and, more reluctantly, negotiations with the Soviet Union. But the intent in all this was diplomatic more than military. The aim was to create a 'peace front' to deter Hitler from further self-aggrandizement, rather than a network of alliances to wage war. The British offered no specific military commitments to any country in Eastern Europe, even those guaranteed.[37]

It is possible that in time the British attitude might have evolved. (After all, the Anglo-Russian convention of 1907, which laid the diplomatic basis of alliance in the First World War, had taken some 14 months to negotiate.) But Stalin was not prepared to wait. Aware of Hitler's plans for the attack on Poland, he allowed the parallel negotiations with Germany (reports of which the British had refused to take seriously) to reach a conclusion. In the pact of 23 August Germany and Russia pledged themselves to refrain from any act of aggression against each other. In the secret protocol they agreed that, 'in the event of a territorial and political transformation' of Eastern Europe, the countries of Latvia, Estonia, and Finland, plus Poland east of the Narev and Vistula rivers, should lie within the Soviet 'sphere of interest'.[38] When the 'territorial and political transformation' of Poland took place in September 1939, the Soviet Union took what had been agreed, though under the revised protocol of 28 September Germany secured more of Poland, while Lithuania was now allocated to the Soviet sphere.

In retrospect, neither Britain nor Russia can take much pride in their diplomacy in 1939. The British tardiness in negotiation, their indifference to the fate of Eastern Europe and their underestimation of German diplomacy seem remarkable, even by the low standards of appeasement. And Stalin's decision to abandon collective security for territorial security—an East European buffer in old tsarist lands—has long been denounced in the West and is now coming under increasing criticism within the Soviet Union as its full details are acknowledged. Yet both policies have a rationality, however cynical, if one admits that neither Chamberlain nor Stalin foresaw the events of 1940. British strategy after Munich was to consolidate an Anglo-French bloc, to build up their strength and to play for time in anticipation that Germany was less able to sustain a long war than they were. Stalin, likewise, probably assumed that if the British and French *did* go to war with Germany, the result would be a protracted struggle in which neither side would be free to pay much attention to the Soviet Union. For Russia no less than Britain, the survival of France was probably the 'unspoken assumption' of 1939.[39] Thus in May 1940 'the whole rationale of Soviet policy since September 1939 was put to the test'. In the words of historian

[37] N. H. Gibbs, *Grand Strategy*, i: *Rearmament Policy* (London, 1976), chs. 17, 19.

[38] *Documents on German Foreign Policy*, Series D, vol. vii (London, 1956), docs. 228, 229.

[39] A concept popularized by James Joll. See his essay '1914: the unspoken assumptions', in H. W. Koch, ed., *The Origins of the First World War: Great Power Rivalry and German War Aims* (London, 1972), 307–28.

Adam Ulam: 'If the war developed into a prolonged stalemate à la World War I, this policy would be vindicated. If a rapid decision was forthcoming, the policy would be revealed as a fatal gamble.'[40]

Gamble it proved to be. Soviet policy played a significant part in the debacle, by freeing Hitler to shift all but ten German divisions from the Eastern Front against France. Once the Western Front had been eliminated, Hitler was then able to mount the next stage of his bid for hegemony. On 31 July 1940 he instructed the military to prepare an invasion of Russia the following spring.

There remains some debate about whether his decision was intended as an end in itself or as a means of forcing Britain to the peace table. After the meeting on 31 July, Army Chief of Staff General Franz Halder summarized Hitler's words in his diary: 'Russia [is] the factor on which England is mainly betting...But if Russia is destroyed, then England's last hope is extinguished.'[41] Hitler took the same line frequently that summer. But it is likely that his intent in so speaking was to reassure the military that by attacking Russia they would not be embarking on a war on two fronts—the great strategic nightmare for German planners, given their country's geographic position. Probably more authentic are his remarks to the League of Nations High Commissioner for Danzig, Carl Burckhardt, on 11 August 1939: 'Everything I undertake is aimed against Russia. If the West is too stupid and too blind to grasp this, then I shall be forced to reach an understanding with the Russians to defeat the West and then, after its downfall, turn with all my concerted forces against the Soviet Union.'[42] For it is clear that throughout his career Hitler kept coming back to the idea of achieving living space in Eastern Europe through the defeat of the Soviet Union—doubly damned in his eyes as both Bolshevik and Jewish. Beyond that were more shadowy, if lurid, dreams of world domination entailing the defeat of the United States, but for most of his life (except briefly in mid-1941) Hitler viewed the American campaign as a matter for his successors.[43] Even the struggle against Russia was initially projected for the mid-1940s after a long war against France had been won, and German rearmament proceeded, albeit chaotically, on that broad assumption.[44] The scenario was therefore that Nazi hegemony would be

[40] Adam B. Ulam, *Expansion and Coexistence: Soviet Foreign Policy, 1917–73* (New York, 1974), 295.

[41] Jürgen Förster, 'Hitlers Entscheidung für den Krieg gegen die Sowjetunion', in Horst Boog et al., *Das Deutsche Reich und der Zweite Weltkrieg*, iv: *Der Angriff auf die Sowjetunion* (Stuttgart, 1983), 14.

[42] Andreas Hillgruber, *Hitlers Strategie: Politik und Kriegführung, 1940–1941* (Frankfurt, 1965), 28–9.

[43] For discussions in English of Hitler's policy see Klaus Hildebrand, *The Foreign Policy of the Third Reich*, trans. by Anthony Fothergill (Berkeley, 1973); Meir Michaelis, 'World power status or world dominion?', *Historical Journal*, 15 (1972), 331–60; Milan Hauner, 'Did Hitler want a world dominion?', *Journal of Contemporary History*, 13 (1978), 15–32.

[44] Wilhelm Deist, *The Wehrmacht and German Rearmament* (London, 1981); R. J. Overy, 'Hitler's war and the German economy: a reinterpretation', *Economic History Review*, 2nd series, 35 (1982), 272–91.

achieved piecemeal, with enemies isolated and their potential allies neutralized, as in the tactical alliance with Russia in 1939.

The 40-day victory over France, however, made a new timetable conceivable. The army commanders, previously sceptical about Hitler's strategic vision and resistant to the idea of expansion far beyond Mitteleuropa, were nonplussed and silenced. Some, like Field Marshal Walther von Brauchitsch, the Army Commander-in-Chief, even became enthusiasts for an invasion of Russia in the autumn of 1940.[45] That was utopian, but the European revolution of 1940 had left Hitler free to embark on the next stage of his 'programme' and to indulge without restraint his racist paranoia about Slavs and Jews.

A 'rather coarse Russian proverb' describes the tightest possible situation in life as one in which a person 'can neither relieve himself nor sigh over the need to do so'. That, comments historian Adam Ulam, 'was close to the Soviet situation' at the end of June 1940.[46] Hastily Russia seized the Baltic states on 15–16 June and began an emergency rearmament programme, but in January 1941 Stalin reportedly said that the Red Army needed at least another 18 months or two years.[47]

There has been much criticism of Stalin's own failings in 1941, especially his repeated dismissal of intelligence warnings, not just from the West but from Soviet sources, about the imminence of German attack.[48] In part his refusal to authorize precautionary measures reflected his evident desire to do nothing that might give Hitler a pretext for attack. But perhaps his almost wilful obtuseness, and his apparent breakdown in the days after 22 June 1941, were indications at a psychological level of a man who simply could not accept that his gamble of August 1939 had gone fatally wrong in June 1940.

We now know that the Soviet Union not only survived the Nazi onslaught but also drove the Wehrmacht right back to Berlin. Yet that was achieved at appalling cost: perhaps a tenth of the pre-war Soviet population and a quarter of national assets. And total victory seemed almost inconceivable in the crisis of 1941. Given the fact that Stalin had already concluded a pact with Hitler in 1939, he might well have considered that option again. Take, for instance, the crisis in Moscow on 15–16 October 1941, when the Germans were a mere 60 miles away, the city was prepared for evacuation, and spontaneous panic seems to have engulfed the public and elements of the Party. Later Soviet revelations strongly suggest that Stalin made overtures to Hitler via the Bulgarians for a compromise peace.[49] Likewise, we need to know more about Soviet

[45] Barry A. Leach, *German Strategy against Russia, 1939–1941* (Oxford, 1973), 28–9, 44–7, 57–8. [46] Ulam, *Expansion and Coexistence*, 296–7.

[47] Earl F. Ziemke, 'The Soviet armed forces in the interwar period', in Millett and Murray, eds., *Military Effectiveness*, ii. 19–20, citing A. I. Eremenko, *Pomni voyny* (Donetsk, 1970), 129.

[48] See Barton Whaley, *Codeword Barbarossa* (Cambridge, Mass., 1973); John Erickson, *The Road to Stalingrad* (London, 1975), chs. 1–2; Gabriel Gorodetsky, *Grand Delusion: Stalin and the German Invasion of Russia* (New Haven, 1999).

[49] Erickson, *Road to Stalingrad*, 305–6. On 7 Oct. 1941 Stalin reportedly instructed his secret police chief, Lavrenti Beria, to ask the Bulgarian ambassador in Moscow to act as go-between.

diplomacy in the winter of 1942–3 as the Red Army won its great victory around Stalingrad. Some Western scholars have inferred from Stalin's speech on 6 November 1942 and from reports of Russo-German contacts in Stockholm in December that there was a Soviet attempt to sound out the possibilities of a negotiated peace at this point, with the German assaults exhausted.[50]

So the Red Army's road to Berlin was probably circuitous, as well as bloody. But the war in the East did continue, and it became clear, after Stalingrad and especially Kursk in the summer of 1943, that the Soviet Union would play a vast role in the future of Europe—because it was the main agent of Nazi Germany's destruction. Between June 1941 and June 1944 as much as 93 per cent of German army battle casualties were inflicted by the Red Army.[51]

Why was the Anglo-American contribution in those years relatively so small? In part, the answer lies in the fact that both countries prepared for war so late: in Britain intense rearmament and the introduction of conscription came only in 1938–9, in the United States not until the crisis of 1940. But there was another important reason for the Anglo-American delay in opening a second front on the mainland of Europe—British and US forces were also deeply engaged against Italy and Japan. To understand how a European conflict became a world war, we need to look at the reaction of the Axis powers to the German victories in 1940.

In retrospect the unity of fascism, of the dictators and of the Rome–Berlin axis have generally been taken for granted. In the 1930s, however, this was not the case. Throughout this period the British and French tried to woo Mussolini, or at least prevent him from complete incorporation in the German camp. This was particularly true of the period 1934–8, when it was hoped that Italy would exert itself to prevent the Austrian *Anschluss*—a move that would give Hitler dominance in Central Europe and a frontier with Italy itself. The conciliatory Anglo-French policy over Abyssinia in 1935–6 and over the Spanish Civil War was formulated with this in mind.[52] But even after the 1938 *Anschluss*, and indeed right into 1940, hopes remained of keeping Rome and Berlin apart.

Deeply pessimistic about the military situation, Stalin said that the Soviet Union needed a 'breathing space' akin to the treaty of Brest-Litovsk with Germany in 1918, and spoke of giving Hitler the Baltic states, Belorussia, Moldavia, and part of the Ukraine. See *Moscow News*, 7 May 1989, p. 9, and *Sunday Times* (London), 28 May 1989, p. A18, based respectively on interviews with Marshal Georgi Zhukov, who was present on 7 Oct. 1941, and Dimitar Peyev, then a junior Bulgarian diplomat.

[50] Vojtech Mastny, *Russia's Road to the Cold War: Diplomacy, Warfare, and the Politics of Communism, 1941–1945* (New York, 1979), 73–6.

[51] Jonathan R. Adelman, *Prelude to Cold War: the Tsarist, Soviet and US Armies in the Two World Wars* (London, 1988), 128.

[52] R. A. C. Parker, 'Great Britain, France and the Ethiopian crisis, 1935–1936', *English Historical Review*, 89 (1974), 293–332; Roy Douglas, *In the Year of Munich* (London, 1977); Anthony Adamthwaite, *France and the Coming of the Second World War, 1936–1939* (London, 1977).

As with the appeasement of Germany, this policy rested on assumptions about an internal policy battle between moderates and extremists which in neither case was soundly based. But in Italy, there was somewhat more justification for thinking in these terms. Mussolini's power even in the late 1930s was never as absolute as Hitler's. In theory and in practice, Italy remained a 'diarchy'— Mussolini could not ignore the political and military authority of the King, Victor Emmanuel III. Nor could he override the reservations of the senior military, notably Marshal Pietro Badoglio, chief of the general staff, about the country's appalling military weakness relative to Britain and France. To Mussolini's son-in-law and foreign minister, Count Galeazzo Ciano, this dictated a cautious policy towards these powers. None of these 'moderates' was averse to Italy improving its position around the Adriatic and Mediterranean where possible, but their opposition to throwing in their lot with Germany and risking a great-power conflict restrained Mussolini in September 1938 and again in September 1939. However, Ciano's resistance came to an end in May 1940. Few of the Italian 'moderates' could remain unimpressed by the speed and extent of the German victories. Mussolini opted for war as early as 13 May, and within a week Ciano, Badoglio, and even the King were coming into line, while anti-war demonstrations in the northern cities were quickly replaced by public enthusiasm to join in a grab for the spoils before it was too late. General Franz Halder, German army chief of staff, noted on 17 May that 'internal resistance to war in Italy is melting... Mussolini has a free hand'.[53] On 11 June Italy declared war on Britain and France.

'Only the German victories in the West unleashed Mussolini to carry King and generals into war with promises that they need not fight...'[54] Within months the reservations of the generals had proved all too well founded. Italy's debacles in North Africa and Greece could only be retrieved because the Germans took over the struggle with Britain in those theatres. But Mussolini's bid for *spazio vitale* around the Mediterranean, made briefly plausible by the fall of France, had opened up a new area of operations, of significant interest to the British, whose easy victories over Italy in 1940–1 were followed by a much tougher struggle against the Germans in 1941–3. Moreover, the Americans were also drawn into that theatre in 1942, because Roosevelt needed to commit US troops somewhere against the Germans to counter the domestic pressure to concentrate on revenge against Japan, and because the British would not risk an invasion of France at that time. Once the Mediterranean theatre had been opened, as US Army Chief of Staff General George C. Marshall feared, operations there developed a logic of their own. It was hard not to capitalize on the victories in North Africa by moving on first to Sicily and then Italy, and it

---

[53] MacGregor Knox, *Mussolini Unleashed, 1939–1941: Politics and Strategy in Fascist Italy's Last War* (Cambridge, 1982), 109. The account given here follows Knox and also Denis Mack Smith, *Mussolini's Roman Empire* (London, 1976), esp. chs. 13–15.

[54] Knox, *Mussolini Unleashed*, 287.

was only in the summer of 1944 that Roosevelt and the Joint Chiefs finally put the lid on the Italian theatre, much to Churchill's anger and frustration.[55]

Not only did the Mediterranean strategy become a bitter issue between London and Washington, it also poisoned their collective relations with Moscow. Nothing did more to arouse Soviet suspicions during the war than the delay in mounting a second front on the continent of Europe. Neither Roosevelt's blandishments nor Churchill's reminders that the Soviet Union had not started a second front to help Britain in 1940 carried much weight. And the delay of operation 'Overlord' until June 1944 made it almost certain that the victorious Russians would play a decisive role in the future of Eastern Europe. Not all of this was foreshadowed in 1940, of course, but Mussolini's bid for a new Roman empire, made possible by the German victories, opened up a Mediterranean theatre which had vast implications for the future Allied conduct of the war.

The fall of France also had profound repercussions in Asia. Japan's foreign policy had been thrown into confusion by the Nazi–Soviet pact of August 1939.[56] Since November 1936 Japan and Germany had been linked in the Anti-Comintern pact, and the Army Ministry, which in 1939 had been agitating for a closer alliance with Germany, was discredited by the Russo-German agreement. Indeed the Hiranuma Cabinet, which had been in the process of negotiation with Germany, resigned at the end of August. During the winter of 1939–40 the initiative in the Abe and, from January, Yonai governments lay with the 'Anglo-American faction', centred in court and business circles, who mainly wanted to end Japan's 'quagmire' war in China and improve relations with the Western democracies. Little of substance was achieved, however, because the aim of improved relations stood in tension with the desire of most Japanese leaders, not least Arita Hachiro, Yonai's foreign minister, for a 'new order in East Asia'—a Japanese sphere of economic and political influence. This posed a clear threat to the 'old order', represented by Britain and the United States, which neither was willing to ignore. Thus as in Italy, the trend of Japanese policy was expansionist, by force if necessary, but foreign policy was a matter of intense political debate in the winter of 1939–40 and the outcome was in no way determined. Although the pro-Axis faction in Tokyo regained some credibility by early 1940, the drying-up of German trade in the European war made the Japanese economy even more dependent on the United States. American refusal to sign a new trade agreement until Japan pulled out of China brought down the Abe government in January. 'Had the European stalemate continued, Tokyo's leaders might have been compelled to undertake a much more drastic re-orientation of their China policy.'[57]

[55] See Michael Howard, *The Mediterranean Strategy in the Second World War* (London, 1968); Mark A. Stoler, *The Politics of the Second Front: American Military Planning and Diplomacy in Coalition Warfare, 1941–1943* (London, 1977).

[56] This account follows particularly Hosoya Chihiro, 'The Tripartite Pact, 1939–1940', in James William Morley, ed., *Deterrent Diplomacy: Japan, Germany and the USSR, 1935–1940* (New York, 1976), 191–257.

[57] Akira Iriye, *The Origins of the Second World War in Asia and the Pacific* (London, 1987), 95.

Instead, the German victories revolutionized the Japanese policy debate much as they had the Italian. Reactions in both countries were very similar—enhanced prestige for Germany and its supporters, and a desire to get in on the spoils before it was too late. The British, French, and Dutch colonial authorities in south-east Asia were in a weak position to resist Japanese demands. The Dutch were pressed for guaranteed supplies of oil, tin, and rubber from the Dutch East Indies, and the British and French agreed to close their supply routes to China, which Tokyo hoped would help end Chinese resistance. But the pro-Axis faction in the army found these moves insufficient. It was now ready for war with Britain and, if necessary, America to achieve the 'New Order in Asia'. In July it withdrew its support from the government and brought to power a new ministry, under Konoe Fumimaro, which was committed to a programme of 'southward advance' and closer links among the Axis powers. First fruit of this was the extension of Japanese control into northern Indo-China in September 1940. More spectacular was the Tripartite Pact signed in Berlin on 27 September—a defensive military alliance between Germany, Italy, and Japan.

The Pact was aimed particularly at the United States. Japan, no less than Germany, wished to deter America from commitment to the British cause, for the United States was now one of only two real obstacles to Japanese expansion in the Pacific. Throughout the 1930s Britain's position in Asia had rested on bluff.[58] The growth of the Japanese navy, in conjunction with new threats from Germany and Italy, meant that Britain could only send a fleet to Singapore to protect its Asian and Australasian possessions if the Mediterranean were quiet. From June 1940 that was impossible. Not only was Britain facing possible German invasion, but the fall of France had also left it without French naval support in the Mediterranean at a time when Italy had now entered the war. Unless Britain controlled the Mediterranean, the Italians might join the Germans in the Atlantic against Britain and its supply lines. Thus on 28 June 1940 the Australian and New Zealand governments were told that Britain could not for the foreseeable future send a fleet to Singapore and that they would have to look for American help.

Since the spring of 1940 President Roosevelt had kept the US fleet, usually based in southern California, at Pearl Harbor, in the Hawaiian islands, as a deterrent against Japan. Despite the European revolution of June 1940, this remained one important restraint on Japanese policy. The other was the attitude of the Soviet Union. Konoe's foreign minister, Matsuoka Yosuke, had been particularly keen to advance the other part of the pro-Axis policy—closer relations with Germany's new associate, the Soviet Union—and in April 1941 he concluded a neutrality treaty in Moscow. This was of only limited scope, however, and Japanese fears of Russia remained extremely strong.

[58] See Paul Haggle, *Britannia at Bay: the Defence of the British Empire against Japan, 1931–1941* (Oxford, 1981).

Then in June 1941 Germany attacked Russia, throwing Japanese policy into confusion. Matsuoka favoured abandoning the neutrality treaty and joining Hitler's war against Russia, but the navy successfully argued that Japan should seize the opportunity to push south with impunity. By 2 July 1941 Japan's leadership was committed to intensifying the southward advance into Indo-China and south-east Asia. 'To obtain these objectives the Empire will not hesitate to engage in war with the United States and Britain.'[59] Alternatives *were* canvassed. Konoe himself argued that Hitler's Russian campaign showed the bankruptcy of the pro-German strategy and the danger that Japan could eventually find itself at war with both the United States and the Soviet Union—an impossible position. But for the military such a U-turn would have meant a complete loss of prestige for themselves and their country. 'It was too late for Japan to change sides, it was argued; what the nation must do was to consider the most appropriate strategy for impending global war.'[60] American trade sanctions in July, intended as a deterrent, only served to confirm that policy.

In the preparations for war that followed, Japanese intelligence completely failed to predict the vehemence of the US reaction to Pearl Harbor, the domestic unity behind America's Pacific war, and the vast discrepancy in economic resources between the two countries. For a country that made such brilliant preparations for offensive war, such obtuseness was remarkable. In a way it was deliberate, almost fatalistic. For 'Japan's dilemma of war or surrender had its roots in her earlier decisions of the summer of 1940 to commence the "Southward Advance" '. In the heady atmosphere of 1940 Japan, like Italy, had jumped aboard the Axis bandwagon. 'Since the only alternative, by 1941, was instant surrender' to American economic pressure, 'Japan's policy-makers elected to ignore contrary indications and believed that a limited and therefore winnable conflict was possible'.[61]

Italy discovered the error of its ways earlier, but Japan's ultimate fate was more appalling. That came in 1945, however. For the first four months after the attack on Pearl Harbor, Japan ran amok in the Pacific. Malaya, Singapore, Hong Kong, the Philippines, the Dutch East Indies and much of Burma fell to its brilliant combined operations. By April 1942 there were fears that India and Australia were in real danger. Moreover, these victories had upset the international economic balance and by the spring of 1942 the Axis controlled over a third of the population and mineral resources of the world.[62] Under such circumstances it is understandable that the British and Americans reviewed their grand strategy.

---

[59] Nagaoka Shinjiro, 'The drive into southern Indochina and Thailand', in James William Morley, ed., *The Fateful Choice: Japan's Advance into Southeast Asia, 1939–1941* (New York, 1980), 236.   [60] Iriye, *Origins*, 141.

[61] Quotations from Michael A. Barnhart, 'Japanese intelligence before the Second World War: "best case" analysis', in Ernest R. May, ed., *Knowing One's Enemies: Intelligence Assessment Before the Two World Wars* (Princeton, 1984), 440, 455.

[62] Alfred E. Eckes, Jr., *The United States and the Global Struggle for Minerals* (Austin, Tex., 1979), 84.

The basic principle, outlined in 1941 and confirmed at the ARCADIA conference in January 1942, was that 'notwithstanding the entry of Japan into the War . . . Germany is still the prime enemy and her defeat is the key to victory. Once Germany is defeated, the collapse of Italy and the defeat of Japan must follow.' In these other theatres 'only the minimum of force necessary for the safeguarding of vital interests' should be used.[63] But, by the spring of 1942, such was the scale of the Japanese victories that even firm 'Germany-Firsters' such as General Sir Alan Brooke, Britain's Chief of the Imperial General Staff, judged that much greater resources had to be diverted to the Pacific to prevent complete disaster. As the British Chiefs of Staff observed on 13 April, the war against Germany 'may be entirely vitiated unless we take the necessary steps to hold Japan in the meantime'.[64] In the first half of 1942 the build-up in the Pacific was intense, simply to hold the line. Then from July, when it was clear that no invasion of France would be mounted that year, US naval planners seized the opportunity to secure crucial munitions, equipment, and shipping for an offensive Pacific war.[65] By 1943 the 'Germany First' principle was being honoured more in the breach than the observance. Thus it was the war against Japan, as much as the conflict with Italy, that dissipated Anglo-American resources and thereby helped to delay the second front.

We have seen that, for all three Axis powers, the fall of France had momentous consequences. It consolidated their relationship and encouraged each to embark on aggression that it might not otherwise have countenanced, at least until better prepared. In consequence, too, the United States and the Soviet Union were drawn into a war from which each, in its different ways, had previously hoped to remain aloof. The Russians were now next on Hitler's list, while for the Americans the alternative to intervention seemed to be alien orders in Europe and the Pacific which would leave them isolated in an increasingly hostile world. Italian, German, and Japanese underestimation of the potential of Russia and America, encouraged by the mood of 1940, were fatal ingredients in the eventual downfall of the Axis. But there was at least one other factor of significance in 1940—one that stands in marked contrast to the general trend of that summer, in which the initiative lay spectacularly with Germany. That was British obduracy.

For most of his career Hitler had assumed that Britain would acquiesce in the continental stages of his bid for world power.[66] Not only did he postulate racial ties of Anglo-Saxonism, but he believed that Britain's ambitions were

---

[63] Memo by US and British Chiefs of Staff, WW 17, annex I, CAB 80/33, COS (42) 75(TNA).

[64] See CAB 80/61, COS (42) 71 (0), esp. memo by Brooke, 21 Mar. 1942; and CAB 80/62, COS (42) 97 (0), 13 Apr. 1942, part II, para. 13.

[65] Cf. Mark A. Stoler, 'The "Pacific-first" alternative in American World War II strategy', *International History Review*, 2 (1980), 432–52.

[66] For what follows see generally Andreas Hillgruber, 'England's place in Hitler's plans for world dominion', *Journal of Contemporary History*, 9 (1974), 5–22.

global and that its stance towards the continent was naturally isolationist. One of his most fundamental criticisms of the Kaiser's foreign policy had been the gratuitous offending of Britain by German naval and imperial rivalry at the same time as Germany was also coping with encirclement by land from France and Russia. In his *Second Book* of 1928 he argued that if Germany adopted a 'new political orientation which no longer contradicts England's sea and trade interests but spends itself in continental aims', then the grounds for Anglo-German hostility would cease to exist.[67] This did not preclude an eventual clash when Germany turned to colonial and global expansion, but by then, he tended to assume, his dominance of Europe would make British resistance ineffectual.

At least until the autumn of 1938, Hitler pursued this bid for British neutrality. Even after Britain's policy reappraisal in 1939, Hitler still seems to have doubted British readiness to go to war for Poland, and his assumption of Britain's acquiescence was strengthened by its inertia during the Phoney War. After the fall of France Hitler could not believe that the British would not see sense and reach a settlement. His armed forces had no plans for invasion, and these were only drawn up belatedly in July when his peace overtures were flung back at him.

Up to a point, Hitler's incredulity was well founded. We have seen that the possibility of a compromise peace was at least aired in the British War Cabinet in May 1940. But in the end Britain did fight on. Carried away by the opportunities of the moment, Hitler accelerated his plans for domination, apparently persuading himself and his military that by defeating Russia he would also bring the British to their senses. He was wrong. British defiance pulled German air- and seapower into bombing and blockade, while the successful resistance to Italy's campaigns in North Africa forced Hitler to take over responsibility for that theatre, further diverting resources from the east. Moreover, had Britain capitulated in 1940, the Americans, while possibly confronting Japan in the Pacific, would not have become drawn into the Atlantic and European conflict in the way they did in 1940–1 when they backed Britain as their own front line. In consequence, Russia would have been denied British, and probably US, logistic support—a small but not insignificant factor in the Red Army's eventual victory. Above all, by attacking Russia with Britain still defiant and in receipt of mounting US support, Hitler was committing the cardinal error of a two-front war for which he had so bitterly criticized the Kaiserreich.

Thus Hitler's miscalculations about Britain proved 'a decisive mistake'[68] From 1941 Russian and American strength was crucial in ensuring Germany's total defeat, but in 1940 British resistance was vital in preventing Germany's total victory.

---

[67] *Hitler's Secret Book*, trans. Salvator Attansio (New York, 1961), 157.
[68] Hildebrand, *Foreign Policy of the Third Reich*, 22.

This chapter has highlighted some of the ways in which the European crisis of 1940 made the Second World War very different from the First, in fact helping to turn it into a genuinely global conflict in a way that was not true of 1914–18. The fall of France, apparently inevitable when viewed in retrospect, revolutionized the perceptions and aspirations of most other powers.

Of course, no event stands in isolation. The other crucial difference from 1914–18, apart from the collapse of the Western Front, is the fact that in 1939–40 there was no eastern front because of the Nazi–Soviet pact. Thus one might say that the First World War analogue to 1940 was 1918, when the Russo-German treaty of Brest-Litovsk left the Kaiser's armies free to concentrate on the spring offensives in the West which nearly brought them victory.

But there the analogy ends, for 1918 was nearly four years into war. By then Britain's economy and manpower were fully mobilized and America's resources were beginning to make a major impression. May 1940, by contrast, was only eight months after war began. Britain was still a military pygmy, and the United States remained aloof. The success of the German *Blitzkrieg*, though no more inevitable than the failure of the Schlieffen Plan in September 1914, found France unsupported, left Britain to fight on alone, presented America with its worst security crisis to date, and offered the Axis powers unanticipated opportunities to build a new international order.

1940 and the events it set in motion also had discernible longer-term consequences. Again nothing is inevitable, and all that is suggested here is the way in which certain outcomes were facilitated by the events of 1940, but four in particular are worth noting.

First, it accelerated the 'rise of the superpowers'. Given the size and population of the United States and Russia, their international dominance had long been predicted, way back to the days of Alexis de Tocqueville. In 1846 the German commentator J. H. Pulte, anticipating the modern vocabulary of bipolarity, predicted that 'both of these extremities of the contemporary political bar-magnet will grow into mighty batteries', each with its own ideological charge.[69] In the 1980s Paul Kennedy, in his study *The Rise and Fall of the Great Powers*, depicted the main theme of the whole period 1885–1943 as 'the coming of a bipolar world'.[70]

But though this was clearly the growing trend, the timing and the degree of bipolarity owed much to the devastating impact of 1940. After the fall of France there was no chance that the rest of Europe could defeat Germany. In effect there was no Europe apart from Germany. By the end of 1941 it was clear that the eventual defeat of Hitler and the Axis would depend substantially on the United

---

[69] J. H. Pulse, *Organon der Weltgeschichte* (1846), quoted in P. F. H. Lauxtermann, *Constantin Frantz: Romantik and Realismus im Werk eines politischen Aussenseiter* (Groningen, 1978), 67. See also Chapter 16.

[70] Kennedy, *Rise and Fall*, chs. 5–6; cf. David Reynolds, 'Power, wealth and war in the modern world', *Historical Journal*, 32 (1989), 475–87.

States and the Soviet Union, and that the Europeans, whether on the winning or losing side, were likely to be reliant upon them. Both ended the war with armed forces of 11 or 12 million. Moreover, the vacuum created by Germany's defeat would leave America and Russia confronting each other in Europe itself. And their triumphs in the war engendered a new confidence in the rightness of their respective ideologies—witness the American enthusiasm for press magnate Henry Luce's assertion that 'the 20th century is the American century' and, in the Soviet Union, the post-war revival of the Communist Party and Marxist-Leninist ideology.[71]

The intensity of Soviet–American confrontation and the precise form of the Cold War were not inevitable. Many recent historians have stressed the fluidity of European politics in the immediate post-war years 1945–6.[72] But the emergence of the superpowers and some kind of friction between them were likely outcomes of the events of 1940–1, assuming the Allies were eventually victorious. And the division of Europe into two opposed alliances was a consequence of that rivalry. It took the Europeans, in East and West, nearly half a century to begin to recover their independence and self-confidence. The collapse of the old Europe in 1940 cast a long shadow.

The main institutional form through which Western Europe has recovered a measure of influence, albeit still under the American security umbrella, has been the European Community. This—and here is my second point—also owes much to legacies of 1940, particularly in the case of France. After both world wars, the main French objective was a punitive peace against Germany. Substantial reparations were demanded to rebuild French industry and Germany was to be castrated by amputation of the economic vital parts (especially the Ruhr and the Saar) to make the country militarily impotent. This was the preferred French policy in 1918 and again in 1945. In neither case was it successful, largely because of British and American opposition. After the French occupation of the Ruhr in 1923, the 'Anglo-Saxons' forced on them a revised German reparations settlement (the Dawes Plan) and a network of territorial guarantees for the Rhineland (Locarno).

Much the same happened in 1945–8.[73] Anglo-American opposition to French territorial demands and their determination to rebuild the German economy in the face of economic collapse and fears of communist resurgence, plus the growing confrontation with Russia, led France by 1948 to accept German

---

[71] Henry R. Luce, 'The American century', *Life*, 17 Feb. 1941, 64; William O. McCagg, *Stalin Embattled, 1943–1948* (Detroit, 1978).

[72] e.g. Wilfried Loth, *The Division of the World, 1941–1955* (London, 1988). For a survey of some of this literature see David Reynolds, 'The origins of the Cold War: the European dimension, 1944–1951', *Historical Journal*, 28 (1985), 497–515.

[73] On the similarities and contrasts see Charles S. Maier, 'The two postwar eras and conditions for stability in twentieth-century Western Europe', *American Historical Review*, 86 (1981), 327–52; Jon Jacobson, 'Is there a new international history of the 1920s?', *American Historical Review*, 88 (1983), 617–45.

economic and political recovery in the form of a new West German state. Yet the old fears remained. They were partially assuaged by the novel American commitment to French security in the form of the North Atlantic Treaty of 1949 and the provision of US troops in 1950, both of which were in principle directed at a resurgent Germany, as well as the Soviet Union.[74] But in this new atmosphere of reluctant yet fearful acquiescence in German recovery, Jean Monnet reached back to ideas originally touted in the mid-1920s for a fusion of the French and German economies to prevent another German government turning its economic power into military strength. In this functionalist form the ideas of European unification, themselves encouraged by the revulsion against the war, took shape as practical politics.[75] Monnet's plan, adopted in May 1950 by French Foreign Minister Robert Schuman—a Lorrainer whose own history was a microcosm of the Franco-German antagonism—led to the European Coal and Steel Community (ECSC) of 1952, which in turn laid the basis for the European Economic Community (EEC) that came into existence in 1958.

For the French the lesson of 1940, albeit slowly and painfully assimilated, was: If you can't beat them, join them. France could not live with the more powerful Germany as a rival nation-state, so both must sacrifice some elements of national sovereignty to ensure peaceful coexistence. For all the six countries that founded the ECSC and EEC—France, West Germany, Italy, and the Benelux states—this was the lesson of the war. The assertion of national sovereignty had either failed (for the defeated of 1940) or had ultimately proved disastrously counterproductive (for Italy and Germany).

For Britain, however—and this is my third point—the lesson of 1940 was very different. Whatever the reasons—whether courage, statesmanship, or luck—the country had survived, and had gone on to play a part in eventual victory. National sovereignty seemed to have been vindicated. Moreover, the prime movers for European integration were either ex-enemies or else allies who, in Britain's view, had let it down pathetically in 1940. The countries who had helped most in the war were the 'English-speaking' nations of the United States and the British Commonwealth.

Thus the 1940 shift from France to America proved for Britain a definitive one. This should not imply that there were no countervailing tendencies. The belief in Anglo-French cooperation which surfaced in 1939–40 was nurtured within the Foreign Office and won support from the Labour Foreign Secretary, Ernest Bevin, after 1945. In March 1947 the British offered the French a military guarantee against Germany in the Treaty of Dunkirk, and the Brussels Treaty of March 1948, involving Britain, France, and Benelux, was more than a mere military alliance and included plans for economic, cultural, and social

[74] Cf. Timothy P. Ireland, *Creating the Entangling Alliance: the Origins of the North Atlantic Treaty Organisation* (London, 1981).

[75] See the essays in Raymond Poidevin, ed., *Histoire de debuts de la construction européenne* (Brussels, 1986).

coordination reminiscent of early 1940.[76] But all this occurred at a time when relations with Russia were deteriorating rapidly, and when American willingness to support Europe was far from clear. By mid-1948, with the Marshall Plan, the Berlin blockade, and negotiations for a North Atlantic Treaty, the American attitude seemed very different. Moreover, even the most francophile of British policy-makers had become disenchanted with France's class conflict and endemic political instability—eight ministries in four years between 1947 and 1951. In January 1949 a Whitehall interdepartmental committee in effect reiterated the 'lessons' of 1940: 'Our policy should be to assist Europe to recover as far as we can...But the concept must be one of limited liability. In no circumstances must we assist them beyond the point at which the assistance leaves us too weak to be a worthwhile ally for U.S.A. if Europe collapses.' The main British object was 'a special relationship with the U.S.A. and Canada...for in the last resort we cannot rely upon the European countries'.[77] These 'gut' feelings, nurtured by 1940, have informed British attitudes to European integration ever since. (It would be interesting-to-know the reactions of a 14-year-old Grantham schoolgirl to the fall of France.)[78]

Finally, the global crisis unleashed by the Nazi victories had its own longer-term implications. Japan seized the opportunities opened up in 1940 and its astonishing victories in the winter of 1941–2, particularly the British surrender of Singapore, left an indelible impression in Asia. 'The British Empire in the Far East depended on prestige', observed the Australian Minister to China in May 1942. 'This prestige has been completely shattered.'[79] An Asiatic power had humiliated the Europeans, and the image of the white man in Asia would never be the same again. Of course, 1945 did not mark the end of the empire. The Europeans returned to most of their Asian colonies, and recent work has shown how, in the case of Britain, the war led to a new effort to organize colonial society and develop its resources.[80] But the very act of mobilization helped create forces—political, economic, and social—that could not always be directed by the colonial government: as the British discovered in India or Egypt.[81]

[76] John W. Young, *Britain, France and the Unity of Europe, 1945–1951* (Leicester, 1984).

[77] Memo on meeting of 5 Jan. 1949, printed in Sir Richard Clarke, *Anglo-American Economic Collaboration in War and Peace, 1942–1949*, ed. Sir Alec Cairncross (Oxford, 1982), 208–9.

[78] For what it is worth as indirect evidence, Margaret Thatcher's revered father observed in 1942 that France was 'corrupt from top to bottom': Hugo Young, *One of Us: a Biography of Margaret Thatcher* (London, 1989), 9. Cf. the speech by Enoch Powell in Liverpool on 5 Jan. 1990: 'Where were the European unity merchants in 1940? I will tell you. They were either writhing under hideous oppression or they were aiding and abetting that oppression. Lucky for Europe that Britain was alone in 1940': *Independent*, 6 Jan. 1990, p.3.   [79] Thorne, *Far Eastern War*, 161–2.

[80] Cf. John Gallagher, *The Decline, Rise and Fall of the British Empire*, ed. Anil Seal (Cambridge, 1982); John Darwin, *Britain and Decolonisation: the Retreat from Empire in the Postwar World* (London, 1988), chs. 2–4.

[81] R. F. Holland, *European Decolonization, 1918–1981: an Introductory Survey* (London, 1985), ch. 2.

Thus one can say that, both in aspirations and capacity, the war hastened the rise of viable anti-colonial nationalist movements, be it in India or Malaya, in the Dutch East Indies or in French Indo-China. The increasingly bitter colonial struggles also interacted with the growing superpower rivalry. America and Russia, with their enhanced power and new sense of ideological mission, moved to fill the vacuums created by the contraction of Europe, treating almost every area of the world as pieces in a zero-sum game. For a generation the Cold War had a global dimension until each superpower began to accept, through painfully learned lessons, particularly Vietnam and Afghanistan, that the world could not easily be shaped in its own image.

None of these developments was, of course, the inevitable consequence of 1940. In some respects the German victories in Europe helped accelerate trends that were already in progress. That would certainly be true of the rise of the superpowers and the global reaction to colonialism. In the movement towards European integration, however, one can make a stronger case for the impact of 1940. And in the case of Anglo-American relations, 1940 is very much a turning point. It is now appropriate to look more closely at the character and dynamics of the wartime alliance.

3

Churchill, Roosevelt, and the Wartime Anglo-American Alliance

The wartime alliance was Winston Churchill's creation. That is a statement about historiography as much as history. Churchill popularized the term 'Special Relationship' in his Fulton speech of 5 March 1946—an eloquent appeal for the USA to perpetuate the wartime Anglo-American alliance into the post-war era.[1] He also used his war memoirs, the six-volume history of *The Second World War* published between 1948 and 1954, in part to develop the same theme by laying 'the lessons of the past before the future'.[2]

In his memoirs Churchill depicted the wartime alliance as the outgrowth of an underlying cultural unity—the 'English-speaking peoples'. Between the world wars improvident leaders and indifferent publics in both countries had thrown away the hard-won victory. But, he argued, following his own accession to power in 1940 at a time when a 'warm-hearted friend' of Britain occupied the White House, a special relationship blossomed. This 'gradually became so close that the chief business between our two countries was virtually conducted by these personal interchanges between him and me. In this way our perfect understanding was gained.'[3] Throughout *The Second World War* Anglo-American relations generally appear in a roseate hue, with little evidence of suspicion or controversy. Indeed Churchill admitted to Eisenhower that the final volume, which appeared in 1954 when the two men headed their respective governments, had been carefully vetted by him to ensure 'that nothing should be published which might seem to others to threaten our current relations in our public duties or impair the sympathy and understanding which exists between our countries'.[4]

Originally presented as a paper at the Woodrow Wilson Center in Washington, DC, this chapter was published in Wm. Roger Louis and Hedley Bull, eds., *The 'Special Relationship': Anglo-American Relations since 1945* (Oxford: Clarendon Press, 1986).

[1] *Winston S. Churchill: His Complete Speeches, 1897–1963*, ed. Robert Rhodes James (8 vols., New York, l974), vi. 7289.

[2] Winston S. Churchill, *The Second World War* (6 vols., London, 1948–54), vol. i, p. vii.

[3] Ibid., ii. 22.

[4] Churchill to Eisenhower, 9 Apr. 1953, Presidential Papers, Whitman File, Box 16 (Dwight D. Eisenhower Library, Abilene, Kansas).

For a generation Sir Winston's interpretation of the Anglo-American relationship was definitive for statesmen, scholars, and publics on both sides of the Atlantic. Historians copied his broad picture even if they differed on details, colour, or tone. Since the 1970s, however, a very different image of the wartime alliance has emerged from the work of specialist scholars who have burrowed into the newly opened archives in both countries. It is in fact a double image, as suggested by the titles of some of their books: 'ambiguous partnership', 'competitive co-operation', 'allies of a kind'.[5] Set against the celebrated story of common cause against the Axis—Lend-Lease, the Battle of the Atlantic, and Operation Overlord—is the more chequered Anglo-American relationship in the Pacific and Middle East. Attention has also been paid to less familiar aspects of the war, such as the negotiations over decolonization or economic policy, which sometimes reveal acrimonious rivalry for long-term position and advantage.

From this perspective the wartime alliance is seen as part of a longer and larger story, namely the decline of Britain and the rise of the United States as major world powers. While Britain sacrificed a quarter of her national wealth and suffered a fatal blow to her Asian empire, the war pulled America out of pro-longed depression, set off a boom in consumer as well as war production, and enabled her to extend her influence in the Pacific, East Asia, and the Middle East—areas where before she had frequently taken second place to Britain. World War II, then, marked a decisive moment in the shift of world power, and each government often formulated policy with one eye on the Axis and the other on its rival ally.

The theme of ambivalence has also been extended into studies of the Roosevelt–Churchill relationship. While not denying its intimacy or impor-tance, recent historians have noted the mutual suspicion that characterized its early stages when neither was sure of the other's fidelity. Later, as the alliance blossomed, it remained an unequal partnership—warmer on Churchill's side than Roosevelt's and reflecting, particularly as the war progressed, the imbal-anced bargaining power of the two nations. 'What do you want me to do—stand up and beg like Fala?' asked the premier at one particularly humiliating moment in 1944, likening himself to the president's dog.[6]

---

[5] Robert M. Hathaway, *Ambiguous Partnership: Britain and America, 1944–1947* (New York, 1981); David Reynolds, *The Creation of the Anglo-American Alliance, 1937–41: A Study in Competitive Co-operation* (London, 1981); Christopher Thorne, *Allies of a Kind: The United States, Great Britain and the War against Japan, 1941–1945* (London, 1978). For a similar approach see James R. Leutze, *Bargaining for Supremacy: Anglo-American Naval Relations, 1937–1941* (Chapel Hill, NC, 1977); Wm. Roger Louis, *Imperialism at Bay, 1941–1945: The United States and the Decolonization of the British Empire* (Oxford, 1977); Mark A. Stoler, *The Politics of the Second Front: American Military Planning and Diplomacy in Coalition Warfare, 1941–1943* (Westport, Conn., 1977).

[6] John M. Blum, *From the Morgenthau Diaries* (3 vols., Boston, 1959–67), iii. 373, during the Octagon conference at Quebec in Sept. 1944. See also Warren F. Kimball, ed., *Churchill and Roosevelt: The Complete Correspondence* (3 vols., Princeton, 1984).

Appreciation of the larger context in which both men operated has also led historians away from the Churchillian preoccupation with the two national leaders. As Lord Halifax once remarked, the Prime Minister was usually 'pretty bored with anything except the actual war',[7] and Roosevelt often got bored even with that. Neither kept close track of economic or imperial issues, and historians enquiring into these humdrum but vital aspects of the alliance have been forced to examine the government departments in Whitehall and Washington and to assess the ideas of middle-level civil servants such as Keynes, Harry White, and Harley Notter who often determined the agenda for transatlantic negotiation. This in turn has necessitated closer study of the policy-making élites in both countries.[8]

Such a divergence from the 'great man' theory of history, often informed by political science analyses of how bureaucracies function, highlights the difficulty of talking about governments pursuing unitary, coherent policies. This is particularly true of the United States, where the coordinating forces usually apparent in British decision-making were generally absent. The presence of a much higher proportion of 'outsiders' in senior American government posts, the lack of a cohesive Cabinet to formulate common policy or of a presidential secretariat to implement it—all these impeded clear decision-making even within the Executive. Add the greater formal powers of Congress over foreign affairs, the relative lack of party discipline, the operations of a multitude of organized lobbyists, and the unrestrained media attention (which led one frustrated British official to complain that in Washington 'you either do no business at all or you do it through the newspapers'[9])—and one has a political system in which it was far more difficult for Roosevelt than for Churchill to translate personal preference into national policy. Frequently American leaders were forced to have a 'public' and a 'private' policy on key issues—one for domestic consumption, the other for diplomatic negotiation—though the two could not always be kept from conflicting, as indicated by the Anglo-American row over Greece in December 1944.[10]

Not that US officials were above citing domestic pressures as a convenient justification for policies they themselves ardently supported—as Neville

---

[7] Halifax to Eden, 5 Jan. 1942, Hickleton Papers, A4.410.4.15 (Churchill College, Cambridge).

[8] Pioneered by D. C. Watt. See his *Personalities and Policies* (London, 1963) and *Succeeding John Bull: America in Britain's Place, 1900–1975* (Cambridge, 1984).

[9] Sir Frederick Phillips, quoted in David Reynolds, *Lord Lothian and Anglo-American Relations, 1939–1940* (Philadelphia, 1983), 52.

[10] On 5 Dec. 1944 the State Dept. issued a press release apparently critical of British intervention in Greece, much to London's fury. In fact, US policy-makers basically agreed with British policy in Greece, as long as it was discreet enough not to offend the US public. Their statement, hastily drafted, was an attempt to appease domestic opinion and remind the British of the need for prior consultation, but it struck a chord in the USA and precipitated sustained American media criticism of Britain, to which the British press replied in kind. See Hathaway, *Ambiguous Partnership*, ch. 6, and Lawrence S. Wittner, *American Intervention in Greece, 1943–1949* (New York, 1982), 22–6.

Chamberlain once observed, Congress was the 'Mr Jorkins' of American negotiators.[11] Nor was British policy-making immune from bureaucratic wrangling, or from domestic political pressures (over the Second Front or Imperial Preference). But even if Whitehall did not always run, as Lord Halifax once suggested, like a smooth passenger train in comparison with Washington's jolting freight train,[12] his contrast was broadly accurate. A good deal of Anglo-American friction, from the 'Destroyers-for-Bases' negotiations of 1940 to the abrupt termination of Lend-Lease in 1945, was attributable to the problem of managing the domestic politics of US foreign policy.

This is a reminder not to push the 'revisionist' interpretation of the alliance too far. Much of the acrimony stemmed from the intense, complex, highly public debate within which transatlantic negotiations were conducted. Diplomacy, after all, is the art of reconciling the inevitably divergent viewpoints of independent, sovereign states. The fact of eventual agreement on common, if compromise, policies is surely as important as the colourful disputes through which those agreements were often reached. That is one point to be emphasized in what follows. The other qualification to 'revisionism' is that we should not permit the story of America's rise and Britain's decline to become overstated. Like many long-range trends it does not always help us understand short- and medium-term events. Neither the closeness of the wartime alliance nor the growing American dominance within it are straightforward guides to the outcome of particular wartime negotiations, let alone to the nature of the relationship in the post-war period. A fuller understanding of the alliance requires analysis of its origins in 1939–41 and then a look at four of its most important facets—strategy, imperialism, economics, and post-war planning—often with a glance ahead into the Cold War era.

As emphasized in the previous chapter, the wartime alliance was the result of an unforeseen and unique crisis: the fall of France in May–June 1940.[13] Prior to that Anglo-American relations had been cool and distant. Chamberlain and his colleagues, disillusioned by the history of American isolationism since 1919, had little faith in the likelihood of speedy and substantial American help. Their appeasement diplomacy and Phoney War strategy were predicated on that assumption. The Prime Minister and some of his Conservative colleagues also feared that dependence on the United States would make Britain vulnerable to American economic pressure and to renewed 'Wilsonian' peacemaking. In the

[11] Chamberlain, memo, Sept. 1934, para. 11, Neville Chamberlain Papers, NC 8/I9/1 (Birmingham University Library). (Mr Jorkins figures briefly in Dickens's *David Copperfield* as the mild but unseen junior partner in the law firm of Spenlow and Jorkins, always cited by Mr Spenlow as a ruthless and obdurate taskmaster who prevented him from showing generosity to clients and staff.)

[12] Halifax to Eden, tel. 865, 21 Feb. 1944, Foreign Office Correspondence, FO 954/30B (TNA).

[13] This section summarizes the argument of Reynolds, *The Creation of the Anglo-American Alliance*.

United States the strength of domestic isolationist opinion and Franklin Roosevelt's own weakened political position ruled out an overtly interventionist policy. In any case FDR, though anxious to see Hitler contained, had no wish to become embroiled in another European war, and his policy was therefore to help Britain and France acquire the munitions they needed to deal with Hitler themselves. Thus, during the winter of 1939–40 neither country sought or expected a close association. In fact, British policy-makers were thinking of a long-term 'special relationship' with France rather than the United States.

All was transformed in 1940. That long, hot spring Hitler overran much of north and north-west Europe in a matter of weeks. Most devastating of all and completely unexpected, despite the outpouring of retrospective wisdom, was the abrupt collapse of France. Allied strategy of holding Germany by land, while strangling her by sea and bombarding her from the air, lay in ruins. Britain was left alone, bereft of significant allies, and her tiny army had abandoned much of its modern equipment on the continent. US assistance was therefore essential— for survival let alone victory—and Britain's new leader, Winston Churchill, deluged Roosevelt with impassioned pleas for munitions, ships, aircraft, raw materials, and even immediate American entry into the war. Yet Washington was not initially receptive. The immediate response to France's collapse was a panic-stricken concern for America's own defences. Even Roosevelt shared the wide-spread scepticism about whether Britain could survive alone—personal doubts and political considerations again pointing in the same direction. It was only after Congress had been bypassed, the Republicans squared, and the British cajoled into a hard bargain that Roosevelt agreed to the Destroyers-for-Bases deal in September 1940. The importance of this was more symbolic than real— neither side was to benefit tangibly for many months—and, despite the striking American gesture of support for Britain, it was not until the November presidential election was over and FDR had won an unprecedented third term that the embryonic alliance took shape.

Between January and March 1941 Roosevelt steered the Lend-Lease bill through a divided Congress. It was a testimony to his imagination and political skill—avoiding a new war debts tangle by offering munitions on terms to be decided later, and eliciting for the first time from Congress a clear commitment to his policy of 'material aid to the opponents of force'. Previously Churchill had entertained doubts about Roosevelt's sincerity and favoured a hard-bargaining approach to the United States involving periodic threats about the possibility of a compromise peace if US aid were not forthcoming. But the announcement of Lend-Lease and the visit of Roosevelt's confidant, Harry Hopkins, in January 1941 convinced him that FDR was indeed Britain's 'best friend'. From then on his tactic for the rest of 1941 was to minimize all peripheral differences with the United States and to provide Roosevelt with the diplomatic 'molasses' he needed to sweeten American opinion. Get America into the war—that was his pre-eminent objective. All else was secondary.

Churchill hoped that the Americans would be drawn in through incidents with German U-boats. From April 1941 FDR cautiously and incrementally extended the US Navy's patrolling operations in the Atlantic until, by September, the Americans were escorting Allied convoys across much of the ocean with instructions to shoot at any Axis vessels seen in the vicinity. Privately Roosevelt warned the British of the persistence of anti-war sentiment in Congress and encouraged Churchill to believe that he was trying to provoke an 'incident' that would take the issue of peace or war out of his hands. Historians disagree about Roosevelt's candour on this point: perhaps he was now anxious to get into the conflict, or perhaps he was just telling the British what they wanted to hear. He may have felt less pressured after the German invasion of Russia in June had relieved the threat to Britain and therefore to the United States. At any rate the situation remained uncertain in early December 1941. Periodic clashes between American and German vessels had led to loss of American lives but no *Lusitania*-style public outcry; American merchant ships were now free, after the close-fought repeal of parts of the Neutrality Act, to go to Britain and Russia, but FDR was not planning to move rapidly. The British were becoming progressively more disenchanted and impatient. But in the end the issue was decided in the Pacific and not the Atlantic.

The crisis of mid-1940 had left a vacuum in the Far East. The European colonial powers were unable to stand up to renewed Japanese pressure and the defence of their Asian interests necessarily devolved on the United States. The Americans had two major weapons at their disposal. One was the main American fleet, which since April 1940 FDR had kept at Pearl Harbor, some 2,000 miles from its West Coast bases. The other was Japan's reliance on raw materials ultimately controlled by the United States, particularly oil, and her supplies were restricted in late summer 1940. American policy was to deter Japan from further expansion while not provoking her into war, it being generally agreed in Washington that Germany was the major threat to American interests. That policy worked until mid-1941, but the German attack on Russia, which reduced the pressure in Europe, intensified the crisis in Asia because the Soviet Union was no longer able to threaten Japan. Again FDR hardened American policy, reinforcing the Philippines with heavy bombers and approving a further cut-back in oil supplies. But it seems that Washington 'hawks' transformed this into a full-scale embargo, thereby accelerating Japan's deadline for turning from diplomacy to war in search of its sphere of influence in East and South-East Asia.

During all this Britain had little say in American policy, yet she would suffer more from an Asian war. For the Americans, preoccupied by the Atlantic and suspicious of British imperialism, would not send their own main fleet west of Hawaii to protect Britain's Asian possessions. It was not until late October 1941 that the firmer American policy in the Atlantic permitted the Royal Navy to dispatch even a token force of capital ships to Singapore. In the end, however, the fundamental cause of the Far Eastern debacle was not the divergence of

Anglo-American interests, but a mutual underestimation of Japan. Though expecting war in South-East Asia by December 1941, virtually no one in London or Washington predicted the vehemence and scope of Japan's onslaught. The attack on Pearl Harbor brought the United States into the war, but it was only the beginning of a sustained and brilliant series of Japanese combined operations across the western Pacific which in six months decimated Western forces and toppled the European empires. It also presented the newly consummated alliance with an unanticipated global crisis that was to confound Allied strategy for the rest of the war.

The broad outline of that strategic debate is familiar and easily summarized.[14] The basic principle in 1942 remained 'Germany First': contain Japan and concentrate on overcoming Hitler, after which Japan's defeat would follow. In April 1942 the two governments agreed on a build-up in Britain (Bolero) with a view to invading the continent in strength in 1943 (Roundup) or even on a small scale later in 1942 (Sledgehammer). After the British vetoed the latter operation, Roosevelt and Churchill revived the idea of invading Morocco and Algeria (Torch) and linking up with British forces from Egypt to drive the Axis out of Africa. Torch began in November 1942 and led on to the invasion of Sicily the following July and of the mainland of Italy in September 1943. But meanwhile the American-dominated Allied forces in the Pacific had regained the initiative from the Japanese whose expansion had been finally checked on the edge of India, the mid-Pacific, and Australasia in mid-1942. MacArthur's forces worked north from Australia, taking two grim years to recapture the Solomons and New Guinea, while Admiral Nimitz gradually won the Pacific islands west of Hawaii. With major theatres of operation in the Mediterranean and the Pacific, each devouring the output of the Allied arsenals, it was not until the summer of 1943, after intense argument, that the two governments firmly committed themselves to invading north-west Europe (Overlord) in the spring of 1944. Even then divergences over operations in Burma, the Balkans, and the south of France distracted from that effort, and once on the continent in June 1944 there were sharp disagreements about the extent, speed, and direction of the thrust into Germany. The Reich surrendered in May 1945, and the Americans, now on the periphery of the Japanese home islands and sceptical about the depth of Britain's commitment to the Pacific, rapidly transferred their forces to Asia. But the final bloody offensive was forestalled by Japan's surrender in August 1945, after belated Russian entry into the Pacific war and the dropping of the two atomic bombs.

---

[14] Basic official histories for the USA are Maurice Matloff and Edwin M. Snell, *Strategic Planning for Coalition Warfare, 1941–1942* (Washington, DC, 1953), and Maurice Matloff, *Strategic Planning for Coalition Warfare, 1943–1944* (Washington, DC, 1959); and, for the British, the series of *Grand Strategy* volumes under the general editorship of Sir James Butler (6 vols.; London, 1956–76). See also Michael Howard, *The Mediterranean Strategy in the Second World War* (London, 1968), and Stoler, *Politics of the Second Front*.

Why did the two governments find it difficult to concert their strategy? In part because each had a fundamentally different approach to winning the war, particularly in the European theatre. Extrapolating from the 'Germany First' principle, the American military planners wished to bring the Nazi forces to an early engagement on the continent. They, and especially General Marshall, the Army Chief of Staff, favoured a concentration in Britain as prelude to Roundup-Overlord and the avoidance of peripheral operations, notably in the Mediterranean, which would dissipate Allied resources. Behind such thinking lay the military traditions of the Civil War and America's abundance of manpower and resources. In contradistinction to the United States' classical strategy of applying overwhelming power to annihilate the enemy's forces, Britain favoured a more indirect approach. Relatively weak in manpower, but richly endowed with naval strength and global economic resources, British strategists had traditionally emphasized a war of seapower and blockade. This inclination was reinforced by memories of the Great War carnage and by the disasters of 1940 which made the prospect of a land victory on the Continent seem remote and Utopian. Better to wear the Axis down, concentrating on Hitler's weaker partner, Italy, and engaging in areas where Britain still had a foothold, notably North Africa, as a way of gradually 'closing the ring'. Underlying this strategy, and now often forgotten, was the assumption that the end would come through not the conquest but the collapse of Hitler's Reich. Bombing and blockade would help break the German war economy; peripheral operations on several fronts and aid to the European resistance movements would facilitate a political collapse. Late into the war the British still entertained hopes that the re-entry of Allied armies on to the Continent would be the *coup de grâce* rather than *guerre à outrance*.

Divergent national interests as well as differing strategies also help explain the conflict of policies. Undoubtedly US suspicions of Britain's imperial preoccupations were exaggerated: the British never had a coherent 'Mediterranean strategy' and Churchill's 1944 flirtations with operations in the Balkans and Aegean were frowned on by his own Chiefs of Staff. Nevertheless, the Middle East *was* an area of particular importance to Britain, commanding the sea route to India and access to vital oil fields, and undoubtedly this influenced strategic thinking in London. Moreover, at heady moments of success in Italy, such as the autumn of 1943 and mid-1944, British leaders did talk as if that was the crucial theatre. Similarly, Britain's emphasis on South-East Asia reflected her interest in recovering lost territory in Burma, Malaya, and above all Singapore, which Churchill described in 1944 as 'the supreme British objective in the whole of the Indian and Far Eastern theatres'.[15] His 1944 advocacy of major operations in Italy and in South-East Asia also owed something to a desire to assert Britain's independence and military prowess in an alliance increasingly dominated by

---

[15] Churchill to Chiefs of Staff, 12 Sept. 1944, Prime Minister's Operational Correspondence, PREM 3, 160/6 (TNA).

American power and propaganda. But the Americans, too, did not formulate strategy in a political vacuum. Nurtured on the idea of a special Sino-American relationship and burning to avenge the humiliation of Pearl Harbor, American planners made it clear that the Pacific and the subsequent Allied occupation of Japan were to be American shows. Despite American mythology *neither* government fought the war without considering its longer-term objectives.

These conflicts of national attitude and interest should not be overstated, however. Some of the rows were intra-national in character: the US Navy, for whom Japan had been the real enemy since 1919 and the war in Europe offered little scope for major naval operations, naturally fought the Army for greater resources in the Pacific; the deadlock over British strategy in South-East Asia in 1944 involved the Prime Minister and his Chiefs of Staff in 'perhaps their most serious disagreement of the war';[16] and British and American bomber commanders often joined forces against both their governments to secure priority for the strategic air offensive against Germany. Nor should one overstate Anglo-American differences in the conduct of warfare. As democracies, placing a high value on individual human life, neither government could contemplate the brutally profligate use of manpower characteristic of Stalin's Russia. In that sense both advocated the 'indirect' approach. Such concern for domestic opinion also played a decisive part in the details of strategy. With many Americans obsessed by Japan, and twenty to thirty per cent inclined towards a negotiated peace with Germany,[17] it is little wonder that FDR was adamant that he needed some kind of military operation in Europe in 1942 to keep 'Germany First' alive. He therefore backed Torch against his military advisers once Sledgehammer was abandoned. Nor should one underrate similar pressures on Churchill at this time for a Second Front to aid Russia and a victory for the persistently humiliated British army.

Though understandable, however, Torch was to cast its shadow over the rest of the war. As Marshall feared, it made a sustained diversion of resources into the Mediterranean inevitable, and the postponement of action in north-west Europe also strengthened the US Navy's argument to concentrate on the Pacific. Had resources been unlimited, conflicts of interest might not have arisen. But even the vast American arsenal could not prevent crucial logistical bottle-necks from emerging, notably in merchant shipping in 1942–3 and landing craft in 1943–4. With insufficient equipment to supply three major theatres and a dozen secondary ones, everyone could not be satisfied. By 1943 the 'Germany First' principle had been significantly eroded, and Marshall's 'strategy of concentration' was replaced by planning for 'a multi-front' war.[18]

[16] John Ehrman, *Grand Strategy*, v: *August 1943–September 1944* (London, 1956), 425.

[17] Richard W. Steele, 'American Popular Opinion and the War against Germany: The Issue of a Negotiated Peace, 1942', *Journal of American History*, 65 (1978), 704–23.

[18] Robert W. Coakley and Richard M. Leighton, *Global Logistics and Strategy, 1943–1945* (Washington, 1968), 798.

Yet Torch and its associated decisions were not entirely to 'blame'. After the fall of France, Germany could not be defeated in the manner of the Great War. After the disasters of the winter of 1941–2 Japan could not be put on the backburner to the extent envisaged before Pearl Harbor. Those who argue that VE Day could have occurred much earlier[19] must ponder not just the intricacy of alliance politics but also the ramifications of global war.

As we have seen, strategic debates were bedevilled by Americans' historic suspicions of the British empire. SEAC (the South-East Asian Command), for instance, was quickly glossed by Americans as 'Save England's Asian Colonies'. Such suspicions were part of an American's birthright, and they were not unwarranted, but, as British policy-makers liked to observe, they went with an ignorance of some colonial realities and also a tendency to assume that the American model was universal in its applicability. A case in point was Secretary of State Cordell Hull's claim that the United States' relationship with the Philippines was 'a perfect example of how a nation should treat a colony or dependency'.[20] Even more profound, however, was the blindness on both sides, perpetuated in some historical writing on the subject, about the complex methods by which great powers influence underdeveloped clients. American sanctimoniousness about imperialism reflected the fact that, apart from the aberration of the Spanish-American war, it had generally eschewed formal rule in overseas dependent territories. By contrast its twentieth-century expansion generally followed 'informal' methods of commercial and financial penetration, most notably in Latin America. Historically this had also been the preferred method of British expansion, particularly in the Victorian era: 'informally if possible, formally if necessary',[21] Egypt being an excellent example. Nevertheless, formal empire-building had been a feature of British policy in the late nineteenth century in Africa and again in the Middle East after World War I, and in general Britain's network of global influence relied much more than America's on direct rule.

As 'informal imperialists' the Roosevelt Administration mounted a sustained and high-sounding challenge in World War II to Europe's formal empires. The Atlantic Charter of August 1941 had been mainly directed towards the European war, but its rhetoric about self-determination was quickly appropriated by American policy-makers for use against colonialism in general. FDR talked about putting all colonies under international trusteeship, while the State Department, though gradualist, tried repeatedly to tie the British to firm

---

[19] e.g. Walter S. Dunn, Jr., *Second Front Now—1943* (University, Ala., 1980); John Grigg, *1943: The Victory that Never Was* (London, 1980).

[20] Cordell Hull to William Phillips, 18 Nov. 1942, Hull Papers, Box 50 (Library of Congress, Washington, DC).

[21] John Gallagher, *The Decline, Revival and Fall of the British Empire*, ed. Anil Seal (Cambridge, 1982), 99.

timetables for independence. The most intense intervention came in India in the spring of 1942. Churchill, a bitter opponent of the 1935 Act extending self-government, wanted to postpone any further transfer of power. But American pressure, combined with the military threat from Japan and demands from within his own Cabinet, necessitated the Cripps mission to negotiate a programme of immediate Indianization and Dominion status promptly after the war. Roosevelt took a personal interest, pressing his own proposals and trying to prevent a breakdown, and in the end only a veiled threat of resignation from Churchill made him desist.[22]

In 1942–3 the American challenge to empire was acute, as the Cripps mission and the July 1943 Declaration on the Colonies attest. But the British were able to ride out the storm. In part they did so through creating several regional consultative commissions on the model of the one proposed by the 1943 Declaration, through which the Americans could be involved in colonial reform and development (and in its financing) without having a significant say. In part, too, they funded development and welfare projects of their own, notably through the 1945 Act under which the Foreign and Colonial Offices prised £120 million from the habitually tight-fisted Treasury. But, in addition to appeasing the Americans by limited concessions, the British also benefited from the fact that the Administration's policy shifted in the last year of war. The Joint Chiefs of Staff (JCS), and especially the Navy, had never liked the trusteeship idea. They were adamant that the United States needed to acquire selected territory of its own—notably the mid-Pacific islands formerly under Japanese control, which would provide a valuable network of sea and air bases for civil and military purposes after the war. Talk of general trusteeship would also complicate relations with Russia, now wooed as an ally in the Pacific war, and would make America's continued possession of Puerto Rico and the Virgin Islands a little difficult to justify. With Roosevelt's backing, therefore, the JCS whittled down the State Department's proposals so that UN trusteeship was simply applied to existing League of Nations mandates and captured enemy territory. Although at Yalta Churchill pontificated, Hong Kong, the Gambia, and other British dependencies were no longer in danger. And after the Prime Minister's warning in 1942 and the ebbing of the Japanese tide, India was never again a crisis issue in Anglo-American relations.[23]

This was, nevertheless, a pyrrhic victory. Two years after Yalta the British were surrendering their troubled mandate in Palestine and preparing to evacuate the

[22] Churchill told Hopkins that 'I could not be responsible for a policy which would throw the whole sub-continent of India into utter confusion while the Japanese invader is at its gate' and that while 'I should personally make no objection at all to retiring into private life' Cabinet and Parliament would take the same view of the matter. Draft tel. to Roosevelt, 12 Apr. 1942, communicated verbally to Hopkins, PREM 4, 48/9 (TNA). On Churchill and India see Thorne, *Allies*; Gary R. Hess, *America Encounters India, 1941–1947* (Baltimore, 1971); and Raymond Callahan, *Churchill: Retreat from Empire* (Wilmington, Del., 1984).   [23] See Louis, *Imperialism at Bay*.

Indian subcontinent, the historic heart of empire. Decolonization resulted not only from indigenous nationalist pressures, often accentuated by Japan's humiliation of white power in the Pacific war, but also from the impact of the whole conflict in undermining the economic foundations of Britain's global power. Since the beginning of the century 'invisible earnings' from shipping, financial services, and foreign assets had balanced Britain's chronic trade deficit. But World War II necessitated a massive programme of external disinvestment, particularly in Latin America, India, and South-East Asia. The flow of invisible earnings abated and former clients were transformed into creditor nations able to buy out British properties. Their willingness to hold their credits as sterling balances in London helped preserve the reserve currency status of sterling, but the costs of global commitments became increasingly difficult to sustain. Often the Americans were the main beneficiaries. The United States supplanted Britain as the dominant Western influence in Saudi Arabia and China, and the Pacific crisis of 1941–2 enabled them to draw Australia and New Zealand into the American defence orbit. Whatever he might assert to the contrary, Churchill *had* presided over a turning-point in the liquidation of the British Empire.

But the picture of an ailing imperial giant overwhelmed by the inexorable tide of decolonization and progress is too simple.[24] For one thing, that was not how British leaders saw the situation. In May 1947 Foreign Secretary Ernest Bevin stated categorically that 'His Majesty's Government do not accept the view... that we have ceased to be a great Power.'[25] They remained determined to hold on to their global position, particularly by less burdensome, informal means. They still hoped, for instance, to utilize the manpower and resources of India—the real disaster in their view was not independence but partition—and the recession of British power in South Asia was counterbalanced by determined programmes of resource development in Britain's African territories.[26] Likewise, despite the loss of Palestine, the search for viable alternative centres of British military power in the Middle East continued in Iraq, Libya, and Egypt.

Of course there was self-delusion aplenty here, but it should not obscure the fact that until the 1960s Britain *did* remain a truly global power. Moreover, that fact was not regarded with unequivocal distaste by the Americans, who still felt ambivalent about Britain's formal empire. Though they often regarded it as the epitome of dated Old World imperialism, it also included bases and natural

[24] As is emphasized by Gallagher, *Decline, Revival and Fall of the British Empire*, 73–153; also R. F. Holland, 'The Imperial Factor in British Strategies from Attlee to Macmillan, 1945–63', *Journal of Imperial and Commonwealth History*, 12 (1984), 165–86.

[25] *Parliamentary Debates* (Commons), 16 May 1947, col. 1965.

[26] On Africa see the important debate in Wm. Roger Louis and Ronald Robinson, 'The United States and the Liquidation of the British Empire in Tropical Africa, 1941–1951', in Prosser Gifford and Wm. Roger Louis, *The Transfer of Power in Africa: Decolonization, 1940–1960* (New Haven, 1982), 31–55; John Flint, 'Planned Decolonization and its Failure in British Africa', *African Affairs*, 82 (1983), 389–411; and Robert Pearce, 'The Colonial Office and Planned Decolonization in Africa', ibid., 83 (1984), 77–93.

resources of inestimable value in containing common enemies. Roosevelt had acknowledged this in the battle against the Axis; Truman took the same line as he sought to contain communism. We shall not appreciate the intricacies of the post-war Anglo-American relationship unless we remember that Britain's role as a world power did not end in 1945, and that this role was regarded by the United States as a blessing as well as a curse.

Economic wealth was the basis of global power and the foundation of grand strategy. Allied victory in the war owed much to the successful mobilization and deployment by the British Empire and the United States of their combined resources. In 1939 the two of them accounted for about sixty per cent of the world's industrial production and controlled roughly three-quarters of its mineral wealth. But the Axis victories of 1940–2 revolutionized the situation, giving them dominion over a third of the population and mineral resources of the globe.[27] In 1942 the British and Americans developed a network of combined committees to handle the economic prosecution of the war. Based in Washington—a sign of where ultimate power lay—and by no means immune from internecine conflicts, these were nevertheless a signal advance on the grudging cooperation of World War I and an unusual instance of inter-allied partnership.

Using their superiority in resources and shipping, Britain and America were able to reconstruct the blockade, shattered in 1940. In particular the USA gradually brought much of Latin America within the Allied orbit, satisfying her own deficiencies in tin and ferro-alloys and denying the Axis crucial supplies such as Chilean copper. On occasions, of course, the operation of the blockade provoked serious Anglo-American disagreement. The case of Argentina proved particularly vexatious in 1944. The State Department considered the Peronist Farrell government to be pro-Nazi and hoped to topple it through a comprehensive trade embargo. The British—having considerable economic interests in the country, needing Argentine beef and wheat, and viewing the regime as nationalist not fascist—wished to sign a long-term meat contract. The issue reached the Roosevelt–Churchill level, and only the retirement of Hull and the imminent end of war facilitated a compromise solution.[28]

Behind the disputes about blockade policy, which mirrored similar arguments about how to treat Franco's Spain, lay a sensitivity to post-war national economic interests, for Argentina was one of the remaining countries of dominant British influence in a Western hemisphere increasingly under US economic control. The

---

[27] Alfred E. Eckes, Jr., *The United States and the Global Struggle for Minerals* (Austin, Tex., 1979), 75, 84.

[28] See Randall B. Woods, *The Roosevelt Foreign Policy Establishment and the 'Good Neighbor'* (Lawrence, Kan.,1979); C. A. MacDonald, 'The Politics of Intervention: The United States and Argentina, 1941–1946', *Journal of Latin American History*, 12 (1980), 365–96; R. A. Humphreys, *Latin America and the Second World War* (2 vols., London, 1981–2), ii, chs. 6–7.

European war had once again enabled the New World to 'fatten on the follies of the Old',[29] and the argument over Argentina was paralleled by similar disputes over commodity agreements, merchant shipping, and commercial aviation.

A good instance of the underlying economic rivalry and of how it was handled diplomatically is the case of Middle Eastern oil.[30] The British had established a dominant position in Iran and Iraq after World War I, but the United States had secured concessions in Saudi Arabia in the 1930s and, as concern mounted in 1943 about declining US oil reserves, so did the rivalry and suspicion between British and American oil companies in which both governments became involved. But their fears proved exaggerated and the two sides found it desirable and possible to reach an agreement, concluded in August 1944. This would expedite the orderly development of Middle Eastern reserves, now vital for the post-war international economy, with mutual respect for each country's concessions and recognition of the potential importance of oil sales for easing Britain's peacetime payments problems. In the event, well-orchestrated opposition from smaller American companies ensured that this agreement was never ratified by Congress—another reminder of the unmanageable domestic politics of US foreign policy. But the fact of the agreement is nevertheless significant. Vociferous rivalry, exaggerated suspicions, eventual compromise that was mutually beneficial but usually closer to American than British goals—this was the general pattern for wartime economic disputes. In most cases, too, it was essentially an Anglo-American framework which was imposed on the other powers.

The most striking example of this pattern derives from the protracted transatlantic discussions about the post-war economic order. In the Depression the multilateral economy had disintegrated into several loose economic blocs, each pegged to a major currency and trading largely within itself. Britain's grouping coalesced around the sterling area and the system of Imperial Preference, established in 1932, which discriminated against imports from outside the British Empire. To parts of the Conservative party and some in the Treasury and Bank of England, this seemed to be a viable long-term policy for promoting British commerce and safeguarding the position of the City in international finance. And even non-ideologues in Whitehall generally believed in 1941–2 that retention of trade and currency controls would be essential, at least temporarily, for Britain's post-war recovery.

---

[29] Merrill D. Peterson, *Thomas Jefferson and the New Nation* (Oxford, 1970), 416, quoting a memo by Jefferson dated 12 July 1790.

[30] Phillip J. Baram, *The Department of State in the Middle East, 1919–1945* (Philadelphia, 1978); Michael B. Stoff, *Oil, War, and American Security: The Search for a National Policy on Foreign Oil, 1941–1947* (New Haven, 1980); Irvine H. Anderson, *Aramco, the United States and Saudi Arabia: A Study of the Dynamics of Foreign Oil Policy, 1933–1950* (Princeton, 1981); John A. DeNovo, 'The Culbertson Economic Mission and Anglo-American Tensions in the Middle East, 1944–1945', *Journal of American History*, 63 (1977), 913–36.

During the 1930s, however, the Roosevelt Administration had repented of its initial economic nationalism, dedicating itself to the re-creation of a multilateral world economy. Henry Morgenthau and the Treasury wanted an early return to convertible currencies and stable exchange rates, while Hull's State Department concentrated on the commercial impediments to multilateralism, with Britain's network of preferential tariffs and quotas at the top of their list. Little was achieved in the 1930s, despite the 1938 Trade Agreement, but real opportunities came with Britain's wartime dependence on the United States.

After prolonged negotiations in 1941–2 the State Department secured a general (and not unambiguous) commitment that part of the repayment for Lend-Lease would be an end to British economic discrimination. Similarly, in 1943–4 London's approval of the largely American drafts for the International Monetary Fund and the World Bank reflected her need to secure the continuation of Lend-Lease after Germany's defeat. And at the end of 1945 Britain's ratification of the Bretton Woods agreements and her commitment to sterling convertibility by 1947 was extracted from a resentful Parliament only because the abrupt termination of Lend-Lease that August (again in response to US domestic pressures) left the UK reliant upon an American loan tied to this ratification.

As one US Treasury official predicted in 1940, in the last analysis the British could only 'stand and deliver' when pressed by the United States.[31] It is also undoubtedly true, as British officials grumbled, that the American conversion to Cobdenite values conveniently fitted the interests of a country able to dominate an open, global market economy. But it would be wrong to depict the Americans as international highwaymen, or the British merely as spiritual descendants of Lord North. For, like Cobden, the Roosevelt Administration believed that thriving world commerce was a vital precondition of peace (and one fatally neglected in 1919). Equally, the majority of British policy-makers favoured a return to multilateralism, *if the terms were right*. This meant the United States should belatedly accept its own responsibilities as the world's leading creditor and a major importing nation. Specifically America should promote international liquidity through gold and dollar loans and reduce its own tariff barriers. In the United States Treasury these obligations were acknowledged in principle. Here, then, was the basis of agreement.

Admittedly the balance of power in the alliance ensured that America's was the decisive voice. Harry White's draft for a fixed-size stabilization fund was adopted as the working basis for negotiation, rather than Keynes's broader idea of an international clearing bank with larger assets and controls over creditor as well as debtor nations. The British were also uneasy at US dominance over the new institutions and their location in Washington. But all this was secondary in

---

[31] Butterworth to Morgenthau, 13 Dec. 1940, Henry Morgenthau, Jr., Diary, 339: 401 (Franklin D. Roosevelt Library, Hyde Park, NY).

the minds of most British policy-makers, haunted by 1919 and 1931, to the fact that the United States had finally committed itself to a policy of economic internationalism through which the world might return to multilateralism *without* exchange fluctuations, payments deficits, and domestic deflation. It was agreement on American terms, but offering real benefits to Britain. And, despite Administration efforts to avoid any hint of a 'Special Relationship', it was essentially a blueprint devised by Washington and London and then imposed by them on everyone else.[32]

But we cannot end this story of conflict and compromise in 1945 with the triumph of multilateralism and the creation of the International Monetary Fund and the World Bank. For the multilateral, one-world economy was still-born. The Soviets abstained, Europe was partitioned. After the abortive British experiment in 1947 even limited currency convertibility was not achieved until 1958, and the Americans encouraged western Europe to form its own economic bloc in the interests of security and containment. Under the circumstances it was the American Government and not the IMF or World Bank which assumed the main responsibility for promoting liquidity and reconstruction within 'the free world' through relief loans, Marshall Aid, and overseas military spending. These issues lie beyond the purview of this chapter. But they remind us again that the significance of the wartime alliance can only be fully evaluated if we look beyond 1945.

In contrast to their equivocations about economic cooperation with the United States, British leaders emerged from the crisis of 1940–1 convinced that sustained American support was essential to secure long-term political stability. This time the United States must involve itself in peace-keeping as well as peace-making, working in close concert with Britain in diplomacy and military policy. Although Lord Halifax in 1940 had predicted a future 'special association' with America (see above p. 30), it was Churchill who adapted and adopted the term as official policy in 1943–4. Nothing should prejudice 'the natural Anglo-American special relationship', he instructed post-war planners in September 1943. The following February he told the Foreign Office: 'It is my deepest conviction that unless Britain and the United States are joined in a special relationship, including Combined Staff organization and a wide measure of reciprocity in the use of bases—all within the ambit of a world organization—another destructive war will come to pass.'[33]

But could such a relationship be achieved? One fear was that the 'betrayal' of 1919–20 would be repeated. Republican and isolationist gains in the 1942

[32] See Richard N. Gardner, *Sterling–Dollar Diplomacy in Current Perspective* (3rd edn., New York, 1980); Alfred E. Eckes, Jr., *A Search for Solvency: Bretton Woods and the International Monetary System, 1941–1971* (Austin, Tex., 1975); Armand Van Dormael, *Bretton Woods: Birth of a Monetary System* (London, 1978); Sir Richard Clarke, *Anglo-American Economic Collaboration in War and Peace, 1942–1949*, ed. Sir Alec Cairncross (Oxford, 1982).

[33] Churchill to Attlee and Eden, 14 Sept. 1943, copied in FO 954/22A, p. 197; Churchill to Richard Law, 16 Feb. 1944, PREM 4, 27/10 (TNA).

mid-term elections appalled British leaders, spurring them to seek agreement on the fundamentals of the post-war order while they still had a basically well-disposed administration in power. And in the Foreign Office some, including Eden, counselled against placing all Britain's eggs in the American basket, calling for closer economic and defence cooperation with western Europe. Nevertheless, even the sceptics agreed that they must try their best to construct a durable Anglo-American partnership.

The other and opposite fear was whether Britain would be swamped in such a relationship. This was a nagging anxiety, but British leaders remained basically optimistic. Victorians and Edwardians, they thought not of Britain the island but Britain the centre of a vast empire, and they still expected to draw on manpower and resources not far short of America's or Russia's. They also comforted themselves with the idea that, although increasingly dwarfed by American power, they still possessed superior skill and experience which would allow them to manage the immature young giant. Eden likened the UK–US relationship to that of Austria with Britain after 1815.[34] Harold Macmillan, in what proved a more popular analogy, invoked classical precedent to explain his conception of the British role in Eisenhower's Allied Force Headquarters (AFHQ) in North Africa. Expansively he told one subordinate:

We, my dear Crossman, are Greeks in this American empire. You will find the Americans much as the Greeks found the Romans—great big, vulgar, bustling people, more vigorous than we are and also more idle, with more unspoiled virtues but also more corrupt. We must run A.F.H.Q. as the Greek slaves ran the operations of the Emperor Claudius.[35]

This concept of an Anglo-American 'Special Relationship' was, however, a largely British invention. It never had the same currency in Washington, let alone among the American public for whom wartime cooperation was counterbalanced by the Revolutionary tradition, ethnic pluralism, and a strident, hypersensitive nationalism. The State Department dedicated itself to creating the United Nations Organization and to ensuring, through a vast public relations campaign, that this time Americans accepted the gospel of idealistic internationalism. Power politics, spheres of influence, and formal alliances were all *passé*—at least for public consumption. Privately FDR himself had little faith in international bodies: their efficacy would depend, he believed, upon cooperation among the great powers in keeping the peace. That was closer to the British position, but by 1943 Roosevelt's world 'policemen' included China and Russia as well as Britain and the USA. China was seen by FDR as a future power and, more immediately, as an American client—a 'faggot vote' in Churchill's contemptuous phrase. And Roosevelt's wooing of Stalin from mid-1943—when it was clear that Russia would survive and would have much to say about the peace

[34] James V. Forrestal Diary, 21 Apr. 1945 (Naval Historical Center, Washington Navy Yard).
[35] Richard Crossman, 'The Making of Macmillan', *Sunday Telegraph*, 9 Feb. 1964, p. 4.

settlement—was particularly alarming to Churchill. The 'Special Relationship' seemed in danger of becoming an eternal triangle. At Teheran and Yalta Roosevelt sedulously avoided the appearance of an Anglo-American front and went out of his way to consult Stalin *à deux*.

Nevertheless, the Anglo-American partnership *was* in a class of its own among wartime alliances, as a glance at two of its facets makes clear. In intelligence matters London and Washington began sharing evaluations in 1940–1, and after American entry into the war an extensive and generally unfettered network of collaboration developed, despite some friction between the Office of Strategic Services and the Secret Intelligence Service. Nothing comparable was achieved or envisaged with the Soviet Union: the Russians distrusted even gratuitous information and by late 1942 the best Western intelligence on the state of Soviet forces came through German intercepts and not information from Moscow.[36]

A similar, though more chequered, partnership blossomed in atomic weapons research. Britain had pioneered this work in the late 1930s, but in 1940–1 the two programmes were pooled and development went ahead in the United States. In 1942–3, as American dominance became apparent, some of FDR's atomic administrators tried to exclude the British, but Churchill resisted and the agreement with Roosevelt at Hyde Park, NY, in September 1944 committed the two countries to continued collaboration in both the military and commercial fields after the war. In all this Britain was increasingly the junior, but she remained a partner. By contrast Roosevelt deliberately held back from offering atomic secrets to Russia, perhaps viewing these as a possible bargaining counter in future diplomatic negotiations.[37]

Indeed, with regard to Russia, both British and American leaders shared fundamentally similar attitudes, and we should not allow Republican 'Yalta mythology' or Churchill's reminiscences, both the product of the Cold War, to obscure this fact. For much of the war Roosevelt and Churchill were primarily concerned to ensure that the Soviet Union, bearing the brunt of the fighting until mid-1944, did not succumb or sign a compromise peace. That was far from certain until the summer of 1943. Even then, Russian support was still essential: Roosevelt was anxious to bring them into the war against Japan and both leaders, fearful of a resurgent Germany, desired continued Big Three cooperation after the war.

In the summer of 1944, as the Russian armies swept west and south into Poland and the Balkans, Churchill became more alarmed about Soviet intentions. The result was not confrontation, however, but a spheres-of-influence

[36] F. H. Hinsley et al., *British Intelligence in the Second World War* (3 vols., London, 1979–84), esp. i. 311–14; ii. 41–66; iii, pt. I, pp. 459–75.

[37] Margaret Gowing, *Britain and Atomic Energy, 1939–1945* (London, 1964); Martin J. Sherwin, *A World Destroyed: The Atomic Bomb and the Grand Alliance* (New York, 1973); Barton J. Bernstein, 'The Uneasy Alliance: Roosevelt, Churchill, and the Atomic Bomb, 1940–1945', *Western Political Quarterly*, 29 (1976), 202–30.

arrangement for South-East Europe, negotiated in Moscow in October. Roosevelt did not protest at this, although it smacked of the 'power politics' deprecated publicly by the State Department, and it was in essentially the same spirit that Roosevelt and Churchill negotiated at Yalta in February 1945. Having little alternative, they conceded Stalin's predominance in Eastern Europe, but the agreements on free elections and the Declaration on Liberated Europe were intended to prevent a Russian sphere of influence becoming a closed Soviet bloc. In his last months the President was determined to hold Stalin to the Yalta accords, without causing unnecessary friction, and Churchill's urgent telegrams to Truman during the spring were not the prelude to Cold War but a demand that the two Western allies try to negotiate their differences with Russia before troop withdrawals sapped their bargaining power.[38]

This gradual convergence of British and American policy into a firm (if still irenic) approach towards the Soviet Union may seem to take us neatly into the beginnings of the Cold War era. But once again it is misleading to extrapolate from the Anglo-American relationship in 1945. For one thing this disintegrated rapidly immediately the war ended. Though the dominant world power, committed unlike in 1919 to upholding the new international order, the United States nevertheless withdrew from Europe to some degree once hostilities ceased. (Roosevelt had predicted as much in 1943–4.[39]) The Truman Administration was intent on establishing its exclusive protectorate over Japan while Congress struggled to restrict overseas spending and to bring the boys home. Not until the economic crisis of 1947 did the United States intervene substantively in Europe, and in the interim Britain was the main adversary of the Soviet Union.

In 1947–8 the Truman Doctrine, the Marshall Plan, and the Berlin airlift all symbolized a new American commitment to Europe and it seemed as if the wartime alliance was being recreated. But appearances were deceptive. For most

---

[38] For discussions from various angles see Robert Dallek, *Franklin D. Roosevelt and American Foreign Policy, 1932–1945* (New York, 1979); Elisabeth Barker, *Churchill and Eden at War* (London, 1978); Eduard Mark, 'American Policy toward Eastern Europe and the Origins of the Cold War, 1941–1946: An Alternative Interpretation', *Journal of American History*, 66 (1981), 313–36; Warren F. Kimball, 'Naked Reverse Right: Roosevelt, Churchill, and Eastern Europe from TOLSTOY to Yalta—and a little beyond', *Diplomatic History*, 9 (1985), 1–24. See also Chapters 13–14.

[39] At Teheran in Nov. 1943 FDR spoke of a one- or two-year occupation of Germany—see *Foreign Relations of the United States [FRUS]: The Conference at Cairo and Tehran, 1943* (Washington, 1961), 256. The following February he told the State Dept.: 'I do not want the United States to have the post-war burden of reconstituting France, Italy and the Balkans. This is not our natural task at a distance of 3,500 miles or more. It is definitely a British task in which the British are far more vitally interested than we are.' Roosevelt to Acting Secretary, 21 Feb. 1944, State Dept. Records, 740.00119 Control (Germany)/2–2144 (National Archives, Washington, RG 59). In Dec. 1944 the President, in conversation with one British diplomat, 'spoke of a United States withdrawal from Europe with a genial kind of fatalism which was somewhat depressing'. (Richard Law, memo, 22 Dec. 1944, Foreign Office General Political Correspondence, FO 371/44595, AN 154/32/45, TNA.) And at Yalta on 5 Feb. 1945 he reiterated 'that he did not believe that American troops would stay in Europe much more than two years'. See *FRUS: The Conferences at Malta and Yalta, 1945* (Washington, 1955), 617.

of the war continental Europe had been under enemy control: the United States and Britain were the only surviving Western democracies and their relationship constituted a main axis of international politics. By the late 1940s, however, France was a significant actor again, and increasingly America's designated partner in the transatlantic alliance was not Britain alone but Western Europe which the US hoped would be under British leadership. Thus, after the mid-40s hiatus a new *Atlantic* alliance had been created of which the Anglo-American axis was only a part. Again the wartime alliance does not point us simply into the Cold War era.

The wartime alliance was neither natural nor inevitable, but the consequence of the unexpected global emergency of 1940–1. It was a marriage of necessity, uniting two major states whose recent history had been one of peaceful rivalry. That rivalry subsisted even during the crisis of global war, and arguments about grand strategy, decolonization, economic blocs, and post-war security all reflected the larger divergence of national interests and ideals. Apart from the profits of direct wartime competition, for example in the Middle East or Latin America, the USA also benefited from the destruction of much of Britain's trading base: exports cut by 40 per cent, shipping by 30 per cent, £4.2 billion external disinvestment.[40] And the war brought the United States near the zenith of her world power, with territory in the Pacific and a dominant influence in East Asia, as well as a monopoly of atomic weapons.

The growing disparity between the two powers was not, however, always reflected in the outcome of specific wartime arguments. In 1940–1 America's war effort had scarcely got going, yet Britain was her suitor because of the desperate international crisis. By 1942 the United States was a co-belligerent and her war industries were in full swing, yet the relationship was at its most equal, and in grand strategy, for instance, the British largely called the tune. In the last year of the war America was the dominant partner, militarily and economically, and she used her leverage to obtain a post-war economic order on her own terms. Yet at the same time the American challenge to Britain's empire, presaged in bitter debates about colonialism, failed to materialize, and the two nations drew closer in their thinking on post-war security and on handling of the Soviet Union. Nevertheless, the broad trend was evident: the United States the dominant power, Britain weakened and increasingly dependent upon her. That was a leading theme of World War II.

Yet, although we can no longer see the wartime alliance in Churchillian terms, there is no denying its remarkable character. Instead of measuring it against the standards of international harmony proclaimed by Utopians or propagandists, we should take our criteria from the real world of alliance politics. No two sovereign states have identical interests; every joint endeavour involves prior

[40] W. K. Hancock and M. M. Cowing, *British War Economy* (London, rev. edn., 1975), 548.

debate and compromise; neither side is totally committed to the common cause but keeps a weather eye open for its own advantage. Accepting, then, that no alliance is perfect, we can acknowledge that this one was much less imperfect than most.

Anglo-American cooperation grew out of a sense of shared threat and mutual need. For Britain after the fall of France American aid was essential for survival, victory, and a stable peace. For disarmed America the British Isles and its fleet were initially the last bastion against Hitler and later the essential base for liberating the continent of Europe. Britain's empire, despite American disquiet, was generally supported as a vital supplier of Britain's needs (and also of some of America's own) as well as a bulwark against further Axis expansion. Similar ideals reinforced similar interests. Despite the legacies of the Revolution and mass immigration, the two countries shared a tradition of liberal, capitalist democracy, and this was all the more apparent in a world of totalitarian states glorifying violent change. Furthermore, the sense of common cause was accentuated by the shared language. Admittedly this had deleterious consequences, because it facilitated highly publicized arguments about the alliance among bureaucrats, soldiers, legislators, pressmen, and opinion leaders. But this was a sign that the relationship was unusually intense and extensive—involving more people and thus offering more scope for disagreement and misunderstanding. Anyone who doubts its remarkable, three-dimensional character should look at wartime alliances that tried to span a language barrier—Britain's with France, America's with China.

What were the legacies of this wartime cooperation? Firstly, it assisted in the reordering of international relations. The Nazi drive for hegemony was mastered. Germany was divided. And all three major Axis powers were democratized and integrated in a new international order directed by the United States along Anglo-American guidelines. The war, and the way it was fought, also facilitated the extension of Soviet power in Europe. Subsequent anxiety about Russian intentions prompted renewed Anglo-American cooperation in the late 1940s when the two countries played a decisive role in creating an Atlantic alliance that has lasted to the present day.

At an intellectual level the wartime alliance profoundly shaped foreign policy attitudes. In a way unimaginable to Neville Chamberlain it predisposed British leaders for a generation to think in terms of a 'Special Relationship' with the United States—not as the sole basis of British policy but as a principal element—and sometimes to romanticize the link. On the American side this was never the case, but the wartime experience did help ensure that, as America emerged to superpower status, her attention was directed primarily not towards the Pacific but Western Europe, with Britain as her main intermediary. For Americans, then, the intellectual legacy of the war was 'Atlanticism'—articulated by pro-Allied publicists in 1941, visualized in the cartographic revolution of the war, institutionalized in NATO in 1949. Atlanticism proved the dominant paradigm for a third of a century. Not until the 1980s was it seriously questioned, with talk of a 'successor generation', the shift in America's centre of gravity to the south and west, and closer US ties with Hispanic America and the Pacific basin.[41]

Finally, the alliance forged enduring and important personal relationships at all levels of the two countries' officialdoms. The contacts at the top, between men such as Macmillan, Eisenhower, Marshall, and Ismay are the most obvious, but connections lower down, among middle-ranking officials later to rise to policy-making positions in the 1950s and early 1960s, were perhaps more significant as well as wider-ranging. These personal links did not guarantee agreement—witness 1956—but they did provide a firm framework for diplomatic interchange, and in the case of intelligence at least there was continuous institutional cooperation through the post-war era.

Nevertheless, we should not treat the wartime alliance as an exact paradigm for what followed. For that alliance was abnormally close—the temporary response to a temporary world crisis. Most of the joint enterprises of the war did not survive its end: the Combined Chiefs of Staff, the other Anglo-American war-making boards, the atomic alliance (strangled by Truman and Congress in 1945–6). Most of the panaceas for the post-war order, concocted jointly though closer to American than British ideals, also fizzled out—One World, the UN, the new multilateral world economy. In part failure was attributable to unforeseen Cold War circumstances, but the formulae were also intrinsically flawed because they grew out of the unusually simple pattern of international relationships in 1940–2, when Britain and the USA were the only major Western democracies left and Russia's future remained uncertain. Through war the two nations were forced together, but in peacetime the scope and complexity of diplomacy increased again for both powers. To American policy-makers, relations with Russia and the reviving countries of western Europe assumed new importance; for the British, despite the seductions of the 'Special Relationship', traditional links with the Empire and the Continent once more had to be taken into account. And Britain was not yet finished as a world power.

The wartime Anglo-American relationship was probably the most remarkable alliance of modern history. No two countries have ever been so completely 'mixed up together ... for mutual and general advantage', to borrow Churchill's felicitous words from 1940.[42] Their cooperation helped reshape the international order at a particularly malleable time and, despite the post-war upheavals, it set durable patterns for future attitudes and institutions (as we shall see in Chapter 17). Yet the wartime relationship was also unusual because never again would the two countries be so closely matched in power and capability. After

---

[41] On cartography see Alan K. Henrikson, 'The Map as an "Idea": The Role of Cartographic Imagery during the Second World War', *American Cartographer*, 2 (1975), 19–53. Stephen F. Szabo, ed., *The Successor Generation: International Perspectives of Postwar Europeans* (London, 1982) is a good study.   [42] *Parliamentary Debates* (Commons), 20 Aug. 1940, col. 1171.

1945 Britain's decline became apparent, even though she remained a genuine world power into the 1960s. And never again would the two nations be thrown so completely upon each other. In the post-war world greater American power and the multiplicity of America's and Britain's peacetime interests meant that each mattered less to the other. In more senses than one, the wartime alliance was truly a 'special' relationship.[43]

---

[43] More recent discussions of the wartime relationship, appearing since this chapter was first published, include Alex Danchev, *Very Special Relationship: Field Marshal Sir John Dill and the Anglo-American Alliance, 1941–1944* (London, 1986); Randall B. Woods, *A Changing of the Guard: Anglo-American Relations, 1941–1946* (Chapel Hill, NC, 1990); Keith Sainsbury, *Churchill and Roosevelt at War: The War They Fought and the Peace They Hoped to Make* (London, 1994); Warren F. Kimball, *Forged in War: Roosevelt, Churchill and the Second World War* (New York, 1997); Mark A. Stoler, *Allies and Adversaries: The Joint Chiefs, the Grand Alliance, and U.S. Strategy in World War II* (Chapel Hill, NC, 2000); David Reynolds, *In Command of History: Churchill Fighting and Writing the Second World War* (London, 2004). The argument of the most iconoclastic works of revisionism, by John Charmley—*Churchill, The End of Glory: A Political Biography* (London, 1993), and *Churchill's Grand Alliance: The Anglo-American Special Relationship, 1940–1957* (London, 1995)—is addressed below, in Chapter 5.

II

CHURCHILL

4

Churchill and the British 'Decision' to Fight on in 1940

Right Policy, Wrong Reasons

The summer of 1940 has gone down in patriotic folklore as Britain's finest hour. After France had collapsed, the British people fought on alone but united, aroused by the miracle of Dunkirk, protected by the heroic RAF, inspired above all by Churchill's bulldog spirit—'victory at all costs', 'blood, toil, tears and sweat', 'we shall fight on the beaches... we shall never surrender'. It is a comforting story—one that is recalled with nostalgia in every national crisis—and its authority was enhanced by Churchill's own categorical statements in his war memoirs. There he wrote: 'Future generations may deem it noteworthy that the supreme question of whether we should fight on alone never found a place upon the War Cabinet agenda' nor was it 'even mentioned in our most private conclaves'. 'It was taken for granted', he assured his readers, that Britain would continue the struggle 'and we were much too busy to waste time upon such unreal, academic issues.'[1]

It is true that the question of fighting on was never listed explicitly as an item on the War Cabinet's agenda. In every other respect, however, Sir Winston's assurances were, to say the least, disingenuous. The question was all too real, and answers to it were certainly not taken for granted, after the world's best army had been shattered in six weeks leaving Britain isolated with only minimal defences.

This chapter originally appeared in a festschrift for my doctoral supervisor, Sir Harry Hinsley. See Richard Langhorne, ed., *Diplomacy and Intelligence during the Second World War: Essays in Honour of F.H. Hinsley* (Cambridge: Cambridge University Press, 1985), 147–67. Earlier versions were given as papers to the Cambridge Historical Society and the London University Seminar in 20th-Century British History—the only occasion when I had the chance to meet A. J. P. Taylor.

The essay aroused considerable comment when first published, including a wonderfully apoplectic blast from Lord Annan in the *London Review of Books*, 1 Aug. 1985, p. 5. Since then the Cabinet debates of May 1940 have become better known. For a dramatic portrayal see John Lukacs, *Five Days in London, May 1940* (New Haven, 1999); cf. the more nuanced picture of Halifax in Andrew Roberts, *'The Holy Fox': A Life of Lord Halifax* (London, 1991), chs 22–4. Neither has altered the essence of my argument, but for further reflections see David Reynolds, *In Command of History: Churchill Fighting and Writing the Second World War* (London, 2004), ch. 11.

[1] Winston S. Churchill, *The Second World War* (6 vols., London, 1948–54), ii. 157, 159.

This chapter re-examines some of the myths about 1940. First it looks at the discussions in Whitehall and Westminster about a negotiated peace and connects them with the fluid political situation during Churchill's early months as premier. Then it considers the reasons why the government, and particularly Churchill, believed that Britain still had a chance of defeating Germany. I shall suggest that those reasons were invalid and that they rested on mistaken perceptions of Germany and the United States. To appreciate all this, we need to forget some familiar developments later in the war—unconditional surrender, the special relationship, Churchill's political pre-eminence. And if we do so we shall also form a rather more complex picture of Churchill than that of the indomitable, single-minded, pro-American hero enshrined in the war memoirs and in national mythology.[2]

To understand the discussions in Britain about a negotiated peace, we must remember Churchill's unusual political position in the summer of 1940. For a decade from 1929 to 1939 he had been in the wilderness—written off by most MPs as a spent and eccentric elder statesman, outside the Tory fold on major issues such as India, rearmament, and the Abdication. In the late thirties Tory opposition to Chamberlain's foreign policy coalesced around Eden rather than Churchill, and although Churchill was brought into the War Cabinet as First Lord of the Admiralty when war broke out in September 1939 he was denied effective control over Britain's war effort. But then, in the Commons vote of confidence about the Norwegian campaign on 8 May 1940, Chamberlain's normal majority slumped from around 200 to 81. He tried in vain to draw Labour and Liberals into a national coalition, and after two days of confused politicking Churchill was asked by the King on the evening of 10 May to form a ministry. That morning the German attack on the Western Front had begun. For Churchill, this was his hour of destiny.

During the course of 1940 Churchill established a position at Westminster and in the country at large that was stronger than Chamberlain had enjoyed even at the pinnacle of his popularity after Munich. But in the early months of his premiership Churchill felt much less secure. He had not been the inside choice to replace Chamberlain. Lord Halifax, the Foreign Secretary, enjoyed the confidence of Chamberlain, the King, and the Tories, and would have been supported by the Labour and Liberal parties.[3] It was Halifax's reluctance which gave Churchill his chance. Even then Churchill's position was anomalous. He was a prime minister without a party. Chamberlain remained the Conservative leader, and Tory backbenchers, somewhat chastened by the effect of their abstentions

---

[2] For a broader discussion of British foreign policy and of Anglo-American relations, on which this chapter draws, see David Reynolds, *The Creation of the Anglo-American Alliance, 1937–1941: A Study in Competitive Co-operation* (London, 1981).

[3] I remain unconvinced by David Carlton's ingenious argument that Chamberlain may have preferred Churchill to Halifax, and stand by the more traditional accounts. See David Carlton, *Anthony Eden: A Biography* (London, 1981), 161–2.

during the Norway debate, ostentatiously rallied behind him immediately after the political crisis. Churchill was keenly aware of these political realities. 'To a large extent I am in y[ou]r hands', he wrote to Chamberlain after being asked to form a government,[4] and that feeling was reflected in the composition of his Cabinet. Despite the addition of the Labour and Liberal leaders, the coalition still contained many of the old guard in key positions. Chamberlain was made Lord President, with effective control over domestic policy, Halifax stayed as Foreign Secretary, together with Chamberlain intimate R. A. Butler as his Parliamentary Under Secretary, and Kingsley Wood became Chancellor of the Exchequer. After Dunkirk, when there was a vigorous press campaign to remove the 'Guilty Men' supposedly responsible for Britain's disasters, it was made very clear to Churchill that if Chamberlain was forced to resign, Simon, Kingsley Wood and several junior ministers, including Butler, would go as well. Calling on the press lords to desist, Churchill gave striking expression to his sense of insecurity:

Churchill said not to forget that a year ago last Christmas they were trying to hound him out of his constituency, and by a succession of events that astounded him he was invited by the practically unanimous vote of both Houses of Parliament to be Prime Minister. But the men who had supported Chamberlain and hounded Churchill were still M.P.s. Chamberlain had got the bigger cheer when they met the House after forming the new administration. A General Election was not possible during a war and so the present House of Commons, however unrepresentative of feeling in the country, had to be reckoned with as the ultimate source of power for the duration. If Churchill trampled on these men, as he could trample on them, they would set themselves against him, and in such internecine strife lay the Germans' best chance of victory.[5]

Churchill's fears were probably unfounded. Although Chamberlain seems initially to have entertained hopes of recovering the premiership after the war, the diagnosis of terminal cancer forced him to retire from politics in the autumn,[6] and Churchill, with the cautionary examples of Lloyd George and MacDonald before him, quickly accepted the Tory leadership when it was offered to him in October. From then on his political position was unassailable. But in the spring and summer—and this is my point—Churchill *felt* insecure, and that is

---

[4] Churchill to Chamberlain, 10 May 1940, Neville Chamberlain papers, NC 7/9/80 (Birmingham University Library).

[5] Cecil H. King, *With Malice toward None: A War Diary*, ed. William Armstrong (London, 1970), 50, entry for 7 June 1940 (quotation by kind permission of Messrs Sidgwick and Jackson, Ltd). Or, as R. A. Butler put it picturesquely in July: 'If intrigue or attacks on the Government grow to any great extent all we have to do is to pull the string of the toy dog of the 1922 Committee and make it bark. After a few staccato utterances it becomes clear that the Government depends upon the Tory squires for its majority.' Butler to Hoare, 20 July 1940, Templewood papers, T/xiii/17 (Cambridge University Library).

[6] After being operated on for cancer Chamberlain wrote in his diary on 9 Sept. 1940 of the need 'to adjust myself to the new life of a partially crippled man which is what I am. Any ideas of another Premiership after the war have gone. I know that is out of the question.' Chamberlain papers, NC 2/24A.

what we must bear in mind as we turn to the War Cabinet discussions about a negotiated peace.

These discussions took place on 26, 27, and 28 May 1940.[7] By the 26th the bulk of the British Expeditionary Force had been trapped around Dunkirk. At this stage it was expected that only 30,000 to 50,000 could be evacuated, without their equipment—hardly the basis of a successful defence against invasion.[8] Moreover, it was feared that invasion might be imminent. For a while in late May British intelligence estimates suggested that Hitler was going to curtail operations in France to mount an immediate attack on the British Isles.[9] The outlook in short was grim as Halifax in particular was well aware. Like most of Whitehall the Foreign Secretary had been stunned by the disintegration of the French army—'the one firm rock on which everybody had been willing to build for the last two years'[10]—and back in December 1939 he had observed in Cabinet that, if ever the French government wanted to make peace, 'we should not be able to carry on the war by ourselves'.[11] Faced now with the inconceivable, he began to look for some way out. It is important to be clear about what Halifax was saying. He was not advocating immediate surrender or anything of the sort. He wanted to use the Italians to ascertain Hitler's likely peace terms. Halifax stressed that he would fight to the end if Britain's integrity and independence were threatened—if, for example, Hitler demanded the fleet or the RAF. However, if terms could be secured to guarantee this independence—even if they involved surrendering part of the empire—then it was senseless, in his opinion, to permit further slaughter and destruction.[12]

Churchill's response was that no satisfactory peace could possibly be achieved until Britain had shown Hitler that she could not be conquered. Only then would a basis of equality have been reached from which negotiation might be possible. Even to inquire about German terms at this stage, Churchill insisted, would be a sign of weakness which would undermine Britain's fighting position at home and abroad.[13] The issue was thrashed out at five long meetings during which the argument became sufficiently heated for Halifax, briefly, to talk of

[7] They have been discussed at some length by several historians, esp. Sir Llewellyn Woodward, *British Foreign Policy in the Second World War* (London, 1970), i. 197–208; P. M. H. Bell, *A Certain Eventuality: Britain and the Fall of France* (Farnborough, Hants, 1974), 38–48; Elisabeth Barker, *Churchill and Eden at War* (London, 1978), 140–6; Eleanor M. Gates, *The End of the Affair: The Collapse of the Anglo-French Alliance, 1939–1940* (London, 1981), 143–52; Martin Gilbert, *Winston S. Churchill* (London, 1983), vi. 402–22. The records are in CAB 65/13, Confidential annexes, WM (40) 139/1, 140, 141/1, 142, 145/1(TNA).

[8] Churchill told junior ministers on 28 May that 'we should certainly be able to get 50,000 away. If we could only get 100,000 away, that would be a magnificent performance.' Hugh Dalton, diary, xxii. 93 (British Library of Political and Economic Science, London).

[9] F. H. Hinsley, *British Intelligence in the Second World War: Its Influence on Strategy and Operations* (London, 1979), i. 165–6.

[10] Halifax, diary, 25 May 1940, Hickleton papers, A 7.8.4 (Borthwick Institute, York).

[11] War Cabinet minutes, WM 107 (40) 2, 7 Dec. 1939, CAB 65/2.

[12] See e.g. CAB 65/13, pp. 149, 151, 179–80.

[13] See e.g. CAB 65/13, pp. 150, 187, and Chamberlain diary, 26 May 1940, NC 2/24A.

resignation.[14] In the end Chamberlain came round to Churchill's point of view, which was also endorsed by the Labour and Liberal members of the War Cabinet and applauded at a meeting of junior ministers. Halifax was therefore isolated and the idea of approaching the Italians was rejected.[15] Moreover, by early June, the military situation seemed much better. To everyone's relief and amazement, 335,000 Allied troops had been evacuated from Dunkirk, and it also became clear that Hitler intended to finish off the French before he turned his attention to Britain. With the immediate crisis averted, a consensus now formed in the Cabinet around the Churchillian position that no question of peace terms could be raised until the Battle of Britain had been won. However, the hope was still that, by continuing the struggle, Britain would eventually secure not total victory but acceptable terms. Halifax and Butler were particularly emphatic on this point, fearing that Churchill would be carried away by emotion and bravado into prolonging the war unnecessarily.[16]

At Westminster, too, doubts were expressed about the wisdom of fighting on. A group of some thirty MPs and ten peers, loosely organized by the Labour businessman, Richard Stokes, believed it would be disastrous for Britain and Germany to continue the war. Whoever won, they argued, Europe would be ravaged and the only beneficiaries would be Russia and the United States. This was not an argument for 'peace at any price' but for serious consideration of any reasonable offer from Hitler that offered a chance of 'a just peace with disarmament'.[17] Stokes' group looked to Lloyd George as its potential leader. In fact, the former PM's attitude was broadly similar to that of the War Cabinet after Dunkirk. He did not advocate an immediate peace but believed that Britain should seek favourable terms once the Battle of Britain had been won.[18] Although we think of Lloyd George by 1940 as a spent force, that was not the opinion of contemporaries. Senility was yet to set in and he remained an influential figure at home and abroad, whom many still saw as a great leader. Churchill certainly had not written him off. On several occasions in May and June he tried to draw Lloyd George into his government, but these efforts were frustrated by Chamberlain, whose bitter hatred of Lloyd George dated back to World War I. However, Churchill persuaded Chamberlain to withdraw his opposition as the price for getting the 'Guilty Men' press campaign called off.

[14] Halifax, diary, 27 May 1940, Hickleton papers, A 7.8.4.

[15] It is interesting to see how Churchill handled the episode in his war memoirs. There it is discussed almost entirely in the context of Anglo-Italian relations—could Mussolini be bought off and prevented from entering the war?—without any reference to its wider implications: *Second World War*, ii.108–11. [16] Cf. Woodward, *British Foreign Policy*, i. 204, note.

[17] e.g. Stokes to Lloyd George and enclosed memo, 17 July 1940, Lloyd George papers, G/19/3 (House of Lords Record Office, London). The basis of Stokes' organization was the 'Parliamentary Peace Aims Group' formed by dissident Labour MPs the previous autumn. For background see Richard R. Stokes papers, files 73 and 76 (Bodleian Library, Oxford).

[18] As stated in e.g. Lloyd George to the Duke of Bedford, 14 Sept. 1940, Lloyd George papers, G/3/4.

Thereafter, Lloyd George was the main obstacle, ostensibly because he would not serve with those he called 'the architects of disaster'—Chamberlain and Halifax.[19] This was not the only reason, however. As Chamberlain and Churchill suspected, Lloyd George also saw himself as a future peacemaking prime minister, ready to take command when the battle for survival had been won and the nation appreciated the impossibility of achieving total victory. As he told his secretary in October 1940: 'I shall wait until Winston is bust.'[20]

Blessed (and burdened) as we are with hindsight, it is easy to stigmatize Halifax, Lloyd George, and their like as appeasers and defeatists, out of touch with the heroic mood of the moment. Talk about a compromise peace seems a far cry from the unconditional surrender of May 1945. It is therefore important to emphasize that the idea of an eventual negotiated settlement was not aberrant and unpatriotic but was in fact the goal with which British leaders had entered the war in 1939. As Chamberlain explained to Roosevelt that October:

My own belief is that we shall win, not by a complete and spectacular victory, which is unlikely under modern conditions, but by convincing the Germans that they cannot win. Once they have arrived at that conclusion, I do not believe they can stand our relentless pressure, for they have not started this war with the enthusiasm or the confidence of 1914.[21]

Convincing the Germans that they could not win meant maintaining the pressure to cause 'a collapse of the German home front' and a coup to overthrow Hitler and the Nazi system.[22] After this it might be possible to negotiate with a new German government, perhaps involving Göring and conservative generals with whom the British government tried to keep open tentative lines of communication during the winter of 1939–40.[23] For Chamberlain and his colleagues this seemed a balanced, realistic goal. Britain's aim was to eliminate the Nazi threat to Europe's security, not to smash the German nation, and after the horrors of 1914–18 no one could be enthusiastic about a war of attrition

---

[19] Lloyd George to Churchill, 29 May 1940, and drafts, Lloyd George papers, G/4/5. See also Chamberlain, diary, 31 May, 4–7, 10–11 June 1940, NC 2/24A, and *Life with Lloyd George: The Diary of A. J. Sylvester, 1931–45*, ed. Colin Cross (London, 1975), 360–70.

[20] Sylvester, diary, 3 Oct. 1940, in *Life with Lloyd George*, 281. See also the interesting discussion in Paul Addison, 'Lloyd George and Compromise Peace in the Second World War' in *Lloyd George: Twelve Essays*, ed. A. J. P. Taylor (London, 1971), 361–84. On the larger question of German peace feelers in the summer of 1940 and the British and American responses, see Bernd Martin, *Friedensinitiativen und Machtpolitik im Zweiten Weltkrieg, 1939–1942* (Düsseldorf, 1974), 234–336. Although tendentious in its view of Roosevelt (as bent on world domination), this rightly notes the disingenuousness of official British accounts, such as those by Churchill and Woodward, on the peace issue (e.g. pp. 298–9).

[21] Chamberlain to Roosevelt, 4 Oct. 1939, PREM 1/366 (TNA).

[22] Neville Chamberlain to Ida Chamberlain, 10 Sept. 1939, Chamberlain papers, NC 18/1/1116.

[23] See Callum A. MacDonald, 'The Venlo Affair', *European Studies Review*, 8 (1978), 443–64 (but cf. Hinsley, *British Intelligence*, i. 56–7); Peter Ludlow, 'Papst Pius XII, die britische Regierung und die deutsche Opposition im Winter 1939/40', *Vierteljahrshefte für Zeitgeschichte*, 22 (1974), 299–341.

particularly in the absence of an Eastern Front. For some right-wingers in the Cabinet, there was a further consideration. Historically British leaders had conceived of a strong but peaceful Germany as a potential source of stability in central Europe. Eliminating the Nazi menace at the cost of exposing the Continent to the Soviet threat was hardly a desirable prospect. Thus Sir Samuel Hoare, Chamberlain's Home Secretary and close associate, wanted an internal collapse in Germany and a moderate, peacemaking government, but not a real revolution which would lead to a Bolshevik Europe.[24]

Where did Churchill stand on this issue? On 13 May he had told the Commons that his policy was 'Victory at all costs, victory in spite of all terror, however long and hard the road may be, for without victory there is no survival.' Privately on 18 May and 1 June he spoke of his conviction that Britain would beat Germany and he rejected the idea of preparing contingency plans to evacuate the royal family and government abroad.[25] But in Cabinet during the Dunkirk crisis he was much less adamant that total victory was the only acceptable result. When asked by Halifax on 26 May 'whether, if he was satisfied that matters vital to the independence of this country were unaffected, he would be prepared to discuss terms', Churchill replied 'that he would be thankful to get out of our present difficulties on such terms, provided we retained the essentials and the elements of our vital strength, even at the cost of some territory'.[26] In Chamberlain's more colourful account of the exchange, Churchill is recorded as saying that 'if we could get out of this jam by giving up Malta and Gibraltar and some African colonies he would jump at it', although he did not see any such prospect.[27] The following day he took a similar line. According to the War Cabinet minutes he commented that 'if Herr Hitler was prepared to make peace on the terms of the restoration of German colonies and the overlordship of Central Europe, that was one thing', but he felt that such an offer was 'most unlikely'.[28] Summing up his position on 28 May, Churchill stressed that in the present crisis they could not get acceptable terms from Italy and Germany:

Signor Mussolini, if he came in as mediator, would take his whack out of us. It was impossible to imagine that Herr Hitler would be so foolish as to let us continue our rearmament. In effect, his terms would put us completely at his mercy. We should get no worse terms if we went on fighting, even if we were beaten, than were open to us now. If, however, we continued the war and Germany attacked us, no doubt we should suffer some damage, but they would also suffer severe losses. Their oil supplies might be reduced. A time might come when we felt that we had to put an end to the struggle, but the terms would not then be more mortal than those offered to us now.[29]

[24] Notes of interview with Hoare, 22 Sept. and 15 Oct. 1939, Kingsley Martin papers, box 30, file 6 (Sussex University Library, Brighton).

[25] House of Commons, *Debates*, 5th series, vol. 360, col. 1502; Gilbert, *Churchill*, vi. 358, 449.

[26] CAB 65/13, pp. 179–80, WM 142 (40) CA, 27 May 1940. Halifax was reminding the PM of a discussion on the previous day, but Churchill made no demurral to this paraphrase of his comments.   [27] Chamberlain, diary, 26 May 1940, NC 2/24A.

[28] CAB 65/13, p. 180.   [29] CAB 65/13, p. 187, WM 145 (40) 1, CA.

In each case the Prime Minister seems to have acknowledged the possibility of an eventual negotiated peace, while emphasizing that this was definitely not the right moment. Certainly his language was a far cry from 'victory at all costs'.

How should we interpret these remarks? Was Churchill simply trying to maintain Cabinet unity by reassuring influential colleagues that he was not a romantic diehard? This argument is certainly plausible, especially when we remember Churchill's relatively weak political position that summer.[30] But before we dismiss his statements as a tactical ploy, we should note that he took a similar line in other, more public situations when one might have expected a pugnacious, optimistic statement to strengthen domestic opinion. For instance, on 29 May, concerned at defeatist talk in London, he issued a general injunction to ministers to maintain 'a high morale in their circles; not minimizing the gravity of events, but showing confidence in our ability and inflexible resolve to continue the war *till we have broken the will of the enemy to bring all Europe under his domination*'.[31] No mention here of total victory.

Yet one might respond that all these remarks by Churchill, like the whole War Cabinet controversy, date from the Dunkirk period, and therefore reflect the extreme but temporary crisis atmosphere before the evacuation succeeded. This interpretation, like the previous one, must be taken seriously, but it is relevant to note that Churchill made similar statements about a negotiated peace at less desperate moments. For instance, after Hitler's peace feelers in late September 1939, Churchill drafted a possible answer. Although negative, he told Chamberlain, it 'does not close the door upon any genuine offer' from Germany.[32] On 6 June 1940 Churchill told Halifax that, before admitting Lloyd George to any Cabinet post, he would put the former PM 'through an inquisition first, as to whether he had the root of the matter in him'. As the criterion, Churchill said he would adopt Halifax's formula 'that any peace terms now, as hereafter, offered must not be destructive of our independence'.[33] And in August 1940, in terms reminiscent of the previous autumn, the Prime Minister insisted that a firm reply to Hitler's current overtures was 'the only chance of extorting from Germany any offers which are not fantastic'.[34]

It seems feasible, therefore, that Churchill did not rule out the possibility of an eventual negotiated peace, even if he judged May 1940 to be an inopportune moment. Like his colleagues his object may not have been total victory, which appeared unrealistic even when France was in the war, but the elimination of

[30] For this argument see J. A. S. Grenville, 'Contemporary trends in the study of the British "appeasement" policies of the 1930s', *Internationales Jahrbuch für Geschichts- und Geographie-Unterricht*, 17 (1976), 245–7; also Jonathan Knight, 'Churchill and the approach to Mussolini and Hitler in May 1940: a note', *British Journal of International Studies*, 3 (1977), 92–6.

[31] Churchill, memo, 29 May 1940, copy in Beaverbrook papers, D 414/3 (House of Lords Record Office, London). Emphasis added.

[32] Churchill to Chamberlain, 9 Oct. 1939, PREM 1/395 (TNA).

[33] Halifax, diary, 6 June 1940, Hickleton papers, A 7.8.4.

[34] Churchill, note, 3 Aug. 1940, PREM 4/100/3, p. 131.

Hitler and Nazism, the evacuation of Germany's conquests and a durable peace with adequate guarantees. After all, more than most Tories he feared the long-term Bolshevik threat, and in August 1941 he talked about his goal of a Germany that was 'fat but impotent'.[35] We should remember, too, that British war aims took shape slowly, and that the 'unconditional surrender' policy of January 1943 grew out of a very different phase of the war. After the Blitz Göring looked much less attractive in British eyes and during 1941 expectations about the German 'moderates' were gradually extinguished. At the same time Russia and America became active allies. By 1943, in other words, total victory seemed both necessary and possible; this was not the case in 1940.

In the end these arguments are speculative: inferences from fragmentary and ambiguous evidence. But there can be little doubt that, contrary to the mythology he himself sedulously cultivated, Churchill succumbed at times to the doubts that plagued British leaders in the summer of 1940. In February 1946, when Churchill was reminiscing about the dark days of the war, he surprised Halifax by saying 'that he had never really believed in invasion. He had been into it all in 1913 [as First Lord of the Admiralty] and realized how difficult it was . . .'[36] But on 4 June 1940 Churchill had scribbled a hasty note to Stanley Baldwin in which his tone was more equivocal: 'We are going through v[er]y hard times & I expect worse to come: but I feel quite sure that better days will come! Though whether we shall live to see them is more doubtful.'[37] In July 1946 the American writer Robert Sherwood was discussing the same period with General Ismay, the PM's wartime military secretary. Ismay recalled a conversation he had with Churchill on 12 June 1940, after their penultimate conference with the demoralized French leaders at Briare. According to Sherwood's notes:

When Churchill went to the airport to return to England, he said to Ismay that, it seems, 'we fight alone'. Ismay said he was glad of it, that 'we'll win the Battle of Britain'. Churchill gave him a look and remarked, 'You and I will be dead in three months time.'[38]

From the evidence set out so far, it is therefore apparent that the question of a negotiated peace *was* aired in Whitehall and Westminster in the summer of 1940. It is also clear that some of those who toyed with the idea, notably Halifax and Lloyd George, were politicians whom Churchill had to take seriously,

---

[35] Dalton, diary, xxv. 57, 26 Aug. 1941.

[36] Churchill added that 'although he didn't entirely appreciate it at the time he had no doubt that the Germans had made an overwhelming error in frittering away their fleet on all the Norwegian business'. Halifax, diary, 10 Feb. 1946, Hickleton papers, A 7.8.18. Cf. Churchill, *Second World War*, ii. 144: 'I was always sure we should win'.

[37] Churchill to Baldwin, 4 June 1940, Stanley Baldwin papers, vol. 174, p. 264 (Cambridge University Library).

[38] 'Ismay said, "Quite possibly, but we'll have a hell of a good time those last seven days." Churchill seemed to feel that this point was well taken.' Robert E. Sherwood, notes of interview with Ismay on 11 July 1946, Sherwood papers, folder 1891 (Houghton Library, Harvard University).

particularly in view of his sense of insecurity at this time. We have seen that Churchill probably shared some of their doubts about Britain's chances and that he spoke privately on a number of occasions about the possibility of an eventual negotiated peace. In public, however, it was obviously essential to strike the most hopeful and inspiring attitude in order to sustain domestic morale in preparation for the expected invasion. Hence Churchill's series of uplifting speeches, phrases from which have justly passed into the treasury of the English language. But rhetoric alone was insufficient. Aside from emotion, there had to be compelling *reasons* for fighting on. And those reasons have been neglected in subsequent historiography.

One of the most cogent statements of the case for an early peace came from the pen of Lloyd George in September 1940. In a long and thoughtful memorandum he laid bare the gravity of Britain's strategic position compared with World War I. Then it had taken four years of dreadful conflict, waged for the most part on two fronts in conjunction with major Continental allies, before Germany had finally succumbed. This time Britain had been driven from the Continent, Russia was neutral, and France conquered. To defeat Germany, he argued, Britain would first have to reestablish herself on the Continent—itself no easy task—and then wage a prolonged war of attrition on the model of 1914–18. The whole process would take from five to ten years, by which time the British Isles would be devastated, depopulated, and bankrupt, with most of her empire and commerce in the hands of America, Russia, and Japan. Nor did Lloyd George place much hope in American intervention. 'She will no doubt help us in all ways short of War', he wrote. 'But I cannot foresee her sending another huge Army to Europe.' And even if she did decide to do so, Lloyd George reckoned from the bitter experiences of 1917–18 that the US Army 'would not be an efficient fighting machine for at least 2 years. It might then take the place of the French Army in the last war—although that is doubtful.'[39]

Lloyd George had put his finger on the two central issues at stake. Could Germany be defeated without another bloody land war across the Continent? And what were the prospects of rapid American help on a sufficiently large scale? Answers to these two questions largely determined one's assessment of Britain's chances. Lloyd George's response was negative on both counts—hence his pessimism. Churchill took a more optimistic view, which he successfully established as official policy. To appreciate this, we must look more closely at British assessments of Germany and then of the United States.

British strategists in 1940–1, and indeed for some time before and after, consistently rejected Lloyd George's first argument—that Germany could not be defeated without a war of attrition across Europe. In their view—and Churchill was outstanding here—the large scale British Expeditionary Force (BEF) of World

---

[39] Lloyd George, memo, 12 Sept. 1940, Lloyd George papers, G/81.

War I had been a disastrous aberration from traditional British policy of the eighteenth and nineteenth centuries. The present war should be fought in the old way, in other words by relying on Britain's economic, financial, and naval strength in conjunction with the manpower of Continental allies. (Or, as the French saw it, the British would fight to the last Frenchman.) Thus, planning papers in 1939 envisaged that the French army, and a token BEF, would resist the initial German onslaught. Then the German economy and morale would be undermined by blockade, supplemented by bombing of industrial centres and intensive propaganda, until the time was ripe for the final offensive.[40] This strategy was all very well during the period of the Anglo-French alliance. But British policy-makers clung to it even after the loss of the French army. In the words of the Chiefs of Staff in September 1940: 'The wearing down of Germany by ever-increasing force of economic pressure should be the foundation of our strategy.'[41] To the triad of blockade, bombing, and propaganda was added a new weapon—subversion. Britain would assist partisan movements in occupied Europe in harassing their Nazi rulers and preparing for eventual uprisings. (It was in July 1940 that Churchill created the Special Operations Executive with its mandate to 'set Europe ablaze'.) The Army would be vital for defending the British Isles and the empire, but its offensive role was still seen as limited. As the Chiefs put it:

It is not our policy to attempt to raise, and land on the continent, an army comparable in size to that of Germany. We should aim nevertheless, as soon as the action of the blockade and air offensive have secured conditions when numerically inferior forces can be employed with good chance of success, to re-establish a striking force on the Continent with which we can enter Germany and impose our terms.[42]

How could this strategy of limited liability still remain credible after June 1940? Part of the answer lies in the growing faith in strategic bombing. In their September memorandum the Chiefs of Staff still placed their principal emphasis on the blockade, but the RAF took a different line, and one that gradually became official orthodoxy thanks in large measure to the advocacy of Churchill. Now that Germany controlled Scandinavia and much of Europe, the Prime Minister observed in July 1940 that the blockade had been 'broken' as an effective weapon. In his view the only one thing that would bring Hitler down was 'an absolutely devastating, exterminating attack by very heavy bombers from this country upon the Nazi homeland'.[43] He spelled out his thinking more fully in a memorandum for the Cabinet on 3 September:

The Navy can lose us the war, but only the Air Force can win it. Therefore our supreme effort must be to gain overwhelming mastery in the Air. The Fighters are our salvation

---

[40] e.g. Chiefs of Staff sub-committee, 'European Appreciation', 20 Feb. 1939, CAB 16/183A, DP (P) 44, esp. paragraphs 27–37, 267–8.
[41] Paper on 'Future Strategy', 4 Sept. 1940, CAB 80/17, COS (40) 683, para. 211.
[42] Ibid., para. 214.
[43] Churchill to Beaverbrook, 8 July 1940, Beaverbrook papers, D 414/36.

[i.e. in protecting the British Isles], but the Bombers alone provide the means of victory. We must therefore develop the power to carry an ever-increasing volume of explosives to Germany, so as to pulverise the entire industry and scientific structure on which the war effort and economic life of the enemy depend, while holding him at arm's length from our Island. In no other way at present visible can we hope to overcome the immense military power of Germany . . . [44]

Churchill continued to stress this strategy over the succeeding months. 'I consider the rapid expansion of the Bomber Force one of the greatest military objectives now before us', he wrote in December 1940. And the following July he instructed that Britain must aim at having nothing less than twice the strength of the *Luftwaffe* by the end of 1942. This was 'the very least that can be contemplated, since no other way of winning the war has yet been proposed'.[45] The RAF's idea that the Army would do little more than 'deliver the coup de grace'[46] was naturally unpopular in the War Office, where opposition mounted during 1941 to this strategy for winning the war.[47] But officially, at the top level, the three services had now come round to Churchill's view. The Chiefs of Staff review of 'General Strategy' on 31 July 1941 allowed the Army only the role of an occupation force in the final stages of Germany's defeat, unless it were decided to accelerate victory by landing forces on the Continent at an earlier stage. Even then, however, these would be modern armoured divisions, engaged in mobile warfare, and not the vast infantry line offensives of World War I. By contrast, the Chiefs spoke of massive bombing as the 'new weapon' on which Britain must principally rely to destroy the German economy and morale. It was to be given top priority in production and no limits would be set on the eventual size of the force required.[48]

But even this excessive faith in strategic bombing during 1940–1 is not sufficient to explain British optimism about defeating Germany at limited cost. The fundamental reason was their grave and persistent underestimation of the strength of the German war economy, a theme suggestively discussed in volume one of Sir Harry Hinsley's official history of *British Intelligence*.[49] On 18 May 1940 'Chips' Channon, a junior minister at the Foreign Office, noted: 'It is now believed that the war will be over in September—the Germans will either win or be exhausted by this terrific effort.'[50] Such thinking was clearly apparent in the

[44] Memo, 'The Munitions Situation', 3 Sept. 1940, WP (40) 352, CAB 66/11. In deference to the Chiefs of Staff Churchill was here a little less pessimistic about the blockade, speaking only of it as having been 'blunted' by the German victories.

[45] Minutes M 485 and M 740/1, 30 Dec. 1940 and 12 July 1941, Ministry of Aircraft Production papers, AVIA 9/5 (TNA).

[46] The phrase used by Sir Cyril Newall, Chief of the Air Staff, on 31 Aug. 1940, SA (J) 3rd mtg, pp. 5–6, CAB 122/59.

[47] Cf. *Chief of Staff: The Diaries of Lieutenant-General Sir Henry Pownall*, ed. Brian Bond (2 vols., London, 1972–4), ii. 38–9, entry for 20 Aug. 1941.

[48] CAB 99/18, COS (R) 14, esp. paragraphs 28–9, 36–8. See also R. J. Overy, *The Air War, 1939–1945* (London, 1980), ch. 5.   [49] Hinsley, *British Intelligence*, i. 63–73, 232–48, 500–4.

[50] *'Chips': The Diaries of Sir Henry Channon*, ed. Robert Rhodes James (London, 1967), 253.

War Cabinet debates of 26 May. There Attlee observed, as a matter of fact, that Hitler 'had to win by the end of the year' while Chamberlain 'thought he would have to win by the beginning of the winter'. Even Halifax shared this belief in Germany's 'internal weakness': he used it to justify his contention that Hitler might not feel strong enough to insist on 'outrageous terms'.[51] The underlying assumption behind such remarks was that German shortages of food and raw materials, especially oil, would soon make themselves felt. On 25 May the Chiefs of Staff submitted their assessment of whether Britain could hope to win alone. (Significantly the exact question posed was: 'Could we ultimately bring sufficient economic pressure to bear on Germany to ensure her defeat?') They argued that if the blockade could be maintained, then, by the winter of 1940–1, inadequate supplies of oil and foodstuffs would weaken German rule in Europe and that by mid-1941 'Germany will have difficulty in replacing military equipments. A large part of the industrial plant of Europe will stand still, throwing upon the German administration an immense unemployment problem to handle.'[52] In a more considered verdict on 4 September the Chiefs predicted that, 'unless Germany can materially improve her position', in 1941 the deficiencies in the crucial areas of oil, food, and textiles 'may prove disastrous'. They went on to draw the remarkable conclusion that although 1941 would be a year of attrition for Britain, her aim *'should be to pass to the general offensive in all spheres and all theatres with the utmost possible strength in the Spring of 1942'*.[53]

Churchill seems to have shared this assumption that the German economy was over-stretched. In fact as early as February 1939, according to an American visitor, Churchill 'felt that Hitler had now reached the peak of his military power. From now on he would grow weaker in relation to England and France.'[54] In May 1940 he was insisting that 'if only we could stick things out for another three months, the position would be entirely different'.[55]And this belief in fundamental German weakness also sheds light on a neglected part of the Prime Minister's 'finest hour' speech to the Commons on 18 June 1940. There he encouraged his countrymen, shocked at the French surrender, by a reminder that:

During the first four years of the last war the Allies experienced nothing but disaster and disappointment . . . During that war we repeatedly asked ourselves the question, 'How are we going to win?' and no one was able ever to answer it with much precision, until, at the end, quite suddenly, quite unexpectedly, our terrible foe collapsed before us, and we were so glutted with victory that in our folly we threw it away.[56]

[51] CAB 65/13, pp. 148–9. Cf. Halifax, secret diary, 16 Mar. 1941, A 7.8.19: 'I remember last May and June everybody was saying "if we can hold out till the autumn we shall be all right".'
[52] CAB 66/7, WP(40) 168, para. 18.
[53] CAB 80/17, COS (40) 683, paras 50, 47, and 218. Emphasis in original.
[54] William S. Wasserman, 'Interview with Mr Winston Churchill', 10 Feb. 1939, p. 3, President's Secretary's File (PSF) 73: 'Agriculture Department' (Franklin D. Roosevelt Library, Hyde Park, New York).   [55] CAB 65/13, p. 147, WM 140 (40) CA, 26 May 1940.
[56] House of Commons, *Debates*, 5th series, vol. 362, cols. 59–60.

As we now know, the idea of a 'taut' Nazi economy, vulnerable to economic pressure and strategic bombing, was an illusion. German munitions production did not reach its peak until July 1944; bombing had only a limited impact on overall industrial output until late in that year; and civilian morale and productivity were, if anything, improved when Allied raids brought the war home to the German people.[57] So why had British policy-makers been so wrong? As Hinsley emphasized the basic error was not one of information but of presuppositions. In fact, several false assumptions may be detected. First there was the conviction that Hitler's pre-eminent goal was the subjugation of Britain rather than expansion to the east. Whitehall policy-makers were coming round to this view by late 1938, and from January 1939 there were recurrent scares that Germany might mount an immediate, devastating air assault on London perhaps without involving the French.[58] Indeed on 4 May 1940, less than a week before the offensive on the Western Front began, the Chiefs of Staff expressed the opinion that an attack on Britain was more likely than an attack on France,[59] and these fears recurred, as we have seen, at the time of Dunkirk. Churchill seems to have shared the conviction that Britain was Hitler's real target. On 26 May, for instance, he observed that France was 'likely to be offered decent terms by Germany, which we should not...There was no limit to the terms which Germany would impose upon us if she had her way.'[60] Yet, through all the historiographical debate about Hitler's war aims, it seems clear that in at least the early phases of his expansionist programme he sought and expected British acquiescence while he consolidated his grip on continental Europe. With the partial exception of the Navy, Nazi rearmament was geared to that assumption, and, when it was falsified in 1938–9, the German armed forces found themselves ill-prepared for the general European war that broke out in September 1939. Even during the summer of 1940 Hitler was still entertaining hopes of an agreement with Britain.[61]

Thus, the British wrongly assumed that Hitler intended war with Britain in 1939. They also believed that he would only have begun such a war when his economy was fully ready. By that they meant an economy completely converted from peace to wartime goals, with concomitant retooling, controls, and organization. In the German case that seemed a particularly reasonable judgement since this was a totalitarian state, supposedly under rigid regimentation. Commented the Chiefs of Staff in September 1940: 'The economic system of Greater Germany has produced spectacular results because it was based on an imposed

[57] Burton H. Klein, *Germany's Economic Preparations for War* (Cambridge, Mass., 1959), 225–35; see also Overy, *The Air War*, 122–5.

[58] Cf. Hinsley, *British Intelligence*, i. 80.   [59] CAB 66/7, WP (40) 145.

[60] CAB 65/13, p. 148.

[61] See Klaus Hildebrand, *The Foreign Policy of the Third Reich* (Berkeley, 1973); Andreas Hillgruber, 'England's place in Hitler's plans for world dominion', *Journal of Contemporary History*, 9 (1974), 5–22; Wilhelm Deist, *The Wehrmacht and German Rearmament* (London, 1981).

discipline covering all activities down to individual transactions.'[62] Yet the British knew that German output and stockpiles were not impressive in absolute terms. They therefore concluded that Hitler had brought the economy to its peak performance, that this was insufficient for a sustained war and that the system was so 'taut' that it might soon collapse under continued British pressure. As the Ministry of Economic Warfare stated in September: 'the Nazi economy is much more brittle than the German economy of 1914–18 which was not so highly integrated. It is not impossible that an acute shortage of oil or a tie-up of the transport system might cause a breakdown of the closely-knit Nazi system with repercussions throughout Germany and German Europe of the utmost importance.'[63]

Two basic misapprehensions are evident here. First, the British thought in terms of an economy geared either to peace or to war: they failed to grasp the intermediate concept of *Blitzkrieg* warfare. In the 1960s Alan Milward argued that this was a calculated response by Hitler to the exigencies of Germany's economic and geopolitical position—short, sharp wars against individual foes for which it was unnecessary to convert the whole economy to war production. This made it possible to avoid another two-front war for Germany and to have guns as well as butter. Later historians such as Richard Overy, Williamson Murray, and Wilhelm Deist have suggested that *Blitzkrieg* was not a well thought out strategy but an ad hoc response to a general war that came several years earlier than German leaders had expected. Either way, the German war economy of 1940 was characterized by rearmament in breadth rather than depth. The Army and Air Force lacked reserves, spares, and above all supplies for a sustained campaign, but they had exceptional short-term striking power, which was amply demonstrated in Poland and in France. The British appreciated this—hence their concern to survive the first few months of a German onslaught—but they believed that it marked the peak of Hitler's capacity. For, in the second place, they did not realize the uncoordinated, inefficient nature of the Nazi war economy in 1939–40. Far from being a highly regimented, totalitarian system, Germany at this time lacked a cohesive central economic administration. The three services competed indiscriminately, German industry displayed a marked reluctance to convert to war needs, and the conservative industrial structure impeded the introduction of automated, mass-production methods. Not until 1942, under Speer, were matters taken in hand, and this helps to explain why Germany did not reach its peak production until 1944. In

---

[62] CAB 80/17, COS (40) 683, 4 Sept. 1940, para. 44. For earlier examples of this assumption see Wesley K. Wark, 'British Intelligence on the German Air Force and Aircraft Industry, 1933–1939', *Historical Journal*, 25 (1982), 644, 646–7.

[63] Ministry of Economic Warfare, note, appendix to CAB 79/6, COS 295 (40) 2, 5 Sept. 1940. From late 1940, however, British oil experts became progressively less sanguine about Germany's position.

other words, the Nazi economy, far from being 'taut' in 1940, still had a large amount of 'slack'.[64]

As Hinsley's work has shown, the crux of good intelligence is often not specific information—the product of spies, decrypts, and the like, so much associated with intelligence operations in the popular imagination—but the paradigms or frameworks of assumptions into which the nuggets of information are set. British estimates of German output and stockpiles were not correct, but they were not wildly inaccurate. What mattered most was the underlying set of beliefs about Hitler's aims, the nature of war economies, and the regimentation of a totalitarian state. British policymakers in 1940 believed that the German war machine was approaching maximum efficiency and that traditional methods of economic pressure, supplemented by the 'new weapon' of the heavy bomber, would bring the struggle to a satisfactory conclusion without another major land war on the Continent. These beliefs were slow to die. They help, for instance, to explain British opposition to America's 'second front' strategy in 1942–3.[65] And they constitute one part of the explanation for Britain's hopefulness in fighting on alone in 1940.

The other part, of course, was British expectations of help from the United States. In assessing Britain's chances alone, the Chiefs of Staff made it clear in May 1940 that their major assumption was that the USA was 'willing to give us full economic and financial support, *without which we do not think we could continue the war with any chance of success*'.[66] They laid particular emphasis on full cooperation from the Western Hemisphere in enforcing the blockade of Germany, on immediate US supplies of aircraft and warships and on naval assistance in the Pacific to restrain Japan. But they still did not envisage another American Expeditionary Force—and not just because that would have been Utopian in the present state of American rearmament. The military planners observed in late June that although American technical personnel would be of very great value, 'we are unlikely to require troops' because Britain's own supplies of manpower should be adequate.[67] Here again is evidence of the pervasive

[64] Alan S. Milward, *The German Economy at War* (London, 1965), esp. chs. 1–2. Cf. R. J. Overy, 'Hitler's war and the German economy: A reinterpretation', *Economic History Review*, 2nd series, 35 (1982), 272–91; see also Deist, *Wehrmacht*, esp. pp. 102–12; Williamson Murray, 'The Luftwaffe before the Second World War: A Mission, A Strategy?', *Journal of Strategic Studies*, 4 (1981), 261–70, and 'Force Strategy, Blitzkrieg Strategy and the Economic Difficulties: Nazi Grand Strategy in the 1930s', *Journal of the Royal United Services Institute*, 128/1 (Mar. 1983), 39–43.

[65] After discussing strategy for the attack on Continental Europe with Churchill on 22 May 1943, Henry Wallace, the US Vice-President, noted: 'Churchill and Cherwell [F. A. Lindemann, the PM's scientific adviser] still think that the job can be done from the air and sea without the help of the land.' *The Price of Vision: The Diary of Henry A. Wallace, 1942–1946*, ed. John M. Blum (Boston, 1973), 210.

[66] Chiefs of Staff, 'British strategy in a certain eventuality', 25 May 1940, WP (40) 168, para. 1, CAB 66/7. Emphasis in original.

[67] Chiefs of Staff, Joint Planning Sub-Commt., draft aide mémoire, 27 June 1940, COS (40) 496, para. 29, CAB 80/13.

belief that an over-stretched Germany could be broken largely by economic pressure.

Above all, British leaders in mid-1940 hoped for an early American declaration of war. Their reasons were twofold. In the long term, they believed only this would arouse the US public and permit all-out economic mobilization. But the immediate and decisive consideration in their view was the likely impact on morale in Britain and overseas. Churchill put the point directly to Roosevelt on 15 June:

When I speak of the United States entering the war I am, of course, not thinking in terms of an expeditionary force, which I know is out of the question. What I have in mind is the tremendous moral effect that such an American decision would produce, not merely in France but also in all the democratic countries of the world, and, in the opposite sense, on the German and Italian peoples.[68]

Churchill's preoccupation there with the psychological effects of American belligerency can only be fully understood when we again remember his belief that this would not be a war of mass armies. If Britain's goal was to promote an internal collapse by destroying Germany's will to fight, then the relative morale of the belligerents would be a decisive factor. This was a point to which Churchill returned frequently. In a talk to newspaper editors on 22 August 1941:

He was very anxious that America should declare war, owing to its psychological effect. He said he would rather have America in and no American supplies for six months, than double the present level of American shipments while she maintained her present position as a neutral. He had come to the conclusion that this was a psychological war and that much depended on whether the Germans could get the inhabitants of Europe to acquiesce in their New Order before we could convince them of our ability to set them free. In this race for time, American participation in the war would be a great psychological point in our favour.[69]

The problem for Churchill in 1940, and much of 1941, was that Americans showed no apparent readiness to declare war. On the contrary their immediate response to the fall of France was a panic-stricken preoccupation with their own defences to the detriment of even the limited material aid they were then offering to Britain. But throughout the summer of 1940 Churchill insisted that American belligerency was a matter of months at the most, and he spread his belief with such determination and skill that it became an axiom of British policy.

As with Churchill's confidence about defeating Germany, his predictions about the United States depended heavily on the assumed impact of the bomber. Essentially his thesis was that German air raids on British cities would arouse American public opinion and lead to a declaration of war. This was a long-standing belief, expressed for instance on several occasions in private and in

---

[68] Churchill to Roosevelt, telegram, 15 June 1940, PREM 3/468, pp. 126–7.
[69] King, *With Malice toward None*, 139, diary entry for 23 Aug. 1941.

public during 1939.[70] And he used it repeatedly in mid-1940 whenever there was talk of defeat or surrender. The precise argument varied. Sometimes he emphasized the effect of bombing itself. In his memoirs, de Gaulle, the Free French leader, recalled:

I can still see him at Chequers, one August day, raising his fists towards the sky as he cried: 'So they won't come!' 'Are you in such a hurry', I said to him, 'to see your towns smashed to bits?' 'You see', he replied, 'the bombing of Oxford, Coventry, Canterbury, will cause such a wave of indignation in the United States that they'll come into the war!'[71]

On other occasions Churchill stressed actual invasion, telling the anxious Dominion prime ministers on 16 June 'that the spectacle of the fierce struggle and carnage in our Island will draw the United States into the war'.[72] But increasingly, after the failure in June to persuade Roosevelt to declare war, Churchill recognized that FDR's hands were tied until the presidential election on 5 November, and it was on this date that he pinned his hopes. On 20 June, just after the French had asked for terms, he addressed a crucial secret session of the House of Commons. Only his notes survive, but they indicate clearly the burden of his remarks:

Attitude of United States.
Nothing will stir them like fighting in England.
No good suggesting to them we are down and out.
The heroic struggle of Britain best chance of bringing them in . . .
All depends upon our resolute bearing and holding out until Election issues are settled there.
If we can do so, I cannot doubt whole English-speaking world will be in line together.[73]

During the early autumn Churchill plugged away at the same theme. In a letter about America on 15 October he told Bevin cryptically: 'I still hope the big event may happen over there.'[74] And on 1 November Churchill said that 'he was sure Roosevelt would win the election by a far greater majority than was supposed,

---

[70] In Feb. 1939 Churchill told an American visitor that if war broke out with Germany and Italy, the main fighting would be in the Mediterranean while the Maginot Line kept Germany out of France. 'In the meanwhile there would be much unpleasantness in the air. London would be bombed. The spectacle of 50,000 English women and children being killed might readily bring the United States into the conflict—especially in view of Mr. Roosevelt's present attitude.' (Wasserman, 'Interview with Mr. Winston Churchill', 10 Feb. 1939, p. 5, cited in note 54). In September he told the British Ambassador in Washington that Hitler might shrink from making a decisive air attack on British factories. 'If however he tried and succeeded, the United States would come into the front line.' (Churchill to Lothian, 24 Sept. 1939, Ge/39/2, FO 800/397.) For similar, if more veiled predictions in print, see his articles 'Bombs don't scare us now', *Colliers*, 17 June 1939, reprinted in *The Collected Essays of Sir Winston Churchill*, ed. Michael Wolff (London, 1976), i. 453; and in *News of the World*, 18 June 1939, quoted in Martin Gilbert, *Winston S. Churchill* (London, 1976), v. 1075.

[71] Charles de Gaulle, *War Memoirs*, trans. Jonathan Griffin (London, 1955), i. 108.

[72] Churchill to Dominion PMs, 16 June 1940, PREM 4/43B/1, p. 278.

[73] Winston S. Churchill, *Secret Session Speeches*, compiled by Charles Eade (London, 1946), 15.

[74] Churchill to Bevin, 15 Oct. 1940, Ernest Bevin papers, 3/1, p. 58 (Churchill College, Cambridge).

and he believed that America would come into the war'.[75] By this stage even cautious specialists in the American Department of the Foreign Office had come round to this view.[76] Indeed, to Admiral Robert Ghormley, the USA's 'Special Naval Observer' in London, it seemed 'that everybody in Great Britain expects the U.S. to enter the war within a few days after . . . the President is re-elected'.[77]

This expectation about the likely effect on US opinion of German bombing helped keep Britain going during the summer of 1940. And one can find warrant for it in the public comments of such distinguished American observers as the journalist Walter Lippmann,[78] and even in a private remark by the President himself, which was reported by King George VI to British leaders, probably including Churchill, in the summer of 1939.[79] Like the belief about an early German collapse, however, it proved to be sadly misplaced. Roosevelt's re-election did not herald a declaration of war. It was only in December 1941, and then in response to Japan and Germany, that the USA became a belligerent.

How can we explain British over-confidence? Part of the answer lies in their too sanguine estimates of the effect of bombing. The Blitz did not prove the holocaust that a generation of Britons had feared.[80] Losses of life were unexpectedly low, compared with the widespread damage to property and essential services, and although German raids did help strengthen pro-British feeling in America, they did not provide the catalyst that Churchill had predicted. Another reason was that Churchill consistently exaggerated the unity of what he called the

[75] Sir John Colville, *Footprints in Time* (London, 1976), 144–5, quoting diary entry for 1 Nov. 1940.

[76] Reynolds, *The Creation of the Anglo-American Alliance*, 108, 149.

[77] Admiral Robert L. Ghormley to Admiral Harold L. Stark, 11 Oct. 1940, US Navy Strategic Plans Division, Box 117: 'Naval Attaché, London' (Naval Historical Division Archives, Washington Navy Yard, Washington, DC).

[78] Lippmann, 'Today and Tomorrow' column, *Washington Post*, 23 Mar. 1939. This was taken seriously by the Foreign Office—see FO 371/22829, A 2439/1292/45.

[79] After talking with Roosevelt on 10–11 June 1939 the King recorded in his notes of their conversations: 'If London was bombed U.S.A. would come in.' Back in London, according to his biographer, the King 'communicated the essence of his talks with the President to the proper quarters'. See John W. Wheeler-Bennett, *King George VI: His Life and Reign* (London, 1958), 391–2. Churchill was definitely told by the King about the naval aspects of his talks with Roosevelt (Churchill to Pound, 7 Sept. 1939, Admiralty papers, ADM 116/3922, p. 255, PD 07892/39) and it is likely that George VI would also have given him the gist of Roosevelt's other remarks at the same time. If so, Churchill's conviction about the effect of bombing must have been greatly strengthened.

[80] A particularly vivid indication of this fear comes in a letter by the historian Arnold Toynbee to an American international lawyer just after Munich: 'It is probably impossible to convey what the imminent expectation of being intensively bombed feels like in a small and densely populated country like this. I couldn't have conveyed it to myself if I hadn't experienced it in London the week before last (we were expecting 30,000 casualties a night in London, and on the Wednesday morning we believed ourselves, I believe correctly, to be within three hours of the zero hour). It was just like facing the end of the world. In a few minutes the clock was going to stop, and life, as we had known it, was coming to an end. This prospect of the horrible destruction of all that is meant to one by "England" and "Europe" was much worse than the mere personal prospect that one's family and oneself would be blown to bits. Seven or eight million people in London went through it.' (Arnold Toynbee to Quincy Wright, 14 Oct. 1938, in Roger S. Greene papers, folder 747, Houghton Library, Harvard University.)

'English-speaking peoples'. Despite his half-American ancestry and frequent visits to the United States, Churchill had little real understanding of America's ethnic diversity or of the anglophobia that many of her European immigrants brought with them from the Old World. For him, the United States was an extension of the British family of nations—bound by ties of kin, culture, and, above all, of language—so that, as he told the French leaders on 31 May 1940, an invasion of England, if it occurred, would have a profound effect, 'especially in those many towns in the New World which bore the same names as towns in the British Isles'.[81] Churchill also underestimated the political constraints still felt by Roosevelt after 5 November. Like most British policy-makers he found it hard to appreciate just how far American political parties lacked the cohesion and discipline of their counterparts at Westminster. Even with large nominal majorities after the 1940 election, the President still had laboriously to build up a consensus among congressmen and the public for any foreign policy initiative, as the 1941 debates over Lend-Lease, convoying, and the renewal of the draft were all to show. And, finally, it is also likely that Churchill was too optimistic about the bellicosity of the President himself. To British leaders FDR was always at his most warlike, implying that, but for public opinion, he would be in the conflict tomorrow. Yet Franklin Roosevelt was a past-master at telling his listeners what they wanted to hear.[82] The real intentions of this deeply secretive man are difficult to divine, but there is evidence to suggest that he was always hopeful of avoiding formal, total US involvement in the war if American security could be safeguarded by aid to the Allies. It is also possible that this hope was given new vitality by Hitler's move east and the successful Russian resistance in the summer of 1941.[83]

All this may serve to confirm the stereotype of Churchill as heroic but uncomplicated, even naive—someone who displayed an uncritical faith in American friendship which was inspiring yet misplaced, the man who, on 20 August 1940, likened Anglo-American cooperation to the great Mississippi, rolling on 'full flood, inexorable, irresistible, benignant, to broader lands and better days'.[84] To assess such statements properly, however, and to reach a balanced judgement on Churchill's publicly-stated confidence in the USA, we

[81] Supreme War Council (39/40) 13th mtg., p. 12, 31 May 1940, CAB 99/3. Cf. this report by the US Ambassador in London: 'Churchill said quite definitely to me he expects the United States will be in right after the election; that when the people in the United States see the towns and cities of England, after which so many American cities and towns have been named, bombed and destroyed they will line up and want war.' (Joseph P. Kennedy to Cordell Hull, tel. 1603, 12 June 1940, State Dept. decimal file, 740.0011 EW 1939/3487 6/10, National Archives, Washington, DC.)

[82] It is quite likely, for instance, that the King was handled in this fashion in June 1939 (see above, note 79). More experienced Roosevelt-watchers in the Foreign Office took such utterances with the necessary grain of salt.

[83] For elaboration of this argument see Reynolds, *The Creation of the Anglo-American Alliance*, ch. 8, esp. pp. 211–12, 217–19.

[84] House of Commons, *Debates*, 5th series, vol. 364, col. 1171. Cf. Correlli Barnett, *The Collapse of British Power* (London, 1972), 588–9.

also need to bear in mind two other considerations—his deep disillusion *in private* that summer at the lack of real American help and the very tough line he adopted towards the USA in transatlantic diplomacy.

Churchill fully shared the general resentment felt in Whitehall at the isolationist panic in Washington and on 27 May 1940 he observed bitterly that the USA 'had given us practically no help in the war, and now that they saw how great was the danger, their attitude was that they wanted to keep everything which would help us for their own defence'.[85] Or, as he put it in a telegram to his old American friend, Bernard Baruch, a month later: 'Am sure we shall be alright here but your people are not doing much.'[86] In these circumstances Churchill believed that America's hand would have to be forced, and throughout the summer he therefore insisted, against the advice of the Foreign Office, that any British concession to the United States should only be made if and when some commensurate benefit was offered by Roosevelt in return. He was adamant, for example, that the Americans should not be given the right to build much-needed bases on British islands in the Caribbean and western Atlantic except as part of a deal in which Britain received destroyers and other munitions. Likewise, he deprecated suggestions that the government should throw its military secrets such as Asdic and Radar into the American lap and then wait to see what they offered in exchange. 'Generally speaking', he wrote on 17 July, 'I am not in a hurry to give our secrets until the United States is much nearer war than she is now.'[87]

Churchill even resorted to diplomatic blackmail in his efforts to prise America out of her shell. There were widespread fears in Washington that summer that the British and French fleets might be sunk or surrendered. These fears were shared by Roosevelt himself, who had received garbled and alarming reports about the Cabinet discussions of late May. At this time America only had a 'one-ocean navy', currently based at Pearl Harbor, two thousand miles from her *west* coast, in an effort to deter Japan, and if Hitler gained control of the Atlantic the east coast of the United States might be extremely vulnerable. Churchill played on these anxieties assiduously as the French collapsed. On 20 May he told Roosevelt that although his own government would never surrender, it might not survive a successful invasion and 'if others came in to parley amid the ruins, you must not be blind to the fact that the sole remaining bargaining counter with Germany would be the fleet, and if this country was left by the United States to its fate no one would have the right to blame those responsible if they made the best terms they could for the surviving inhabitants'.[88] This was also the burden of several other telegrams he sent to the President in May and June.

[85] Cabinet minutes, WM 141 (40) 9, CAB 65/7.

[86] Churchill to Baruch, telegram, 28 June 1940, Selected Correspondence, vol. 47, Bernard M. Baruch papers (Seeley G. Mudd Library, Princeton University).

[87] Churchill to Ismay, 17 July 1940, PREM 3/475/1. For fuller discussion of material in this and the next two paragraphs see Reynolds, *The Creation of the Anglo-American Alliance*, esp. pp. 113–32, 158–60, 167–8.   [88] Churchill to Roosevelt, tel., 20 May 1940, FO 371/24192, A3261/1/51.

Churchill's mood was not fundamentally changed by the Destroyers Deal of September 1940, nor by Roosevelt's re-election two months later. On the contrary, the Prime Minister confessed himself on 2 December 'rather chilled' by the US attitude over the previous month,[89] and on the 20th he complained: 'We have not had anything from the United States that we have not paid for, and what we have had has not played an essential part in our resistance.'[90] The decisive change seems to have come in January 1941. Roosevelt's submission of the Lend-Lease bill to Congress and then the visit to London by his close friend and emissary, Harry Hopkins, convinced Churchill that the President was indeed Britain's 'best friend' and that he meant what he said about helping to the limits of his ability. But in mid-1940, as we have seen, Churchill was much less optimistic. Although he did tend at times to romanticize the Anglo-American relationship, his publicly-stated confidence in 1940 about American generosity and imminent belligerency was not the blind faith of an indomitable but ingenuous man. It reflected calculation as much as conviction. As with his statements about victory at all costs, Churchill forced himself to speak publicly in 1940 with an optimism that he often did not feel.

This leads us to the first of the two general conclusions from this chapter—that the Churchill of myth (and of the war memoirs) is not always the Churchill of history. Scholars working on the 1930s and World War II have long been aware of this discrepancy, but it deserves to be underlined in view of the dogged rearguard action fought by popular biographers and television producers. Contrary to national folklore, Churchill did not stand in complete and heroic antithesis to his pusillanimous, small-minded political colleagues. British leaders of the 1930s and World War II all faced the same basic problem of how to protect their country's extended global interests with insufficient means at their disposal. The various policies they advanced are not to be divided into separate camps—appeasers and the rest—but rather marked on different points of a single spectrum, with no one as near either extreme as is often believed. This is true of the Chamberlain era; it is also true, as I have argued here, of 1940. In private, Churchill often acknowledged that the chances of survival, let alone victory, were slim. He also expressed acceptance, in principle, of the idea of an eventual negotiated peace, on terms guaranteeing the independence of the British Isles, even if that meant sacrificing parts of the empire and leaving Germany in command of Central Europe. And, far from already being part of an Anglo-American special relationship, his attitude to the United States in 1940 was frequently one of disillusion and suspicion, as he utilized every diplomatic weapon, including the threat of British surrender, to bludgeon a hesitant Roosevelt into providing real help. But in public, Churchill's stance on all these

---

[89] Cabinet minutes, CAB 65/10, WM 299 (40) 4.
[90] Churchill to Foreign Secretary, 20 Dec. 1940, PREM 4/25/8, p. 502.

matters was very different. In public he maintained a mood of indefatigable optimism, insisting that Britain would settle for nothing less than total victory and arguing to sceptics at home and abroad that the USA would soon be in the war. This is not in any sense to belittle Churchill's greatness. On the contrary. My contention is that the popular stereotype of almost blind, apolitical pugnacity ignores the complexity of this remarkable man and sets him on an unreal pedestal. A not unskilful politician, handling the same issues in different ways for domestic and foreign audiences, privately wrestling with his own doubts and fears, yet transcending them to offer inspiring national and international leadership—that is surely a more impressive as well as a more accurate figure than the gutsy bulldog of popular mythology.

Equally misleading are the conventional beliefs about Britain's 'finest hour'. There was no formal 'decision' to fight on in June 1940, but it was far from being a foregone conclusion, as Churchill suggested. In Cabinet at the time of Dunkirk, and among a small group of MPs and peers, there was considerable debate about Britain's future chances and about the possibility of a satisfactory negotiated peace, immediately or when the threat of invasion had passed. Among those associated with such ideas were Halifax and Lloyd George—the former Churchill's rival for the premiership, the latter the would-be leader of a future peacemaking government. At this time Churchill was a prime minister without a party, acutely conscious of his recent years of exclusion not only from office but also from the affections of the Tory party. In the early months of his premiership he had therefore to take very seriously the possible threat posed by these senior colleagues and the policies they espoused, and it is surely significant that when the post of Ambassador to the USA fell vacant in December 1940 Churchill offered it first to Lloyd George, who refused on grounds of age, and then, successfully, to the reluctant Halifax. (It was not the first or the last time that the Washington Embassy was treated by British prime ministers as a convenient political dustbin.)[91] To counter the plausible case developed by these advocates of an early peace, Churchill and other British policy-makers of like mind argued that if Britain could survive 1940 then she could win the war. They believed that the German economy was already 'taut' and vulnerable to British bombing, and that Hitler had to defeat Britain by the winter if he was to win at all. If Britain could hang on until then it was also likely that German attempts at invasion, and particularly the merciless bombing of British cities, would have outraged opinion in the USA and brought her into the war after the November election. Churchill put the two points together in his crucial speech of 20 June to the secret session

---

[91] In May 1923 Stanley Baldwin had urged his predecessor as Tory leader, Austen Chamberlain, to take the post. See Keith Middlemas and John Barnes, *Baldwin: A Biography* (London, 1969), pp. 175–6; Sir Charles Petrie, *The Life and Letters of the Right Hon. Sir Austen Chamberlain* (London, 1940), ii, pp. 221–2. In May 1979 Margaret Thatcher offered the Washington Embassy to the former Conservative leader, Edward Heath.

of the Commons. His notes read:

If Hitler fails to invade or destroy Britain he has lost the war.
I do not consider only the severities of the winter in Europe.
I look to superiority in Air power in the future.
Transatlantic reinforcements.
If [we] get through next 3 months [we] get through next 3 years.[92]

British expectations about Germany and about the USA were almost entirely erroneous. Their hopes of survival, let alone of victory, might also have proved too optimistic, but for Hitler himself. Their best reason for fighting on was one of which they had no knowledge at this time: namely that as early as July 1940 Hitler was already thinking of turning against Russia in 1941. Of this, no prediction can be found in the British intelligence reports and strategic assessments of 1940. Throughout that year, and for much of the next, the British still assumed that Hitler's main target was the British Isles. His Balkan campaigns in the spring of 1941 were therefore seen as part of a peripheral strategy to sever Britain's imperial lifelines as prelude to eventual invasion later in the year. And in April many British strategists accepted that Germany could create a bridge-head on the South Coast any time she was willing to make the sacrifice. A visiting US general noted: 'Dill, Beaverbrook, Freeman and Sinclair all believe that it can be done and will be tried.' Their hopes were pinned not on preventing an invasion but on stopping a German breakout from the beach-head.[93] As Hinsley's official history showed, it was not until early June 1941 that most of Whitehall accepted that Hitler really intended to invade the Soviet Union. Even then, such were the doubts about Russian military capabilities that when Operation 'Barbarossa' began on 22 June most British policy-makers reckoned that Germany would win in three to six weeks without heavy losses.[94] Not surprisingly Churchill ordered on 25 June 1941 that anti-invasion preparations in the British Isles should be 'at concert pitch' by 1 September.[95] Had Hitler not turned east, had the Russians not survived, had Hitler not then compounded his folly by joining Japan against the United States, the outcome of the war would probably have been very different. In 1940 Churchill and his colleagues made the right decision—but they did so for the wrong reasons.

---

[92] Churchill, *Secret Session Speeches*, p. 14. A few days later Churchill recalled: 'I was strongly pressed in the House of Commons in the Secret Session to give assurances that the present Government and all its Members were resolved to fight on to the death, and I did so, taking personal responsibility for the resolve of all.' (Churchill to Halifax, 26 June 1940, FO 800/322, p. 277.)

[93] General Henry H. Arnold, diary of visit to England, 24 April 1941, p. 20, Arnold papers, box 271 (Library of Congress, Washington, DC). Beaverbrook was often prone to defeatist moods, but the same cannot be said of the others. (Sir John Dill was Chief of the Imperial General Staff, Sir Wilfred Freeman was Vice-Chief of the Air Staff, and Sir Archibald Sinclair was Secretary of State for Air.) Similar views had been expressed to Arnold a few days before by, among others, the First Lord of the Admiralty, A. V. Alexander (ibid., 14, 21 April).

[94] Hinsley, *British Intelligence*, i, chs. 8, 11, 13, 14, esp. pp. 248–9, 347, 355, 429, 470–83.

[95] As he put it in a telegram to Roosevelt on 1 July (PREM 3/469, p. 212).

5

Churchill the Appeaser?

Between Hitler, Roosevelt, and Stalin, 1940–1944

On Bonfire Night, 5 November 1944, a German V-1 'flying bomb' landed in Sussex. Nothing surprising in that: southern England had been under fire since June. But this V-1 carried propaganda not explosives. Its four-page leaflet explaining why Britain should sue for peace ended with a V-1 shaped crossword. The clues and answers included the following:

He is your enemy, too. *Bolshevik.*
He wants all you have got. *Roosevelt.*
Britain has none at inter-Allied conferences. *Voice.*
At Tehran, Churchill practically did this before Stalin. *Knelt.*[1]

The claim that Churchill had sold out Britain to America and Russia was a staple of Nazi wartime propaganda. As the Yalta conference was beginning in February 1945, Hitler denounced Churchill for living in the past:

The crucial new factor is the existence of these two giants, the United States and Russia. Pitt's England ensured the balance of world power by preventing the hegemony of Europe—by preventing Napoleon, that is, from attaining his goal.... If fate had granted to an ageing and enfeebled Britain a new Pitt instead of this Jew-ridden, half-American drunkard, the new Pitt would at once have recognised that Britain's traditional policy of balance of power would now have to be applied on a different scale, and this time on a world scale. Instead of maintaining, creating and adding fuel to European rivalries Britain ought to do her utmost to encourage and bring about a unification of Europe.

In these final outpourings, Hitler argued that he had given Churchill plenty of opportunity for 'grasping the truth of this great policy' and allowing Germany a free hand on the Continent. Britain 'could have pulled her chestnuts out of the fire' after the defeat of Poland or the fall of France. 'At the beginning of 1941,' Hitler claimed, 'after her success in North Africa had re-established her prestige,

Apart from a few cuts to avoid overlap with Chapters 4 and 6, this chapter appears as first published in a festschrift for Zara Steiner—see Michael Dockrill and Brian McKercher, eds., *Diplomacy and World Power: Studies in British Foreign Policy, 1900–1950* (Cambridge, 1996), 197–220. The editors and Prof. Peter Clarke kindly commented on a draft version.

[1] CAB 66/57, WP (44) 642 (TNA); cf. *Sunday Dispatch*, 13 Jan. 1945, p. 4.

she had an even more favourable opportunity of withdrawing from the game and concluding negotiated peace with us.' But instead she preferred 'to obey the orders of her Jewish and American allies, people, indeed, who were more voracious than even the worst of her enemies'.[2]

Accusations similar in substance, if not tone, were also voiced at times in wartime London, especially in 1944–5. It was, for instance, a widespread feeling in the Foreign Office in December 1944 that Churchill was erroneously pursuing a 'policy of appeasement' towards Moscow and Washington. This was a time of acute transatlantic friction and even the normally pro-American weekly *The Economist* demanded publicly: 'let an end be put to the policy of appeasement which, at Mr Churchill's personal bidding, has been followed, with all the humiliations and abasements it has brought in its train, ever since Pearl Harbor removed the need for it'. On the political right, there were many who viewed Churchill's policy towards Stalin in the same light by 1945. The Yalta agreement on Poland prompted four government ministers to abstain in the Commons. Two resigned their posts. Ironically, some of the sternest critics of Poland's treatment were men such as Lord Dunglass (later Lord Home) who had been Chamberlain loyalists in 1938. And Churchill himself sounded distinctly like Chamberlain when he told the Commons that he returned from Yalta with the impression that Stalin wished 'to live in honourable friendship and equality with the Western democracies' and added: 'I know of no Government which stands to its obligations, even in its own despite, more solidly than the Russian Soviet Government.' It seemed that the wheel had come full circle. To quote MP and diarist Harold Nicolson, 'the warmongers of the Munich period have now become the appeasers, while the appeasers have become the warmongers'.[3]

After the archives were opened, some historians and commentators developed these wartime criticisms. At the end of his book *The Collapse of British Power* (1972), Correlli Barnett argued that in 1940 'Churchill and his government quite deliberately, if in their view inevitably, chose to sacrifice England's existence as an independent power, a power living and waging war on her resources, for the sake of "victory".' The options of peace with Hitler or a limited war to hold the Axis at bay were dismissed, Barnett argued, in favour of a quixotic policy of 'victory at all costs' which ran down Britain's wealth and made her dependent on the United States. Thus 'Lend-Lease gradually consummated the policy that Churchill had begun of transforming England into an American satellite warrior-state.'[4]

---

[2] François Genoud, ed., *The Testament of Adolf Hitler*, trans. R. H. Stevens (London, 1961), 30–5.
[3] Basil Liddell Hart Papers, LH 11/1944/65 (Liddell Hart Centre for Military Archives, King's College, London) (henceforth KCL); *Economist*, 30 Dec. 1944, p. 858; Commons, *Debates*, 408: 1284, 27 Feb. 1945; Churchill to Roosevelt, 10 Mar. 1945, in Warren F. Kimball, ed., *Churchill and Roosevelt: Their Complete Correspondence*, 3 vols. (Princeton, 1985), iii. 552 (henceforth *C-R*); Harold Nicolson, *Diaries and Letters, 1939–1945*, ed. Nigel Nicolson (London, 1967), 437.
[4] Correlli Barnett, *The Collapse of British Power* (London, 1972), 588, 592.

In 1993, biographer John Charmley fused the wartime grumblings of left and right to suggest that Churchill overestimated both the altruism of America and the fidelity of Russia, thereby sacrificing what was left of British power and independence. He implied that Chamberlain's own, derided version of appeasement—aimed at Germany—in fact 'offered the only way of preserving what was left of British power; if 1945 represented "victory", it was, as Chamberlain had foreseen, for the Soviets and the Americans'. Turning Charmley's insinuations into verities, former Tory government minister Alan Clark claimed in *The Times* that, but for Churchill, peace could have been obtained on 'reasonable' terms in 1940 and on 'excellent' terms in 1941. This piece was perhaps a midwinter *jeu d'esprit*, by an ex-politician whose generous sense of mischief was matched by a certain stinginess with the *actualité*. But it (and a bad week for serious news) helped make Charmley's book a *cause célèbre*. The extent to which such assertions have solidified as certitudes is suggested by a *Guardian* columnist who wrote in 1994 that Churchill 'sold every stick of family silver to his American cousins along with his beloved empire, class and party. All went bust in 1945. Oh yes, and the Russians ended up with half Europe, as Churchill spotted too late.' Despite the flippant tone, these are presented as matters of fact.[5]

But *are* they true? Even in the more scholarly books, where not delivered tongue in cheek, they are offered more as lament than argument. At root, they seem to rest on an implicit syllogism. In 1945 Britain was weaker than in 1940. Churchill was leader from 1940 to 1945. Ergo, Churchill was the guilty man. The alternatives are not seriously examined: indeed they cannot be from the limited vantage point of biography. Like most swings of the historiographical pendulum, Churchillian revisionism is a reaction to the heroic orthodoxy that prevailed for so long. It is, up to a point, much needed because that orthodoxy, pioneered in Churchill's own war memoirs, has often been fawningly claustrophobic. It requires little time in the archives and diaries of the war to discover that Churchill's self-portrait was not a snapshot of real life. But to replace a hero with an anti-hero, or at least a more recognizably flawed figure, is of limited utility. The approach is still biographical: one man fills the picture, the background is obscured. It is certainly ironic that Churchill, of all people, presided over a decline in British power. But irony is not causality; *post hoc* does not mean *propter hoc*.

The issues involved here are large and intricate, far beyond the compass of a short essay. But, as a contribution to an important debate, I offer some reflections on three central questions. Was there any hope of a viable modus vivendi with Hitler in 1940–1? What did Britain *gain* from its alliance with the Soviet

---

[5] John Charmley, *Churchill: The End of Glory. A Political Biography* (London, 1993), 2, 559–61; *The Times*, 2 Jan. 1993, p. 12; *The Guardian*, 24 Mar. 1994, sec. 2, p. 11. See also John Charmley, 'The Price of Victory', *Times Literary Supplement*, 13 May 1994, p. 8.

Union and the United States? And what exactly was Britain's strategy during the dark middle of the war from the fall of France to the dawning of D-Day? Only with these issues in mind can Churchill's wartime diplomacy be justly evaluated.

First, then, what should be made of claims, or insinuations, that Britain could have reached a modus vivendi with Hitler in 1940–1—either through a nego-tiated peace or a war of limited liability that would have kept the Nazis at bay across the Channel? To respond, we must examine German intentions and capabilities, a move rarely made by proponents of these arguments.

Some scholars of Nazi foreign policy, such as Gerhard Weinberg, have insisted that Britain was a prime target of Hitler's malevolence and that the Führer showed no readiness to take account of British interests. Certainly Hitler sometimes spoke in this way—'I want to beat England whatever it costs,' he told Goebbels in December 1939. But most authorities take the view that Hitler's oft-stated animosity towards Bolshevik Russia should be considered the lode-star of his policies and that, at least in the medium term, he sought an accom-modation (*Ausgleich*) with Britain that would have given him a 'free hand' on the Continent. Germany's failure to do this in the decade before 1914 was Hitler's fundamental criticism of the Kaiser's foreign policy, set out at length in his so-called Second Book of 1928. There is little doubt that Hitler tried to avoid this error after he came to power or that, by 1939, he had actually repeated it. The result was a war in the west that he had neither expected nor wanted at this stage. His famous remark to the Swiss diplomat Carl Burckhardt in August 1939 can probably be taken at face value: 'Everything I undertake is directed against Russia; if the West is too stupid and blind to grasp this, I shall be forced to reach an understanding with the Russians to defeat the West and then, after its downfall, turn with all my concerted forces against the Soviet Union.'[6]

After the defeat of Poland and the fall of France Hitler made speeches in the Reichstag offering peace to Britain, on 6 October 1939 and 19 July 1940. Both were aimed at least partly at domestic opinion, but the British Foreign Office judged that 'these offers were seriously meant' and that 'Hitler was disappointed at the decisive manner in which they were rejected.' Certainly there is little doubt that Hitler was surprised and perplexed at British intransigence in mid-1940. He had assumed that victory in the west would end the war with Britain as well as France, leaving Germany free to turn east with impunity. When these hopes proved wrong, the Wehrmacht hastily improvised attempts to force Britain to make peace, by bombing or invasion, but, to quote historian Williamson Murray, 'the task facing the Germans in the summer of 1940 was beyond their

---

[6] Gerhard L. Weinberg, 'Hitler and England, 1933–1945: Pretense and Reality', *German Studies Review*, 8 (1985), 299–309; *Hitler's Secret Book*, trans. Salvator Attanasio (New York, 1961), ch. 14; Andreas Hillgruber, *Hitlers Strategie: Politik und Kriegführung, 1940–1941* (Frankfurt a.M., 1965), 29. For a survey of the literature see Marie-Luise Recker, *Die Aussenpolitik des Dritten Reiches* (Munich, 1990).

capabilities'. The Army High Command was preoccupied with Eastern Europe and the Mediterranean; the *Luftwaffe* lacked both doctrine and aircraft for strategic bombing; and the Navy warned that lack of air supremacy meant that any landing must be regarded as a 'last resort'. As the summer wore on, the general hope in Berlin was that bombing would force the British to their senses, perhaps via a change of government. In the words of the German official military historians, 'the preparations for landing were predominantly an instrument of psychological warfare; at times Hitler did not rule out the operation . . . but soon he again lost interest in an enterprise for which the indispensable prerequisites seemed unattainable'.[7]

As shown in Chapter 4, some British government ministers in mid-1940 wanted at least to find out what Hitler's terms would be, notably Lord Halifax, the foreign secretary, and his parliamentary under-secretary R. A. Butler. The most intense debate occurred at the end of May, before the 'miracle' of Dunkirk was assured, but Halifax and Butler remained of this view throughout the summer. Churchill did not rule out an eventual negotiated peace treaty, but argued that 'we should get no worse terms if we went on fighting' and that 'the position would be entirely different when Germany had made an unsuccessful attempt to invade this country'.[8]

Such remarks shift the debate on to early 1941 which, in retrospect, both Adolf Hitler and Alan Clark regarded as the critical moment. By then the Battle of Britain had been won and the Italian assault on Egypt decisively repulsed. By this time, too, Hitler's plans for invading Russia were well advanced. Hence the continuing fascination with the dramatic arrival in Britain of Hitler's deputy Rudolf Hess on 11 May 1941 and his proposals for a compromise peace. Thanks to the sustained disingenuousness of the British government, the full story of the 'Hess Mission' remains to be told. But whether it was sanctioned by Hitler or, as is more probable, a lone mission by a deranged man, is not material here.[9] Two points *are* germane to our argument. On the one hand, what Hess proposed was broadly what his leader had long desired. On the other hand, in May 1941, as a year before, a viable compromise peace was, *for Britain*, still unobtainable.

[7] PREM 4/100/8 (TNA): FO memo on peace feelers, 1 July 1942, para. 2; Williamson Murray, *Luftwaffe: Strategy for Defeat, 1933–1945* (London, 1988), 81; Hans Umbreit in K. A. Maier, H. Rohde, B. Stegemann, and H. Umbreit, *Germany and the Second World War, II* (Oxford, 1991), 369.

[8] Churchill quoted from CAB 65/13, folios 180, 184. See generally, e.g. Christopher Hill, *Cabinet Decisions on Foreign Policy: The British Experience, October 1938–June 1941* (Cambridge, 1991), ch. 6; Thomas Munch-Petersen, ' "Common Sense not Bravado": The Butler–Prytz Interview of 17 June 1940', Scandia, 52: 1 (1986), 73–114. On Churchill's first ten months in office see also Sheila Lawlor, *Churchill and the Politics of War, 1940–1941* (Cambridge, 1994).

[9] Bernd Martin, *Friedensinitiativen und Machtpolitik im Zweiten Weltkrieg, 1939–1942* (Düsseldorf, 1974), 425–47; John Costello, *Ten Days to Destiny* (New York, 1991), chs. 1, 16–17; Ulrich Schlie, *Kein Friede mit Deutschland: Die geheimen Gespräche im Zweiten Weltkrieg, 1939–1941* (Munich, 1994), 290–324.

One reason, quite obviously, was the difficulty of taking Hitler at his word. Here the takeover of Bohemia and Moravia in March 1939 had been a watershed. Previously it had been possible to believe Hitler's protestations that he was only redressing the inequities of Versailles and bringing all Germans within the Reich. But Munich was a bilateral agreement with the British prime minister; Prague was its brutal revocation and a clear step beyond *Grossdeutsch* limits. British perceptions of Hitler changed fundamentally. When the government officially rejected his peace offer of October 1939, a central argument was that 'assurances given by the German Government in the past have on so many occasions proved worthless that something more than words will be required today to establish confidence which must be the essential basis of peace'. And henceforth, although Chamberlain and Halifax equivocated at times, most British policy-makers felt that 'something more than words' entailed at the very least a new German government. As Sir Alexander Cadogan, permanent under-secretary at the Foreign Office, put it in October 1939, the line should be 'that *we won't make peace with Hitler*. Get rid of Hitler: that is my *war* aim—not peace aim. Do that first: then you will win the war.'[10]

Aside from the basic question of trust, it is also clear now that Hitler's desire for accommodation with Britain was a tactical expedient. His larger aims remain the subject of controversy. Did he want world domination (*Weltherrschaft*) or 'merely' world power status (*Weltmachtstellung*)? Did he have a coherent *Programm* or phased *Stufenplan*? These debates, which still revolve around the 1960s work of Günter Moltmann, Andreas Hillgruber, and Klaus Hildebrand, are beyond our compass here, but three points may be made. First, most of Hitler's statements on these matters were at the level of what Ian Kershaw calls 'vague and visionary orientations for action'. When Hitler talked of a global conflict with America, for instance, this was usually identified as a task for his successors. But, secondly, at moments of triumph in 1940–1 they assumed greater priority. After France fell and again on the eve of Barbarossa, Hitler sanctioned major naval building programmes aimed at control of the Atlantic. The fact that these plans were subsequently reversed does not undermine the basic point: when Hitler *thought* he had a free hand on the Continent, he started flexing his muscles on the world stage. On 14 July 1941, for instance, he urged the Japanese ambassador that, with Russia apparently routed, their two countries should combine to 'destroy' America as well as Britain. At other times, admittedly, he spoke of Britain as (junior) partner in the struggle with America, and that may have remained his hope. But, thirdly, there is no doubt that his larger aspirations included colonial territories for Germany as well as an Atlantic imperium. And it is hard to see how Britain could have remained indifferent (let alone independent) as these developed. In May 1940 General Franz Halder, chief of the

---

[10] Lothar Kettenacker, ed., *Das 'Andere Deutschland' im Zweiten Weltkrieg* (Stuttgart, 1977), 144; David Dilks, ed., *The Diaries of Sir Alexander Cadogan, OM, 1938–1945* (London, 1971), 221.

army general staff, noted in his diary: 'We are seeking contact with Britain on the basis of partitioning the world.'[11] Given Hitler's larger aims, that partition was likely to be as temporary as the Nazi–Soviet pact.

In considering the prospects for an Anglo-German modus vivendi in 1940–1, it is also worth noting the voices around Hitler clamouring for a *more* anti-British policy. Another feature of recent historiography has been the attack on a classic totalitarian image of Nazi Germany, in which all policy supposedly emanated from one man. Instead, scholars have talked of a Nazi 'polycracy' with bureaucratic rivalries inadequately restrained by the Führer and of a 'plurality of conceptions' in foreign policy. One such historian, Wolfgang Michalka, notes that the 'wooing of Great Britain, which for Hitler was of central importance for future German policy, was viewed by conservative politicians with much more sceptical and dubious eyes'. Within the German Foreign Office and among economic policy-makers, notably Hjalmar Schacht before the war, colonial and commercial expansion were priorities, while Admiral Raeder and the Navy entertained Tirpitzian aspirations for Germany as a naval world power. For both groups, Britain was a major and immediate threat. Their ideas were given coherence and weight by Joachim von Ribbentrop, Nazi foreign minister from 1938, who envisaged a tripartite Axis alliance aimed at Britain. To this end he masterminded the pact with Russia in 1939. Now it remains true that the crucial foreign policy decisions of the Third Reich were Hitler's: the totalitarian thesis is not completely without foundation. But the *Konzeption-Pluralismus* underlying German foreign policy is relevant when we recall the hopeful British scenario of negotiating with a non-Hitler German government. Some of those around the Führer regarded Britain as a more immediate enemy than did their leader.[12]

The Raeder–Ribbentrop anti-British policy is particularly relevant to our thinking about 1940–1. When the Wehrmacht started improvising military plans to make Britain seek peace in June 1940, General Alfred Jodl, chief of its operations staff, outlined two possible strategies. One was the direct approach of bombing and eventual landing, the other was an indirect strategy to seal off the Mediterranean, including capture of Gibraltar and the Suez Canal. Underlying both was the idea of long-term pressure through blockade of Britain's imports. This policy was warmly supported by the Navy who also hoped to enhance its reach by acquiring bases on Spanish and Portuguese islands in the Atlantic. Hitler toyed with this strategy in the autumn of 1940, courting Franco and

---

[11] Ian Kershaw, *The Nazi Dictatorship: Problems and Perspectives of Interpretation* (3rd edn., London, 1993), 129; Klaus Hildebrand, *The Foreign Policy of the Third Reich, 1933–1945* (London, 1973), 96, 100, 109, 112–13; Meir Michaelis, 'World Power Status or World Dominion?', *Historical Journal*, 15 (1972), 331–60; Milan Hauner, 'Did Hitler Want a World Dominion?', *Journal of Contemporary History*, 13 (1978), 15–32.

[12] Wolfgang Michalka, 'Conflicts within the German Leadership on the Objectives and Tactics of German Foreign Policy, 1933–9', in Wolfgang J. Mommsen and Lothar Kettenacker, eds., *The Fascist Challenge and the Policy of Appeasement* (London, 1983), 52; Hildebrand, *Foreign Policy of the Third Reich*, 58–9, 96–9.

Pétain, before confirming plans to attack Russia in 1941. But he justified that decision (which reflected his own deepest desires) by insisting that Britain was placing its remaining hopes in Russia and so a successful war in the east would end the war in the west as well. It seems reasonable to suppose, therefore, that, had Hitler vanquished Russia in 1941, he would have resumed the endgame against Britain. And the indirect strategy of demolishing Britain's empire and strangling her supply routes offered an attractive alternative to the hazards of direct assault by air and land.[13]

To sense what might have happened, we need only look at the evolution of the Battle of the Atlantic in 1941–2. This, it should be noted, was waged by a German navy that had not begun preparing for war with Britain until 1938, which lacked its own reconnaissance aircraft, and whose resources were split between surface raiders (Hitler's obsession) and submarines (the preference of Raeder and Dönitz, the U-boat commander). Despite these weaknesses, in 1942 Nazi depredations neared the 700,000 tons a month target that Dönitz claimed would offset new construction by the Allies and force Britain to sue for peace. In November 1942, U-boats alone destroyed 729,000 tons of shipping—their best month of the war. The 1942 crisis coincided with (and was partly caused by) the German addition of a fourth wheel to their Enigma coding machines, rendering them unbreakable by the Allies between February and December. Only the codebreakers' success in regaining the initiative (and the introduction of High Frequency Direction Finders on Allied vessels from the summer) prevented the crisis from becoming a catastrophe. As it was, victory over the U-boat was not secured until the summer of 1943. Historian John Keegan suggests that if each U-boat had sunk only one more merchant ship in the summer of 1942, when losses already exceeded launchings by 10 per cent, 'the course, perhaps even the outcome, of the Second World War would have been entirely otherwise'.[14]

Even so, the consequences for Britain were grave. Imports in the first year of war were 44.2 million tons, compared with 50–60 million in the last years of peace. By calendar year 1942 they had dropped to 22.9 million tons. (The figure for 1917, with a smaller population to support, had been 29.8 million.) Churchill never forgot the import crisis. He claimed in his memoirs that he had been basically optimistic about invasion and the air threat and that the 'only thing that ever really frightened me during the war was the U-boat peril'. His writings at the time bear out this claim. His long letter to Roosevelt on 8 December 1940 is usually cited as the stimulus for Lend-Lease. In fact, finance took up only about one-tenth of this 4,000-word letter. 'I wish to focus on shipping', Churchill insisted to advisers, and he devoted over half the letter, plus

[13] Maier, *Germany and the Second World War*, ii. 367, 404–15, 419; G. Schreiber, B. Stegemann, and D. Vogel, *Das Deutsche Reich und der Zweite Weltkrieg*, iii (Stuttgart, 1984), 178–222.

[14] S. W. Roskill, *The War at Sea, 1939–1945*, ii (London, 1956), 94, 218, 485–6; H. Boog, W. Rahn, R. Stumpf, and B. Wagner, *Das Deutsche Reich and der Zweite Weltkrieg*, vi (Stuttgart, 1990), III/2–3, esp. p. 301; John Keegan, *The Second World War* (London, 1989), 123.

a long appendix, to the problem. He told the president that it was 'in shipping and in the power to transport across the oceans, particularly the Atlantic Ocean, that in 1941 the crunch of the whole war will be found'. In a similar strategic *tour d'horizon* dated 31 October 1942, Churchill told Roosevelt: 'First of all, I put the U-boat menace', insisting 'I cannot cut the food consumption here beyond its present level.' At the Casablanca conference the following January, the combined chiefs of staff stated: 'The defeat of the U-boat must remain a first charge on the resources of the United Nations.' They placed this ahead of all other desiderata: aiding Russia, invading Sicily, bombing Germany, and liberating France.[15]

Of course, Britain's exact import requirements are hard to establish. What constituted an essential minimum was keenly debated in Whitehall and, in fact, belt-tightening went much further than the prophets of doom believed possible. Moreover, some of the imports were required for offensive action, or to free British industry for war production, and this might not have been needed on such a scale if the fortress-Britain or limited-war scenarios had been adopted. It is also true that some of the losses of 1942 were due to the bloody minded slowness of (anglophobe) US Admiral Ernest R. King in adopting a (British) convoy policy for merchantmen in American waters.[16] None of these qualifications, however, invalidates the basic point: Britain was an island geographically but not economically. Its 'independence' could be threatened indirectly as well as directly. Even if the British could have resisted direct assault, by air or land, they were acutely vulnerable to blockade, particularly after 1940 when Germany acquired bases along the north and west coasts of France. In estimating the chances of the British reaching a viable peace or at least an armed modus vivendi with Hitler, one must take account of the Battle of the Atlantic as well as the Battle of Britain.

There are, then, cogent reasons for believing that Britain's 'independence' could not have been preserved, except in the very short term, while Hitler dominated continental Europe. Even if direct invasion had been repulsed or deterred, even if the *Luftwaffe* had been neutralized by successful defence and the threat of massive retaliation on Germany, there still remained the danger of death by strangulation. It is against this background that we must ponder Churchill's aphorism that 'there is only one thing worse than fighting with allies, and that is fighting without them!'[17]

---

[15] C. B. A. Behrens, *Merchant Shipping and the Demands of War* (2nd edn., London, 1978), 37–8, 190, 201; Winston S. Churchill, *The Second World War*, 6 vols. (London, 1948–54), ii. 529; David Reynolds, *Lord Lothian and Anglo-American Relations, 1939–1940* (Philadelphia, 1983), 46–7; Kimball, ed., *C-R*, ii. 103, 648, 650; Michael Howard, *Grand Strategy*, iv (London, 1970), 621.

[16] For a more sympathetic view of Admiral King see Eliot A. Cohen and John Gooch, *Military Misfortunes: The Anatomy of Failure in War* (New York, 1991), ch. 4.

[17] e.g. Alanbrooke diaries, 5/10, 1 Apr. 1945 (KCL).

The year 1940 had ended in stalemate. The British had been evicted from the Continent and the Germans held at bay above and around the British Isles. But the British military faced the spring of 1941 with new anxiety. During his visit to London in April 1941, General 'Hap' Arnold, head of the US Army Air Corps, found many British policy-makers admitting that the Germans could establish a beachhead on the south coast any time they were willing to make the sacrifice. He noted: 'Dill, Beaverbrook, Freeman and Sinclair all believe it can be done and will be tried.' Sir John Dill, chief of the imperial general staff, went so far as to send Churchill a formal memo on 6 May, warning against further diversion of troops to the Middle East. He argued that Germany could concentrate resources fairly quickly for an invasion and claimed that 'we have gone to the limit, if not beyond it, in respect of the security of Great Britain'. It was not until early June that British intelligence concluded that an attack on the Soviet Union was imminent, but, even then, most British policy-makers reckoned that Germany would win in three to six weeks. On 22 June Barbarossa began with devastating effect. On 1 July Churchill told Roosevelt: 'I am asking that everything here shall be at concert pitch for invasion from September 1st'.[18]

We know now that the Russians survived and eventually reversed the German onslaught, in a struggle that ended four years later amid the ruins of Berlin. But in 1941 Churchill and his colleagues would have needed a crystal ball (and one of particularly roseate hue) to foresee such an outcome. The stubborn Russian resistance in July 1941 enabled relaxation of anti-invasion plans on 2 August, when the British armed forces were told they would have one month's notice of any renewed threat. The Red Army's counter-attack in midwinter 1941–2 was heartening, but the new German offensive of June 1942 revived the previous year's anxieties, particularly in the Joint Planning Staff, who on 17 July were talking of 'the possibility of Russian defeat'. Much of the debate about Anglo-American strategy in mid-1942 revolved around this issue. By September the mood was more optimistic and in 1943, after the Russian victory at Stalingrad, the Joint Intelligence Committee advised that 'the prospect of a German defeat of Russia has receded to vanishing point'.[19]

On the other hand, the danger of another Nazi–Soviet pact seemed greater. At the end of January 1943, for example, the British ambassador in Moscow, Sir Archibald Clark Kerr, thought 'Stalin may make a separate peace if we do not help him.' We now know that the Soviet-German peace feelers via Stockholm were at their most active in the first half of 1943 and it seems likely that, at this stage, they reflected genuine interest on Stalin's part. After all, Russia was safe from defeat, but the Red Army was 1,000 miles from Berlin and

[18] Gen. H. H. Arnold, diary of visit to England, 21, 24 Apr. 1941, Arnold papers, box 271, Library of Congress, Washington, DC; WO 216/5 (TNA): Dill to Churchill, 6 May 1941; F. H. Hinsley et al., *British Intelligence in the Second World War* (4 vols., London, 1979–88), 470–83; Churchill to Roosevelt, 1 July 1941, in Kimball, ed., *C-R*, i. 216.

[19] Hinsley et al., *British Intelligence*, ii. 78–9, 101, 105, 615.

Anglo-American commitment to invading France was still uncertain. The details of these contacts remain unclear but they exercised British and US intelligence during the summer, at a time when Stalin was venting his fury at the May 1943 decision to defer a cross-Channel attack until the following year.[20]

For at least two years after Barbarossa, therefore, the possibility could not be ruled out of Hitler turning back to intensify the war against Britain and its sea lanes. During this period, too, the British had become dependent on the United States for economic survival against the German blockade. The most celebrated feature was Lend-Lease, in March 1941, when America was still neutral, under which Britain could receive essential goods and materials without need for immediate payment. This was not pure altruism—Roosevelt considered Britain to be America's front line of defence, giving his country time to rearm—and Churchill's description of Lend-Lease as 'the most unsordid act in history of any nation' was for public consumption. But the more sordid bargaining in private should not detract from the essential point. Even allowing for British reciprocal aid, Lend-Lease covered a staggering 54 per cent of the British balance of payments deficit in the war years 1939–45. A second facet of American aid, though less well known, was the president's commitment in November 1942 to alleviate Britain's supply crisis by promising that in 1943, 7 million tons of imports (a quarter of the estimated total) would be carried in US vessels. He told his advisers: 'If we are going to keep England in the war at anything like this maximum capacity, we must consider the supplementing of their merchant fleet as one of the top military necessities of the war.' Although Roosevelt, characteristically, had made the promise without squaring his own bureaucracy, causing a messy squabble in Washington, he did honour his commitment. What the US official historians called the 'gamble' of this 'massive shift of American shipping into British services' eventually paid off, because of victory in the Atlantic (and in the shipyards), but at the time it was a real gamble.[21]

Roosevelt's support for Britain was sustained against considerable domestic opposition. Lend-Lease required a bruising two-month battle in Congress—one of the longest legislative struggles of his whole presidency and as bitter as the Supreme Court furore of 1937. Even after America entered the war, priority for Britain remained controversial. The humiliations of Pearl Harbor and the Philippines left Americans most concerned for revenge against Japan. Polls in 1942 indicated that about 30 per cent of the American population favoured a

---

[20] Clark Kerr is quoted in Harold Nicolson, *Diaries and Letters, 1939–1945* (London, 1967), 277. See generally Vojtech Mastny, *Russia's Road to the Cold War* (New York, 1979), 73–85; Bernd Martin, 'Deutsch-sowjetische Sondierungen über einen separaten Friedensschluss im Zweiten Weltkrieg', in I. Auerbach, A. Hillgruber, and G. Schramm, eds., *Felder und Vorfelder Russischer Geschichte* (Freiburg, 1985), esp. pp. 281, 284–7; Ingeborg Fleischhauer, *Die Chance des Sonderfriedens: Deutsch-sowjetische Geheimgespräche, 1941–1945* (Berlin, 1986), esp. pp. 286–7.

[21] R. S. Sayers, *Financial Policy, 1939–1945* (London, 1956), 498; Richard M. Leighton and Robert W. Coakley, *Global Logistics and Strategy, 1940–1943* (Washington, DC, 1955), 679, 702.

compromise peace with Germany. Even in April 1944, after the campaigns in Tunisia and Italy, 20 per cent were willing to discuss peace with Hitler. And, among policy-makers, the 'Pacific First' strategy was consistently advanced by the US Navy and by some interested generals such as MacArthur. Their bureaucratic clout was evident in late summer 1942, during the policy deadlock about operations in Europe, as they swung idle manpower and resources into the Pacific war. At the end of the year more American troops were deployed against Japan than against Germany and Italy. Little wonder that Roosevelt was so anxious to get US troops into action in Europe in 1942. Otherwise the political and bureaucratic pressures against the 'Germany First' policy might have become overwhelming.[22]

For three years from June 1941, the Russians bore the brunt of the war against Germany. At the same time, Britain's economic survival came to depend heavily on American finance, shipping, and supplies. The Russians diverted the Nazi threat away from Britain; the Americans sustained the British against the German blockade. Whether or not Churchill paid too high a price at times, whether Britain had leverage of its own that could have been used more effectively, are important issues, but they require case-by-case analysis on a scale beyond the scope of a short essay. What I am emphasizing here is simply that Russian and American aid was vital to Britain in the dark middle years of the war. And it could not be taken for granted.

There was a third benefit of 'fighting with allies' that should also be noted. Russia and America were, in their separate ways, important for Britain's survival in 1940–3; jointly they were also essential to ensure victory in 1944–5. No separate peace had occurred. Nor had Germany collapsed. The battle had to be carried right into Berlin. The Russian contribution to victory was, of course, overwhelmingly the greatest. Between June 1941 and June 1944, 93 per cent of German Army battle casualties (4.2 million men) were inflicted by the Red Army. Even after D-Day, the Russians were facing about two-thirds of the Wehrmacht, except during the Battle of the Bulge. But the American contribution in Europe was significant in the last nine months of the war. Although only 43 per cent of the troops who hit the Normandy beaches on D-Day were American, the proportion grew inexorably over the ensuing months. At the end of the war 65 per cent of the 4 million Allied soldiers in Western Europe were American, only 20 per cent were British. Not surprisingly, the British Army Group in northern Germany became, by the spring of 1945, a marginal factor in the strategy and conduct of the final campaign.[23]

---

[22] Richard W. Steele, 'American Popular Opinion and the War against Germany: The Issue of a Negotiated Peace, 1942', *Journal of American History*, 65 (1978), esp. 705, 709, 722; Mark A. Stoler, 'The "Pacific First" Alternative in American World War II Strategy', *International History Review*, 2 (1980), 432–52; Leighton and Coakley, *Global Logistics*, 662.

[23] Jonathan R. Adelman, *Prelude to the Cold War: The Tsarist, Soviet, and US Armies in the Two World Wars* (London, 1988), 128, 176, 180; L. F. Ellis, *Victory in the West*, 2 vols. (London, 1962–8), ii. 406.

I have suggested so far that a compromise peace (or limited war) with a Hitler-dominated European continent would have been neither tenable nor desirable for Britain in the long run. I have also argued that Russian and American help was significant in averting British defeat and ensuring eventual victory. These were tasks that Britain could not achieve alone, as is clear if we look at the evolution of British strategy after 1940.

What must be emphasized is that Britain alone never had a credible policy for defeating Nazi Germany. It was assumed, when war began in September 1939, that Britain probably faced a long conflict, to be waged in the manner of the Hanoverians in the eighteenth and nineteenth centuries. That meant relying on Britain's economic, financial, and naval strength in conjunction with the manpower of continental allies—or, as the French put it, 'the British would fight to the last Frenchman'. Planning papers in 1939 envisaged that the French army, plus a token British Expeditionary Force, would resist the initial German onslaught. Then Germany's economy and morale would be undermined by blockade, bombing, and intensive propaganda, until the time was ripe for the final offensive.[24] The scenario was not dissimilar to that of 1914–18—a war of attrition which would end in the enemy's political and economic collapse, not a war of manoeuvre culminating in Germany's military defeat.

Even in 1939 this scenario was optimistic. The naval blockade had been of limited utility against Napoleonic France, a country significantly reliant on maritime trade. It was much less credible against Nazi Germany, which could draw on the resources of hinterland Central and Eastern Europe. And by the 1930s Britain itself was newly vulnerable to direct attack because, in the age of airpower, an enemy could leapfrog what Shakespeare called the 'moat defensive' and menace London—centre of government, commerce, and finance and home to one-fifth of the country's population. When Britain started to rearm in 1934, the government concentrated on creating a bombing force to match Germany's. After his famous warning that 'the bomber will always get through', Baldwin added that 'the only defence is in offence, which means that you have to kill more women and children more quickly than the enemy if you want to save yourselves'.[25] Although chances of defence against the bomber improved in the late 1930s, with fast monoplane fighters and the advent of radar, Britain's defence spending all through the war was shaped by this commitment to the bomber from the early 1930s. Equally important, during this time the army remained of minor concern. Unlike the continental powers since Bismarck's era, Britain had always eschewed peacetime conscription, counting on its empire (especially India) for global military manpower and on the French army nearer

---

[24] CAB 16/183A, DP(P) 44 (TNA): COS sub-commt., 'European Appreciation', 20 Feb. 1939, esp. paras 27–37, 267–8.
[25] Keith Middlemas and John Barnes, *Baldwin: A Biography* (London, 1969), p. 735; for the argument in this para. see generally David Reynolds, *Britannia Overruled: British Policy and World Power in the 20th Century* (London, 1991), ch. 5.

home. Fitting out a BEF was the lowest priority for defence spending in the late 1930s and in May 1940 Britain had only 10 divisions on the Western Front, compared with 104 French, 22 Belgian, and 8 Dutch.

The debacle of 1940 exposed and exacerbated the weaknesses of this strategy. Hitler's lightning conquests of Scandinavia and western Europe, coupled with his economic pact with Russia, made nonsense of any naval blockade. Italy's entry into the war opened up new dangers in the Mediterranean, at a time when France's collapse left the Royal Navy to face them alone. And Britain had only a tiny army (nearly lost at Dunkirk) with which to plan re-entry on to the continent of Europe, always assuming it could survive Nazi bombing, invasion, or blockade. Yet Churchill believed (rightly, I have argued) that a modus vivendi with Hitler would not guarantee security. How, after June 1940, did he expect to win the war?

Here historians have been too ready to take at face value his oratory, such as the famous words on 13 May 1940 about 'victory at all costs'. For traditionalists, they epitomize his 'indomitable stoutness'; for revisionists, they are proof of his self-delusion.[26] Both take them as a statement of policy. It would be more accurate, I think, to consider his words on 13 May as a rhetorical trope, designed to hearten Commons and country in his first speech as prime minister. Churchill knew that talk of victory was essential to head off talk of defeat. But total military victory over Germany had never been a British aim in 1939, let alone after France fell. We need to look more closely at Churchill's war aims and strategy as they evolved in the middle of the war.

Taking war aims first: left to itself in 1939–40, the British government assumed some kind of eventual negotiated peace. This was clearly Churchill's position, though Establishment figures have ridiculed such suggestions as 'rubbish'. In the Cabinet discussions during the Dunkirk crisis, Churchill left open the possibility of future negotiations: 'A time might come when we felt that we had to put an end to the struggle, but the terms would not then be more mortal than those offered to us now.' While this was partly intended to disabuse Halifax of the idea that he was a diehard, it reflects his position at other times. In August 1940 (as in October 1939) he argued that firm rejection of Hitler's peace offers was 'the only chance of extorting from Germany any offers which are not fantastic'.[27]

The British position in mid-1940 can be discerned more clearly in the light of discussions a year later. In a speech on 5 July 1941 Anthony Eden, the Foreign Secretary, stated that 'we were not prepared to negotiate with Hitler at any time on any subject'. (The previous December the Foreign Office had baulked at such a categorical statement. Frank Roberts of the Central Department had advised

---

[26] Cf. Isaiah Berlin, *Mr Churchill in 1940* (London, 1964), 15, 26; Charmley, *Churchill*, 401–2, 465–8, 596.

[27] David Reynolds, 'Churchill and the British "Decision" to Fight On in 1940: Right Policy, Wrong Reasons', in Richard Langhorne, ed., *Diplomacy and Intelligence during the Second World War* (Cambridge, 1985), esp. pp. 152–4; cf. Lord Annan in *London Review of Books*, 1 Aug. 1985, p. 5.

against a public commitment about 'never undertaking negotiations in any circumstances with Herr Hitler'.) On 7 July 1941 Churchill drew the War Cabinet's attention to Eden's words: 'While this statement expressed the opinion of the whole War Cabinet, it was perhaps the most explicit public declaration on the subject that had been made. Such a declaration had been necessary at this moment in order to forestall any peace offensive by Hitler in the near future.' The Cabinet minute concluded: 'The War Cabinet took note, with approval, of this declaration.'[28] Churchill's remarks (and the care taken to record Cabinet approval) suggest awareness that this was a significant policy step.

This firming up of policy reflected the need to reassure the Soviet Union, where London's secrecy about the Hess mission had strengthened fears of an Anglo-German deal against Russia. One of Stalin's first demands from his new British ally was a pledge not to sign a separate peace with Germany. But Russia's own resistance could not be guaranteed and Churchill told the Cabinet on 5 September that he 'had the feeling that the possibility of a separate peace by Stalin could not be altogether excluded'. By then Churchill also had America to consider, having agreed what became known as the Atlantic Charter at his meeting with Roosevelt in August. Although he had hoped for a declaration of war not of war aims, the moral identification of America with the Allied cause was significant. The Charter did, however, allude to 'the final destruction of the Nazi tyranny' and, more generally, implied that British diplomacy towards Germany would henceforth take account of America as well as Russia. Churchill's frame of reference by the autumn of 1941 is shown by his insistence on 10 September that there should not be 'the slightest contact' with any German peace feelers. 'Nothing would be more disturbing to our friends in the United States or more dangerous with our new ally, Russia, than the suggestion that we were entertaining such ideas.'[29]

Yet this did not mean that an eventual negotiated peace had now been ruled out. In November 1941 Eden was keen about 'exorcising certain suspicions in Stalin's mind', including the idea that Britain would 'be prepared to make peace with a Germany controlled by the Army, if they were to overthrow the Party'. It is interesting to note that Churchill did not rule out this idea. According to the Cabinet minutes for 27 November 1941, he said that

we had made a public statement that we would not negotiate with Hitler or with the Nazi *regime*; but he thought it would be going too far to say that we would not negotiate with a

[28] CAB 65/19, WM 66 (41) 5 (TNA), 7 July 1941; cf. FO 371/24362, C13729/7/62 (TNA), minute by Roberts, 18 Dec. 1940, noted without contradiction by Strang and Cadogan.
[29] CAB 65/23, WM 90 (41) 3 CA (TNA), 5 Sept 1941; PREM 4/100/8 (TNA): Churchill to Eden, M888/1, 10 Sept 1941. Cf. Gabriel Gorodetsky, 'The Hess Affair and Anglo-Soviet Relations on the Eve of "Barbarossa"', *English Historical Review*, 101 (1986), 405–20; and David Reynolds, 'The Atlantic "Flop": British Foreign Policy and the Churchill–Roosevelt Meeting of August 1941', in Douglas Brinkley and David Facey-Crowther, eds., *The Atlantic Charter* (New York, 1994), 129–50.

Germany controlled by the Army. It was impossible to forecast what form of Government there might be in Germany at a time when their resistance weakened and they wished to negotiate.[30]

How was this eventual negotiated peace to be achieved? Not, it should be stressed, by invading the Continent and smashing a way to Berlin. This was even less likely after the fall of France than it had been in 1939: the Allies no longer had even a beachhead on the Continent. As befitted a state that had consistently placed its army last in defence priorities, Churchill's government always assumed that invading Fortress Europe would be the final *coup de grâce* rather than the central *coup de main*. To quote the Chiefs of Staff in September 1940:

It is not our policy to attempt to raise, and land on the continent, an army comparable in size to that of Germany. We should aim nevertheless, as soon as the action of the blockade and the air offensive have secured conditions when numerically inferior forces can be employed with good chance of success, to re-establish a striking force on the Continent with which we can enter Germany and impose our terms.

Churchill certainly saw the army in this essentially auxiliary role. The humiliating disasters of 1940–2—from Norway and Dunkirk to Singapore and Tobruk—cast a permanent shadow over his evaluation of German and British military capabilities. 'I am ashamed. I cannot understand why Tobruk gave in,' he told his physician in June 1942. 'More than 30,000 of our men put their hands up. If they won't fight . . .' He stopped, abruptly. Reviewing the war situation the following month, he placed first among its 'salient features' what he called 'the immense power of the German military machine'. Bearing in mind what two panzer divisions and one light division had done in North Africa 'against our greatly superior numbers and resources,' he wrote, 'we have no excuse for underrating German military power in 1943 and 1944. It will always be possible for them to set up a holding front against Russia and bring back fifty or sixty, or even more, divisions to the West.'[31] This was why he adamantly opposed plans for invading France before German power was broken.

How, then, did Churchill imagine that Germans would be brought to overthrow Nazism and seek peace? Frankly, he was not sure but, like most strategists, he sought guidance from the previous war. This was evident in his speech of 18 June 1940, quoted in Chapter 4, when he reminded the Commons of the suddenness with which the apparently formidable Kaiserreich had disintegrated in 1918. This scenario underpinned British strategic thinking through the middle of the Second World War, as evidenced by the steady flow of reports to

---

[30] CAB 65/24, WM 120 (41) 5 CA (TNA), 27 Nov. 1941; cf. Eden's paper printed as CAB 66/20, WP (41) 288.

[31] CAB 80/17, COS (40) 683 (TNA), 4 Sept. 1940, para 214; Lord Moran, *Churchill: The Struggle for Survival, 1940–1965* (London, 1968), 21 June 1942, p. 55; CAB 66/26, WP (42) 311 (TNA), 21 July 1942; cf. Joseph L. Strange, 'The British Rejection of Operation SLEDGEHAMMER: An Alternative Motive', *Military Affairs*, 46: 1 (Feb. 1982), 6–14.

the Cabinet and chiefs of staff on the state of economy and morale, both in Germany and the extended Reich. In these the prediction of a 1918-style collapse of 'startling rapidity' recurred at times of particular optimism.[32]

The disintegration of 1918 had begun with Germany's allies and this is one reason why Churchill was so keen to support subversion within the Third Reich. The Special Operations Executive that he created in the summer of 1940 was intended to help 'set Europe ablaze', exploding timely 'detonators' to set off resistance movements across Europe. His celebrated 'peripheral strategy' into the Baltic and the Mediterranean always had this in mind. Invasion of Italy in 1943, for example, was predicated on the (eventually erroneous) assumption that Hitler would evacuate most of the peninsula up to the Alps. This campaign was therefore expected to knock one member of the Axis out of the war quickly, at little cost. It would also allow the Allies to aid the partisan struggles in Greece and Yugoslavia. Churchill told Eisenhower in July 1943, 'if we can get hold of the mouth of the Adriatic so as to be able to run even a few ships into Dalmatian and Greek ports, the whole of the Western Balkans might flare up with far-reaching results'.[33]

The main assumption behind British hopes of a Nazi collapse lay in the supposed tautness of Germany's economy and morale, as we saw in Chapter 4. This was an axiom of British thinking in 1940–2, reflecting the erroneous belief that Germany's economy was already fully mobilized for war, and it gave apparent credibility to the strategy of maintaining economic pressure on the enemy. The problem was how to keep up that pressure, given Hitler's vast conquests in 1940. Although the MEW talked in September 1940 of the blockade henceforth as 'a stiletto rather than a bludgeon', Churchill himself had no doubt that the blockade had been 'blunted and rendered largely ineffectual'.[34] *Faute de mieux,* he looked to the skies not the seas. Hence his assertion to the Cabinet that the Fighters were Britain's 'salvation' in 1940, but the Bombers alone provided 'the means of victory'.[35] As we have seen, this remained the foundation of his strategy right through 1941.

During 1942, any hope of an alternative German government faded. In part, this reflected a hardening of opinion in Whitehall as Nazi atrocities became evident and convictions strengthened about the incorrigibility of Germany as a whole. Over the 'last 70 years', Eden told the Commons in December 1942, 'successive German Governments have consciously and consistently pursued a policy of world domination' and it would therefore be 'sheer folly to allow some

---

[32] Commons, *Debates*, 5s, 362: 59–60, 18 June 1940; cf. Hinsley et al., *British Intelligence*, ii. 98, 114, 159.

[33] David Stafford, 'The Detonator Concept: British Strategy, SOE and European Resistance after the Fall of France', *Journal of Contemporary History*, 10 (1975), 185–212; Hinsley et al., *British Intelligence*, 3/1, pp. 5, 14; Michael Howard, *Grand Strategy*, iv (London, 1970), 501.

[34] CAB 79/6, COS (40) 295th mtg.(TNA), 5 Sept. 1940, esp. item 2, annex and appendix.

[35] CAB 66/11, WP (40) 352, (TNA).

non-Nazi German Government to be set up, and then, so to speak, to trust to luck'. Although the term 'unconditional surrender' was only unveiled publicly by Roosevelt and Churchill at Casablanca in January 1943, it had been circulating privately in Whitehall for some months before. Equally significant in the hardening of attitudes were the constraints of alliance politics, once both Russia and America were formally in the war. As early as January 1942, the United Nations declaration pledged signatories to 'complete victory over their enemies'. Sensitivity to the views of Washington and Moscow (and also of the minor European allies) dictated a continued policy of 'absolute silence' to peace feelers and encouraged the preference for a blank-slate approach to peacemaking rather than haggling with numerous allies over possible terms. Moreover, the entry of Russia and America now made military victory more likely. Unconditional surrender therefore seemed both desirable and possible—the two aspects were reciprocally related.[36]

Although Britain's prospects and goals were gradually transformed during 1942, it is noteworthy that Churchill's strategic framework remained essentially the same: the new wine was poured into old bottles. For instance, in his paper on 'The Campaign of 1943', written in December 1941 after Pearl Harbor, Churchill suggested that, as the growing power of the three allies was brought to bear on Germany, 'an internal collapse is always possible, but we must not count on this'. The alternative scenario was therefore 'the defeat in Europe of the German armies'. But 'it need not be assumed that great numbers of men would be required'; rather 'armies of liberation', spearheaded by 'armoured and mechanised forces', in conjunction with popular revolt. 'We have therefore to prepare for the liberation of the captive countries of Western and Southern Europe by the landing at suitable points, successively or simultaneously, of British and American armies strong enough to enable the conquered populations to revolt.'[37]

Reviewing the war position on 21 July 1942, Churchill appeared to recognize the dubiousness of strategic bombing and the new strategic position following American entry. He wrote:

In the days when we were fighting alone, we answered the question: 'How are you going to win the war?' by saying: 'We will shatter Germany by bombing.' Since then the enormous injuries inflicted on the German Army and man-power by the Russians, and the accession of the man-power and munitions of the United States, have rendered other possibilities open.

But these 'other possibilities' were actually variations on the old theme: 'We look forward to mass invasion of the Continent by liberating armies, and the general

---

[36] Commons, *Debates*, 5s, 385: 1238, 2 Dec. 1942; Rainer A. Blasius, 'Waiting for Action: The Debate on the "Other Germany" in Great Britain and the Reaction of the Foreign Office to German "Peace-Feelers", 1942', in Francis R. Nicosia and Lawrence D. Stokes, eds., *Germans against Nazism: Nonconformity, Opposition and Resistance in the Third Reich* (New York, 1990), esp. pp. 296–300.   [37] J. R. M. Butler, *Grand Stategy*, iii, part 1 (London, 1964), 334–5.

revolt of the populations against the Hitler tyranny.' Moreover, he added,

it would be a mistake to cast aside our original thought which, it may be mentioned, is also strong in American minds, namely, that the severe ruthless bombing of Germany on an ever-increasing scale will not only cripple her war effort including U-boat and aircraft production, but will also create conditions intolerable to the mass of the German population.

This memo was intended for widespread official consumption, in Washington as well as London. In private, Churchill was even more categorical. He told Clement Attlee, the deputy prime minister, on 29 July 1942:

Continuous reflection leaves me with the conclusion that, upon the whole, our best chance of winning the war is with the big Bombers. It certainly will be several years before British and American land forces will be capable of beating the Germans on even terms in the open field.[38]

Even in 1942–3 British policy continued to hope for a German internal collapse. In June 1942, with the Nazis' Russian offensive in full cry, the Cabinet's Joint Intelligence Committee advised that, between August and October, 'events may move to a climax . . . and it may be touch and go which of the two adversaries collapses first'. The JIC acknowledged that 'we cannot rule out the possibility of Russia collapsing', but was more hopeful about the Axis crumbling first. 'If the Germans realise that they cannot avoid another winter campaign in Russia and are faced with the threat of Anglo-American invasion in the West, they may collapse with unprecedented rapidity as they did in 1918.' The Chiefs of Staff thought that the picture was 'painted in rather too rosy a hue for Russia'. But Churchill considered it 'a very good appreciation'. Perhaps the high-water mark of the 1918 scenario came in September 1943. On the day after the Italian surrender, the JIC produced a paper which it went so far as to entitle 'Probabilities of a German Collapse'. This was a historical comparison between the current situation and the dramatic finale of the Great War. The JIC concluded that 'Germany is if anything, in a worse position to-day than she was in the same period of 1918.' But for the fact that the country was this time under a brutal, totalitarian regime, 'we should unhesitatingly predict that Germany would sue for an armistice before the end of the year'. In this connection, the JIC noted, 'great weight must again attach to the view taken by Germany's Allies'. Churchill had the paper circulated to the War Cabinet.[39]

At the same time, he had still not modified his opposition to a premature invasion of the Continent (as will be seen in more detail in Chapter 6).

---

[38] CAB 66/26, WP (42) 311(TNA), memo of 21 July 1942, para 6; PREM 3/499/9 (TNA): Churchill to Attlee, 29 July 1942. A copy of WP 311 was passed, for instance, to the US War Dept.—see George C. Marshall Library, Lexington, VA: Verifax 1278.
[39] PREM 3/395/13: JIC (42) 200, 1 June 1942, paras 69–71(TNA); Hollis to Churchill, 5 June 1942; Churchill to Ismay, 7 June; CAB 66/42, WP (43) 479, JIC (43) 367(TNA), 9 Sept. 1943.

But Churchill was no longer able to shape Allied strategy. This was demonstrated by his coerced commitment at Teheran in November 1943 to invade France the following spring. American military planners (outside the Army Air Force) had never shared the British concept of a war of attrition, using the army only for the knock-out blow when Germany was about to collapse. They saw this as 'a confession of bankruptcy', a strategy 'derived from British weakness'.[40] More exactly, it was derived from general weakness and specific strengths, particularly the 1930s concentration on the bomber. If not quite a case of making bricks without straw, certainly grasping at whatever straws were blowing in the wind, such as the persistent hope that Germany was over-stretched.

By the autumn of 1943, the bankruptcy of British strategy was evident. Churchill had lost faith in strategic bombing, as photographic and economic intelligence cast doubts on the RAF's claims. Even in December 1942 he was speaking of the bombing offensive not as the winning weapon but only as 'our principal effort in the air'. Meanwhile, the peripheral approach had resulted in lengthy wars of attrition in Tunisia and Italy, in which it was far from clear whether the Allies were pinning down the Germans or vice versa. Nor had European resistance been detonated; instead, notes David Stafford, the dynamite proved 'a rather damp squib'. Robert Keyserlingk observes that this whole strategy rested on a misplaced faith in the 'essential decency (*Anständigkeit*) and power of historic European nationalism' and yielded 'no tangible results'. In fact, after the JIC's heady optimism of September 1943 evaporated, Churchill became increasingly sceptical about a German collapse. On 5 January 1944, he expected Hitler still to be in power on the fifth anniversary of the war, 3 September 1944. A few days later, the JIC admitted in response to Churchill's questioning that they now saw no prospect of Germany crumbling from within and acknowledged that the Russian advance into the Balkans would probably prompt Nazi occupation rather than Axis collapse.[41]

At the same time, however, the idea of a compromise peace with Hitler remained unacceptable. The threat, direct and indirect, remained. There was the looming menace of Nazi V-weapons, eventually unleashed in June 1944 and developed by Hitler at great expense to the strained Nazi war economy as terror weapons against Britain. Moreover, the battle of the Atlantic had only just been turned and Raeder made a new effort with modernized U-boats in 1944. Here we have reached the heart of Churchill's strategic dilemma. Britain was right to

[40] Leighton and Coakley, *Global Logistics*, 119; Theodore A. Wilson, *The First Summit: Roosevelt and Churchill at Placentia Bay, 1941*, 2nd edn. (Lawrence, Kan, 1991), 122.

[41] CAB 66/32, WP (42) 580 (TNA): Churchill, note on 'Air Policy', 16 Dec. 1942; Stafford, 'The Detonator Concept', 210; Robert H. Keyserlingk, 'Die Deutsche Komponente in Churchills Strategie der Nationalen Erhebungen, 1940–1942', *Vierteljahrshefte für Zeitgeschichte*, 31 (1983), 625, 634; John Colville, *The Fringes of Power: Downing Street Diaries, 1939–1955* (London, 1985), 433; PREM 3/396/10 (TNA): esp. JIC interim report in Ismay to Hollis, 14 Jan. 1944. See also the insightful discussion in Tuvia Ben-Moshe, *Churchill: Strategy and History* (Boulder, Colo. 1992), ch. 9.

fight on in 1940 but, alone, she had no viable strategy for eliminating the Hitler threat. Churchill complained privately in April 1944 that *Overlord* had been 'forced upon us by the Russians and the United States military authorities'.[42] But D-Day was also tacit recognition that British strategy had reached the end of the road. Only military victory would force a German collapse—not blockade, bombing, subversion or peripheral operations. And this victory could only be won by Russian and American arms.

What some critics, then and later, saw as Churchill's growing 'appeasement' of America and Russia was the diplomatic consequence of that strategic reality. This is not to suggest that he had absolutely no room for manoeuvre—as indicated by his occasional disputes with Eden, particularly over France and de Gaulle. Nor is it to imply that his vision was unclouded by sentiment. Today his talk in September 1943 about 'common citizenship' between the United States and the United Kingdom seems Utopian, as do his remarks to Eden in January 1944 about 'the deep-seated changes which have taken place in the character of the Russian State and Government' and 'the new confidence which has grown in our hearts towards Stalin'. But Churchill's differences with Eden were matters of emphasis not substance: the foreign secretary's francophilia hardly offered the prospect of 'some control for Britain over an independent foreign policy'. And while it is neat and, up to a point, apt, to compare Churchill and Chamberlain as 'appeasers', the 'man of Yalta' and the 'man of Munich'—one writing off the Poles, the other sacrificing the Czechs—there remains a fundamental difference.[43] Churchill had his blind spots about Roosevelt and Stalin, whereas Chamberlain's vision was clouded about Hitler. Misjudging one's allies is dangerous, but misjudging one's enemies can be fatal.

Churchill's 'policy' was not 'glory'. It was not even 'victory at all costs'. Less elegantly but more accurately his aim is encapsulated in his private motto of 1940–1: 'KBO' or 'Keep Buggering On'.[44] He was right that Britain could not be secure as long as Nazi Germany controlled continental Europe, but his strategy for security was largely wishful thinking. Ultimately, this is not a comment on Churchill's mind but on Britain's power. The country never had a capacity alone for waging a continental war, in the nineteenth century let alone the twentieth. Its global power had assumed a continental balance maintained by other means. In defeating Hitler—as with Napoleon and the Kaiser, not to mention Philip II of Spain or Louis XIV—allies were needed to enhance Britain's strength. And, where these were lacking, appeasement was a long-standing method of adjusting policy to the limits of power—'in a sense,'

---

[42] PREM 3/197/2(TNA): Churchill to Cadogan, 19 Apr. 1944.

[43] Charmley, *Churchill*, 541, 551, 556, 561, 612; cf. David Reynolds, 'Great Britain: Imperial Diplomacy', in Reynolds, W. F. Kimball, and A. O. Chubarian, eds., *Allies at War: The Soviet, American, and British Experience, 1939–1945* (New York, 1994), 333–53.

[44] Charmley, *Churchill*, 560; M. Gilbert, *Churchill*, vii. 1273.

Paul Kennedy has observed, 'the "natural" policy for a small island state gradually losing its place in world affairs'.[45]

This reminds us also of the limits of biography. Although there has not been space here for detailed examination of Churchill's wartime diplomacy, I have argued that it must be set in its proper context. That means not only the international situation and the strategic calculus, but also the long-term dilemmas of British power. Near the end of her classic study of *Britain and the Origins of the First World War*, Zara Steiner quoted Lord Salisbury's observation of 1895: 'Power has passed from the hands of Statesmen, but I should be very much puzzled to say into whose hands it has passed.'[46] Half a century later, Churchill would have understood. He *is* open to the label of appeaser, particularly when taken in its historical context. But one could equally remark on the power he was able to conjure out of impotence—how much he made out of so little for so long.

[45] Paul Kennedy, *Strategy and Diplomacy, 1870–1945* (London, 1984), 38; Reynolds, *Britannia Overruled*, 19–25, 61–2.

[46] Zara S. Steiner, *Britain and the Origins of the First World War* (London, 1977), 250.

6

Churchill and Allied Grand Strategy in Europe, 1944–1945

The Erosion of British Influence

Winston Churchill did not always get his way: British grand strategy in the last year of the war was not simply a mirror of his mind. But the prime minister played a more active, hands-on role in the daily making of policy than did Franklin D. Roosevelt. The US Army chief of staff, General George C. Marshall, confessed after the war that 'sometimes I didn't see the President for a month'.[1] Marshall's British counterpart, Sir Alan Brooke, would often have regarded even a week without Churchill as paradise. Roosevelt was generally content to set the course and leave the details to Marshall and the Joint Chiefs, whereas British strategy, grand or operational, in 1944–45 bears Churchill's imprint at every stage.

A second contrast with Roosevelt is that Churchill left his own interpretation of that strategy for posterity. Even if FDR had not died before the war was over, it is hard to imagine him grinding away at Hyde Park on tomes of self-vindication. Some fireside chats with Harry Hopkins, serialized in the *Saturday Evening Post*, would probably have been all he left by way of disinformation. Churchill, in contrast, set out his account of the war in six volumes, buttressed by selective but massive quotation from his own papers. As he said in September 1944, after losing the argument over landings in southern France, he would leave the controversy to history but would himself be one of the historians. In the later volumes of memoirs he was intent on providing his wisdom as grand strategist in two respects. First, he wished to 'dispose of the many American legends that I was inveterately opposed to the plan of a large-scale Channel crossing'. Second, he wanted to demonstrate his early recognition 'that Soviet Russia had become

---

This chapter was first presented at a conference to mark the fiftieth anniversary of D-Day at the Roosevelt Study Center in Middelburg, the Netherlands. It was subsequently published in the conference volume: Charles F. Brower, ed., *World War II in Europe: The Final Year* (New York, St Martin's, 1998), 39–54. Although I used and have cited the manuscript version of Alanbrooke's diaries and 'notes on my life', these have now been published as Field Marshal Lord Alanbrooke, *War Diaries, 1939–1945*, ed. Alex Danchev and Daniel Todman (London, 2001).

[1] Larry I. Bland, ed., *George C. Marshall Interviews and Reminiscences for Forrest C. Pogue*, 2nd edn. (Lexington, Va., 1991), 321.

a mortal danger to the free world', requiring the projection of Allied troops 'as far east as possible' to achieve a settlement with the Russians 'before the armies of democracy had melted'. He was particularly scathing about the American decision to emasculate the Allied army in Italy, which was thereby 'deprived of its opportunity to strike a most formidable blow at the Germans, and very possibly to reach Vienna before the Russians, with all that might have followed there from'.[2]

These claims indicate the three broad themes of this chapter: Churchill's attitude to Overlord and the campaign in northwest Europe, his preoccupation with the Italian theatre, and, related to both of these, the place of the Russians in his grand strategy. In addition, we need to consider how he kept one eye on the balance of power with the Americans as well. For the last year of the war saw the weight of the alliance shift dramatically away from Britain, as Russian victories and American manpower came to dominate events. At Teheran in November 1943 Churchill claimed to have sensed 'for the first time what a small nation we are'. He spoke of 'the poor little English donkey' caught between 'the great Russian bear' and 'the great American buffalo'.[3] This became a familiar refrain: the animals varied, but not the idea of Britain trying to hold its own in an international *ménage à trois*. In terms of grand strategy this meant that command was as important as strategy, and who got the credit mattered as much as what was done.

Did Churchill accept that an invasion of France would be necessary? To that the answer is 'yes'. Did he want Overlord in 1944? Here the answer is 'no'. Ever since 1939 British grand strategy had been to wage a war of attrition until the Germans collapsed from within. This policy was confirmed by the fall of France, which left Britain without a foothold on the Continent and with no major land power as ally. Even when the Battle of Russia had run its course in 1941–43 and US manpower was mobilized, Churchill and his chiefs of staff remained doubtful about invading France except as a *coup de grâce*. They were still awed by the Wehrmacht, doubtful of their own army after the disasters of 1940–42, and sceptical about the quality of the GIs. Churchill noted in the autumn of 1943 that Overlord should be 'a knock-out blow, the timing of which must be settled in relation to the condition and dispositions of the enemy'. He told FDR: 'Unless there is a German collapse the campaign of 1944 will be far the most dangerous we have undertaken and personally I am more anxious about its success than I was about 1941, 1942, or 1943.'[4]

By implication, this put 1944 on a par with 1940; indeed, that was Churchill's deepest nightmare. Although he occasionally spoke in lurid terms about the

---

[2] John Colville, *The Fringes of Power: Downing Street Diaries, 1939–1955* (London, 1985), 509; Winston S. Churchill, *The Second World War*, 6 vols. (London, 1948–54), iv. 584, vi. 90, 400.

[3] John Charmley, *Churchill: The End of Glory* (London, 1993), 548.

[4] CAB 66/44, WP (43) 586 (TNA): Churchill, memo, 26 November 1943; Churchill to FDR, 17 October 1943, in Warren F. Kimball, ed., *Churchill and Roosevelt: The Complete Correspondence*, 3 vols. (Princeton, 1984), ii. 541. See also Tuvia Ben-Moshe, *Churchill: Strategy and History* (Boulder, Colo., 1992), 245–76.

Channel running with blood, his real fear was not another Dieppe but a second Dunkirk. He told the chiefs of staff in October 1943 that he 'felt that we should probably effect a lodgement and in the first instance we might make progress. It was the later stages of the operation which worried him.' He feared that Germany might shift troops rapidly across the Continent and 'inflict on us a military disaster greater than that of Dunkirk' that would lead to 'the resuscitation of Hitler and the Nazi regime'.[5]

Throughout 1943, Churchill tried to block or postpone Overlord. At Teheran, the combined weight of Roosevelt and Stalin compelled acquiescence, but, as his official biographer observes, the lassitude and despondency that so many noted in early 1944 was the result not merely of recent illness but also of trepidation at what was to come. Characteristically, the adrenalin began to flow as D-Day approached and he assured Eisenhower and others that he was 'hardening' to the enterprise. Although attempts have been made to explain away this remark, it accurately reflects his attitude that spring—private doubts but public fortitude. On 9 April he told Sir Alexander Cadogan of the Foreign Office (who had exclaimed the previous autumn that 'all this "Overlord" folly must be thrown "Overboard" '): 'This battle has been forced upon us by the Russians and the United States military authorities. We have gone in wholeheartedly, and I would not raise a timorous cry before a decision in the field has been taken.'[6]

The successful landings on 6 June were a relief. But, as he had told Stalin the previous November, Churchill 'was not afraid of going on shore, but what would happen on the 30th, 40th or 50th day?' Like Eisenhower, he did not expect that the Allied deception campaign, Operation Fortitude, threatening a main attack around Calais, would distract the Germans from a major counter-offensive for as long as it did. He wrote to one member of Parliament with a mixture of hope and foreboding on 15 June: 'Very heavy fighting lies ahead in France but I expect our power to reinforce is greater than the enemy's—at any rate for some time.' He therefore viewed with mounting misgivings the stalemate on the Allied front, especially around Caen, which Montgomery had talked of capturing on or soon after D-Day.[7]

Exacerbating Churchill's anxiety in midsummer was the collapse of the Italian campaign. As Michael Howard has shown, Churchill did not have a coherent Mediterranean strategy. Talk of targeting the 'soft underbelly' of the Axis originated in a desperate ploy to persuade Stalin in August 1942 that the invasion of North Africa *was* the second front. It was a slogan not a strategy. The moves into northwest Africa, Sicily, and Italy were successive improvisations, taking advantage of events and employing troops and ships that were temporarily idle.

[5] CAB 79/66, COS (43) 254 (0) (TNA), 19 October 1943, item 4.

[6] Martin Gilbert, *Winston S. Churchill*, vii: *1941–1945* (London, 1986), 738, 746, 760; Colville, *Fringes of Power*, 483; Carlo d'Este, *Decision in Normandy* (New York, 1991), 87–90; David Dilks, ed., *The Diaries of Sir Alexander Cadogan, OM, 1938–1945* (London, 1971), 26 October 1943, 570; PREM 3/197/2 (TNA): Churchill to Cadogan, M 446/4, 19 April 1944.

[7] CAB 66/45, WP (44) 9 (TNA); Churchill to Shinwell, 15 June 1944, CHAR 20/146 (CAC).

But they did have some strategic rationale. In the case of Italy in 1943, British intelligence assumed on the basis of Ultra that the Germans would evacuate most of the country and withdraw to the Maritime Alps. Churchill was therefore hoping for a relatively easy victory, but one that would have dramatic effect on the political balance across southeast Europe. At the Algiers Conference in June 1943, he was emphatic 'that he was not advocating sending any army into the Balkans now or in the near future'. But he expected to use Italy as a base to aid the partisan struggles in Yugoslavia and Greece. He told Eisenhower on 7 July that 'if we can get hold of the mouth of the Adriatic' then 'the whole of the Western Balkans might flare up with far reaching results'. This was the old concept of Allied aid as 'detonator' for explosive forces within the German empire. Churchill had not forgotten that the collapse in 1918 began with the Bulgarian armistice. And he kept one eye on Turkey, whom he forever hoped to entice into the Allied camp, where it would form a vital hinge between British and Russian operations.[8]

This was a grandiose vision. *If* one accepted British assumptions about how the war should be fought and won, it made some sense. And, if it had been realized, the balance of power in southern Europe would have been dramatically changed. But the Americans did not accept the basic assumptions. And, on 4 October 1943, the gamble of an easy victory failed when Hitler reversed his policy and directed Kesselring to hold on south of Rome. A similar decision by Hitler in November 1942 to fight for Tunisia had led to a long and bloody battle, thereby playing havoc with strategic timetables for 1943. As Churchill grimly observed then: 'I never wanted the Anglo-American Army to be stuck in North Africa. It is a spring-board not a sofa.' Likewise, in the autumn of 1943, a similar misreading of Hitler's obduracy turned Italy into a quagmire, in which, as Marshall feared, the Allied troops became bogged down.[9]

The Anzio landing of January 1944 was a desperate, half-baked, and ill-supplied effort by Churchill to regain the initiative. He hoped, in his favoured phrase, 'to land a wild cat that would tear out the bowels' of the Germans, but instead he 'stranded a vast whale with its tail flopping about in the water!' Failure at Anzio left him even more pessimistic about a similar landing in France and it condemned the Allied forces to stalemate throughout the winter. Even talk of tying down Germans rang hollow. With two or even threefold Allied preponderance, historian Alex Danchev asks, was 'Alexander containing Kesselring, or Kesselring containing Alexander?' The narrow, mountainous Italian peninsula overwhelmingly favoured the defence. As Marshall observed after the war, 'the soft underbelly had chrome-steel baseboards'.[10]

[8] Michael Howard, *The Mediterranean Strategy in the Second World War* (London, 1968), 2, 69; F. H. Hinsley et al., *British Intelligence in the Second World War*, 4 vols. (London, 1979–88), iii/1. 5, 14; Michael Howard, *Grand Strategy*, vol. iv (London, 1970), 499, 501.

[9] Hinsley et al., *British Intelligence*, iii/1. 173; Gilbert, *Churchill*, vii. 260.

[10] Brooke, diary, 29 February 1944, Alanbrooke Papers, 5/8, Liddell Hart Centre, King's College, London; Alex Danchev, 'Great Britain: The Indirect Strategy', in David Reynolds,

Why, then, did Churchill persist in his Italian obsession? Partly because it fitted his strategic vision for an ultimate German collapse and because he remained hopeful of a decisive breakthrough once summer campaigning began. But alliance politics were equally important. Italy was a theatre in which the British had preponderance. Churchill told Stalin at Teheran that 'there were three or four times more British troops than American' in the Mediterranean, and that roughly 10 of the 14 divisions in Italy were British. This was reflected in the command structure. Churchill said he had accepted a US commander for Normandy because the Americans 'would soon have a preponderance in "Overlord" and their stake would be greater after the first few months'. On the other hand, as the British were more numerous in the Mediterranean, they were able to choose the commander and, Churchill added, he 'had his own ideas about the war there'. Moreover, he did not scruple to intervene directly, bypassing the Americans (and sometimes his own Chiefs of Staff). He told General Sir Henry Maitland Wilson in February 1944: 'While I do not wish to interfere with your direct communications to the Combined Chiefs of Staff, you are free if you wish to let me see privately beforehand what you propose to send', by using secret intelligence channels.[11]

The combination of British predominance and British commanders meant that success would be credited largely to Britain. Alanbrooke noted after the war Churchill's underlying 'desire to form a purely British theatre when the laurels would be all ours'. And, as Michael Howard remarks, this 'element of sheer chauvinism' became 'an ever stronger factor in his strategic thinking as time went on'. This was surely a response to Britain's diminishing contribution to the alliance. In 1942 the British had been able to determine second-front strategy because they would provide most of the manpower for a cross-Channel attack. By 1944, however, America's belated but massive mobilization had taken effect, while Britain's had passed its peak. Churchill admitted in November 1943 that 'our man-power is now fully mobilized for the war effort; on the contrary, it is already dwindling'. That meant, he said, that 'if the war against Germany continues after the end of 1944 we shall have to rely increasingly on United States resources to make up for the declining scale of our own effort'. Even in Italy, American troops and logistics were of growing importance.[12]

The Italian campaign is, therefore, a good illustration of how strategic principles and alliance politics conjoined in Churchill's grand strategy. So much was at issue, in his opinion, that the campaign sparked perhaps the most acrimonious

Warren F. Kimball, and A. O. Chubarian, eds., *Allies at War: The Soviet, American, and British Experience, 1939–1945* (New York, 1994), 13–14; Bland, ed., *Marshall Reminiscences*, 612.

[11] CAB 66/45, WP (44) 9 (TNA): Churchill memo on talk on 30 November 1943; Churchill to Wilson, T253/4, 8 February 1944, CHAR 20/156; cf. 'Notes on My Life', Alanbrooke Papers, 3/B/XIV, 1070.

[12] Howard, *Mediterranean Strategy*, 57 (including Brooke); CAB 66/42, WP (43) 490 (TNA): Churchill memo, 1 November 1943.

Anglo-American row of the war. In the autumn of 1943 Churchill had fumed when seven crack divisions, three of them British, were moved from Italy to Britain in preparation for Overlord. In the early months of 1944 there was a long debate about an invasion of southern France (code-named Anvil) to coincide with the Normandy landings. Churchill persuaded first Eisenhower and then the Joint Chiefs of Staff (JCS) that this would divert scarce landing craft from Normandy, but his success proved only temporary and argument resumed once D-Day was over. On the one hand, there was a vital need to break out in France. On the other, Rome had finally been captured just before D-Day and Alexander had ambitious plans for further advance.

In Washington as well as London, strategic principles were intertwined with nationalist sentiments. The JCS took their stand mainly on the firm decision of the Teheran Conference and on the current need for extra port capacity to nourish Overlord. But Marshall was also determined to utilize the additional 30 or more divisions trained and ready in the United States and to do so under American leadership. Against this, the British deployed all their persuasive powers. In June, Alexander, with Churchill's encouragement, held out the prospect of a drive northeast towards Vienna. In August Churchill tried at the eleventh hour to have the Anvil invasion force diverted 1,600 miles to the Brittany ports. The Balkan strategy, as we shall see later, was chimerical; the Brittany idea, as even the official British historian admits, was totally inconceivable. Both were really desperate ploys to maintain momentum in Italy.[13]

With the Combined Chiefs deadlocked, the basic issue was thrashed out in direct communication between Roosevelt and Churchill at the end of June 1944—much as happened in the debate over France or North Africa two summers before. But the balance of the alliance had now tipped to the United States. And, in further contrast with the decision for Torch, Roosevelt backed the JCS to the hilt. Privately Churchill called Arnold, King, and Marshall 'one of the stupidest strategic teams ever seen'. But he added: 'they are good fellows and there is no need to tell them this'. He also drafted a cable to Roosevelt threatening resignation at this 'absolutely perverse strategy'. Significantly, it was not sent. Instead he promised FDR to 'do our best to make a success of anything that is undertaken', while lamenting what he called 'the first major strategic and political error for which we two have to be responsible'.[14] The consequences were felt immediately. In June and July the Fifth US Army in Italy lost almost 40 per cent of its strength, including its most experienced mountain troops. Air support was also cut back and the existing forces, after long and heavy fighting, were starved of replacements and ammunition through the winter. Chances of a rapid advance in Italy remain debatable, given the terrain and the German resistance. But

[13] John Ehrman, *Grand Strategy*, v (London, 1956), 345–67.
[14] CHAR 20/153: Churchill to Ismay, minute D218/4, 6 July 1944; Kimball, *Churchill and Roosevelt*, 2: 225–9.

undoubtedly they were reduced further by the diversions to France. When the Russians entered Vienna on 7 April 1945, Alexander had still not crossed the Po.

In both strategic ideas and national influence, therefore, Churchill had little to offer in 1944–45 as the Allies mounted what he deemed a premature invasion of 'Fortress Europe' and as Britain's prime theatre, Italy, was emasculated in consequence. At times his grand strategy was really an exercise in damage limitation. Above all, that meant trying to maximize British influence in what became the main western European theatre—France.

Conscious of America's eventual manpower superiority, Churchill was anxious to ensure parity during the landings themselves, when international attention would be at its peak. He wrote to the War Office in November 1943 that he wanted to tell the Americans 'we will match you man for man and gun for gun on the battlefront' and, to that end, sanctioned 'considerable risks with what is left in the island'. Referring to the rows over Italy, he noted that 'we have carried the present trouble entirely by maintaining that we had preponderance on the battlefront. We ought to have at least equality in this other most critical task.' Significantly, when he wrote his war memoirs he made much of this Anglo-American parity in June 1944.[15]

In the long run, Churchill knew, Britain would lose the numbers game in France. But he also hoped that British brains could guide American brawn. This was basic British policy (or conceit) in the last part of the war: the aim, in the words of one Foreign Office memorandum, was 'to make use of American power for purposes which we regard as good'. In military terms, that entailed continuance of the so-called stratosphere policy, which the British felt had succeeded in the Mediterranean. To quote Brooke, they had accepted an inexperienced American, Eisenhower, at the very top to 'devote his time to political and inter-allied problems, whilst we inserted under him one of our own commanders to deal with the military situations'. In 1944, similarly, Ike as supreme commander for Overlord was balanced by British officers in charge of land, air, and sea operations.[16]

This, it should be noted, was not total chauvinism. The British were genuinely disturbed by the late change of command in December 1943 from Marshall to Eisenhower. Churchill said he has 'the greatest confidence in General Marshall both as a man and a soldier', but he could only call Ike 'an acceptable alternative'. The War Cabinet believed that 'public opinion here will be surprised and rather uneasy at the substitution' and 'felt very strongly' that if Ike's name were announced in isolation the effect on public opinion would be 'deplorable'. British operational commanders were therefore deemed essential, not merely for patriotic reasons but to enhance confidence in the assault. Most important was

---

[15] PREM 3/342/5 (TNA): Churchill, minute M786/3, 6 November 1943; cf. Churchill, *Second World War*, ii. 4–7.

[16] 'Notes on My Life', Alanbrooke Papers, 3/A/VIII, 609. FO 371/38523,AN1538 (TNA): N. American Department memo, 21 March 1944.

the role of Montgomery, victor of Alamein and British national hero, as commander of *all* Allied land forces during the assault phase.[17]

Monty was really Brooke's favourite, not Churchill's, and soon became the butt of the PM's anger as the battle bogged down before Caen. There was also more than a hint of Churchillian jealousy about a man whose popularity (and populism) rivalled his own. But, as a totem of British status, Monty received Churchill's full support. At the end of August, under pressure from Washington, Eisenhower implemented previous plans and assumed operational command of land forces. Monty, previously Bradley's de facto superior, was now on a par with him as an army group commander. With the British press as clamorously nationalistic as the American about the command issue, Churchill moved rapidly to balance the perceived 'demotion' for Monty by elevating him to field marshal. He told Ike: 'I considered this step necessary from the point of view of the British nation with whom Montgomery's name is a household word.'[18]

Monty's own hopes of regaining operational command were destroyed by his press conference during the Battle of the Bulge, when he had temporary command of two of Bradley's armies. Monty's insensitivity, exacerbated by misinformation on both sides, created Ike's worst command-diplomacy headache of the war. Monty was never forgiven by the Americans, and Churchill, privately, believed his remarks were 'most unfortunate'. But the PM raised the idea of a deputy theatre commander again in February, pressing on Ike the claims of his own favourite, Alexander, by then becalmed in the Mediterranean as it became a strategic backwater. Churchill complained huffily that 'I am sure you would not wish to deny us the kind of representation on your Staff in respect of military matters which is our due', but desisted when Ike made it clear that Alexander would only be allowed a political and logistical role. Ike (and Marshall) intended that Americans would command in fact as well as name. The stratosphere policy had vanished into thin air.[19]

In Monty's mind the cause for a ground commander was bound up with unhappiness about Ike's broad-front strategy. Since August he had argued intermittently for a concentrated northern thrust towards the Ruhr and, ultimately, Berlin. Churchill, however, seems to have raised the command issue largely as a matter of national status. Although expressing doubts to FDR in December 1944 about the position in the west, he did not start clamouring for a northern thrust to Berlin until well into 1945. To understand this, we need to appreciate that Churchill never really came to terms with the speed and mobility of modern war.

[17] PREM 3/336/1 (TNA): Churchill to Attlee, 2 September and 14 December 1943, Grigg to CIGS, 15 December and Attlee to Churchill, 22 December; see also CAB 65/40, WM 170 (43) 1 CA (TNA).

[18] Churchill to Eisenhower, 31 August 1944, Dwight D. Eisenhower Library (DDEL), Abilene, Kan., 16/52 file, box 22.

[19] Churchill, minute, D20/5, 10 January 1945, CHAR 20/209; Churchill to Eisenhower, 22 February 1945, DDEL 16/52 file, box 22.

Take, for instance, his protests about the invasion of southern France. In a lengthy note for the cabinet on 28 June 1944, which he copied to Roosevelt, a central part of his case was the remoteness of Marseilles. It was, he said, 600 miles 'as the crow flies' from Cherbourg, and 400 miles from Paris. He spoke of 'a march' of 355 miles to the Normandy battlefront, which would 'present a flank to any German forces to the northward'. The country, he argued, 'is most formidable' and the Germans could easily withdraw troops from Italy to block the advance. 'Without the enemy withdrawing a single division from the OVERLORD battle, we could be confronted with superior forces at every step we advance up the Rhone valley.' In short, he doubted that the operation 'would have any tactical relation to the battle we have to fight now and throughout this summer and autumn for OVERLORD'.[20]

Despite its special pleading, this memorandum tells us much, I think, about Churchill's underlying conception of warfare. The idea of static fronts suggests analogies with the war of 1914–18. The repeated references to 'marches' smacks of the era of Napoleon or even Churchill's ancestor, Marlborough, of whose campaigns he had written at length in the 1930s. It is significant that Churchill had repeatedly disparaged the US Army's use of motor transport. In February 1944 he was scathing about the 18,000 vehicles in the Anzio beachhead: 'We must have a great superiority of chauffeurs.' Over dinner on 14 June he let rip in similar vein about Normandy. 'What we wanted, he said, were combatants and fighting men instead of a mass of non-combatants.' Brooke argued that 'fighting men without food, ammunition and petrol were useless', but the PM 'was not open to conviction'. What mattered, insisted Churchill, were what he called, again significantly, 'bayonets'.[21]

Churchill's essentially foot-slogging concept of land warfare also helps explain his doubts about the Normandy campaign. Of course, no one anticipated the direction and the pace of the Allied breakout when it finally came at the end of July. The aim of Overlord was to gain a 'lodgement' on the Continent, as a basis for future campaigns, for which the prime need was Cherbourg and the Britanny ports to the *west*. And even Patton, who led the eventual eastward dash across France, had lamented in England on 19 June that the Allies would probably not be able to 'repeat the armored drives the Germans had achieved in 1940' and that they would 'have to go back to 1918 methods' with the infantry bearing the brunt. But Churchill was more conservative than most. Overlord planners hoped to push the Germans back to the Seine and Loire in 90 days, and there regroup for a month before further advance. But in July 1944 Churchill privately felt that crossing the Seine would be 'next season's campaign'—in other words, the agenda for 1945. The velocity of the American breakout astonished him.

[20] Kimball, *Churchill and Roosevelt*, ii. 217–19.
[21] Churchill to Wilson, T277/4, 10 February 1944, CHAR 20/156; Brooke, diary, 14 June 1944, Alanbrooke papers, 5/9.

Learning on 7 August 1944 that 12 US divisions were well through the Avranches gap, he exclaimed, 'Good heavens, how do you feed them?' Bradley told him that they were running trucks up to the front 'bumper to bumper, 24 hours a day'. By the spring of 1945 every American division could motorize all its infantry. In congratulating Ike in March 1945 on the 'destruction of all the Germans west of the Rhine', Churchill remarked particularly that 'no one who studies war can fail to be impressed by the admirable speed and flexibility of the American Armies'.[22]

Perhaps, as Russell Weigley has argued, the US Army never properly fused mobility with firepower into an integrated military doctrine. But in 1944–45 its mobility was far superior to that of the Wehrmacht, still reliant on horse transport, while the American combination of tactical air support with time-on-target artillery proved devastating. Britain's artillery was also superb, but, in general, the British lacked both the firepower and the mobility of the Americans. The impact of their forces, in any case smaller than the GIs, was further weakened by being divided between two main European fronts. And, only weeks after D-Day, the War Office warned that future replacements could only be provided by breaking up existing divisions. This, as much as Monty's temperament, helps explain his caution during the battle for Caen and thereafter. In short, from Churchill's perspective, outright military victory over the Germans still seemed remote. He assumed a continued war of attrition until the enemy collapsed from within, rather than the decisive blow that the Americans favoured *and* could deliver. It was still a policy of KBO rather than KO.[23]

In the light of this discussion, we are now better able to understand what historian Tuvia Ben-Moshe rightly notes as Churchill's remarkable non-involvement in the crucial stage of the broad- versus narrow-front argument between Ike and Monty in August 1944. Unlike later rounds in the argument, this occurred at a point when German resistance seemed to be collapsing. The British official historian called the three weeks from 15 August to 5 September 1944 'among the most dramatic of the European war, equalling in intensity those of May and June 1940'. Contrary to Churchill's fears, the Rhone valley had proved a highway not a cul-de-sac and by 3 September the Allies had driven 150 miles to Lyon. Meanwhile, Ike's armies had not paused, as planned, for logistical breath at the Seine but had raced on to the German border and the Moselle River, covering in 19 days what 'should' have taken them another 260. In other words, on 12 September 1944 they occupied positions not anticipated

    [22] Roland G. Ruppenthall, *Logistical Support of the Armies*, vol. i (Washington, 1953), 188–9; Liddell Hart Papers, KCL, 11/1944/39–40: Patton; d'Este, *Decision in Normandy*, 305; Omar N. Bradley, *A Soldier's Story* (New York, 1951), 368–9; Churchill to Eisenhower, 9 March 1945, DDEL, 16/52 file, box 22.
    [23] Russell F. Weigley, *Eisenhower's Lieutenants* (London, 1981), 727–30; d'Este, *Decision in Normandy*, 258–60; KBO was Churchill's motto in 1940–1: 'Keep Buggering On.'

by Allied planners until 21 May 1945. For a while the German armies were close to disintegration.[24]

Monty's case for a British-led northern thrust to the Ruhr, and ultimately Berlin, may not have been feasible for diplomatic or logistical reasons, but that is beside the point here. What is interesting is why Churchill kept quiet in such a momentous strategic argument. It probably owed something to his awareness of diminished British leverage. As he told Jan Smuts in December 1944, 'our armies are only about one-half the size of the American and will soon be little more than one-third', so that 'it is not so easy as it used to be for me to get things done'. But his silence also reflects the strategic priorities already identified. Unlike the cabinet's Joint Intelligence Committee, he did not believe in late summer that Germany was close to defeat. He considered it 'at least as likely that Hitler will be fighting on the 1st January as that he will collapse before then. If he does collapse before then,' Churchill added revealingly, 'the reasons will be political rather than military.' In any case, Churchill's attention at this time was devoted to south-eastern Europe. As Ben-Moshe notes, he was in Italy for much of August— willing on the British troops to a victory beyond their grasp—when the crucial Ike–Monty arguments were taking place. And, after conferences in North America, he returned there in October. Significantly, this trip was sandwiched around his visit to Moscow to confer with Stalin about southeastern Europe.[25] For August 1944 was an equally dramatic moment on the eastern front, as Russian troops surged into Poland and the Balkans, knocking Romania and Bulgaria out of the Axis. In short, Churchill's strategic attention at this critical moment was directed to dangers in the east rather than opportunities in the west.

What, then, *was* the place of Russia in the endgame of Churchill's grand strategy? In retrospect, one can find many occasions during the war when Churchill bemoaned the dangers of Soviet expansion. One night at Teheran in November 1943, for instance, he was bleakly despondent about future relations, predicting 'a more bloody war'. But his view of Russia was typically mercurial. In January 1944 he wrote to his foreign secretary about 'the deep-seated changes' in the character of the Russian state and 'the new confidence which has grown in our hearts towards Stalin'. As the official historians have argued, in 1943–44 Churchill's Italian strategy had little to do with forestalling the Soviets. In June 1944 talk of a drive to Vienna was mainly an attempt by Alexander and Churchill to persuade the Americans that Italy had strategic prospects. Only in August 1944 did Churchill—prompted by Smuts, by the sweeping Russian victories, and perhaps by the agony of Warsaw—introduce the idea of beating the Russians into central Europe. He told the sceptical Chiefs of Staff on

---

[24] Ben-Moshe, *Churchill*, 301–3; Ehrman, *Grand Strategy*, v. 377; Ruppenthal, *Logistical Support*, i. 481–8.

[25] Michael Carver, 'Montgomery', in John Keegan, ed., *Churchill's Generals* (London, 1992), 161–3; Churchill to Smuts, T2235/4, 3 December 1944, CHAR 20/176; Ehrman, *Grand Strategy*, v. 402; Ben-Moshe, *Churchill*, 301.

9 September that Britain should have 'powerful forces in Austria and from Trieste northwards at the close of the German war, and should not yield central and southern Europe entirely to Soviet ascendancy or domination'.[26]

There can be little doubt, I think, that in the *very last* months of the war, Churchill was more prescient than Roosevelt about future relations with the Soviets. But fears are not the same as strategy. Churchill's problem was that, in 1944–45, any ability he might have had to forestall the Russians had been negated by previous decision. On diplomacy, for instance, Churchill had come round to the Foreign Office's strategy of trying to pin Stalin down to a clear sphere of influence in eastern Europe. For three years after Barbarossa, discussions centred on the status of former Tsarist territory recovered by Stalin under his pacts with Hitler in 1939–40. As the Red Army surged into the Balkans, the geographical scope of this policy necessarily enlarged, and it was to conclude a spheres-of-influence agreement for the Balkans as a whole that Churchill travelled to Moscow in October 1944. In the same spirit he sought agreement over Poland at Yalta in February 1945, as we shall see in Chapter 13.

Churchill's Russian policy, then, was not confrontation but negotiation from strength. Until at least August 1944, when the Allied offensive in the west developed a momentum of its own, Russian military help was essential. And there was still the Asian war, where Soviet entry might prompt a quick Japanese surrender and, to quote Churchill before Yalta, 'save us many thousands of millions of pounds'. In any case, the chances of gaining a position of strength by military means were dashed by previous strategic decisions. Only an earlier invasion of the Continent might have given the prospect of forestalling the Russians in Europe. By D-Day the issue of the Russo-German war had already been decided and the Russians were poised for their decisive breakout into eastern and southeastern Europe. Moreover, when Churchill *did* perceive a danger, he looked to the wrong theatre for remedies. As noted by subsequent historians, and by the Chiefs of Staff in 1944, Vienna was 600 miles beyond Rome—times the distance from Naples that had taken the Allies six months to cover. And the route lay in winter over mountainous country with poor roads: the much-cited 'Ljubljana Gap', for instance, was a plateau 2,000 feet high and 30 miles wide commanding all the surrounding terrain. Little wonder Brooke termed the Vienna scenario 'Winston's strategic ravings'. By this stage, the only possible hope of penetrating central Europe before the Russians lay in France in August 1944. And, as we have seen, the logistical and diplomatic obstacles there were enormous, even if Allied leaders, always scanning the casualty lists, had been willing to bear the human costs.[27]

---

[26] Lord Moran, *Winston Churchill: The Struggle for Survival, 1940–1965* (London, 1968), 160; PREM 3/399/6: Churchill to Eden, M(S)31/4, 16 January 1944; Ehrman, *Grand Strategy*, v. 392–4; CAB 120/144 (TNA): Churchill, minute, D(0)4/4A, 9 September 1944, printed at end of COS 7th mtg.

[27] CAB 120/714 (TNA): Churchill, minute, M127/5, 28 January 1945; Ben-Moshe, *Churchill*, 320–4; Howard, *Mediterranean Strategy*, 65–8; Brooke, diary, 5/9, 23 June 1944.

The final Anglo-American controversy in April 1945 about capturing Berlin and Prague sums up the themes of this essay. A race for Berlin was diplomatically difficult, given the general need to keep in with the Russians and also the prior agreement on occupation zones, pushed by the Foreign Office. The Joint Chiefs would not brook any interference in Ike's operational decisions and he believed, on military grounds, that the main thrust should be in the centre and south. This meant that the Ninth US Army, hitherto attached to Monty's army group and vital to helping him gain his objectives, was withdrawn to bolster Bradley's final push. The PM complained about the 'relegation of His Majesty's Armies to an unexpected restricted sphere'. But, unlike Anvil the previous summer, he did not turn this dispute into a crisis. 'I hope,' he told the Chiefs of Staff, 'we shall realize that we have only a quarter of the forces invading Germany and that the situation has thus changed remarkably from the days of June.'[28] In the middle of the war, the British had decisively shaped Allied policy for the defeat of Germany. But the last year of the European conflict had seen the progressive marginalization of Churchill's grand strategy.

[28] Churchill to Eisenhower, 31 March 1945, DDEL 16/52 file, box 22; Ehrman, *Grand Strategy*, vi. 135.

III

ROOSEVELT

7

The President and the King

The Diplomacy of the British Royal Visit of 1939

Late on June 7, 1939, a reigning British sovereign set foot on American soil for the first time. King George VI and Queen Elizabeth crossed the border into the United States at Niagara after a three-week tour of Canada. Behind the scenes there were many misgivings. This was only the second state visit that the shy young monarch had made since he succeeded his brother, Edward VIII, in December 1936. Some isolationist senators denounced the trip as British propaganda for the impending European war, and there were disturbing reports of Irish Republican extremists in Detroit and New York. But official fears quickly evaporated as the royal party plunged into a hectic whirl of social engagements. The first two days were spent in the ninety-degree heat of Washington, with visits to the Capitol, Mount Vernon, and Arlington Cemetery, a formal state dinner at the White House, and a large garden party and another dinner at the British Embassy. Saturday, 10 June, saw the king and queen in New York, where they looked at the Battery and the World's Fair and lunched at Columbia University. Plans for a parade through Manhattan had been abandoned because it was felt that New Yorkers had 'cheapened' their famous tradition of hospitality. 'They used to throw down ticker tape, but now they drop telephone directories,' President Roosevelt observed drily.[1] Finally a weary royal party journeyed up the Hudson River to the Roosevelt estate at Hyde Park. There they spent the rest of the weekend informally with the President's family before setting out for Canada on Sunday evening en route back to London.

The royal couple had received almost unqualified praise in America. Huge crowds had turned out to welcome them, their charm and sincerity had made an excellent impression, and press comment proved almost entirely favourable. Roosevelt, who had adopted an avuncular attitude towards the young King and Queen, found them not only 'delightful and understanding people' but also

---

This chapter was first published in *The Historian*, 45 (1983), 461–72.
[1] Lindsay to Cadogan, despatch, 1 Nov. 1938, FO 371/21548, A8828/76737/45 (TNA).

surprisingly well informed on national and international problems.[2] As for George VI, the visit was a profoundly maturing experience from which he derived new confidence and inspiration. It was also a turning point in the character of British royal tours abroad. Instead of being dominated by formality and protocol—what the King called 'that high-hat business, the kind of thing that my father and those of his day regarded as essential'—there had been contact with ordinary people, much more of 'the common touch'. For George VI, this represented 'a new idea of kingship'.[3]

The British side of the royal visit has been discussed by the King's biographer, Sir John Wheeler-Bennett. Benjamin Rhodes has argued that the Foreign Office envisaged the trip as a safe but effective way to strengthen American sympathies for Britain at a time when Europe was sliding rapidly into war.[4] Less attention, however, has been paid to President Roosevelt's thinking, and in particular to his evolving conception of the visit's precise character. FDR had come to believe that the occasion could serve a number of important foreign policy goals, *if* it were handled correctly. His idiosyncratic ideas were not always grasped by the British, but they helped to ensure the visit's success.

Roosevelt first extended an invitation at the time of George VI's coronation in May 1937. Knowing that Mackenzie King, the Canadian premier, was trying to arrange a royal tour of Canada, FDR instructed his special envoy to the coronation, James W. Gerard, to convey his hope that 'if and when the King and Queen paid an official visit to Canada, they would find it possible also to pay a private and unofficial visit to President Roosevelt at Hyde Park'.[5] There were no plans at this stage for a Canadian visit, but Sir Ronald Lindsay the British ambassador in Washington, and Anthony Eden, the Foreign Secretary, both felt that if one were arranged it would be both inevitable and highly desirable that the USA be included in the itinerary. Coming at the right time, they believed, this could have an excellent effect on Anglo-American relations.[6] The persistent Gerard was therefore given a noncommittal but encouraging reply, and when Mackenzie King secured agreement in August 1938 for the royal couple to visit Canada, FDR renewed his invitation, this time in a personal letter to George VI, which was formally accepted on 3 November.

[2] FDR to Nicholas Roosevelt, 15 June 1939, in *F.D.R.: His Personal Letters, 1928–1945*, ed. Elliott Roosevelt with Joseph P. Lash, 2 vols. (New York, 1950), ii. 893.

[3] W. L. Mackenzie King, diary, 12 June 1939, 3, Public Archives of Canada, Ottawa (cited hereafter as Mackenzie King diary).

[4] John W. Wheeler-Bennett, *King George VI: His Life and Reign* (London, 1958), 371–94; Benjamin D. Rhodes, 'The British Royal Visit of 1939 and the "Psychological Approach" to the United States', *Diplomatic History* 2 (1978), 197–211. For criticism of Rhodes, stressing FO fears of an isolationist backlash to the visit, see Peter Bell, 'The Foreign Office and the 1939 Royal Visit to America: Courting the USA in an Era of Isolationism', *Journal of Contemporary History*, 37 (2002), 599–616.   [5] Eden to Lindsay, tel 157, 11 May 1937, FO 954/29A, 6 (TNA).

[6] Lindsay to Eden, tel. 128, 11 May 1937, and Hoyer Millar to Hardinge, 20 May 1937, FO 954/29A, 7, 11–13 (TNA).

In his invitation, the President said that the visit would give him the greatest personal pleasure and added, 'Frankly, I think it would be an excellent thing for Anglo-American relations.'[7] What exactly did Roosevelt have in mind? As collective security collapsed during the mid-1930s, he had been moving closer to Britain and France, but it was only after the Czech crisis in September 1938 that his foreign policy took on a firm and precise character. To borrow the language of post-war diplomacy, he hoped to contain Hitler by deterrence, or at worst a limited European war in which the USA would not have to be directly involved. Britain and France would be America's 'front line' against Germany. During the winter of 1938–39 he wanted to 'stiffen the backbones' of British and French leaders by assurances of American material support, to warn Hitler that the USA would not remain forever indifferent to aggression, and to educate his own countrymen out of what he saw as the shibboleths of isolationism. This was the thinking behind two major speeches to Congress in January 1939 about the threat to world peace and the need for rearmament. It also underlay his messages to Germany and Italy in April asking them to guarantee the integrity of specified European and Middle Eastern states and his repeated conversations with British diplomats and public figures about his efforts to assist the European democracies.[8] As the royal visit drew near, the President probably saw it as another opportunity to advance these basic foreign policy goals. It would symbolize the shared interests and ideals of Britain and the USA in an unmistakable but apolitical manner. FDR made the point explicitly in his toast at the White House dinner for the royal guests on 8 June 1939. He held out as an example to the world the way in which the two countries conducted their mutual relations— peacefully resolving disagreements without resort to force or an arms race. As evidence, he cited the recent settlement of their dispute over ownership of two tiny Pacific islands—Canton and Enderbury—which had assumed considerable significance as potential bases for trans-Pacific commercial aviation.[9]

Originally, Lord Halifax, Eden's successor as Foreign Secretary, had hoped to accompany the King. It was customary for royalty touring abroad to have a 'minister-in-attendance', and Halifax had intended to use this as a cloak for talks

---

[7] FDR to George VI, 25 Aug. 1938, President's Secretary's File (PSF), box 49: Great Britain, King and Queen, 1938–1942, Franklin D. Roosevelt Library, Hyde Park, NY (cited hereafter as PSF 49: GB, K&Q).

[8] See David Reynolds, *The Creation of the Anglo-American Alliance, 1937–1941: A Study in Competitive Co-operation* (London, 1981), 40–4.

[9] The toast is printed in *The Public Papers and Addresses of Franklin D. Roosevelt*, comp. Samuel I. Rosenman, 13 vols. (New York, 1939–1950), ix. *War and Neutrality, 1939*, 364–65. In fact, this text is the formal press release; the actual toast was given extemporaneously, embodying all the general thoughts in the official version. FDR had scrapped most of the original State Department draft, but he did preserve the general theme. The example of the Pacific Islands was his own. See FDR, memo, 15 June 1939, and Welles to FDR, 27 May 1939, enclosing draft, PSF 49: GB, K&Q. In his toast FDR addressed the king and queen as 'Great Gentleman' and 'Gallant and Gracious Lady'. He told Mackenzie King that this broke all the rules of protocol, but he was determined to do it. Mackenzie King diary, 8 June 1939, 4.

with Roosevelt and Cordell Hull, the Secretary of State. When Lindsay broached the idea to Sumner Welles, FDR's friend and Undersecretary of State, on 1 March 1939, Welles's initial reaction was favourable.[10] But strong opposition was expressed by Henry Stimson, formerly Hoover's Secretary of State, whose advice Lindsay greatly valued, on the grounds that Halifax's presence would play into the hands of Roosevelt's isolationist critics. This was also the President's opinion. He told Lindsay on 5 March that if Halifax accompanied the king it

would excite a lot of talk about an alliance. Lord Halifax would greatly attract the attention of the press. They would dog his steps. If he had three minutes with Mr. Hull or ten minutes with himself the press would pick it up, and the center of public interest would be diverted from the King to political matters, which was just what it was desired to avoid.

Halifax, who had foreseen such an objection, quickly agreed,[11] and there is little doubt that FDR was right. Without Halifax, even anglophobe, isolationist papers such as the *Chicago Tribune* found their hands tied. Although warning its readers to be on their guard for pro-British propaganda and for signs of an incipient alliance, the *Tribune* appreciated that to attack the royal visitors themselves would seem tactless and inhospitable.[12] Some of the President's supporters felt that the mere presence of the King and Queen in the USA had aroused public suspicions,[13] but further vindication of Roosevelt's strategy came in an opinion poll the following September. Although nearly 24 per cent of those questioned felt that the visit had been designed to entice the USA into a wartime alliance, 58 per cent agreed that it was 'no more than a token of friendship among English speaking peoples'.[14]

Although he did not want Halifax or any British minister to accompany the royal party, Roosevelt told Mackenzie King, the Canadian Prime Minister, on 18 January 1939, 'I hope much that The King will bring you with him as his "Minister-in-Attendance" or whatever they call it. . . . I am very certain that this coming visit is going to do much good here and it would really help if you can arrange to come too.'[15] Back in August 1938, in a speech at Kingston, Ontario, FDR had publicly emphasized the USA's interest in Canada's security, and for some time he had been cultivating the sensitive Canadian leader, who in turn

[10] Welles, memo of conversation with Lindsay, 1 Mar. 1939, Department of State papers, 841.001 George VI/347 1/2, National Archives, Washington, DC.

[11] Notes by Lindsay and Halifax, 6 and 17 Mar. 1939, FO 800/324, 25–26, 22 (TNA); cf. Henry L. Stimson diary, 29: 4–5, Sterling Library, Yale University.

[12] *Chicago Tribune*, 7 and 9 June 1939; cf. Jerome E. Edwards, *The Foreign Policy of Col. McCormick's Tribune, 1929–1941* (Reno, Nev. 1971), 131. The generally enthusiastic reception by the American press, even in the Midwest, is documented in Lindsay to Halifax, desp. 677, 20 June 1939, FO 371/22801, A4441/27/45 (TNA).

[13] e.g., William Allen White to Lord Lothian, 19 June 1939, William Allen White Papers, C-318, Library of Congress, Washington, DC.

[14] *Public Opinion Quarterly* 4 (1940), 96–7.

[15] FDR to Mackenzie King, 18 Jan. 1939, PSF 49: GB, K&Q.

considered himself the lynch pin in the Anglo-American relationship. Clearly FDR saw the visit as a convenient way to strengthen ties with Canada as well as Britain. For his part, Mackenzie King was very enthusiastic about the idea. He had already insisted that he and not the British Governor-General, Lord Tweedsmuir, should meet the royal party on their arrival in Quebec and also that he should accompany them as minister-in-attendance throughout their tour of Canada. Personal pride played a part here, as did his feeling that the royal advisers were Conservatives, hostile to his Liberal government, but at root the Canadian Prime Minister was convinced that a major constitutional issue was at stake. He believed that the English court was 'still living in the reign of the Stuarts'—that it continued to see Canada as a colonial outpost rather than as an independent and equal member of the British Commonwealth of Nations. A proper place for him in the royal visit to North America would symbolize these new international realities.[16]

Consequently, Mackenzie King turned the question of who should accompany the royal party in the USA into a top-level diplomatic controversy. At his prompting, Tweedsmuir had sent the gist of FDR's 18 January letter to London, but King learned at the end of February that this was being disregarded and that Buckingham Palace, guided by Lindsay, believed that the American authorities opposed his presence in the USA. Convinced that he was the victim of a British Old Guard conspiracy, headed by the Palace and the Washington Embassy, King phoned the White House on 4 March to ask the President to intervene. 'This is outrageous,' Roosevelt exploded when he was told what the Palace believed. 'I thought this had all been settled. You are certainly coming. I am looking forward tremendously to that.' He promised that he would sort it all out with Lindsay the following day.[17] But when he saw the British Ambassador on 5 March, FDR raised the matter in typically oblique fashion. During their conversation he casually observed that although Halifax should not accompany George VI, 'as regards Mackenzie King it would be easier. He has been down here often and I could represent his presence as the visit of an old friend.'[18]

Was this an offhand remark, or had the President stated a firm policy preference? As so often with Roosevelt, the British found it hard to decide. They tried to pin him down, but it seems that FDR had no desire to become further embroiled in this delicate controversy which was actually outside his own sphere of authority. When approached on 8 March by Alan Lascelles, George VI's private secretary who was then in Washington to finalize arrangements, he therefore 'resolutely refused to be drawn' even though Lascelles deliberately gave

[16] See Mackenzie King diary, 21 Feb. 1939, 3 (quotation) and 28 Feb. 1939, 2–10. His views were most clearly stated to the British Government in King to Chamberlain, tel. 22, 14 Mar. 1939, Dominions Office correspondence, DO 121/65 (TNA).

[17] Mackenzie King diary, 4 Mar. 1939, 3; see also 28 Feb. 1939, 6–7, 1 Mar. 1939, 2–3, and 3 Mar. 1939, 1–2.

[18] Lindsay, note, 6 Mar. 1939, FO 800/324, 26 (TNA).

him several opportunities to pronounce on the question.[19] Meanwhile, however, Mackenzie King had communicated directly with Chamberlain, who accepted his interpretation of the political and constitutional issues involved, and on 10 April King received an official request from George VI to act as minister-in-attendance for the whole North American tour. Roosevelt wrote to King to express his pleasure, adding that 'I had done my best in several conversations'. The Prime Minister later recorded that throughout the American visit the President 'made it a point of having me always in evidence along with the King and himself'.[20] After the visit was over, FDR told the US minister in Ottawa that it had been 'a piece of great good fortune' that Mackenzie King had been able to accompany George VI 'for it made all the difference in the world not only in the United States but also, I think, in providing for the King himself a sort of interpreter of the close relationship between Canada and the United States, without detracting in anyway [*sic*] from the loyalty of Canada to the British Empire.'[21]

The President also had strong feelings about the royal party's itinerary. His initial invitation in 1937 had spoken of 'a private and unofficial visit' to the Roosevelt family home at Hyde Park,[22] and this remained throughout the central feature of his plan. Lindsay questioned the idea—'in my opinion it would emphasize the personal nature of the visit to the President too much for American opinion'—and he made his reservations known to London on several occasions.[23] But Lindsay was a career diplomat of the old school. Quite deliberately FDR wanted to avoid a traditional state visit. The British monarchy was, after all, the symbol of all that *divided* the two countries—a reminder of the colonial past and the stratified Old World society that Americans were proud to have repudiated. Roosevelt was therefore anxious to display the royal couple in the best possible light—to show that fundamentally Britain and the USA shared the same political ideals. He told George VI that 'to the American people, the

[19] Lascelles to Hardinge, 9 Mar. 1939, FO 800/324, 27–9, and similarly Cadogan, minute, 24 Mar. 1939, FO 371/22800, A2137/27/45 (TNA). But in his diary in April 1940, after a meeting with FDR, Mackenzie King recorded that the president 'told me he had written the King in a letter, in his own hand, saying that he hoped that the King would bring me with him to the US on account of our being such good friends, etc. That he had not sent this message through Lindsay knowing how hostile Lindsay was and had not sent it through Kennedy [US Ambassador in London] as he did not want Kennedy to have to do with the matter.' (Mackenzie King diary, 23–24 Apr. 1940, 14.) There is no record of such a letter in Roosevelt's papers, and British officials at the Palace and the Foreign Office seem to have known nothing about it.
[20] FDR to Mackenzie King, 16 Apr. 1939, PSF 35: Canada; Mackenzie King diary, 11 June 1939, 1. [21] FDR to Daniel Roper, 10 July 1939, PSF 35: Canada, Roper.
[22] Eden to Lindsay, tel. 157, 11 May 1937, FO 954/29A, 6 (TNA). Writing later for the historical record, FDR simply said that he had asked Gerard to suggest that if George VI 'ever went to Canada he should come to visit us in Washington'. FDR to Gerard, 6 July 1939, PSF 46: Great Britain. Nevertheless, his emphasis on Hyde Park is quite clear throughout the arrangements.
[23] Lindsay to FO, tel. 389, 25 Oct. 1938, FO 371/21548, A8061/7673/45 (TNA). See also Lindsay's despatch, 1 Nov. 1938, and letters to Cadogan, 22 Nov. 1938, and to Oliphant, 29 Dec. 1938, *ibid.*, A8828, A9293, A9777 (TNA).

essential democracy of yourself and the Queen makes the greatest impression of all' and that 'if you could stay with us at Hyde Park for two or three days, the simplicity and naturalness of such a visit would produce a most excellent effect'.[24] Although the President conceded that some official functions in Washington and New York were unfortunate necessities of protocol, a weekend at Hyde Park became a fixed part of the itinerary. There George VI dined informally with the President's family, worshipped at the local Episcopal church, enjoyed a picnic lunch and a swim, and toured the Roosevelt properties with the President. The keynote throughout was informality, and as British officials later admitted, reports of the King lunching on beer and hot dogs and swimming on Roosevelt's estate undoubtedly revealed a new and appealing side of royalty to the American public.[25]

The visit to Hyde Park also gave Roosevelt another opportunity to try to 'stiffen Britain's backbone'. Throughout the winter he had stressed to British visitors that they could expect the material help of the United States if war broke out, hoping thereby to encourage them to 'stand up' to Hitler. This was also the theme of the two long conversations he had with the King at Hyde Park. In his breeziest manner, the President explained all he was doing to educate his own countrymen and impede Hitler. One point was his belief, often stated in private, that the Canadians could get round the US Neutrality Act by importing aircraft parts from the USA which they could then assemble into warplanes for Britain. He also dwelt on his fears about German bases and naval raiding in South America and talked of his plan for a western hemisphere naval patrol involving the use of bases in the British West Indies, which he raised formally with the British government a few weeks later. (Although this plan was not realized in 1939, it constituted a precedent for the Anglo-American Destroyers-for-Bases deal of September 1940.) All in all, the King found Roosevelt 'terribly keen. If he saw a U-boat he would sink her at once and wait for the consequences. If London was bombed U.S.A. would come in.'[26]

George VI, earnest and rather naive, was much cheered by Roosevelt's conversation and reported the President's comments to his principal ministers. Churchill, for instance, was told by the King about the western hemisphere patrol plan when he became First Lord of the Admiralty in September 1939.[27] But the Foreign Office was less impressed. Officials there were used to FDR's habit of

[24] FDR to George VI, 2 Nov. 1938, and draft, PSF 49: GB, K&Q; FDR told the governor general of Canada, 'the American people admire the essential democracy of the King and Queen, and it would help if the formal "functions" could be supplemented by a peaceful and simple visit to a peaceful and simple American country home.' FDR to Tweedsmuir, 3 Nov. 1938, PSF 35: Canada. Of course, FDR also recognized that 'a nice, quiet 24 hours' at Hyde Park would make a welcome break for the king and queen on a strenuous tour. Mackenzie King diary, 4 Mar. 1939, 4.

[25] Godfrey Haggard (British consul-general in New York) to Lindsay, desp. 211, 14 June 1939, FO 371/22801, A4435/27/45 (TNA).

[26] George VI, memo of talks with FDR, 12 June 1939, printed in Wheeler-Bennett, *George VI*, 391–2. See also Mackenzie King diary, 10 June 1939, 3–4, and 12 June 1939, 2–6.

[27] Cf. Churchill to Pound, 7 Sept. 1939, ADM 1167/3922, 255 (TNA).

telling his listeners what they wanted to hear and always took his bellicose statements with a pinch of salt.[28] They saw little chance of Congress and the American public supporting more than a policy of 'benevolent neutrality', whatever the President might wish or claim. Mackenzie King also came round to a more cynical view of Roosevelt. He had sat in on one of the Hyde Park conversations and went away convinced 'that the President was anxious to do everything he possibly could to be of help, short of committing his country to a war'. Consequently, FDR's prompt and comprehensive declarations of US neutrality at the beginning of the European war in September left King disgusted and 'really ashamed'.[29]

One final observation on Roosevelt's conception of the royal visit should be made. For FDR, diplomacy was in large measure the art of personal relationships. Throughout his presidency he tried to create informal and intimate ties with foreign leaders, either directly or through trusted intermediaries such as Norman Davis, Harry Hopkins, and Averell Harriman. Such contacts were particularly important in the case of Britain because most of FDR's personal links dated from his years in Washington during World War I. Old friends such as Sir Arthur Murray and Sir Arthur Willert were of limited importance in Britain in the 1930s and FDR knew virtually none of the country's current leadership. When he came to power in 1933, he had been able to build a good relationship with the then Prime Minister, Ramsay MacDonald, who responded promptly to FDR's invitation to visit the USA. But relations were cool with MacDonald's successor, Stanley Baldwin, and when Neville Chamberlain became premier in May 1937, Roosevelt made determined and repeated overtures through Norman Davis about an early visit to the USA. These Chamberlain rebuffed. Similar efforts in the autumn of 1938 in conjunction with the signing of the Anglo-American Trade Agreement proved unavailing, and the following February Chamberlain briskly dismissed suggestions in Parliament that, after his recent trips to Germany and Italy, an American visit might now be appropriate. Chamberlain's reluctance is, in part, readily understandable. Well aware of the US phobia about propaganda, he believed that 'the sure way . . . to lose the Americans is to run after them too hard'.[30] Furthermore, in an era before regular transatlantic air travel, a visit to the USA would take him away from Britain for several weeks. In 1937 he was just finding his feet as premier; beginning with August 1938, the continued European crisis made a

---

[28] For instance, Hugh Dalton, Labour party spokesman on foreign affairs, talked with R. A. Butler of the Foreign Office about the USA on September 18, 1939. Dalton recorded, 'The President has said [to Lothian, the British ambassador in Washington] "we shall come right in before long", but this was rather typical of the President's way of speaking loosely and optimistically in private conversation.' Hugh Dalton, diary, xxi. 62, British Library of Political and Economic Science, London (cited hereafter as Dalton diary). See also J. V. Perowne, minute, 9 Sept 1939, on similar comments by FDR which the Foreign Office attributed to 'wishful thinking'. FO 371/22816, A6085/98/45 (TNA).   [29] Mackenzie King diary, 12 June and 3 Sept. 1939.
[30] Dalton diary, 28 June 1939.

long absence unthinkable. But Chamberlain also placed a relatively low priority on Anglo-American cooperation. He did not believe that the USA would act effectively and quickly in the event of a European war, and he was aware that American help would make Britain more dependent on the USA. In addition, he feared that a visit might exacerbate the dictators' sense of encirclement by the democracies and make it harder to reach the European settlement that he so ardently desired.[31]

Whatever Chamberlain's reasons, it must have been apparent to FDR by the spring of 1939 that his hopes of building a close personal relationship with the British Prime Minister were vain.[32] When war began in Europe in September 1939, Roosevelt sent an unprecedented invitation to Churchill, Britain's most celebrated opponent of Hitler and the new First Lord of the Admiralty, to write to him personally about anything of interest or importance. This was not done behind Chamberlain's back—a similar letter was addressed to the premier himself and Churchill punctiliously sought the approval of Chamberlain and the Cabinet for his messages to the President.[33] But this was clearly an attempt by Roosevelt to open up new and more fruitful lines of communication with British leaders. There may have been a similar motive behind Roosevelt's handling of the royal visit the previous June, which would help to explain the remarkable energy and attention he expended on George VI. One of his sons commented, 'As a practitioner of the arts of persuasion, Father wanted the welcome he planned for the King and Queen of England to act as a symbol of American affinity for a country whose present political leadership he did not trust.'[34] Likewise, Roosevelt's cultivation of Mackenzie King probably had a definite diplomatic purpose. When FDR talked of the Canadian Prime Minister as 'the official interpreter between the President and the King in relation to the affairs of the United States and Great Britain', Mackenzie King believed Roosevelt 'was making it perfectly clear that he intended not to discuss matters with the [British] embassy but rather in a more immediate and direct way where it served his purpose'.[35] In the summer of 1940, under very different circumstances, FDR used King extensively in his efforts to extract from Churchill a promise that if Britain was in danger, she would send the Royal Navy to North American ports rather than let it fall into German hands. Such pressure came more fittingly from

---

[31] For fuller discussion of Chamberlain's policy and of Anglo-American relations in general during this period, see Reynolds, *Creation of the Anglo-American Alliance*, chs. 2–3.

[32] Willert recalled that when they talked in March 1939 FDR 'had no use for Chamberlain' or his senior ministers. See Sir Arthur Willert, *Washington and Other Memories* (Boston, 1972), 215.

[33] Churchill immediately sent Chamberlain FDR's invitation, commenting that there were 'many things we want him to do for the Admiralty' and that the offer of 'a liaison must be used to the full'. Churchill to Chamberlain, 4 Oct. 1939, Neville Chamberlain papers, NC 7/9/64, Birmingham University Library. See also FDR's letters of 11 Sept. to Churchill and to Chamberlain, respectively in ADM 199/1928 and PREM 1/366 (TNA).

[34] Elliott Roosevelt and James Brough, *A Rendezvous with Destiny: The Roosevelts of the White House* (New York, 1975), 230.   [35] Mackenzie King diary, 11 June 1939, 1.

a Commonwealth leader and co-belligerent than from a neutral president whose lack of tangible support was bitterly resented in London.[36]

In exploring at length some of Roosevelt's ingenious ideas, I do not imply that all his objectives were realized. Far from it. For instance, the long-term effect of the royal visit on American opinion is difficult to assess. Some members of the royal party did believe it had a decisive impact. The King's private secretary called the American crowds 'genuinely friendly, and loyal—there is no other word to describe it, for their attitude seemed to me exactly similar to that of H[is] M[ajesty]'s subjects in this country'.[37] Such a ridiculous comment clearly reflects the enthusiasms of the moment. More detached observers in the British diplomatic corps, although delighted with the visit's success, took a cautious line. Their evaluation was that American emotions, which they judged to be extremely important in determining relations with Britain, had been profoundly stirred and that the good feelings aroused by the visit might help tip the balance in Britain's favour at a time of real crisis. But the Foreign Office did not anticipate any immediate, concrete diplomatic benefits, such as the repeal of the US embargo on arms sales to belligerent powers, and its attitude was vindicated by the negative votes on this question in Congress a few weeks later.[38]

Nor should we read too much into Roosevelt's intentions. In view of the imminence of war in Europe, the future use of Mackenzie King, and the possible links between Roosevelt's attitude to the royal visit and the beginnings of his correspondence with Churchill, it is tempting to think that in 1938–39 FDR was already trying to build the special relationship that was finally consummated after Pearl Harbor.[39] But that, it seems to me, is an anachronistic assumption. The turning point in Anglo-American relations came not in September 1939 but in mid-1940. Until the fall of France neither government sought more than strictly limited cooperation. Roosevelt remained determined to keep his country out of war and to help the British and French to contain Hitler themselves by diplomatic and material assistance from the USA. For their part, the British had learned from bitter experience—of which the summer 1939 fiasco over the arms embargo was only the most recent example—that it was unwise to place much faith in American reliability, and they also feared that large-scale US help could undermine their own independence. Only after the European balance had

[36] See J. L. Granatstein, *Canada's War: The Politics of the Mackenzie King Government, 1939–1945* (Toronto, 1975), 119–32; Fred E. Pollock, 'Roosevelt, the Ogdensburg Agreement, and the British Fleet: All Done with Mirrors', *Diplomatic History* 5 (1981), 203–19.

[37] Lascelles to Grigg, 27 June 1939, Altrincham papers, Bodleian Library, Oxford, MSS. 1005.

[38] Lindsay to Halifax, despatch 679, 20 June 1939, and minutes by Gage and Scott, 3 and 4 July 1939, FO 371/22801, A4443/27/45 (TNA). See also Reynolds, *Creation of the Anglo-American Alliance*, 57–8.

[39] As suggested by Richard A. Harrison, 'A Presidential *Démarche*: Franklin D. Roosevelt's Personal Diplomacy and Great Britain, 1936–37', *Diplomatic History* 5 (1981), 271, 272.

shifted with devastating suddenness in May–June 1940 was an alliance sought by London and, much more cautiously and tentatively, by the President.[40]

Roosevelt's interest in the British royal visit of June 1939—encompassing even minutiae such as seating plans for the various functions—is attributable in part to his fascination with historic occasions. But, on a deeper level, it is clear that this ostensibly ceremonial event was gradually invested by the President with considerable diplomatic significance. It is, in fact, a good illustration of some of FDR's major foreign policy goals of the late 1930s and of the subtlety of his efforts—successful or not—to achieve them in an uncongenial domestic environment. Between the original invitation in May 1937 and its realization over two years later, Roosevelt's conception of the visit had become character- istically complex and many-sided. He wanted it to symbolize Anglo-American amity in a striking way for his countrymen, the British, and the dictators, while not laying himself open to isolationist critics at home. He saw it as a means of strengthening ties with Canada and of helping to make the British monarchy more human and democratic in American eyes. He also used the talks with George VI to continue his attempt to toughen Britain's policy and to develop new contacts with her leaders. In short, the British royal visit of 1939 provides an interesting and instructive vignette of Roosevelt the diplomatist.

[40] This argument is developed in Reynolds, *Creation of the Anglo-American Alliance*, esp. 95–6, 143–4, 293–4.

8

The President and the British Left

The Appointment of John Winant as US Ambassador in 1941

Little that Franklin Roosevelt did was ever simple or straightforward. 'A man who would never tell the truth when a lie would serve him just as well,' was Douglas MacArthur's bitter epitaph.[1] The President's closest associates often despaired of his deviousness. 'You won't talk frankly even with people who are loyal to you and of whose loyalty you are fully convinced,' complained Harold Ickes. 'You keep your cards close up against your belly. You never put them on the table.'[2] Few of FDR's actions stemmed from a single motive. Beneath the surface bonhomie and the inspiring rhetoric lay a secretive, complex, calculating mind. Sometimes he was too clever by half, but even in failure, Roosevelt's ingenuity is a subject of enduring fascination for historians. A small but intriguing example is his choice in February 1941 of John Gilbert Winant as US Ambassador to Great Britain.

The Winant appointment is of interest for another reason. Many studies of Anglo-American diplomacy during the Second World War have concentrated on Roosevelt and Churchill. In large measure this is only right. As Churchill himself observed: 'My relations with the President gradually became so close that the chief business between our two countries was virtually conducted by these personal interchanges between him and me';[3] and the rich mass of official records subsequently opened on both sides of the Atlantic has given scholars ample opportunity to document the relationship between the two leaders and

This chapter first appeared in *The International History Review*, 4 (1982), 393–413. Helpful comments on a draft version were provided by John Thompson, Henry Pelling, and particularly Garry Clifford, who kindly drew my attention to additional evidence. More recent literature of relevance includes Kevin Jefferys, *The Churchill Coalition and Wartime Politics, 1940–1945* (Manchester, 1991), and Nicholas John Cull, *Selling War: The British Propaganda Campaign against American 'Neutrality' in World War II* (Oxford, 1995).

[1] William Manchester, *American Caesar: Douglas MacArthur, 1880–1964* (Boston, 1978), 240.

[2] *The Secret Diary of Harold L. Ickes* (3 vols., New York, 1954), ii. 659, recording conversation with FDR on 21 June 1939.

[3] Winston S. Churchill, *The Second World War* (6 vols., London, 1948–54), ii. 22. For a comprehensive edition of their exchanges see *Churchill and Roosevelt: Their Complete Correspondence, 1939–45*, ed. Warren F. Kimball (3 vols., Princeton NJ, 1982).

their immediate advisers. But the undoubted importance of these top-level exchanges should not blind us to the complexity of the wartime Anglo-American relationship. The enforced 'mixing-up' of the two countries from mid-1940 encompassed a variety of social groups apart from government leaders. Another strand in the web, spun out concurrently in 1940–1 with the emerging Roosevelt–Churchill connection, was the growing contact between the President and the British Labour Party. Winant's appointment was a central part of that story.[4]

Roosevelt nominated 'Gil' Winant on 6 February 1941. Four days later the Senate gave its approval and the new ambassador arrived in London on 1 March. Part of Roosevelt's reasoning is obvious. By early 1941, he was publicly committed to Britain as the US's front line against Hitler. That commitment was expressed in the Destroyers-Bases deal of September 1940 and then in the Lend-Lease bill which he submitted to Congress on 10 January 1941 and finally signed into law two months later. But the US Ambassador in London until November 1940 was Joseph P. Kennedy, who had long been out of step with Roosevelt's foreign policy. After France fell in June 1940, Kennedy concluded that the British had 'not got a Chinaman's chance' without US help and that the USA would be better advised to concentrate on defending the Western Hemisphere rather than frittering away its scarce resources to an unreliable client across the Atlantic.[5] Neglected by the President and openly critical of his diplomacy, Kennedy had no desire to stay on in London after Roosevelt's re-election in November 1940. For his part, FDR naturally wanted someone who would represent his policy enthusiastically, and Winant, a vehement anti-Nazi with considerable experience of Europe, seemed an appropriate choice. As historian Robert Dallek observed, the appointment 'reflected the President's commitment to Britain's triumph over Berlin'.[6]

Winant also fitted FDR's social criteria for an ambassador. Like any President, Roosevelt treated many diplomatic posts as patronage plums. Robert Bingham, Claude Bowers, and Breckinridge Long went to London, Madrid, and Rome in

---

[4] Four decades ago, Professor Donald Watt noted that work on British attitudes to the USA had generally concentrated on movements in mass opinion or on 'the radical and politically "nonconformist" elements in British political society', to the neglect of the 'foreign-policy-making elite'. Donald C. Watt, *Personalities and Policies* (London, 1965), 19. With the subsequent opening of the official records in both countries the balance swung dramatically the other way.

[5] Kennedy to Hull, tel. 2535, 2 Aug. 1940, State Department Decimal File, 740.0011 EW 1939/4929 3/4, Record Group 59, National Archives, Washington, DC. On Kennedy's ambassadorship see David E. Koskoff, *Joseph P. Kennedy: A Life and Times* (Englewood Cliffs, NJ, 1974), 114–295; and Michael R. Beschloss, *Kennedy and Roosevelt: The Uneasy Alliance* (New York, 1980), chs. 6–7.

[6] Robert Dallek, *Franklin D. Roosevelt and American Foreign Policy, 1932–1945* (New York, 1979), 533. For background on Anglo-American relations in this period see David Reynolds, *The Creation of the Anglo-American Alliance, 1937–1941: A Study in Competitive Co-operation* (London, 1981).

1933 in return for their support during the 1932 election campaign. And FDR also had to balance the claims of the career diplomats. They received about half the 1933 appointments, with veterans such as Joseph Grew and William Phillips given due recognition by their fellow alumnus of Groton and Harvard.[7] But wealth and professional expertise were not for Roosevelt the ideal credentials for an ambassador. Time and again he spoke of wanting men who embodied New Deal ideology. He told the Canadian Prime Minister in April 1940 'that the real trouble that he had was that most of the career men in diplomatic service were Republicans. They were not sympathetic with his policies.'[8] Another failing was that they tended to lose touch with their own country and its values. In 1936, Roosevelt had Ray Atherton transferred from his post as Counsellor at the London Embassy after King Edward VIII had said he would like to see the USA represented by Americans, not imitation Englishmen.[9] Sometimes Roosevelt hoped that his political appointees would prove immune to the charms of the Old World; that was certainly his expectation when he sent Kennedy to Britain in February 1938. But the new ambassador was quickly seduced by London high society and overwhelmed by the general fear of war, becoming in Roosevelt's view a tool of British appeasement. 'Who would have thought the English could take into camp a red-haired Irishman?' he complained soon after Munich.[10] Again, Winant seemed a better bet. He had sound liberal credentials, a former progressive Republican Governor of New Hampshire who had become an enthusiastic New Dealer and Chairman of the Social Security Board in 1935–7. He was also a shy, idealistic, and informal man with an aversion to ceremony, who therefore seemed likely to prove more resistant than Kennedy to British blandishments. Probably Roosevelt chose Winant in part as a good representative of New Deal America and one who was likely to remain an American.

But contemporaries discerned a further motive for the selection, one that forms the substance of this chapter. Briefly in 1935 and again from 1937, Winant was Roosevelt's nominee to the International Labour Organization in Geneva, serving first as Assistant Director and then, from February 1939, as Director. In this capacity, Winant had become acquainted with many British trade union leaders, and newspaper reports at the time of his appointment to London suggested that Roosevelt had made the choice at the suggestion of Supreme Court Justice Felix Frankfurter in order to build bridges with the British left. As confirmatory evidence they sometimes cited the concurrent selection—as Winant's 'legal adviser'—of Benjamin V. Cohen, a Frankfurter protégé, notorious in Republican polemic as one of the 'scarlet-fever boys from

---

[7] On the 1933 appointments see Frank Freidel, *Franklin D. Roosevelt: Launching the New Deal* (Boston, 1973), 144, 359–62.

[8] W. L. Mackenzie King, Diary, 23–24 Apr. 1940, p. 14, Public Archives of Canada, Ottawa.

[9] Martin Weil, *A Pretty Good Club: The Founding Fathers of the US Foreign Service* (New York, 1978), pp. 82–3; cf. *Franklin D. Roosevelt and Foreign Affairs*, ed. Edgar B. Nixon (Cambridge, Mass. 1969), iii. 234, 507–8. Among Atherton's 'sins' was his marriage to an Englishwoman.

[10] John M. Blum, *From the Morgenthau Diaries* (Boston, 1959), i. 518.

the little red house in Georgetown' who had helped draft the 'communist' legislation of the early New Deal.[11]

This interpretation of Winant's appointment first surfaced publicly in Joseph Alsop's and Robert Kintner's newspaper column on 6 February. They stated that 'the President is authoritatively understood to have been much influenced by intimations from London that Mr. Winant's appointment would be extremely agreeable to British labor leaders. In the course of his work at Geneva Mr. Winant became particularly intimate with the famous British Minister of Labor, Ernest Bevin, and the New Dealers here hopefully anticipate that having a crony at the American Embassy will strength[en] Mr. Bevin's hand in British politics.'[12] The following day this theme was developed by the columnist Arthur Krock, who suggested that the explanation for this 'mysterious' appointment lay in a series of connections: Winant's friendship with Bevin through the ILO; Bevin's admiration for the New Deal and his likely role in implementing similar reforms in Britain; and the respect supposedly felt for Bevin by the British Marxist intellectual Harold Laski who kept in close touch with both Roosevelt and Frankfurter. 'So,' Krock concluded, 'Mr. Winant will supply an official tie to those now unofficially linking a powerful trans-Atlantic group of economic and social reformers.'[13]

The story quickly hardened into received opinion and was widely reported by the press and by British officials in Washington. At its heart was the belief that Winant's appointment had been engineered by Frankfurter and Laski, and that it was intended to align the United States with the social changes then occurring in Britain. Winant's biographer gave some credence to the latter hypothesis, but, apparently on the basis of an interview with Frankfurter in 1959, he asserted that 'contrary to speculation, neither Laski nor his close friend, Felix Frankfurter, exerted influence in the selection of this new envoy'.[14] The biography was published in 1968 and since then new evidence has become available in Britain and the United States, which suggests strongly that direct requests from Laski and possibly Bevin may well have determined Roosevelt's decision. It also confirms that FDR believed that a 'social revolution' was underway in Britain in 1940–1 and that he wanted to open contacts with the Labour leaders who would probably form her post-war government.

To understand why the Labour party wanted Winant as Ambassador we must look first at British attitudes towards Roosevelt's America during the 1930s. In general, the New Deal had little impact on Britain. The media paid scant

[11] Cf. William E. Leuchtenburg, *Franklin D. Roosevelt and the New Deal, 1932–1940* (New York, 1963), 149.   [12] *New York Herald Tribune*, 6 Feb. 1941, p. 2.

[13] *New York Times*, 7 Feb. 1941, p. 18.

[14] Bernard Bellush, *He Walked Alone: A Biography of John Gilbert Winant* (The Hague, 1968), 157, 160. There is no mention of this question in Winant's autobiography *A Letter from Grosvenor Square* (London, 1947), ch. 1, or in the essay by Bert R. Whittemore, 'A Quiet Triumph: The Mission of John Gilbert Winant to London, 1941', *Historical New Hampshire*, 30 (1975), 1–11.

attention to the United States, except as a source of sensationalized human interest stories, and the schools taught virtually nothing to correct the distorted images of Hollywood. In so far as Britons understood what was happening across the Atlantic, they believed that Roosevelt was belatedly pulling his country out of the era of nineteenth-century individualism through reforms of the sort enacted in Britain by Asquith's Liberal Government before the Great War. On both ends of the British political spectrum, the US experience seemed largely irrelevant. For the Right, the Depression represented the failure of capitalists rather than capitalism, while the dogmatic left, taking the opposite view, reaffirmed its commitment to radical socialism. But, on the centre-left of British politics, men such as Lloyd George and Harold Macmillan showed considerable interest in New Deal experiments in planning, notably the Tennessee Valley Authority, while critics of the Tory-dominated National Governments of Stanley Baldwin and Neville Chamberlain used the example of America's dynamic President as a convenient stick with which to attack official lethargy. In the minds of the British public Roosevelt grew into a larger-than-life figure, his exploits thrown into relief against the dark background of British ignorance about the United States, and their respect grew with the international crisis of the late 1930s, when the President's outspoken denunciations of fascism, although accompanied by little in the way of decisive action, evoked approval from all who despaired of the policy of appeasement.[15]

For most of the 1930s, since the collapse of Ramsay MacDonald's Labour government in the financial crisis of 1931, the left had been out of power in Britain. But, in May 1940, when Chamberlain was forced from office, Churchill formed a coalition government, and his near-total preoccupation with diplomacy and strategy soon left Labour with almost a free hand in domestic policy. At the same time the civil service was expanded by an influx of temporary staff from the universities, journalism, and the professions, many of whom had been advocates of planned reform during the 1930s. The acceptance of Keynes and Keynesian ideas by the Treasury in 1940–1 was an early and striking instance of this new influence. And there was also a discernible swing to the left in popular attitudes. Anger at Chamberlain and the 'Guilty Men' supposedly responsible for Britain's desperate plight spilled over into a widespread conviction that this was a 'people's war', fought for a better world at home as well as abroad.

In Whitehall and in the country at large, therefore, the time seemed ripe for reform. But the Labour party was divided on the question of how best to exploit its new opportunity. Doctrinaire left-wingers, notably Harold Laski, Aneurin

---

[15] For British attitudes to the New Deal, see Henry Pelling, *America and the British Left: From Bright to Bevan* (London, 1956), ch. 8; R. H. Pear, 'The Impact of the New Deal on British Economic and Political Ideas', *Bulletin of the British Association for American Studies*, NS, 4 (1962), 17–28; Barbara Malament,'British Labour and Roosevelt's New Deal: The Response to the Left and the Unions', *Journal of British Studies*, 17 (1978), 136–67; and John Dizikes, *Britain, Roosevelt and the New Deal: British Opinion, 1932–1938* (New York, 1979) [a reprint of a 1964 Harvard University Ph.D. dissertation]. On British ignorance of the USA see also Chapter 10.

Bevan, and Emanuel Shinwell, called for immediate implementation of radical policies, including the nationalization of land, banking, and transportation. However, the Labour ministers, led by the party leader, Clement Attlee, took a more moderate view. They argued that victory was the overriding priority, but that quiet, piecemeal wartime reforms could lay the basis for more systematic progress once the war had been won. Despite this persistent divergence of opinion, both wings of the party did agree, against Churchill, that the war must do more than eliminate Nazism and restore the 1930s *status quo*. They insisted that the roots of conflict could only be eradicated by social and economic change in Britain and overseas; that, to use a contemporary cliché, international security and social security were two sides of the same coin. And like British liberals in the First World War, they felt that the United States could play an important role in establishing a just, progressive peace. When Roosevelt was re-elected for a third term in November 1940, Attlee wrote jubilantly to Laski: 'Is not the result in the USA magnificent? Quite apart from the fact that any change of personnel at the White House would have meant confusion and delay for months in the war effort, the retention of Roosevelt means that we have there a man with real understanding of European problems, strategic and economic as well as political and perhaps above all ideological. Only a man who sees the interrelationship between home policy and foreign policy can really give the hand required.'[16] This enthusiasm was common to both wings of the Labour party. And it helps to explain the requests each made for Winant's appointment.

Although Attlee was party leader, the most influential of the Labour ministers was bulky, bespectacled Ernest Bevin. The illegitimate son of a Somerset midwife, Bevin had left school at 11 and, after working his way up the dockers' union, had become the General Secretary of the Transport and General Workers Union from its foundation in 1921. Then, in May 1940 at the age of 59, Churchill had appointed him Minister of Labour and National Service. Although Bevin had scant formal education and no experience of Parliament or Government, he was a shrewd and able man with wide practical knowledge of industrial problems in many Western countries. He was also the pre-eminent British union leader of his day, who provided an essential bridge between Government and workers as the new Prime Minister strove desperately to mobilize all the country's resources in defence against possible invasion. Bevin rapidly made his mark on the public mind, becoming the most popular politician in the country after Churchill, and by virtue of his ability and of his crucial job he was made a member of the inner War Cabinet in October 1940.[17]

[16] Attlee to Laski, 7 Nov. 1940, enclosed with Laski to Roosevelt, 18 Feb. 1941, President's Personal File (henceforth PPF) 3014: Laski, Franklin D. Roosevelt Library, Hyde Park, NY. See generally Paul Addison, *The Road to 1945: British Politics and the Second World War* (London, 1975), chs. 4 and 5; T. D. Burridge, *British Labour and Hitler's War* (London, 1976), ch. 3.

[17] The standard biography is Alan Bullock, *The Life and Times of Ernest Bevin* (2 vols., London, 1960, 1967).

Bevin was a patriot who shared the Prime Minister's determination to win the war. His years in the docks had also turned him into an ardent anti-communist. But although repudiating the extreme ideas of Labour left-wingers, Bevin shared their belief that the war should bring about a better world, and in the autumn of 1940 he was saying in public and in private that a basic war aim must be social security for all based on full employment and the proper development of national resources without obstruction by vested private interests. One such speech, on 20 November 1940, drew a 'very friendly hint' from Churchill to avoid political controversy in the interests of wartime unity 'till the Hun is beat'.[18] Bevin also believed that domestic reform had a crucial international dimension. Since attending his first ILO conference in 1928, he had been a firm supporter of its work in promoting international agreements on complex labour problems and in drafting resolutions which had gradually gained acceptance as the basis of an international labour code. He drew particular attention to this in a long memorandum he prepared for the Foreign Office in the autumn of 1940 about the reform of the diplomatic service. In it he argued that British diplomacy had long been out of touch with working people and with the rising force of trade unionism and socialist ideas. Had Britain reformed her social system during the interwar years and then given a lead to progressive democratic forces on the Continent, Bevin argued that the spread of fascism probably could have been resisted. He was particularly critical of the 'aloof attitude' of the British Government to the ILO. 'The one institution that came out of the last war, which had within it great possibilities, had it been encouraged, was the International Labour Office and, if, in conjunction with that, there had been some real attempt at economic organisation internationally, the whole course of events, particularly in middle Europe, would have been different.'[19]

During 1940, Bevin also developed some of his ideas in correspondence with an old New York friend, Spencer Miller, who was Director of the Workers Education Bureau of America. In a letter of 28 August, he suggested that wartime innovations, such as the Ministry's factory welfare schemes, were part of 'the making of a World Order'. Miller, who was enthusiastic about what he called the 'socializing' of British democracy,[20] was also in contact with Arthur Young, the Christian industrialist who was then Director of the Labour Supply Committee in Bevin's ministry. On 6 November 1940, Young sent Miller a long letter which began by expressing the 'delight' felt by Bevin and himself at Roosevelt's re-election. He went on:

Last weekend I had the great pleasure of entertaining Ernest Bevin at my home in Kenilworth. He mentioned during the course of many long talks one important matter

[18] Churchill to Bevin, 25 Nov. 1940, Prime Minister's Confidential Correspondence, PREM 4/83/1A, pp. 66–7 (TNA).

[19] Bevin, memorandum, 'Diplomatic Service', [Dec. 1940], Bevin. MSS, 2/1, Churchill College, Cambridge University. On Bevin and the ILO see Bullock, *Bevin*, i. 407–11, 576–9, 653.

[20] Bevin to Miller, 28 Aug. 1940, and Miller to Bevin, 10 Sept. 1940, Bevin MSS, 6/45.

on which he would like to have your personal and immediate opinion . . . The point is this. Would in your opinion J. G. Winant prove to be a good Ambassador, representing your country at the Court of St. James? Clearly E.B. has been thinking of this possibility and his own view is that if from your knowledge of Winant he would be a suitable man in all other respects it would be a striking vindication of the good work that the I.L.O. has done at Geneva over many years if the great American republic appointed to such an important post a man who had been so closely identified with this work . . . [I]mplicit in this recognition [would be] their ardent desire that this kind of work should be continued in the future.[21]

To ensure receipt of the letter, Young sent two copies. The original went with Whitelaw Reid, son of the owners of the *New York Herald Tribune*, who was returning by air to New York after a visit to London. The other copy was sent by ordinary mail in a Ministry of Labour envelope.

Presumably Young thought that the official envelope would ensure secrecy. If so, he was wrong. The letter was opened in the normal course of wartime censorship and a copy was sent to the Foreign Office for comment. Officials there did not take Bevin's idea very seriously. They believed that, although 'honourable, upright and intelligent', Winant was too shy to make an effective ambassador. R. A. Butler, the Conservative MP and Parliamentary Under-Secretary at the FO, was the only one to know Winant personally. He cautioned against underestimating Winant's subtlety and his 'taste for politics', but generally agreed with the official view: 'Whitehall would find him quite incomprehensible. His very ill wife would continue to distract his attention. He would be more interested in personalities than in business, and would certainly get into messes with Labour. Personally I find him most attractive & worthy of study. His sense of honour is pronounced, but I cannot envisage him as ambassador.'[22] Accordingly the Foreign Office dismissed the idea and by early January had other names in mind as the likely short list for Kennedy's replacement.[23]

Young did not receive a reply from Spencer Miller. But at the end of November, a report appeared in the British press that Winant's name was under consideration by the President, and Young sent the article to Bevin commenting: 'It may be, therefore, that he [Miller] has induced others to "fly a kite."'[24] Had word of Bevin's suggestion reached the White House? No indication can be found in Roosevelt's papers, although both Miller and Helen Rogers Reid, Whitelaw Reid's mother, were occasional correspondents of the President. One

---

[21] A. P. Young to Miller, 6 Nov. 1940, copy in FO 371/26263, A4898/4898/45.

[22] Ibid., minutes by David Scott and R. A. Butler, 20 and 23 Nov. 1940.

[23] Particularly the career diplomat Norman Armour, then Ambassador to Argentina. See minutes on FO 371/26179, A101/101/45.

[24] Young to Bevin, 30 Nov. 1940, Bevin MSS, 6/56. In 1937–9 Young had been in contact with Carl Goerdeler, one of the leading German 'moderates', and in the winter after Munich had passed material from Goerdeler to the Roosevelt Administration via George Messersmith in the State Department. See C. A. MacDonald, *The United States, Britain and Appeasement, 1936–1939* (London, 1981), 93, 150.

might surmise that a direct statement of preference from a major British political figure was unlikely to remain a secret, but no firm judgement can be made.

However, the President was definitely the recipient of an explicit request from the other wing of the Labour party. If Bevin symbolized the pragmatic reformism of the Labour ministers, Harold Laski was the intellectual leader of the Labour left as well as the party's principal authority on the United States. Laski had taught at Harvard from 1916 to 1920, where he made firm friends of Holmes, Brandeis, and Frankfurter, before becoming Professor of Political Science at the London School of Economics in 1926. The depression of the early 1930s converted him to Marxism, and thereafter his attitude to the United States was always painfully ambivalent. On strict ideological grounds, he considered the United States to be the embodiment of capitalism and believed the New Deal was a mere palliative, doomed to failure. Yet, as an Americophile, and as a democrat in the fascist-ridden Europe of the 1930s, Laski drew new confidence from the capacity of US democracy to reform and revitalize itself. In October 1935, the US Ambassador in London reported that Laski 'said he was convinced that our country now had the greatest leader and the surest-footed statesman in the world'.[25] As the decade progressed, that conviction was strengthened by Roosevelt's denunciations of fascism, and Laski became a regular and adulatory correspondent of the President and of their mutual friend Felix Frankfurter. For Laski, war in 1939 was an ideological conflict. Military victory had to be complemented by immediate nationalization and social reconstruction. What was needed, he urged again and again from 1940, was 'a revolution by consent', so that Britain could evolve peacefully into a socialist state; and he became increasingly critical of the Labour ministers' apparent acquiescence in Churchill's conservatism. Laski told Roosevelt on 20 October 1940 that a 'British New Deal' was the precondition for real victory and lasting peace. He believed that Churchill was too obsessed with wartime strategy to see this, and asked FDR to bring his own influence to bear.[26]

For Laski, as for Bevin, then, the United States had a part to play in reforming Britain. As soon as Roosevelt had been re-elected, Laski sent a further message to the President. 'I feel as though we had won a victory comparable in magnitude to what we lost in the defeat of France. It is grand, grand, grand,' he told FDR. Then, at the end, he added a brief paragraph: 'And send us John Winant as ambassador. That would complete my American devotion.'[27] To ensure that his message got through, Laski sent a supplementary request on 24 November in a letter to Frankfurter. After commenting on the election and on Kennedy's return to America, Laski added: 'I hope F.D.R. will take seriously my suggestion that

[25] Robert W. Bingham, diary, 24 Oct. 1935, Bingham papers, box 1, Library of Congress. For background see Pelling, *America and the British Left*, 143–5; Kingsley Martin, *Harold Laski, 1893–1950: A Biographical Memoir* (London, 1953), esp. chs. 7 and 11.

[26] Laski to Roosevelt, 20 Oct. 1940, President's Secretary's File (PSF) 53: Great Britain, Laski, Roosevelt Library.   [27] Laski to Roosevelt, 6 Nov. 1940, PPF 3014.

the ideal Ambassador to London is John Winant.'[28] The motive for Laski's initiative is evident in another letter, written the following February, after the selection of Winant as Ambassador and Cohen as legal adviser had been announced. 'They are noble appointments,' he told the President, '—the expression of that in American democracy the possession of which I covet for this country. And I think they come at an hour ripe for learning what they can teach ... If liberal America makes England speak the right word and *do the right acts* even this agony may in the end be worth the blood and tears that will have been shed.'[29]

As with Bevin's proposal, no direct causal connection can be traced between Laski's letter and Roosevelt's decision to appoint Winant. Nevertheless, Roosevelt and Frankfurter definitely received Laski's request, and circumstantial evidence suggests that it did play a significant part. The President's first choice to replace Kennedy had been William C. Bullitt, an old associate who had served as Ambassador in Moscow and later in Paris until the French collapse in June 1940. Twice in November 1940, Bullitt was offered the London embassy. Twice he refused. He wished to remain in the United States with his motherless teenage daughter, but it was also rumoured that he sought a Cabinet post;[30] and privately Bullitt alluded to his bitter rivalry with Sumner Welles, the Under-Secretary of State, saying that 'he could not go to London with W[elles] at his back with a knife'.[31] Laski's letter therefore arrived at an opportune moment. There was no shortage of would-be ambassadors, but by 20 December, after a recuperative Caribbean cruise and a conversation with Frankfurter, FDR was definitely settling on Winant.[32] According to Treasury Secretary Henry Morgenthau, who talked with Roosevelt on the 30th, this was 'because he thought his [Winant's] labor connections were such that it would be helpful in England'.[33] Of course Laski was not the only person to propose Winant. As early as 8 November, his name had been advanced by Eleanor Roosevelt's old friend, Esther Lape.[34] But Morgenthau's record, taken in conjunction with Laski's letters to Roosevelt and Frankfurter, gives credibility to the widespread rumours that Laski and Frankfurter decisively influenced the President. And those rumours are further strengthened if we look more closely at Roosevelt's own reasons for making the Winant appointment.

To understand FDR'S thinking, we need to remember the American view of Britain in 1940. Whereas the British regarded the USA as an adolescent, bastardized version of the mother country, Americans tended to see Britain as

[28] Laski to Frankfurter, 24 Nov. 1940, Felix Frankfurter MSS, box 74, folder 1502: Laski, Library of Congress.   [29] Laski to Roosevelt, 18 Feb. 1941, PPF 3014.

[30] Ickes, *Secret Diary*, iii. 369–70, 374.

[31] Memorandum, 'WCB', 20 Dec. 1940, Joseph W. Alsop MSS, box 32: General memos, Library of Congress.   [32] Ickes, *Secret Diary*, iii. 398.

[33] Presidential Diary, iii. 755, Henry Morgenthau, Jr., MSS, Roosevelt Library.

[34] See papers in Official File (OF) 48/12: Ambassador to Great Britain, Roosevelt Library.

a democracy manqué, which had pioneered the ideals of political liberalism but on the insecure foundations of an archaic if fascinating social system. This evaluation was of more than mere historical interest. It lay at the basis of national myth, because the New World had defined its identity self-consciously in antithesis to the values of the Old. And Britain, as the 'parent' from whom the US had broken away, and as the most readily accessible of European cultures, served as the embodiment of Old World traditions. American commentators were therefore preoccupied with the distinction between what one called 'old-school-tie England' and 'cap-in-hand England'.[35] And in late 1940, they seized eagerly on signs that this distinction was being blurred by the war.

In September and October 1940, American newspapers and radio were dominated by the Battle of Britain. Their reports grossly exaggerated the destructive effect of German bombing, but they helped to arouse unprecedented American admiration for the British people. They also prompted considerable discussion, particularly in the East Coast metropolitan press, about the way in which total war seemed to be undermining the foundations of British society. The issue was examined, for instance, in a *New York Times* editorial on 20 September, and the following day the paper printed a special dispatch from James Reston, then a correspondent in London, in which he stated: 'The democratization of Great Britain goes on apace. What centuries of history have not done for this country, Chancellor Hitler is doing now. He is breaking down the class structure of England every night his bombers come over . . . Why, it has even got so now that total strangers speak to each other on the streets, a completely un-English thing to do. Many people think they are seeing the start of a great movement here at last.'[36]

Apart from the social mixing caused by bombing and evacuation, several other themes recurred in American comment. One was the marked extension of governmental powers over economy and society as a result of the wartime emergency. This took on added significance in view of the role of the Labour party, especially the well-publicized figure of Bevin, in the coalition. Another topic of discussion was the general social levelling caused by the combined effects of rationing, high taxation on the rich, and rising wages for the workers. But it was not only the Eastern press which commented on these upheavals. They were the subject of a detailed analysis prepared in the US Treasury Department in December 1940. Although emphasizing that 'it is too early to say whether the social ferment and changes that have occurred and are occurring constitute as yet a social revolution', the Department predicted that 'the longer the war lasts, the greater the possibility of profound economic and social change'.[37]

---

[35] Samuel Grafton, *New York Post* column, 8 Aug. 1939, quoted in Grafton, *An American Diary* (New York, 1943), 5.   [36] *New York Times*, 20 Sept. 1940, p. 22, and 21 Sept., p. 2.
[37] Harry Dexter White to Morgenthau, memo, 11 Dec. 1940, Morgenthau Diary, vol. 338, pp. 276–88 (FDRL).

In fact, judgements about the British shift to the left were distinctly mixed. Liberals and New Dealers were pleased to see the erosion of Britain's social distinctions, but in business and Republican circles there was concern at the prospects of a radical upheaval. With no effective social democratic tradition of their own, many Americans found it difficult to distinguish socialism from communism or to realize that the roots of British radicalism lay less in Marxist ideology than in practical trade-unionism and Protestant nonconformity. They took Laski as the epitome of the British Labour movement, and judged Bevin to be a fiery demagogue, without appreciating that a realistic, subtle negotiator lay behind the forceful rhetorical style. The limited influence of Laski in British politics and the vehement anti-communism of most Labour leaders, including Bevin, therefore came as a revelation to most Americans visiting Britain during the war. As an instructive example, here are the impressions of Wendell Willkie, FDR's Republican challenger in 1940 who quickly buried the hatchet and travelled with Roosevelt's blessing to Britain in January 1941. On his return Willkie talked with Joseph Alsop, whose paraphrase of their conversation reads in part as follows:

There is only one leader in England and he is Churchill. Aside of him Bevin pales into insignificance. Bevin's role in England is exaggerated in this country. He is a John L. Lewis type of fellow, with William Green's conservatism and Willkie says 'compared to Bevin I am a Socialist.' The people really follow Churchill and Bevin could not lead them away if he wanted to. Willkie doubts that Bevin will be Churchill's successor and thinks that Eden is the better guess...

Willkie doesn't think there is much danger of a socialization of England. Bevin himself is extremely conservative. Laski has no real influence in England, not even with the labor groups. Churchill says frankly that Laski is an unimportant person and probably has more influence in America than he does in England. Morrison and Atwood [*sic*—Attlee] seemed to be stronger persons. Willkie was emphatic that Laski in England did not have near the influence of Frankfurter in this country. While socialization of England seems improbable there are obviously going to be some changes after the war. The titled and very rich landed class realizes that it is finished. Willkie spent an evening at the estate of Lord Derby, the richest man in England who has 400 people employed in his stables alone. Derby told him very frankly that the era of people like him was over. Willkie says of course after the war there will be increased social benefits for the workers, better public housing and a continuation of the reforms that England has long been a pioneer in but he doubted that labor would take over the government or that England would move very far to the left.[38]

Of course, these comments are not to be taken as an authoritative verdict on developments in Britain. Willkie clearly underestimated Bevin's reforming

[38] Interview with Willkie, n.d. [Jan. 1941], Alsop MSS, box 32: General memos. (Throughout, the name 'Bevan' is used, but from context this is clearly an error, and I have therefore substituted 'Bevin'. This, and the mistaken 'Atwood' for 'Attlee', are themselves evidence of American ignorance of the British Labour movement in 1940.) Green was the circumspect President of the American Federation of Labor—comprising craft unions. Lewis was the demagogic leader of the industrial unions in the Congress of Industrial Organizations.

passions, and his remark that 'compared to Bevin I am a Socialist' is nonsense. But the conversation is interesting for what it reveals about Willkie's assumptions *before* he visited Britain. The importance of Bevin and particularly of Laski, and the prospects for social revolution in Britain, were clearly much exaggerated in Washington and New York in 1940.

The President himself was probably also inclined to exaggeration. He had long been critical of Britain's social structure—'too much Eton and Oxford' as he liked to put it[39]—and his reaction to the wartime upheavals is indicated in this interesting letter from Lord Halifax, British Ambassador in Washington, in April 1941. Halifax told the Foreign Office:

I think it is certainly true that there is much anxiety here as to the future evolution of politics in England after the war, and particularly lest these should move too violently and too fast to the Left. I shouldn't have thought, however, that this was a fear particularly in the President's mind. From various talks I have had with him, and from what I have heard from others, I would have guessed that his fear, if he had one, would have been the other way, that we should be sufficiently ready to rebuild on new lines . . . The last time I saw the President . . . he did say something about supposing that what he called Eton and Oxford would no longer hold the place they had previously done in public life.[40]

Roosevelt apparently wanted a replacement for Kennedy who could understand this 'new' Britain. He said as much on 28 January 1941 to Sir Walter Citrine, General Secretary of Britain's Trades Union Congress and a good friend of Bevin, who was then in the USA on a speaking tour. According to Citrine's diary, the President explained the choice of Winant in this way: 'I thought to myself he has had experience in the I.L.O. I sent him there and I believe he made a good job of it. I read of war changes which were taking place in England. They are taking place here also. We are a long way behind. But eight years ago we tried to make up some of the lee-way. So I wanted somebody who could measure these changes and keep me informed.'[41] Citrine's testimony is corroborated by one of Winant's early dispatches from London. Cabling Roosevelt on 3 April 1941, he headed one paragraph 'Social Matters' and then continued: 'When you first spoke to me about the Ambassadorship you told me there were certain phenomena which you wanted to know and which were seldom reported to you.' He went on to discuss the effect of the bombing on local communities and

[39] Memo of conversations with Roosevelt, 25–6 Mar. 1939, Sir Arthur Willert MSS, 14/61, Sterling Library, Yale University. FDR made the comment with particular reference to Anthony Eden, of whom he and many of his associates did not have a high opinion at this time.

[40] Halifax—himself a product of Eton and Oxford—responded that 'provided there was a sufficient basis of merit', they would retain their traditional influence. He told the Foreign Office: 'The truth is that even the most intelligent people here find it very difficult to understand how essentially opposed the ordinary Englishman is to abstract ideologies, and how he always seeks to form his life on the basis of making certain broad principles work without too much regard to logic.' Halifax to Sir David Scott, 24 Apr. 1941, FO 371/26250, A3774/2215/45.

[41] Citrine, Diary of American visit, vol. iv 28 Jan. 1941, Citrine MSS, III/1/12, British Library of Political and Economic Science, London.

on ordinary life.[42] To aid Winant in his analysis of social and economic developments, he took with him Professor P. Sargent Florence—a British economist—and Florence's American wife, Lella, who were specialists on labour and production problems with good contacts in the British Labour movement.

But the President wanted more than an observer. On 17 February 1941, Halifax recorded in his diary a conversation with Wendell Willkie, after the latter had returned from England and had talked with FDR. According to Halifax, Willkie 'had a good deal to say about the President, who, he said, was definitely looking forward to something like a socialist government and community in England after the war, and said from his point of view he had not liked my [i.e. Halifax's] appointment before I had arrived'.[43] Earlier in London, Willkie had linked FDR's expectation directly to the Winant appointment. One British official noted: 'Willkie told me that Roosevelt had seen him before he left and said that he was appointing Winant as Ambassador because he expected a social revolution in England and he thought Winant was, therefore, a suitable choice as Ambassador. ([Walton] Butterworth, [a US Treasury official based in London who had just returned there after a visit to Washington] confirmed this and says that he thinks it is chiefly due to wishful thinking on the part of the more ardent New Dealers who are Roosevelt's advisers).'[44] From within the State Department came similar reports. Pierrepont Moffat, US Minister in Ottawa, was in Washington in late January 1941, and one of his conversations was with Jimmy Dunn, the State Department's Political Adviser on European Affairs. Moffat recorded that Dunn was 'very unhappy' about the department's diminishing influence. 'The power behind the throne was Felix Frankfurter. He was placing his men in key positions everywhere. Winant was his selection...F.F., persuaded by Laski, is convinced that Labor is going to run England after the war and has in turn convinced the President... Winant's appointment was made on that premise and on that premise only. It is not a popular appointment.'[45] Most intriguing of all is the assessment of Breckinridge Long, who was then one of the Assistant Secretaries of State. Long mulled over the choice of Winant, Cohen, and the Florences, and then set down his own interpretation as follows:

Roosevelt had his own contacts with Churchill and has the formal and customary contacts with the old style British Government and important people through our formal diplomatic establishment. However, he sees the possibility (even probability) of a 'new order' in England. The Country Gentlemen type, the landed and industrial aristocracy of England, are being jolted out of position. If Churchill should fall, a new Government would be drafted from a new type—not the McDonald [*sic*] type but more wholly

[42] Winant to Roosevelt, tel. 1309, 3 Apr. 1941, PSF (Safe), Box 9: Winant.
[43] Halifax, 'Secret Diary', 17 Feb. 1941, Hickleton MSS, A 7.8.19, Borthwick Institute, York.
[44] Memo by Tommy Brand, 11 Jan. 1941, FO 371/26200, A716/252/45.
[45] J. Pierrepont Moffat, notes on Washington visit, 31 Jan. 1941, Moffat diary, vol. 46, Houghton Library, Harvard University. On State's obsessive feud with Frankfurter see Weil, *A Pretty Good Club*, 108–13.

composed of popular interests and definitely labor groups, among whom could be persons now considered radical and with Bevan [Bevin] as the possible head of the Government. In other words, a Government out of sympathy with the present and past influences in controlling groups—a new set-up. Roosevelt sees this possibility and is establishing contacts with what may be the Government in the future.[46]

Admittedly, the State Department was obsessed with Frankfurter's supposedly ubiquitous influence in early 1941, and this must be taken into account when weighing the testimony of Long and particularly of Dunn, a close friend of the Secretary of State, Cordell Hull. However, their judgements were corroborated by two other observers—Butterworth and Willkie—the second of whom was apparently drawing on an explicit statement from Roosevelt himself. It therefore seems reasonable to argue that FDR did indeed expect a social revolution in Britain and that he chose Winant in part to make contact with the Labour leaders who might well form the post-war government.

However, with Franklin Roosevelt one can never be categorical. It would be misleading to imply that the Winant appointment reflected a firm, consistent policy of wooing the British left. Domestic US politics probably played a part in the decision. Since the beginning of the European war, FDR had been trying to broaden the political base of his administration. In September 1939, he had made overtures to Alf London and Frank Knox, his Republican opponents in the 1936 election. Although these proved unsuccessful, Roosevelt still had in mind to form a 'National Cabinet' in the event of an international crisis, and in April 1940 he even spoke of Winant as a possible Secretary of War.[47] When the French collapsed in June, Roosevelt was able to appoint Knox and Henry Stimson, Hoover's Secretary of State between 1929 and 1933, to run the Navy and War Departments, a shrewd political move in an election year. In early 1941, Winant went to London, Willkie became a valued and well-publicized supporter of US foreign policy and, in the summer, William Donovan, another Republican whose name had been mentioned in 1939–40, was put in charge of foreign intelligence operations. The Winant appointment therefore seems to be part of a larger pattern: Roosevelt's choice of progressive Republicans of interventionist persuasion to enhance his administration's political appeal and to establish a bipartisan foreign policy in the way Wilson had so disastrously failed to do in 1918.[48]

---

[46] Breckinridge Long, Diary, 15 Feb. 1941, pp. 23–4, Library of Congress, also printed in *The War Diary of Breckinridge Long: Selections from the War Years, 1939–1944*, ed. Fred L. Israel (Lincoln, Nebraska, 1966), 181. 'McDonald' is a reference to J. Ramsay MacDonald, the Labour Prime Minister who formed a coalition in the financial crisis of 1931 and was henceforth excommunicated by the Labour movement as a traitor to class and party.

[47] Morgenthau, Presidential Diary, ii. 466, 18 Apr. 1940, Roosevelt Library.

[48] Garry Clifford points out that in 1941 FDR also brought two other New Hampshire Republicans into the middle levels of his Administration—Ernest M. Hopkins, President of Dartmouth College, and Robert P. Bass, the veteran progressive and former Governor of the state.

In evaluating the appointment, we should also note that the President did not consider Winant ideal. 'I know he's not a good administrator,' FDR admitted to Morgenthau in April 1940,[49] and these doubts had not disappeared by the winter. We have seen that Winant was not Roosevelt's first choice for the London embassy. It was only when Bullitt proved unreceptive that FDR looked elsewhere, and, on his own admission to Sir Walter Citrine on 28 January 1941, choosing Winant was something of an experiment: ' " Most of the fellows I have to deal with are career diplomats" said the President, "and Hull wanted me to appoint one of them. I said No, some of the fellows I have appointed are men of business and those active in public work, and I have had about as much luck with one set as with the other." '[50] A few days later, when Winant's name was announced, Adolf Berle, another Assistant Secretary of State, noted in his diary: 'It is said that the State Department opposed the appointment. This is untrue. The President did not consider Winant's appointment ideal; asked us if we could think of anyone better. We couldn't.'[51]

Furthermore, Winant's appointment did not prove as important as its proponents on both sides of the Atlantic had expected or desired. For the first few months the new ambassador saw a good deal of Churchill, but thereafter major business was increasingly handled by President and Prime Minister directly or through trusted emissaries such as Harry Hopkins and Averell Harriman. Soon Winant was complaining, in tones characteristic of many of Roosevelt's ambassadors, that he rarely saw government leaders and that the work he was given could have been transacted by an efficient career diplomat.[52] Nor did the predictions current in 1940 about a British social revolution prove accurate. Certainly political attitudes in Britain shifted leftwards, particularly in 1940–2, and Churchill himself admitted to Stalin at Teheran in November 1943 that the complexions of the British people were very definitely becoming 'a trifle pinker'.[53] But, whatever American observers might have feared, Labour's election triumph in July 1945 was a victory not for Laski's ideology of 'peaceful revolution' but for the gradualism of Attlee and Bevin. During the war, government powers were enhanced, social services extended, and a mixed economy developed, but no fundamental changes in social structure ensued. Moreover, the principal architects of these changes were not the Labour radicals or even the union leaders but upper middle-class liberals such as Beveridge and Keynes who

---

[49] Morgenthau, Presidential Diary, 18 Apr. 1940.

[50] Citrine, Diary, 28 Jan. 1941, cited in note 41. Cf. this comment by the biographer of one of FDR's career ambassadors: 'he liked to drive an ill-assorted team to see which horse pulled the hardest.' Waldo H. Heinrichs, Jr., *American Ambassador: Joseph C. Grew and the Development of the United States Diplomatic Tradition* (Boston, 1966), 190.

[51] Adolf A. Berle, Diary, 6 Feb. 1941, Berle MSS, Roosevelt Library.

[52] e.g., Martin to Churchill, 26 Aug. 1942, PREM 4/26/10, p. 1224; Winant to Hopkins, 16 Oct. 1943, Map Room papers, box 13: Hopkins, Roosevelt Library.

[53] To which Stalin instantly responded: 'That is a sign of good health!' Minutes of dinner on 30 Nov. 1943 in *Foreign Relations of the United States: The Conferences at Cairo and Tehran, 1943* (Washington, 1961), 584.

helped create a consensus which endured in British politics for a generation.[54] To that process Winant made an insignificant contribution.[55]

However, Winant's relatively minor role in subsequent Anglo-American relations does not alter the circumstances of his selection as Ambassador to Britain in the winter of 1940–1. British Labour leaders believed that the USA had a part to play in wartime reform. Laski envisaged Winant as additional pressure on Churchill to promote an immediate 'British New Deal', while Bevin, more moderate in his approach, felt that the appointment would vindicate the work of the International Labour Office and spotlight the need to include socioeconomic problems within the purview of British diplomacy. Laski's request, and possibly Bevin's too, reached Roosevelt at a time when he was intrigued with reports of an incipient 'social revolution' in Britain; when his first choice, Bill Bullitt, had declined; and when he was anxious to strengthen the administration's bipartisan image. The President was a pragmatist about diplomatic appointments. His only requirements in this case were an anti-Nazi and a red-blooded American. He had no ideal alternative to Bullitt, and, encouraged by Frankfurter, he decided that Winant would be a suitable observer of British social changes and also an early link with the Labour party which might well form a post-war government. As in 1939, when he began courting Churchill, so in 1941 with his overture to the British left; FDR was following his customary tactic of keeping open several options without investing too much faith in any one of them. The appointment of John G. Winant reminds us again of the subtlety of Roosevelt's diplomacy and casts an interesting sidelight on the complexity of Anglo-American relations during the Second World War.

[54] The precise extent of wartime changes remains a matter of debate among historians. See Angus Calder, *The People's War: Britain, 1939–1945* (London, 1969), esp. pp. 21–2, 674–6; Henry Pelling, *Britain and the Second World War* (London, 1970), esp. ch. 12; Addison, *The Road to 1945* (cited in note 16), 275–8; Arthur Marwick, *The Home Front: The British and the Second World War* (London, 1976), esp. pp. 10–12, 180–4.

[55] Nor did much come of Roosevelt's desire, as expressed to Citrine and Winant, to observe and learn from British wartime reforms. With the partial exception of major events such as the Beveridge report on social security (December 1942), American interest was spasmodic and low-level, and direct borrowing was impeded by the large institutional, legal, and political differences between the two societies. For the example of urban planning see Philip J. Funigello, *The Challenge to Urban Liberalism: Federal-City Relations during World War II* (Knoxville, Tenn., 1978), 187–216.

9

The Wheelchair President and his Special Relationships

The British royal visit of 1939 and Winant's appointment as Ambassador in 1941 provide two case studies in the intricacies of Roosevelt's diplomacy. They also offer a telling contrast with Churchill's style as war leader. Whereas the Prime Minister loved the dramatic public gesture, the President preferred the nudge here and the wink there. This was partly because of the political constraints imposed on him before Pearl Harbor by congressional and public opinion but it also reflected his machiavellian nature, which revelled in plots and schemes. 'Never let your right hand know what your left is doing,' he told Henry Morgenthau, his Treasury Secretary and a close friend since 1915. 'Which hand am I, Mr President?' Morgenthau asked. 'My right hand' came the reply. 'But I keep my left under the table.'[1] Moreover, Churchill liked nothing better than to dictate broad surveys of grand strategy, thereby leaving a detailed paper trail for historians. Of course, those documents need careful analysis: as we have seen, they involved a good deal of wishful thinking. But Churchill left scholars much more to go on than did the secretive FDR, who avoided committing himself on paper. To the frustration of the State Department, he rarely dictated a record of his conversations with foreign statesmen and stated that 'no notes should have been kept' of President Wilson's discussions at the Paris Peace Conference.[2]

These differences of style touch on a deeper issue. Not only did Churchill outline sweeping plans, he loved racing around the world trying to implement them. During the war he travelled more than 107,000 miles—checking out the war fronts from North Africa to the Rhine, browbeating or even sacking recalcitrant generals, visiting the troops (as close to the frontline as possible), and haranguing other heads of government. During his visit to Moscow in October 1944, someone remarked that Churchill, Roosevelt, and Stalin were like the Trinity. 'If that is so,' quipped Stalin, 'Churchill must be the Holy Ghost. He

---

This chapter develops some ideas outlined in the *London Review of Books*, 2 June 2005, 29–31.

[1] John Morton Blum, *From the Morgenthau Diaries: Years of Crisis, 1928–1938* (Boston, 1959), 254, entry for 20 May 1935.

[2] Warren F. Kimball, *The Juggler: Franklin Roosevelt as Wartime Statesman* (Princeton, 1991), 203.

flies around so much.'[3] Most of those journeys were hazardous in the extreme, using unheated and unpressurized planes flying close to enemy air space. After one such trip, to Cairo, Teheran, and Moscow in August 1942, General Douglas MacArthur, no anglophile, commented that the Prime Minister deserved a Victoria Cross just for undertaking the flights.[4] Of course, Roosevelt did not sit at home for the whole war. In 1943 he journeyed to summits at Casablanca and Teheran; in February 1945 he ventured to Yalta. But he travelled far less than Churchill and the trips he did make were enormously costly: his health never recovered from Teheran, and Yalta finished him off. But that points up the most important and oft-forgotten contrast with Churchill. Stated bluntly, the President was a cripple.

FDR was the longest-serving president in American history: twelve years and one month. He triumphed in four elections and forged a Democratic majority in Congress that lasted into the 1960s. When he took office in March 1933 America's banking system had collapsed, GDP was two-thirds of what it had been in 1929, and a quarter of the country's workforce was unemployed. When he died in April 1945 Americans enjoyed unprecedented prosperity and victory in the war had catapulted the country from the margins of international politics to the rank of global superpower. These were some of the most dramatic years in American history and FDR was always centre stage. Cartoonists regularly depicted him walking a tightrope, striding into battle, or slugging it out in the boxing ring. The image was one of perpetual motion, yet in reality the man could not move unaided. FDR was the wheelchair president.

It is important to spell out what his disability entailed. Roosevelt was stricken by polio in August 1921 and never recovered the use of his legs. Every day of his life thereafter he had to be dressed and undressed, helped onto the toilet and heaved into bed. 'Rubberlegs'—the nickname given him by General 'Vinegar' Joe Stilwell—was characteristically nasty yet entirely apt.[5] All the pictures of a smiling, jaunty Roosevelt at wartime conferences were carefully staged, with the President wheeled into position, lifted onto his chair and settled in place before the other leaders arrived and the cameras started to click. FDR could not stand erect without heavy metal braces on each leg; he could move only with the aid of a cane and the arm of an aide or family member, looking like a man walking on stilts. For a deeply private person, each day must have been pricked with a dozen minor humiliations, yet Roosevelt's demeanour was almost always chatty and confident. Brushing aside his mother's pleas to spend the rest of his days as a gentlemanly invalid, he exercised daily to strengthen his torso and thereby heave his lower body around. To the end of his life, he seems to have persuaded himself

[3] W. Averell Harriman and Elie Abel, *Special Envoy to Churchill and Stalin, 1941–1946* (New York, 1975), 362; travel figures from the Churchill Museum, Cabinet War Rooms, London.

[4] Martin Gilbert, *Winston S. Churchill*, vol. vii (London, 1986), 217.

[5] Barbara W. Tuchman, *Stilwell and the American Experience in China, 1911–1945* (London, 1970), 398.

that full recovery was possible. That, perhaps, is why Winston Churchill could say on several occasions 'I really loved that man'.[6] Churchill reserved his deepest admiration for men of courage and FDR, despite all his duplicity, was brave beyond measure.

Our present generation is inclined to take a more open and positive attitude to disability. In the Roosevelt era there was still a real stigma attached and, if the full extent of his incapacity had become known, it would surely have undermined his political credibility. There was a good deal of deception involved in FDR's rehabilitation, calibrated by his performance at the Democratic Conventions of 1924 and 1928. On both occasions, FDR gave a rousing speech nominating the New York Governor Al Smith for the presidency. But in 1924 he lumbered painfully to the podium on crutches, sweating profusely, whereas in 1928 he walked with the aid of a stick, leaning on his son's arm. Under the trousers, of course, were the iron braces that held his useless legs erect but, to political observers in 1928, FDR no longer seemed crippled, merely 'lame'. This was how his disability was publicly understood thereafter.[7] He also persuaded the media not to highlight his physical state and few such pictures appeared. During his presidency, Secret Servicemen usually confiscated the film of errant cameramen. Only very rarely did FDR display his handicap, and then for good reason. In July 1944, visiting a hospital in Hawaii that looked after veterans who had lost arms or legs, he asked to be wheeled slowly through the wards, stopping for a cheery word at every bed. The message was clear: if a cripple could become President, there was hope for these young amputees. Most of his staff were in tears.[8]

Roosevelt's health has fascinated historians, but their main focus has been on whether his deteriorating condition in 1944–5 affected his conduct of diplomacy, particularly at Yalta. Robert H. Ferrell even speculated that 'a more alert Roosevelt might have prevented the debacle of the Vietnam War'.[9] Much less attention has been paid to how Roosevelt's disability shaped his whole diplomatic style. As a child, FDR had visited Europe most years between 1885 and 1896 and he honeymooned there in 1905. He crossed the Atlantic twice in 1918–19 as Assistant Secretary to the Navy but then polio intervened and his only other visit to Europe was a brief one in 1931 when his mother was hospitalized there with pneumonia.[10] In other words, Roosevelt's direct experience of Europe (including Britain) was essentially pre-1914. Less able than

[6] Quoted in *Life*, 16 Nov. 1953, 92.

[7] A contrast brought out well in Patrick Renshaw, *Franklin D. Roosevelt* (London, 2004), 40, 50, 54, 67.

[8] Doris Kearns Goodwin, *No Ordinary Time. Franklin and Eleanor Roosevelt: The Home Front in World War II* (New York, 1994), 532.

[9] e.g. Jim Bishop, *FDR's Last Year, April 1944–April 1945* (New York, 1974); Robert H. Ferrell, *The Dying President: Franklin D. Roosevelt, 1944–1945* (Columbia, Mo. 1998), 149.

[10] Apart from a brief stopover in Palermo en route from Teheran in Dec. 1943. See John Lamberton Harper, *American Visions of Europe: Franklin D. Roosevelt, George F. Kennan, and Dean G. Acheson* (Cambridge, 1994), 13–14, 19.

the flying Prime Minister to get to the centre of the action, the wheelchair President needed the action to come to him. One way was through foreign visitors, such as the King in 1939. More frequently, however, Roosevelt used personal emissaries, bypassing what he called the 'striped-pants set' from the State Department, of whom he was deeply sceptical. These trusted envoys acted as his eyes and ears, just as his wife had been around the United States in the 1930s;[11] they were Roosevelt's special relationships. To gain some sense of their importance, this chapter looks at how FDR used his personal contacts to get a handle on Hitler in 1938, Churchill in 1940–1, and Stalin from 1941 to 1943.

The young Franklin was particularly well acquainted with Germany. His family vacationed every summer from 1891 to 1895 at the Rhineland spa of Bad Nauheim on account of his father's deteriorating health. In school there, FDR became fluent in German and he spent the summer of 1896, aged 14, on a cycling holiday in the upper Rhineland. These memorable years became a staple part of FDR's self-mythology, to which he often returned in later life to explain his rooted suspicion of German militarism. One old chestnut was the story of how, as a bright and lanky foreigner, he was always picked on by playground bullies for wrestling matches. But, said Roosevelt, if he could hold out for five minutes or so, they always cracked for some inexplicable reason. 'There was a yellow streak in the German nature.'[12] Because of such experiences, said FDR privately in 1940, he had 'little patience with those who seek to draw a clear distinction between the German Government and the German people'. He recalled how in 1893 his school class started on 'Heimatkunde'—geography lessons centred on home. The first year, they moved out from the village to the neighbouring towns and finally covered the whole province of Hesse-Darmstadt. The following year they were told about what could be seen 'on the way to the French border'. He did not take the course the following year, but understood that the class was 'conducted' to France—'all roads leading to Paris'.[13]

Exaggerated or not, these childhood experiences created the intellectual capital on which FDR drew as war leader. The Roosevelt Presidency and the Third Reich synchronized almost exactly: Hitler became Chancellor on 30 January 1933, little over a month before the President took the oath of office on 4 March, and FDR died on 12 April 1945, less than three weeks before the Führer committed suicide. Roosevelt read the abridged English edition of *Mein Kampf* soon after entering the White House, writing caustically on the flyleaf: 'This translation is so expurgated as to give a wholly false view of what Hitler

---

[11] Eleanor Roosevelt travelled more than 280,000 miles around the United States in seven years up to the spring of 1940. Goodwin, *No Ordinary Time*, 27–8.

[12] Sir Arthur Willert, memo of conversations with FDR in Jan. and Mar. 1936, 14 Apr. 1936, p. 5, Willert papers, 14/59 (Sterling Library, Yale University).

[13] FDR to Arthur Murray, 4 Mar. 1940, Elibank papers, National Library of Edinburgh, Scotland, MSS. 8809, p. 229.

really is or says. The German original would make a different story.'[14] Despite his suspicions of German militarism in general and Hitler in particular, however, Roosevelt initially viewed Nazi Germany as a problem primarily for Britain and France. With American opinion focused on the Depression and fearful of entanglement in another European war, he kept his distance from the growing crisis. Domestic affairs took centre-stage in his first term. But as the international scene darkened with the Spanish civil war from 1936 and renewed Japanese aggression in China in 1937, he began to engage more closely in world affairs. In October 1937 the President spoke publicly of the need to 'quarantine' aggressor states. Although drawing back from any concrete action, he was airing an idea that would underpin his whole approach to global security. And in the winter of 1937–8, he toyed with hopes that Hitler's revisionist demands could be addressed through a new international conference, brokered by the United States.

The Czech crisis of September 1938 marked a fundamental shift in Roosevelt's attitude, which was prompted largely by the vivid reports he received from his emissaries in Europe, especially his old friend William C. Bullitt, whom he had sent as US Ambassador in Paris.[15] From the French leaders, via Bullitt, FDR derived a vivid impression of Hitler's style and mental state during the crisis meetings over Czechoslovakia that culminated at Munich. The Führer's intransigence over Czechoslovakia seemed clearly to go beyond the bounds of normal diplomacy. His bellicose rantings suggested someone who was psychologically deranged. Citing these diplomatic reports off the record to Senators in January 1939, FDR was quite blunt, referring to Hitler as a 'wild man', walking up and down the room for hours on end, 'pounding the table and making speeches'. He seemed, said the President, to believe himself 'a reincarnation of Julius Caesar and Jesus Christ. What can we people do about a personality like that? We would call him a "nut". But there isn't any use in calling him a "nut" because he is a power and we have to recognize that.'[16]

In other words, power had to be met by power, which led on to the other big lesson FDR derived from the diplomatic reports. Hitler had got his way, it seemed, because of Germany's advantage, or perceived advantage, in airpower. This had been crucial in intimidating the British and French leaders, fearful of bombing on an appalling scale. Within weeks Roosevelt was outlining grandiose plans for a massive air force. 'When I write to foreign countries', he told advisers

[14] Adolf Hitler, *My Battle*, abridged and translated by E. T. S. Dugdale (Boston, 1933)—copy in FDRL, with inscription on flyleaf: 'Franklin Delano Roosevelt. The White House. 1933.'
[15] As argued by Barbara Reardon Farnham, *Roosevelt and the Munich Crisis: A Study in Political Decision-Making* (Princeton, 1997), esp. ch. 5. See also David Reynolds, *From Munich to Pearl Harbor: Roosevelt's America and the Origins of the Second World War* (Chicago, 2001), chs. 2 and 3.
[16] Transcript of conference with Senate Military Affairs Committee, 31 Jan. 1939, in Donald B. Schewe, ed., *Franklin D. Roosevelt and Foreign Affairs, Jan. 1937–Aug. 1939* (14 vols., New York, 1979–83), xiii. 203–4.

on 14 November, 'I must have something to back up my words. Had we this summer 5,000 planes and the capacity immediately to produce 10,000 a year . . . Hitler would not have dared to take the stand he did.'[17]

October 1938, therefore, saw a fundamental change in Roosevelt's foreign policy, based largely on his reading of and reflection on the diplomatic cables from trusted ambassadors such as Bullitt. And the effects were lasting. His conviction that Hitler was a 'nut', supplemented by his rooted suspicion of the German character, not only led the President into a deepening confrontation with Hitler but also prompted his demand by 1943 for Germany's 'unconditional surrender'. One could not do business with such a man, or such a people. The animosity was mutual: the eugenicist Führer despised the American President as the crippled leader of a mongrel race. In fact, Roosevelt versus Hitler became a personal grudge match (much more so than Churchill against Hitler: the Prime Minister's focus remained on German militarism and autocracy). And FDR's belief that he could only talk loudly if he carried a big stick led him into a steadily increasing arms build-up, especially from 1940. By the time the war ended, the United States was the greatest air and naval power in world history, with a monopoly of atomic weapons. Power had become superpower, as will be explored more fully in Chapter 16.

By early 1939 FDR was talking privately about Britain and France as America's front line of defence. But he still assumed that theirs was the primary responsibility for containing Hitler. 'What the British need today', he wrote in February 1939, 'is a good stiff grog, inducing not only the desire to save civilization but the continued belief that they can do it. In such an event they will have a lot more support from their American cousins.'[18] America's rearmament, coupled with a repeal of the arms embargo that he eventually got through Congress in November 1939, was intended to strengthen their hand. But Roosevelt had little confidence in Neville Chamberlain, which is why, on the outbreak of war in Europe, he opened up contacts with Churchill, now First Lord of the Admiralty, inviting him to write personally and outside normal channels concerning 'anything you want me to know about'.[19] The two men had met only once before, at a dinner in London in 1918. In the first volume of his memoirs, published in 1948, Churchill wrote that, although there had been 'no opportunity for anything but salutations', he had been 'struck' by Roosevelt's 'magnificent presence in all his youth and strength'. In fact, he had completely forgotten the episode, asserting before the Atlantic Conference in 1941 that he had never previously met Roosevelt. FDR actually recalled the evening in 1918

---

[17] Herman Oliphant, memo, 14 Nov. 1938, in Henry Morgenthau, Jr., Diary, vol. 150, p. 338 (FDRL).

[18] FDR to Roger B. Merriman, 15 Feb. 1939, PSF 46: Great Britain, 1939 (FDRL).

[19] FDR to Churchill, 11 Sept. 1939, in Warren F. Kimball, ed., *Churchill and Roosevelt: The Complete Correspondence* (3 vols., Princeton, 1984), i. 24. This was not done behind the back of Ten Downing Street: FDR issued a similar invitation to Chamberlain.

with considerable resentment, telling Joseph Kennedy in December 1939 that Churchill had 'acted like a stinker . . . lording it all over us'. Despite his lingering irritation, however, Roosevelt recognized the desirability of opening contacts with a man who was Britain's most bellicose opponent of Hitler and, quite possibly, a future Prime Minister.[20]

But the conflict did not develop as Roosevelt had expected; throughout the winter, both sides engaged in a 'phoney war'. So in February 1940, Roosevelt sent his old friend Sumner Welles to Europe. Welles was part of a group in the State Department keen to explore the chances of a viable compromise peace before what seemed the inevitable spring offensive. Roosevelt told Breckinridge Long of the State Department that, as far as he was concerned, one aim of the trip was to get the 'low down on Hitler and get Mussolini's point of view'. The President claimed he already knew what London and Paris thought and that the visits there were only 'window dressing', but this was probably disingenuous.[21] Welles's reports provided the gossipy, revealing portraits that FDR liked. For instance, Welles commented that, talking with Chamberlain, 'one obtains none of the "puzzled hen" effect of which one hears so much, and which photographs emphasize. The dominating features are a pair of large, very dark and piercing eyes, and a low incisive voice.'[22]

Welles also provided a colourful account of his meeting with the First Lord of the Admiralty. 'When I was shown into his office, Mr. Churchill was sitting in front of the fire, smoking a 24-inch cigar and drinking a whisky and soda. It was obvious that he had consumed a good many whiskeys before I arrived.' Churchill then embarked on a speech that lasted one hour and fifty minutes, in the course of which, said Welles, 'he became quite sober'.[23] Learning from the US Embassy that the President's emissary had claimed Churchill was one of the most fascinating personalities he had ever met, Sir Alexander Cadogan, the Permanent Under-Secretary at the Foreign Office, felt 'some delicacy' about asking Chamberlain or Halifax, the Foreign Secretary, for authority to tell Churchill that he had made 'a unique impression on Mr. Welles'. But, added Cadogan waspishly, 'I take comfort from the fact that Mr. C. will already have that conviction, so nothing is lost.'[24]

---

[20] Winston S. Churchill, *The Second World War* (6 vols., London, 1948–54), i. 345; Michael Beschloss, *Kennedy and Roosevelt: The Uneasy Alliance* (New York, 1980), 200; David Reynolds, *In Command of History: Churchill Fighting and Writing the Second World War* (London, 2004), 112–13, 260, 555.

[21] Fred L. Israel, ed., *The War Diary of Breckinridge Long: Selections from the War Years, 1939–1944* (Lincoln, Neb., 1966), 64. For fuller discussion of the Welles mission see David Reynolds, *The Creation of the Anglo-American Alliance, 1937–1941: A Study in Competitive Cooperation* (London, 1981), 69–72.

[22] Welles, report of meeting with Chamberlain on 12 Mar. 1940, *FRUS 1940*, i. 74–5.

[23] Welles, report of meeting with Churchill on 11 Mar 1940, pp. 1–2, in PSF (Safe), box 9: Welles Reports, 1940. These passages were omitted by the State Dept. from the published version in *FRUS 1940*, i. 83–4.

[24] Cadogan, minute, 30 Mar. 1940, FO 371/24407, C4618/89/18 (TNA).

Welles's caustic comments on Churchill reflected more general reservations about him in Washington, even after he became Prime Minister. Adolf Berle of the State Department referred to him as one of 'the old war horses, behaving as well as he can, but no longer the young Churchill'. As a diehard on India and the Empire, he also seemed a long way from the ideology of the New Deal. His American friends were 'definitely . . . not on our team', as Kennedy put it to FDR.[25] Welles's comments about Churchill's propensity for alcohol also fitted a common Washington stereotype. When FDR met the Canadian premier, Mackenzie King, in April 1940, they gossiped about Churchill being 'tight most of the time'. And on hearing news of Churchill's appointment as premier, according to Interior Secretary Harold Ickes, FDR told his Cabinet 'that he supposed Churchill was the best man England had, even if he was drunk half of his time'. Ickes added that Churchill was reputedly 'very unreliable when under the influence of drink'.[26]

The truth of these perceptions is less important here than their pervasiveness and persistence. Whatever FDR said about Britain in public, he was not sure in private in 1940 about how to regard Churchill. During the election campaign, the Republican candidate, Wendell Willkie made play with some critical comments by Churchill years before of how the early New Deal had alienated American business. Although disconcerted, the Prime Minister decided to make no public response, on the principle 'least said, soonest mended', but it is possible that all this rankled in the White House.[27] As soon as Roosevelt's victory was announced, Churchill sent the President a fulsome telegram of congratulations. He was most disturbed not to receive a reply, and pressed the British Embassy to ascertain what had happened. The official line from the White House was that the telegram had got lost in the deluge of post-election mail—a somewhat implausible claim, even allowing for the disorder of the presidential office. It is striking that after FDR's fourth-term victory in November 1944, Churchill took the trouble to send him a copy of the 1940 message, 'as you may have forgotten it'.[28]

Snub or not, this episode is further evidence of the uncertainties in the Roosevelt–Churchill relationship in 1940. The President remarked in December that a lot of the problems between the two countries 'could be solved if Churchill

[25] Adolf A. Berle, diary, 18 May 1940; Joseph P. Kennedy to FDR, 2 Nov. 1939, PSF (Confidential) 53: Great Britain, Kennedy (both FDRL).
[26] Mackenzie King diary, quoted in J. L. Granatstein, *Canada's War: The Politics of the Mackenzie King Government, 1939–1945* (Toronto, 1975), 117; Harold L. Ickes, diary, vol. 31, p. 4380, 12 May 1940 (Library of Congress). The reference to drink is omitted from the published version—see *The Secret Diary of Harold L. Ickes* (3 vols., New York, 1953–4), iii. 176.
[27] See FO 371/24234, A4279/39/45, quoting from Colville to Whitehead, 4 Nov. 1940; also Joseph P. Lash, *Roosevelt and Churchill: The Partnership That Saved the West* (New York, 1976), 246–7.
[28] FDR assured Churchill he had not forgotten it. For the messages see Kimball, ed., *Churchill and Roosevelt*, i. 80–1 and iii. 382–5. For fuller evidence and discussion see Reynolds, *Creation of the Anglo-American Alliance*, 179, 341–2.

and I could just sit down together for a while'. This was clearly impossible at the time, so Roosevelt sent his most trusted confidant, Harry Hopkins, to serve as what Hopkins called 'a catalytic agent between two prima donnas'. On the face of it, Hopkins was an unlikely figure to warm to Churchill—a deeply committed New Dealer with a large dose of Midwestern suspicion about the aristocratic Old World. That was probably an asset in the eyes of FDR, irritated at the way that Kennedy had 'gone native' in his support of British appeasement. In fact, Hopkins set out very sceptical about all the adulation of the new British Prime Minister—'I suppose Churchill is convinced that he's the greatest man in the world'—so much so that one friend told him to stop behaving like 'a damned little small-town chauvinist' with a big chip on his shoulder.[29]

Hopkins arrived in London on 9 January 1941. Next day, in his first encounter with the Prime Minister, he came straight to the point, saying 'there was a feeling in some quarters that he, Churchill, did not like America, Americans or Roosevelt'. This sparked vehement denials from the PM.[30] For his part, Hopkins admitted to one of Churchill's secretaries that for years he had strongly disliked the British but claimed that these prejudices had been dispelled by the kindness of Queen Elizabeth towards his infant daughter during the royal visit of 1939.[31] Over the next month, Hopkins was treated to a relentless diet of Churchill—in Cabinet, at Chequers, preparing speeches and on inspection trips—all at full throttle and lubricated by a steady consumption of alcohol that clearly made little difference to his capacities. Hopkins's initial suspicions were quickly dispelled. As early as 13 January he reported to the President that '*Churchill* is the gov[ernmen]t in every sense—he controls the grand strategy and often the details—labor trusts him—the army, navy, air force are behind him to a man . . . I cannot emphasize too strongly that he is the one and only person over here with whom you need to have a full meeting of minds.' Hopkins also told FDR: 'I cannot believe that it is true that Churchill dislikes either you or America—it just doesn't make any sense.'[32] After one all-day odyssey, finishing at 2 a.m., Churchill went off to do some dictation and his American visitor slumped into an armchair muttering, 'Jesus Christ! What a man!'[33]

Near the end of his visit, Hopkins dined with Churchill and a few of his entourage at the Station Hotel in Glasgow. During the meal he stood up, turned to the Prime Minister and raised the matter that had been on all the minds of his British hosts in the last few weeks—what he would tell Roosevelt on his return. Hopkins said he simply intended to quote one verse from the Old Testament book of Ruth: 'Whither thou goest, I will go; and where thou lodgest, I will

[29] Quotations from Robert E. Sherwood, *Roosevelt and Hopkins: An Intimate History* (New York, 1948), respectively pp. 230, 236, 232. [30] Sherwood, *Roosevelt and Hopkins*, 238.
[31] Recalled by Colville to Ismay, 23 June 1958, pp. 6–7, Ismay papers, 1/14/31/3 (Liddell Hart Centre for Military Archives, King's College, London).
[32] Sherwood, *Roosevelt and Hopkins*, 243.
[33] Cadogan, minute, 29 Jan. 1941, FO 371/26179, A101/101/45 (TNA), quoting a story told by Oliver Lyttelton, President of the Board of Trade.

lodge: thy people shall be my people, and thy God my God.' In a whisper he
added: 'Even to the end.' Churchill's eyes filled with tears.[34]

Hopkins's visit put relations between Roosevelt and Churchill on a new footing
and also paved the way for their first summit, off Newfoundland in August 1941.
Before that, however, Hopkins had been sent on an equally important and far
more hazardous mission—to Moscow.

On 22 June Hitler mounted the biggest offensive in history, Operation
Barbarossa, deploying 3.5 million men along a front of 1,000 miles. Most of the
Red Airforce was destroyed on the ground, and the Wehrmacht gained over 200
miles in the first five days. Echoing Churchill, Roosevelt said publicly on 24 June
that the United States would 'give all the aid we possibly can to Russia'—which
sounded forthcoming while also leaving room for manoeuvre. The big question
was whether this would be aid down the drain: the War Department, for
instance, reckoned that Moscow would fall in one to three months. Roosevelt's
gut instinct was more optimistic. 'Now comes this Russian diversion', he wrote
to his Ambassador in Vichy France on 26 June. 'If it is more than just that it will
mean the liberation of Europe from Nazi domination—and at the same time I
do not think we need worry about any possibility of Russian domination.'[35] But
these were no more than hunches and, if wrong, the consequences would be
profound. Aid to Russia would be at Britain's expense, as Hopkins was reminded
when he came to London in mid-July for further discussions. So on 25 July he
cabled Roosevelt asking for permission to visit Moscow (the RAF had just
opened a flyingboat route from Scotland around Norway to Archangel). FDR
immediately agreed, and sent Hopkins a letter of introduction for Stalin.

The Soviet leader rarely met foreign ambassadors, but Hopkins was granted
two long meetings at the Kremlin on 30 and 31 July. As the President's personal
emissary, he was able to go right to the top, just as when visiting England in
January. He returned home deeply impressed with Stalin—terse, controlled, and
totally determined to win. 'Give us anti-aircraft guns and the aluminum and we
can fight for three or four years', was an exclamation that particularly stuck
in Hopkins's memory. Stalin also employed language surely tailored to fit
Roosevelt's ideological mindset, talking, for instance, of the need for 'a minimum moral standard between all nations' and asserting that 'the President and
the United States had more influence with the common people of the world
than any other force'.[36]

Although cabling FDR on 1 August he was 'ever so confident about this
front', Hopkins actually saw nothing of the fighting; his confidence in Soviet

---

[34] Lord Moran, *Winston Churchill: The Struggle for Survival* (London, pbk edn., 1968), 20.
[35] FDR quotations from Edward M. Bennett, *Franklin D. Roosevelt and the Search for Victory:
American-Soviet Relations, 1939–1945* (Wilmington, Del., 1990), 26, 28.
[36] Sherwood, *Roosevelt and Hopkins*, ch. 15, esp. pp. 327, 328, 343. The records of these two
meetings are available in full in the Harry L. Hopkins papers, box 306: Moscow (FDRL).

survival derived mostly from these encounters with Stalin. More than any formal intelligence data, his reports persuaded FDR to move decisively on his hunch about aid to Russia. On 1 August an angry President lectured his Cabinet for forty-five minutes, accusing the War Department in particular of foot-dragging. Already forced to share America's still limited war production with the British, the armed forces objected strongly to a three-way cut. When told that, with Hopkins away, there was no one able to cut through the red tape, FDR charged Wayne Coy of the Office of Emergency Management with a rare written directive: 'Act as a burr under the saddle and get things moving.'[37]

In September 1941 a supply mission to Moscow filled out the details and its head—another trusted Roosevelt middleman, Averell Harriman—reinforced Hopkins's optimism about Soviet resistance. It also strengthened the impression that Stalin was a man with whom you could negotiate, even though he was no pushover. Roosevelt started his own correspondence with Stalin, assuring Churchill breezily (on absolutely no evidence) in March 1942 that 'I think I can personally handle Stalin better than either your Foreign Office or my State Department. Stalin hates the guts of all your top people. He thinks he likes me better, and I hope he will continue to do so.'[38] During 1942 FDR remained dependent on second-hand impressions of Stalin, such as those from Churchill after his own mission to Moscow in August but, after the epic turning of the tide at Stalingrad, the President was determined to develop direct American contacts with the leader who would clearly be a force in post-war Europe. The result, in May 1943, was another mission to Moscow, this time by Joseph E. Davies.

Davies was an old Roosevelt crony, dating back to their days together in Wilson's Washington. A wealthy corporate lawyer who helped bankroll FDR's election campaigns, he was rewarded in 1937 with the post of Ambassador to Moscow. Davies was ideal for Roosevelt's purposes, critical of the starchy diplomats with their hardline anti-Bolshevism, and an enthusiast for improved Soviet-American relations. His 1941 memoir, *Mission to Moscow*, and the ensuing movie made Davies a celebrity and, after Barbarossa, he cultivated close links with the Soviet Embassy in Washington, acting as an informal backchannel between it and the White House. By the spring of 1943, Roosevelt felt deeply anxious at the deterioration in Soviet–American relations following the failure of the Western Allies to mount a Second Front in France. He told Davies (in language very similar to his conversation with Hopkins about Churchill in December 1940) that if he could have 'a face to face talk' with Stalin, they could clear up a lot of misunderstandings. 'Three's a crowd', said Roosevelt; 'we can arrange for the Big Three to get together thereafter. Churchill will understand. I will take care of that.' He particularly wanted Davies

---

[37] Waldo Heinrichs, *Threshold of War: Franklin D. Roosevelt and the American Entry into World War II* (New York, 1988), 140.
[38] FDR to Churchill, 18 Mar. 1942, in Kimball, ed., *Churchill and Roosevelt*, i. 421.

to convey the message that Stalin was not caught in the 'nutcracker' of a firm Anglo-American axis.[39]

At the Kremlin on 20 May, Davies emphasized that Roosevelt and Churchill did not see eye to eye on everything, for instance colonialism, and invited Stalin to a bilateral meeting with the President in Alaska. Although this never materialized—Stalin was preoccupied throughout the summer of 1943 with the great Soviet counter-offensive at Kursk—what is interesting is how FDR conducted the business behind Churchill's back. When the Prime Minister got wind of the proposed bilateral meeting and raised it with FDR, the President lied blatantly, telling Churchill 'I did not suggest to U[ncle] J[oe] that we meet alone', claiming that the suggestion had come from Stalin.[40] Churchill knew this was untrue and the deception probably rankled. It also signalled the big shift in Anglo-American relations from the bilateral axis of 1940–2 into the triangular relationship of the last half of the war, in which the British became increasingly the junior partner.

The case studies described in this chapter—Bullitt in 1938, Welles in 1939, Hopkins in 1941, and Davies in 1943—are examples of a larger and longer pattern, of how the wheelchair president used personal emissaries to be his eyes, ears, and sometimes mouthpiece. Even after establishing direct contact with Stalin at Teheran in November 1943, the President continued to rely heavily on Harriman in Soviet–American relations. The content of those relations and the way they broke down in the mid-1940s is the theme of Part V. But first we should look more closely at the changing texture of Anglo-American relations during the later part of war. In August 1940, Churchill rightly predicted that the two countries would become increasingly 'mixed up together in some of their affairs'.[41] This happened not only in top-level diplomacy but also at the grass roots. Nearly three million American soldiers passed through Britain in 1942–5: their impact takes us into cultural and social dimensions of international history.

---

[39] Elizabeth Kimball Maclean, 'Joseph E. Davies and Soviet-American Relations, 1941–43', *Diplomatic History*, 4 (1980), 73–93, quoting pp. 86, 87, 89.

[40] FDR to Churchill, 28 June 1943, in Kimball, ed., *Churchill and Roosevelt*, ii. 283; see also pp. 233, 244–5, 277–9.

[41] House of Commons, Debates, 5th series, 364: 1171, 20 Aug. 1940.

IV

'MIXED UP TOGETHER'

10

Whitehall, Washington, and the Promotion of American Studies in Britain, 1941–1943

Most of Britain seems to believe that nothing happens in America except 'gangster shootings, rapes and kidnappings'. That was the complaint of Joseph P. Kennedy, the US Ambassador, in a speech in Liverpool in May 1939. Kennedy blamed this perception on the British belief that American 'home life, history, and even legal practice are typified by motion pictures'. He appealed for better press coverage of the United States and for the study of American history in British schools and universities.[1]

Kennedy's appeal fell on deaf ears in 1939. This was not because of its rich irony—the Ambassador was a 'compulsive philanderer' who had made his fortune from movies, liquor, and insider trading.[2] More important, the time was not yet ripe. But two years later, in the spring of 1941, the British Government decided to mount an ambitious campaign to promote the study of America throughout the British education system and this was implemented, particularly in schools, with remarkable alacrity. The originators of the campaign—the Ministry of Information and the Board of Education—were not exactly 'heavy hitters' in Whitehall but they received consistent support from the Foreign Office and the BBC. On the American side, Kennedy's successor as Ambassador, John Winant, was equally enthusiastic. The story constitutes an important and neglected episode in the development of American studies in Britain. It also offers an interesting sidelight on the place of cultural relations in British and American wartime diplomacy.

Kennedy's strictures were justified. Well over half the British population between the ages of fifteen and sixty-five attended the cinema every week, in the

This chapter was originally published in *Journal of American Studies*, 16 (1982), 165–88. It is reproduced here with a slightly reordered opening and the removal of most of one paragraph to avoid duplication with earlier chapters.

[1] *The Times*, 19 May 1939, 18.
[2] Quotation from Robert Dallek, *John F. Kennedy: An Unfinished Life, 1917–1963* (London, 2003), 23.

late 1930s and American films took about 80 per cent of screen time.[3] From them it was easy to derive the impression that the United States was populated by cowboys, Chicago gangsters, and Park Avenue socialites, that its politics were rotten with corruption and that it was a land of unbelievable wealth for those with brains, brawn, and a pliant conscience. Such stereotypes were not dispelled by the British press. One survey in 1936–37 estimated that in 'the more sober morning newspapers' the USA received only 8 to 16 per cent of the total space allotted to foreign news. Of this a quarter was devoted to government and politics, 15 per cent to finance and commerce, and between 30 and 40 per cent to sensation, sex, and crime.[4] Another study, conducted in January 1939, concluded that America was still being treated in the Northcliffe tradition—as a convenient source of salacious human interest stories. Serious news appeared intermittently, at times of crisis, without suitable background or interpretation, and coverage was concentrated on New York, Washington, and Hollywood where most of the correspondents and news agencies were based.[5]

But, despite Kennedy's pleas, the British educational system did little to correct the media's distortions. 'American work in the schools of the inter-war period had the character of scattered experiments, dependent on interested individuals, and limited in effect by lack of co-ordination.'[6] Geography received only superficial treatment and literature was almost totally neglected. Despite greater interest in US history, significant progress was made only at isolated schools, usually private, under the aegis of enthusiasts such as Robert Birley at Charterhouse and J. Howard Whitehouse at Bembridge. In the universities the situation was a little better. Again American literature was largely ignored, but there were two permanent chairs of US history—the Harmsworth professorship at Oxford, to be held by an American scholar, and the Commonwealth Fund chair at University College, London, which had been occupied by H. Hale Bellot since its establishment in 1930. In addition to these two universities, only four others offered courses largely or wholly on US history—Birmingham, Bristol, Aberystwyth, and St Andrews—and there was also a course on US economic history at Liverpool.[7] Outside Oxford and London there was a grave shortage of suitable books, and teaching depended on the enthusiasm of individual lecturers such as John Hawgood at Birmingham or Sidney Herbert at Aberystwyth.

---

[3] Paul Smith, ed., *The Historian and Film* (London, 1976), 112; Bruce M. Russett, *Community and Contention: Britain and America in the Twentieth Century* (Cambridge, Mass., 1963), 123.

[4] Richard Heathcote Heindel, *The American Impact on Great Britain, 1898–1914: A Study of the United States in World History* (Philadelphia, 1940), 15–18.

[5] *Planning* [Broadsheet of the Political and Economic Planning group], No. 148, 30 May 1939.

[6] Sigmund Skard, *American Studies in Europe: Their History and Present Organization*, 2 vols. (Philadelphia, 1958), i. 59. Ch. 2 of this vol., esp. pp. 57–71, provides the background for much of this paragraph.

[7] See 'Interim report submitted by Mr Joseph Scott', July 1937, and Hubert Howard to W. G. Humphrey, 14 Nov. 1938, papers of the Carnegie Endowment for International Peace, 24192 and 24182 (Columbia University Library, New York). The Endowment's London office conducted a thorough survey of American studies in the summer of 1937.

Nowhere was US history a required course, and, in the form of a special subject, for example on the American Revolution at Oxford, it tended to attract weaker candidates lured by the absence of a language requirement.[8] Post-graduate students, from whose ranks would come the next generation of university teachers, showed little interest—only eight D.Phil. theses on American subjects were completed in Oxford between 1925 and 1940.[9] And at the very top it proved extremely difficult to entice distinguished US scholars over to teach. Thus, after the pioneering efforts of Samuel Eliot Morison, the first Harmsworth professor from 1922 to 1925, US history atrophied at Oxford under his charming but ineffectual successor, Robert McElroy, who occupied the chair until 1939. Vigorous efforts in 1935–37 to find an appropriate replacement were unavailing, because no eminent American historian would countenance the prospects of professional isolation and a steep drop in salary. 'Consequently,' Morison told Felix Frankfurter, 'the danger is that nobody can be found for the chair but failures, misfits, ex-diplomats, and the like.'[10]

The state of American studies attracted virtually no official attention. The Board of Education provided oversight and guidance rather than direct interference in the running of the schools, and it had minimal control over the universities, whose financial connection with the Government was through the University Grants Committee. In any case, British leaders of the 1930s generally displayed little interest in things American, and most shared the prevailing distaste for the United States as a land of violence, materialism, and what Harold Nicolson called 'eternal superficiality'.[11] Their foreign policy was directed towards a settlement with the European dictators, and, embittered by their experience of Woodrow Wilson and of inter-war American isolationism, they considered, in Chamberlain's notorious phrase, that it was 'always best and safest to count on *nothing* from the Americans except words'.[12]

On the American side, Kennedy's periodic outbursts did not reflect a determined official policy of trying to explain the United States to the British. Throughout the inter-war years American efforts to promote better cultural relations between nations were almost entirely in the hands of the great New York philanthropic foundations such as the Commonwealth Fund, the Carnegie Endowment, the Rockefeller Foundation and the American Council of Learned Societies. The creation of the State Department's Division of Cultural Relations

---

[8] D. W. Brogan to Joseph Scott, 8 July 1937, Carnegie Endowment Papers, 24305.

[9] Skard, *American Studies*, ii. 70.

[10] Morison to Frankfurter, 1 Mar. 1937, Felix Frankfurter Papers, 85/1751 (Library of Congress, Washington, DC). For the mid-1930s efforts see Frankfurter to Roosevelt, 24 Jan. and 5 Feb. 1935, ibid., 98/2004, and Robert W. Bingham, diary, 11 May 1935 and 16 May 1936, Bingham Papers, box I (LC).

[11] Harold Nicolson, *Diaries and Letters, 1930–1939*, ed. Nigel Nicolson (London, 1966), p. 189—Letter of Nov. 1934.

[12] Neville Chamberlain to Hilda Chamberlain, 17 Dec. 1937, Neville Chamberlain Papers, NC 18/1/1032 (Birmingham University Library).

in July 1938 did not mark any major departure. The Division's role was merely to stimulate and coordinate existing private programmes for cultural and educational exchange between the USA and Latin America. There was little support for suggestions in 1934 and again in 1938 that the State Department should set up an official library of information in London to help educate British opinion about the United States.[13]

In the absence of governmental interest in either country, the growth of American studies in Britain in the 1930s depended on the activities of private organizations. In London the English-Speaking Union arranged exchanges of school teachers and took a keen interest in the question of an American library. But the most active body in the last years before war was the Carnegie Endowment for International Peace, which had to curtail its operations in continental Europe because of the extension of Nazi power and concentrated instead on making 'American history and policies better understood by the English-speaking peoples.'[14] During 1937–38, after a comprehensive survey of the state of American studies in Britain, the Endowment provided grants of about £100 apiece to the Universities of Birmingham, Bristol, St Andrews, and Aberystwyth for the purchase of books. In 1939 it held a small but very successful conference of university teachers of US history, and it also tried to promote American studies at the secondary level by allocating £400 for public schools and teacher training colleges to obtain books, films, and visiting lecturers. Further expansion was planned but all these activities were brought to an end by the outbreak of war.

There was also some public discussion in Britain in the late 1930s about the state of American studies. The spring and summer of 1937 saw a long and spirited correspondence in *The Times*, and the problem was analysed in more detail in several scholarly essays published in 1937 and 1938. Occasionally the case for studying America was presented on purely educational grounds. Hale Bellot, for instance, was already expounding the concept of 'Atlantic history' which became popular in the 1950s, namely that the development of Britain, continental Europe, and North America had become so entangled in the nineteenth century that they could only be properly studied as part of a single Atlantic economy.[15] But most apostles of American studies were concerned with current diplomacy rather than past history. Their thesis, to quote Howard

[13] See documents in the papers of the US Department of State, Record Group (RG) 59, Decimal File for 1930–39, 841.43/30 (NA). For background on US cultural diplomacy see Frank A. Ninkovich, *The Diplomacy of Ideas: U.S. Foreign Policy and Cultural Relations, 1938–1950* (Cambridge, 1981), ch. 1.

[14] Nicholas Murray Butler to Hubert Howard, 27 July 1938, Carnegie Endowment Papers, 22492. The rest of this paragraph draws on the records of the Endowment's London office, box 98, esp. papers 24145, 24192, and 22494.

[15] H. Hale Bellot, 'The Place of American History in English Education', *History*, 21 (1937), 331–9. For subsequent development see e.g. Frank Thistlethwaite, *The Anglo-American Connection in the Early Nineteenth Century* (Philadelphia, 1959), esp. ch. 1.

Whitehouse, was 'that a close friendship and understanding between the two great English-speaking countries is of supreme importance to the world to-day' and 'that this friendship and understanding can be greatly helped by the intelligent study of American history in our schools'.[16] As we have seen, however, official policy-makers placed much less emphasis on the USA and, in general, British enthusiasts for America, the New Deal and Anglo-American cooperation tended to come from the centre-left of the political spectrum, which had little influence over the National Government of the 1930s[17]. That the justification for expanding American studies was political rather than educational was confirmed by the Carnegie Endowment. Its 1937 survey concluded that, on the basis of present demand, there was no reason to increase the number of courses, research programmes and the like. The main requirement was to provide better resources in the existing facilities—hence its emphasis on book grants. The survey concluded that any further expansion would probably depend on political developments: if Anglo-American relations became closer and the USA took a more forceful role on the world stage, this would stimulate British interest in the United States and, consequently, demand for American studies at all levels of the educational system.[18] It was a shrewd prediction—and one that events would eventually confirm.

There was no immediate strengthening of Anglo-American relations after the outbreak of hostilities in Europe in September 1939.[19] Throughout the 'phoney war' Chamberlain and his colleagues continued to expect little more from the United States than 'benevolent neutrality'. There was also a recognition, particularly in the Tory party, that dependence on the USA might further undermine Britain's increasingly precarious international position, as it had in 1914–19. 'Heaven knows I don't want the Americans to fight for us,' Chamberlain wrote in January 1940. 'We should have to pay too dearly for that if they had a right to be in on the peace terms.'[20]

The mood changed dramatically in May–June 1940, after Churchill became Prime Minister and France was overrun. What Lord Halifax called 'a special association with the United States'[21] became the top priority of British policy, as we saw in Chapter 2. But a comparable American commitment to Britain was slower to materialize, even after Roosevelt's re-election in November. Churchill

---

[16] J. Howard Whitehouse, *America and Our Schools* (London, 1939), 2. For other examples see Sir Josiah Stamp, *The Times*, 25 June 1937, p. 18, and Frank Darvall, 'American Interest in Britain versus British Interest in America', *The Universities Review*, 9 (1937), 114–15.

[17] Cf. Henry Pelling, *America and the British Left: From Bright to Bevan* (London, 1956), ch. 8.

[18] Scott, 'Interim report', July 1937, Carnegie Endowment Papers, 24192.

[19] This paragraph summarizes part of the argument of David Reynolds, *The Creation of the Anglo-American Alliance, 1937–1941: A Study in Competitive Cooperation* (London, 1981), chs. 3–6.

[20] Neville Chamberlain to Ida Chamberlain, 27 Jan. 1940, Chamberlain Papers, NC 18/1/1140.

[21] Halifax to Hankey, 15 July 1940, Hankey Papers, HNKY 5/4 (CAC).

confessed himself 'rather chilled' by the American response.[22] Feelings in London did not change until the New Year, when the President sent the Lend-Lease bill to Congress and fought a difficult, two-month battle to secure its acceptance. Here at last was a public commitment of sustained material aid to Britain, backed by clear legislative support. By the time the bill became law on 11 March 1941 Whitehall could at last see an Anglo-American alliance in embryo.

The passage of Lend-Lease had a similar effect on British public opinion. In 1940 there had been considerable popular resentment at the lack of American help. When the survey group Mass-Observation polled its panel of 1,500 voluntary observers in October 1940 only 27 per cent were favourably disposed towards the USA. This placed America lower in esteem than the Greeks, Poles, or Jews. But when the panel was questioned again in April 1941 the United States was the most popular foreign nation, with 60 per cent approval.[23] With this new enthusiasm came a new curiosity. The United States mattered to Britain far more than ever before, and the press, radio, and the newsreels reflected and reinforced the unprecedented interest. One survey of BBC listeners in July 'detected a genuine realisation on the part of ordinary people that, despite all the output of Hollywood, they know very little about the American as a human being and they want to know more'.[24] Not surprisingly one commentator called 1941 the year of the British 'discovery of America'.[25]

But public opinion did not change completely. There was still much impatience at the slowness of US help, and the old stereotypes about American selfishness and materialism persisted—much to the disquiet of the British Ministry of Information. The MOI was concerned about the state of domestic morale, particularly in the first half of 1941 before Russian involvement in the war eased the pressure in the west and reduced the threat of invasion. The Ministry feared that public enthusiasm for the USA would wane disastrously when it became clear that Lend-Lease did not herald an immediate outpouring of American material aid, let alone US entry into the war. It seemed important to explain the inevitable lead-time in converting an economy to war production and to educate the British public about the political problems of building a foreign-policy consensus in a federal system with loose party discipline and immense sectional and ethnic diversity. There was also a general concern to dispel the unflattering movie image of the United States by providing a more balanced picture of everyday American life.[26]

[22] War Cabinet minutes, 2 Dec. 1940, CAB 65/10, WM 299 (40) 4 (TNA).

[23] Mass-Observation file report 759, 27 June 1941, Mass-Observation Archive (University of Sussex, Brighton).

[24] Listener Research Report, LR/296, 8 July 1941, copy in Ministry of Information Papers, INF 1/292 (TNA).

[25] John Murray, 'The Discovery of America', The Contemporary Review, 159 (1941), 396–403. Murray was Principal of the University College of the South-West at Exeter.

[26] e.g., Sir Kenneth Clark, 'Publicity about the U.S.A. in Britain', 21 June 1941, copy in INF 1/312.

These became the objectives of a large-scale MOI campaign which got underway in July 1941. But, at a less public level, they had been official goals of Ministry policy since the previous January when the MOI's Home Planning Committee had discussed the disturbing ambivalence of popular attitudes and had approved a programme of 'quiet activities over a long period' to explain the USA to the British public.[27] Among these activities were lectures, newspaper articles, and special radio talks. But schools and universities were also to be involved, and in March 1941 Duff Cooper, the Minister of Information, made a series of far-reaching proposals. Specifically, Cooper asked the Board of Education, as the responsible government department, to issue a circular urging greater emphasis on US history, literature, and politics in schools, and to introduce references to US history in British school and college textbooks. He also made the remarkable suggestion that all British universities should have chairs of US history, perhaps even Regius professorships endowed by the government.[28]

The response in Whitehall to Cooper's letter was quick and unanimous— indicating the new persuasiveness of the political argument for American studies. Thus, Arthur Greenwood, the minister responsible for post-war planning, agreed that 'only education' could build up 'a mutual understanding between our two democracies who will carry the common burdens of the future'.[29] Similar sentiments were expressed in the Foreign Office, where T. North Whitehead, a temporary member of the American Department who had previously worked for many years in the USA, had already been urging the importance of greater British awareness of American life and attitudes. In a letter prepared by Whitehead in April 1941, R. A. Butler, then Parliamentary Under Secretary at the FO, wrote to support the idea of American studies in schools. The FO believed, he said, 'that in the long run this may be of the greatest importance in helping to promote a closer co-operation between the English-speaking nations—without which it hardly seems likely that the peace of the world can be maintained'.[30]

The Board of Education needed little encouragement. Its President, Herwald Ramsbotham, warmly welcomed Cooper's ideas and quickly set his staff to work. Within a fortnight the Board's 'History Panel' had evolved a three-point pro- gramme, involving guidance memoranda, new textbooks, and short courses for teachers. Although Ramsbotham lost his job in the Cabinet reshuffle of July 1941, his successor as President of the Board of Education was R. A. Butler, who enthusiastically supervised the programme's implementation. Meanwhile,

[27] Home Planning Commt. minutes, items 516, 528, 545 (quotation), 13, 16 and 20 Jan. 1941, INF 1/249.

[28] Cooper to Ramsbotham, 18 Mar. 1941, ED 121/3. The Board of Education was renamed the 'Ministry of Education' in the 1944 Education Act.

[29] Greenwood to Ramsbotham, 17 June 1941, Cabinet Office Papers, CAB 117/95 (TNA).

[30] R. A. Butler to Ramsbotham, 9 Apr. 1941, Foreign Office general political correspondence, FO 371/26228, A2469 (TNA).

the University Grants Committee took up Cooper's proposal about new chairs of US history, and within a few months had prepared its own proposals. The work done in the spring of 1941 laid the basis for a major campaign to promote American studies in Britain, which we shall examine first in the schools and then at the university level.

The Board of Education's first task was to inform schools of its new interest in the United States. In July 1941 and February 1942 it issued two short guidance memoranda about the teaching of US history in, respectively, elementary and secondary schools. These contained general advice about methods of instruction and short lists of suitable books. A purely bibliographical leaflet about the study of US geography followed in June 1942, and the Scottish Education Department produced its own memorandum 'America and the Schools' in November 1941.[31] The essentially political justification for this sudden interest in American studies was acknowledged and emphasized. As the Scottish memo put it: 'The promotion of mutual understanding between the peoples of Great Britain and the United States is of fundamental importance for the future of the world. Those who can contribute towards it have no time to lose.' Particular stress was placed on correcting the cinema's projection of America, both by providing balanced, detailed instruction and by underlining the common tradition of liberal democracy which both countries shared. But there was more to these memos than hands-across-the-sea propaganda. The first one warned: 'It is essential . . . that we should rid ourselves of the tendency to assess the history of the U.S.A. according to an English scale of values, to look at America for English traits and within a framework of English political ideas.' The object, then, was to dispel popular misconceptions and to illuminate both the similarities and the differences between British and American life—'to make children realize that Hollywood, hot music and slang are not the most important features of the life of the U.S.A.; they should come to appreciate the great American leaders and the generous idealism actuating this nation, that speaks the same tongue as we do but is otherwise different in tradition and outlook.' As to methods, the memoranda advised that for younger children the best approach was through stories about great Americans such as Washington, Lincoln, and Edison. At the secondary level political developments could be studied, and a chronological presentation was appropriate for the ante-bellum period. But thereafter the absence of a vigorous political narrative between 1865 and 1901 and the lack of perspective on recent events probably dictated a thematic approach. This, the memos stressed, offered much opportunity for inter-disciplinary collaboration, particularly between

---

[31] Board of Education, *The schools in war-time*, memos 26 and 28: *The teaching of the history of the United States of America*—I (July 1941), II (Feb. 1942) and 31: *A list of books dealing with some of the aspects of the Geography of the United States of America* (June 1942). Scottish Education Department, memo 234: *America and the Schools* (Nov. 1941). (Copies of the Board memos can be found in ED 138/27.)

history and geography teachers in examining themes such as sectionalism and isolationism. Integrated methods could also be used for such topics as American art, architecture, and literature, while, for primary children, the 'history stories' could be enlivened by learning songs and reading classic novels such as *Little Women* or *The Adventures of Huckleberry Finn*.

But these memoranda only highlighted the paucity of suitable reading material for British schoolchildren. US textbooks were too long and assumed too great a knowledge of American life, while British writing, by scholars such as Laski or Brogan, was more suited to undergraduates. Special texts were therefore needed, and here the Board was assisted by Oxford University Press, which had discovered America long before Whitehall,[32] and particularly by the US Ambassador in London, John G. Winant, who arrived in March 1941. As we saw in Chapter 8, his brief from FDR was to promote progressive tendencies in wartime Britain. Winant was in fact a former history teacher and he took a keen interest in the Board's programme. After considerable discussion it was decided to approach Allan Nevins, the distinguished historian of the Civil War and the Gilded Age, who was spending a sabbatical from Columbia University as Harmsworth professor at Oxford. He was commissioned in May 1941 to produce a very short survey of US history which would be placed in secondary schools throughout the country. Nevins worked on the text through the summer and completed it in mid-August, after his return to the USA. To speed up its delivery to England the manuscript was sent via the White House's special diplomatic pouch.[33] Winant himself contributed a foreword on the importance of US history and the book was published early in 1942 under the title *A Brief History of the United States*. It ran to about 40,000 words and covered the period from the 1770s to 1941, with roughly two-thirds devoted to the ante-bellum era. In places the book was rather compressed and lacking in colour, and occasionally there were tendentious generalizations—'the Negro and carpet-bagger governments [in the South after the Civil War] were probably the worst that had ever been known in any English-speaking land'[34]—but, given the word restriction and the speed with which it was composed, it was undoubtedly a remarkable achievement. OUP considered it 'a brilliant success'[35] and they asked Nevins and his Columbia colleague, Henry Steele Commager, to write a longer study of about 100,000 words, which they published in December 1942.[36]

However, guidance on paper and the provision of new textbooks were clearly insufficient. Most teachers knew as little as the public at large about the USA and

[32] Cf. correspondence of autumn 1940 in FO 371/24249, A4533/434/45.

[33] Nevins to Stephen Early, 15 Aug. 1941, Franklin D. Roosevelt Papers, Official File (OF) 4281: Winant; Nevins to Winant, same date, John G. Winant Papers, box 210: Nevins (both Franklin D. Roosevelt Library, Hyde Park, NY).

[34] Allan Nevins, *A Brief History of the United States* (Oxford, 1942), 103.

[35] A. P. Norrington to Winant, 17 Jan. 1942, Winant Papers, box 191: Clarendon Press.

[36] Allan Nevins and Henry Steele Commager, *America: The Story of a Free People* (Oxford, 1942).

its history and so the Board of Education arranged a series of week-long training courses around the country. The first of these was inaugurated in London on 21 July 1941 by Ambassador Winant and it was followed by five others in various parts of England during the summer. In all 1,102 teachers attended— 775 elementary, 237 secondary, 59 from technical schools, and 21 staff of training colleges. The courses obviously answered a need—a large proportion of the primary school teachers proved 'almost completely ignorant of the most elementary facts of American History'[37]—and there was general satisfaction in Whitehall at what had been achieved. The Foreign Secretary, Anthony Eden, considered the courses an 'excellent' idea, and R. A. Butler, the newly-appointed President of the Board of Education, punned exuberantly: 'This initiative is one which will "make history".'[38] Accordingly further weeks were arranged for the coming academic year and by the time the series ended in the autumn of 1942 sixteen courses had been held in England and two in Wales, attended by more than 3,000 teachers.[39] The Board urged local education authorities to follow up with periodic lectures and discussion groups of their own to bring the subject to the attention of an even larger number.[40] The format of the courses combined lectures from distinguished specialists with discussion groups led by HM Inspectors who had particular knowledge of the USA. Speakers included D. W. Brogan, Robert Birley, H. G. Nicholas, and North Whitehead of the Foreign Office, while Allan Nevins came over specially from the USA at his own expense to lecture to some of the summer courses in 1942. When the Board's History Panel evaluated the whole programme in February 1943 it was felt that the courses, if not an outstanding success, had justified the money and time devoted to them. Reports from District Inspectors made it 'quite clear that the volume of American studies in this country is already much larger than most of us thought' and that, although the Board's courses could not take all the credit for this, 'they have been a very considerable factor'.[41]

The short courses also spotlighted some of the problems involved in introducing America into the classroom, particularly at the secondary level. As long as School Certificate papers concentrated on British and European history, it would be difficult to justify much emphasis on the USA in the basic curriculum. Furthermore, the global scope of the war by 1942 had strengthened demands for

[37] Statistics and quotation from report on 'American History Courses; July–September, 1941', ED 121/4. This file is the main source for this paragraph.

[38] Eden to Ramsbotham, 20 June 1941, ED 121/3; R. A. Butler, minute, 18 Nov. 1941, ED 121/4.

[39] The exact total was 3,026. The detailed breakdown was as follows: 1941: London—278; Newcastle—158; Bingley—161; Oxford—167; Exeter—164; Maidstone—184; Birmingham— 240; Cheltenham—126; Bishop's Stortford—137; Aberystwyth—119. 1942: Loughborough— 214; Manchester—261; Bingley—152; Chichester—117; Darlington—138; Liverpool—197; Culford—120; Aberystwyth—93. Figures from Board memo, Aug. 1944, ED 121/102.

[40] Inspectorate memo, 37 (Gen), 9 Dec. 1941, ED 135/1.

[41] D. B. Adams, 'Report on USA Courses, 1941–42', Feb. 1943, ED 121/4.

studying other non-European countries apart from the United States. Thus Lord Elton, Secretary to the Rhodes Trust, complained in the House of Lords in July 1942 that the Board was unfairly neglecting the history of the Commonwealth.[42] To some extent the exam syllabuses did try to accommodate these new concerns. As President of the Board of Education, R. A. Butler noted that imperial history was occasionally offered as an alternative paper to European history and that almost all the examination boards believed 'that attention must be given to British Imperial History and sometimes to American history'.[43] However, none of this was obligatory and the Board of Education had no intention of breaching its customary policy of guidance without interference by trying to insist on compulsory questions. In practice, then, as the short courses and memoranda indicate, the Board accepted that the primary focus of the exam syllabus would be on Britain but it urged teachers to make 'significant excursions' into American history at points where the two countries' affairs were particularly entangled.[44] The Revolutionary era was the obvious example, but others were suggested. The Scottish memo, for instance, proposed that the Highland clearances could be linked to a study of transatlantic emigration.[45] Outside the exam syllabus it was hoped that more systematic attention could be devoted to the USA, particularly in the last years before the School Certificate course. The Nevins *Brief History* was primarily designed for this age group. And it was here, too, that there seemed the most scope for special inter-disciplinary projects on American themes, as outlined in the official memoranda.

Whitehall's programme to promote American studies was complemented by the activities of other influential bodies. *The Times* lent its august support with a leading article in June 1941. This argued that the United States was now supplanting Britain as world leader, but that its leadership would 'take forms rooted in the American past, and largely unfamiliar to the Eastern hemisphere. In every sense a world in which American leadership is effective will be a new world. That is one of many reasons,' *The Times* concluded, 'why the study of American history, American institutions, and above all American traditions is of prime importance to the rising generation in this country.'[46] Likewise, teachers' periodicals gave increasing prominence to the question. Encouraged by OUP, the *Journal of Education* editorialized about the subject in June 1941 and went on to publish a 'Special American Number' in November. This contained articles on education in the USA, the geography of the Americas and methods of teaching US history in schools, together with detailed bibliographical essays by Robert Birley and Hale Bellot.[47] And the new emphasis was reflected in BBC

---

[42] House of Lords, *Debates*, 5th series, Vol. 123, Col. 872, 15 July 1942.

[43] R. A. Butler to Lord Elton, 12 May 1942, ED 121/145. The Oxford and Cambridge Joint Board set a special subject on the growth of the USA from 1815 to 1865, and both the Oxford and Cambridge Local Boards offered a paper on The History of the British Empire since the Tudors as an alternative to European history.   [44] Report cited in note 37.

[45] Memo 234 cited in note 31.   [46] 'Studying America', *The Times*, 17 June 1941, p. 5.

[47] *Journal of Education*, 73 (1941), 223, 476–92.

radio broadcasts for schools. During the autumn term of 1941 prominent Britons from various walks of life were asked to speculate on their lives 'If I Were American', and at the same time the USA was the subject of the senior schools geography series and one of the themes running through the senior history course.[48] The following autumn a special series, aimed at 11–14 year olds, followed the growth of America through dramatized episodes and commentary, dealing with such themes as the pioneer, Lincoln, the railroads, and Andrew Carnegie. The last programme, on the American ideal, included a brief message from Eleanor Roosevelt who was then in Britain visiting the US troops.[49]

Nor did American government representatives in Britain fail to respond. Ambassador Winant's enthusiastic involvement in the Nevins textbook and the short courses has already been mentioned. From mid-1942 the London section of the Office of War Information (OWI) devoted some of its attention to what was called the 'slow media' including education. Late that year, after prolonged debate, the OWI set up an official US reference library in London. Its director, the historian Richard Heindel, began operations in December 'sitting on one case of books' in a house next door to the US Embassy, but by September 1944 the library had expanded into larger quarters and contained some 6,000 volumes and 10,000 pamphlets and documents, especially tailored to fill gaps in British holdings and to meet the interests of regular 'clients' in government, the media, schools, and universities.[50] The OWI also arranged a very successful exhibition giving an unvarnished account of the life of children and adolescents in contemporary America. This was first shown in Westminster at Easter 1944 and then, transported in a US Army truck, it toured schools all over England from Bridlington to Barnstaple, usually being presented as part of a special 'American Day' in conjunction with lectures, films, and question times. By March 1945 the 'Young America' exhibition had made 194 visits and had been seen by more than 37,000 people.[51] Meanwhile, US consular officials around the country were being faced with many appeals for advice and help from local schools. Some took little interest, arguing that this would involve them in 'political' activity outside their official brief. Thus, in February 1942 the US Consul General in Belfast sent only a curt rejection when asked to preside over the first of nine special lectures on America to be given for local schoolteachers by the Northern Ireland Ministry of Education. Yet the following August he complained caustically to Washington about British ignorance of the USA and what he considered the failure of the authorities to present a truer picture of America

[48] F. W. Ogilvie to Winant, 3 Dec. 1941, Winant Papers, box 187: Broadcasting House; Ogilvie to Ramsbotham, 13 June 1941, ED 121/3.

[49] Mary Somerville to Dorsey Fisher, 6 Nov. 1942, with enclosures, Eleanor Roosevelt Papers, box 2975 (Roosevelt Library).

[50] See documents in RG 59, decimal file 1940–44, 841.28, esp. Heindel's report of Sept. 1944, 841.28/11–2844. For Heindel's academic work see above, note 4.

[51] See papers in ED 121/77, esp. report by Louise J. Riley, 17 Mar. 1945.

through the schools.[52] At the other extreme was George Armstrong, US Consul in Manchester, an avuncular widower who liked Britain and loved children. Armstrong gave numerous informal talks on American history and life to schools in his district. He encouraged and helped coordinate pen pal correspondence with American schools especially in Manchester's namesake towns. And he built up a close and cordial relationship with schools that took an active interest in American studies, such as William Hulme Grammar School, where he initiated an annual prize essay competition on the United States.[53]

In its later stages the British Government's campaign was sustained and enlivened by the American GIs. The first of them started to arrive in Northern Ireland in late January 1942, followed by a steady build-up there and in southern England through the spring and summer. After the decision in July to invade North Africa numbers stabilized through the winter of 1942–43 at around a quarter of a million, until a new wave began to arrive from mid-1943 in preparation for the invasion of France. On the eve of D-Day there were some 1,650,000 US service personnel in Britain, most of them concentrated in the south and south-west of England and in East Anglia. The Board of Education took advantage of this new opportunity and commissioned the poet Louis MacNeice to write a booklet which was entitled *Meet the U.S. Army*. 100,000 were printed and a copy was sent to every school in July 1943 for use in preparing lessons or talks for pupils. MacNeice's aim was to transform the GIs from a vague stereotype 'and set them in a perspective from which they will appear as human beings—like us *and* unlike us, but more the former than the latter'. He discussed the history and traditions of the US army, surveyed the regions of the United States with particular though discreet comment on the problems of the South, emphasized the country's ethnic diversity and devoted several pages to American customs, language, and sports—'You will get a good mark if you have heard of Babe Ruth (the W.G. Grace of baseball)'[54] Such stilted advice was quite unnecessary. For most English children the GI was the first 'real' American they had met. Not only was their curiosity aroused in everyday matters—such as the ubiquitous chewing gum or the mysterious 'balloons' littering the more secluded parts of English towns the morning after an American 'liberty run'. It was also channelled into formal educational activities. Some soldiers, who had been history teachers in civilian life, gave special lessons in schools near their bases. Others simply came to talk about their home town and its way of life. Children around High Wycombe in the autumn of 1942 particularly enjoyed a talk on American Indians given in two local schools by an Air Corps captain attired in

---

[52] Parker W. Buhrman to R. S. Brownell, 5 Feb. 1942, and Buhrman to SecState, desp. 127, 5 Aug. 1942, Records of US Foreign Service Posts, RG 84, Belfast, files 841 and 842 (NA).

[53] This section is based on the mass of papers in RG 84, Manchester, file 842 (1942–45). See also RG 59, 123 AR/56.

[54] Board of Education, *Meet the U.S. Army* (London, 1943), quotations from pp. 6 and 20. Cf. FO 371/34118, A6944.

full Indian costume and accompanied by traditional Indian songs.[55] Such encounters—in school or more often outside—did as much as conventional classroom lessons to enlarge the children's image of the USA.

The overall effect of Whitehall's campaign is difficult to measure. There were clearly wide local variations, because memoranda, textbooks, teachers' courses, and official help were no substitute for keen and interested staff. Where these existed, much could be achieved despite limited resources. Thus, Blackley Senior and Junior schools, in a working-class area north of Manchester, developed an imaginative series of classroom projects in 1942 on US history, geography, economics, and cultural life, using such everyday items as money, postage stamps, and the labels from American canned goods.[56] Because of the constraints of the exam syllabus, America was usually studied not through a sustained, formal course on US history but in the form of inter-disciplinary projects over a specific period of time. For instance, Birmingham Central Boys Grammar School mounted a special programme during the spring term of 1944, engaging 'as many boys as possible on as many aspects of American life as possible', which culminated in an exhibition at the end of April. The US Consul in Birmingham helped arrange a series of speakers from an American army service unit stationed in nearby Lichfield.[57] Generalizations about the national extent of American studies must be tentative, for no good statistical evidence exists. But one HM Inspector estimated very roughly in September 1942 that one-third of secondary schools would include some American history, either in the fourth or fifth year, during 1942–43.[58] And in February 1943 the History Panel felt that, whereas in 1940–41 no more than a dozen schools made a systematic study of US history, now the figure ran into hundreds if not thousands. It concluded 'that in most parts of the country it appears to be now the rule rather than the exception for some emphasis to be given to the study of the U.S.A. at some stage of the senior school curriculum'.[59] The Board of Education could feel well pleased with its response to Duff Cooper's letter of March 1941.

But Cooper had also called for greater study of the USA in British universities, and here the effects of his letter were less impressive. Since the Board of Education was responsible only for schools, the Ministry of Information took this question up with Sir Walter Moberly, chairman of the University Grants Committee. After consulting several Vice-Chancellors Moberly presented a report on 23 July 1941. In it he argued that the 'shameful' and 'disastrous' ignorance of US affairs could only be remedied by a widespread study of American history in British schools, but that this was impossible until competent

[55] J. W. Moss to Gen. Ira C. Eaker, 23 Nov. 1942, Carl A. Spaatz Papers, box 322 (LC).

[56] See RG 84, Manchester, file 842 (1942): Blackley, esp. report of 18 July 1942.

[57] RG 84, Birmingham, file 842, esp. Pasley to Wilkinson, 29 Nov. 1943 and Wilkinson to Col. Killian, 13 Dec. 1943.   [58] Minute by E. E. Y. Hales, 2 Sept. 1942, ED 121/7.

[59] Adams, report, Feb. 1943, ED121/4.

staff had been trained. Since teachers in secondary and central schools came from the universities it was there that a start had to be made. Accordingly Moberly proposed that the Treasury should endow three new permanent chairs in US history, say at Cambridge, Glasgow, and Manchester or Liverpool, to be held initially by American academics until qualified British scholars were available. He also suggested that six fellowships should be endowed for existing staff at other universities to spend a year in the USA and thereby prepare themselves to teach US history.[60]

Moberly's report was cogent and thorough, but there was one insuperable objection. The cost would be about a quarter of a million pounds—the equivalent of approximately 11 per cent of the Treasury's total annual grant to the universities via the UGC.[61] As a temporary wartime department, without much bureaucratic clout in Whitehall, the MOI was always starved of money for its own schemes and saw little prospect of prising that sort of money from the Treasury. The idea therefore lapsed until the end of 1941, when it was revived by Professor Harold Laski of the LSE in a personal letter to Churchill. The Prime Minister expressed his interest and referred the matter to the Foreign Office, who shared his enthusiasm until it discovered the cost. Although far more influential than the MOI, FO officials recognized that they could not make out a case for this kind of expenditure in wartime.[62] At least for the moment, therefore, it seemed better for the Board of Education to do the necessary 'spade work' in secondary schools before more 'spectacular' innovations at the university level.[63]

Shortage of funds also killed off a proposal in 1941 for a privately-endowed chair of American affairs. This was to have been in memory of Lord Lothian, the commentator on Anglo-American relations and former Secretary to the Rhodes Trust who had served briefly but with great distinction as British Ambassador in Washington from August 1939 until his sudden death in December 1940.[64] Stimulated by the British Government's campaign in the schools, some of Lothian's friends, led by Lord Astor, hoped to found a research professorship attached to the Royal Institute of International Affairs in London. In the autumn of 1941 Astor approached Norman H. Davis and others of Lothian's old contacts associated with the Council on Foreign Relations in New York. Most were anglophiles, with a keen sense of the need to educate Britain about the United States. As one of them, the Wall Street banker Thomas Lamont, commented in 1942: 'The British as a whole are abysmally ignorant of everything American, even of our origins in history. They have generally looked upon us as perhaps the

---

[60] Sir Walter Moberly, memo, 'American Studies in British Universities', ED 121/7.

[61] Cf. P. H. J. H. Gosden, *Education in the Second World War: A Study in Policy and Administration* (London, 1976), 152.

[62] This account is based on FO 371/30679, A650, A1342, A1863, and on papers in ED 121/7.

[63] R. A. Butler, minute, 18 May 1942, ED 136/668.

[64] On Lothian's ambassadorial career see David Reynolds, *Lord Lothian and Anglo-American Relations, 1939–1940* (Philadelphia, 1983).

higher type of colonials, but nothing more. They have thought of us in terms of Hollywood and of gangsterdom.'[65] But Lamont, Davis, and others agreed that although the project was a worthy one, there was no chance at the present time of raising a sufficient endowment in the USA. Reluctantly Astor had to drop the idea.[66]

Nevertheless, the changed state of Anglo-American relations encouraged the universities to undertake their own reforms. As early as October 1941 the University of Manchester was considering the re-establishment of its chair of US history, which had been defunct for some years, and by 1944 plans were being formulated for the American Studies programme that was eventually begun in 1948.[67] At Oxford, Nevins' presence in 1940–41 set in motion important reforms in the History School. With a committee chaired by the Regius Professor, F. M. Powicke, he successfully proposed that questions on US history should be set in the final exam and that a new special subject, 'Slavery and Secession', should replace Morison's old paper on the American Revolution.[68] In recognition of the persistent difficulties of attracting eminent American scholars for long periods of time, the Harmsworth chair became, de facto, an annual appointment, nominated by a committee of American historians rather than by the US Ambassador.[69] But the most spectacular, if belated, innovation came at Cambridge. Back in February 1866 the Conservative, Anglican University Senate had rejected an offer of Harvard money to set up a visiting lectureship in US history. It feared the undergraduates would be corrupted by American vulgarity and by Harvard's republican, Unitarian ideas.[70] But from 1942–43, encouraged by E. A. Benians and George Kitson Clark, a paper on US history since 1774 became part of the Tripos, and the History Faculty was shaken and invigorated by the presence, for the first half of that year, of Henry Steele Commager. Atonement was also made for the error of 1866. In July 1943 it was announced that Cambridge would establish a visiting Professorship of American History and Institutions, endowed, after a fruitless worldwide search for funds, by £44,000 from the University Press,

[65] Thomas W. Lamont to Archibald MacLeish, 1 Oct. 1942, Lamont Papers 61–28 (Baker Library, Harvard University Business School).

[66] This paragraph is based on correspondence of Sept.–Nov. 1941 in Norman H. Davis Papers, box 2: Astor (LC).

[67] George A. Armstrong to Glenn A. Abbey, 25 Oct. 1941, RG 84, Manchester, file 800 (Confidential); John S. B. Stopford to Richard A. Johnson, 10 Jan. 1944, RG 59, decimal file for 1940–44, 841.42/140. The Chair of American History and Institutions was filled in 1948 and in the early 1960s a Department of American Studies was established.

[68] Nevins, diary, 28 Apr. 1941, Allan Nevins Papers, box 32 (Butler Library, Columbia University); Allan Nevins, 'Report', 30 June 1941, Carnegie Endowment Papers, box 14, report 940.

[69] See RG 84, London, 842: Harmsworth Professor (1942–45), esp. minutes of meeting of 27 Nov. 1945. For wartime changes at Oxford see also Herbert Nicholas, 'The Education of an Americanist', *Journal of American Studies*, 14 (1980), 19–20.

[70] Ged Martin, 'The Cambridge Lectureship of 1866: A False Start in American Studies', *Journal of American Studies*, 7 (1973), 17–29.

and in 1945–46 Dexter Perkins of the University of Rochester became first incumbent.[71]

These Cambridge reforms prompted Whitehall to reopen the question of government-endowed professorships. In March 1943, when Cambridge was seeking funds for its proposed new chair, Kitson Clark asked R. A. Butler whether the Government had any plans to place the university teaching of US history on a more permanent footing. His enquiry led to renewed consultation between Butler, Moberly, and the Foreign Office. Ideally, the FO would have preferred chairs in American *studies* rather than *history*, because its concern was to deepen British knowledge of *modern* America, but it warmly endorsed the proposal drawn up by Moberly in May for the creation of two temporary five-year chairs of US history at Liverpool and Glasgow. Since no permanent endowment was required, unlike Moberly's earlier scheme, the total cost would be only about £15,000 for the professorial salaries. The Board felt that this had a chance of passing the Treasury, and a formal request was prepared in July. But the letter was not sent, partly because Butler was already deeply involved in financial negotiations about his major reform of the educational system, partly because of reports of the new Cambridge chair. The Board felt 'that the Cambridge windfall might have queered our pitch with the Treasury!' who would use it to argue that the universities could and should raise the money themselves. Nothing came of the breezy assurance from Brendan Bracken, the Minister of Information, that he could probably raise the sum from private sources, and the matter dropped out of sight from August 1943 amid the pressure of more urgent business.[72]

In Britain, of course, professors are only the apex of a university system in which the main teaching burden is borne by lecturers or, at Oxford and Cambridge, by college fellows. The collapse of the scheme for new chairs was consequently not a complete setback to the cause of American studies. Nevertheless, it is one of several indications that the British Government's campaign had lost momentum by 1943. Several reasons may be adduced for this. One, of course, was that there were very real limits to what the Board of Education could do in wartime, when there were prior claims on the nation's manpower and financial resources. Its budget and staff had been slashed and the remaining employees were pre-occupied with basic administration. Conscription seriously reduced the number of teachers in schools and universities, and by 1943 university arts courses were

---

[71] Cambridge University Faculty Board of History: Lectures and Finance Commt., minutes, 30 Jan., 20 Mar., 19 June and 1 Dec. 1942 (Seeley Historical Library, Cambridge); *The Historical Register of the University of Cambridge: Supplement, 1941–50* (Cambridge: Cambridge University Press, 1952), p. 4; G. Kitson Clark, 'A Hundred Years of the Teaching of History at Cambridge, 1873–1973', *Historical Journal*, 16 (1973), 550–1.

[72] Sources for this paragraph are FO 371/34190, A5131, and ED 121/7, quotation from Sylvia Goodfellow to B. C. Sendall, 14 Aug. 1943.

almost entirely attended by female undergraduates and service cadets because able-bodied young men were no longer allowed any deferment. The upheavals of the war also seriously affected teaching. City schools were disrupted by bombings and by evacuation into country areas, and much time was spent simply catering for the physical needs of the children. And the new interest in world history—particularly of Russia and the Commonwealth—limited the time available for studying the United States. All in all the Board felt it had done as much as could reasonably be expected to promote American studies. As the head of its History Panel concluded in February 1943: 'If sixteen courses, spread all over the whole country, have failed to call the attention of the schools to the Board's view as to the importance of some knowledge of the U.S.A., the task would seem to me to be an impossible one.'[73]

Furthermore, by 1943 top-level interest in the campaign had waned. Its originators had been Duff Cooper at the Ministry of Information and Herwald Ramsbotham at the Board of Education. Both men lost their jobs in July 1941, after plans had been laid but before their implementation. Bracken, the new Minister of Information, although sympathetic, did not share Cooper's pressing concern to eradicate British prejudice and ignorance about the USA. Butler, on the other hand, did, and a few days after becoming President of the Board of Education he told Winant: 'I am convinced that Ramsbotham has made a thoroughly sound move in starting this work to encourage understanding of America and the Americans in the schools of this country, and I mean to carry the work on and give it every encouragement.'[74] He was true to his word in 1941–42, but thereafter his attention was increasingly taken up with the drafting and passage of the 1944 Education Act. His pre-occupation—and Bracken's relative indifference—partially explain the abandonment of the 1943 proposal for new chairs and the Board's failure to capitalize on the campaign in the schools.

In any case, the original stimulus for the campaign no longer existed. The 1941 proposals were formulated because the MOI feared that British ignorance and prejudice about the USA were causing dangerous pessimism about US aid and might also strengthen anti-British feeling in the States, thereby retarding American entry into the war. The worst of these fears were dispelled by Pearl Harbor in December 1941. Although Whitehall continued to see Anglo-American amity as the basis of British policy, it no longer placed the same emphasis on public education. In fact, the American studies drive was only one—albeit the most important—of several brief propaganda campaigns to enhance public understanding and appreciation of Britain's allies. During the short-lived Anglo-French alliance of the 'phoney war', the Board started what would have been a large-scale attempt to promote the study of France. Likewise, the alliance with the USSR in June 1941 led to an MOI domestic propaganda

---

[73] Adams, report, Feb. 1943, ED 121/4.
[74] R. A. Butler to Winant, 25 July 1941, copy in Winant Papers, box 200: Hopkins.

campaign about Russia, in which the Board arranged a short course of lectures in April 1942 and issued a guidance memorandum the following August.[75] Among the public, too, the intense interest in these and other of Britain's allies was ephemeral. It was a response to events that were currently in the headlines or impinged directly on their lives. In the case of the United States, the catalyst in 1941 was the debate and passage of Lend-Lease, followed by the Battle of the Atlantic. Subsequently interest was kept alive by the presence of the GIs, but their numbers diminished rapidly after D-Day. With the war over, curiosity about the United States declined and one survey in April 1947 concluded that the wartime experience, including the GIs, 'appears to have had relatively little effect' on people's preconceived ideas about America and its inhabitants.[76]

One final reason may be advanced for the running down of the British campaign to promote American studies. The enthusiastic support offered by Winant, London staff of the OWI, and American consuls such as George Armstrong was not reflected in official attitudes in Washington.[77] The late 1930s, as previously mentioned, had seen the beginnings of the US Government's involvement in cultural relations, and that trend was vastly accelerated by the war. In the winter of 1941–42 the State Department gave serious consideration to developing a programme in Europe, and its European desk advised that 'efforts should be made without delay' to encourage the unprecedented British interest in the USA and to assist what it called the 'very far reaching' programme then underway in the schools.[78] But the American Government's priorities lay elsewhere. Its wartime propaganda and cultural diplomacy concentrated on Latin America, China, and also, from 1943, the Middle East. The goal was to counteract Axis subversion and to project the USA into new and promising areas of influence. In early 1945, as the war drew to a close, American diplomats on the spot again emphasized the needs and opportunities existing in Britain. The US Embassy in London produced a plan for a cultural relations division, while George Armstrong in Manchester, carried away by his enthusiasm, submitted a twelve-page, single-spaced memorandum arguing the case for three regional cultural attachés spread around the country.[79] But these proposals had little effect. Not until the autumn of 1945 did the State

---

[75] See guidance memos 18 (Apr. 1940) and 33 (Aug. 1942) in ED 138/27.

[76] Mass-Observation Bulletin, new series, No. 7 (Apr. 1947), 3 (Mass-Observation Archive).

[77] For background to this paragraph see Helen R. Pinkney, 'The Division of Cultural Cooperation', unpublished TS, Dec. 1945, in RG 59, War History Branch Studies, box 10: CU file; also Ninkovich, *Diplomacy of Ideas*, and J. Manuel Espinosa, *Inter-American Beginnings of U.S. Cultural Diplomacy, 1936–1948* (Washington, DC 1976).

[78] Theodore Achilles, memo, 'Cultural Relations with Great Britain', 22 Jan. 1942, RG 59, decimal file 1940–44, 811.42741/120. Cf. RG 59, War History Branch Studies, box 55, folder 9: RC—Extension of Activities—British Empire.

[79] Richard A. Johnson, 'An American Cultural Relations Program for Great Britain', 26 Jan. 1945, RG 84, London, file 842: Cultural Relations; George A. Armstrong, 'Opportunity for a Cultural Program in the Manchester-Sheffield Consular Area', 5 Feb. 1945, RG 84, Manchester, file 842.

Department begin to direct much attention or money to cultural diplomacy in the Old World, and even then it was mainly concerned with programmes for denazification and rehabilitating the educational and cultural life of continental Europe. And by the late 1940s the emphasis had shifted to the Cold War and the ideological battle with European communism. At each stage the strengthening of pro-American feeling in Britain—a secure ally relatively well-disposed to the United States—was naturally a low priority. It was not until the early 1950s that a minor but significant initiative was taken. Following a proposal in October 1948 from the historian Joseph Charles, then cultural attaché in London, the Fulbright Commission arranged four summer conferences between 1952 and 1955 for British Americanists, out of which originated the British Association for American Studies. This provided the institutional framework for the slow but steady growth of the next quarter century, much of it assisted by private and governmental funds from the United States.[80]

After 1943, therefore, the surge of British official interest in the USA was not sustained. Committed teachers and lecturers were left to carry on the progress made as best they could, and even when American studies in Britain 'took off' in the 1950s the principal governmental support came from Washington not Whitehall. Nevertheless, it would be quite wrong to ignore the wartime developments, for the result of the British Government's campaign was undoubtedly a significant expansion in the study of America at all levels of the educational system. As the US Embassy observed in 1945: 'There has been an appreciable improvement in teacher training in United States history during the past three years, a marked increase in the amount of time given to United States history in secondary schools and public fora, and a definite improvement in the facilities school and public libraries offer to students of United States history.'[81] And it is difficult to believe that all the 3,000 teachers who attended the Board's short courses on America lost their interest in the subject, or that the greater emphasis on the USA in exam papers in schools and universities had no effect on students' awareness of the United States. Intellectually, then, 1941 did mark the British 'discovery of America'—even if it took another decade or so to put the United States firmly on the educational map.

---

[80] Walter Johnson and Francis J. Colligan, *The Fulbright Program: A History* (Chicago, 1965). For discussion of later developments see Skard, *American Studies*, i. 74–127; H. C. Allen, *American History in Britain* (London, 1956); and three articles entitled 'American Studies in Britain', by Howard Temperley, *American Quarterly* 18 (1966), 251–69; by J. E. Morpurgo, *American Studies*, 10 (1971), 18–22; and by Dennis Welland, *American Studies International*, 16 (1977) 38–46.

[81] Richard A. Johnson, 'Cultural Exchanges between the United States and the United Kingdom', 18 Mar. 1944, part I, p. 7. An edited version of this report was published under the title 'Teaching of American History in Great Britain', *American Historical Review*, 50 (1944), 73–81.

11

Churchill's Government and the Black GIs, 1942–1943

Just before lunch on Tuesday 13 October 1942 the British War Cabinet assembled for a hasty meeting in the Prime Minister's room in the House of Commons. Sandwiched on the agenda between discussion of the impending visit of the South African premier and the arrangements for celebrating Armistice Day was a unique item, one on which no less than six different Cabinet ministers had submitted papers. The subject was the treatment of the black soldiers who were in Britain as members of the US Army's expeditionary force. The American policy was to segregate them as much as possible from white troops. The Cabinet had now to make up its mind about a War Office proposal that British troops should be encouraged to adopt a similar attitude to the black GIs. The issue, bluntly stated, was whether the British Government should approve a discreet colour bar.[1]

To understand British policy towards the black Americans, we need to look first at the Government's attitude to British colonial manpower. In World War I the Army had avoided using West Indian troops in combat, except against non-whites in the Middle East, and they were mostly employed in labour battalions. Indian troops were used in action in France, but care was taken to minimize their

---

This chapter appears here virtually as first published in the *Transactions of the Royal Historical Society*, 5th series, 35 (1985), 113–33, except for some cuts to the final paragraph. For further discussion of these issues see Graham Smith, *When Jim Crow Met John Bull: Black American Soldiers in World War II Britain* (London, 1987), and David Reynolds, *Rich Relations: The American Occupation of Britain 1942–1945* (London, 1995), chs. 14 and 18.

[1] Aspects of this subject have been dealt with in Thomas E. Hachey, 'Jim Crow with a British accent: Attitudes of London Government officials toward American negro soldiers in England during World War II', *Journal of Negro History*, 59 (1974), 65–77 (a collection of edited documents); Christopher Thorpe, 'Britain and the black G.I.s: Racial issues and Anglo-American relations in 1942', *New Community*, 3 (1974), 262–71; Graham A. Smith, 'Jim Crow on the home front, 1942–1945', *New Community*, 8 (1980). 317–28; J. E. Flint, 'Scandal at the Bristol Hotel: Some thoughts on racial discrimination in Britain and West Africa and its relationship to the planning of decolonisation, 1939–47', *Journal of Imperial and Commonwealth History*, 12 (1983), 74–93. This chapter concentrates on the policy of the British government rather than the wider questions of the race issue in transatlantic diplomacy, colonial policy, or wartime Britain, as discussed by Thorne, Flint, and Smith.

contact with white women and to keep them out of Britain.² Similar policies were adopted at the beginning of World War II. Although black pressure groups forced the Government to announce in October 1939 that British citizens 'not of pure European descent' could volunteer for the armed forces and be considered for commissions on the same basis as whites, this was only a temporary measure 'during the present emergency'.³ And in practice the Cabinet intended that black volunteers should be mainly used in labour units in their home territories.⁴ Part of the reason was logistic: the Government lacked the equipment to fit out any additional combat divisions in the foreseeable future. But the Colonial and War Offices also agreed that black West Indians 'would be of doubtful military value for combat service overseas, especially against German troops in Europe', citing the Great War as precedent and evidence. And they also quite explicitly noted that 'for obvious reasons it is not desired to encourage coloured British subjects to come to this country for direct enlistment in the Imperial forces'—whereas that was the approved method for applicants 'of pure European descent'.⁵ This policy was enunciated in January 1940.When manpower needs became more acute that summer after the fall of France selective modifications were made in order to secure certain skilled workers: 600 foresters were brought from British Honduras to the Edinburgh area in late summer 1941, followed by another 400 a year later, while some 350 engineering and electrical technicians came to Merseyside between February 1941 and January 1943.⁶ These schemes did not, however, represent any fundamental change in policy on non-white immigration. As one Foreign Office official recorded in January 1942, after interdepartmental consultation: 'It became evident that, during discussions on the subject of overseas manpower, the recruitment to the United Kingdom of coloured British subjects, whose remaining in the United Kingdom after the war might create a social problem, was not considered desirable.' This, he said, was 'the accepted view' in Whitehall.⁷

This same desire to minimize the non-white presence in Britain led the Government to oppose the entry of black Americans. Although the USA did not enter the war until December 1941, the issue had first emerged in the middle of that year when Britain was appealing for volunteer doctors from North America to supplement army medical teams in bomb-damaged British cities. Faced with

---

² C. L. Joseph, 'The British West Indies Regiment, 1914–1918', *Journal of Caribbean History*, 2 (1971), 94–124; Jeffrey Greenhut, 'Race, sex, and war: The impact of race and sex on morale and health services for the Indian Corps on the Western Front, 1914', *Military Affairs*, 45 (1981), 71–4.
³ House of Commons, *Debates*, 5th series, vol. 352, columns 1083–4, 19 Oct. 1939.
⁴ War Cabinet minutes, 25 Jan. 1940, CAB 65/5, WM 23 (40) 3 (TNA).
⁵ Malcolm MacDonald, memo, 22 Jan. 1940, War Cabinet papers, CAB 67/4, WP(G) 4015 (TNA).
⁶ See Colonial Office papers, CO 876/41–43 (TNA), and Anthony H. Richmond, *Colour prejudice in Britain: A study of West Indian workers in Liverpool, 1941–1951* (London, 1954).
⁷ F. E. Evans, minute, 22 Jan. 1942, Foreign Office General Political correspondence FO 371/ 26206, A 10036/257/45 (TNA).

the offer of help from a negro physician in New York the War Office procras-
tinated until, under pressure from the Foreign Office, it agreed to accept what it
termed 'one token negro doctor as evidence of co-operation', but for service in
West Africa and not Britain.[8] Two weeks later, however, the War Office was able
to reject the volunteer outright when it was discovered that he was over the
age-limit for service in the Royal Army Medical Corps.[9] Likewise in 1942 the
Government expressed discreet but firm opposition to US plans to send black
troops to Britain. The British Chiefs of Staff told Washington in April that
they did not favour the use of coloured troops, but, although supported by the
US army command in Britain, their preferences were overruled by the US War
Department, who decreed that 'in planning for shipment of troops to the
British Isles, including Northern Ireland, Colored Troops may be included in
reasonable proportion for any type of Service Unit'.[10] In July 1942 the issue was
discussed by the War Cabinet, with Anthony Eden, the Foreign Secretary,
expressing fears of trouble between GIs and British civilians, particularly
'through certain sections of our people showing more effusiveness to the
coloured people than the Americans would readily understand'.[11] The problem
was raised with General George C. Marshall, the US Army Chief of Staff, and
Harry Hopkins, Roosevelt's confidant, who were both in London at the time,
and it seems likely that Churchill personally told Hopkins that they did not want
any more black GIs.[12] But once again the British were rebuffed. When Marshall
returned to Washington he reiterated that the need in Britain for labour units,
most of which were black, and the exigencies of US domestic politics necessitated
maintenance of the existing policy. When Eden took up the matter again with
Winant on 31 August, he even argued that the cold and damp of an English
winter was 'badly suited to negroes' and would damage their health. The
Ambassador, however, was unmoved.[13]

As Marshall indicated, this was an essentially political issue. The US Army
wanted to minimize the use of black troops. It ensured that segregation was
maintained, that blacks were used mainly as non-combatants, and that few negro
officers were appointed. But since 1940 President Roosevelt had been obliged to

[8] War Office to Military Attaché, Washington, tel. 78528, 17 July 1941, War Office papers,
WO 193/321 (TNA).
[9] Col. S. Arnott to V. Cavendish-Bentinck, 2 Aug. 1941, FO 371/26227, A 8364/538/45(TNA).
[10] See Cabinet Office papers, CAB 79/20, COS 126 (42) 11, 21 April 1942, and CAB 80/62,
COS (42) 104 (0); Chancy to War Dept., tel., 25 April 1942, in US War Dept., Operations Div.,
Diary, copy in Dwight D. Eisenhower Library, Abilene, Kansas, USA; Eisenhower, memo, 25 April
1942, US National Archives, Record Group RG 165, Operations Division, OPD 291.2.
[11] E. Bridges to J. Martin, 21 July 1942, in Franklin D. Roosevelt Library, Hyde Park,
New York, USA, Harry Hopkins papers, box 136.
[12] Cf. Angus Malcolm, minute, 28 Dec. 1942, FO 371/30680, A 11903/990/45.
[13] Sir Ronald Campbell to FO, tel. 4086, 12 Aug. 1942, FO 954/30A, f. 151; Eden to Halifax,
1 Sept. 1942, FO 954/298, US/42/158. On US policy see Ulysses Lee, *The employment of negro
troops* (Washington, 1966) in the series 'US Army in World War II: Special studies'; and Morris J.
MacGregor, Jr., *Integration of the Armed Forces, 1940–1965* (Washington, 1981).

make concessions to the demand of black pressure groups, now increasingly important within the Democratic coalition, for greater participation in the country's war effort. Consequently it was agreed that the percentage of blacks in the American army would be roughly equal to the proportion of blacks in the US population as a whole, namely ten per cent, and that some black troops would be allowed to serve abroad. The first of them landed in Britain in May 1942 and by late summer about 12,000 had arrived.

Britain was certainly not devoid of race prejudice. On the contrary. One anecdote going the rounds in London in the summer of 1942 concerned a grand English lady who decided to do her bit for the war effort by writing to the local American commander and inviting him to send half-a-dozen of his men to join her for Sunday lunch. But, she added on the invitation, 'No Jews, please'. At Sunday lunchtime there was a knock at the door. She opened it and discovered six huge black GIs standing outside. Horrified, she exclaimed that there must be some mistake. 'Oh no, ma'am', one of them replied, 'Colonel Cohen no make any mistakes.'[14] This story may be apocryphal, but racial discrimination was definitely evident in parts of Britain. In port cities, such as Cardiff, Liverpool, and London, the black communities had grown steadily after World War I, when many colonial seamen who had served in the wartime Merchant Navy decided to settle in Britain. Racial clashes had occurred in 1919, notably in Liverpool, and the Depression had aggravated the high unemployment of these areas, where pioneering sociological studies revealed established patterns of discrimination in housing, employment, and social relationships.[15]

But Britain's black community was minute at this time—probably no more than seven or eight thousand in 1939[16]—and most British people, particularly in rural areas, had never met a non-white. Moreover, the black GI was a temporary visitor. He did not pose the same 'threat' to jobs, housing, and womenfolk as the black Britons were felt to do. Consequently, British people on the whole treated him well, as reports from all sources concur. Frequently the black GI's courtesy was contrasted favourably with the brashness of the whites. There was little sense of a colour bar: blacks were often invited into British homes and were popular with many British women, particularly mid-teenagers. Yet this kind of inter-racial contact, especially across the sexes, was anathema to white GIs from the South, where a clear code of 'racial etiquette' kept the races apart and the blacks 'in their place'. They vented their fury on blacks, vilified British women who associated with them, and tried to persuade hoteliers and publicans to exclude

---

[14] Cf. *New Statesman and Nation*, 26 Sept. 1942, p. 202.

[15] See James Walvin, *Black and white: The negro English society, 1555–1945* (London,1973), esp. chap. 13; Roy May and Robin Cohen, 'The interaction between race and colonialism: A case study of the Liverpool race riots of 1919', *Race and Class*, 16 (1974), 111–126; K. L. Little, *Negroes in Britain: A study of racial relations in English society* (London, 1947), based on research done in Cardiff in 1941.

[16] See Colonial Office memo, Aug. 1942, CO 879/14, f.4. Harold A. Moody, *The Colour Bar* (1944), 8, suggests a figure of at least 10,000 for 1939, which is probably too high.

black customers. Again the reports concur that British people, though disliking black–white contact across the sexes, generally repudiated this kind of overt discrimination and often took the blacks' side in fracas with whites and even with US military police.[17]

The US army command in Britain did its best to limit such incidents. Basic policy was laid down by General Dwight D. Eisenhower, the Commander of the European Theater of Operations (ETO) from June 1942.[18] On arrival in Britain troops were to be warned against making any racial slurs. They were also told about the lack of a colour bar in Britain and the need to respect this custom. But as far as possible black and white troops were kept apart, both on bases and in leave accommodation. In an attempt to eliminate contact in local towns the principle of 'rotating passes' was used, whereby blacks used the town, or selected pubs and dance halls, on one night and whites on another. (To avoid imputations of racial discrimination the passes were ostensibly allocated by unit, but since units were racially homogeneous the result was the same.) Eisenhower also tried to restrict black troops to certain defined areas of the country, particularly around the western ports where the black British population was concentrated.

Although the British Cabinet was still unhappy about the influx of black GIs,[19] it was well pleased with Eisenhower's policy of segregation. This promised to reduce contacts between black GIs and British civilians. However, the Government was at pains to distance itself officially from the US Army's policy. The Home Office issued a circular to all Chief Constables on 4 September 1942. This stated that:

It is not the policy of His Majesty's Government that any discrimination as regards the treatment of coloured troops should be made by the British authorities. The Secretary of State, therefore, would be glad if you would be good enough to take steps to ensure that the police do not make any approach to the proprietors of public houses, restaurants, cinemas or other places of entertainment with a view to discriminating against coloured troops.

Should the US Army wish to put certain places out of bounds to coloured troops, the circular stressed, this was their own decision and was to be implemented by them. British police 'should not make themselves in any way responsible for the enforcement of such orders'.[20]

Not everyone in Whitehall, however, was content to leave the matter in the hands of the US Army. It was agreed at a conference in the War Office on 5 August that British officers should explain the American attitude so that their own troops, especially women of the Auxiliary Territorial Service (ATS), might

[17] e.g., James Warburg to Elmer Davis, 1 Sept. 1942, National Archives, Washington, RG 107/47, box 124, ASW 291.2; extracts from Regional Commissioners' reports, Jul.–Nov. 1942, FO 371/34123, A 866/33/45.

[18] See Eisenhower's directives of 16 July and 5 Sept. 1942, US National Archives, RG 332: European Theater of Operations, US Army (ETOUSA), Adjutant General records, (AG), Classified General Correspondence (CGC) 291.2.

[19] Cf. War Cabinet minutes, 10 and 31 Aug. 1942, CAB 65/27, WM (42) 109/6 and 119/6.

[20] Home Office circular, 4 Sept. 1942, annex to CAB 66/29, WP (42) 456.

avoid contact with the black GIs. The War Office injunction was to use only oral instructions because of the delicacy of the subject, but two days later the senior administrative officer in Southern Command, where most of the black troops were stationed, issued his own written advice to district commanders and civilian regional commissioners. This document depicted the history of American blacks in a roseate hue, following the presentation by a US officer at the 5 August meeting. Blacks were portrayed as inherently the intellectual and moral inferiors of whites, having 'a simple mental outlook' and lacking 'the white man's ability to think and act to a plan'. In the USA, particularly in the South, they lived their own separate lives but, according to the paper, 'they are sympathetically treated by the white man' who 'feels his moral duty to them as it were to a child'. After this disingenuous, not to say inaccurate, account of race relations in the American South, the paper suggested ways for British men and women soldiers 'to adjust their attitude so that it conforms to that of the white American citizen'. While showing sympathy for blacks, 'soldiers should not make intimate friends with them, taking them to cinemas or bars'. And 'white women should not associate with coloured men'. This meant that 'they should not walk out, dance, or drink with them'. Any attempt by 'political extremists' to stir up trouble on the race question must be ignored, and British troops should scotch all inflammatory stories and rumours of racial friction.[21]

This document was intended for the guidance of British soldiers. But some local military commanders and their civilian counterparts wanted to 'guide' civilian behaviour as well. In July the GOC of Western Command complained to the city authorities of Chester that black GI truck drivers stationed near the city had been walking around with white women. He pointed out 'that this sort of thing is not customary in America and that we do not want to infringe American customs'. (The Lord Mayor of Chester replied that Indians and West Indians could be described as coloured and asked what was to be done about them.)[22] At an inter-departmental meeting in Whitehall on 12 August it was proposed that British women might be warned off association with black GIs 'by an open statement on the danger of venereal disease'. That idea, and a related one for 'a whispering campaign on the same lines', were blocked by the Foreign Office.[23] But whispering campaigns of a less pointed character were undoubtedly fostered. On the same day, the Ministry of Information's advisory committee for the West Region, centred on Bristol, discussed with concern the association of black GIs and British girls. The suggestion of an admonitory broadcast was rejected because the problem was 'dynamite', but the BBC's regional director recorded:

Probably the best means of approach is that individual and unofficial warnings should be spread about by members of such services as the A.R.P. [Air Raid Precautions Service],

---

[21] 'Notes on relations with coloured troops', annex to CAB 66/29, WP (42) 441.
[22] Quoted in report by Regional Information Officer, Manchester, 23 July 1942, in CAB 123/176.
[23] Minutes of BC (L) (42) Misc. 3, 1st mtg., 12 Aug. 1942, in CO 876/14.

W.V.S. [Womens' Voluntary Service], and Housewives Committees. This, I know, is the view of the Regional Commissioner here.[24]

This discussion presumably explains the action of the wife of the vicar of Worle in Somerset, who, the *Sunday Pictorial* reported on 6 September, had proposed to local women a six-point code of behaviour. This included crossing to the other side of a street if a black soldier was coming towards her, moving immediately to another seat in a cinema if he sat next to her and leaving a shop as quickly as possible if he entered. On no account were coloured troops to be invited into the homes of white women or to have a 'relationship' with any of them.[25]

It is unlikely that the vicar's wife was acting off her own bat. One may assume that her homily was an example of the characteristic MOI policy of using the right sort of people to foster discreetly the right sort of attitudes among the general public. But, inevitably on such a contentious issue, word about the official policy leaked out in late summer. Not only did the *Sunday Pictorial* publicize the story of the vicar's wife, the *New Statesman* reported a British soldier's account of his unit's guidance about non-fraternization with black GIs and also noted 'on fairly good authority that the ruling in one area is that if an A.T.S. girl is seen walking with a coloured soldier "she should be removed to another district for another reason" '.[26] The issue was also raised by backbench MPs in the House of Commons on 29 September. Responding, Churchill regretted the 'unfortunate question' and expressed the hope 'that, without any action on my part the points of view of all concerned will be mutually understood and respected'.[27] Most significantly, the Southern Command memo fell into the hands of the Colonial Office who took the matter up with the Army. According to the Ministry of Defence, the War Office's papers on the subject have been destroyed (no doubt an unfortunate mistake!),[28] but from documents that have survived in the Colonial Office files it would seem that the War Office had previously hoped to handle the problem in its own way without official fuss. Forced out into the open, the Secretary of State for War, Sir James Grigg, apparently decided to request Cabinet sanction for the policy he and his officials had been following. By 8 September a draft War Office paper for the Cabinet was circulating in Whitehall.[29]

In this paper, Grigg presented himself as 'on a razor's edge' between US racial practices and British public resentment of them. He argued that as far as possible the Government should rely on the US Army to keep white and black GIs apart, but that where its fiat did not apply, for example in British railway canteens,

[24] BBC West Regional Director, memo, 14 Aug. 1942, in BBC Written Archives, Caversham Park, Reading, R 34/912/1. Quoted by permission.   [25] *Sunday Pictorial*, 6 Sept.1942, p. 3.
[26] *New Statesman and Nation*, 22 Aug. 1942, p. 121, and 19 Sept. 1942, p. 184.
[27] *H. C. Debs.*, 5s, 383: 670, 29 Sept. 1942.
[28] Letters to author from Mrs J. C. North, Ministry of Defence, 29 July 1983, and Dr M. J. Jubb, Public Record Office, 7 June 1982 (on relevant FO papers also destroyed).
[29] This account reconstructed from the draft WO paper in CO 876/14, esp. para. 12.

there should be no discrimination against black GIs. In addition Grigg wanted to give British soldiers information about 'the facts and history of the colour question' in the USA and the American army. To this end he proposed a special article in 'Current Affairs', the organ of ABCA (the Army Bureau of Current Affairs) which used weekly pamphlets as the basis for officer-led group discussion. In addition, Grigg wanted Army officers, 'without the issue of overt or written instructions', to 'interpret these facts to the personnel of the Army including the A.T.S. and so educate them to adopt towards the U.S.A. coloured troops the attitude of the U.S.A. Army authorities'.[30]

Over the next month the question was debated intensively around Whitehall. Papers were submitted by the Home and Colonial Offices, the Ministry of Information, the Lord Chancellor and the Lord Privy Seal. But the final discussion in Cabinet proved something of an anti-climax. Not only were ministers in a rush to get away for lunch, Churchill had just returned from Scotland and had not read the relevant papers. While he did so the debate ebbed and flowed around him in turbulent fashion, which, as so often, is artfully concealed in the orderly minutes distilled by the Cabinet Secretary.[31] One is reminded of the anonymous verse by one harried civil servant:[32]

> And so while the great ones depart to their dinner
> The secretary stays, growing thinner and thinner,
> Racking his brains to record and report
> What he thinks that they think that they ought to have thought.

The main opposition to the War Office paper had come, not surprisingly, from the Colonial Office. John Keith, head of the CO's Student Department, called the Southern Command memo 'puerile and prejudiced stuff' and condemned Grigg's paper as 'full of special pleading'.[33] His superiors were less incensed, but all agreed that the interests of black British subjects in Britain had to be safeguarded and that an overt colour bar against black GIs would arouse deep resentment at home and in the colonies. The Colonial Secretary, Viscount Cranborne, therefore put up a Cabinet paper arguing that while information should be provided to British troops about the US race problem, they should be left to draw their own conclusions about how to behave towards black GIs. Equally, the different British attitude to race relations should be explained to the Americans and the US Army must be asked to respect the rights of black Britons.[34] Cranborne was supported by the Lord Chancellor, Viscount Simon. Although usually stigmatized as an amoral appeaser, Simon was a veteran Liberal

---

[30] CAB 66/29, WP (42) 441.
[31] CAB 65/28, WM 140 (42) 4, 13 Oct. 1942; cf. *The Diaries of Sir Alexander Cadogan, 1938–1945*, ed. David Dilks (London, 1971), 483.
[32] Sir Arthur Bryant, *The Turn of the Tide, 1939–1943* (London, 1957), 320.
[33] Minute, 12 Sept. 1942, CO 876/14.
[34] Memo of 2 Oct. 1942, CAB 66/29, WP (42) 442.

with a long record as an advocate of civil liberties, who had resigned from the Asquith Cabinet in 1916 over conscription. Unlike some of his colleagues, he knew the USA, made no secret of his distaste for the 'Jim Crow' South, and argued that Grigg's proposals could be the thin end of the wedge towards a general colour bar.[35] Cranborne raised these concerns about black British subjects in the Cabinet meeting on 13 October. He instanced one of his own black officials who had been recently barred from his habitual restaurant at the instigation of the US officers who now frequented it. The Prime Minister, however, was unsympathetic. 'That's all right', he said. 'If he takes a banjo with him they'll think he's one of the band.'[36]

As Churchill's flippancy suggests, Cranborne's concerns were not taken all that seriously by the War Cabinet. In fact on the major issues Grigg got his way. Ministers accepted that the US Army's attitude 'was a factor of great importance' when determining British policy towards black GIs, and, in the words of the Cabinet minutes, 'it was generally agreed that it was desirable that the people of this country should avoid becoming too friendly with coloured American troops'. On specifics, there was no objection, even from the Colonial Office, to the double-standard policy of covertly supporting US Army segregation as long as the British authorities were not involved in enforcing it, and the War Cabinet also agreed that information on US race policies should be provided to British troops through ABCA. On Cranborne's request that the flow of information should be two-way, the Cabinet minutes did note the feeling that 'it was equally important that the Americans should recognise that we had a different problem as regards our coloured people and that a modus vivendi between the two points of view should be found'.[37] But no specific action on this point was recommended in the Cabinet conclusions, and this fact was used by the War Office to justify their failure to make any approach to Eisenhower and his staff. Keith's consequent remonstrances within the Colonial Office were not supported by his superiors who felt that any pressure to have the British attitude explained to GIs would get them 'into very deep water indeed'.[38]

The main modification to Grigg's proposals was on the question of whether troops should not merely be informed but 'educated' into adopting US Army attitudes to black troops. Some ministers outside the War Office supported this view. Richard Law, son of the former Conservative prime minister and Parliamentary Under Secretary at the Foreign Office, approved of the WO paper and the Southern Command memo, arguing that 'the really important thing is

---

[35] Memo of 9 Oct. 1942, ibid., WP (42) 455. Back in 1934 Simon's wife had greatly angered the US Ambassador by interrogating him at an official luncheon as to 'when you southern people are going to stop your hideous, horrible lynching of negroes'. Robert W. Bingham, diary, 30 Oct. 1934, Library of Congress, Washington, DC.   [36] Cadogan, *Diaries*, 483.
[37] WM 140 (42) 4.
[38] See Keith, min., 24 Oct. 1942, min. by Sir Arthur Dawe (quotation) and letter from Col. Rolleston, 31 Oct. 1942, CO 876/14.

that we should not have avoidable friction between the two armies, and that the American troops should not go back to their homes with the view that we are a decadent and unspeakable race'. But Anthony Eden, the Foreign Secretary, thought that Grigg's proposal went 'much too far'[39] and most of his Cabinet colleagues agreed that it should be toned down. Many liked the amendments proposed by Sir Stafford Cripps and he was invited, in consultation with Grigg and Herbert Morrison, the Home Secretary, to prepare a revised memo to guide senior officers. This was approved by the Cabinet on 20 October. Presentation of the US racial situation was somewhat more complex than in the original Southern Command version, and the patronizing appraisal of negro character was omitted. But the account of race relations in the South was still partial and disingenuous—on Churchill's instructions the revised document had been shown by Cripps to Eisenhower before the Cabinet discussed it[40]—and although British troops were to be told that there was no reason for them to 'adopt the American attitude . . . they should respect it and avoid making it a subject for argument and dispute'. The drift of the specific advice was to avoid contact with black GIs as far as possible, whether in a bar or particularly in the company of white women, because this would lead to 'controversy and ill-feeling'.[41]

The guidance memo and the related ABCA article were issued in early December 1942, and their contents widely but cautiously disseminated among troops. That caution is one reason for the lack of public fuss on the matter during the winter of 1942–3. Another is the influence probably exerted on the press. To forestall embarrassing publicity the memo had been framed in deliberately blander terms than either the Southern Command's original or Cripps' first revision. And the Cabinet agreed that, in the best British lobby tradition of press management, the Minister of Information should give copies of the memo and the ABCA article 'to such editors as he thought appropriate, for their confidential information'. Probably they were advised, as Cripps suggested, that they should not 'feature' the ABCA article or make any reference to the guidance memo.[42] I have not been able to discover direct evidence of these briefings—the War Office files have been destroyed and in any case the whole emphasis of Government policy was now on the avoidance of written instructions—but such cosy briefings, encouraging a sense of special privilege and appealing to editors' public spiritedness, were characteristic MOI techniques for promoting press self-censorship. An extant example of what was done is the record of a briefing of editors in Belfast in August 1942. After a US officer had explained American racial attitudes, the editors were asked to help in 'playing down' racial incidents

[39] Law, min., 5 Oct. 1942, Eden, notes, FO 371/30680, A 9731/990/45.
[40] Cf. Prime Minister's papers, PREM 4, 26/9, f. 864 (TNA).
[41] CAB 65/28, WM 143 (42) 3, and CAB 66/30, WP (42) 473.
[42] WM 143 (42) 3, and Cripps, memo, WP (42) 473. My interpretation differs somewhat from that of Ian McLaine, *Ministry of Morale: Home front morale and the Ministry of Information in World War II* (London, 1979), 271–3, who suggests that little was done to guide opinion.

on the grounds that publicity might be exploited by enemy propaganda. The editors offered assurances that they would handle such stories 'with great discretion' and do 'everything possible to encourage a better understanding' between GIs, British troops, and civilians.[43]

A further reason for the lack of fuss in 1942–3 was the tailing-off of the US influx into Britain. Plans for an invasion of the continent in 1943 or even late 1942 were abandoned in favour of the Anglo-American assault on North Africa. This began a prolonged diversion of US manpower into the Mediterranean, while, at the same time, the Pacific theatre received far more troops and supplies in 1942–3 than envisaged in original Allied plans. The casualty in all this was operation Bolero—the projected build-up in Britain.[44] By early 1943 there were little more than 100,000 US troops in Britain, only 7,000 of whom were black.[45] Not until mid-1943, with the go-ahead for operation Overlord in spring 1944, did the build-up resume.

This new wave of GIs gave rise to further racial friction, as white and black troops unfamiliar with the situation in Britain came into contact with each other and with a larger number of British civilians. On the whole the British and US army authorities were happy with their mutual collaboration and with the guidance given to British troops. But in the autumn of 1943 renewed thought was given to an issue skirted the previous year, namely what if any 'advice' should be offered to British civilians. The Commander of the Southern Base Section of ETO was concerned at the number of incidents in which British civilians took the side of black GIs abused by whites, and his British counterpart, the GOC Southern Command, suggested to the War Office in September that guidance should be given to civilians along the lines of the army memo of the previous year. A possible method was through the informal network of influence available to the MOI through the civil defence services, the WVS, and other voluntary organizations who met regularly with MOI staff. The whole idea was rejected as impractical by the Home Office's Southern Regional Commissioner, who pointed out that most of the incidents stemmed not from British civilians' ignorance about the American colour problem but from resentment at 'what they regard as unfair and bullying treatment'.[46] But Churchill's roving eye had,

[43] C. L. Frankland, memo, 21 Aug. 1942, in Public Record Office, Belfast, Northern Ireland, Cabinet Secretariat files, CAB 9CD/225/19. (Quoted by permission of the Deputy Keeper.)

[44] Because of the diminishing number of incidents and the desire to avoid Anglo-American controversy at the time of the North African invasion, by late Oct. 1942 Grigg wanted to postpone issuing the guidance memo until further trouble occurred. It would seem that he was trying to return to the covert and more extreme guidance policy that the WO had been following until drawn out into the open by the Colonial Office. But the Cabinet Office was aware of Grigg's foot-dragging, and Cripps successfully argued that the papers should be issued to avert renewed incidents rather than in the wake of them. (See papers in CAB 120/727 and CAB 127/62.)

[45] See Roland G. Ruppenthal, *Logistical Support of the Armies*, vol. I (Washington, DC, 1953), 100, 129; Lee, *Negro Troops*, 433; statistical summaries in National Archives, Washington, RG 332: ETOUSA, Admin. 424.

[46] Sir Harry Haig, memo, 6 Sept. 1943, FO 371/34126, A 10199/33/45.

temporarily, lighted on the papers, directed there in part by his cousin, the Duke of Marlborough, who was a liaison officer with ETO. And Sir James Grigg in the War Office took advantage of the prime minister's attention to argue the case for wider civilian education: 'I expect that the British soldier [abroad] who fears for the safety or faithfulness of his women-folk at home would not feel so keenly as the B.B.C. and the public at home appear to do in favour of a policy of no colour bar and complete equality of treatment of negro troops.' And he warned that 'there is a danger that grave mischief will be done to Anglo-American relations unless we realise that before the problem can be solved we may have to face the question of changing our attitude to the colour question'.[47]

Grigg's concern for good relations with the USA was echoed in the Foreign Office. In fact the FO's attitude to this whole question is worthy of particular comment. In July 1941, when the War Office attempted to bar the volunteer black doctor from New York, the FO wished 'a fuss to be made', telling the War Office: 'on political grounds we urge that this negro doctor should be accepted as the effect of insisting on a colour bar in this matter might well have serious repercussions in the United States at the moment'.[48] The FO presumably had in mind the 'March on Washington' threatened by American black leaders and only recently headed off when Roosevelt ordered an end to discrimination among defence contractors. With this illustration of black muscle, at a time when the USA was not in the war and much of the pro-allied pressure came from American liberals, the FO evidently felt it unwise to affront black aspirations. By 1942–3, however, the balance of power in Washington had shifted. Conservative Democrats from the South, whose underlying sympathy for Britain had previously been held in check by antagonism to Roosevelt's New Deal, now rallied around the President's war policies and constituted the most reliable supporters of Britain in Congress. Nevile Butler, head of the FO's North American Department from late summer 1941, was a cautious career diplomat whose previous post had been at the Washington Embassy. He was therefore well aware of the importance of the Southern Democrats and also of their intense racism. Butler feared an anti-British backlash in Southern states if Britain was accused of 'undue kindness to the negroes' or of arousing black expectations which then led to trouble in post-war America, and he argued that there were consequently 'strong incentives for trying to do something' to educate British civilians 'and for letting the Americans know we have tried to do something, even if our action is ineffective'.[49] For the FO, the primary concern was the maintenance of Anglo-American amity and its continuance into the post-war world. What Butler called

[47] Grigg to Churchill, 2 Dec. 1943, PREM 4, 26/9, ff. 804–10.

[48] Quotations from Evans, min., 21 July 1941, and Cavendish-Bentinck to Brigadier P. G. Whitefoorde, 11 July 1941, FO 371/26227, A 8364/538/45.

[49] Quotations from Butler, min., 12 Feb. 1944, FO 371/38623, f. 120 ('kindness'), and mins. of 24 Nov. 1943, FO 371/34126, ff. 231, 236. Butler's juniors in the North American Dept. disagreed with him about 'educating' civilians.

'our Southern friends'[50] would have far more say about that than American blacks, and the FO determined its policy on race relations accordingly.

In the event nothing resulted officially from this debate about guidance for British civilians. Churchill's interest reverted to grand strategy and the War Office concentrated on improving relations between British and American soldiers.[51] Furthermore, the record of black GIs began to improve perceptibly in late 1943, as the US Army commanders in Britain, shaken by several serious incidents that summer, took positive measures to ameliorate the blacks' lot through better recreational facilities and proper health education. Recognizing that incompetent, racist white officers were often at the root of the problem, ETO and the Eighth Air Force also selected many new unit commanders who combined strict discipline with genuine sympathy for their men. Following these and other reforms (such as the increasing use of joint black–white military police patrols) there was a distinct improvement in black performance, conduct, and morale, and Churchill and the War Office decided to drop the idea of further guidance for British civilians.

It would be wrong, however, to treat the decisions taken or not taken in Whitehall as definitive guides to what British officials actually did. For it is clear that local army and police authorities frequently exceeded their written instructions. For instance, there is considerable evidence to suggest that, as the *New Statesman* reported in August 1942, ATS women soldiers continued to be disciplined for associating with black GIs. The guidance memo approved by the Cabinet that October simply advised that 'for a white woman to go about in the company of a negro American is likely to lead to controversy and ill-feeling'. But the original Southern Command memo had firmly instructed soldiers that 'white women should not associate with coloured men',[52] and it would seem that this bore closer relationship to the line actually adopted. For local police forces seem to have routinely reported women soldiers found in the company of black GIs, and in January 1944 William Leach, the Labour MP for Bradford Central, asked Grigg in the House of Commons 'who is responsible for a recent issue of an order to the A.T.S. forbidding its members to speak with coloured American soldiers except in the presence of a white'. When Grigg professed no knowledge of such an order, Leach responded with the inevitable supplementary: 'If I send the right hon. gentleman a copy of this order, will he go further into the matter?' A furious Grigg replied: 'Yes, and I shall be very grateful if the hon. Member will tell me how he got hold of it too.' Nowhere in the exchange or in the Foreign and War Office minutes on the question was there any denial that such an order had been issued.[53]

It is also clear that British officials were more involved in enforcing segregation than Government policy statements permitted. In the summer of 1942, for

---

[50] Butler to Michael Wright, 14 Mar. 1944, FO 371/38609, AN 587/159/45.
[51] See Chapter 12.   [52] CAB 66/29, WP (42) 441, annex.
[53] *H. C. Debs*, 5s, 397: 3–4, 15 Feb. 1944; FO 371/38623, AN 738/275/45.

instance, the US Army lacked sufficient hospital space of its own and would have had to use British facilities in the event of an early invasion of the continent. Officials of the Bolero committee handling US requirements agreed in principle that, although black GIs should be transferred as quickly as possible to American army hospitals, if they had to be treated in British hospitals 'separate lavatory accommodation should be provided for them, even though it might not be possible to provide treatment in separate wards'.[54] This policy never had to be implemented and it was enunciated before the War Cabinet's discussions in autumn 1942. But in June 1943, when the Bolero committee agreed to billet GIs in British homes to ease the accommodation shortage, it was 'definitely agreed with the U.S. authorities that no coloured troops should be billeted'.[55] Likewise, black troops were excluded from the exchanges between British and US units which were arranged on a large scale in the winter of 1943–4.[56] And there is also evidence that the British police infringed Home Office instructions that they should in no way help to enforce US segregation policy. For instance, the Dorothy Dance Hall in Cambridge was out of bounds to black troops in 1943–4. The proprietor's stated reason was that his floor would not stand the strain of jitterbugging, but in fact he was acting on verbal advice from the Chief Constable of Cambridge who had apparently reached an informal understanding with the local US Provost Marshal about how to divide the city's recreational facilities between black and white GIs.[57]

Local police and magistrates in some areas also found legal pretext to come down very hard on British civilian women found in the company of black GIs. In June 1943 the Derbyshire county police reported: 'The association of U.S.A. coloured troops with British women is still continuing at Hilton. Prosecutions under the Defence (General) Regulations are pending in this connection, with a view to stopping this practice.' The Foreign Office and Ministry of Home Security privately admitted that they could not understand how the wartime Defence Regulations could be invoked in this way. Nevertheless the Derbyshire police continued to do so. The following month they were prosecuting racially mixed couples on account of the damage they caused to growing crops. And in Melton Mowbray in Leicestershire five young women were imprisoned in June for one month 'for trespassing on premises in the occupation of coloured troops'. The police report noted: 'There is no doubt that the young women were on these premises for an immoral purpose, undoubtedly attracted by the amount of money these troops can either give them or spend on them.'[58] The following

---

[54] CAB 81/48, BC(L) 15 (42) 6, 29 July 1942.
[55] QMC 10 (43) 6, 11 June 1943, copy in FO 371/34117, A 5706/32/45.
[56] AAR/M 2 (44) 10, 6 Feb. 1944, WO 163/222.
[57] National Archives, Washington, RG 332, ETOUSA, AG, CGC, 291.2, 'Report of Investigation', esp. exhibit G; Hq ETO to CG, ETO, 27 Feb. 1944, copy in Library of Congress, Washington, National Association for the Advancement of Colored People papers, II/A, box 587: 'White's European tour'.   [58] All quotations from reports in FO 371/34126, A 6556/33/45.

January, in the city of Leicester two young women of 20 and 22, cotton hands from Preston, were found sleeping in a hut on a US Army camp where black GIs were stationed. They were sentenced to three months hard labour for 'trespassing on a Military Camp'.[59]

It is therefore apparent, despite the destruction of much of the official archival evidence, that the British authorities during World War II did try to regulate the behaviour not merely of soldiers but also civilians towards the black GIs.[60] In part, the Cabinet determined policy, but frequently Whitehall departments and local officials went farther than it decreed, and, as Grigg's conduct in 1942 suggests, Cabinet 'decisions' could be used to throw a seemly but loose veil of authority over departmental actions. Thus efforts to influence civilian mores continued, even though the Cabinet had officially declined to 'educate' public opinion, as shown by the evidence of 'whispering campaigns' in 1942 and the activities of Derbyshire and Leicester police in 1943–4. Likewise, within the British army, where a general non-fraternization policy was approved by the Cabinet, far more rigid controls were imposed by the Army on the conduct of women soldiers. On occasions when infractions of the Cabinet guidelines were discovered, Whitehall departments were frequently ready to turn a blind eye, assisted by the lack of media fuss thanks to effective government management of the press.

Official British policy towards the black American troops was determined by three principal considerations. First, and not always consciously recognized, were certain basic assumptions about non-whites. The British Government wanted neither black colonials nor black Americans in Britain. Their own manpower policies could control the influx of British colonial subjects, but, unable to dissuade the Roosevelt Administration from sending black GIs, the Government was happy to connive at the US Army's policy of de facto segregation in order to minimize black–white contacts. Unlike the Americans, the British did not deny privately that this was racial discrimination. Their particular legal fiction was to claim that segregation was purely an American matter, though in fact they approved of it and local British officials often helped covertly to enforce it. Underpinning British policy was a set of racial stereotypes, formed in the late nineteenth century as the development of anthropology, comparative anatomy and other fields of post-Darwinian scholarship fostered pseudo-scientific justifications for the belief that there were definable 'races' with fixed, inherited

---

[59] Police report, Leicester city, 15 Jan. 1944, FO 371/38624, AN 2089/275/45.' "Hard labour" at this time meant that the prisoner performed whatever labour he or she was medically fit to do, and also went without a mattress during the first fourteen days of the sentence.' Edward Smithies, *Crime in Wartime: A Social History of Crime in World War II* (London, 1982), 7.

[60] It is interesting to note that when US units were moved to Britain again in large numbers during the Korean War, the Foreign Office once more did its best to discourage the sending of black troops. Among the reasons given were the likelihood of 'numerous black babies', the danger that discrimination by white GIs against blacks would arouse anti-American feeling among the British public, and the opportunities thereby provided for communist propaganda. FO 371/90966, esp. AU 1194/20, J. N. O. Curle, min., 7 Nov. 1951.

differences of moral and intellectual capacity.[61] In particular, the assumption of aggressive black sexuality was deeply ingrained. Fears about this lay at the root of official efforts to keep black GIs away from British civilians, efforts which far outstripped their concern for the consequences of white GI indiscretions and which reflected an abhorrence of interracial sexual contact. This was frankly admitted, for example in the ABCA memo of December 1942 where soldiers were told that 'in our present society such unions are not desirable, since the children resulting from them are neither one thing nor the other and are thus badly handicapped in the struggle for life'.[62] In fact the number of illegitimate children fathered by black GIs proved to be considerably less than the authorities feared or sensationalist press reports of 10,000–20,000 suggested. Authoritative estimates placed the total at 1,200 to 1,700, a proportion comparable with what seem to be reliable figures of 22,000 children born out of wedlock to white GIs in Britain.[63]

In addition to a basic prejudice against non-whites, the British Government was motivated by a concern for public order. Racial friction was almost inevitable when white and black GIs were transported to a freer social milieu, and, in a compact island with British women the (often eager) object of competition, the local populace was naturally drawn in. Even General Benjamin O. Davis, Roosevelt's token black general who took a keen interest in the situation in Britain, did not seriously contest the need to keep black and white GIs apart as much as possible.[64] Nor did the Colonial Office, despite its concern for the consequences of segregation on British and colonial race relations. It should also be noted that much of the debate took place in a fraught atmosphere. This was in part due to the intense emotions raised by white–black contact: many reports of black GIs' sexual exploits were little more than gossip and evaporated under investigation. One US diplomat in London in late summer 1942 found the city 'filled with stories of the black and white problem, many of which are exaggerated'.[65] What added to the frenzy in 1942 was the erroneous British conviction that by April 1943 100,000 black GIs would be in Britain. This figure, which recurred in official discussions, was an extrapolation from the Bolero plan, with its target of one million GIs in Britain by April 1943, and from the US Government's principle of ten per cent black representation. The fear that a totally

[61] Cf. Douglas A. Lorimer, *Colour, Class and the Victorians: English Attitudes to the Negro in the Mid-Nineteeth Century* (Leicester, 1978).   [62] *Current Affairs*, 32 (5 Dec. 1942), 11.

[63] George Padmore to Walter White, 29 Apr. 1947 and enclosed memo of 24 Apr., in NAACP papers, II/A, box 631: 'US Army—brown babies'; *Ebony*, 4 (Mar. 1949), 22; *Life*, 23 Aug. 1948, p. 41 (22,000). To give some sense of proportion: about three million US servicemen passed through Britain in the years 1942–5 (cf. TSFET, Transportation Corps, Progress report, 30 Sept. 1945, Table I, in RG 332, ETOUSA, Admin. 452.)

[64] e.g. Davis, memo, 24 Dec. 1942, National Archives, Washington, RG 107/47, box 123, ASW 291.2.

[65] William Phillips, diary, vol. 28, 28 Aug. and 18 Sept. 1942 (quotation), Houghton Library, Harvard University, Cambridge, Mass. Cf. *The War Diaries of Oliver Harvey*, ed. John Harvey (London, 1978), 21 July 1942, p. 141.

unprepared country would have to deal in six months with that size of racial minority helps to account for something of the panicky atmosphere of autumn 1942. In fact, thanks to the invasion of North Africa, the dreaded 100,000 mark was not reached until a year later, in the spring of 1944, by which time official policies had been developed and the US Army in Britain had begun to reform itself, thereby helping ensure that the anticipated disasters did not happen.

The third main consideration defining British official attitudes was the importance of good relations with the USA. It was vital in the short term to maintain harmony between the British and US armies who would have to fight together in the Mediterranean and continental Europe. But, as we have seen, the Foreign Office, and the British Government as a whole, also considered it essential that the wartime alliance be perpetuated into the post-war world as one of the foundations of British foreign policy. Churchill called it 'my deepest conviction that unless Britain and the United States are joined in a special relationship . . . another destructive war will come to pass'.[66] Moreover, British leaders did not take that post-war relationship for granted—rightly, as events later proved—and there were protracted official debates about the possibility of renewed US isolationism once the war was over. Convinced that 'public opinion' largely determined US foreign policy, the British Government spent a huge amount of time, money, and effort in welcoming and entertaining the GIs—far more than they did on less important allies such as the very numerous Canadian troops—and it was hoped that this hospitality would pay dividends when the GIs returned home. Likewise it was important to conciliate the power brokers in Congress, notably the Southern Democrats who would help decide whether the alliance would persist and whether Britain would receive essential financial aid after the war. In both cases the British Government deemed it vital not to offend American racial sensitivities. By comparison, solicitude for colonial feelings or the civil rights of black Britons was far less salient. The Colonial Office did articulate these concerns, but its achievements were limited to toning down the official statements of guidance for troops and ensuring that British policy operated more circumspectly than might otherwise have been the case.[67]

Racial prejudice, a panicky concern for public order, and a determination not to upset the US Government—these were the underlying reasons for British policy, both as stated and as implemented. What is striking throughout the debate is the lack of reference to any fundamental moral issues, or the dismissal of these as tangential.[68] In part that is because the treatment of the black GIs was

---

[66] Churchill to Law, 16 Feb. 1944, PREM 4, 27/10, f. 1261.

[67] Throughout the war, Colonial Office staff continued to protest against what they called the 'blimpish' attitude of other departments on race questions, especially that of the War Office, e.g., A. H. Poynton, min., 17 Mar. 1944, CO 537/1223.

[68] Cf. this comment by a junior FO official on 'educating' civilians to shun black GIs: 'Apart altogether from the ethical aspect, even to attempt to proceed as the Americans suggested would obviously be political dynamite for ourselves in most parts of the Colonial Empire.' J. Donnelly, min., 16 Nov. 1943, FO 371/34126, A 10199/33/45.

an American matter. But the Government could have refused to cooperate with segregation, or requested, as the Colonial Office wished, that British views of race relations be explained more directly to the GIs. It chose not to do so, for reasons that I have tried to elucidate. Keeping in with America was seen as essential for winning the war and securing a peace that would benefit *all* peoples in their search for justice. For harassed British officials, faced with a multitude of simultaneous problems at a time of declining national power and influence, victory was the ultimate morality.

12

GIs and Tommies

The Army 'Inter-attachment' Programme of 1943–1944

Winston Churchill once observed that 'there is only one thing worse than fighting with allies, and that is fighting without them'.[1] The history of warfare is replete with examples of his maxim, from the days of the Athenian League, through the wars of Marlborough and the coalitions against Napoleon. The Anglo-American alliance of 1941–45 provides particularly rich evidence of the difficulty of harmonizing the interests, objectives, and methods of two sovereign states. Numerous military historians have examined the debates over grand strategy, the rivalries between senior commanders, the painstaking creation of combined staffs in the Mediterranean and north-west Europe and the divergent national military doctrines and traditions which impeded combined operations. Less attention, however, has been paid to the problem of inter-Allied military cooperation at the grass roots—the need to promote understanding between the ordinary fighting men. This became a serious concern of British and American planners in 1943–44 as they prepared for the combined invasion of Europe, because relations between soldiers of the two nations were not only bad but were also deteriorating. To improve matters they devised a series of exchanges between the two armies, which was an immense success, but which has attracted little attention from historians. The origins and execution of this programme of 'inter-attachment' are the main subjects of this chapter, but we shall also see that the reports by British and US participants about their experiences provide interesting insights into the characteristics of the two armies. More generally, this programme, taken in conjunction with earlier precedents in both world wars, illuminates more recent discussion about 'inter-operability' in NATO.

This chapter appears as first published in the *Journal of Strategic Studies*, 7 (1984), 406–22, except for a few cuts to eliminate overlap with Chapter 11. It was originally presented to the London University seminar in military history. Brian Bond, Robert K. Griffith, Hew Strachan, and John A. Thompson kindly commented on a draft version.

[1] Quoted in David Reynolds, *The Creation of the Anglo-American Alliance, 1937–1941: A Study in Competitive Cooperation* (London, 1981), 283.

Long before Pearl Harbor, US officers had been slipping into Britain as observers and planners, but the influx of ordinary GIs did not commence until late January 1942. During the spring and summer there was a steady build-up of US forces in Northern Ireland, East Anglia, the Midlands, and south-west England, and by mid-October over 225,000 American soldiers and airmen were in the British Isles. Their morale, conduct, and relations with the local inhabitants were anxiously monitored by British government departments, particularly the War Office, Foreign Office, and Ministry of Information, and by the headquarters of the US Army command in Britain, known from midsummer as the European Theater of Operations (ETO). The reports they compiled all pointed in roughly the same direction. It seemed that the GIs were generally well received by the British public, although a minority gave their fellow countrymen a bad name through boastfulness, drunkenness, and promiscuity. On the other hand, relations with British troops were usually less than satisfactory. At best there was only superficial cordiality, and a good deal of mutual resentment was often detected.

The causes of this tension were obvious to anyone who saw a British and an American soldier side by side off duty. The GI wore a lightweight, tailored uniform, complete with collar, tie, and all-important raincoat—a marked contrast with his British counterpart's thick, bulky battledress and khaki jacket buttoned up to the neck. Equally noticeable was the GI's array of medals, which, in the opinion of the British, were awarded far too readily for nothing in particular. This was all the more galling in view of America's belated entry into the war, a grievance for Britons of all social levels, and the GIs' propensity, nonetheless, to assume that the quaint little island would have sunk under the waves but for US help. The American troops arrived at a time when Britain's military reputation had declined to its nadir with the surrender of Singapore, and the famous GI line—'Give me a beer as quickly as you guys got out of Dunkirk'—became notorious. Another American gibe in 1942 was to ask British soldiers the colours of their flag. To the reply, 'Red, white, and blue,' they would respond that it had a fourth colour 'Yellow'. The British soldier's riposte to these jokes included derisory comments about Pearl Harbor, and it was noted by government reports in February 1943 that the American reverses at Kasserine in Tunisia were greeted with a good deal of quiet satisfaction by British troops.[2]

Personal envy and interservice rivalry were part of the problem, but its root cause was pay. Direct comparison is very difficult because virtually no soldier was paid at the base rates. Family allotments, overseas allowances (for the GIs but not for British troops abroad), bonuses for long service or specialist skills—all these

[2] Extract from Army mail censorship report 61, 11–25 Feb. 1943, Foreign Office General Political Correspondence, FO 371/34124, A 2391/33/45 (TNA). After Kasserine, 'groups of young IRA men' in Belfast walked the streets singing 'The Yanks are Running' to the tune of the Great War song, 'The Yanks are Coming'. Lieutenant Commander Robert E. Vining, USN, report on situation in Ireland, p. 4, 26 Apr. 1943 (Stanford University, California: Hoover Institution on War, Revolution and Peace; TS Ireland V 785).

make it almost impossible to identify the 'average' soldier in each army. As a rough rule of thumb, however, one can say that the disposable pay of a newly enlisted GI in England in June 1942 was £3. 10s.(£3.50 or $14) while his British counterpart drew 17s. 6d. (£0.87½ or $3.50).[3] In other words, the British soldier received about a quarter of the American rate. The disparity was less for married soldiers, and British base rates improved in September 1942, but even allowing for this and for the increasingly successful savings campaign mounted by the US army to mop up surplus cash, the GIs must have had at least two or three times the expendable pay of British troops. One must also bear in mind that the US soldier could purchase 'essentials' such as razor blades and cleaning materials for substantially less than could the British, while cigarettes were available to the GI at about a quarter of the price. Furthermore, the discrepancy in pay rates was accentuated by the fact that the GI was paid monthly (later bimonthly) whereas the British soldier drew his pay every week. This meant that the GI had a good deal more money to throw around, especially on his first 'liberty run' after pay day.

And it was on 'liberty runs' that the pay issue caused the most trouble. The US troops could outspend their British rivals whenever they went into town. Even friendly contact was often embarrassing—reciprocating an American round of drinks in a pub could clean out a British private—while it became notorious that British girls flocked like bees to a honey pot around the free-spending Yanks. Not that the GIs had it all their own way. There was a common, and justified, complaint that many shops and pubs had a covert two-price tariff—with substantially higher charges for the Yanks, many of whom could not master the intricacies of the currency. Quipped one GI in Chester: 'The only thing that is cheap in England is the women.'[4] Nor was it really fair to blame the US soldiers or their government. As the American army privately observed, and many British officials acknowledged, the fault lay ultimately with the British government and the low rates of service pay, compared not only with Allied troops but even British civilian workers. Whatever the rights and wrongs, however, the substantial difference in purchasing power lay at the root of much of the ill-feeling between British and US troops. Usually these feelings were suppressed: British forces groused and kept their distance, GIs spent, socialized, and felt confirmed in their impression of British army stuffiness. But where tact was lacking and too much alcohol had been consumed, unpleasant and bitterly resented incidents could occur, as exemplified in this extract about the GIs from a British soldier's letter in late summer 1942:

One of them turned to one of our Lance Corporals and said: 'Say, Tommy, what do they pay you a day?' Fred replied, 'Three and six.' At this he laughs loud and calls to all his

---

[3] House of Commons, *Debates*, 5th series, 10 Feb. 1942, Vol. 377, cols. 1,376–7; US War Department, Finance Department, *Army Pay Tables* (Washington, 1942), 50. The British base rate was raised to 21s. in Sept. 1942. US Army pay had increased in 1940 after remaining the same since 1922. See Robert K. Griffith, *Men Wanted for the US Army: America's experience with an All-Volunteer Army between the World Wars* (Westport, Conn., 1982), 237.

[4] War Office DQMG, Digest of Nov. 1942 reports, War Office papers WO 32/10267 (TNA).

gang . . . says that British soldiers would work for a dime if the big shots paid it to 'em. When we came outside after the place had closed there was an army lorry waiting for the Yanks. We stood there and watched them pile in. Then the one who had been doing all the shouting put his hand in his pocket and as the lorry pulled away, threw about a bob's worth of coppers at us and shouted above the others' laughter, 'Get y'self a cup of tea each of you poor little———.' If I could have laid my hands on him, I, like many more, would have busted his pan. I think they *stink*.

A War Office official commented gratuitously: 'Such incidents do little to inspire respect and friendship for US Troops.'[5]

Official reports regularly noted these problems in relations between British and US troops from the onset of the American 'occupation', but throughout 1942 and into the spring of 1943 there did not seem cause for serious disquiet. Although the planners had been preparing for an American force of over a million men by April 1943, the invasion of North Africa in November 1942 siphoned off many of the troops based in or originally intended for Britain. From a peak of some 228,000 during October 1942 the number of GIs declined to little over 100,000 by the following February, and in the early months of 1943 reports on GI–British relations were generally encouraging. From May 1943, however, as the Allied leaders committed themselves to an invasion of Europe the following spring, the American presence in Britain began to increase rapidly. The total reached 250,000 during July 1943, half a million before the end of November and nearly 1.7 million on the eve of D-Day.[6] The scale of this influx posed problems in itself: contact and friction with British troops was much more likely. Moreover, these GIs were almost all new to Britain and it took time to indoctrinate them into the conditions of British life and the delicacy of inter-Allied relations. After polling 3,000 representative GIs in November 1943, US staff officers estimated that 'nearly one half of the soldiers in this theater attach little or no importance to Anglo-American understanding'.[7] Not surprisingly, therefore, in the summer and autumn of 1943 British authorities became increasingly concerned about the state of relations between the two armies and expressed with growing conviction the belief that existing arrangements were no longer adequate.

The underlying problem was that in Britain US and British soldiers generally came into contact only in off-duty social situations. There—in pubs, at dances,

[5] WO, Q(AL), Conclusions from recent MOI reports on Anglo-American relations, 13 Nov. 1942, p. 7, copy in records of European Theater of Operations, US Army, World War II (ETOUSA), Adjutant General (AG), General Records, Classified General Correspondence (CGC), box 611, decimal file 336.2 (US National Archives, Record Group, RG 332).

[6] Troop figures from Roland G. Ruppenthal, *Logistical Support of the Armies*, vol. i (Washington, 1953), 100, 129, 232 (volume in series 'United States Army in World War II: The European Theater of Operations').

[7] Hq, Services of Supply (SOS), ETO to General Devers, 14 Dec. 1943, 'Soldier Attitudes towards the English', copy in papers of General Carl A. Spaatz, box 324 (Library of Congress, Washington DC).

or around the cinemas—the contrast in pay and dress were most likely to cause offence as soldiers let off steam and competed for scarce drink, entertainment, and female company. Reports from combat areas abroad, however, indicated that where the two armies had to work and fight together the differences in quality of life became much less contentious. As one War Office memo observed in March 1943: 'It is still rare to see the members of the two armies fraternizing much in the UK, but it is clear, as always, that when the British and American troops get together (mainly overseas) and work side by side on the same job, the relations between them are probably 75 per cent good.'[8] Or, as another report put it, more pithily, in June: 'British and American soldiers evidently get on better together when they are out side by side on the same job than when they are side by side in the same bar.'[9]

The main source of these judgements was the experience of the Allied armies in North Africa. During the early fighting in Tunisia, between mid-November 1942 and late February 1943, British, French, and US units were committed as soon as they arrived in the combat zone and were integrated piecemeal, even as far down as company level. There had been virtually no preparation for such combined operations between troops with different languages, training, and equipment, and chaos often resulted, with damaging effects on mutual respect among the allies at all levels. Friction between the British and US Army Commanders, Generals Anderson and Fredendall, was paralleled lower down by premature British condemnation of the GIs after the setback at Kasserine, which was due in part to this wholesale integration, while the performance of the French colonial troops revived the bitter Anglo-French recriminations of 1940. The Supreme Allied Commander in North Africa, General Eisenhower, set about building a unified Allied force. An integrated Allied Force headquarters staff (AFHQ) was created, a common Battle School for all Allied troops in General Alexander's 18th Army Group helped promote uniform combat methods, and, after the Tunisian disasters, it was decided that henceforth combat integration should only take place at or above the divisional level.[10]

The later North African record showed that with proper preparation inter-Allied cooperation in battle was not only possible but could also facilitate greater harmony among troops of various nationalities. Britain of course was not an active theatre. Indeed, this was part of the problem because bored and frustrated troops had excess energy which they directed into their off-duty hours. The War Office saw a possible answer in AFHQ's occasional practice of attaching

---

[8] WO, DQMG, Digest of March 1943 reports, FO 371/34125, A 3961/33/45.

[9] WO, Morale Report for Feb.–Apr. 1943, 19 June 1943, p. 8, MC/P (43) 8, WO 163/161. The solidarity engendered by a sense of shared danger is of course a phenomenon often noted by writers on the psychology of war—e.g. J. Glenn Gray, *The Warriors: Reflections on Men in Battle* (New York, second edition, 1970), esp. ch. 2.

[10] John Hixson and Benjamin Franklin Cooling, 'Combined Operations in Peace and War' (TS., US Army Military History Institute, Carlisle Barracks, Pennsylvania, revised edition, 1982), 96–123.

small parties of troops of one nationality, usually administrative or technical personnel, to equivalent units of the other army. In a combat theatre this was difficult to effect on a large scale; in Britain, by contrast, the obstacles were much less and the need much greater.

The idea of mutual exchanges was not unknown in Britain. In November 1942, for instance, 22 US officers were attached to British anti-gas schools, 26 were attending the schools of military engineering, eight were on commando courses, seven at Intelligence schools and ten at medical schools, in addition to individual local attachments.[11] And by the following April the ETO's Deputy Theater Commander noted that 'twelve junior officers from an American division are exchanged every two weeks with an equal number from one of the British divisions'.[12] But these exchanges were mainly confined to officers, usually on specialist duties, and were generally one-way—attaching Americans to British units—rather than reciprocal. The War Office took little interest in the matter and calls for a more extensive programme by one Conservative MP elicited only a bland Commons answer from the Prime Minister in September 1942.[13] It was not until the summer of 1943 that the War Office, concerned at the new friction in Britain and encouraged by the North African example, took up the idea of exchanges in a serious way.

The initiative came from the Army's Council's 'Committee on Morale in the Army'. At its meeting on 23 July 1943 it decided to appoint a special sub-committee on relations between British and US troops, charged as its first task with the development of an 'inter-attachment' programme. Pilot schemes had been tried in Northern Ireland and in Southern Command and the result confirmed the evidence from North Africa.[14] The subcommittee met for the first time on 4 August, with representatives from the American liaison section of the War Office and various home commands, under the chairmanship of Brigadier E. H. A. J. O'Donnell. While preliminary plans were being made the scheme received a great fillip from the intervention of the Foreign Office. It too had been increasingly disturbed at the state of troop relations, partly because of insistent pressure from Colonel Brian Rowe, who handled American liaison in the War Office. Rowe argued that little improvement could be expected until British and particularly US commanders were clearly told from on high that this was a matter of real importance, rather than a peripheral 'social' issue unrelated to the central problems of building an invasion force. The Foreign Office agreed, and it raised the matter at the Roosevelt–Churchill 'Quadrant' conference in Quebec in August 1943. The minutes record: 'It was agreed between the President and

[11] Drew to Watson, 2 Nov. 1942, Prime Minister's Confidential Papers, PREM 4/26/10, pp. 1167–8 (TNA).
[12] Hq, ETO, Ingles to Gribble, 26 Apr. 1943, ETO; AG, CGC, box 474, 091.711. (5,000 American volunteers were still serving in the British forces, about half the peak figure of earlier in the war.) [13] House of Commons, *Debates*, 383: 26, 8, Sept. 1942.
[14] WO 163/161, MC/M, minutes 51(x), 57, 61, 68.

Prime Minister that all possible steps should be taken to promote fraternization between the US and British forces in the British Isles.'[15] Armed with this brief but invaluable authority the Foreign Office and War Office were able to press ETO for action on the American side. US representatives started attending the subcommittee at its third meeting on 1 October, and from 19 November it was reconstituted as a separate, combined body—'The Anglo-American (Army) Relations Committee' (AARC). With proper administrative machinery and top-level endorsement, the inter-attachment scheme was able to get under way.

The formal announcement came in parallel letters from the Army Council on 9 October 1943 and from General Jacob L. Devers, Commanding General of the ETO, on the 15th.[16] In similar terms they instructed subordinates to promote exchanges between small groups of British and US troops. These were to last about two weeks with an optimum size of one officer and ten 'other ranks', or 'enlisted men' in American parlance. Troops were to be swapped with equivalent units from the other army—engineers, armour, AA units, and so on—so that they could learn as much as possible about their opposite numbers' work and virtually replace those who had been attached to their own units. Part of the object of the scheme was therefore to familiarize British and American troops with the other army's equipment, procedures, and training. This would be essential, as an earlier memorandum by Rowe had pointed out, if the two armies were to work together effectively on the continent where administrative troops would certainly be 'mixed up' and supply troops might well be servicing a joint line of communication, which would require knowledge of each army's jargon, *matériel*, and methods.[17] But much of this familiarization could be and was being done in specialist training schemes. As Devers' letter stressed, 'the primary aim of this programme is the intermingling of American and British soldiers'.[18] They were simply to get acquainted as human beings, to break down stereotypes and create mutual respect. For this reason troops were to be billeted individually with their hosts, and commanders were instructed to exchange parties not from existing sub-units, which might then club together, but from specially selected personnel who would mix more readily.

The programme was intended in the short term to prepare for the invasion of continental Europe. Stressing 'the urgent operational importance of this matter now', the Army Council observed: 'Troops who have learnt to know and appreciate each other's qualities, methods and weapons will cooperate all the more efficiently in battle.'[19] But the British at least kept one eye on the

[15] US Department of State, *Foreign Relations of the United States: The Conferences at Washington and Quebec, 1943* (Washington, 1970), 932, meeting of 22 Aug.

[16] Circular letters from Sir Frederick Bovenschen, WO, 9 Oct. 1943, and General Jacob L. Devers, 15 Oct. 1943, copies in ETO, AG, CGC, box 474, 091.711.

[17] Rowe, WO, 'Note on the Integration of the US and British Armed Forces', no date [mid-1943], copy in FO 371/34126, A 6417/33/45. [18] Devers, letter of 15 Oct. 1943.

[19] Bovenschen, letter of 9 Oct. 1943.

longer-term future. The Army Council's letter alluded to 'the obvious benefits which must result after war from better understanding and mutual esteem between the armed forces of the two peoples'. This reflected the concerns not only of those in the War Office directly involved in Anglo-American integration, such as O'Donnell and Rowe, but also some very senior officers including Sir Ronald Adam, the Adjutant General.[20] Similar considerations were always in the mind of the Foreign Office who viewed the GIs' presence in Britain as a supreme opportunity to foster a post-war Anglo-American alliance which they felt essential for peace and stability. As one typical Foreign Office memo noted: 'Before the end of the war many hundreds of thousands of Americans will have spent months or even years in the United Kingdom, and will return to the United States with an impression of this country which will be an important, possibly the most important, factor in colouring, for many years to come, American opinion of us and our ways.'[21] Some Americans placed a similar emphasis on the enduring value of Anglo-American understanding. Devers told his subordinates that this was 'supremely important' for America and that it must be appreciated by the whole of ETO.[22] For most Americans, however, a transatlantic special relationship never assumed the same importance as it did for British leaders; many in fact had considerable reservations about the idea. But, for the British authorities at least, considerations of post-war diplomacy as well as wartime military operations played a part in their enthusiasm for the inter-attachment scheme.

The first exchange began in November and initial reports were highly satisfactory. Encouraged, the AARC urged more general adoption of the scheme and also pressed for informal exchanges of small groups between messes over the Christmas holiday. In the New Year the inter-attachments really got going, with the participation of major combat commands such as the British 21st Army Group, and they reached peak activity in the late winter and early spring. In the period 5–18 January 1944, for instance, 28 parties of 11 were exchanged by the First US Army (FUSA) with units from the British Second Army and Southern Command. Units involved included the Guards Armoured Division which exchanged five parties with the 2nd US Armored Division, and the 15th Scottish which swapped a similar number with the 28th US Infantry Division.[23] The fullest statistics on the programme were compiled in the spring. On 10 May 1944 the AARC learnt that 338 officers and 3,080 other ranks had been sent from British to American units, and 915 officers and 4,726 enlisted men from the US Army had been attached to British forces.[24] Thereafter the scheme ran down, as US troops

---

[20] For Adam's concern see his TS. memoirs, no date, ch. 10, in Sir Ronald Adam papers, section VIII (Liddell Hart Centre for Military Archives, King's College, London).

[21] F. E. Evans, Memo, 10 July 1943, FO 371/34119, A 7757/32/45.

[22] Devers to Eaker, 22 Dec. 1943, in Spaatz papers, box 324.

[23] Hq FUSA to CG, ETO, 8 Feb. 1944, RG 332, ETO, AG, General Correspondence (GC), box 59, 092 (1944), vol. i.

[24] A total of 9,059 personnel. AAR/M (44) 5th Meeting, Minute 20, 10 May 1944, WO 163/222. In addition, shorter visits were arranged for air-force personnel: by 4 May 1944, 4,620 troops

were engaged in pre-invasion preparations and then left for the continent, and it became more of a British to American flow, especially in static commands such as anti-aircraft. By August 1944 it was almost in abeyance except among troops in British and US convalescent hospitals and even here the exchanges were limited because of American fears that soldiers might ascribe slow or incomplete recuperation to the inadequate medical skills of the other nation![25]

Inevitably a few snags were encountered. Sometimes units were not appropriately matched; occasionally officers felt that the exchanges lasted too long. A few commanders protested that the scheme interfered with training. To this the AARC responded that on the contrary it should be regarded as an integral part of training because mutual confidence was essential for successful combined operations.[26] More substantial was the pay problem, because British soldiers sometimes felt unable to reciprocate hospitality. When this issue was first raised in January 1944 the AARC rejected proposals for a special hospitality allowance. This, it felt, would inject an official element into a scheme successful precisely because of its informality, and one US member of the committee emphasized the importance of letting the GI see that the British soldier did the same job as himself for less remuneration. But the issue recurred and, following further discussion just after D-Day, the British Treasury agreed in July to provide an expense allowance of 1s. (5p) per man per day for British units entertaining or visiting US troops.[27] Another sensitive matter was the involvement of black US troops in the exchanges, given the US Army's policy of segregation (Chapter 11). At its meeting on 16 February 1944 the AARC discussed the question of exchanges in districts where large numbers of coloured troops were stationed. The minutes record:

There are obvious difficulties about arranging inter-attachments with coloured units, and, if exchanges were made with white units in these districts and not with coloured units, accusations of discrimination might be made. It was agreed that no inter-attachments in these districts would be made until the matter had been referred to high level on both US and British sides.[28]

Thereafter the question was quietly dropped, and no exchanges with black units were arranged even though by D-Day they constituted about nine per cent of the US Army in Britain.

Despite these difficulties, the verdict on the programme as a whole was overwhelmingly favourable. Often the effects were long-term: subsequent social

---

of the 8th Air Force had visited British units for an average of 24 hours; 3,638 soldiers of the 9th Air Force had paid visits averaging six hours; and 383 troops of the Air Service Command had been attached to British units for periods of two to three days. Two-thirds of those involved were flying personnel. Four-fifths visited RAF units, the rest visited units of the British Army. See RG 332, ETO, AG, GC, box 59, 091.711 (1944), vol. i.

[25] Hq Chief Surgeon, ETO to AARC, 1 June 1944, RG 332, ETO, G-1, box 7, 092, and AAR/M (44) Minutes 28, 32, 39 and 46, WO 163/222.

[26] AAR/M (44) 3rd Meeting, Minute 15, 15 Mar. 1944.

[27] Ibid., Minutes 35, 39 and 46.   [28] Ibid., Minute 10.

visits between those exchanged, and even requests by men to spend their 48 hours' leave with the units to which they had been attached. Sporting events and reciprocal invitations to special shows and entertainments also maintained and developed the initial contacts. The War Office and ETO received numerous reports testifying to the good effects of the scheme. For example, a captain, lieutenant, and five men from an American truck company were attached to a British transport company on the Upper Malone Road in Belfast. 'The British Officers stated, on more than one occasion, that the exchange of personnel is an excellent practice, which should have been adopted long ago, and which should be continued for the duration, at least.' As for the GIs, they were 'unanimous in saying that their attitude toward the British Army in general and toward the individual British soldier, was changed completely by their exchange tour of duty'.[29] Higher echelons echoed this opinion. FUSA HQ judged the scheme 'the best means yet attempted to create a better understanding between soldiers of the two armies and to promote better Anglo-American relations'.[30] In Northern Ireland, the US commander, General Wade H. Haislip, had welcomed the exchanges in January as an 'excellent' idea which would 'result in a great improvement in the mutual understanding between our two armies'; by mid-February his staff were already pronouncing it 'a great success' on the basis of censorship reports of soldiers' letters; and in April Haislip's British counterpart, General Sir Alan Cunningham, concurred 'that on our side too we know from all available sources that the feelings of the British troops towards the Americans are proceeding rapidly towards comradeship and admiration'.[31] For its part, the War Office was delighted. Sir Ronald Adam commended the exchanges to the commander of British forces in the Middle East, where relations between British and US soldiers were strained in early 1944. On 2 February he wrote: 'As you know, we have had similar troubles among troops in the UK, but things are much better now here, and I think this is very largely due to the scheme of inter-attachments', which was proving 'a far greater success than we ever hoped for'. Those involved, he said, 'invariably have not only a far better knowledge but a far friendlier opinion of their opposite numbers.... In fact, there is general agreement here that the thing is a 100 per cent success.'[32]

From the reports we can also learn something of the character of the two armies. The soldiers involved were probably struck most of all by the contrasting degrees of hierarchy. The US Army was in many ways an 'unAmerican'

[29] Hq, Co. 'I', 513th QM Truck Regiment, report, 23 Dec. 1943, RG 332, ETO, AG, CGC, box 474, 092.   [30] FUSA report cited in note 23.
[31] Haislip to Cunningham, 21 Jan. 1944, and Cunningham to Haislip, 1 Apr. 1944, Wade H. Haislip papers, box 1 (Hoover Institution, Stanford Univ.); Base Censor Office 1 to Theater Censor, ETO, 'Digest of Morale Reports', 1–15 Feb. 1944, RG 332, ETO, Administrative History Collection (Adm.) 212.
[32] Adam to General Sir Bernard Paget, 28 Feb. 1944, WO 32/10268.

institution: regimented, stratified and calibrated with special privileges for particular ranks, it contrasted strikingly with the values of American civilian life. Nevertheless, these features were far less marked than in the British army, and Americans participating in the attachment programme commented frequently on the greater distinctions made between officers, NCOs, and 'other ranks' (enlisted men). Even officers found British military etiquette bizarre and sometimes trying. One American, attached to a British military hospital near Southampton, held forth in a letter home about the officers' mess:[33]

In the Mess at supper I mentioned how beautiful Ingrid Bergman was. 'Be careful, sir,' someone said. 'There is a fine of drinks all round if you mention girls in this Mess, simply not done.'! I could write a paper on the formal English Army Mess. Other topics which are taboo are religion and money, which limits the discourse to polo, cricket, dogs and the war. You may tell jokes, but they must be from Punch and you must always quote Punch as your authority. This morning I dunked my toast and the chappie alongside said, 'I remember so well 8 years ago seeing a man who had been to America doing that in the mess—bit of a shock you know!' He hadn't gotten over it yet . . . . There is no loud talking and laughter, only after being here a month now is anyone speaking to me voluntarily. I have learned to eat in silence and my digestion is excellent. I have lost 11 lbs on British food. In justice to these men I must say that the Colonel was a prisoner in Italy, my chief returned from Africa after his hospital had been blown up, another officer escaped from Germany, many went through Calais and Dunkirk, and during air-raids they show no emotion—really excellent officers, my experience here has heightened my respect for their sterling qualities. In their way the English are all right.

The customs of the service evoked most comment in connection with the place of the NCO (or non-com, as the Americans called him). By early 1944 nearly 40 per cent of enlisted men in the US army were non-coms—about 2.5 million out of 6.5 million—and by the end of the war the figure was nearly half.[34] Not only was the proportion of NCOs to privates far less in the British army, but NCOs were also quartered and messed separately from their men—a further, striking contrast with American practice. In consequence, British NCOs played a different role in their units from that of their American counterparts. One report, from the 5th US Infantry Division in Northern Ireland noted: 'The British non-commissioned officer is highly trained, commands great respect and performs many of the duties normally done by a commissioned officer in the US Army.'[35] An American staff sergeant observed after two weeks with a British Ambulance Car Company near St Ives in Cornwall: 'I think the non-coms in the British Army have more responsibility than we do. A corporal has to set up and take care of a section, which includes drawing rations, picking his camping site,

[33] MI12 report on US soldiers' mail, 1–20 Sept. 1943, FO 371/34126, A 9114/33/45.

[34] Samuel A. Stouffer, et al., *The American Soldier: I, Adjustment during Army Life* (Princeton, 1949), 238–9.

[35] Extract from report by Commander, 5th US Infantry Division, WO 163/53, AC/G (44) 19, Appendix A.

preparing of food, camouflage and paying his men.'[36] On the merits of the British procedure, opinion was more divided than one might expect. Some British soldiers commented favourably about the lack of 'class distinction' in the US Army, but others felt that the mixing of NCOs and men placed the former in an invidious position and led to casualness and disrespect.[37] Quite a few GIs seem to have approved of the British practice and felt it contributed to good discipline and morale, but there was also a feeling that it stifled initiative—'They never tell them anything. The [men] rely too much on the NCOs.'[38] On the whole this seems to have been the general American judgement. Despite greater respect for and understanding of British army organization, they preferred their own and felt that US Army methods were more flexible and fostered greater individual enterprise.

Other features of army life provoked outspoken comment. British sanitation got low marks from the GIs, especially in the messes. 'It was felt that mess gear could not be kept properly clean because of the lack of adequate or hot wash waters.' One US lieutenant, who took his men to a British signals unit at High Wycombe, concluded: 'I think without exception no medical officer of the American Army would pass any of the mess facilities, either those in permanent camps or in the field of the British Army.'[39] On the other hand, the GIs felt that the British had a more civilized working day. Not only was it somewhat shorter, but there were also half-hour breaks mid-morning and a longer lunch hour (one and a half hours instead of one).[40] In addition, passes were issued on a more liberal basis. On food, comparisons were generally in the Americans' favour. The GI's ration was substantially larger than that of his British counterpart, and it was renowned for the availability of fruit, fruit juices, and sweetstuffs. A US captain felt moved to provide extra cookies for one of his men 'who hasn't been able to get enough to eat after spending two weeks with the British'.[41] But British army cooking received good marks, at least from GIs in Northern Ireland. The report from the 5th Infantry summed up in the words of one lieutenant: 'Although their food ration lacks variety and quality such as we have, their preparation is superior and the food is served in an appetizing manner.' The report added 'The same opinion was expressed regarding the enlisted men's messes.'[42]

[36] Staff Sergeant Herman A. Sordyl, 564th Amb. Co., Motor., report, enclosed in Lieutenant William H. Godfrey to CG, FUSA, 14 Mar. 1944, Records of 1st US Army, World War II, RG 338, AG, GC, box 94, 092/50 (National Archives, Washington, DC).

[37] Report of Head Censor, Military Base Censorship, Northern Ireland, on mail of British units, Feb. 1944, WO 163/53, AC/G (44) 19, Appendix B.

[38] PFC John J. Buckley, report, enclosed in Godfrey to CG, FUSA, cited in note 36.

[39] 5th US Infantry Division report, p. 3, cited in note 35; Lieutenant Albert Wootten, Hq, 17th Signal Operation Battalion, report, 24 Jan. 1944, RG 338, FUSA, AG, GC, box 94, 092/50.

[40] Wootten, report, p. 2. Cf. Hq, 29th Infantry Division, General Order 43, 20 Nov. 1942, RG 332, ETO, AG, CGC, 250.1 (1943, Vol. I).

[41] Captain Theodore H. Fossieck to Janice Fossieck, 26 Feb. 1944, p. 4 (Fossieck papers, US Army Military History Institute, Carlisle Barracks, Pennsylvania).

[42] 5th Infantry Division report, p. 1.

Pay, of course, provided the most glaring contrast. The GIs were usually instructed to avoid the topic, but it was almost invariably raised by their British counterparts in a forthright though usually not hostile manner. Though the Tommies sometimes blamed the British government, they told the GIs frankly about the discrepancy and about the way American openhandedness had caused offence. Indeed, visits to US camps sometimes exacerbated the problem, because the British discovered the very low price, relatively, that GIs paid for cigarettes in their post-exchanges.[43] On the other hand, the GIs were able to explain the extent of Army savings schemes and the higher cost of living in the USA, and a survey of mail from British units taking part in inter-attachment schemes in Northern Ireland concluded that 'It would seem that much good has been done by free and friendly discussions on the vexed question of pay.'[44]

This, overall, seems to have been the effect of the programme. Sometimes it aggravated differences and suggested new grievances; occasionally it confirmed existing stereotypes. In general, however, it vindicated the expectation that familiarity would breed understanding, that prejudices and grouses could be aired and dispelled as soldiers lived and worked together. Seeing the GIs in tough training helped the British to transcend stereotypes of American luxury and self-indulgence derived from the movies and reinforced by off-duty contact in pubs. Conversely, the US soldiers learned to penetrate behind British reserve and social nuance and to respect British practices even if they concluded that ultimately they preferred their own. Sometimes conversion could be total, as indicated by these comments from the US lieutenant stationed near High Wycombe:

My men were very frankly told about a week after they arrived that the [British] soldiers had not looked forward particularly to our being attached. They said that most Americans they had observed were very rowdy and loud and seemed only intent on bragging about what they were doing to win the war. They then qualified this by saying that their opinion had been changed completely after living so closely together with our men.[45]

Many reports also concluded that fundamentally the similarities were more striking than the differences. According to the commander of an American engineer battalion, interviews with soldiers exchanged revealed 'that the characteristics of the British and American soldier are *basically* the same and that underneath the individual and national idiosyncracies there is a foundation for mutual understanding and friendship in arms'.[46]

Although only about 10,000 troops took part in the full scheme, the shorter visits and social contacts that it spawned added considerably to the number affected, and there must have been a further ripple effect as participants shared

[43] e.g. AAR/M (44) 1st Meeting, Minute 3, 12 Jan. 1944, WO 163/222.
[44] Head Censor's report, cited in note 37.   [45] Wootten, report, p. 2, cited in note 39.
[46] Major Robert O. Haas, Hq, 86th Engineers Heavy Pontoon Battalion to CG, FUSA, 22 Jan. 1944, RG 338, FUSA, AG, box 94, 092/50.

experiences and conclusions with their compatriots. Other schemes in 1943–44 were also designed to improve relations between British and US troops, such as the 'Anglo-American Legion' and the development of allied servicemen's clubs, but inter-attachment was probably the most successful. As the War Office's report on the morale of British Home Forces for the late winter of 1943–44 concluded:

There has been a steady improvement in relations between British and US troops, and the interchange of visits between personnel of the two Forces has helped considerably. A consencus [sic] of opinion reveals that the interchange of visits has been highly satisfactory both educationally and socially and is one of the most profitable means of promoting better Anglo-American relations.[47]

It is instructive to identify precedents for the inter-attachment programme of 1943–44. For instance, between March and August 1918 troops from some ten US divisions were trained for combat with British units in France. The Americans were attached by battalion to British brigades for about ten weeks at a time. They used British weapons and ammunition and were fed on the Tommy's rations (except that the rum allowance was omitted).[48] The US War Department had intended to include the 92nd Infantry Division—a black unit—but in May 1918 it heard through the British Military Attaché in Washington 'that the British War Office is strongly against the attachment of any battalion of coloured infantry for training with the British', and despite representations from General Pershing, the Commander of the American Expeditionary Force, the idea was dropped and the 92nd attached to the French instead.[49] Another Great War precursor of inter-attachment was the programme of training for US aircrews and mechanics at RFC and RAF depots in England. At its peak in September 1918 some 16,000 men were involved. Initially the Americans messed with the British, but differences in taste, such as American preferences for a big evening meal, their dislike of heavy puddings and the notorious Australian rabbits, and the unbridgeable gulf between tea drinkers and coffee drinkers gradually led to separate messes.[50]

In both these instances from World War I the primary emphasis was on training rather than fraternization. A predecessor of inter-attachment that is closer both in time and spirit to the scheme of 1943–44 involved the British

[47] Morale report, Home Forces, Feb.–April 1944, MC/P (44) 5, WO 163/162. All in all, the evidence does not bear out Norman Longmate's assertion that the exchanges 'seem to have strengthened existing prejudices rather than removed them'. Norman Longmate, *The GIs: The Americans in Britain, 1942–1945* (London, 1975), 100.

[48] USA, Department of the Army, Historical Division, *United States Army in the World War, 1917–1919* (Washington, 1948), 1–237; C/S, AEF to Colonel George S. Simonds, 20 Feb. 1918, records of the American Expeditionary Force, World War I, RG 120, AEF, GHQ, AG file, entry 6, file 12856-G (National Archives, Washington, DC).

[49] Ibid., file 16637: quotation from War Department to GHQ, AEF, tel. 1237, 3 May 1918.

[50] 'History of the Operations of Base Section 3' (TS., 7 vols), ch. 15, RG 120, entry 2473.

Expeditionary Force (BEF) in France in the winter of 1939–40. There, it is interesting to note, the British troops stood in much the same relationship to the French soldiers and civilians as the GIs to the British a few years later. Exuberant behaviour by off-duty Tommies, complaints about drunkenness and occasional molesting of French women—these are recurrent themes of reports from British consuls around France. Above all, there was much ill-feeling about the disparity in pay between British and French troops—'*les quinze francs des Anglais and les quinze sous des Français*'.[51] (All this, incidentally, is a reminder that we are dealing with problems that afflict every army, particularly on foreign soil, rather than vices peculiar to the American character, as some Britons liked to think.) The desire to reduce Anglo-French friction led to the attachment of British brigades for three-week periods to the French 3rd Army on the Saar front. This scheme began at the end of November 1939 and nine brigades took part before the whole 51st Division was moved in at the beginning of May 1940, just before the German offensive began.

The BEF showed great foresight in preparing for the exchanges—'Some knowledge of French is desirable,' it reminded commanders!—and it was well pleased by the results. The British Liaison Officer with the 3rd Army reported in January 1940 that already the scheme 'has been a great success from the point of view of instruction to our troops, and of liaison between the Armies'. He explained that since a brigade 'was only a small and not tactically an independent unit, the contact between British and French troops has necessarily been extremely intimate with the best possible results on both sides'. Similarly General Condé, the 3rd Army Commander, told General Gamelin that '*le séjour d'une brigade anglaise dans mon secteur a eu les meilleurs résultats.... La vie côte à côte, dans une ambiance de guerre véritable, a créé, aussi bien entre les officiers qu'entre les soldats des deux nations, des liens très puissants de camaraderie de combat et de confiance réciproque du plus haut intérêt.*'[52]

There is no indication, however, that in 1943–44 the War Office recalled these precedents from 1918 and 1940. The evidence available suggests that it was most influenced by AFHQ's experiences in the Western Desert. Later in 1944 there was talk of a similar inter-attachment programme for British and US troops on the continent of Europe. An Anglo-American Relations Committee was set up there under the control of SHAEF (Supreme Headquarters, Allied Expeditionary Force) and at its first meeting on 1 November 1944 there was general agreement that if possible the exchange programme should be repeated among troops on the continent. In an active theatre, however, this proved difficult, particularly after the chaos caused by the German Ardennes

[51] 'Note on the Morale of French Soldiers', 18 Apr. 1940, FO 371/24310, C 6306/65/17.

[52] Quotations from DCGS, GHQ, BEF to I and II Corps, 17 Nov. 1939, Major W.D.E. Williams to DCGS, 11 Jan. 1940, and Condé to Général d'Armée, 18 Jan. 1940, in WO 197/33. For fuller details on the scheme see this file, WO 197/43 and L. F. Ellis, *The War in France and Flanders, 1939–1940* (London, 1953), 20, 249–52, 262–93.

counter-offensive of December 1944. By the time the committee considered the matter again, on 7 March 1945, the alliance structure was beginning to disintegrate in the face of impending victory, redeployment, and demobilization, and nothing further was done.[53]

Wartime alliance was the precondition for all these exchange schemes. After World War II, just as happened after the Great War, the erstwhile allies went their own ways, reverting to the norm of preparing for individual national wars. But the commitment of UN troops to Korea in 1950 again created similar problems and necessitated similar solutions. For instance, in South Korea in October 1950 the Americans set up a special UN Reception Centre (UNRC) to process units from such diverse allies as Thailand, France, Greece, and Turkey. Apart from retraining and weapons familiarization, the UNRC confronted delicate cultural problems. A meat-less ration had to be devised for Moslem Turks, and it was discovered that US-made boots and clothing would not fit the smaller-sized Thais.[54] But this time the lessons of coalition war were not entirely lost. In the wake of the North Korean attack and the concurrent alarm about Soviet intentions in Europe, the North Atlantic Treaty Organization was transformed into a full-scale military alliance. There was even talk in the early 1950s about an integrated NATO army and, although little came of this idea, permanent arrangements were evolved to promote cooperation between allied forces. From the beginning of NATO both US and British authorities were enthusiastic about exchanges of officers among their units in Germany.[55] It became standard practice to exchange US and British officers between staffs, colleges, and training courses right down to company commander level.

Nevertheless, it would seem that the inter-attachment scheme of 1943–44 was unusual in two respects. It was aimed mainly at other ranks rather than officers, and its principal object was not training but the promotion of mutual understanding and respect. In part the story of the scheme is an interesting sidelight on Anglo-American relations in World War II. But it also has a larger significance. Since 1950 the development of NATO and the use of UN and other 'peace-keeping' forces have made national governments more sensitive to the need for 'inter-operability'. The central obstacles are those of language, close liaison and standardization of codes, organization, doctrine and equipment—issues that have to be solved primarily at the command and staff levels. But the inter-attachment programme of 1943–44 reminds us of the grass-roots aspect of inter-operability: alliances have to be forged at the bottom as well as the top.

[53] See Minutes in WO 219/1424.

[54] See Hixson and Cooling, 'Combined Operations', ch.8, esp. pp. 231–3.

[55] FO 371/97625, esp. AU 10202/2. 'I am all for these exchanges', wrote Anthony Eden, the Foreign Secretary, on 5 July 1952. Eden had also headed the Foreign Office during the period of the World War II scheme.

V

COLD WAR

13

Churchill, Roosevelt, and the Stalin Enigma, 1941–1945

As the Second World War progressed, the Anglo-American couple became part of a *ménage à trois*. But the Soviet Union proved a difficult and unpredictable bedfellow. In a radio broadcast on 1 October 1939, Churchill described Russian foreign policy as 'a riddle wrapped in a mystery inside an enigma'. In September 1944, the American diplomat George F. Kennan felt no wiser, writing that 'Russia remains today, more than ever, an enigma for the western world'.[1] In the early twenty-first century, such puzzlement may seem surprising. The rise of the superpowers seems inevitable, their ideological enmity axiomatic, and the brutality of Stalinism all too clear. Yet we need to recall the uncertainties about Russia that bedevilled the wartime alliance. At the heart of the enigma was the personality of Stalin himself.

During the Cold War, Roosevelt and Churchill attracted frequent criticism in the West for their handling of Stalin. The Yalta conference, February 1945, became the wartime analogue of Munich, September 1938, as a synonym for appeasement.[2] However, the pass had already been sold by early 1945, because a Soviet presence in Eastern Europe was the result not of diplomacy (an Anglo-American sellout) but of strategy (the delayed second front). The war of attrition that Churchill persuaded Roosevelt to wage in 1942–3 plus the unanticipated delays in taking North Africa and then Italy meant that the land war in Europe was largely decided on the Eastern Front. Between June 1941 and June 1944 (from Barbarossa to D-Day), 93 per cent of the German armed forces' combat losses were inflicted by the Soviets. In cold figures that meant 4.2 million dead,

---

This chapter was originally presented to a conference on 'Stalin and the Cold War' at Yale University in September 1999, held under the aegis of the Cold War International History Project. For a fuller study of British assumptions, published after this essay was written, see Martin H. Folly, *Churchill, Whitehall and the Soviet Union, 1940–45* (London, 2000).

[1] Winston S. Churchill, *Into Battle* (London, 1941), 131; George F. Kennan, memo, 'Russia—Seven Years Later', Sept. 1944, in *FRUS*, 1944, iv. 911.

[2] On the American side, the classic study is Athan G. Theoharis, *The Yalta Myths, 1945–1955: An Issue in U.S. Politics, 1945–1955* (Columbia, Mo., 1970).

wounded, or missing on the Eastern Front, against 329,000 elsewhere.[3] Once the Soviets won that titanic battle, it was likely that they would end up deep in Eastern and East-Central Europe. That did not make the Cold War inevitable, but it shaped the geopolitical position after 1945.

Since all that seems evident in retrospect, one might ask why Roosevelt and Churchill were not more concerned. In part, the answer is sheer necessity. Waging war was the priority in 1942–3. If, as Churchill believed and Roosevelt accepted, an early cross-Channel attack was impossible, that meant keeping the Russians going as Allied proxies. The fears in London and Washington in mid-1943 that Moscow might again do a deal with Berlin made them more willing to acknowledge Stalin's territorial concerns at Teheran in November.[4] On the other hand, as we saw in Chapter 5, in the middle of the war Churchill did not rule out a negotiated peace with an alternative, non-Nazi German government following a German collapse akin to the end of the Great War. Roosevelt also recalled the 1918 precedent in March 1943, during talks with Anthony Eden, the British Foreign Secretary, which centred on policy after 'the collapse of Germany'.[5] FDR's desire at this time for an early meeting with Stalin reflected the same concern. A draft telegram prepared by the President in December 1942 stressed the need to formulate 'emergency policies we should be ready with if and when Germany collapses'.[6]

In January 1943, however, at Casablanca Roosevelt articulated a doctrine of total victory. And by the summer of 1943, with the Red Army surging into the Ukraine and Anglo-American forces about to land in Italy, it was likely that the war would end in enforced occupation of Germany. The need to concert policy became urgent: hence the conferences of Foreign Ministers in Moscow in October and of the Big Three at Teheran at the end of November. Britain and America now had to face up to the prospect of the Soviet Union as a force in European politics.

Broadly, there were two contrasting perceptions of the post-war Russian question: that the Soviet Union would be an expansionist threat driven by a mixture of ideology and imperialism, or that it would be an obstreperous but essentially cooperative partner, concerned for some years primarily with security and reconstruction. In Washington in early 1943 the first position was identified particularly with the former Ambassador to Moscow, William C. Bullitt. His ideas were taken up by the Joint Chiefs of Staff to add weight to their calls for an early cross-Channel attack. Admiral Ernest J. King, the Chief of Naval Operations, warned his colleagues that, unless London and Washington made 'some definite moves toward the defeat of Germany, Russia would dominate the peace table'.[7]

---

[3] Jonathan R. Adelman, *Prelude to the Cold War: The Tsarist, Soviet, and U.S. Armies in the Two World Wars* (Boulder, Colo., 1988), 128.

[4] Vojtech Mastny, *Russia's Road to the Cold War: Diplomacy, Warfare and the Politics of Communism, 1941–1945* (New York, 1979), 84–5.   [5] *FRUS* 1943, iii. 42, cf. pp. 17, 34, 36.

[6] Draft telegram, 8 Dec. 1942, Map Room papers, box 8 (FDRL). The version eventually sent to Stalin read '. . . if and when conditions in Germany permit'.

[7] Mark A. Stoler, *The Politics of the Second Front: American Planning and Diplomacy in Coalition Warfare, 1941–1943* (Westport, Conn., 1977), 85–91, quoting p. 88. Bullitt's key memos are

In London fears of a long-term Russian threat were articulated in the summer of 1944 by parts of the military, notably the Post-Hostilities Planning Staff, based largely on an assessment of potential Soviet capabilities. These fears were echoed by the Chiefs of Staff, who warned in July 1944 that, despite the concern to keep Germany down after the war, 'the more remote, but more dangerous, possibility of a hostile Russia making use of the resources of Germany must not be lost sight of'. Sir Alan Brooke, Chief of the Imperial General Staff, noted in his diary:

Germany is no longer the dominating power of Europe, Russia is. Unfortunately Russia is not entirely European. She has however vast resources and cannot fail to become the main threat in 15 years from now. Therefore foster Germany, gradually build her up, bring her into a federation of Western Europe. Unfortunately this must all be done under the cloak of a holy alliance between England, Russia and America.[8]

Roosevelt, however, consistently dismissed what he called 'the Bullitt thesis that the Soviet Government was determined to dominate all of Europe by force of arms or by force of communist propaganda'. Instead, as historian Warren F. Kimball has emphasized, the President sought to draw the Soviet Union into what he called 'the family circle' and to make it one of the 'policemen' who would ensure peace and stability in the post-war world. In London, the cooperative instinct was embodied in Anthony Eden and many senior Foreign Office officials, who believed it imperative to create a working relationship with the Soviet Union. In February 1943, Eden told the Ambassador in Moscow that 'to facilitate and encourage Soviet co-operation in the post-war settlement ... it is essential that His Majesty's Government should treat the Soviet Government as partners.'[9]

Churchill oscillated between these two positions. A vehement critic after the 1917 Revolution of what he called 'the foul baboonery of Bolshevism', he never entirely lost his hatred of Soviet ideology or his fears of Russian imperialism. 'It would be a measureless disaster,' he told Eden in November 1942, 'if Russian barbarism overlaid the culture and independence of the ancient States of Europe.'[10] By 1943 he acknowledged that Britain would have to live in a Europe in which 'the overwhelming preponderance of Russia' would be 'the dominant

---

printed in large part in Orville H. Bullitt, ed., *For the President, Personal and Secret: Correspondence between Franklin D. Roosevelt and William C. Bullitt* (London, 1973), ch. 31.

[8] 'Comments by the Chiefs of Staff on Policy towards Western Europe', 27 July 1944, FO 371/ 40725, folio 102 (TNA); Field-Marshal Lord Alanbrooke, *War Diaries, 1939–1945*, ed. Alex Danchev and Daniel Todman (London, 2001), 575, entry for 27 July 1944.

[9] Warren F. Kimball, *The Juggler: Franklin Roosevelt as Wartime Statesman* (Princeton, 1991), 83 ff.; Graham Ross, ed., *The Foreign Office and the Kremlin: British Documents on Anglo-Soviet Relations, 1941–1945* (Cambridge, 1984), 121. For overviews see Edward M. Bennett, *Franklin D. Roosevelt and the Search for Victory: American-Soviet Relations, 1939–1945* (Wilmington, Del., 1990); Martin Kitchen, *British Policy towards the Soviet Union during the Second World War* (London, 1986).

[10] Speech of 19 Feb. 1919, quoted in Martin Gilbert, *Winston S. Churchill*, vol. iv (London, 1975), 257; Churchill to Eden, M474/2, 21 Oct. 1942, PREM 4/100/7 (TNA).

fact of the future' but asserted 'we shall certainly try to live on good terms with her'.[11] Despite abrupt shifts of mood, that remained his objective. Even in the last months of the European war, when he urged redeployment of forces in northern Germany and north-east Italy to pre-empt Russian territorial gains (the thrusts toward Berlin and Vienna discussed in Chapter 6), this was to strengthen his hand for the peace conference rather than to embark on military confrontation.[12]

Thus, the majority of leading policy-makers in London and Washington, particularly politicians and diplomats, inclined toward a policy of cooperation rather than confrontation during that second half of the wartime alliance. There were, of course, tactical differences between those favouring an open-handed approach as opposed to tough quid pro quo bargaining as the better way to achieve a working partnership. In the United States, Roosevelt exemplified the first, Averell Harriman the second; in Britain, one might counterpose Eden against Brooke. Churchill, again, wavered between the two poles. With regard to Central and Eastern Europe, as is well known, cooperationists advocated an understanding on 'spheres of influence', in fact if not name (because these were dirty words in the State Department and on Capitol Hill). Churchill's percentages agreement in Moscow in October 1944, after the Red Army's spectacular summer offensive, was an attempt to reach a deal on the Balkans before it was too late, building on an earlier understanding in May about the relative significance of Romania to the Soviet Union and of Greece to Great Britain. He and FDR made their gruelling journeys to Yalta the following February in the same spirit. The President, unconsciously anticipating the famous words of Stalin to Milovan Djilas, is recorded as telling Senators before he left Washington that

although spheres of influence had been mulled over at Teheran the idea kept coming up because the occupying forces had the power in the areas where their arms were present and each knew that the others could not force things to an issue. He stated that the Russians had the power in Eastern Europe, that it was obviously impossible to have a break with them and that, therefore, the only practicable course was to use what influence we had to ameliorate the situation.[13]

It is also widely accepted by historians that British and American policy-makers, again with different degrees of emphasis, hoped for spheres that were 'open' rather than 'exclusive', to quote the distinction popularized by Eduard Mark based on the ideas of State Department officials such as

[11] Note by Prime Minister, probably 12 Apr. 1943, PREM 4/30/11 (TNA).
[12] My view of Churchill contrasts with that of David Carlton, *Churchill and the Soviet Union* (Manchester, 2000), esp. 200, 204–14, that Churchill's wartime 'appeasement' of Stalin was largely a tactical ploy by a consistent ideological opponent of the Soviet Union.
[13] Memo of 11 Jan. 1945, in Thomas M. Campbell and George C. Herring, eds., *The Diaries of Edward R. Stettinius, Jr., 1943–1946* (New York, 1975), 214. In April 1945 Stalin told Djilas: 'This war is not as in the past; whoever occupies a territory also imposes on it his own social system. Everyone imposes his own system as far as his army has the power to do so. It cannot be otherwise.' Milovan Djilas, *Conversations with Stalin*, trans. Michael B. Petrovich (London, 1962), 105.

Charles E. Bohlen.[14] Tolerably free elections, plus some degree of openness to trade and ideas, were the minimum conditions. Hence the Declaration on Liberated Europe at Yalta and the deal on reconstructing the Polish government. Even hard-headed diplomats such as Sir Alexander Cadogan, the Permanent Under-Secretary at the Foreign Office, returned from Yalta genuinely hopeful: 'We have got an agreement on Poland which may heal differences, for some time at least, and assure some degree of independence to the Poles.'[15]

Historians have shown more interest in the unravelling of the Yalta agreements in 1945 than in the assumptions on which they were based. Yet it is worth asking why policy-makers in London and Washington were so hopeful that Stalin could be co-opted into a post-war concert, based on an open sphere of influence for the Soviet Union in Eastern Europe. Three Anglo-American assumptions, spoken or tacit, should be noted.

The first was the expectation that there would be no long-term American presence in Europe after the war. Since this runs counter to the whole history of the Cold War, it deserves to be underlined. In April 1943, for instance, Churchill observed: 'We must not expect that the United States will keep large armies in Europe for long after the war. Indeed, I doubt whether there will be any American troops in Europe four years after the "Cease Firing".'[16] Roosevelt made the point explicitly on several occasions. Asked by General George C. Marshall in November 1943 how long it would be necessary to keep an occupation force in Germany, he said 'for at least one year, maybe two'. That same month, at Teheran, when discussing with Stalin the application of his policemen concept to Europe, the President said that 'England and the Soviet Union would have to handle the land armies in the event of any future threat to the peace' because he 'only envisaged the sending of American planes and ships to Europe'.[17] And he told Churchill in February 1944: 'I am absolutely unwilling to police France and possibly Italy and the Balkans as well. After all, France is your baby and will take a lot of nursing in order to bring it to the point of walking alone.'[18] The implications of such comments were not lost in Whitehall (or presumably the Kremlin). They disposed British policy-makers to seek cooperation because of the superiority of Russian power, particularly on land and in Europe. To adapt Churchill at Teheran: 'the poor little English donkey' was in no position alone to stand up to 'the great Russian bear'.[19]

---

[14] Eduard Mark, 'American Policy toward Eastern Europe and the Origins of the Cold War, 1941–1946: An Alternative Interpretation', *Journal of American History*, 68 (1981), esp. 319–20.

[15] David Dilks, ed., *The Diaries of Sir Alexander Cadogan, OM, 1938–1945* (London, 1971), 709.

[16] Note by Prime Minister, probably 12 Apr. 1943, PREM 4/30/11 (TNA).

[17] *FRUS: The Conferences at Cairo and Tehran, 1943* (1961), 256, 531.

[18] Roosevelt to Churchill, 7 Feb. 1944, R-457, in Warren F. Kimball, ed., *Churchill and Roosevelt: The Complete Correspondence* (3 vols., Princeton, 1984), ii, 709.

[19] John Wheeler-Bennett, ed., *Action this Day: Working with Churchill* (London, 1968), 96.

The assumption of American disengagement, at least from heartland Europe, may explain why there seemed little choice but to concede a Soviet sphere of influence. But it does not explain the expectation that this sphere would be tolerably open. Here we need to adduce two other assumptions: about Stalin as a person and 'Stalinism' as a system.

During the wartime alliance, the conviction grew—to borrow the phrase famously used by Margaret Thatcher after her first meeting with Mikhail Gorbachev in 1984—that Stalin was a man with whom you could do business. One needs to remember how remote the Kremlin leadership was to Western observers before 1941. Diplomatic staff had minimal opportunity for contacts with Russian officials, let alone the ordinary population; even Ambassadors rarely had meetings with Stalin; and the Soviet press provided virtually no useful political information, in stark contrast with the hothouse atmosphere of the media in Washington. Then, suddenly, the doors to the Kremlin opened. Harry Hopkins and Averell Harriman, Max Beaverbrook and Anthony Eden all spent hours with Stalin in the second half of 1941. Churchill met him for extended summits on four occasions before VE-Day and Roosevelt for two. Of course, Stalin was a difficult, often truculent, interlocutor. In 1941–2 Harriman and Beaverbrook, Eden and then Churchill were all subject to the one, two, three treatment, in which a bruising middle meeting was sandwiched between cordial opening and closing sessions. But, equally important, what William Taubman calls 'the nasty second-session ploy' became familiar to Stalin's visitors and was accepted as one of his negotiating tactics.[20] It was less evident in the conferences in the second phase of the wartime alliance, from Teheran onward, and this in itself was taken as a sign of deepening trust.

Most visitors also developed a real respect for Stalin, while never entirely forgetting the terror on which his regime rested. 'I am sold on Stalin', noted Roosevelt's son-in-law John Boettiger, who accompanied the President to Teheran and who attended the social events. 'This comes from me after many years in which I have distrusted the Soviets, feared what they would try to do after the war is over. Stalin is not at all a colorful man, he has no magnetism, but he talks in a quiet, earthy manner which is convincing . . . And to have witnessed a beginning of molding friendship between him and FDR, with very obvious proofs of their liking for each other, gives me a greater sense of security for the future.'[21] Boettinger was not a seasoned observer, but here is a comment about Yalta from the diplomat Sir Alexander Cadogan, innately cynical about politicians in general and foreigners in particular:

I have never known the Russians so easy and accommodating. In particular Joe has been extremely good. He *is* a great man, and showed up very impressively against the

---

[20] William Taubman, *Stalin's American Policy: From Entente to Détente to Cold War* (New York, 1982), 46; cf. Ian Jacob, diary, 13 Aug. 1942, JACB 1/17 and Cadogan to Lady Theo, 14 Aug. 1942, ACAD 3/13 (both CAC).

[21] Diary entry, 30 Nov. 1943, in John Boettiger papers, box 13, p. 112 (FDRL).

background of the other two ageing statesmen . . . On the first day, he sat for the first hour and a half without saying a word—there was no call for him to do so! The President flapped about and the P[rime] M[inister] boomed, but Joe just sat taking it all in and being rather amused. When he did chip in, he never used a superfluous word, and spoke very much to the point. He's obviously got a very good sense of humour—and a rather quick temper.[22]

The terms 'Joe' or 'Uncle Joe' deserve comment. They had entered the private vocabulary of Roosevelt and Churchill by August 1942, before either man had met 'the Bear' for the first time.[23] Such nicknames suggest, of course, familiarity and approachability—the avuncular, pipe-smoking image of Soviet wartime propaganda. (A matching sobriquet, 'Auntie Mol', did not catch on in the Foreign Office because Molotov made himself so disagreeable.) The nicknames also sound faintly patronizing: British officials never referred to FDR as 'Franklin' let alone 'Uncle Frank'. At times, the condescension was explicit. In Moscow in August 1942, for instance, Churchill spoke privately (though also, we may presume, to NKVD bugs) about Stalin being 'a peasant' whom he, Churchill, knew exactly how to handle. The connotations of the first part of that remark are as important as the hubris of the second.[24]

The peasant image was partly the result of Stalin's attire in this phase of the war. One of the British party in Moscow in 1942, Colonel Ian Jacob, after describing Stalin's 'lilac-coloured tunic, buttoned up to the neck, his cotton trousers stuffed into long boots' and 'rather shambling walk', referred to him as 'this little peasant, who would not have looked at all out of place in a country lane with a pickaxe over his shoulder'.[25] In reality, Stalin was wearing standard party dress, but the idea that the Soviet leader was a provincial yokel who had hacked his way to the top helped British interlocutors to explain away his periodic roughness and vituperation. As one Foreign Office official put it, not entirely tongue-in-cheek: 'It's too bad that Stalin and Mol[otov] were not at Eton and Harrow, but what can we do about it?'[26]

Later in the war, Stalin's image changed dramatically. In his memoirs, Air Marshal Sir Arthur Tedder recalled his visit to the Kremlin in January 1945, having last been there with Churchill in August 1942:

I noticed one change in Stalin's office. On one wall, there were three or four life-sized paintings. In 1942, the portraits had been those of Karl Marx, Engels, and others. In 1945, they were of four field-marshals from Russian military history, including Suvarov [Suvorov]. There had also been a change as regards Stalin himself. In 1942, he had been

---

[22] Letters to his wife, in Dilks, ed., *Cadogan Diaries*, 708–9 and 706.

[23] Kimball, ed., *Churchill and Roosevelt*, i. 553.

[24] Lord Tedder, *With Prejudice: The War Memoirs of Marshal of the Royal Air Force Lord Tedder GCB* (London, 1966), 330.

[25] Diary, 14 Aug. 1942, printed in Charles Richardson, *From Churchill's Secret Circle to the BBC: The Biography of Lieutenant General Sir Ian Jacob, GBE, CB, DL* (London, 1991), 139.

[26] Geoffrey Wilson to Sir Archibald Clark Kerr, 15 May 1944, p. 3, FO 800/302 (TNA).

very much a civilian in his grey smock, breeches, and field boots. In 1945 he was in full sail as a field-marshal, suitably hung with red stars and similar appropriate decoration.[27]

Sir Archibald Clark Kerr, the British Ambassador in Moscow, dated the iconographic revolution more precisely to the summer of 1943, after the great tank battle at Kursk, which began the Soviet drive to Berlin. Reporting a meeting with Stalin on 13 August, he wrote: 'I was interested to notice that over the table at which we sat hung huge portraits of Suverov [*sic*] and Kutuzov. They had pushed enlarged photographs of Marx and Engels into a corner.'[28] As for the sartorial shift, Sir Alexander Cadogan, another member of Churchill's retinue in August 1942, had noted this at Teheran in November 1943, commenting that Stalin 'now wears a marshal's uniform which doesn't fit him or suit him ... he doesn't look at ease in it.'[29]

Stalin's adoption of military dress was part of his identification with the army after the successes of Stalingrad and Kursk. The use of heroes from the 'Patriotic War' against Napoleon reflected the deliberate evocation of Russian nationalism in the 'Great Patriotic War' against Hitler. Yet this transformation of Stalin from 'Boss' to 'Generalissimo' was not unsettling to his Western allies. Whereas Hitler in military uniform looked sinister, and Mussolini comical, Stalin's manner in conferences remained calm and often humorous. There was no sign of the Hitler rants or Mussolini bombast that many British diplomats had endured before the war. Even in uniform, Stalin did not seem like a dictator.

In other words, Stalin could probably be trusted—that became the axiom of summit diplomacy. Churchill made the point most remarkably after Yalta when he told junior ministers: 'Poor Neville Chamberlain believed he could trust Hitler. He was wrong. But I don't think I'm wrong about Stalin.'[30] Preparing an account of Yalta for the Commons, he wrote: 'Soviet Russia seeks not only peace, but peace with honour.' His private secretary Jock Colville scribbled against that phrase—'? omit. Echo of Munich.' Churchill did leave it out but he told the Commons on 27 February he was sure Stalin and the Soviet leaders wished 'to live in honourable friendship and equality with the Western democracies. I feel also that their word is their bond.'[31]

Like Chamberlain in September 1938, Churchill in February 1945 fell victim to the seductions of summitry, persuading himself that he had forged a genuine

---

[27] Tedder, *With Prejudice*, 646. Cf. Dmitri Volkogonov, *Stalin: Triumph and Tragedy*, trans. Harold Shukman (London, 1991), 464, who says that the military pictures were hung 'at the beginning of the war'. But Ian Jacob's record for 13 August 1942 is similar to Tedder's. He noted three pictures: 'one of Lenin making a speech, one of Lenin sitting at his desk, and one of Karl Marx.' Richardson, ed., *From Churchill's Secret Circle*, 136.

[28] Clark Kerr to FO, tel. 760, 13 Aug. 1943, copied in PREM 3/396/13 (TNA).

[29] Letter to his wife, 30 Nov. 1943, in Cadogan papers, ACAD 3/13 (CAC).

[30] Ben Pimlott, ed., *The Second World War Diary of Hugh Dalton, 1940–45* (London, 1986), 836, entry for 23 Feb. 1945.

[31] Winston S. Churchill, *The Second World War* (6 vols., London, 1948–54), vi. 351. For the amendment to speech draft see CHAR 9/206/126 (CAC).

personal relationship. The parallels with pre-war appeasement do not end there. One of the axioms of British policy-makers in the 1930s was an assumed polarity between 'moderates' and 'extremists' in Nazi Germany. Chamberlain, in particular, believed Hitler was teetering between the two and was therefore susceptible to diplomatic blandishments.[32] One can detect hints of the same typology in wartime thinking about Soviet policy. To appreciate this, one needs to remember that academic Sovietology was a creature of the Cold War. Little was known during the war about the structure of Soviet government, and assumptions about it were rudimentary in the extreme. As Stalin emerged into the rosy-hued spotlight of personal acquaintance, this threw into relief the sinister political gloom that surrounded him.

Consider, for instance, Churchill's interpretation of the bruising second session in Moscow in August 1942, in contrast with the constructive mood of their opening encounter. 'I think the most probable [explanation]', he told Roosevelt, 'is that his council of commissars did not take the news I brought [about no second front in Europe in 1942] as well as he did. They perhaps have more power than we suppose and less knowledge.'[33] Also instructive is his reaction to two messages from the Kremlin sent on the same day, 15 March 1943. The first spoke in warm terms about the British bombing of Germany and welcomed Churchill's offer of a new film about the recent successes of the 8th Army in the Western Desert. In return, Stalin promised a personal copy of the recent Soviet movie on Stalingrad. The second message, by contrast, was a formal and cold reiteration of the urgent need for a Second Front in 1943, ending with 'apprehension' about the 'vagueness' of Churchill's statements on the subject. Churchill called the first message 'the friendly personal telegram which Stalin sent evidently to take the edge off the official one'. He told Eden: 'Stalin's two telegrams to me of the 15th emphasize the feeling which has for some time been growing in my mind that there are two forces to be reckoned with in Russia: (a) Stalin himself, personally cordial to me. (b) Stalin in council, a grim thing behind him, which we and he have both to reckon with.'[34]

The image of Stalin as a relative moderate buffeted by dark and powerful political forces became a recurrent motif. On 16 October 1943, for instance,

---

[32] C. A. MacDonald, 'Economic Appeasement and the German "Moderates," 1937–1939: An Introductory Essay', *Past and Present*, 56 (1972), 105–35.

[33] Message C-131, 15 Aug. 1942, in Kimball, ed., *Churchill and Roosevelt*, i. 566.

[34] PM to Foreign Secretary, telegrams T318/2 and T320/3, 17 and 18 Feb. 1943, in CHAR 20/ 108 (CAC); cf. USSR Ministry of Foreign Affairs, *Correspondence between the Chairman of the Council of Ministers of the USSR and the Presidents of the USA and the Prime Ministers of Great Britain during the Great Patriotic War of 1941–1945* (2 vols., Moscow, 1957), vol. i, docs. 128 and 129. In line with Churchill's view of Kremlin politics as volatile and not monolithic, it is interesting that, in the first volume of his war memoirs, published in 1948, Churchill defied his research assistants and depicted the 1937 purges as Stalin's reaction to a genuine 'military and Old-Guard-Communist conspiracy to overthrow Stalin, and introduce a new regime based on a pro-German policy'. For details see David Reynolds, 'Churchill and *The Gathering Storm*', in David Cannadine and Roland Quinault, eds., *Winston Churchill in the Twenty-First Century* (Cambridge, 2004), 135–6.

Churchill copied to Roosevelt a long and fractious telegram from Stalin about convoys to Russia. The Prime Minister commented: 'I think or at least I hope this message came from the machine rather than from Stalin as it took 12 days to prepare. The Soviet machine is quite convinced it can get everything by bullying and I am sure it is a matter of some importance to show that this is not necessarily always true.'[35] During his 'percentages' meeting in Moscow in October 1944, Churchill cabled home: 'There is no doubt that in our narrow circle we have talked with an ease, freedom and beau gest[e] never before attained between our two countries. Stalin has made several expressions of personal regard which I feel sure were sincere. But I repeat my conviction that he is by no means alone. "Behind the horseman sits dull care." '[36]

Nor was this a peculiarly British way of thinking. During 1944 Harriman, as Ambassador to Moscow, developed his own two-camps theory of Soviet policy-making. 'Many of Stalin's counsellors', he told the State Department in September, 'see things to a degree at least as we do, whereas others are opposed. The Soviet Government is not of one mind. Through our actions we should attempt to encourage his [i.e. Stalin's] confidence in the advice of the former group and make him realize that the others get him into trouble when he follows their advice.'[37] Both Harriman and Roosevelt were prone to blame Soviet displays of truculence on unfriendly factions in the Politburo or on the failure of Molotov, Vyshinsky, or Soviet intelligence to provide Stalin with accurate information.[38]

This supposed dichotomy in the Kremlin helped British leaders to explain the deterioration in relations in the spring of 1945. Ernest Bevin, soon to become Foreign Secretary in the post-war Labour government, suggested in March that Molotov, not Stalin, might be responsible for Moscow's tougher line on the Polish government.[39] After reading Stalin's angry telegrams about German peace feelers to the Western allies, Churchill commented that *'the Soviet leaders, whoever they are*, are surprised and disconcerted at the rapid advance of the Allied armies in the west...'[40] And in mid-May Sir Orme Sargent, Deputy Under-Secretary at the Foreign Office, speculated that the new Soviet hard line in Eastern Europe stemmed from 'influences in Russia working independently of Stalin. These may either emanate from the Party bosses behind the scenes or

---

[35] Printed as message C-459 in Kimball, ed., *Churchill and Roosevelt*, ii. 553.

[36] PM to War Cabinet, tel. Hearty 167, 17 Oct. 1944, in CHAR 20/181 (CAC). The message is reproduced in Churchill, *Second World War*, vi. 208, with the final words rendered as 'black care'. This is possibly an allusion to the 19th-century poet, Charles Calverley, whose 'Ode to Tobacco' includes the lines: 'Thou, who when fears attack, Bidst them avaunt, and Black Care, at the horseman's back Perching, unseatest...' Or perhaps Churchill remembered the original words from one of Horace's Roman Odes.

[37] Harriman to SecState, 20 Sept. 1944, *FRUS 1944*, iv. 997–8, cf. p. 989.

[38] Dennis J. Dunn, *Caught between Roosevelt and Stalin: America's Ambassadors to Moscow* (Lexington, Ky. 1998), 139.

[39] War Cabinet, 6 Mar. 1945, WM 26 (45) 5 CA, CAB 65/51 (TNA).

[40] Message C-934, 5 Apr. 1945, in Kimball, ed., *Churchill and Roosevelt*, iii. 613 (my italics).

from the Army Marshals at the front' who wished to run their own shows without any Allied interference.[41]

The wartime alliance, therefore, was founded on faith in Stalin. But, and this takes me to the third assumption, it was also founded on hopes about 'Stalinism'. As with the other assumptions I have mentioned—about American neo-isolationism and Stalin's trustworthiness—we need to disabuse ourselves of Cold War hindsight. The term 'Stalinism' was in use in the United States by the mid-1930s, in a neutral sense, to denote the cumulative changes that distinguished Stalin's version of communism from that of Lenin. One theme was that the Bolshevik ideology of world revolution was now passé and that the West was dealing with something like a conventional great power. How benevolently to evaluate that power's intentions was a matter of debate, but the consensus during wartime was that Marxism itself, to quote the US Embassy in Moscow in early 1944, was 'an honored tradition rather than a living philosophy'.[42]

Hence the significance attached in public in America and Britain to the formal abolition of the Comintern in May 1943. A British government directive to the BBC described this as 'by far the most important political event of the war', signifying that international cooperation rather than class war would be the Soviet method for securing the peace.[43] Behind the scenes, officialdom was more sceptical about the Comintern's supposed demise, but it *was* impressed by signs of religious tolerance, particularly Stalin's decision in September 1943 to allow the Russian Orthodox Church to convene a Synod and appoint a new patriarch. This 'new religious freedom' was played up by sympathetic visiting clerics from the Church of England, commentators such as the BBC's Moscow correspondent Alexander Werth, and *Life* magazine's influential photojournalist Margaret Bourke-White.[44]

At the official level, appraisals of Soviet policy increasingly assumed a post-revolutionary and, in that sense, an increasingly 'normal' state. In January 1942, after his first visit to Moscow, Eden considered Stalin 'a political descendant of Peter the Great rather than Lenin'.[45] Similarly, a Foreign Office paper of April 1944 on post-war Soviet security policy stated: 'Externally the fixed point will be

[41] Sir Orme Sargent to Prime Minister, 14 May 1945, in PREM 3/396/14 (TNA).

[42] Eduard Mark, 'October or Thermidor?: Interpretations of Stalinism and the Perception of Soviet Foreign Policy in the United States, 1927–1947', *American Historical Review*, 94 (1989), 938 and 946 (quotation).

[43] Quoted in P. M. H. Bell, *John Bull and the Bear: British Public Opinion, Foreign Policy and the Soviet Union, 1941–1945* (London, 1990), 70. See John Lewis Gaddis, *The United States and the Origins of the Cold War, 1941–1947* (New York, 1972), 47–56; Kitchen, *British Policy toward the Soviet Union*, 157–8; Victor Rothwell, *Britain and the Cold War, 1941–1947* (London, 1982), 104–5.

[44] In reality, Stalin's sudden encouragement of Russian Orthodoxy, apart from its public relations value in the West, was prompted by the desire to use the Church as a convenient instrument for Russification as the Red Army advanced into the Ukraine and Poland, where the Uniate and Catholic churches acted as bastions of anti-Russian nationalism. See Steven Merritt Miner, *Stalin's Holy War: Religion, Nationalism, and Alliance Politics, 1941–1945* (Chapel Hill, NC, 2003), esp. chs. 4 and 8.   [45] Eden to Halifax, 22 Jan. 1942, FO 954/29A, fo. 361 (TNA).

in the future, as it has been in the past (at any rate, since Stalin's victory over Trotsky), the search for security against any Power or combination of Powers which might threaten her while she was organising and developing her own domain.'[46] This concept of 'Russia redux' helped resolve the Soviet enigma for many policy-makers and buttressed the idea that one could do business with Stalin.

But one should also consider 'Stalinism' from the angle of domestic policy because it betokened the related idea that, internally, the Soviet Union was developing from revolutionary uniqueness into a society more recognizable to British or American eyes. Roosevelt spoke of the USSR evolving 'from the original form of Soviet Communism...toward a modified form of state socialism.'[47] In April 1943 he expressed his belief that 'the revolutionary currents of 1917 may be spent in this war,...with progress following evolutionary constitutional lines' in the future. And he told a British diplomat in December 1944 'that he was not afraid of Communism as such. There were many varieties of Communism and not all of them were necessarily harmful.'[48] In similar vein, Speakers' Notes disseminated by the British Ministry of Information in February 1943 asserted that communism in the USSR was 'not a malignant Marxist bogey, but much more a Russian answer to a Russian problem' and that Stalin's reforms showed that 'while Russia is certainly not a democratic state as we understand it, it is a state moving towards the democracies'.[49]

Viewed from a post-Cold War vantage point, of course, this theory of convergence can easily seem ludicrous.[50] Undoubtedly it rested on serious myopia, ignorance, and wishful thinking about the Soviet Union. But, as historians, we need to look at the 1940s through the eyes of people who had just managed to survive the Great Depression rather than from the stance of those who had triumphantly won the Cold War. Convergence theory was not simply a statement about how the Soviets were becoming more like us; it was also about how 'we' in some respects were becoming more like them. The Depression had a devastating effect on faith in unfettered private enterprise. This was particularly true in Britain where interest in some form of state planning extended well beyond the Labour left. At the height of wartime good feeling, the success of the Russian war effort could not be dissociated in the public mind from admiration for some aspects of the Soviet system, and this may have played a part, despite the Labour leadership's detestation of communism, in the party's victory in the election of July 1945. As one Conservative candidate declared afterwards: 'At meeting after meeting questioners would get up and say: "Look what

---

[46] FO paper of 29 Apr. 1944, in Ross, ed., *Foreign Office and the Kremlin*, 147.
[47] According to Sumner Welles, quoted in Gaddis, *The United States and the Origins*, 41.
[48] Forrest Davis, 'Roosevelt's World Blueprint', *Saturday Evening Post*, 10 Apr. 1943, 21; Richard Law, minute of meeting with FDR, 22 Dec. 1944, FO 371/44595, AN 155/32/45 (TNA).
[49] Quoted in Bell, *John Bull and the Bear*, 69–70.
[50] As in Dunn, *Caught between Roosevelt and Stalin*.

nationalization has done for Russia, and how great she has become . . . " '[51] Even Churchill, that fervent anti-Red, had to acknowledge to Stalin at Teheran that the political complexion of the British people was 'becoming a trifle pinker'. (To which Stalin shot back: 'That is a sign of good health.')[52]

In the United States, unlike most of Europe, there was not a significant wartime swing to the left—if anything the opposite. But the New Deal, however one interprets it, had clearly been a modification of liberal capitalism, involving a more corporatist society, greater governmental direction to the economy and an enlarged Federal bureaucracy. The total engrossment of society by the state was, of course, anathema: use of the term 'totalitarianism' peaked in the United States between the Nazi–Soviet pact and Barbarossa and embraced Germany, Italy, and the Soviet Union. It was to become a staple of the Cold War manichean worldview from 1946. But we should not forget that, in the intervening period, one of the most influential American writers of the 1940s on political economy, James Burnham, argued in his 1941 best-seller *The Managerial Revolution* that, although liberal capitalism was declining, recent Soviet history suggested that the victor would not be socialism but a new, centralized society controlled by 'managers'. In Britain, the term totalitarian was even appropriated by some writers in this period to describe the ubiquitous erosion of individualism and privacy by large organizations. The scientific popularizer C. H. Waddington insisted in 1941: 'The Totalitarians of today have taken, with the wrong foot foremost, a step which we shall all have to take tomorrow.' The author George Orwell, anticipating his Cold War novel *1984*, told a BBC radio audience in June 1941: 'When one mentions totalitarianism one thinks immediately of Germany, Russia, Italy, but I think that one must face the risk that this phenomenon is going to be world-wide.' The pervasive acceptance among intellectuals that the modern state would have to direct more of economy and society helps to explain the passion of Friedrich von Hayek's classic denunciation in 1944 of these ideas as *The Road to Serfdom*.[53]

I am not implying that busy policy-makers had time to pore over Burnham or Waddington, or that such writers were necessarily widely representative. I offer these examples to suggest that the theory of convergence worked both ways: there was frequent recognition that the liberal capitalism was changing and not just Soviet communism. Rather than assuming that the great bipolar divide in political economy was set in stone by 1945, we should recognize that this was contested terrain at the heart of the early Cold War.

I have suggested that British and American hopes of a working relationship with the Soviet Union reflected three important assumptions—expectations of a

---

[51] Aubrey Jones, in Paul Addison, *The Road to 1945: British Politics and the Second World War* (London, 1975), 141; cf. Bell, *John Bull and the Bear*, 74–5.
[52] Dinner on 30 Nov. 1943, in *FRUS: Cairo and Teheran*, 584.
[53] See discussion in Abbott Gleason, *Totalitarianism: The Inner History of the Cold War* (New York, 1995), ch. 3, quoting from pp. 58 and 59.

limited American role in post-war Europe, confidence in Stalin himself as a man with whom one could do business, and hopes that 'Stalinism' betokened a shift from revolutionary ideology at home and abroad towards a more 'normal' state. I have outlined these three assumptions very briefly; a fuller account would show greater sensitivity to nuances within and between Great Britain and the United States. Nevertheless, I believe these ideas offer clues toward explaining why leading British and American policy-makers hoped that the policy of cooperation with the Soviet Union could outlast the war. How and why those hopes evaporated is the theme of the next two chapters.

14

Churchill, Stalin, and the 'Iron Curtain'

Churchill's speech at Fulton, Missouri, on 5 March 1946 is perhaps the most celebrated of his long and distinguished oratorical career. The claim that 'an iron curtain' had descended across the Continent echoed around the world, becoming one of the most famous and influential soundbites of the Cold War. It also created an enduring image of Churchill as Cold Warrior that has obscured the complexity of his thinking on relations with the Soviet Union. This chapter looks closely at Churchill's speech, arguing that the way it was received did not entirely square with what he had intended. To understand this, we need to appreciate the volatility of his attitude to the Soviet Union in 1945–6 and also, paradoxically, the remarkable persistence of his wartime optimism about Stalin.

The term 'iron curtain' has a long prehistory. It dates back at least to the First World War, and Churchill had used it a good deal in 1945–6 before it hit the headlines at Fulton. On 12 May, four days after Victory in Europe had been declared, Churchill cabled President Truman warning that 'an iron curtain is drawn down upon their front. We do not know what is going on behind. There seems little doubt that the whole of the regions east of Lübeck-Trieste-Corfu will soon be completely in their hands.' Churchill was probably reminded of the phrase 'iron curtain' by Nazi propaganda in the dying days of the Third Reich, but the underlying idea had taken shape in his mind weeks before as he struggled for diplomatic access to Poland. To Roosevelt on 16 March he referred to 'an impenetrable veil'; on 1 April he complained to Stalin that 'a veil of secrecy' had been 'drawn over the Polish scene'. Both these telegrams are quoted in his war memoirs.[1] On 18 May he spoke of an 'iron screen' during a brisk dressing down of Feodor Gusev, the Soviet Ambassador. Common to all these references is the theme of concealment: the Western Allies did not know what the Soviets were

Earlier versions of this chapter were presented at Churchill College, Cambridge, in 1996 (a lecture to mark the fiftieth anniversary of the Fulton Speech); at Rutgers University, New Brunswick, New Jersey in 2001; and at Westminster College, Fulton, Missouri, in 2002. I am grateful to Piers Brendon, Allen Packwood, Lloyd Gardner, Warren F. Kimball, Jerry D. Morelock, and John Hensley for these opportunities.

[1] Winston S. Churchill, *The Second World War* (6 vols., London, 1948–1954), vi. 377, 383, 498–9.

up to in their areas of occupation, especially Poland. But during the spring the imagery had gradually hardened—from 'veil' to 'curtain' and then to 'screen'— and by May the 'iron' had entered Churchill's rhetoric, and his soul. He told Gusev bluntly that the British 'refused to be pushed about' and that they had postponed the demobilization of the Royal Air Force so as 'to enter upon discussions about the future of Europe with all the strength they had'.[2]

A few days later Churchill recalled all copies of the record of this 18 May meeting. Ostensibly this was because the coalition government was now breaking up, but it is likely that he had second thoughts about drawing attention to his reference about delaying demobilization of the RAF. For Churchill had secretly instructed his military planners to examine 'Operation Unthinkable': how to 'impose upon Russia the will of the United States and British Empire' in order to get 'a square deal for Poland'. The hypothetical date for the start of hostilities against the Red Army was 1 July 1945.[3]

The planners were told to assume that such a war would have 'the full support' of British and American public opinion and that they could 'count on the use of German manpower and what remains of German industrial capacity'. Attacking a popular ally just three months after the end of the war, using the troops of the former enemy, was, of course, truly unthinkable, but the planners made the best of an impossible brief, highlighting the strength of the Allied navies and strategic bombers. But they had to acknowledge massive Soviet superiority on land, of roughly four to one in infantry and two to one in tanks. They proposed a surprise attack by forty-seven American and British divisions around Dresden and envisaged achieving a limited political objective, such as a more acceptable Polish government. But this, they admitted, could not be 'a lasting result'. The Allies would have to accept the prospect of 'total war', which could only be won by penetrating far more deeply and durably into the Soviet Union than the Wehrmacht had managed briefly in 1942. Even if up to 100,000 Germans were mobilized in the long term as part of the Allied armies, this would make no substantial difference to the imbalance of forces. And, added the Chiefs of Staff on 8 June, if the Americans wearied of the struggle and turned to the Pacific War then the odds would change from 'heavy' to 'fanciful'. Sir Alan Brooke, the Chief of the Imperial General Staff, wrote in his diary that the whole idea was 'fantastic and the chances of success quite impossible. There is no doubt that from now onwards Russia is all powerful in Europe.'[4]

[2] Sir Archibald Clark Kerr, note of discussion on 18 May 1945, PREM 3/396/12, fos. 363–5 (TNA).

[3] Even in 1998, when 'discovered' in the British National Archives, the plan caused a sensation—e.g. *Daily Telegraph*, 1 Oct. 1998, pp. 1, 8–9. The full text was printed in the Russian journal *Modern and Contemporary History*—O. A. Rzheshevsky, 'Secretnye Voinye Plani u Cherchillia protin USSR v May 1945 g', *Novaia i Noveishaia Istoriia* (May 1999), 98–123.

[4] Report by the Joint Planning Staff, 'Operation "Unthinkable"', 22 May 1945, and COS to PM, 8 June 1945, CAB 120/691 (TNA); Field-Marshal Lord Alanbrooke, *War Diaries, 1939–1945*, ed. Alex Danchev and Daniel Todman (London, 2001), 693, entry for 24 May 1945.

Faced with this grim scenario, Churchill not only conceded defeat but performed a complete somersault. Abandoning any idea of the West imposing its will on Russia, on 9 June 1945 he told the planners to consider how 'we could defend our Island' if the Americans withdrew to the Pacific leaving the Russians with 'the power to advance to the North Sea and the Atlantic'. By retaining the codeword 'Unthinkable', he added, 'the Staffs will realise that this remains a precautionary study of what, I hope, is still a purely hypothetical contingency.'[5]

'Unthinkable' was so unmentionable that Churchill made no reference to it in the text or drafts of his war memoirs. It did, however, come out indirectly in 1954. On 23 November, in a speech to his constituents at Woodford in Essex, Churchill claimed credit for anticipating the current plans to bring West Germany into NATO: 'Even before the war had ended and while the Germans were surrendering by hundreds of thousands, and our streets were crowded with cheering people, I telegraphed to Lord Montgomery directing him to be careful in collecting the German arms, to stack them so they could easily be issued again to the German soldiers whom we should have to work with if the Soviet advance continued.'[6] The ensuing furore in the press and parliament proved deeply embarrassing for Churchill. Asked to produce the text of the message, he initially said that it was in his war memoirs but this was erroneous and he had to eat humble pie. 'I shall be very glad to give that to the House—when I find it', he told MPs, conceding 'I might have been confused in my mind' and mixed up one telegram with another. Over the next week the newspapers were full of 'hunt the telegram' articles and cartoons, but nothing ever turned up. 'I made a goose of myself at Woodford,' Churchill admitted privately.[7]

The Woodford affair has often been taken as sign of Churchill's senility but that is not the whole story. Contrary to the impression sometimes created, this was not a brief, off-the-cuff speech but a long, carefully crafted address.[8] And the central, bombshell claim was one Churchill had tried to verify years before. In March 1950 he asked his research assistants for 'a telegram sent by him to Montgomery in 1945 telling M. to stack German equipment and arms in case they should be needed'. Nothing could be found at Chartwell or in the Cabinet Office files, except for an exchange between Churchill and Eisenhower on 9–10 May 1945 about not destroying German planes; this was later printed in volume

[5] PM to Chiefs of Staff, 9 June 1945, CAB 120/691. Churchill substituted 'a purely hypothetical contingency' for the phrase in the original draft by one of his military secretaries, Jo Hollis—'a highly improbable event'.

[6] *Winston Churchill: His Complete Speeches*, ed. Robert Rhodes James (8 vols., New York, 1974), viii. 8604–5.

[7] Ibid. viii. 8609–20; Lord Moran, *Winston S. Churchill: The Struggle for Survival* (London, pbk edn., 1968), 649.

[8] The collected edition of Churchill's addresses calls it 'a brief speech' and quotes only the passages on foreign affairs—probably following the carefully expurgated version in Winston S. Churchill, *The Unwritten Alliance: Speeches 1953 to 1959*, ed. Randolph S. Churchill (London, 1961), 196–7. For the full text and drafts see CHUR 5/56A (CAC).

six of the memoirs. After the Woodford speech, the Cabinet Secretary, Norman Brook, initiated an extensive search of official papers but again drew a blank.[9]

Churchill might well have been mistaken about the whole business; he had several other erroneous *idées fixes* about wartime events. But the file on Operation Unthinkable puts the speech in a rather different light, as does supporting evidence from Montgomery's papers. Monty was in the United States when the Woodford row erupted and his first, public reaction was to state that he had indeed received such a telegram. Back home, and unable to find anything in his files, he told Churchill that his wartime intelligence chief remembered seeing the message but said it had come on 'the very secret link' (via the Secret Intelligence Service) and was therefore destroyed after being read. Then in June 1959 Monty wrote a private memorandum for the record saying that he had met Churchill at Downing Street on 14 May 1945 to discuss the military government of Germany. Churchill 'got steamed up about the Russians' and told Monty not to destroy the weapons of the one million Germans who had surrendered to him a week before because 'we might have to fight the Russians with German help'. This was a verbal order, Monty noted in his memo, with 'no written confirmation'. On 14 June 1945, concerned at the number of troops thereby diverted to guarding weapons dumps, he asked the War Office to confirm or rescind these instructions. A week later, having received no reply, he gave orders for the destruction of the German weapons. Monty heard nothing more about the matter until Churchill's Woodford speech. 'He said he had sent me a telegram. It could not be found. There was no telegram!! The true facts are as above.'[10] Monty was not the most reliable of witnesses—and he had changed his tune since his private message to Churchill in December 1954—but his statement fits the other evidence of the Prime Minister's near panic about a third world war in mid-May 1945.

The panic, it must be stressed, was temporary and did not betoken all-out hostility towards the Soviet Union. Churchill's comments about veils and curtains were mostly directed to the situation in Poland, where the Soviets were dragging their feet in the spring of 1945 on the reconstruction of the existing communist government, agreed in outline at Yalta, while non-communists in Poland were being quietly eliminated. Once that process was complete, at the end of June Stalin was happy to welcome Truman's emissary, Harry Hopkins, and include a few token non-communists in a new Polish government. After the Americans had agreed, Churchill had no choice but to acquiesce. At the same time he had to accept the American decision to pull back their troops to the occupation zones previously agreed between the Allies. Churchill had wanted them to remain, at least for the moment, in the heart of defeated Germany, including Magdeburg and Leipzig, right up to the middle Elbe. Although that

---

[9] See CHUR 4/390/62–6 (for 1950) and CAB 21/3775 (for 1954).

[10] Montgomery papers (Imperial War Museum, London), BLM 162, esp. Monty to Churchill, 6 Dec. 1954, and 'The truth about the telegram', MS, June 1959.

might have provided a platform for an offensive, as in Operation Unthinkable, Churchill's main reason was diplomatic rather than military. He wanted to retain the most eastwardly positions possible as bargaining counters for a new summit. As he told Truman in his 'iron curtain' telegram of 12 May: 'Surely it is vital now to come to an understanding with Russia, or to see where we are with her before we weaken our armies mortally or retire to the zones of occupation.'[11] Even though the Americans decided to withdraw, this remained Churchill's strategy: a new summit with the Russians at which, he hoped, the outstanding differences could be resolved or at least reduced. The summit eventually convened at Potsdam on 17 July, considerably later than Churchill wanted, and he spent only a week there before being evicted from office by the British electorate.

Churchill's behaviour during the spring of 1945 remains puzzling. It is sometimes argued that Stalin's breach of the Yalta agreement showed it was no longer possible to trust the Soviets and that, as in the 1930s, Churchill was now offering prescient warnings of the new danger.[12] The new evidence, presented here, about Operation Unthinkable could be fitted into this interpretation, as a sign that an alarmed Churchill examined the prospect of war with Russia, realized it was impossible even with American support, and therefore sought a diplomatic rather than a military showdown. This train of argument would lead us on naturally to Fulton where he deployed the 'Iron Curtain' theme publicly in an effort to win American backing.

Yet that is not the only way to look at the evidence. Churchill's faith in Yalta and in Stalin, as we saw in the last chapter, rested on a tissue of optimistic assumptions that were eerily reminiscent, even to Churchill at the time, of Neville Chamberlain. Roosevelt's attitude was even more hopeful, of course, but his diplomacy remained consistent and in March and early April he batted back Churchill's increasingly frenzied telegrams about Poland with advice not to react to each day's crisis because 'most of them straighten out' after a few weeks.[13] If one accepts the basic assumptions of both leaders about the importance of working with the Soviets, Roosevelt's stance was probably more logical than Churchill's. It is certainly possible to read Churchill's frenzy—including the truly ludicrous Operation Unthinkable—as evidence that he was mentally and physically exhausted by his titanic exertions over the previous five years. When he had a week's vacation in July, just before Potsdam, he did no work in preparation for the conference, even though on his own scenario it was the critical showdown with the Soviets.

[11] Churchill, *Second World War*, vi. 499. For fuller discussion see David Reynolds, *In Command of History: Churchill Fighting and Writing the Second World War* (London, 2004), ch. 30.

[12] Often the wise Churchill is set against the naïve and appeasing Roosevelt. See for instance Amos Perlmutter, *FDR and Stalin: A Not So Grand Alliance, 1943–1945* (Columbia, Mo., 1993), 209–10.

[13] Roosevelt to Churchill, 11 Apr. 1945, in Warren F. Kimball (ed.), *Churchill and Roosevelt: The Complete Correspondence* (3 vols., Princeton, 1984), iii. 630.

In other words, Churchill's alarm in spring 1945, though significant, should not necessarily be taken to imply a radical change in policy. This becomes clearer if we look carefully at the Fulton speech. A close examination of its genesis in the months after Churchill's election defeat calls into question the familiar Cold War framework.

For five years Churchill had been Britain's war leader and also a pre-eminent world statesman. In July 1945 he still wanted to win victory against Japan and preside over the anticipated peace conference—a new and better version of Paris in 1919. He returned to London from Potsdam on 25 July expecting a substantial Tory majority; his daughter and his doctor both left half their luggage at Potsdam.[14] It was only on the morning of the 26th that he awoke, 'with a sharp stab of almost physical pain', to the conviction that he had lost. The language he uses to convey that conviction is striking. 'All the pressure of great events, on and against which I had mentally so long maintained my "flying speed", would cease and I should fall. The power to shape the future would be denied me.' By noon, the extent of Labour's victory was clear. 'It may well be a blessing in disguise,' his wife remarked consolingly, aware of his immense fatigue. 'At the moment,' grunted Churchill, 'it seems quite effectively disguised.'[15]

In Britain, the verdicts of the electorate are executed with brutal suddenness. Unlike the United States, there is no transition period of two and a half months—or four months as it was until after the disastrous governmental paralysis during the Depression of 1932–3. On Friday 27 July, the day after the result was declared, the Churchills vacated Ten Downing Street. Speaking to his wartime Foreign Secretary, Anthony Eden, in the Cabinet room, Churchill said morosely: 'Thirty years of my life have been passed in this room. I shall never sit in it again. You will, but I shall not.'[16] His Map Room was empty, his private secretaries had gone, and there were no more 'red boxes', full of secret messages from around the world. After five years at the heart of government, Churchill was suddenly cut off from the arteries of power; the effect was almost physical. (When Konrad Adenauer, the veteran West German Chancellor, was finally forced from office in 1963 at the age of 87, he likened it to having his arms and legs chopped off.[17]) After a lachrymose farewell dinner at Chequers, the Prime Minister's official country residence, Churchill asked everyone to sign the visitors' book. He entered his name last of all and underneath wrote a single word: 'Finis'.[18]

On a purely domestic level, the loss of power caused acute problems because the Churchills no longer had anywhere to live in London. Having disposed of

[14] Richard Lovell, *Churchill's Doctor: A Biography of Lord Moran* (London, 1991), 271; author's interview with Lady Soames, 27 July 2004.   [15] Churchill, *Second World War*, vi. 583.

[16] Anthony Eden, *The Reckoning* (London, 1965), 551.

[17] Hans-Peter Schwarz, *Adenauer: Der Staatsmann, 1952–1967* (Munich, 1991), 839.

[18] Mary Soames, *Clementine Churchill* (2nd edn., London, 2002), 426.

their apartment in Morpeth Mansions, near Victoria Station, at the beginning of the war, they spent the first week or so in Claridge's Hotel, before their daughter and son-in-law Diana and Duncan Sandys generously vacated their own apartment for temporary use. While looking for a place of their own in London, Churchill's wife, Clementine, tried to restore their country house—Chartwell in Kent—which had been much neglected during the war. She, too, was exhausted by the war years and personal relations became very strained. On 26 August, Clementine wrote to her daughter Mary: 'I cannot explain how it is but in our misery we seem, instead of clinging to each other to be always having rows. I'm sure it is all my fault, but I'm finding life more than I can bear. He is so unhappy & that makes him very difficult.'[19]

Fortunately, Churchill's favourite general, Field-Marshal Sir Harold Alexander, the British commander in Italy, invited Churchill to use his official villa on Lake Como. Winston and a small entourage, including his doctor Lord Moran, flew there on 2 September, leaving Clementine behind to recover and to prepare their new London home in Hyde Park Gate. At Como, Churchill threw himself into painting, an absorbing hobby that he had put aside during the war. On 8 September, he told Moran: 'With my painting I have recovered my balance.' In a rare allusion to the election, he added: 'I'm damned glad now to be out of it.' Churchill looked out for a long time over the lake and then said: 'I shall paint for the rest of my days. I've never painted so well before. The [news]papers seem to bore me; I just glance at them.' This was also his line in letters home. 'I feel a great sense of relief, which grows steadily, others having to face the hideous problems of the aftermath,' he told his wife. Echoing her words on the day of the election result, he declared: 'It may well indeed be "a blessing in disguise".'[20]

Although gratified at Churchill's unaccustomed serenity, Moran did not expect it to last. In the New Year of 1946, he looked back on the previous few months, likening the effect of the election result on Churchill to major surgery. During his convalescence in Italy, the election had been banished from thought and discussion, allowing the wound partially to heal. But what Moran called 'an ugly scar' remained and, once back in London, it flared up again as colleagues and friends kept returning to the election and its political significance. Behind the scenes, there were mutterings in the Conservative party that Winston should make a graceful exit. Given his stature as war leader, it was clear that he could not be pushed, but 1945 had been the worst Conservative defeat since 1906 and, before that, 1832: radical changes were clearly needed. There was a widespread assumption, voiced at times in whispering campaigns in the press, that the 71-year-old Churchill would soon resign as Conservative leader and leave the

---

[19] Ibid. 429.
[20] Moran, *Churchill*, 328, entry for 8 Sept. 1945; Churchill to Clementine, 5 Sept. 1945, in Mary Soames, ed., *Speaking for Themselves: The Personal Letters of Winston and Clementine Churchill* (London, 1998), 535.

post to his heir apparent, Anthony Eden. Churchill was aware of the speculation, and it pushed his mind back to the still incredible defeat of July 1945. Moran scribbled in his diary the words, 'delayed shock'.[21]

There were times in late 1945 when Churchill came close to bowing out as Leader of the Opposition. He certainly had little interest or energy for routine party affairs, and left much of Commons business to Eden. On 15 December he told the Duke of Windsor: 'The difficulties of leading the opposition are very great and I increasingly wonder whether the game is worth the candle.'[22] Yet what else might he do? The obvious answer was writing. He was contracted to the publishers, Cassell's, to complete his monumental *History of the English-Speaking Peoples*, which he had laid aside in the spring of 1940. And he was mulling over whether and when to write his war memoirs. But no decisions had been made and Churchill was in no condition for serious work. His doctor noted in January 1946: 'Winston—incredible as it may seem—is out of a job, looking for something to do, anything to keep his mind away from the past.' And that meant getting away from Britain.[23]

The first three months of 1946 were spent in the United States, much of it at the Florida vacation home of a Canadian admirer, Frank Clarke. Before he left Churchill told Moran: 'There are a lot of flies buzzing around this old decaying carcass. I want something to keep them away.' Sun, solitude, and the sybaritic life in Miami would be ideal. But, as the doctor readily divined, Churchill yearned for more than a winter vacation. 'I think I can be of some use over there; they will take things from me . . . It may be that Congress will ask me to address them. I'd like that.'[24]

Although Moran does not allude to it, the germ of this idea had been sown back in October and was already sprouting by the time Churchill left Britain. When Churchill returned from his Italian vacation in October, amid the mass of invitations awaiting him was one from a small college in the middle of Missouri. On 3 October 1945, Dr Franc L. McLuer, the President of Westminster College in Fulton, sent a letter inviting Churchill to give the annual Green Foundation lectures, usually a series of three or four talks. In the normal course of events, such a letter would have received the standard polite refusal from Churchill's secretaries, but on the bottom was a postscript. 'This is a wonderful school in my home state. Hope you can do it. I'll introduce you. Best regards—Harry S. Truman.' McLuer had secured Truman's involvement via the President's military aide, General Harry H. Vaughan, who was a Westminster alumnus, and it was the presidential postscript that made all the difference to Churchill. He told Truman that he was planning a winter visit to Florida for 'rest and

[21] Moran, *Churchill*, 332–4, entry for 4 Jan. 1946; cf. John Ramsden, 'Winston Churchill and the Conservative Party, 1940–1951', *Contemporary Record*, 9 (1995), 106–7.

[22] Churchill to Duke of Windsor, 15 Dec. 1945, quoted in Martin Gilbert, *Winston S. Churchill, 1945–1965* (London, 1988), 174.   [23] Moran, *Churchill*, 332, entry for 4 Jan. 1946.

[24] Ibid.

recuperation' and would certainly not be able to contemplate the effort of composing and delivering four lectures. But, he told Truman, 'if you, as you suggest in your postscript, would like me to visit your home State and would introduce me, I should feel it my duty—and it would also be a great pleasure— to deliver an Address to the Westminster University [*sic*] on the world situation, under your aegis. This might possibly be advantageous from several points of view.' He added that it was the only public-speaking engagement he had in mind and 'the explanation for it would be my respect for you and your wishes'.[25]

Truman was given notice that his presence at Fulton was what mattered. For Churchill it ensured that his words would be given special attention. In due course, he arranged several other lectures and the trip became far more than the reclusive convalescence he implied in his letter. But Fulton was always repres-ented as a command performance for the President. And the combination of Churchill and Truman ensured that on 5 March 1946 this tiny college town (population 8,000, average student class of 350) was overrun by the international media, as Churchill's words were broadcast across America and around the world. Afterwards Churchill told McLuer he hoped he had 'started some thinking that would make history'. On the train back to Washington, he said to Frank Clarke that Fulton had been 'the most important speech' of his career.[26]

It is clear, therefore, that Churchill went to Fulton to hit the headlines. Depressed by his election defeat, angry at being marginalized from public affairs, he wanted to say something that would attract attention. Those were his motives. But what exactly did he want to say? We need to look more closely at the contents of his speech.[27]

Churchill's essential message can be summed up in four soundbites. The first, of course, is 'iron curtain'. I have already noted how he was playing with this idea in the spring of 1945, but that was in private conversations or messages. And at this time phrases like 'iron veil' or 'iron screen' connoted primarily secrecy and exclusion, albeit exclusion that implied sinister ends. By the time Churchill used the term publicly on 16 August in the House of Commons, that implication was explicit: 'it is not impossible that tragedy on a prodigious scale is unfolding itself behind the iron curtain which at the moment divides Europe in twain.'[28] Yet this Commons statement attracted little attention. It was not until Fulton that

[25] McLuer to Churchill, 3 Oct. 1945, CHUR 2/230/350 (CAC) and Churchill to Truman, 8 Nov. 1945, CHUR 2/230/166–7; cf. *Kansas City Star*, 20 Jan. 1946, C1.

[26] William E. Parrish, *Westminster College: An Informal History, 1851–1969* (Fulton, Mo., 1971), 211; Charles G. Ross diary, 7 Mar. 1946, Ross papers, box 22 (Harry S. Truman Library, Independence, Mo.).

[27] References in what follows are to the published text in Churchill, *Speeches*, vii. 7285–93 and the drafts in CHUR 5/4. Two valuable interpretations of the speech are Henry B. Ryan, 'A New Look at Churchill's "Iron Curtain" Speech', *Historical Journal*, 22 (1979), 895–920, and John Ramsden, 'Mr. Churchill Goes to Fulton', in James W. Muller (ed.), *Churchill's 'Iron Curtain' Speech Fifty Years Later* (Columbia, Mo., 1999), 15–47—though my account differs in important respects from each of these. [28] Churchill, *Speeches*, vii. 7214, 16 Aug. 1945.

the phrase was popularized and its meaning hammered home: 'From Stettin in the Baltic to Trieste in the Adriatic, an iron curtain has descended across the Continent.' East of that line, in 'the Soviet sphere', said Churchill, the people were subject 'not only to Soviet influence but to a very high and, in many cases, increasing measure of Soviet control'. Communist parties were 'seeking everywhere to obtain totalitarian control' and, except in Czechoslovakia, 'there is no true democracy'.

Churchill also warned his audience that problems with the Soviet Union would not be removed 'by a policy of appeasement'. Here was his second famous soundbite from Fulton. In retrospect, the so-called 'lessons of appeasement' are a familiar feature of post-1945 diplomacy, from Korea to Vietnam, from Suez to the Iraq wars. But Fulton was probably the first time that Churchill or any notable British public figure had used the term 'appeasement' so deliberately in public about the Soviet Union.[29] It complemented his tendency in the speech to equate communism and fascism, for instance as he warned of a third world war if, as in the 1930s, his advice was not heeded. 'Last time I saw it all coming and cried aloud to my own fellow-countrymen and to the world, but no one paid any attention.' And so, he said, 'one by one we were all sucked into the awful whirlpool. We surely must not let that happen again.'

Churchill's alternative to appeasement was summed up in his third theme, the need for the 'fraternal association of the English-speaking peoples' based on 'a special relationship between the British Commonwealth and Empire and the United States'. Insisting that this relationship depended not only on special affinities, such as language, but on special institutions, he talked of military cooperation, interchangeable weaponry, the sharing of bases, and eventually even common citizenship. These were ideas Churchill had espoused for most of the war. At Harvard in September 1943 he had spoken in similar terms about a 'fraternal association' between the two countries. As we saw in Chapter 3, he started using the term 'special relationship' in private that autumn and publicized it in a long speech to the Commons in November 1945.[30] But, as with the phrase 'iron curtain' it took the special circumstances of Fulton to bring it firmly to the attention of America and the world. From there it also passed into the lexicon of international politics.

Churchill's thesis about a special relationship was the most contentious part of his speech in the United States. In the first few days it provoked strenuous criticism from liberals and the left, such as Eleanor Roosevelt and Henry Wallace, on the grounds that Churchill was calling for a transatlantic 'military alliance' that would break up the new United Nations. 'Winnie, Winnie, go away, UNO is here to stay' chanted demonstrators outside Churchill's hotel

---

[29] See Alan Foster, 'The British Press and the Coming of the Cold War', in Anne Deighton, ed., *Britain and the First Cold War* (London, 1990), 13.

[30] Churchill, *Speeches*, vii. 6287 (6 Sept. 1943) and 7248 (7 Nov. 1945).

when he arrived in New York a week later.[31] This helped distract attention from Churchill's fourth major soundbite. Although the Fulton address is now almost universally known as the Iron Curtain speech, that was not Churchill's title. Instead he called it 'The Sinews of Peace'.

What did Churchill mean by this variant on the old adage that money was the sinews of war? Essentially he was saying that Anglo-American unity constituted the sinews of peace. He dismissed talk that war with the Soviet Union was inevitable, asserting of the Russians that 'there is nothing they admire more than strength, and nothing for which they have less respect than weakness, especially military weakness'. When he talked of a margin of strength going beyond the balance of power, he was sketching what we would now recognize as a concept of containment. But he did not use such word, because it would have been too static: Churchill wanted to transcend the deadlock, not entrench it. He urged negotiation from a position of strength—provided in large measure by the 'special relationship'—as the only way to prevent another war. What was needed was 'a good understanding on all points with Russia under the general authority of the United Nations Organization' backed by 'the whole strength of the English-speaking world'. This, said Churchill in a sentence added on the train en route to Fulton, 'is the solution which I respectfully offer to you in this Address to which I have given the title "The Sinews of Peace".'

Of the four soundbites, the most important for Churchill was the special relationship. That, he told his audience, was 'the crux' of his message. Three weeks before, he had visited Washington to discuss the speech with President Truman and Secretary of State James Byrnes. Afterwards he told Prime Minister Clement Attlee that it would be 'in the same direction as the one I made at Harvard two years ago, namely fraternal association in the build-up and maintenance of U.N.O., and inter-mingling of necessary arrangements for mutual safety in case of danger, in full loyalty to the Charter. I tried this on both the President and Byrnes, who seemed to like it very well.' The most pressing international issue for Britain at the time was not the Cold War but whether a cost-cutting and increasingly anglophobe US Congress would approve a massive post-war loan to save the country from bankruptcy. Byrnes flew down to Florida specially for a meeting with Churchill about this. Churchill was also conscious that Britain had now been cut out of the atomic bomb and that the Combined Chiefs of Staff were withering away. The growing coolness in Anglo-American relations in 1945–6 was the background to his speech.[32]

The structure of Churchill's address confirms the impression that its prime focus was on the special relationship. He spoke first of 'the two great dangers which menace the homes of the people, War and Tyranny'. He argued that war

[31] John Lewis Gaddis, *The United States and the Origins of the Cold War, 1941–1947* (New York, 1972), 309.

[32] Churchill to Attlee, 17 Feb. 1946, CHUR 2/210; Halifax diary, 10 and 11 Feb. 1946, Hickleton papers, A 7.8.18 (Borthwick Institute, York).

could not be prevented, or the UN made to work effectively, without a special relationship. Only then did he introduce the 'iron curtain' theme, to justify his contention that 'time may be short' and that the 'fraternal association' should be formed soon. The alternative was to learn these lessons yet again 'for a third time in a school of war'. Rather than proposing an Anglo-American axis to wage the Cold War, Churchill was invoking the threat of a Third World War to justify a special relationship.

Why, then, has the Fulton speech been understood as the clarion call to Cold War? Churchill himself was partly to blame. For a man so attuned to words, he was surprisingly indecisive about titles. His speech was originally billed as being simply about 'World Affairs'. By mid-February 1946 President McLuer of Westminster College wanted something more precise. Churchill replied that he had still not made up his mind but that the speech would probably be called 'World Peace'. Only the day before Churchill spoke was the title changed to 'The Sinews of Peace'. Many of the advance texts for the press did not use this title and that affected the balance of some reporting.[33]

Context mattered even more than content in explaining reaction to the Fulton speech. By the time Churchill spoke, the Soviets and Americans were facing off at the UN about the Red Army's failure to withdraw, as agreed, from northern Iran. His comments on Russia were therefore likely to hit the headlines, particularly when packaged in such a compelling phrase. What's more, Moscow unleashed a massive counter-attack on Churchill. A three-column front-page editorial in the party newspaper, *Pravda*, on 11 March was followed next day by a lengthy article in the government paper, *Izvestia*. On 13 March, most remarkably, *Pravda* printed a question and answer session with Stalin himself about Churchill's speech. The drama of the moment is vividly conveyed by the *New York Times* banner headlines on Thursday 14 March:

STALIN SAYS CHURCHILL STIRS WAR
AND FLOUTS ANGLO-RUSSIAN PACT;
SOVIET TANKS APPROACH TEHERAN

SEES RACE THEORY

Russian Leader Likens Churchill to Hitler for Plea to U.S.

SAYS SOVIETS CAN WIN WAR

The full text of the interview, printed on page four of the *New York Times*, amplified these points. Stalin castigated the Fulton speech as 'a call to war with the Soviet Union'. Churchill, he said, was arguing that the English-speaking

---

[33] Churchill to McLuer, 14 Feb. 1946, CHUR 2/230B; cf. *Daily Telegraph*, 5 Mar. 1946, copy in Churchill Press Cuttings, CHPC 23 (CAC). The official British Information Services advance text of the speech, given to the press, does not contain this sentence: see copy in W. Averell Harriman papers, box 991 (Library of Congress).

peoples, 'being the only valuable nations, should rule over the remaining nations of the world'. This was a 'racial theory' based on language—'one is reminded remarkably of Hitler and his friends'.[34]

This was an astonishing outburst, but Churchill had been in Stalin's sights for a while. A few months before, *Pravda* had published excerpts from a speech by Churchill on 7 November praising Stalin ('this truly great man') and the 'noble Russian people' for their contribution to Allied victory. Stalin sent his Politburo colleagues a stinging rebuke: Churchill 'needs these eulogies to soothe his guilty conscience and in particular to camouflage his hostile attitude towards the USSR'. Publicity for his words was 'a mistake'; Stalin warned against 'servility and fawning' whenever Russia was praised by foreigners. Here perhaps was an intimation of his subsequent campaign to eliminate 'cosmopolitan' tendencies that had taken root in the Soviet Union during the wartime alliance.[35] Stalin's apparently emotional denunciation of Fulton was also carefully calculated. As a good Marxist-Leninist, he assumed that contradictions between the capitalist powers ruled out a durable Anglo-American alliance, but Fulton could be used to make propaganda points. Historian William Taubman has speculated on Stalin's motives: 'By exaggerating Churchill's warnings, by treating them as a fully-fledged "call to war", he would alarm the Western masses while mobilizing the Soviet people.' And perhaps, as David Holloway implies, his forceful response was intended as further evidence that Moscow would not be intimidated by the West, even though America possessed the atomic bomb.[36] Whatever Stalin's motivation, his high-profile response as much as Churchill's own words ensured that the Fulton speech went down as one of the opening salvoes in the Cold War.

The delicacy of the Iran crisis and the vehement Soviet reaction prompted the British and American governments to dissociate themselves from the Fulton speech. On 11 March two Labour MPs put down a Commons motion asking Attlee to repudiate Churchill's tone and content. This was signed by over a hundred others, including a future Prime Minister, James Callaghan. Attlee declined to comment, stating that Churchill had spoken in 'an individual capacity' in a foreign country. What Churchill said was, however, broadly in line with official policy and Attlee, given the gist of Churchill's argument in advance, had told him, 'I am sure your Fulton speech will do good.'[37]

---

[34] *New York Times*, 14 Mar. 1946, 1 and 4.

[35] Stalin to Molotov, 10 Nov. 1945, printed with commentary in Alexander O. Chubarian and Vladimir O. Pechatnov, 'Molotov "the Liberal": Stalin's 1945 Criticism of his Deputy', *Cold War History*, 1 (2000), 129–32.

[36] William Taubman, *Stalin's American Policy: From Entente to Détente to Cold War* (New York, 1982), quoting 141, 144; David Holloway, *Stalin and the Bomb* (London, 1994), 168–71. See also Vladislav Zubok and Constantine Pleshakov, *Inside the Kremlin's Cold War: From Stalin to Khrushchev* (Cambridge, Mass., 1996), 123–5.

[37] House of Commons, *Debates*, 5th series, vol. 420, cols. 759–61, 11 Mar. 1946; cf. Attlee to WSC, 25 Feb. 1946, CHUR 2/210.

The Truman Administration had been much more closely consulted. Not only did Churchill discuss the speech with the President for ninety minutes on 10 February, he also solicited comment on the almost final text from Admiral William Leahy, the White House Chief of Staff. 'I can find no fault in his proposed address,' Leahy wrote in his diary. Truman read a copy during their train journey from Washington to Fulton and, according to Churchill, said 'he thought it was admirable and would do nothing but good, though it would make a stir. He seemed equally pleased during and after.' Given all this consultation, historian Fraser Harbutt has argued that the Truman Administration willingly used the Fulton speech as the centrepiece of its new campaign to shift public opinion behind a posture of confrontation toward the Soviet Union. It was the anti-Soviet thrust of Churchill's remarks more than their Anglo-American theme that attracted the budding Cold Warriors in Washington. But given the intensity of comment in both the United States and the Soviet Union, the Truman Administration, like the Attlee government, found it prudent to distance itself from Churchill.[38]

The Fulton speech also ruffled feathers among his Tory colleagues, who had not been consulted in advance. Anthony Eden, his professional heir apparent and the party's foreign affairs spokesman, was severely embarrassed. Not only was he still taking a more conciliatory line in public toward the Soviet Union, he had, that very day in the Commons, denied the claim by a Labour MP that his party leader was about to make 'a sensational speech in America' putting Russia 'on the spot'. Eden responded: 'I certainly have not heard anything of the kind from my right hon. friend and, may I add, I do not believe it for one single moment.' Lord Salisbury, the Tory elder statesman, feared that Fulton could wreck Britain's bipartisan policy of firmness towards Russia by persuading Labour left-wingers that it was really 'the policy of the Right'. Salisbury felt that the speech strengthened the case for Churchill retiring from the Tory leadership: then 'he could say what he liked, without associating the party with it'. Eden also entertained hopes that Churchill would 'now be less anxious to lead' and would 'want to pursue an anti-Russian crusade, independent of us'.[39]

And so official circles in America and Britain distanced themselves from the controversy that Churchill had stirred up. In consequence, as Fulton moved rapidly from notoriety to celebrity—a visionary warning rather than a reckless polemic—Churchill gained sole credit for a speech that the British and particularly American governments had been happy to facilitate. Stalin's vituperation did not upset him; on the contrary. Words deleted at the last minute from a

[38] Leahy diary, 10 Feb. and 3 Mar. 1946, William D. Leahy papers (LC); Churchill to Attlee, 7 Mar. 1946, CHUR 2/4; Fraser J. Harbutt, *The Iron Curtain: Churchill, America, and the Origins of the Cold War* (New York, 1986), 280–5.

[39] House of Commons, *Debates*, vol. 420, cols. 231, 236, 5 Mar. 1946; Salisbury to Eden, 13 Mar. 1946, and Eden to Salisbury, 15 Mar. 1946, Avon Papers AP 20/43/17 and/17A (Birmingham University Library).

speech in New York on 15 March betray his glee at hitting the headlines:

It is extraordinary that the head of a mighty, victorious government should descend from his august seat of power to enter into personal controversy with a man who has no official position of any kind and had been particularly careful to say that he spoke without the authority of any government. I shall not let the implied compliment turn my head. Nor am I dismayed by harsh words, even from the most powerful of dictators. Indeed I had years of it from Hitler and managed to get along all right.[40]

Fulton had served its purpose. The American President had sat alongside him as he spoke; the leader of the Soviet Union blasted him for what he had said; his words had echoed around the world. Buoyed up by being the centre of attention again, Churchill dealt firmly with press speculation about his imminent retirement as Tory party leader. A statement from New York declared: 'I have no intention whatsoever of ceasing to lead the Conservative Party until I am satisfied that they can see their way clear ahead and make better arrangements.'[41] By the summer of 1946 Churchill's zest for politics had returned, fired by a belief that the Labour party was selling off the empire and selling out the country. He told his doctor on 27 June: 'A short time ago I was ready to retire and die gracefully. Now I'm going to stay and have them out.' With great vehemence, he snarled: 'I'll tear their bleeding entrails out of them.' His crony Brendan Bracken summed up the new mood in typically vivid terms. Churchill, he said, was 'determined to continue to lead the Tory party till be becomes Prime Minister on earth or Minister of Defence in Heaven.'[42]

I have suggested that Churchill went to Fulton to hit the headlines with a clarion call about the special relationship but that the reaction to his speech, particularly from Moscow, made him seem more of a Cold Warrior than he had intended. Support for this argument may be found in Churchill's attitude to Stalin: despite the explosive rejoinder from the Kremlin, Churchill seems to have retained a remarkable faith in the Soviet dictator.

His public praise of Stalin on 7 November 1945 was not an isolated incident. Churchill continued his wartime habit of sending Stalin birthday greetings. A telegram in December 1945 wishing 'Many happy returns of the day' received a belated but cordial acknowledgement. Nor did Churchill allow the Fulton furore to interrupt his pattern. On 21 December 1946 he asked the Soviet Ambassador in London to transmit a brief message to Stalin: 'All personal good wishes on your birthday, my wartime comrade.' Three days later came the reply: 'My warm thanks for your good wishes on my birthday.' With Moscow's

---

[40] Second draft of 15 Mar. 1946 speech, p. A2, in CHUR 5/4.

[41] *Evening News*, 15 Mar. 1946, *Daily Mail* and *The Star*, 18 Mar. 1946—all in Churchill Press Cuttings, CHPC 23.

[42] Moran, *Churchill*, 339; Bracken to Beaverbrook, 16 Oct. 1946, Beaverbrook papers, C/56 (House of Lords Record Office).

consent, Churchill duly published his message to Stalin, which was printed in several British papers, often featuring the phrase 'My wartime comrade.'[43]

In January 1947 Field-Marshal Montgomery visited Moscow, picking up a long-standing invitation in the hope of reducing what Attlee called 'the cloud of suspicion' hanging over Anglo-Soviet relations. Monty spent a cordial and constructive evening with Stalin on 10 January, parts of which he duly reported in a letter to Churchill. Stalin had inquired as to Churchill's health and 'then said that you disagreed with him now on many political matters, but he would always have the happiest memories of his work with you as the great war leader of Britain; he added that he had the greatest respect and admiration for what you had done during the war years.' Stalin said he would be 'delighted' if Monty would convey these words to Churchill.[44]

'I shall endeavour to write to him in a similar spirit', Churchill told Monty, and on 3 February 1947 he replied as follows:

My dear Stalin

I was very glad to receive your kind message through Field-Marshal Montgomery. About political differences, I was never very good at Karl Marx.

I always look back on our comradeship together, when so much was at stake, and you can always count on me where the safety of Russia and the fame of its armies are concerned.

I was also delighted to hear from Montgomery of your good health. Your life is not only precious to your country, which you saved, but to the friendship between Soviet Russia and the English-speaking world.

Believe me,
Yours very sincerely,
Winston S. Churchill[45]

Of course, too much should not be made of such diplomatic pleasantries. Nevertheless, these exchanges remind us that the Fulton speech was not intended as a personal attack on Stalin and suggest that Churchill had retained something of his wartime faith in the Soviet leader. It is also striking that throughout his war memoirs, written from 1946 to 1953, Churchill avoided personal attacks on Stalin. Even where he was bluntly critical of Soviet wartime conduct, as over the Warsaw Rising in 1944, he referred to 'men in the Kremlin who were governed by calculation and not by emotion'. In notes for volume six, Churchill suggested that the breach of the Yalta agreements 'probably was due not to bad faith on the part of Stalin and Molotov, but that when they got back home they were held up by their colleagues'. This intriguing observation echoes his wartime comments

---

[43] See CHUR 2/142/139–40 (for 1945) and CHUR 2/156/90–102 (for 1946).

[44] Montgomery to Churchill, 21 Jan. 1947, CHUR 2/143/95. Monty gave an account of the visit in *The Memoirs of Field-Marshal the Viscount Montgomery of Alamein, KG* (London, 1958), 446–56, quoting Attlee on p. 446.

[45] Churchill to Montgomery, 23 Jan. 1947, and to Stalin, 3 Feb. 1947, CHUR 2/143, fos. 96, 100.

about Stalin not being an entirely free agent.[46] Volume six actually contains some very positive asides about the Soviet leader. In 'Prelude to a Moscow Visit', drafted in November 1950 at the nadir of the Korean war, Churchill wrote: 'I felt acutely the need to see Stalin, with whom I always considered one could talk as one human being to another.' And at the end of May 1951, revising his account of Stalin at Potsdam, he added that July 1945 'was the last time I saw this amazing and gigantic personality'.[47]

Churchill never did see Stalin again, but this was not for want of trying. On 4 November 1951, little over a week after returning to Downing Street for a second term, Churchill sent a cable to the Soviet leader. 'Now that I am again in charge of His Majesty's Government, let me reply to your farewell telegram from Potsdam in 1945, "Greetings. Winston Churchill." ' Stalin replied next day with a short note of thanks, and Churchill cabled Truman, 'we are again on speaking terms'. On 6 November, he read to MPs a message he had sent to Stalin on 29 April 1945, warning that a quarrel between 'the English-speaking peoples' and 'you and the countries you dominate' would 'tear the world to pieces'. He then promised 'a supreme effort to bridge the gulf between the two worlds, so that each can live its life, if not in friendship at least without the fear, the hatreds and the frightful waste of the "cold war".'[48]

The 1945 documents were live in his mind from working on the memoirs, and his 4 November 1951 message to Stalin was almost saying: 'Let us resume from where we were so rudely interrupted six years ago.' Back in February 1950, Churchill had called for another 'parley at the summit'—coining a further slogan for the diplomatic lexicon to complement 'iron curtain' and 'special relationship'.[49] Summitry was the overriding passion of his second term and on several occasions during 1952 Churchill spoke privately of his desire for a joint Anglo-American approach to Stalin, leading perhaps to a modern Congress of Vienna at which the Potsdam conference would be reopened and concluded. He also observed in June 1952 that 'while Stalin was alive we were safer from attack than if he died and his lieutenants started scrambling for the succession'. Reminiscing with Soviet Ambassador Andrei Gromyko in February 1953 about wartime summits, he said his 'percentages' meeting with Stalin in Moscow in October 1944 was 'the highest level we ever reached'.[50]

There are signs, however, that Churchill's hopes of doing business with the Soviet dictator had waned by early 1953. He was shaken by the purges in Eastern Europe and declared that 'under these conditions the chances of achieving

---

[46] 'Notes on Volume VI', p. 15, Ismay papers, 2/3/296 (Liddell Hart Centre, King's College, London).

[47] Churchill, *Second World War*, 6: 186; cf. CHUR 4/355/8. On Potsdam see CHUR 4/380B/187.

[48] Gilbert, *Churchill, 1945–65*, 659; Churchill, *Speeches*, 8: 8296–7; John W. Young, *Winston Churchill's Last Campaign: Britain and the Cold War, 1951–5* (Oxford, 1996), 46–7.

[49] Speech in Edinburgh, 14 Feb. 1950, in Churchill, *Speeches*, viii. 7944.

[50] John Colville, *The Fringes of Power: Downing Street Diaries, 1939–1955* (London, 1985), 650, 655; Young, *Churchill's Last Campaign*, 130.

anything with Stalin were almost nil, whereas the dangers of failure would be very great'.[51] He responded with alacrity to the sudden news of Stalin's death on 5 March, sensing a relaxation of tension under the new reformist leadership. And in his Woodford speech in November 1954, remarking on the transformation of Germany in a decade from enemy to ally, he said that this 'vast reversal of British, American and of European opinion was brought about only by the policy of Soviet Russia itself and above all by Stalin, the Dictator, who was carried away by the triumphs of victory and acted as if he thought he could secure for Russia and Communism the domination of the world.' This was his most direct personal attack on Stalin.[52]

Yet in April 1956, he told President Eisenhower that 'Stalin always kept his word with me', again recalling the percentages meeting of 1944 when he told the Soviet leader 'You keep Rumania and Bulgaria in your sphere of influence, but let me have Greece.' To this bargain, said Churchill, 'he scrupulously adhered during months of fighting with the Greek Communists'. This was Churchill's abiding refrain in later life, that Stalin 'never broke his personal word to me'. Years later Churchill's private secretary was still puzzled by what he termed this 'remarkable blind spot in judging Stalin'.[53]

Although this discussion has taken us into the 1950s, it is relevant to understanding Churchill's Fulton speech. In 1945, it seemed that Churchill, now 70, was finished. During a low in the election campaign, he told his doctor sadly: 'I have no message for them now.' After his defeat, President Truman could only wish him 'the happiest possible existence from now to the last call'.[54] But in the spring of 1946 Churchill found a new voice, indeed a new life. He had gone to Fulton—a place he would not otherwise have been caught dead in—because Truman's presence ensured that his words would be heard. Arguably his main aim was to give a speech about the need for a post-war Anglo-American alliance, using the Soviet presence in Eastern Europe as justification. But Stalin's denunciation ensured that what hit the headlines was the 'iron curtain' rather than the 'special relationship' or 'the sinews of peace'. Yet Churchill's persistent faith in Stalin as a man of his word reminds us of that basic message of Fulton. And it also underlines the fact that, even for one of the most prophetic figures of twentieth-century diplomacy, the road to the Cold War was more circuitous than hindsight suggests. That is a major theme of the next chapter.

---

[51] Klaus Larres, *Churchill's Cold War: The Politics of Personal Diplomacy* (New Haven, Conn., 2002), 181.   [52] Churchill, *Speeches*, viii. 8604; also CHUR 5/56A/156.
[53] Churchill to Eisenhower, 16 Apr. 1956, CHUR 2/217/98–9; Anthony Montague Browne, *Long Sunset* (London, 1996), 158.
[54] Moran, *Churchill*, 277, entry for 22 June 1945; Truman to Churchill, 30 July 1945, CHUR 2/142/212.

15

The 'Big Three' and the Division
of Europe, 1945–1948

Winston Churchill called the Second World War 'the unnecessary war'.[1] In the first volume of his war memoirs he set out to show how it could have been avoided if the allies of 1914–18 had maintained their unity and had enforced the peace treaties agreed in Paris. It would be going too far to depict the Cold War as 'unnecessary', but it was definitely unwanted and unintended. In 1945 all the 'Big Three'—Great Britain, the Soviet Union, and the United States—wished to maintain their wartime alliance as the basis for post-war international cooperation, even though each understood cooperation in different ways. This chapter suggests why the 'Grand Alliance' of 1945 crumbled into a polarized Europe by 1948.

Looking at the broad sweep of modern history, it is not perhaps surprising that the wartime alliance between the United States and the Soviet Union was soon under strain.[2]

In 1917 the US entry into the World War and the Bolshevik revolution in Russia heralded the appearance on the European stage of two novel ideologies, embodied in Woodrow Wilson and V. I. Lenin. Each challenged the existing structure of international relations based on the rivalry of heavily armed empires. American and Bolshevik ideologies also challenged each other—the first the vanguard of liberal, capitalist democracy, the other dedicated to the overthrow of

This chapter started out as a paper about recent Western scholarship on the origins of the Cold War at a colloquium in the Institute of General History, Academy of Sciences, Moscow, in 1988. The presentation and discussion, at the height of *glasnost*, was one of the most exciting seminars I have experienced. A revised version was then published in *Diplomacy and Statecraft*, 1 (1990), 111–36, and it appears here with minor changes of wording and the deletion of some remarks that are no longer topical, because I feel the general argument is still correct. But there has been an explosion of research since the end of the Cold War and I indicate some of the more important literature at the end of the chapter.

[1] Winston S. Churchill, *The Second World War* (6 vols., London, 1948–54), p. viii.

[2] For surveys of the Russian–American relationship by US and Soviet historians see John Lewis Gaddis, *Russia, the Soviet Union, and the United States: An Interpretive History* (New York, 1978); Nikolai V. Sivachev and Nikolai N. Yakovlev (trans. Olga Adler Titelbaum), *Russia and the United States* (Chicago, 1979).

capitalism by revolutionary socialism. The early post-war years deepened their antipathy. The Bolsheviks never forgot the Allied intervention during the Civil War, intended initially to foster a new eastern front against Germany but eventually to help crush a revolution that was spreading to Hungary and Germany. In the USA, anti-communism began to take root. Socialism was killed off in the war and the Red Scare and thereafter Americans, denied any experience of the sort of left-of-centre politics that was normal in Europe, had no indigenous criteria against which to check their crude stereotypes of socialism, communism, and totalitarianism. Although the Bolshevik government adopted a dual policy in the early 1920s—playing the imperialist game of diplomacy while working to promote revolution (a dualism institutionalized in the Foreign Ministry and Comintern)—the United States kept aloof. Despite some commercial contacts it delayed diplomatic recognition until 1933, and up to 1941 US–Soviet relations remained distant and suspicious.

The wartime alliance was therefore a deviation from the trend of recent history. The British, supported by the USA, had sought an agreement with Hitler up to 1939; the Soviet Union signed a pact of non-aggression and a deal to divide Poland in August of that same year. Only when all three were the victims of Nazi aggression, from 1941, were they ready to cooperate. As Churchill observed grimly in 1945, it was hard to avoid the conclusion that 'the only bond of the victors is their common hate'.[3] Throughout the war the Western Allies harboured deep suspicions of Stalin's territorial aims in Eastern Europe, encouraged by the secretive and often truculent methods of Soviet diplomacy, while the Soviet Union repeatedly demanded a second front in Continental Europe to relieve the Red Army, which was doing the bulk of the fighting.

Not only did Anglo-American strategy disturb the Soviet Union, it also helped determine the balance of power in Europe after the war. The delay in D-Day made it likely, assuming Stalin did not conclude a negotiated peace, that the Red Army would end the war established in Eastern and Central Europe. That would be the baseline for the post-war settlement—a very different story from 1918. In the West, Hitler's occupation of Continental Europe in 1940 and the growing dependence of Britain on US economic and military help meant that when the war ended the United States would be in a dominant position. Thus the defeat of Hitler's Reich left two new 'superpowers' straddling the Continent, viewing each other through the lenses of ideological suspicion.

In Asia, too, America and Russia were vying for influence. The USA was determined to dominate the occupation of Japan and to turn the country into an American-style client. The Soviet Union, entering the war during its last days, wanted effective control of the adjacent regions of Mongolia, Sinkiang, and Manchuria as well as the Kuril and Sakhalin islands north of Japan. In Korea the

---

[3] Though he added: 'We ought to think of something better'. Churchill, notes, 8 Feb. 1945, Prime Minister's Confidential Correspondence, PREM 4/30/8, fo. 355 (TNA).

two powers had taken the Japanese surrender—the Americans in the south, the Russians in the north. Unable to agree on a peace treaty, they allowed two separate states to emerge, each claiming control over the whole peninsula. And in China, the renewed civil war between Nationalists and Communists saw increasing Soviet support for the latter, under Mao Tse-tung, and, reluctantly, some $3.5 billion of US aid to his rival, Chiang Kai-shek, between 1945 and 1949. Behind all this lurked the spectre of the atomic bomb, exploded by America on Japan in August 1945, which the Russians were now racing to develop for themselves.

Against this background, it is therefore not surprising that what Churchill called 'the Grand Alliance' soon crumbled. But if Soviet–American friction was predictable in 1945, the precise form that it took in Europe was not. Various options were possible, including all-out war, mutual isolation in two spheres of influence, and American indifference to European affairs. Why did the particular relationship that we call the 'Cold War' emerge?—a bitter but peaceful struggle for influence and position, played out as a zero-sum game in which one side's gain was automatically regarded as the other side's loss. And why, given the extent of Soviet–American friction in Asia, did the Cold War begin in earnest first in Europe, before spreading to the Far East and much of the world?[4]

Let us look first at the Soviet attitude in Europe at the end of the war.

Recent work has moved us away from depictions of Stalin as having a fixed 'blueprint' for expansion.[5] Instead, Western scholars are now more inclined to a schema in which the Soviet leader is seen as having a spectrum of minimum to maximum aims. The minimum aims, on which Stalin was adamant, amounted effectively to a Soviet sphere of influence in Eastern Europe, including recovery of old Tsarist lands lost at the end of the First World War and communist dominance in the politics of key states such as Poland, Romania, and Bulgaria, where action was taken promptly with the arrival of the Red Army in 1944. This *glacis* in Eastern Europe was considered essential protection against renewed German attack—Stalin's greatest concern in 1945. His policy for Germany itself centred immediately on substantial reparations to compensate a country that had

---

[4] Robert J. McMahon summarizes scholarship on American policy in China as follows: 'U.S. policymakers never viewed China as a vital interest during the 1940s. Instead, the Truman administration's Cold War strategy always gave precedence to Europe, where American interests were judged more critical and the Soviet threat appeared more pressing.' Robert J. McMahon, 'The Cold War in Asia: Towards a New Synthesis', *Diplomatic History*, 12 (1988), 310.

[5] For instance, Albert Resis, 'Spheres of Influence in Soviet Wartime Diplomacy', *Journal of Modern History*, 53 (1981), 417–39; William O. McCagg, Jr., *Stalin Embattled, 1943–1948* (Detroit, 1978); Vojtech Mastny, *Russia's Road to the Cold War: Diplomacy, Warfare, and the Politics of Communism* (New York, 1979); William Taubman, *Stalin's American Policy: From Entente to Detente to Cold War* (New York, 1982); Martin McCauley, *The Origins of the Cold War* (London, 1983). These historians have different emphases: McCauley and Resis tend to see Stalin as a cautious spheres-of-influence man; Mastny and Taubman believe he entertained larger aims that were vague but expansionist; while McCagg argues for the primacy of domestic politics in shaping his foreign policy.

lost over a tenth of its population and a quarter of its capital assets. Beyond that, from March 1945 the USSR came out firmly against German dismemberment, probably to ensure access to reparations from the Western zones. It refused, however, to proceed quickly to a new German state until proper controls had been established on German economic and military strength which would ensure that Germany could never again threaten Soviet security. Behind this policy may have been the hope that a communist government for a united Germany was an eventual possibility.

At this point minimum aims blur into larger objectives. The language of class struggle and impending capitalist collapse was proclaimed anew from post-war Moscow and, at a time when most communist parties around the world were closely controlled by the USSR, there is no reason to suppose that Soviet leaders had abandoned the ultimate revolutionary aspirations that had been a strain in national policy since 1917. To foreign communist leaders Stalin talked in 1946 about an international economic crisis and a new war in perhaps fifteen years' time.[6] But whatever Stalin's long-term aims, his immediate intentions were not confrontational. The Soviet Union had suffered too much to risk another war.[7]

Stalin's immediate objective was therefore to secure as much as he could *within* a framework of collaboration with America and Britain. It seems likely that, from the percentages deal with Churchill in Moscow in October 1944 and the Yalta agreements of February 1945, he concluded that the West would concede him the sphere of influence he wanted in much of Eastern Europe.[8] In return he would not fuss about areas that he acknowledged to be in the Western sphere, especially Greece—Churchill's main concern in Moscow. Subsequent evidence suggests that Stalin honoured this pledge and that the support for the communists in the Greek civil war came from Yugoslavia and Albania, not from the USSR. Outside Eastern Europe Stalin's pressure was largely confined to areas adjacent to the USSR against which Russia had historic claims, particularly Turkey and Iran.[9] Reflecting his general reluctance to challenge the Western

---

[6] Cf. Taubman, *Stalin's American Policy*, 78, 134–5.

[7] For further reading, see the works cited at the end of these notes.

[8] Yalta lies at the heart of divergent national interpretations of the origins of the Cold War. Soviet scholars generally treated Yalta and Potsdam as definitive agreements which laid the basis for the post-war peace and stability, going on to interpret Western policy thereafter as a series of attempts to renege on them. Cf. Vilnis Sipols, *The Road to Great Victory, 1941–1945* (Moscow, 1985), esp. pp. 249, 271, and 317. For the Republican right in the Cold War Yalta was a symbol of Roosevelt's supposed sell-out of Eastern Europe to the Soviet Union. Cf. Athan Theoharis, *The Yalta Myths: An Issue in U.S. Politics, 1945–1955* (Columbia, Mo. 1970). For the French Yalta became a synonym for the division of Europe by the two superpowers, with France deliberately excluded by Roosevelt. Cf. Denis Lacorne, Jacques Rupnik, and Marie-France Toinet, eds., *L'Amerique dans les têtes: un siècle de fascinations et d'aversions* (Paris, 1986), 25.

[9] Even total communist control of Poland may not have been inevitable, had Stalin been faced with an abler and more flexible Polish leadership in London, ready to compromise on the issue of frontiers and concentrate on the struggle for political power. For this argument see the important article by Antony Polonsky, 'Stalin and the Poles, 1941–7', *European History Quarterly*, 17 (1987), 453–92.

powers, Stalin had dissolved Comintern in 1943 and, more significantly, in 1944–5 instructed communist leaders in Eastern and Western Europe not to promote revolution but to enter into coalition governments with bourgeois parties. To doubters such as the Yugoslavs Stalin pointed to the success of the British Labour party: 'Today socialism is possible even under the English monarchy. Revolution is no longer necessary everywhere.'[10]

Stalin's spheres-of-influence and coalitionist policies can be seen either as a sincere change of heart or as merely preparing the ground for eventual armed struggle. In trying to adjudicate, some Western historians—moving further from the 'totalitarian dictatorship' stereotype of the USSR that was once a staple of Cold War studies[11]—have tried to discern the scale and character of the domestic power struggle going on in the shadows behind Stalin between Andreii Zhdanov and Georgii Malenkov. Should the revival of party control and Marxist-Leninist orthodoxy under Zhdanov be seen as uncontrollable forces which necessarily shaped Soviet foreign policy, or were they instruments used by Stalin in his battle to tame the triumphant Red Army and Malenkov's industrial complex that had supported it?[12] Alternatively, did the Zhdanov–Malenkov struggle pit 'moderates' against 'extremists', with the Zhadanovites' fall in 1948–9 a symptom of the growing Cold War chauvinism and paranoia.[13] Or was that struggle merely a factional battle between two power-hungry 'clans', with ideology and foreign policy largely the fallout from domestic politics? And was Stalin recuperating on the sidelines in 1945–7 after a succession of serious heart problems?[14]

That last suggestion probably goes too far. Most scholars agree that Stalin remained firmly in overall control of Soviet policy, but we need to recognize that Soviet policy was no monolith. And whether Stalin was a power-politician or an ideologue, it seems clear that in 1945 he did not seek conflict with America and Britain and that he was hopeful that his minimum aims at least could be met within a framework of shrewd negotiation.[15] In other words, the initial arena for the post-war duel between the USA and USSR was diplomatic.

What was the US position?[16] Roosevelt himself shared certain Wilsonian objectives: ideally he wanted an international peacekeeping organization, decolonized empires, and liberalized trade. But he believed that the realities of

[10] Milovan Djilas (trans. Michael B. Petrovich), *Conversations with Stalin* (Harmondsworth, 1962), 90.

[11] Cf. Stephen F. Cohen, *Rethinking the Soviet Experience: Politics and History since 1917* (Oxford, 1985), esp. ch. 1.   [12] McCagg, *Stalin Embattled*, argues the latter.

[13] Werner G. Hahn, *Postwar Soviet Politics: The Fall of Zhdanov and the Defeat of Moderation, 1946–53* (Ithaca, NY, 1982).

[14] Gavriel D. Ra'anan, *International Policy Formation in the USSR: Factional 'Debates' during the Zhdanovschina* (Hamden, Conn., 1983).

[15] For further reading, see the works cited at the end of these notes.

[16] Basic books on FDR's thinking are Willard Range, *Franklin D. Roosevelt's World Order* (Athens, Ga., 1959); Robert A. Divine, *Roosevelt and World War II* (Baltimore, 1969); Robert Dallek, *Franklin D. Roosevelt and American Foreign Policy, 1932–1945* (New York, 1979).

power had to be taken into account. Within the new United Nations peace would have to be kept by the big powers, the 'policemen', acting in concert as far as possible. Particularly important was the relationship with the USSR, Roosevelt's principal concern from mid-1943. The President believed that this could best be secured through patient diplomacy, generous Lend-Lease aid and, in particular, good ties with the Soviet leader.[17] To achieve this he resisted Churchill's pressure for a joint Anglo-American diplomatic front against Stalin at conferences like Teheran and Yalta. FDR was hopeful that Soviet objectives in Eastern Europe could be accommodated within the framework of Allied war aims and American interests. He argued that, given legitimate Soviet security interests and the presence of the Red Army, there was little that the West could or should do to deny the USSR an effective sphere of influence. Few senior US policy-makers disagreed, but in 1944–5 only George Kennan, Counsellor at the US Embassy in Moscow, believed that the Americans should go as far as to write off Eastern Europe and accept a clean division of the Continent. Most agreed with Roosevelt that, to satisfy US public opinion and realize war aims such as the Atlantic Charter, Soviet influence in Eastern Europe must be ameliorated by democracy and basic freedoms—hence the Declaration on Liberated Europe and the determination to reconstruct the Polish government dominated by Moscow-backed communists. By the autumn of 1945 'Chip' Bohlen, senior Soviet specialist at the State Department, was developing a distinction between 'open' and 'exclusive' spheres, between 'legitimate' Soviet influence over a neighbour's security policy on the one hand and effective domination of its politics on the other.[18]

Stalin probably understood all this as ideological window-dressing, but the Americans took it very seriously. The Soviet-backed establishment of communist control in Poland, Romania, and Bulgaria became a deeply contentious issue. Even before his death in April 1945 Roosevelt may have been reassessing his policy of patience. His successor, Harry Truman, inexperienced and insecure but with a penchant for toughness, inclined towards the 'firm but friendly' line advocated by Averell Harriman, US Ambassador in Moscow. His 'lecture' to Soviet Foreign Minister V. M. Molotov within two weeks of taking office may have been read by the USSR as evidence of a turn of policy. In reality Truman was thrashing around, somewhat out of his depth. In May he shifted back to conciliatory diplomatic tactics and sent Harry Hopkins, FDR's former confidant, to Moscow in a successful effort to settle the Polish question. After a new flurry of firmness at the Foreign Ministers' conference in London in September,

---

[17] A theme explored above, Chs. 9–10.

[18] For good accounts of America's limited but real aims in Eastern Europe see Geir Lundestad, *The American Non-Policy towards Eastern Europe, 1943–1947: Universalism in an Area not of Essential Interest to the United States* (Oslo, 1978); Eduard Mark, 'American Policy toward Eastern Europe and the Origins of the Cold War, 1941–1946: An Alternative Interpretation', *Journal of American History*, 68 (1981), 313–36.

Truman's Secretary of State, James F. Byrnes, also swung around and finessed the Romanian and Bulgarian issues in Moscow in December. In all three cases, the existing governments had been modified by token non-communist additions.[19]

Despite apparent agreement, however, the arguments over Eastern Europe had left deep scars. Both sides believed that the Yalta agreement had been broken. Stalin, having probably assumed a crude sphere-of-influence agreement, was alarmed to see the West pressing on areas of major Soviet concern. The Americans viewed these rows in conjunction with Soviet pressure for a base in Turkey, a trusteeship in Italian North Africa, and vast reparations in Germany as part of an equally sinister pattern. The Soviet failure to withdraw from northern Iran was especially controversial, causing a direct confrontation in the UN in the spring of 1946 and prompting American assistance for anti-Soviet elements in the country—both significant new departures in US policy.[20]

John Gaddis and others have argued that the pieces fell clearly into place for many US policy-makers after February 1946, with George Kennan's 'Long Telegram' from the US Embassy in Moscow. This depicted Soviet foreign policy as 'not based on any objective analysis of [the] situation beyond Russia's borders' but as driven inexorably from within by a volatile mixture of historic insecurities and Marxist ideology.[21] But although Kennan's survey was required reading in the Pentagon, it probably did not have much influence on Truman and Byrnes. Certainly it did not betoken a shift in America's *public* policy, which was still the Rooseveltian one of trying to find grounds for agreement with the USSR, even if the tactics were now those of quid pro quo negotiation rather than patient friendliness.[22] Throughout 1946 US diplomacy remained in a state of flux. To understand the development of the Cold War, we need to consider other factors as well.

Conventionally US historiography, whether 'traditionalist', 'revisionist', or 'post-revisionist', has focused on the two superpowers. According to Hans Morgenthau in 1954, 'the international situation is reduced to the primitive spectacle of two giants eying [*sic*] each other with watchful suspicion'. In Europe in 1945 there were 'two superpowers separated only by a power vacuum', stated John Gaddis in 1978.[23] Since the 1980s however, various European scholars

---

[19] Important American accounts of the 1945–7 period in US–Soviet relations include John L. Gaddis, *The United States and the Origins of the Cold War, 1941–1947* (New York, 1972); Daniel Yergin, *Shattered Peace: The Origins of the Cold War and the National Security State* (Boston, 1977); Deborah Welch Larson, *Origins of Containment: A Psychological Explanation* (Princeton, 1985).

[20] Cf. Robert L. Messer, *The End of an Alliance: James F. Byrnes, Roosevelt, Truman, and the Origins of the Cold War* (Chapel Hill, NC, 1982); Fraser J. Harbutt, *The Iron Curtain: Churchill, America, and the Origins of the Cold War* (New York, 1986).

[21] Telegram of 22 Feb. 1946 in Thomas H. Etzold and John L. Gaddis, eds., *Containment: Documents on American Policy and Strategy, 1945–1950* (New York, 1978), 53.

[22] I follow Larson, *Origins of Containment*, 259–60; cf. Gaddis, *The US and the Origins of the Cold War*, 284, 312–15, and Yergin, *Shattered Peace*, 163–4.

[23] Hans J. Morgenthau, *Politics among Nations: The Struggle for Power and Peace* (2nd edn., New York, 1954), 339; Gaddis, *Russia, the Soviet Union, and the US*, 180. For surveys of recent

have stressed that European problems and pressures played a decisive part in shaping the US–Soviet confrontation.[24]

One distinctive feature of the European scene after the war was the swing to the left politically. If inter-war politics were dominated by fascism and the conservative right, the immediate post-war years saw the triumph of socialism in Britain and Scandinavia. Even more significant was the growth of communist parties, benefiting from their role in leading the resistance movements in many of the occupied countries. In France CP membership reached over one million in 1946; in Italy 1.7 million by the end of 1945. In both these countries the communists were in coalition governments in 1945–7. Eastern Europe saw even more spectacular increases, from a few hundred CP members to half a million in Hungary in 1945 and from 28,000 to 1.2 million in Czechoslovakia in the year from May 1945. In neither of these two cases can Soviet pressure be considered an all-sufficient explanation: the Hungarians were largely Catholic and historically anti-Slav, while the Red Army pulled out from Czechoslovakia in agreement with the Western Allies in November 1945.

This swing to the left posed a real dilemma for the USA and Great Britain, who had little doubt that, whatever the immediate coalitionist tactics of the communists, their gains would ultimately redound to Stalin's benefit. But the communist expansion also posed problems for Stalin. After the oppressions of fascist and Nazi rule, the demand for revolution was strong in many of these communist parties and Moscow's coalitionist line proved unpalatable. Leaders like the Czech communist Klement Gottwald found it hard to persuade his activists that 'in spite of the favourable situation the immediate target is not soviets and socialization but the really consistent working out of the democratic and national revolution'.[25] Although Stalin was able, in the interests of maintaining the Grand Alliance, to restrain the communists in Western states like France and Italy, there was enough deviation to imperil his overall policy. China was to be a particular problem later, but in the mid-1940s it was Tito's Yugoslavia (the scene of an indigenous revolution largely unassisted by the Red Army) which did him the most damage. Tito's demands for Trieste, his funnelling of support to the Greek communists and his shooting-down of two

American historiography see J. Samuel Walker, 'Historians and Cold War Origins: The New Consensus', in Gerald K. Haines and J. Samuel Walker, eds., *American Foreign Relations: A Historiographical Review* (Westport, Conn., 1981), 207–36; John L. Gaddis, 'The Emerging Post-Revisionist Synthesis and the Origins of the Cold War', *Diplomatic History*, 7 (1983), 171–90, and discussion, pp. 191–204.

[24] See Geir Lundestad, 'Empire by Invitation: The United States and Western Europe, 1945–1952', *Journal of Peace Research*, 23 (1986), 263–77; also David Reynolds, 'The Origins of the Cold War: The European Dimension, 1944–51', *Historical Journal*, 28 (1985), 497–515. The policies of the leading Western European powers are conveniently summarized in the essays in Josef Becker and Franz Knipping, eds., *Power in Europe?: Great Britain, France, Italy and Germany in a Postwar World 1945–1950* (Berlin, 1986).

[25] Remarks of April 1945, in Adam Westoby, *Communism since World War II* (Brighton, 1981), 49.

US transport planes in August 1946 were among the actions that the Western powers readily but erroneously assumed were orchestrated by Stalin.

In 1945–7 neither so-called superpower could therefore control Europe's post-war swing to the left. Nor, secondly, could they order Eastern Europe in a mutually acceptable form. In some Slavic areas, such as Bulgaria and the Serbian parts of Yugoslavia, the Russians were not unwelcome, but in much of Eastern Europe, such as Romania, Hungary, and Poland, it was a different story. Historic antagonisms, dating back over many centuries, were exacerbated by ethnic rivalries and territorial disputes. Poland, for instance, had been partitioned by the great powers for much of the previous two centuries. It re-emerged after 1918 mainly at the expense of Russia, and the two countries fought a bloody war in 1920–1. In 1939 Poland was partitioned anew, and relations deteriorated even further over the Katyn massacre, exposed in 1943, and the Warsaw rising of 1944. In these circumstances security became a zero-sum game—an either-or situation for Poles and Russians.

In many of these countries, the communist party, despite increased support, was fundamentally compromised by identification with the Russians. Furthermore, in Germany and Austria in particular, Red Army brutality (partly in revenge for Nazi atrocities in the USSR) quickly turned public feeling against the communists.[26] The upshot was that where free elections were permitted, the communists usually did very badly compared with socialist or agrarian parties—as shown by the votes in Austria and Hungary in November 1945 or the elections in Berlin in October 1946.

These circumstances—anti-Russian feeling and lack of overwhelming voluntary support for the communist party—suggest that in the long run the American policy of trying to harmonize Soviet security with Western demands for openness was unlikely to succeed. In much of Eastern Europe an 'open sphere' would simply not produce governments and policies sympathetic to Soviet interests.[27] Yet the alternative—exclusive Soviet control—was unacceptable to US political and public opinion. In any case, given Stalin's attitude to political pluralism at home—from the elimination of left and right in the 1920s, through the brutal collectivization of agriculture, to the purges of the later 1930s—it is unlikely that he could have lived with openness on American terms. There is no doubt that in 1945–6 Hungary, Czechoslovakia, and even the Soviet zone of Germany were following their own distinctive paths leftward,[28] but, even

[26] Thomas T. Hammond, ed., *Witnesses to the Origins of the Cold War* (Seattle, 1982), 185, 233–4.

[27] The main exception was Czechoslovakia, where Benes tried to maintain democracy and independence while conciliating Moscow, which was a major reason why the communist takeover there in February 1948 was regarded as so significant by the West.

[28] See N. G. Papp, 'The Democratic Struggle for Power in Hungary: Party Strategies, 1945–46', *East Central Europe*, 6 (1979), 1–19; Martin R. Myant, *Socialism and Democracy in Czechoslovakia, 1945–1948* (Cambridge, 1981); Gregory W. Sandford, *From Hitler to Ulbricht: The Communist Reconstruction of East Germany, 1945–1946* (Princeton, 1983).

if superpower relations had not deteriorated as badly as they did in 1947, Stalin would probably have consolidated his hold eventually.

A third semi-autonomous European problem was Germany—in fact the key issue in the emerging Cold War. At stake for the USA and the USSR was control of the country that had started two world wars and might, it was feared, start a third if the victors did not make the right decisions this time. In principle both superpowers inclined to a unified German state, under satisfactory guarantees. It was the French who wanted, as after the First World War, to amputate Germany's economic vital parts, particularly the Ruhr and the Saar, and place them under French or else international control. For the Russians the crucial issue was the settlement of Germany's reparations payments, including substantial amounts from the industrialized western zones controlled by the Allies. In reacting to this stalemate, Washington was initially divided in 1945–6. The State Department's European desk, anxious to restore French power, was sympathetic to their arguments, but the War Department and the occupation authorities under General Lucius Clay wanted to get Germany back on its feet economically and end the military regime. Clay's decision to stop reparations payments from the US zone to the USSR (May 1946) was not aimed exclusively at the Soviet Union but was also intended to force the German deadlock to a head in the Allied counsels.[29]

Behind American disputes with France and the USSR was mounting domestic pressure to get back to normal. Dean Acheson, Under-Secretary of State, declared in November 1945: 'I can state in three sentences what the "popular" attitude is toward foreign policy today. 1. Bring the boys home. 2. Don't be a Santa Claus. 3. Don't be pushed around.'[30] Although the US government was determined to shape post-war Japan in its own image, excluding all the other allies from any effective say in General Douglas MacArthur's occupation regime, it never intended to play a major role in post-war Europe. At all the wartime conferences Roosevelt had insisted that US troops would not stay in Europe for more than two years after the conflict. He knew that a large peacetime presence would not be practical politics in a country where the desire to 'bring the boys home' and cut back on foreign aid and overseas commitments would be overwhelming. (It is important to note that the abrupt end of Lend-Lease and the opposition to foreign credits, which aggravated US–Soviet relations in 1945–6, were also reproduced in America's relations with Britain, its closest wartime ally, in the same period.) For Roosevelt and his immediate policy-making successors, Europe would be 'policed' primarily by Britain and the USSR, albeit

[29] The French dimension of America's German policy is emphasized (and probably exaggerated) in John Gimbel, *The Origins of the Marshall Plan* (Stanford, Calif., 1976). On Germany in general there are useful essays in Roland G. Foerster, et al., *Anfänge westdeutscher Sicherheitspolitik, 1945–1956*, i: *Von der Kapitulation bis zum Pleven-Plan* (Munich, 1982); Josef Foschepoth, ed., *Kalter Krieg und Deutsche Frage: Deutschland im Widerstreit der Mächte, 1945–1952* (Göttingen, 1985).

[30] Walter Isaacson and Evan Thomas, *The Wise Men: Six Friends and the World They Made. Acheson, Bohlen, Harriman, Kennan, Lovett, McCloy* (New York, 1986), 338.

in harmony with US policy, and American sympathy for a revived role for France was a reflection of this recognition that Washington would not have primary responsibility for European affairs. Behind the Army's demands to sort out the German problem lay this mounting irritation in Congress and the public. Demands increased to reduce the costs of the US occupation of Germany by making the country self-sufficient economically and thus able to pay for its own imports and reconstruction.

The implications of American resistance to European commitments bring us naturally to a fourth facet of the European dimension—the place of Britain. Although it is easy to neglect its importance today, Britain in the late 1940s was unquestionably the strongest Western European state, economically and militarily, retaining worldwide commitments and interests. Despite the loss of a quarter of her national wealth in the war, Britain's Labour leaders, no less than Churchill and Eden, were determined to maintain her position as a world power. Their view of the United States was ambivalent: the Americans, by language and culture, were seen as natural allies, but they were also rivals for Britain's trade and critics of her empire. More to the point in 1945, although the British would have liked to see firm American commitments to Europe, they recognized that this was unlikely. Consequently it was important to maintain the best possible relationship with the Soviet Union, because together they would have to keep the European peace against a revived Germany.[31]

Despite his reputation as a notorious anti-communist, Churchill shared these convictions, as we saw in the previous two chapters. Like Roosevelt, he acknowledged privately the inevitability of a Soviet sphere of influence in Eastern Europe, but wanted to prevent it becoming a closed Stalinist bloc. (Britain felt particular obligations to the Poles because they had been the immediate cause of her declaration of war against Germany in 1939.) Churchill therefore wanted to maintain the wartime alliance. Though he favoured more of a quid pro quo approach than Roosevelt, not least in pushing the Anglo-American armies as far east as possible in the spring of 1945, this was not as a prelude to renewed war but as the basis for negotiation from a position of strength. Similar views were also held by the new Labour government headed by Clement Attlee, with Ernest Bevin as Foreign Secretary. Bevin, like Churchill, was ready to 'talk tough' to Molotov, but in 1945–6 he still had not abandoned the attempt to reach negotiated agreements. As late as December 1947 he could still express doubt in private about 'whether Russia was as great a danger as a resurgent Germany might become'.[32]

---

[31] For background see Graham Ross, ed., *The Foreign Office and the Kremlin: British Documents on Anglo-Soviet Relations, 1941–1945* (Cambridge, 1985), which includes a useful introduction; Martin Kitchen, *British Policy towards the Soviet Union during the Second World War* (London, 1986).

[32] Alan Bullock, *Ernest Bevin: Foreign Secretary, 1945–1951* (London, 1983), 269. On Churchill see Elisabeth Barker, *Churchill and Eden at War* (London, 1978).

Beneath this official policy, however, Whitehall, like Washington, was uncertain about Soviet intentions. The leading hardliners were the Chiefs of Staff, particularly in the form of their Post-Hostilities Planners, who by 1944 were already talking of the USSR as the only likely enemy for Britain in the future. The Chiefs and the Foreign Office were particularly disturbed about the Eastern Mediterranean—a major area of British interest and historically a centre of Anglo-Russian rivalry. In 1945–6 the Soviet Union's pressure on Turkey, its slowness to withdraw from northern Iran and the communist insurgency on Greece all took on sinister significance for many in Whitehall. Another aspect of Soviet policy that alarmed the British more than the Americans was the new and intense anti-imperialist propaganda campaign in the Soviet press, which was directed particularly at Britain and which contrasted strongly with the restrained tone of the Soviet media during the war. Despite the growing doubts, however, the British political leadership in 1945–6 remained anxious for agreement. Attlee argued tenaciously that the Russian threat in the Mediterranean was exaggerated and that, in any case, Britain was unnecessarily over-extended in the area. Bevin, like Eden, discouraged talk of a Western European bloc, centred on Anglo-French cooperation, for fear that it would arouse Soviet fears of Western encirclement. Nor would he go along with calls from the FO's Russia Committee (set up in the spring of 1946) for a propaganda counter-attack on communism and for the provision of moral and material support to anti-communist social democrats.[33]

The nearest Bevin came to an overt breach with the USSR was the decision in July 1946 to fuse the British and US zones of occupation in Germany. Without economic recovery, Bevin feared disaster. Not only would communism increase its appeal among discontented and impoverished people, but the burden of running the zone would become unbearable for Britain's weakened economy. The Treasury was anxious for cuts and, as public anger mounted about 'British reparations to Germany', the Cabinet in July 1946 was forced to impose bread rationing (a course not adopted even in the darkest days of the war) to help maintain a flow of grain to Germany. Politically, such a situation could not continue. With British and US perceptions in line on the issue, the two governments agreed to fuse their zones, to reduce costs. This came into operation in January 1947.[34]

But although the 'Bizone' proved a significant development, it did not make inevitable the crisis events of 1947. To understand their full significance, we

[33] For themes touched on in this paragraph see Victor Rothwell, *Britain and the Cold War, 1941–1947* (London, 1982)—a digest of FO opinion; John W. Young, *Britain, France and the Unity of Europe, 1945–1951* (Leicester, 1984); the important article by Raymond Smith and John Zametica, 'The Cold Warrior: Clement Attlee Reconsidered, 1945–1947', *International Affairs*, 61 (1985), 237–52; and Ray Merrick, 'The Russia Committee of the British Foreign Office and the Cold War, 1946–1947', *Journal of Contemporary History*, 20 (1985), 453–68.

[34] For the argument that Britain forced the pace over Germany, see Anne Deighton, 'The "Frozen Front": The Labour Government, the Division of Germany and the Origins of the Cold War, 1945–1947', *International Affairs*, 53 (1987), 449–65.

need to look now at the underlying perceptions of the three allies. Some of these have already emerged in the foregoing discussion, but it is time to pull them together. For the Cold War developed not so much from the actions of the three powers as from the way these actions were interpreted, or misinterpreted.[35]

One fundamental problem was the 'universalist' ideologies publicly espoused by the United States and the Soviet Union. In practice, as we have seen, both countries may well have been adopting a sphere of influence policy, which on Eastern and Western Europe (if not on Germany) involved some acknowledgement of the other's interests and sensitivities. But that is not what they said in public. Privately Roosevelt spoke the language of spheres of influence,[36] but official US foreign policy was couched in terms of one world, open to democratic values, in which, to quote Secretary of State Cordell Hull, 'there will no longer be need for spheres of influence, for alliances, for balance of power, or any other of the special arrangements through which, in the unhappy past, the nations strove to safeguard their security or to promote their interests.'[37] Roosevelt and Truman believed that the American public would not tolerate the language of the old diplomacy, but by encouraging misleading, even Utopian, expectations they paved the way for growing US disenchantment with what the Soviet Union was doing, as well as intensifying Moscow's suspicions. Conversely, the renewed rhetoric of Marxism-Leninism had its effect in the USA. Whether Stalin sincerely supported it or merely utilized this attack on 'cosmopolitanism' as part of his domestic battles, it had a deeply unsettling effect in Britain and the USA. Particularly perplexing in Washington was Stalin's election speech of 9 February 1946 which began with a Leninist interpretation of the origins of the Second World War. To many in the West it seemed to confirm that ideology was back in favour in the Kremlin and, at a time when the communist movement was assumed to be under Stalin's control, the actions of Pieck in eastern Germany or Tito in Yugoslavia were easily conflated into a single pattern.

Readings of recent history also played their part. In the United States Soviet actions were fitted into an image of totalitarian regimes. Repression at home implied aggression abroad—from the Kaiser, through Hitler, to Stalin. As Truman observed in May 1947: 'There isn't any difference in totalitarian states . . . Nazi, Communist or Fascist, or Franco, or anything else—they are all alike . . . '.[38]

[35] A useful German textbook on the Cold War that embodies this approach is Wilfried Loth, *The Division of the World, 1941–1955* (London, 1988).

[36] For instance, he told US Senators in January 1945 'that the Russians had the power in Eastern Europe, that it was obviously impossible to have a break with them and that, therefore, the only practicable course was to use what influence we had to ameliorate the situation'. Dallek, *Roosevelt and American Foreign Policy*, 507–8.

[37] Address to Joint Session of Congress, 18 Nov. 1943, in *The Memoirs of Cordell Hull* (New York, 1948), ii. 1314–15.

[38] John Lewis Gaddis, *The Long Peace: Inquiries into the History of the Cold War* (New York, 1987), 36.

Equally important were the 'lessons' of appeasement. Both in Washington and London there was sensitivity about the Western failure to react quickly and effectively against Hitler's build-up in the 1930s. Thus, Secretary of the Navy James Forrestal in September 1945 dismissed the idea 'that we should endeavor to buy their [Soviet] understanding and sympathy. We tried that once with Hitler. There are no returns on appeasement.'[39] Given these views of totalitarianism and of appeasement, there was a tendency for Western observers to focus on those aspects of Soviet conduct in 1945–6 that fitted the paradigm—Poland, Romania, Bulgaria, for instance, rather than Finland, Czechoslovakia, or Greece. They saw these as the first steps, 1930s-style, to expansion over all of Europe. Though perhaps imperceptive, such an appraisal was understandable if one remembers their view of Stalin as, above all, the architect of the great purges of 1936–9 when perhaps four to five million were eliminated, half a million of them summarily shot, and in which an apparently paranoid dictator disposed of half his own officer corps including his best commanders, thus laying his country open to the disasters of 1941.[40]

If Western leaders may have been ill-tuned to possible nuances in Stalin's policy, the Soviet leadership seems fatally to have misread the relationship between the other two members of the Big Three. Stalin's ideological justification for a policy of collaboration was that he could exploit the inevitable conflicts between the imperialist powers to maximize Soviet advantages. The Anglo-American disagreements during the war over oil, colonies, and trade, and the rifts between FDR and Churchill, at Teheran and Yalta (intended by Roosevelt to demonstrate that Stalin was not the victim of capitalist encirclement) seemed to prove the wisdom of such a Leninist analysis. In 1945–6 Stalin and Molotov repeatedly tried to play off the two Western powers in an effort to gain Soviet objectives. Up to a point they were successful, for instance at Moscow in December 1945 where Byrnes settled Romania and Bulgaria unilaterally with little reference to an angry Bevin, but fundamentally Stalin had misunderstood the ambivalent 'special relationship' of 'competitive cooperation'.[41] If the British were too prone to assume underlying Anglo-American harmony, the Soviet Union, guided by Leninism, was too ready to assume inevitable Anglo-American discord. Britain and America were in certain respects economic and power-political rivals, but they also shared common liberal values and common interests in the stability of Europe. When those values and interests were threatened in 1940, cooperation overrode competition. When a similar threat seemed to emerge in 1946–7 another rapprochement occurred. Stalin and Molotov had pushed them too far.

It is possible, then, that a spheres-of-influence arrangement might have worked for Eastern and Western Europe, if both sides had not been (often

---

[39] Ernest R. May, *'Lessons' of the Past: The Use and Misuse of History in American Foreign Policy* (New York, 1973), 33.

[40] Cf. Roy A. Medvedev, *Let History Judge: The Origins and Consequences of Stalinism* (London, 1972), ch. 6.   [41] See above, Ch. 3.

willing) prisoners of their ideologies and had they not been heavily influenced by their reading of recent history. On Germany, however, the issues were almost intractable. The Soviet Union had suffered too much in two wars to be able to compromise readily on this matter, and the French, also a continental state easily threatened by Germany, had similar fears. Britain and the United States had suffered much less (750,000 dead compared with the USSR's 20–30 million) and they were protected from German aggression by the English Channel and the Atlantic Ocean. For the British and Americans the historical resonance of Germany was economic as much as military—echoing back to the 1920s, when, as they interpreted it, an impossible burden of reparations had fuelled inflation and undermined the international monetary system.

By 1946 they considered that the overriding issues were to reduce the high costs on them of German relief and to revive Germany before discontent played into the hands of the communists. As Clay put it in March 1946, 'there is no choice between becoming a Communist on 1500 calories and a believer in democracy on 1000 calories'.[42] They simply could not comprehend the visceral fears of Germany that gnawed at Soviet leaders—the importance of a secure Eastern European buffer and a reliable German settlement to guard against repetition of the traumatic 'surprise' attack of 1941. Nor could they fully grasp how their efforts to rehabilitate Germany, made necessary in their view by Soviet intransigence, fed Moscow's anxieties. This was particularly true in 1948 when Stalin blockaded Berlin in a counter-productive effort to head off the creation of a West German state.

But why was the USA so concerned about events in Europe? That, after all, was the big contrast with earlier American foreign policy, when US security was not deemed to be inextricably linked to that of Europe. The 1940s saw a greatly expanded definition of US interests, drawing on two main lines of thought. First, Hitler's victories seemed to show that Americans could not allow a potential foe to control Western Europe—the leading economic centre outside the USA. If that happened the Americas might be forced into economic isolation and their security eventually eroded by enemy control of Europe's industrial resources. 'The greatest danger to the security of the United States', warned the CIA in 1947, 'is the possibility of economic collapse in Western Europe and the consequent accession to power of Communist elements.'[43] Linked to this new concern for the European balance was the conviction that air power had revolutionized security. The long-range bomber had 'shrunk' the world, the atomic

[42] Clay to War Dept., 27 Mar. 1946, in Jean Edward Smith, ed., *The Papers of General Lucius D. Clay: Germany, 1945–1949* (2 vols., Bloomington, Ind., 1974), i. 184.

[43] CIA review of world situation, Sept. 1947, quoted in Melvyn P. Leffler, 'The American Conception of National Security and the Beginnings of the Cold War, 1945–48', *American Historical Review*, 89 (1984), 364. For material in this paragraph see Leffler's article and also Yergin, *Shattered Peace*, ch. 8; Richard Best, *'Co-operation with Like-Minded Peoples': British Influences on American Security Policy, 1945–1949* (Westport, Conn., 1986), chs. 2–3; Gregg Herken, *The Winning Weapon: The Atomic Bomb in the Cold War, 1945–1950* (New York, 1982), ch. 10.

bomb heralded undreamt-of destructive force, and exponents of air power such as Generals 'Hap' Arnold and Carl Spaatz argued that the USA now needed an extended defence perimeter with bases across the Atlantic and in Germany and Britain.

These claims had only limited support in 1945–6, even within the Pentagon, and they were partly advanced for bureaucratic reasons, to strengthen the case for a US Air Force independent of the Army. The direct threat to the security of the United States remained extremely remote, particularly before the Soviet A-bomb (1949) and intercontinental missile (1957). It was ideology as much as interests that underpinned America's new 'gospel of national security'—the Wilsonian conviction that the USA could and should use its enhanced power to export liberal, capitalist, democratic, and anti-colonial values for the benefit of a European-dominated world that had torn itself to pieces once again. If 1945 seemed to some communist leaders the cue for revolution, many Americans believed that it demonstrated the need for US-led reform. Though not envisaging major commitments in Europe, the United States expected the post-war international order to conform to its worldview. Harry Hopkins remarked in 1945:

I have often been asked what interests we have in Poland, Greece, Iran, or Korea. Well, I think we have the most important business in the world—and indeed, the only business worthy of our traditions. And that is this—to do everything within our diplomatic power to foster and encourage democratic government throughout the world. We should not be timid, about blazoning to the world our desire for the right of all peoples to have a genuine civil liberty. We believe our dynamic democracy is the best in the world . . . [44]

Bearing in mind what we have just examined—the deteriorating US–Soviet relationship in 1945–6, the European dimension, and the Big Three's underlying perceptions—we are now better able to understand the decisive crisis of 1947. It was a process of action and reaction in which the catalysts came from within Europe. Of particular importance was the abrupt British collapse amid economic crisis in February 1947. Unable to sustain the foreign exchange costs of Britain's overseas commitments, the Treasury, supported by Attlee, forced Bevin and the Chiefs of Staff to abandon the Palestine mandate, pull out of India quickly, and end financial aid to Greece and Turkey. Bevin used the last decision to put the ball firmly in the American court, asking them to assume responsibility for the Eastern Mediterranean.[45]

The State Department, guided particularly by Under-Secretary Dean Acheson, was already coming round to this view, but the urgency of the British request posed a major political problem for Truman. The 80th Congress was controlled by the Republicans, whose anti-communist election rhetoric was

---

[44] Thomas G. Paterson, *On Every Front: The Making of the Cold War* (New York, 1979), 72–3.

[45] For British influences on US policy see Terry H. Anderson, *The United States, Great Britain, and the Cold War, 1944–1947* (Columbia, Mo., 1981); Robin Edmonds, *Setting the Mould: The United States and Britain, 1945–1950* (Oxford, 1986).

balanced by an intense concern to reduce government spending. Sounding out Congressmen, Acheson found them unsympathetic to 'pulling British chestnuts out of the fire' but shocked by warnings that Greece was like a 'rotten apple in the barrel' from which decay would soon spread through southern Europe. Also effective were presentations of the Greek-Turkish issue in terms of a broader struggle between the democratic and totalitarian ways of life, reminiscent of the Second World War. It was therefore in this universalist language that Truman appealed to Congress on 12 March 1947 for money for Greece and Turkey—'at the present moment in world history nearly every nation must choose between alternative ways of life. The choice is too often not a free one.'[46]

The ideological rhetoric of the Truman Doctrine, though exaggerated for political reasons, provided a new statement of policy which then helped shape the US outlook. The strategy of 'containment' gradually evolved.[47] At the same time the economic crisis had brought the German problem to a head. Unable to reach agreement at the Moscow Foreign Ministers Conference, the US Secretary of State, George C. Marshall, guided by Acheson and Kennan, offered American aid for a joint European recovery programme in his speech on 5 June.[48] The central object was the revival of Germany, but the Europe-wide package was intended to make it more palatable to the French and to the Soviet Union, even though the US and Britain were determined not to let the USSR frustrate further progress. Although Soviet rejection was likely, the attitude of the East European governments was less predictable. Poland, Czechoslovakia, Hungary, and Romania were among those interested in participating, but Stalin, after some indecision, warned them off. That has been described as 'a blunder of major proportions that had a profound effect on the future course of European politics'.[49] Eastern European participation could have relieved the subsequent economic burden on the USSR, or, at least, made the Marshall Plan much harder to get through Congress. Stalin undoubtedly regarded Eastern European interest as a further threat to his security zone, but the result of the American offer and the Soviet response was the economic polarization of Europe.

Soviet reaction to the Truman Doctrine had been restrained, but the Szklarska Poreba conference of communist parties in September 1947, at which Cominform

---

[46] *Public Papers of the Presidents of the United States: Harry S. Truman, 1947* (Washington, DC, 1963), 176–80.

[47] Cf. John Lewis Gaddis, *Strategies of Containment: A Critical Appraisal of Postwar American National Security Policy* (New York, 1982).

[48] For useful overviews see Scott Jackson, 'Prologue to the Marshall Plan: The Origins of the American Commitment for a European Recovery Program', *Journal of American History*, 65 (1979), 1043–68; Melvyn P. Leffler, 'The United States and the Strategic Dimensions of the Marshall Plan', *Diplomatic History*, 12 (1988), 277–306. Two very important monographs are Alan S. Milward, *The Reconstruction of Western Europe, 1945–1951* (London, 1984), and Michael J. Hogan, *The Marshall Plan: America, Britain and the Reconstruction of Western Europe, 1947–1952* (New York, 1987).

[49] Joseph L. Nogee and Robert H. Donaldson, *Soviet Foreign Policy since World War II* (New York, 1981), 65–6. Cf. Taubman, *Stalin's American Policy*, 172–3.

was created, saw a firm response to American actions and rhetoric. Zhdanov's 'two camps' statement and the encouragement of the French and Italian communist parties to repent their coalitionist past and mount a programme of industrial and political challenge to the bourgeois order represented significant shifts of policy. In Eastern Europe Stalin's over-reaction to the Marshall Plan helped precipitate the shift from coalitionist tactics to the tried and tested techniques of Stalinization. From late 1947 the popular front governments in Eastern Europe were quickly replaced by communist rule. Independent-minded Communist leaders who had espoused the earlier doctrine of non-revolutionary roads to socialism, such as Gomulka in Poland, were replaced by Stalinists of unquestioned loyalty, and the collectivization of the economy proceeded apace. It was at this point, *pace* Churchill's Fulton speech of March 1946, that the 'Iron Curtain' truly came down.

The break-up of the Grand Alliance in Europe did not occur immediately in 1945, but developed gradually up to the turning-point of 1947. 'Policy-makers' were not following confrontational blueprints from an early stage; they gradually lost faith in the strategy of collaboration without having anything clear to put in its place. In the process of breakdown it is perhaps helpful to distinguish *assumptions, perceptions, actions,* and *policies.*[50]

In all three major protagonists the underlying assumptions were sceptical. The Soviet Union assumed fundamental capitalist antipathy; America and Britain assumed that Soviet intentions were ultimately revolutionary. At root neither side found it easy to accept that peaceful coexistence was possible or even desirable, with so much of the world apparently at stake in the turbulent aftermath of the Second World War. Nevertheless, the form, timing, and intensity of their confrontation were not predetermined. A policy of collaboration was initially adopted, with hopes that differences might be managed by diplomacy and the wartime concert perpetuated into the peacetime world.

In both the USA and Britain perceptions of the Soviet Union were changing in 1945–6, but, although sections of both bureaucracies urged a shift of policy from negotiation to confrontation, the political leaderships were unready to go that far, particularly in public. It was the force of events as much as changing perceptions that drove the British and US governments into action—especially over the problem of communism in their sphere of influence and over the deadlock in Germany. In order to take action, a ringing ideological statement (the Truman Doctrine) was required to overcome US domestic doubts, and this laid the framework for a public policy of containment. Although the British may have been, if anything, keener than the USA to force the pace over Germany, as well as more concerned over the Eastern Mediterranean, their shift in declaratory

---

[50] I am developing here the suggestive approach in Larson, *Origins of Containment*, where the last three concepts are articulated and deployed.

policy did not come until January 1948. Only then did Bevin accept the Russia Committee's long-standing demands and call publicly for Western European union. Simultaneously the Cabinet accepted plans for a moral and material consolidation of Western Europe, a vigorous propaganda counter-attack on international communism and negotiations for a defence pact with France and the Benelux countries which, Bevin hoped, could be extended to include the USA. Thus began the negotiations leading to the North Atlantic Treaty of April 1949.

At what point Stalin moved from changed perceptions to changed policies is harder to say. Scholars still lack access to the Soviet archives, and Stalin's own public statements, in marked contrast to the pre-war period, were few and far between. But as the Marshall Plan took off in the summer and autumn of 1947 he clearly felt obliged to act, for fear that his whole security programme was in danger, and it may be that the Cominform statement represented policy catching up with perceptions and actions.

The shape of Cold War Europe was still not fully defined. 1948 saw the start of a protracted debate on the form of the new Western Europe, with the French promoting economic and political integration as a way of controlling German recovery while the British resisted US pressure to take the lead.[51] Likewise, the decisions to turn NATO into a military alliance and to rearm West Germany were not taken until after the Korean War began in the summer of 1950, when a Soviet offensive in Europe was believed to be a real possibility.[52] The breakdown in Europe also affected Soviet–American relations in Asia. The 1947 crisis provoked a reversal of US policy in Japan, with economic recovery and the containment of communism replacing the creation of a liberal-democratic state as the top American priority. And the successful 1948–9 face-off over Berlin may have led Washington to believe that similar tactics would work in Korea, encouraging the fateful decision in the autumn of 1950 to drive north of the 38th parallel up to the Chinese border to reunify the country. This brought China into the war and helped freeze Sino-American relations in Cold War animosity until the 1970s.[53]

Nevertheless, the crucial developments in the Cold War had occurred in 1945–8, predominantly in Europe. Soviet–American rivalry was apparent in Asia, intensified by the wartime collapse of European influence and the growth of nationalist movements. But the stakes were highest in Europe, whose industrial and military importance centred above all on Germany. At the end of

---

[51] See the useful essays in Raymond Poidevin, ed., *Histoire des débuts de la construction européenne, mars 1948–mai 1950* (Brussels, 1986).

[52] Cf. Robert Jervis, 'The Impact of the Korean War on the Cold War', *Journal of Conflict Resolution*, 24 (1980), 563–92.

[53] Michael Schaller, *The American Occupation of Japan: The Origins of the Cold War in Asia* (New York, 1985); Russell D. Buhite, *Soviet-American Relations in Asia, 1945–1954* (Norman, Okla., 1981), esp. pp. 221–35.

the war it would seem that the 'Big Three' had hoped for some kind of loose spheres of influence arrangement in Europe—but only up to a point. The British still treated much of the Balkans and Middle East as a vital interest, despite dissenting noises from Attlee, and were anxious to contain the expansion of Soviet and communist influence there. American tolerance for spheres was compromised by a universalist ideology and by their newly extended definition of US security to include the stability of Eurasia. The USSR, in its turn, unsettled the British and Americans by its revival of the universalist language of Marxist-Leninist revolution. An even graver problem was Stalinism itself. Given their recent experiences with 'totalitarian' regimes, Britain and the USA feared the worst from a leader for whom security was always closely linked to repression—at home or in Eastern Europe.

Even if the wartime allies had been willing to limit their geopolitical and ideological aspirations, however, the problems of Germany made a secure sphere of influence agreement—mutual tolerance of eastern and western blocs—an unlikely eventuality. The aftermath of Hitler's war was too profound, too unsettling. For the Western powers the economic dislocation of Germany and the emergence of communism, whatever Stalin's immediate policy, were unacceptable. For the Soviet Union, any attempt to rehabilitate its mortal enemy, Germany, without security and reparations was equally intolerable. The struggle for mastery of Germany lay at the heart of the Grand Alliance and also of the Cold War. As Lenin, adapting Clausewitz, had observed thirty years before: 'War is the continuation of the policies of peace and peace the continuation of the policies of war.'[54]

SOME ADDITIONAL READING

John Lewis Gaddis, *We Now Know: Rethinking Cold War History* (Oxford, 1997) offers an analytical synthesis of scholarship from both sides of the Iron Curtain since the end of the Cold War. For the Soviet side see the pioneering study by David Holloway, *Stalin and the Bomb* (New Haven, 1994), and the contrasting interpretations of Stalin by Vladislav Zubok and Constantine Pleshakov, *Inside the Kremlin's Cold War: From Stalin to Khrushchev* (Cambridge, Mass., 1996), and Vojtech Mastny, *The Cold War and Soviet Insecurity: The Stalin Years* (New York, 1996). The extensive American work includes Melvyn P. Leffler, *A Preponderance of Power: National Security, the Truman Administration, and the Cold War* (Stanford, Calif., 1992), and Arnold A. Offner, *Another Such Victory: President Truman and the Cold War, 1945–1953* (Stanford, Calif., 2002). For the European dimension, see David Reynolds, ed., *The Origins of the Cold War in Europe: International Perspectives* (New Haven, 1994), and Norman Naimark and Leonid Gibianskii, eds., *Establishment of Communist Regimes in Eastern Europe, 1944–1949* (Boulder, Colo., 1997). For divergent views of the Big Three and the German question

---

[54] 'Bourgeois Pacificism and Socialist Pacificism' (1 Jan. 1917), in V. I. Lenin, *Collected Works*, xxiii (Moscow, 1964), 192.

see Anne Deighton, *The Impossible Peace: Britain, the Division of Germany, and the Origins of the Cold War* (Oxford, 1990); Norman M. Naimark, *The Russians in Germany: A History of the Soviet Zone of Occupation, 1945–1949* (Cambridge, Mass., 1995); and Carolyn Woods Eisenberg, *Drawing the Line: The American Decision to Divide Germany, 1944–1949* (Cambridge, 1996).

VI

PERSPECTIVES

16

Power and Superpower

The Impact of the Second World War on America's International Role

The emergence of the United States as a 'superpower' was a phenomenon of the mid-twentieth century, yet it had been predicted long before. Perhaps the most distinguished prophet was Alexis de Tocqueville in 1835, who concluded the first volume of *Democracy in America* with the forecast that one day the United States and Russia would each 'hold in its hands the destinies of half the world'. But many others spoke in the same vein. In 1866, for instance, de Tocqueville's compatriot, the economist Michel Chevalier, urged Europe to unify in the face of the 'political colossus that has been created on the other side of the Atlantic' and foresaw future armed conflict between the two continents. In 1882, Constantin Frantz, the German political commentator, considered it virtually inevitable 'that the New World would outstrip the Old World in the not far distant future', while the English historian J. R. Seeley predicted two years later that within the lifetime of his students, 'Russia and the United States will surpass in power the states now called great as much as the great country-states of the sixteenth century surpassed Florence.'[1]

In fact, the idea that the future lay with the 'world powers' became almost commonplace in late-nineteenth-century thought about international relations. For much of the century, America and Russia had been spoken of in the same breath as the two great land powers whose vast size and population guaranteed them eventual supremacy. In the last third of the century, however, America's

This chapter was originally given as a conference paper at Rutgers University, Newark, New Jersey, in 1986. It reflected my attempts to grapple with the ideas of Paul Kennedy about international power, later developed in his book *The Rise and Fall of the Great Powers* (New York, 1988), and he kindly commented on a draft. The text appears here as published in Warren F. Kimball, ed., *America Unbound: World War II and the Making of a Superpower* (New York, 1992) except for omission of three paragraphs near the end relating to the 1970s and 1980s.

[1] Alexis de Tocqueville, *Democracy in America*, ed. J. P. Mayer (New York, 1969), 413; Michel Chevalier, 'La Guerre et la crise européenne', *Revue des Deux Mondes*, 1 June 1866, pp. 784–5; Constantin Frantz, *Die Weltpolitik unter besonderer Bezugnahme auf Deutschland* (Osnabruck, reprint edn., 1966), i. 89; J. R. Seeley, *The Expansion of England* (London, 1884), 301.

promise seemed the greater. The Civil War had removed the possibility that the Union would disintegrate, and America's rapid industrialization closed the gap between its economy and those of Britain, hitherto the dominant industrial power, and Germany, Britain's other main rival. In 1913 the United States produced one-third of the world's manufactures, its coal output equalled that of Britain and Germany combined, and its iron and steel production surpassed that of the entire continent of Europe.[2] The trend seemed clear. Indeed, it is easy to conclude, bearing in mind America's population, natural resources, industrial might, and geographical security, that 'there was a virtual inevitability about the process of American expansion; that is to say, only persistent human ineptitude, or near-constant civil war, or a climatic disaster could have checked this rise to global economic (and, by extension, military) influence.'[3]

That Braudelian judgement is understandable and to a large extent appropriate. In the long run there is an apparent ineluctability about America's rise to globalism. It is, after all, a characteristic of industrial as against premodern societies that 'economic wealth and military power became increasingly synonymous'.[4] Yet that is not the whole story. Some modern states with significant economic strength have not translated this into comparable military influence—think of post-war Japan or, more recently, Saudi Arabia. Theorists of international relations agree that the power of a state cannot be simply equated with crude capabilities such as population, gross national product, or total steel output.[5] What is striking about the history of the twentieth century is surely the relative slowness with which America evolved into a superpower, given its industrial strength by 1914.

In addition to economic power, four other explanatory concepts are suggested here to help us understand America's changing international role during the first half of that century: 'environment', 'intentions', 'interests', and 'institutions'. By 'environment' is meant the general pattern of international relations. This provides the context and opportunity for extending national power and influence. But a favourable environment must be exploited: there must be appropriate 'intentions', a determination to bring the country's resources to bear on international events. That determination can be rooted in morality or ideology, but to be fully effective it usually also requires a concept of national 'interests'— the conviction that the nation's prosperity and security depend on shaping world affairs to one's own advantage. But this can only be done if a country has the appropriate 'institutions' to harness national power and project it internationally. These institutions include not only a diplomatic service and armed forces, but also a coordinated government bureaucracy.

---

[2] A. J. P. Taylor, *The Struggle for Mastery in Europe, 1848–1918* (London, 1954), p. xxxi.

[3] Paul M. Kennedy, 'The First World War and the International Power System', *International Security* 9 (1984), 35.

[4] Robert Gilpin, *War and Change in World Politics* (Cambridge, 1981), 124.

[5] For example, Joseph Frankel, *International Relations in a Changing World* (Oxford, 1979), especially pp. 100–5.

These four concepts will be used to help explain America's rise to superpower status and the place of World War I and, in particular, of World War II in that process. The concepts function like transparencies on an overhead projector—successive overlays help us build up a more complete picture. The object is not to deny the validity of the long-run geoeconomic explanation but to build on it. The underlying 'structures' of geography and economics do much to explain why America rose, but they tell us less about the timing and the form of its emergence as a superpower. And those questions about 'when' and 'how' are as important as 'why' if we wish to understand the course and impact of the two world wars.

In 1914 the United States, although an economic giant, was a military pygmy—a largely regional power in the Western Hemisphere with negligible armed forces who showed little desire to become involved in the European conflict. But the belligerents failed to win their expected quick victory. They were obliged to mobilize their economies for an all-out war in which the industrial and financial resources of the United States soon assumed decisive importance. By 1916 the British were dependent on America for munitions, raw materials, and no less than $9 million of the $22 million per day that they needed to keep fighting.[6] The German High Command decided in January 1917 that cutting the Allies' transatlantic lifeline was the precondition of victory, and its unrestricted submarine warfare pushed a still reluctant president into war.

Woodrow Wilson was now determined to crush German militarism, but he also intended to eliminate the imperialism and armaments of the Allies, which he saw as an impediment to a new world order centred on the League of Nations. He believed that America's economic power was the instrument of international influence. As he wrote in July 1917, 'England and France have not the same views with regard to peace that we have by any means. When the war is over we can force them to our way of thinking, because by that time they will, among other things, be financially in our hands.'[7] His prediction apparently came true in November 1918. Wilson was able to conclude an armistice with the Germans based on his own peace aims and to impose it on the Allies by threatening that America might otherwise sign a separate peace and leave Britain, France, and Italy to fight on as best they could. Intent by now on creating a 'world safe for democracy', Wilson could exploit the favourable environment provided by Europe's self-destruction and its reliance on American economic power.

But the window of opportunity soon began to close. Once the fighting stopped, the Allies were less dependent on the United States, and Wilson expended much of his now diminished influence at the Paris peace conference in securing the League of Nations. With Germany defeated and disarmed, with

[6] See Kathleen Burk, *Britain, America and the Sinews of War, 1914–1918* (Boston, 1985), 81.
[7] Woodrow Wilson to Colonel House, 21 July 1917, in Arthur S. Link, ed., *The Papers of Woodrow Wilson*, vol. xliii (Princeton, 1983), 238.

Britain and France expanding in the Middle East on the ruins of the Ottoman Empire, the wartime shifts in world power seemed to have been redressed and the old European order at least superficially restored.

Meanwhile, at home Wilson failed to convince Americans that it was in the interest of the United States to undertake automatic global commitments to collective security, and he refused to make sufficient concessions to break the Republicans' hold over the Senate. America's will to power, its wartime crusading idealism, evaporated in the bitter fight over the Covenant, and in the 1920s the United States refused to join either the League or its ancillary bodies.

Immediately after the armistice, Wilson and Congress started dismantling the institutions of power. Railroads were returned to private ownership, the vast government-owned shipping fleet sold off, and the wartime draft abandoned. The army, which had grown from less than 100,000 personnel in 1914 to 2.4 million by the armistice, stabilized at 130,000 to 140,000 by the mid-1920s.[8] Only the navy's status had permanently changed. The war enabled the General Board to argue for a 'navy second to none', citing as justification Japan's Asian ambitions and its alliance with Britain, still the world's greatest navy. The threat of a naval race against the United States at a time of economic recession obliged the British to abandon the Anglo-Japanese alliance in 1921 and to accept 'parity' with the United States. Yet throughout the interwar years America did not build up to treaty limits, and Britain, although also restricting its naval construction, remained the world's principal sea power.

Despite Wilson's failure and the dismantling of US military power after the war, the President nevertheless had been right in 1917 to claim that America's new financial strength could be a powerful lever of future international influence. In 1914 America was still a net debtor nation, its trade largely financed by the City of London, and it was not until the Federal Reserve Act of 1913 that US banks were even permitted to establish foreign branches. The war transformed the situation. Substantial European disinvestment and the channelling of US capital into private and governmental loans to the Allies turned America into a net creditor nation of $3.7 billion, exactly reversing the amount of its debt in 1914.[9] Although Britain's total investment abroad still exceeded America's throughout the interwar period, the United States was henceforth the main source of new investment capital. During the war, J. P. Morgan and the National City Bank in particular took advantage of new federal legislation and Europe's preoccupation with war to expand their foreign operations. And in the 1920s Wall Street's new financial power was directed, with Administration encouragement, into loans to restructure German finances, fund the reparations debt, and stabilize the European economy. The Dawes Plan of 1924 and the Young

    [8] US Department of Commerce, Bureau of the Census, *Historical Statistics of the United States: Colonial Times to 1970* (Washington, DC, 1975), 1141.
    [9] Mira Wilkins, *The Maturing of Multinational Enterprise: American Business Abroad from 1914 to 1970* (Cambridge, Mass., 1974), 29–30.

Plan of 1929 illustrate how the United States was now using its enhanced financial power for political ends to support a European settlement that checked France, rehabilitated Germany, and revived world trade.

Yet the institutions of US financial diplomacy were crude and ineffective. In the words of Sir William Wiseman, wartime British diplomat turned Wall Street banker, in 1921: 'America now sits impotent among her money bags. Her merchants and her financiers have learnt that it needs something more than cash to secure an international hegemony.'[10] The federal government exerted only limited direct control over US financial relations with the rest of the world. It could not dissuade Congress from insisting on the Allies' repayment of their war debts (some $11 billion), a heavy burden on international recovery and European governmental finances. Not was it possible to restrain Congress from progressive escalations of US tariffs, which made it ever harder for the Europeans to repay their debts through normal trade. And the US loans to Europe, on which depended the cycle of German reparations to the Allies and Allied debt payments to the United States, did not originate from the US government. They were private loans, mostly short-term—in other words, speculative capital from the overheating American economy that moved around in response to changing investment opportunities. With the collapse of the US stock market from October 1929 the flow of funds dried up, and the rapid withdrawal of existing loans in mid-1931 was an important cause of the German and Austrian bank crises and the British decision to go off gold.[11]

The 1930s were a period when the United States turned in on itself. The international economy broke up into loose economic blocs, centred on Britain, Germany, America, and France. Although the United States was the strongest economic power and thus the potential motor of economic recovery, it adopted insular, protectionist policies. Unlike Britain in late-nineteenth-century depressions, it did not engage in countercyclical foreign lending or significantly reduce domestic tariffs to help revive world investment and trade. In the early 1930s only two powers might have been able to alleviate the Depression. But, in Charles Kindleberger's words, 'the British couldn't and the United States wouldn't.' The former was 'feeble, the other irresponsible.'[12]

Yet the problem went deeper than intentions and institutions. It was more fundamental than an unreadiness to use economic power 'responsibly' in

---

[10] Sir William Wiseman, memo for Foreign Office, May 1921, Wiseman papers 1/4/110 (Sterling Library, Yale University, New Haven, Conn.).

[11] David S. Landes, *The Unbound Prometheus: Technological Change and Industrial Development in Western Europe from 1750 to the Present* (Cambridge, 1969), 371–2. In recent years, however, economic historians have also employed 'endogenous' explanations as well, for example, T. Balderston, 'The Beginning of the Depression in Germany, 1927–30: Investment and the Capital Market', *Economic History Review* 36 (1983), 395–415.

[12] Charles P. Kindleberger, *The World in Depression, 1929–1939* (Berkeley, 1973), 292, 303. For a modification of this argument see David A. Lake, 'International Economic Structures and American Foreign Economic Policy, 1887–1934', *World Politics* 35 (1983), 517–43.

international affairs or the inability of the Executive Branch to direct Congress and the private economy. America lacked the self-interest of Victorian Britain in the health of the world economy. The US boom of the 1920s, like its late-nineteenth-century growth, was largely fuelled by the continent-wide, tariff-free domestic market and not by foreign demand. Britain in its heyday, by contrast, had depended on markets and raw materials around the world, and therefore needed to promote world trade and investment, especially at times of depression. 'Britain's empire is abroad; America's is at home,' one Chicago banker put it succinctly in 1921.[13] And the statistics bear him out. In 1928 the United States was the world's largest exporter, with 15.8 per cent of global exports, yet those exports were a mere 6.3 per cent of national income. Britain's exports that year amounted to 20.8 per cent of its national income. Other figures tell a similar story. In 1928 the ratio of imports to national income was 5 per cent for the United States and 28.8 per cent for the United Kingdom, yet America was second only to Britain as the world's leading importer. And, despite an average of some $900 million per annum invested overseas by Americans in the 1920s, foreign investment was only 3.8 per cent of gross capital formation, compared with about 40 to 50 per cent in the case of Britain at its peak in 1870–1913.[14] The inference is clear: interest reinforced intentions as America retreated into its shell.

This insight can be extended into the military sphere as well. For security as well as prosperity the world needed America more than America needed the world. The growing challenge from Germany, Italy, and Japan to Britain and France and to the existing balance of world power evoked little direct response from an America preoccupied with chronic depression and a sharp pacifist backlash against involvement in the Great War. The prevailing opinion was that in future Europe could stew in its own juice. The peace movement was therefore able to push through a series of Neutrality Acts from 1935. These were intended to ensure that next time America's industrial, financial, and naval power would not be used to affect the course of any European war. On the contrary, by forgoing rights of trade, travel, and investment Americans would 'insulate' themselves from possible entanglement in such a conflict.

In the later 1930s the Roosevelt administration tried to redirect American policy through agreements to reduce trade barriers, diplomatic initiatives to foster a European settlement, and, especially after Munich, covert material assistance to Anglo-French rearmament. But whatever the intentions, the result was little more than 'pin pricks and righteous protest'.[15] Naval cooperation with the British remained tentative and limited, and it was not until after war began

[13] David M. Kennedy, *Over Here: The First World War and American Society* (New York, 1980), 345, quoting C. H. Crennan.

[14] John Braeman, 'The New Left and American Foreign Policy during the Age of Normalcy: A Re-examination', *Business History Review* 57 (1983), 82–6; cf. L. J. Williams, *Britain and the World Economy, 1919–1970* (London, 1971), 67.

[15] James MacGregor Burns, *Roosevelt: The Lion and the Fox, 1882–1940* (New York, 1956), 385.

in Europe in the autumn of 1939 that Roosevelt was able to repeal the arms embargo. Even then US trade with the Allies remained on a 'cash and carry' basis.

Roosevelt's problems were partly the result of public attitudes. Mindful of Wilson's mistakes he felt unable to move far in the face of strong anti-interventionist sentiment on Capitol Hill and in the country at large. As he observed in 1937, 'It is a terrible thing to look over your shoulder when you are trying to lead—and to find no one there.'[16] But he also lacked effective institutions for exercising presidential influence. There was no presidential staff to control the sprawling, bickering bureaucracy; all he had to show for the protracted battle over executive reorganization was the weak 1939 act that set up the executive office of the president with six assistants. Even this covered only domestic policy, and attempts at formalized coordination of external policy, such as the State-War-Navy liaison committee or the Cabinet Defense council in 1941, proved ineffectual. Similarly, after Roosevelt lost the struggle with Congress in 1937 over his attempt to 'pack' the Supreme Court with pro-New Deal judges, FDR lost his hold over Capitol Hill. Essential preconditions for the New Deal legislation of the first term had been Congress's unusual receptivity to Executive wishes and the remarkable dominance and unity of the Democratic party. During the second term, normality was restored—incessant feuding between White House and Capitol Hill and chronic factionalism within the Democratic party. (Periods of firm executive leadership are the exception, not the rule, in US politics: Wilson in 1913–14, Roosevelt in 1933–35, Johnson in 1964–65, and Reagan in 1981–82 stand out in the twentieth century.)

Attitudes and institutions were only part of the story. More fundamentally, US interests did not dictate large-scale intervention. For one thing, Britain was an economic rival of the United States; its 'Imperial Preferences' and financial agreements impeded the revival of US trade. One Anglophobe American diplomat wondered in 1936 why Britain should think 'she can count on our help politically, and yet hit us below the belt commercially all over the world'.[17] Moreover, Roosevelt shared the general desire to keep out of another war and seems to have believed that a firm Allied policy with limited US support would suffice to contain Hitler.[18]

The President was still operating in what C. Vann Woodward, adapting Frederick Jackson Turner, called 'the age of free security'.[19] The term is in some ways a misnomer. In the early nineteenth century the new nation feared a British counter-revolutionary war and later struggled hard to evict the British and other Europeans from the North American continent. But after the Civil War the

---

[16] Quoted in Gloria J. Barron, *Leadership in Crisis: FDR and the Path to Intervention* (Port Washington, NY, 1973), 22.

[17] J. Pierrepont Moffat to Norman Davis, 7 Oct. 1936, Davis papers, box 41 (Library of Congress, Washington, DC).

[18] See David Reynolds, *The Creation of the Anglo-American Alliance, 1937–1941: A Study in Competitive Cooperation* (London, 1981), 43–4.

[19] C. Vann Woodward, 'The Age of Reinterpretation', *American Historical Review* 66 (1960), 3.

United States did enjoy an unusually privileged position. It was highly self-sufficient economically, protected in an era of sea power by the Atlantic and Pacific oceans and shielded in addition by Britain's own self-interest in maintaining the European balance of power. Well into the twentieth century the United States could therefore afford the luxury of low defence expenditure, relative to its vast wealth and to the outlays of more vulnerable European powers. Until the 1930s, US peacetime spending on defence had usually been less than 1 per cent of national income. In 1937 the figure had risen to 1.5 per cent, but the comparable percentages for Japan were 28.2 per cent, Russia 26.4, Germany 23.5, and France 9.1. The lowest spender of the European powers was Britain at 5.7 per cent, but significantly it enjoyed geographical immunity similar in kind, if not degree, to that of the United States. Protected by water, both could avoid the necessity of large conscript armies. US security might not have been totally 'free', but it came at bargain rates.[20]

When the European war broke out in September 1939, therefore, the United States remained a world power in potential but not actuality. It had not translated economic strength into effective institutions of international influence, and moreover it showed an intention not to do so. That was not mere myopia. Although the wider world was increasingly affected by American action or inaction, the United States could afford to turn inward for much of the Great Depression decade because its prosperity and security seemed relatively independent of events overseas. By 1945, however, the situation had been transformed. Bearing in mind this interwar background, we can now use the four concepts of 'environment', 'intention', 'interest', and 'institutions' to explore the impact of World War II.

The two years after April 1940 saw a revolution in the distribution of world power that was more profound than any other in the twentieth century. The decisive actors were Germany and Japan, the decisive moments the spring of 1940 and the early months of 1942.

Between April and June 1940, Hitler conquered Denmark, Norway, the Low Countries, and, above all, France in a mere two-and-a-half months. He succeeded where the Kaiser had just failed in 1918 to bring most of continental Europe under German control. Britain alone was left, but although it survived 1940 it was far from clear that it could continue indefinitely against blockade by sea. The German invasion of Russia in June 1941 and the successful Russian resistance provided a respite, but the chances of a durable Eastern Front were not rated highly by Western observers until well into 1942.

By then, however, the conflict had become a truly world war. For the German successes of 1940–41 gave Japan an unprecedented opportunity to establish its

---

[20] Quincy Wright, *A Study of War* (2 vols., Chicago, 1942), i. 666–72, Appendix XXII, especially tables 58–59.

own sphere of influence in Asia. The European colonial powers were unable to defend their southeast Asian possessions, and after June 1941 Russia, Japan's greatest Asian rival, could do little to intervene. Unable to obtain their aims diplomatically, the Japanese resorted to war in December 1941. Their pre-emptive strike on the US Pacific Fleet at Pearl Harbor was the prelude to a remarkable series of combined operations which led to the conquest of Hong Kong, Malaya, Singapore, the Philippines, the Dutch East Indies, and Burma in only four months. By April 1942 India and Australia seemed in danger. Like the fall of France, this came as a devastating surprise. US planners had expected the Japanese to be only a nuisance—trade raiding, some local conquests, but not much more. In fact, they had upset the balance of power in Asia as dramatically as Hitler in Europe two years before.

The United States could not remain immune from the international revolution of 1940–42. World War II was taking a very different course from its predecessor, and America's role was necessarily very different as well. After June 1940 there was no Western Front in Europe. Britain assumed a critical importance for the United States—first as the front line while a near-defenceless America rearmed, later as the forward base for bombing and then invading Hitler's Europe. But the British required massive US economic and financial aid—as did the Russians from summer 1941 and the campaigns against Japan after Pearl Harbor. By 1944 the United States was producing some 40 per cent of world armaments and 60 per cent of the combat munitions used by the Allies,[21] in the process finally pulling the country out of the Depression and setting off a remarkable boom in consumer production as well. To defeat the Axis in this truly global war—with fronts in the Pacific, Mediterranean, and, eventually, Europe—the United States also constructed a 'two-ocean navy' and drafted, trained, and serviced huge armed forces—12.1 million by May 1945 compared with 2.9 million in November 1918.[22]

At the end of World War I America's opportunity for world power proved only temporary, in part because of the rapid recovery of the Europeans once the fighting stopped. In 1945 Europe's predicament again eased to some extent. The Western Europeans embarked on the longest economic boom in their history and re-entered their colonies wrested back, with US help, from Japan. But this time the cost of victory was all too apparent. France had been occupied and never again achieved great power status, while Britain had lost a quarter of its national wealth and was transformed from the world's second-largest creditor nation to its greatest debtor. The contraction of Anglo-French power and that of the Axis left a vacuum for the United States to fill: sharing in the occupation of Germany, dominating post-war Japan, and projecting its influence into China and the Middle East. But the United States was not the war's only beneficiary. Victory

[21] Alan S. Milward, *War, Economy and Society, 1939–1945* (Berkeley, 1977), 67, 70.
[22] *Historical Statistics*, 1141. Total US population in 1918 was about 105 million, in 1945 about 140 million. (Ibid., 8.)

cost Russia far more—perhaps 17,000,000 dead compared with America's 323,000, a devastated country rather than a boom economy unscathed by enemy action.[23] But Russia also benefited—particularly in Eastern Europe where its control extended farther than at any time since the Napoleonic Wars.

Two great themes of the twentieth century have been Germany's double bid for continental and world power and the nationalist challenge to European empires stimulated by Japan. In World War II these themes intertwined and also intersected with a third, perhaps the greatest theme: the emergence of America and Russia as the dominant world powers. For such was the success of Germany and Japan in 1940–42 that they shattered the old order and allowed these two new superpowers to shape a new one. This new order may have been predicted for more than a century, but the extent and pace of the transition were nothing short of revolutionary.

But 1918 had also been America's moment, and the United States had not exploited that opportunity—admittedly a less dramatic one—for an enhanced world role. In 1945, however, America's 'intentions' were different; there was a new will to power. To talk of a country's 'intentions' is, of course, a shorthand, often a dangerous one which ignores the diversity of national opinion and bureaucratic positions, not to mention the underlying public apathy about foreign affairs which studies recurrently reveal. Nevertheless, one can reasonably claim that the war saw a profound and durable change in the broad consensus about foreign policy in the United States, a shift, to use the classic concepts, from 'isolationism' to 'internationalism'. (It is instructive to note that at least two post-war presidents of the United States—John Kennedy and Gerald Ford—had supported and contributed to the anti-interventionist 'America First' organization in 1940–41.[24]) The process was not as simple or automatic as might be suggested by Senator Arthur Vandenberg's famous remark that Pearl Harbor 'ended isolationism for any realist'.[25] It was the consequence not merely of events but of a protracted national debate in which the anti-interventionists were discredited and frequently vilified as 'isolationists', 'fascists', anti-Semites, or, at best, 'illustrious dunderheads', to quote the title of Rex Stout's 1942 anthology of their 'wisdom, vision and statesmanship'.[26]

This did not mean that foreign policy would no longer be controversial or that US diplomacy between the wars had been as 'isolationist' as the internationalists' caricatures suggested. (The United States had never cut itself off from world affairs in the manner, say, of Tokugawa Japan, and the term 'isolationist' was more a political polemic than an accurate definition.) But before 1940 the burden of proof had lain with those who wished to depart from the non-entanglement

---

[23] Figures from Milward, *War, Economy and Society*, 211.

[24] Justus D. Doenecke, *Not to the Swift: The Old Isolationists in the Cold War Era* (London, 1979), 21.

[25] Arthur H. Vandenberg, Jr., and Joe A. Morris, eds., *The Private Papers of Senator Vandenberg* (Boston, 1952), 1.   [26] Rex Stout, ed., *The Illustrious Dunderheads* (New York, 1942).

tradition of the Founding Fathers. Roosevelt, for instance, in 1941 felt obliged to justify US naval operations in the Atlantic as merely extensions of the Monroe Doctrine. By 1945 the onus of justification was on those who argued that the United States should and could preserve its autonomy regardless of events overseas.

On an 'idealistic' level the national debate focused on the concept of 'one world', popularized by Wendell Willkie in what became the greatest nonfiction bestseller to date in US publishing history. His account of his seven-week, 31,000-mile tour, published in April 1943, sold over 1.5 million copies in the first four months.[27] In his book the Republican presidential candidate of 1940 argued that air travel had abolished distance and that all people had to live together in the interests of peace. America's task was to eschew isolationism and imperialism and set an example of international cooperation in a world ripe for US leadership. Appeals like Willkie's provided the moral context for the campaign to ensure US membership in a new international organization. Sympathetic pressure groups gradually rehabilitated the reputation of Woodrow Wilson, identified US repudiation of the league as a major cause of the present war, and urged that America had a providential 'second chance' to secure lasting peace through collective security. The State Department mounted a massive publicity campaign to help sell the idea to the American public, while Roosevelt, remembering Wilson's failings in 1918–19, enlisted the support of cooperative Republicans such as Vandenberg. In 1945 the United States became a founding member of the new United Nations, with a permanent seat on the Security Council. This time Senate approval was overwhelming—89 to 2.

But anti-interventionism had been based not only on morality, a belief that the Old World was beyond redemption, but on necessity, the argument that the United States need not undertake foreign commitments because the 'Western Hemisphere' was secure and invulnerable. Such ideas were also discredited during World War II—again partly by events and partly by interpretations of those events that became the new orthodoxy. For the first time America's 'foreign-policy public' shared a set of ideas justifying international commitments as a matter of US self-interest.

This new orthodoxy had three main elements (at risk of oversimplification). First, and central, was the importance of Western Europe for future US security. One of the most influential exponents of this theme was the political commentator Walter Lippmann. His *U.S. Foreign Policy: Shield of the Republic*, also published in April 1943, was the 'realist' counterpart to Willkie's 'one world' idealistic internationalism (or 'globaloney', as sceptics called it). The book sold half a million copies, as well as being popularized in condensed versions and even in a seven-page cartoon strip in the *Ladies Home Journal*.[28] In it Lippmann

---

[27] Wendell Willkie, *One World* (New York, 1943); Ellsworth Barnard, *Wendell Willkie: Fighter for Freedom* (Marquette, Mich., 1966), 412.

[28] Walter Lippmann, *U.S. Foreign Policy: Shield of the Republic* (Boston, 1943); Ronald Steel, *Walter Lippmann and the American Century* (New York, 1980), 406.

argued that Hitler's victories in 1940 showed that the United States could not allow a potential foe to control the industrial resources of Western Europe. In the past the Atlantic Ocean, the Royal Navy, and the balance of power had kept America inviolate. But the advent of air power and the weakening of the Europeans, particularly Britain, forced a radical reassessment, in Lippmann's view. The United States must acknowledge its membership of what he had long been calling an 'Atlantic Community', and it must pay its membership dues.

Although Europe was the major concern, experience of worldwide war in the air age had inspired a truly global conception of security. If Japan could strike 3,500 miles from Tokyo against the US fleet, then America's defence perimeter must be extended far across the Pacific. If aircraft could fly the South Atlantic and Caribbean, then West Africa and all of South America were inextricably related to US security. The series of influential works from 1942 by 'geopoliticians' such as Hans Weigert, Robert Strausz-Hupé, and Nicholas Spykman, was assisted by what has been called a veritable 'Copernican revolution' in cartography.[29] Conventional maps based on Mercator's projection had distorted distances and encouraged the idea of self-contained 'hemispheres'. A common depiction of the United States in pre-war atlases centred on a 'Western Hemisphere' with apparently limitless ocean disappearing on either side. But wartime cartographers, notably Richard Edes Harrison and their geopolitical collaborators promoted 'air-age globalism'.[30] Their new azimuthal projections, centred on various parts of the world, demonstrated that distance had indeed been revolutionized by aviation and encouraged the idea of a unified international community.

This new idea of global security was vividly illustrated by President Roosevelt in one of his most effective fireside chats on 23 February 1942. Asking Americans to study their maps as he talked, he introduced them to the truly global nature of the war and to the vital logistic links binding the United States to its new allies in Britain, Australia, China, and the Soviet Union. Pearl Harbor, he argued, had disproved those isolationists who 'wanted the American eagle to imitate the tactics of the ostrich', burying its head in the sand in a futile effort to ignore danger. The geography of modern global war demonstrated the error of those neo-isolationists who, 'afraid that we may be sticking our necks out, want our national bird to be turned into a turtle. But,' the President concluded, 'we prefer to retain the eagle as it is—flying high and striking hard.'[31]

The other main feature of the new US thinking about 'national security' was the belief that peace depended on prosperity. This belief was not new. The third

[29] Alan K. Henrikson, 'America's Changing place in the World: From "Periphery" to "Centre"?' in Jean Gottmann, ed., *Centre and Periphery: Spatial Variations in Politics* (London, 1980), 83.

[30] Alan K. Henrikson, 'The Map as an "Idea": The Role of Cartographic Imagery during the Second World War', *The American Cartographers* (1975), 24.

[31] *The Public Papers and Addresses of Franklin D. Roosevelt*, comp. Samuel I. Rosenman, vol. xi, *1942* (New York, 1950), 105–17, especially 107–8. Alerted by the White House, many US newspapers had printed large maps to help radio listeners follow the President's talk.

of President Wilson's Fourteen Points talked of reducing economic barriers and establishing equal trading conditions, and, after the insular protectionism of the early 1930s, the State Department under Cordell Hull worked energetically for trade agreements to realize these Wilsonian goals. But Congress and the White House were lukewarm and Hull's achievements limited. It was not until the war that Wilsonian economics became official orthodoxy. By 1942 the State, Treasury, and Commerce departments gave priority to promoting world economic growth and re-creating an international economy based on convertible currencies, stable exchange rates, and nondiscriminatory trade.

Clearly it was in America's narrow self-interest to break down commercial and financial barriers to trade such as Britain's Imperial Preference. Now the world's strongest economy, it was best able to profit from an open market. And although post-war exports still ran at less than 10 per cent of the total GNP, certain key sectors relied heavily on foreign markets. In 1947, nearly 20 per cent of US coal and steel was exported, half of US wheat, and 10 per cent of the total output of General Motors.[32] Wartime demands also made the United States less self-sufficient in crucial raw materials. Having been a leading exporter of lead and zinc before the war, America was importing 35 per cent of its consumption of each in 1943, and by 1948 it was a net importer of petroleum for the first time since the late 1910s.[33] Although their fears were exaggerated, post-war US policy-makers showed an understandable concern for access to markets and raw materials.

But prosperity was not seen as a zero-sum game. Increased trade would benefit all nations, encouraging economic growth and reducing the commercial rivalries that, it was argued, lay at the root of war. 'Nations which act as enemies in the marketplace cannot long be friends at the council table,' as Assistant Secretary of State Will Clayton put it in May 1945.[34] Growth was also expected to alleviate conflicts within as well as between nations, by reducing pressure for radical change. It was hoped that 'the politics of productivity'[35] would replace the politics of revolution as well as the politics of war.

By the summer of 1945 the term 'national security' (popularized by Walter Lippmann) had become something of a commonplace in Washington.[36] The independence of Western Europe, the extended air defence of the United States, and the revival of a prosperous world economy—these were the main characteristics of America's new self-interested 'internationalism'. And at the same time the United States was developing new institutions to ensure that US capabilities matched its defined 'interests'.

[32] Thomas G. Paterson, *On Every Front: The Making of the Cold War* (New York, 1979), 78.
[33] Alfred E. Eckes, Jr., *The United States and the Global Struggle for Minerals* (Austin, Tex, 1979), 122, 147. [34] Paterson, *On Every Front*, 71.
[35] The phrase coined by Charles S. Maier in 'The Politics of Productivity: Foundations of American International Economic Policy after World War II', *International Organization* 31 (1977), 607–33.
[36] See Daniel Yergin, *Shattered Peace; The Origins of the Cold War and the National Security State* (London, 1977), 194–5.

In Europe the accent was on diplomacy. This time the United States took an active and continuing share in the planning and negotiations for a European peace settlement, not bowing out as after 1919. The lesson of two world wars was that Europe was too important to be left to the Europeans. In particular, the future of Germany was of fundamental significance for the United States. On the one hand, it must not be allowed to become a great power again, nor must its industrial resources fall into the hands of a potential foe.

On the other hand, those resources were essential for the economic recovery of Western Europe, still one of the powerhouses of the world. These contradictory concerns about Germany as both a potential military threat and a potential economic benefit provoked substantial intragovernmental argument in Washington in 1946–47 and growing friction with the Soviet Union. But in 1944–45 it was hoped that compromise could be reached through great-power collaboration under the auspices of the United Nations. For Roosevelt, America, Britain, and Russia were to act as judges and 'policemen' of Europe.

The 'institution' of global security was a new military establishment centred on air power. This did not happen immediately: an independent US Air Force was not created until 1947 after an intense bureaucratic battle between admirals and airmen. But by 1944 the US Navy had accepted that the battleship era was over. It based its claim for a leading role on 'sea-air power'—the aircraft carrier—while the embryonic air force insisted that the new long-range bomber (the B-36) should have pride of place in future budgets. The airmen's case was strengthened by the efficacy of the new atomic bomb dropped on Hiroshima and Nagasaki in August 1945 and, by that autumn, aviators such as Generals Spaatz, Arnold, and LeMay were already talking of an 'air-atomic' strategy requiring a seventy-group air force.

But the American eagle, in Roosevelt's words, could only 'fly high and strike hard' if it had safe perches around the globe. Since the mid-1930s Roosevelt had been assiduously acquiring Pacific and Atlantic islands for naval and air bases to enlarge America's defence perimeter and in 1940 negotiated rights on eight British possessions in the Western Atlantic and Caribbean in return for fifty old US destroyers. By 1943 the policy was being systematized. The Joint Chiefs of Staff drew up plans for a grid of bases from the Philippines to the Azores that would provide defence in depth and would enable the United States to strike fast and hard at any enemy. Supplementing these were transit and landing rights negotiated with private airlines and foreign governments which would allow bases to be reinforced promptly in any emergency.[37]

Air power from bases on land and sea was envisaged as the guarantor of US security in the air-atomic age, deterring attack or, in the event of war, retaliating quickly while keeping the enemy at arm's length. Despite changes in the balance

[37] Melvyn P. Leffler, 'The American Conception of National Security and the Beginnings of the Cold War, 1945–48', *American Historical Review* 89 (1984), 349–56.

of power and the technology of war, the United States would thereby still be able 'to fight our wars, if they be necessary, in someone else's territory'.[38]

The underlying objective was to prevent war breaking out. Here new economic institutions were intended to play a significant part. One major change from the 1920s was the acknowledgment of federal government responsibility for foreign economic policy. This would no longer be left to private interests, particularly bankers, acting with the blessing of Washington. The monetary crisis of 1929–31 had shown the folly of that. As Henry Morgenthau, Treasury Secretary for nearly all of Roosevelt's presidency, remarked in 1946, his primary goal while in office had been to 'move the financial center of the world from London and Wall Street to the United States Treasury and to create a new concept between the nations of international finance'.[39]

That 'new concept' testified to another fundamental change from the 1920s: the acceptance of American responsibility for the health of the world economy. Since 1942 US Treasury officials, led by Harry White, drafted and negotiated plans for new world financial institutions which would help reflate world trade through increased liquidity. These were approved at the Bretton Woods conference in July 1944. The International Monetary Fund in particular was to assist nations in overcoming their balance of payments problems through short-term loans, and 36 per cent of the Fund's original $8.8 billion resources were provided by the United States.[40] These new financial institutions were intended as a framework for gradual reversion to multilateral trade once the immediate period of post-war reconstruction was over. In this way the US government began to acknowledge its 'responsibilities' in the international economy.

Industrial power and world influence had been gradually shifting toward the United States throughout the twentieth century, but I have suggested in this brief sketch that World War II saw a very rapid acceleration of the process. During the crisis years 1940–45 America developed an enhanced awareness of its global reach and a new conviction that its own self-interest required a greater managerial role in world affairs. At the same time the capacity of the federal government to harness national power and to use it internationally was greatly enlarged.

This is necessarily a very schematized interpretation intended to highlight broad changes in America's international role. It is therefore appropriate in conclusion to note briefly a few qualifications which help to blur the sharp edges of the silhouette.

The previous account may, for instance, suggest an excessively 'rationalist' view of foreign policy-making—that a nation state can be conceived of as

---

[38] Gen. Charles H. Bonesteel, 28 August 1945, quoted in Michael S. Sherry, *Preparing for the Next War: America's Plans for Postwar Defense, 1941–45* (New Haven, 1977), 205.

[39] Letter to President Truman, March 1946, quoted in David Rees, *Harry Dexter White: A Study in Paradox* (London, 1973), 138.

[40] Richard N. Gardner, *Sterling-Dollar Diplomacy in Current Perspective: The Origins and Prospects of Our International Economic Order* (New York, 1980), 112–13.

analogous to a rational human being.[41] He reacts to major crises by adapting his philosophy, reassessing his personal interests, and finding more appropriate means to achieve them. In other words, 'environment' changes 'intentions' and 'interests' which in turn affect 'institutions'. Of course, that belies the reality of human as well as social life: the dynamics of change are more complex, its directions more erratic.

For example, institutions may create interests as much as the reverse. The debate about air power illustrates this. To establish themselves as a separate service the airmen exaggerated the wartime effectiveness of strategic bombing and the contribution of the atomic bomb to ending the war against Japan.[42] On a more general level, different parts of the federal government tended to stress different clusters of 'national security' ideas in line with their own bureaucratic interests. The US Treasury emphasized the goals and institutions of economic recovery, while the JCS focused on military measures, including a demand for universal military training. This reminds us that it may be misleading to refer to the new wartime ideas about 'national security' as a unified 'doctrine' or 'concept'.

But my outline needs to be modified in another way. We have to look forward as well as back if we wish to appreciate the true significance of World War II, for the immediate post-war period saw a reduction of US power and influence reminiscent in kind, if not degree, to that after World War I. The armed forces were cut from 12.1 million to 1.6 million in two years. In the same period America's 'international expenditure' (defence, foreign military aid, foreign economic aid) dropped from 88 per cent of the federal budget to 51 per cent and from 39 per cent of GNP to 8.43 per cent.[43] Domestic preoccupations were again paramount—getting the boys home, combating inflation, coping with pent-up labour discontent—and between April 1947 and August 1948 the draft was abandoned. There was a tendency to assume that the new international institutions, such as the United Nations and the International Monetary Fund, backed by great-power cooperation, would provide the necessary framework for peace and prosperity. The Russians were initially seen as difficult rather than dangerous, the weakness of Europe underestimated.

What really confirmed the wartime shift in America's role was the Cold War. By 1947 'one world' internationalism was discredited and the Soviet Union regarded as the new 'totalitarian' threat to peace, capitalism, and democracy. This 'threat' took various forms: the menace of communism in an impoverished Western Europe from 1946 to 1947; the imbalance of conventional forces in Europe in 1948; the

---

[41] Ernest May has suggested 'proclivities' as a more appropriate word than 'intentions'. See Ernest R. May, ed., *Knowing One's Enemies: Intelligence Assessment before the Two World Wars* (Princeton, 1986), 503.

[42] Gregg Herken, *The Winning Weapon: The Atomic Bomb in the Cold War, 1945–1950* (New York, 1981), 209–10.

[43] Robert A. Pollard, *Economic Security and the Origins of the Cold War, 1945–50* (New York, 1985), 256, 258.

'fall of China' and the loss of atomic monopoly in 1949; and then the outbreak of war in Korea in 1950 that, it was feared, presaged war in Europe by 1952.

The Cold War gave a focus for America's new notions of 'national security'— its specific aim became the containment of Russian power and, increasingly, of international communism as a whole. In the process, the 'institutions' changed: diplomacy and economic aid gave place to military power, with the development of large land forces again from 1950. The first serious efforts were also made to coordinate the nation's external policies. The year 1947 saw the creation of the Central Intelligence Agency, the National Security Council, and a 'unified' Department of Defense. As in 1940–45, the dynamics of policy change were complex. Up to a point the United States was reacting to a new and unexpected situation caused by the wartime extension of Soviet influence. But that expansion was unacceptable in part because of the greatly enlarged definition of US security needs. Institutional self-aggrandizement was again an element, encouraging airmen and later soldiers to exaggerate the Soviet 'threat'.

But what one can say in general is that cold war and world war have to be taken together in understanding the revolution in America's international role in the 1940s. In retrospect, the decade can be seen as a dual crisis, with the second phase being viewed as a possible replay of the first unless the 'lessons of the past' were heeded.[44] Together they form the context for America's emergence as a superpower.

Nevertheless, our attention to World War II is surely warranted. The expansion of Russian power was a direct consequence of that conflict, and the 'Soviet threat' gave a specific referent to ideas about peace and security formulated in wartime. By the end of the war the United States was undoubtedly a 'superpower' on the criteria used by William Fox, who probably coined that term in 1944. For him 'superpower' meant 'great power plus great mobility of power'.[45] By 1945 the US government had harnessed national power to national ends, creating a permanent naval and air power establishment and essaying for the first time a US foreign economic policy. This revolution was grounded in novel ideas about how national security was related to world peace, political stability, and capitalist prosperity. The development of the US Navy and the Army Air Forces, linked to a network of bases, gave the United States 'great mobility of power' for influencing and responding to a greatly changed world order, in which the powers of Europe, hitherto the creators and sustainers of the modern international system, had been displaced. The remarkable economic

[44] Ernest R. May, *'Lessons' of the Past: The Use and Misuse of History in American Foreign Policy* (New York, 1973), 49–51. For the elision of the New Deal and World War II in historiography about domestic change in twentieth century America, see Gerald D. Nash, *The Great Depression and World War II: Organizing America, 1933–45* (New York, 1979).

[45] William T. R. Fox, *The Superpowers* (New York, 1944), 21. It is worth noting that Fox included Britain with the United States and Russia among the 'superpowers' in this work. For Fox's claim to have invented the term see his article 'The Super-powers Then and Now', *International Journal* 35 (1980), 417–36.

growth of the United States may constitute much of the long-term explanation for its rise to globalism, but America's transformation from power to superpower was very much the consequence of World War II.

The late emergence of the United States as a superpower has also posed problems for the domestic management of external policy. Here the American experience was very different from that of much of continental Europe, where the national security state had long been in existence, since the era of 'enlightened despotism' in the eighteenth century. The institutions of strong national governments—effective taxation, enlarged bureaucracies, standing armies, and the official promotion of strategic industries—were gradually created by European monarchs in the interests of defence and internal security.[46] Subsequently, most of these autocratic governments were gradually forced to concede domestic liberties to their subjects, but in many cases not until the twentieth century.

In the United States the pattern was reversed: democratization preceded state-building. The legacy of 1776 was a reaction against anything that purported to be a strong central government: under the constitution of 1787 the powers of the federal government were divided and balanced, the rights of the individual states safeguarded. By the 1830s local autonomy was reinforced by the prevalence of democracy for most white adult males, not just in local elections but in choosing their head of state (inconceivable in Europe). This combination of extremes— highly developed democratic politics without a concentrated governing capacity—made early America the great anomaly among western states.[47] In the era of 'free security' there was no external threat to impel statebuilding in the European sense. Not until the twentieth century was a serious attempt made to create stronger institutions of national government, intermittently in the progressive era and the New Deal, intensively in the dual crises of the 1940s (world war and cold war), the era in which national security seemed seriously at issue for the first time.

Thus, unlike most of Europe, the United States was a democracy long before it became a state, let alone a superpower.[48] Yet, since the 1940s, it has exercised that superpower role through democratic and antistatist institutions. These may be suited, perhaps, to its own domestic needs as a vast, continent-size complex of interest groups, but they are at odds with the historical experiences of most other countries who have risen to the rank of great powers. And this is one reason why America's allies, not least Britain, have found the United States an erratic partner.

[46] See E. N. Williams, *The Ancient Regime in Europe: Government and Society in the Major States, 1648–1789* (Harmondsworth, 1972), 32–4.

[47] Stephen Skowronek, *Building a New American State: The Expansion of National Administrative Capacities, 1877–1920* (New York, 1982), 8. A fascinating study. Elsewhere I have noted the parallels in this respect between America and Britain, both essentially 'liberal' polities. See David Dimbleby and David Reynolds, *An Ocean Apart: The Relationship between Britain and America in the Twentieth Century* (New York, 1988), especially, ch. 2 and conclusion.

[48] See Zara Steiner, 'Decision-making in American and British Foreign Policy: An Open and Shut Case', *Review of International Studies* 13 (1987), 16.

17

A 'Special Relationship'?

America, Britain and the International Order since the Second World War

A fortnight after Pearl Harbor, Winston Churchill arrived in the United States. For much of his three-week visit he stayed in the White House itself, engaged in lengthy and informal conversations with the President. On one occasion, so the story goes, Roosevelt was wheeled into his guest's room only to discover Churchill emerging from the bath—wet, glowing, and completely naked. Disconcerted, FDR made as if to withdraw, but Churchill waved him back. 'The Prime Minister of Great Britain', he announced, 'has nothing to conceal from the President of the United States.'[1]

Sir Winston denied the anecdote, but, true or not, it captures something of what is meant by the concept of an Anglo-American 'special relationship': an intimate, harmonious bond between the two nations celebrated on state occasions with suitably hyperbolic prose. Leaders as diverse as Churchill and Richard Nixon have used the term. Harold Wilson preferred to talk of a 'close relationship' while Margaret Thatcher has reaffirmed the 'extraordinary alliance'. Others, however, have dissented. Historian Max Beloff, for instance, portrayed the notion of a special relationship as an agreeable British 'myth' to help cushion the shock of national decline, while Dean Acheson, the former US Secretary of State, denounced it as a dangerous intellectual obstacle to acceptance of Britain's largely European role.[2]

The argument of this chapter was first outlined to a conference at the Woodrow Wilson Center in Washington in 1985 and developed as an article in *International Affairs*, 62 (1986), 1–20. Three-quarters of that essay are reprinted here, with a new ending taking the story from 1973 to 2005. This draws on ideas about cultural relations set out in 'Rethinking Anglo-American Relations', *International Affairs,* 65 (1989), 89–111.

[1] Robert E. Sherwood, *Roosevelt and Hopkins: An Intimate History* (New York, 1948), 442.

[2] For examples of these and other views see the selections in Ian S. McDonald, ed., *Anglo-American Relations since the Second World War* (New York, 1974). On the 'myth' see Max Beloff, 'The special relationship: an Anglo-American myth', in Martin Gilbert, ed., *A Century of Conflict, 1850–1950: essays for A. J. P. Taylor* (London, 1966), 151–71. Other discussions of the 'special relationship' include Coral Bell, *The Debatable Alliance: an Essay in Anglo-American Relations* (London, 1964); Bell, 'The "special relationship"', in Michael Leifer, ed., *Constraints and Adjustments in British Foreign Policy* (London, 1972), 103–19; and A. E. Campbell, 'The United

Sixty years on from 1945, what meaning, if any, should be attached to the concept of a post-war Anglo-American special relationship?

Although used on both sides of the Atlantic, the term has been very much more prevalent in Britain than America. Churchill popularized and perhaps coined it in the winter of 1945–6 but as an objective of British foreign policy it has been in continuous existence since early in the century. In September 1917, for instance, Lord Robert Cecil emphasized in a memo for his Cabinet colleagues that the Americans were at last 'taking a part in international European affairs' and 'they will soon begin to realise what vast power they have'. He noted that 'there is undoubtedly a difference between the British and the Continental view in international matters' and argued that 'if America accepts our point of view in these matters, it will mean the dominance of that point of view in all international affairs.' Cecil was hopeful this could be achieved because, 'though the American people are very largely foreign, both in origin and in modes of thought, their rulers are almost exclusively Anglo-Saxons, and share our political ideals'.[3] Perhaps the most engaging formulation of what British policy-makers have really meant by the 'special relationship' is contained in an anonymous verse of 1945, when Britain was soliciting a post-war US loan:

> In Washington Lord Halifax
> Once whispered to Lord Keynes:
> It's true *they* have the money bags
> But *we* have all the brains.[4]

In this sense, the notion of an Anglo-American special relationship has been a device used by a declining power for trying to harness a rising power to serve its own ends. Avoid public confrontation; seek private influence. Propitiate openly; manipulate secretly. Never say 'No'; say 'Yes, but' —with the 'Yes' said loudly in public and the 'but' urged quietly behind closed doors. These are the preferred tactics for this form of alliance politics. Not every British policy-maker agreed, particularly in the interwar years. Maurice Hankey, the influential Cabinet Secretary, complained in 1927: 'Time after time we have been told that, if we make this concession or that concession, we should secure the goodwill in America. We gave up the Anglo-Japanese alliance. We agreed to pay our [war] debts . . . I have never seen any permanent result follow from a policy of concessions. I believe we are less popular and more abused in America than ever because they think us weak.'[5] Lord Curzon and Neville Chamberlain were

States and Great Britain: uneasy allies', in John Braeman, Robert H. Bremner, and David Brody, eds., *Twentieth Century American Foreign Policy* (Columbus, 1971), 471–501.

    [3] Cecil, memo, 18 Sept. 1917, GT 2074, CAB 24/26 (TNA).

    [4] Richard N. Gardner, *Sterling-Dollar Diplomacy in Current Perspective* (3rd edn., New York, 1980), xiii.

    [5] Hankey to Balfour, 29 June 1927, copy in Stanley Baldwin papers, vol. 130, fo. 61 (Cambridge University Library).

among those British leaders who shared his doubts about 'appeasing' the Americans. But others, from Joseph Chamberlain to Winston Churchill, were more hopeful. And after 1940 the cultivation of a special relationship with the United States has been the dominant theme of British policy, right down to the days of Tony Blair.

Recognizing that the 'special relationship' has been in part a deliberate British creation—a 'tradition' invented as a tool of diplomacy—helps us appreciate the artifice that has often lain behind fulsome official British rhetoric about America, its leaders and its ties with Britain. Nevertheless, exploration of that tradition is not the purpose of this chapter. Instead it seeks to ask whether the concept of a special relationship is an accurate description of the place of Anglo-American relations in world affairs since the Second World War. Stated more succinctly: whatever London might say, was the relationship *really* 'special'?

I will talk in what follows of 'Britain' and 'America' even though these can only be shorthand terms for complex political organisms. Works of theory and history by students of international relations have made us well aware of the danger of talking of countries as if they are 'unitary, purposive actors', without attention to domestic politics, bureaucratic interplay, and the impact of 'opinion makers' and the 'foreign policy public'.[6] This is particularly true in the case of pluralist democracies, of which the United States is the supreme example. In America the management of foreign policy is peculiarly difficult, given the extent of congressional power, the uncontrolled bureaucracy, the influence of lobbyists, and the freedom of the media. US relations with Britain have therefore never been the exclusive preserve of government departments, insulated from the currents of larger public debate—witness the loan negotiations of 1945–6. Certain ethnic groups have exercised particular influence. In 1945–8, Jewish-American opinion helped shape Truman's policy towards Palestine/Israel, while the Irish-American lobby helped propagate a generally sceptical American attitude towards British policy in Northern Ireland for many decades.

Britain, by contrast, has a more cohesive political and administrative system—susceptible to greater control by the government of the day—but even here relations between the two countries have been affected by internal differences of view. A notable example has been the anti-Americanism of the Labour left—from the 'Keep Left' movement of 1946–7, through the critics of the Vietnam war, to the nuclear disarmers of the 1980s, and opponents of the 2003 Iraq War.

In international relations states might therefore be conceived of not as billiard balls—solid, clearly-defined entities cannoning off each other—but as distinct, swirling masses of gas—more diffuse but with no less potential energy. This should be remembered when reading the shorthand expressions 'Britain' and

---

[6] e.g. Graham Allison, *Essence of Decision: Explaining the Cuban Missile Crisis* (Boston, 1971); Bernard Cohen, *The Public's Impact on Foreign Policy* (Boston, 1973); David Vital, *The Making of British Foreign Policy* (London, 1968).

'America' used below. Nevertheless, my justification for paying less attention to domestic factors is that these have rarely made a decisive difference to the pattern of Anglo-American relations—consider, for example, the basic continuity in policy between Labour and Conservative governments, whatever the Labour left might demand in 1945–6 or 1964–5. Fundamentally the post-war relationship has been shaped by the power and international position of the two countries. This is where we must look for what, if anything, has made it 'special'.

Whatever the term might mean, it clearly cannot connote perfection or pure harmony. Numerous books have exposed the friction and controversy beneath the surface of Anglo-American cooperation in the Second World War and after. The most important source of argument was Britain's empire—formal and informal—and the US challenge to the British imperial position from both an ideological and self-interested standpoint. Decolonization, oil, and the battle to dominate civil aviation were among the specific issues at stake. And the development of the relationship since the Second World War is part of a larger story of the decline of British power against that of America—with the United States sometimes giving the British Empire a push down the slippery slope.[7]

Furthermore, the concept of a special relationship is not uniquely Anglo-American. It has also been applied to ties between the United States and others of its allies (usually, it might be noted, by the ally rather than by the United States). Israel, Brazil, pre-communist China, and the Federal Republic of Germany are among the examples of this usage.[8]

These considerations suggest some guidelines for our thinking. If the Anglo-American relationship *can* be termed 'special' it is not by reference to some idealized standard of international amity. We must bear in mind the elements of tension and hostility that are evident in this as in any other diplomatic relationship. And we have to assess its 'specialness' against the character of the relationships between the United States and its other close allies. Was the cooperation, however imperfect and flawed, different in degree and extent from that of any other alliance?

But *quality* is not the only criterion for judging the specialness of the relationship. *Importance* provides another touchstone: is or was this bilateral relationship especially important for each country and, indeed, for the world at large? That also seems to have been part of what was meant by the concept of a special relationship. For Churchill at Fulton in 1946 it was no less than guarantor of 'the safety and welfare, the freedom and progress of all the homes and families of all the men and women in all the lands . . .' Conversely Harold

---

[7] See William Roger Louis, 'American Anti-Colonialism and the Dissolution of the British Empire', *International Affairs*, 61 (1985), 395–420.

[8] e.g. Nadav Safran, *Israel: the Embattled Ally* (Cambridge, Mass., 1978), 571, on the ' "special" American connection with Israel'; John D. Martz and Lars Schoultz, eds., *Latin America, the United States, and the Inter-American System* (Boulder, Colo., 1980), 80–1; Michael H. Hunt, *The Making of a Special Relationship: the United States and China to 1914* (New York, 1983); Hans W. Gatzke, *Germany and the United States: a Special Relationship?* (Cambridge, Mass., 1980).

Wilson, a quarter-century later, recalled an aphorism of Charles Lamb, the nineteenth-century essayist, that 'there is nothing so irrelevant as a poor relation'.[9] One may still be fond of the aged relative, the ties may still be unusually close, but the relationship has diminished in value to oneself and to the family fortunes (though not, of course, to its importunate beneficiary).

It may be helpful, then, to judge the specialness of the Anglo-American relationship in two ways. Was or is it special in *quality* from other bilateral alliances? Was or is it of special *importance* for the two countries and for the international order as a whole? These provide criteria for the general survey that follows.

During the 1940s and 1950s, perhaps until the end of Macmillan's premiership, the Anglo-American relationship was special in both quality and importance.

Of course, that cannot be a blanket generalization—as a glance at the ups and downs will show.[10] Brought together by the crisis of 1940, Britain and America entered into a unique alliance, but one in which the United States was clearly the dominant partner by the last year of the war. In 1945–6, however, the partnership disintegrated in many areas, of which nuclear disentanglement was the most notorious, and relations were never again as close or as equal. Nevertheless, the ties were partially reconstructed from 1947 in the deepening Cold War. The Korean war and the challenge of Middle Eastern nationalism gave the relationship a global dimension, but then it faced one of its gravest twentieth-century crises in the Suez debacle of 1956. Even the intelligence artery, the closest link, was nearly ruptured. Yet within a year or two the wounds had healed, as Macmillan recreated a special nuclear relationship with his old wartime ally, Eisenhower, and played a significant part in efforts to thaw out superpower relations. Remarkably he achieved a similar personal rapport with Ike's successor, despite an age difference of twenty-three years, but the extent of British dependence was dramatically demonstrated during the Cuban missile crisis of October 1962.

Despite the uneven texture of the relationship, overall it was unusually close. Its special quality derived from three salient characteristics. First of all, the two countries shared similar interests which became apparent in the sustained international crisis of the 1940s. Both wished to maintain the independence of Western Europe in the face of powers apparently intent on continental domination, first Hitler's Germany and then Stalin's Russia and Cominform. In a much more qualified way they also discerned a common interest in preventing violent, sudden change in Asia and the Middle East, which might threaten their economic interests and the general distribution of power. Hence their cooperation against Japan during the war and, from the late 1940s, against the

[9] Quoted in McDonald, ed., *Anglo-American Relations*, 35, 220.

[10] Surveys of the post-war period include H. G. Nicholas, *Britain and the United States* (London, 1963); John Baylis, *Anglo-American Defence Relations, 1939–84: the Special Relationship* (London, 2nd edn., 1984); and later chapters of D. Cameron Watt, *Succeeding John Bull: America in Britain's Place, 1900–75* (Cambridge, 1984).

spread of radical nationalist or communist movements in Asia and the Middle East associated with Moscow or Beijing.

Similar interests were reinforced by similar ideology. Again the point cannot be pressed too far on the American side. The United States has always seen itself as the New World in antithesis to many of the values of the Old, especially colonialism and such 'feudal' anachronisms as monarchy and aristocracy. Nevertheless, in the 1940s, the similarities between British and US values seemed more apparent to Americans than the differences in a world threatened by 'totalitarianism'. Both were liberal, capitalist democracies, sharing common beliefs in the rule of law and the principle of peaceful change.

And for the British the ideological legacy of 1940 was profound. After the Anglo-French entente of the Phoney War, which many senior policy-makers saw as the basis of a permanent post-war alliance, the French were felt to have betrayed them in 1940. Britain therefore turned away from the perfidious continentals to its kin across the seas—the Commonwealth and the United States. Together, so it was felt, they won the war, and it was only natural to look in the same direction for support and cooperation in peacetime. Such deeply held beliefs coloured British attitudes towards the continent for a generation.

These ties of interest and ideology were institutionalized thirdly, in a network of close personal contacts and friendships. These were forged during the war, as the two sets of policy-makers became 'mixed up together', to borrow Churchill's famous phrase.[11] The Roosevelt–Churchill connection was the most celebrated, but more important in the long run were contacts between men lower down their respective hierarchies who would rise to positions of prominence in the 1950s. For them consultation with colleagues in the other capital became easy and natural.

These personal links were facilitated by the shared language. Admittedly this was not without its problems: Churchill alludes in his war memoirs to the confusion caused at one conference by the diametrically opposite British and US usages of the verb 'to table'.[12] And the similarities of language and culture can encourage policy-makers to conceive of transatlantic counterparts in their own image—sometimes with disastrous results, as during the Suez or Skybolt crises.[13] Nevertheless, the common language permitted more extensive and more intensive communication than would otherwise have been possible, since, in principle, any Briton or American could participate at a depth usually permitted only to skilled linguists. Compare the wartime United States–United Kingdom relationship in this respect to that of Britain and France or America and China.

Here was what made the relationship especially close—the community of interests, values, and personal ties in the face of common threat. But this was not of itself sufficient to make the relationship especially important. That depended on an additional factor—Britain's continued role as a world power.

[11] *House of Commons Debates (Hansard)*, 5th ser., Vol. 364, col. 1171, 20 Aug. 1940.
[12] Winston S. Churchill, *The Second World War* (London, 1948–54, 6 vols.), iii. 609. For the British, 'to table' denoted putting a document forward for discussion; for Americans it meant withdrawing it.   [13] Richard E. Neustadt, *Alliance Politics* (New York, 1970).

What had brought the two countries together in 1940 was a sense of mutual need. After France fell, Britain and its empire needed US support for survival, let alone victory. But the United States, disarmed and disorganized at that time, also needed Britain. The Royal Navy was regarded as America's 'front line' against German expansion into the Atlantic, and Britain's empire was acknowledged, albeit more ambivalently, as a source of key raw materials and a bulwark against Japanese aggression in Asia. From 1942 the British Isles became the essential base for bombing and then invading Hitler's Europe.

Britain ended the war reduced in power and resources. The conflict had cost perhaps a quarter of its national wealth, and Britain's position in the Indian subcontinent never recovered from wartime protests and the humiliation of Japan's Asian victories. For a century India had been the cornerstone of empire—the source of much of its wealth and armed manpower—and the defence of India was the original *raison d'être* for many of Britain's other territorial acquisitions. When India became independent in August 1947 it must have seemed like a grim realization of Curzon's warning at the beginning of the century: 'As long as we rule India we are the greatest power in the world. If we lose it we shall drop straight away to a third-rate power.' And the rest of Britain's colonies and protectorates would become redundant—in his picturesque phrase, 'the toll-gates and barbicans of an Empire that has vanished'.[14]

Sixty years after the end of the Second World War, Curzon's prediction seems all too accurate. The imperial crown lost much of its value after the central jewel had gone. Yet the Labour and Conservative governments of the 1940s and 1950s were more sanguine. Clearly Britain was no longer in the same league as the United States and the Soviet Union—sometimes, to quote one senior diplomat, it seemed to be in 'the position of Lepidus in the triumvirate with Mark Antony and Augustus'.[15] But Bevin firmly denied in 1947 'that we have ceased to be a great Power', insisting that Britain 'was one of the Powers most vital to the peace of the world'.[16] The strategy now was to transform the barbican of empire, the Middle East, into its new keep and stronghold, and to develop the resources of British Africa and south-east Asia for the benefit of the sterling area. The form of the relationship was to be negotiated partnership, not imperial subordination—Commonwealth replaced Empire—but, behind the enlightened rhetoric, the determination to maintain Britain's world role remained positively Churchillian.[17]

[14] Quoted in Michael Howard, *The Continental Commitment: the Dilemma of British Defence Policy in the Era of Two World Wars* (Harmondsworth, 1974), 14.

[15] Sir Orme Sargent, minute, 1 Oct. 1945 FO 371/44557, AN 2560/22/45.

[16] *Hansard* (Commons), Vol. 437, 16 May 1947.

[17] As emphasized: John Gallagher (ed. Anil Seal), *The Decline, Revival and Fall of the British Empire* (Cambridge, 1982); Wm. Roger Louis, *The British Empire in the Middle East, 1945–51* (Oxford, 1984); and the essays by R. F. Holland, 'The imperial factor in British strategies from Attlee to Macmillan, 1945–63', and John Darwin, 'British decolonization since 1945: a pattern or a puzzle?', in the *Journal of Imperial and Commonwealth History*, 12 (1984), 165–86 and 187–209.

The persistence of this global outlook needs to be stressed, in view of the tendency (both popular and scholarly) to write Britain off as a world power after 1945. Nor was the outlook unreasonable even if it did breed some illusions. For Britain was still the world's third major state in the 1940s and 1950s— economically, militarily, and in nuclear capability. As such it remained a valuable ally for the United States. Although the wartime alliance was unique, the mutual need that had cemented it continued to hold the two countries close in the late 1940s and 1950s. And their role as the principal non-communist world powers gave their relationship a special importance in shaping the post-1945 international order as it evolved from World War to Cold War.

The special importance of the relationship—for the two allies and for international relations—can be seen by glancing at four of its aspects in the period from 1945 to about 1963: the world economic order, European security, Cold War diplomacy, and global containment.

First of all the economic connection. Here the ties were least close because of fundamental policy disagreement. Since the Ottawa Conference of 1932, the British had inclined towards a protectionist policy, seeking to consolidate their trading position within countries of the empire and especially the sterling area. But from 1934, successive US governments sought to dismantle trading barriers, especially those of a discriminatory nature, and Britain's Imperial Preference was at the top of their list. British economic policy was the natural response of a declining trading power to the depression and to the 'imperialism' of American free trade. It was also an ironic reversal of the two countries' policies in the late nineteenth century, when emerging America was still vehemently protectionist and dominant Britain preached *laissez faire*. The basic division of outlook was also apparent during the Second World War, and in the post-war era the British resisted as premature US attempts to restore currency convertibility and did their best to build up the dollar-earning power of the sterling area. Adherence to the European Free Trade Association and finally the European Economic Community was part of the same pattern—Britain could not survive economically without maximizing trade, but it could no longer afford the costs of open competition within a multilateral economy dominated by the United States. Hence the British predilection for extensive but protected free trade areas.

This basic divergence in policy precluded special cooperation between the two countries in economic matters. Nevertheless, the differences were not unbridgeable: in principle most British policy-makers favoured a multilateral world economy, *if* British interests were protected and *if* the United States assumed the responsibilities for world stability incumbent upon it as the major exporter and creditor nation. And US leaders in the Second World War did seem ready to accept those responsibilities. This was the basis of the hard-won agreements associated with the Bretton Woods conference of July 1944, from which originated the International Monetary Fund, the World Bank and the

General Agreement on Tariffs and Trade. They were achieved by a small group of British and US economists and civil servants—men such as Keynes, Harry White, James Meade, and Harry Hawkins—against extensive opposition within their respective political systems (an example of how the Anglo-American relationship has been partially insulated from these larger political currents). And, although the two nations increasingly diverged in their basic policies, these agreements constituted the framework for the post-war economic order for a quarter-century.[18]

Even in economic affairs, then, where the relationship was hardly special in quality, it was of special importance at a crucial point in the shaping of the post-war world. Turning to cooperation in European security in the 1940s and 1950s, we find a relationship that was special in both quality and importance. The development of the Marshall Plan and the creation of NATO were very much a joint enterprise, with Bevin playing a major role alongside Marshall and Acheson.[19] Later, in 1954, the Foreign Office made a significant contribution to solving the crisis over German rearmament. Western European Union, German membership of NATO, and the British commitment to German defence date from this time. The Atlantic alliance as we know it today was in many ways an *Anglo*-American creation.

US economic and military help in Europe was, of course, vital for the British government. Less familiar is the degree to which Britain mattered to the United States. At every stage of his European commitment in the 1940s, Truman faced sustained congressional opposition—to Marshall Aid, to the Military Assistance programme, to his desire by 1950 for substantial US rearmament. In each case it required a major international crisis (the Czech coup, the Soviet atomic test, and the onset of the Korean War) to mobilize the necessary support on Capitol Hill. Consequently, the administration did not intend to assume unlimited obligations. Even the US troop commitment to NATO was expected to be a short-term venture. The general philosophy, as expressed by Marshall Aid administrator Paul Hoffman, was 'to get Europe on its feet and off our backs'.[20]

Allies were therefore invaluable to share the burdens of containment. And Britain was still America's principal ally. In the early 1950s Britain's arms production exceeded that of all the other European partners combined, and it manufactured thirty per cent of the industrial production of non-communist Europe.[21] Britain's four divisions and tactical air force were essential components of NATO's Central Front at a time when Germany was disarmed and France preoccupied first with Indochina and then Algeria. In the late 1940s the United States also wanted Britain to lead an integrated Western Europe—a hope soon

---

[18] The classic study remains Gardner, *Sterling–Dollar Diplomacy*.

[19] e.g. Alan Bullock, *Ernest Bevin: Foreign Secretary, 1945–51* (London, 1983); Avi Shlaim, 'Britain, the Berlin blockade and the cold war', *International Affairs*, 60 (1984), 1–14.

[20] See David Reynolds, 'The origins of the cold war: the European dimension, 1944–51', *Historical Journal*, 28 (1985), 512.   [21] Baylis, *Anglo-American Defence Relations*, 43.

dashed but later revived with the advent of de Gaulle. And from July 1948 Britain provided essential bases for Strategic Air Command's B–29s. These became a vital element of US nuclear strategy in what was still the pre-missile era. Use of these bases (and others in the British Middle East) enabled the United States to threaten the Soviet Union in a way that was not possible in return (hence, in part, Khrushchev's later Cuban gamble).

Britain also played a part in trying to thaw out the Cold War. Churchill's attempts in 1953–4 to arrange a summit meeting after Stalin's death laid the groundwork for the Geneva Conference of 1955. This failed, however, and in the mid-1950s the strained relationships between Eden and Eisenhower, and Dulles's close ties with Adenauer, limited the effectiveness of the Anglo-American diplomatic axis. But Macmillan, Eden's successor from January 1957, was an old friend of Eisenhower. They had worked closely together in 1943–4 when Macmillan was British minister attached to Ike's Allied Force Headquarters in North Africa and Italy. And, although Eisenhower was always in ultimate command of US policy, the vacuum created in 1959–60 by Dulles's death and the President's ill health permitted the British to play a more influential international role. Macmillan's visit to Moscow in February–March 1959—the first by a Western head of government since the end of the war—helped modify the Soviet position on Berlin and paved the way for the Eisenhower–Khrushchev meeting in September. Despite the failure of the Paris summit of May 1960, Macmillan maintained his peace-making efforts through a cordial if surprising friendship with Kennedy, and the British were active participants in the negotiations leading to the Partial Test Ban Treaty of August 1963. In these years Britain's self-image as a broker or intermediary, helping to bring the two superpowers together, was not mere self-delusion.

In the Cold War, as in the Second World War, the convergence of Anglo-American security interests was generally closer in Europe than in Asia. The British, pressed by India and the Commonwealth, refused to take the extreme US line over China in 1949–50. They also feared American escalation of the Korean war, including the possible use of atomic weapons, and in the winter of 1950–1 these issues led to intense friction. But the British, whatever their doubts, supported US intervention in Korea with forces of their own, and the American view of the British Empire remained ambivalent. For the British provided a valued network of bases, intelligence, and indigenous clients which would assist in the global containment of communism. Here post-war British determination to retain its world role was of particular importance to the alliance, especially given Indian independence and Britain's subsequent willingness to talk the language of partnership rather than domination. After the Korean War there was periodic US prodding over decolonization (for example, Central Africa under Macmillan) and occasional British objections to American Cold War extremism (such as abstinence from the total trade embargo on Castro's Cuba). But freedom to differ occasionally was built into the relationship, and it rarely imperilled the general cooperation in the 1940s and 1950s between the two world powers in global containment.

The one great exception to that generalization is of course the Middle East. In 1945–8 relations had been strained over Palestine, and in Iran in 1951–4 the United States exploited the oil nationalization crisis to establish Anglo-American parity in what had been Britain's last oil stronghold. Then in 1956 came Suez— the worst crisis between the two countries in the twentieth century. The military operation seemed to the Americans like old-fashioned gunboat diplomacy—all the more contemptible because it was inept as well as imperialist. Eisenhower refused to support the embattled pound until Britain withdrew, and one cannot underestimate the shock caused by the whole episode to British illusions about their independence and about American friendship.

Nevertheless the US objections were mainly about means (military intervention in defiance of international law) and timing (the simultaneous presidential election and the Russian invasion of Hungary). Both governments agreed that Nasserism was a threat to their common interests in the Middle East. When their major ally, the Nuri Said regime in Iraq, was toppled in July 1958, Britain and America mounted a carefully planned, combined operation to shore up client states in Jordan and Lebanon. Coming as it did less than two years after Suez, this is a reminder that the crisis of autumn 1956 should not be exaggerated.

From the late 1940s to the early 1960s the Anglo-American relationship was not without its frictions, but it was nevertheless uniquely close and uniquely important to both governments and to the shaping of the post-war world. Three specific areas of functional cooperation are worthy of closer attention: intelligence, nuclear weapons, and diplomatic consultation. These might be termed the *specialités* of the relationship.

The habit of diplomatic and bureaucratic consultation is the most fundamental. Officials in each government tended naturally and readily to consult with their opposite numbers. Some of this contact was institutionalized through transatlantic committees, but much of it was informal, building on the network of personal contacts and the facility of the common language. The point was to keep abreast of what one's opposite numbers in London or Washington were thinking—to have a sense not just of official policy but of the background debates and the alternative options.

This was particularly important in Washington given the fragmented nature of the US policy-making process. Lord Halifax, British ambassador in America during the war, likened it to 'a disorderly line of beaters out shooting; they do put the rabbits out of the bracken, but they don't come out where you expect.'[22] Washington was (and is) unusual in the limited control and coordination exercised by diplomats—the State Department—over the various strands of

[22] Halifax to Lord Simon, 21 Mar. 1941, Hickleton papers, A4.410.4.14 (CAC).

America's external relations. It was therefore essential to keep tabs on a whole variety of governmental agencies and, because of the independence and power of Congress, to 'work the Hill' assiduously. This the British generally did with subtlety and skill: the failures of consultation, such as Suez or Skybolt, usually came in situations when normal diplomatic channels had been bypassed.

Consultation did not guarantee consensus, of course. Policy towards China in the 1950s or over the Indo-Pakistani dispute in the 1960s and 1970s are cases in point. But these are also instances of how the relationship could accommodate unresolved differences. A member of the Foreign Office's North American Department wrote presciently in 1944 that the Anglo-American partnership 'implies full consultation on all major and many minor issues, but it is perfectly compatible with the view that if consultation fails to produce an agreed policy, each partner should be free to follow that policy which it thinks best, taking due account of the other's special interests or susceptibilities.'[23] Consultation sometimes produced agreement, sometimes agreement to differ.

From this practice of prior discussion each side derived substantial benefits. The British were frequently able to feed their views into the US decision-making process at an early stage before the bureaucratic and political trade-offs that make up American policy had set firm. By that latter point—the moment at which a policy might be offered for formal diplomatic negotiation with allies—it is often too late to effect any significant changes. In return the United States had a natural ally—whose support could generally be assumed because of the similarity of interests and values and the habit of advance consultation.

In a sense the intelligence relationship is only one instance of this 'consultative relationship'. But it is also at the heart of what makes the Anglo-American tie so different from other alliances. In the Second World War the two countries pooled their resources on an unprecedented scale, and the collaboration, in attenuated and secret form, survived the general severing of links in 1945–6. With the onset of the Cold War, mutual need dictated renewed cooperation. Britain had an intelligence network on a scale that it could no longer afford; the United States had dismantled the wartime Office of Strategic Services and was beginning again in 1947 with the Central Intelligence Agency (CIA). America could therefore use British expertise, staff, and installations; Britain needed US financial support.

The outcome was the 1947 UKUSA agreement which created a global division of labour in communications intelligence between the two governments (plus Canada, Australia, and New Zealand). Liaison offices were established in both capitals and in the central intelligence-gathering installations (Government Communications Headquarters (GCHQ) near Cheltenham and the National Security Agency (NSA) headquarters at Fort Meade, Maryland). GCHQ and other British intelligence operations also received significant US funding from

---

[23] P. Mason, minute, 16 May 1944 FO 371/38508, AN 1886/6/45.

the NSA budget. In due course NSA set up its own gathering and relay stations in Britain, at Chicksands, Bedfordshire (from 1950), Menwith Hill near Harrogate (from 1956), and, in Scotland, Kirknewton (1952–66) and Edzell near Montrose (since 1960). And during the 1950s, from the outbreak of the Korean War, the two air forces cooperated in overflights of Soviet Europe using combined crews flying from British and Continental bases. This allowed NATO to maintain surveillance even after the shooting down of Gary Powers in May 1960 obliged Eisenhower to end US-manned U–2 flights over Russia.[24]

The intelligence relationship has experienced frequent friction, for example CIA mistrust of the Secret Intelligence Service after the defection of Burgess and Maclean in May 1951. Nevertheless, its evolution has been relatively smooth compared to the nuclear relationship. In 1939–40 British atomic research was further advanced than American, and the sharing of information and personnel in 1940–1 significantly accelerated the pace of the US 'Manhattan' project. In September 1944 Roosevelt and Churchill concluded a secret agreement that 'full collaboration' in atomic development 'for military and commercial purposes should continue after the defeat of Japan unless and until terminated by joint agreement'.[25] But many in Washington, including Truman, were unaware of the agreement and in August 1946 a nationalistic, secrecy-conscious Congress, anxious that the United States alone should control the 'superbomb', passed the McMahon Act which prohibited the transfer of any atomic information to a foreign government. Subsequent Anglo-American agreements in 1948 and 1955 did little to change the basic position. Britain had been virtually excluded from nuclear collaboration—a source of deep and abiding bitterness in Whitehall and an aberration from the general close Anglo-American relationship in the late 1940s and 1950s.

The shift came in October 1957. Sputnik demonstrated that the Soviet Union now had a missile capable of intercontinental range which could therefore threaten the United States directly, at a time when America's own intercontinental ballistic missile programme was behind that of the Soviet Union. America was shaken and nervy—Macmillan judged the impact of Sputnik to be 'something equivalent to Pearl Harbour'[26]—and felt in need of all the help it could get. Britain was the obvious ally. The British had developed their own nuclear weapons programme over the previous decade, testing a hydrogen bomb in May 1957. Within three weeks of Sputnik, Macmillan had been invited to Washington, where Eisenhower committed himself to seek amendment of the McMahon Act, and in July 1958 and May 1959 new agreements were signed to permit a much fuller exchange of information, technology, and fissile materials.

[24] Duncan Campbell, *The Unsinkable Aircraft Carrier: American Military Power in Britain* (London, 1984), ch. 5; Christopher Andrew, *Secret Service* (London, 1985), 491–9.
[25] Aide-mémoire, 18 Sept. 1944, PREM 3, 139/9.
[26] Harold Macmillan, *Riding the Storm, 1955–9* (London, 1971), 320, quoting diary for 23 Oct. 1957.

In March 1960 collaboration was extended to weapons systems. At Camp David the British were offered the US Skybolt air-to-ground missile on advantageous terms, and Macmillan agreed that the United States could establish a Polaris submarine base at Holy Loch on the Clyde. There was no explicit 'deal', but it was generally understood that the two agreements were implicitly related. There were echoes here of the 'Destroyers-for-Bases' deal of August 1940. Indeed one might call this the 'Missiles-for-Bases' deal. Nearly twenty years had elapsed and the military technology had changed out of all recognition. But once again each country required the other's help at a time of global insecurity. Mutual need, more than Eisenhower's genuine feeling that the British had been badly treated, was at the root of the revived nuclear special relationship.

In one sense, the Polaris agreement at Nassau on 21 December 1962 was only an extension of this relationship. Once Defense Secretary Robert McNamara had decided to cut Skybolt on grounds of cost-effectiveness, Macmillan could justifiably argue that the 1960 'deal' obliged Kennedy to provide Polaris instead. The defusing of the crisis and the continuance of Britain's uniquely privileged access to US nuclear technology were further instances of the specialness of the Anglo-American relationship. Macmillan talked on his return of how Nassau had preserved 'both the concepts of independence and interdependence' that lay at the heart of what he meant by the special relationship.[27]

But, more profoundly, the Nassau agreement permanently altered that relationship. Skybolt was a stopgap—an air-to-ground device that would be carried by Britain's V-bomber force. It was already obsolescent in the impending era of long-range missiles such as Minuteman and Polaris. But neither the RAF nor the Admiralty had been seriously interested in Polaris during the late 1950s, for it would destroy the rationale of both the V-bombers and the blue-water navy. And within Macmillan's Cabinet there were some who doubted whether Britain should remain a nuclear power in the new and massively more costly missile age. Others felt that, if it did, an 'entente nucléaire' with France might be a better option in view of Britain's current interest in the EEC. These debates were terminated by the Skybolt crisis, the sudden switch by Macmillan to Polaris, and his deal with Kennedy at Nassau—which the Cabinet could only rubber-stamp. Britain would now remain in the nuclear game, but using American technology. The nuclear relationship re-established between 1957 and 1962 was special in more ways than one: Britain enjoyed uniquely privileged access to US nuclear secrets and weapons, but was to be the only nuclear power without a delivery system of its own.

Distinguishing historical periods is an agreeable academic exercise, but it rarely corresponds to the confusions of the real world. It is nevertheless fair to say that

---

[27] Andrew J. Pierre, *Nuclear Politics: the British Experience with an Independent Strategic Force 1939–70* (London, 1972), 314. On the Macmillan–JFK relationship, see David Nunnerley, *President Kennedy and Britain* (London, 1972).

the decade after Macmillan's resignation in October 1963 saw a pronounced decline in Britain's special importance to the United States. In part, this was a matter of personalities: Wilson and Heath never established rapports with Johnson and Nixon comparable to Macmillan's relations with Eisenhower and Kennedy. But the decline had set in during the last chaotic months of the Macmillan premiership and the final Macmillan–Kennedy meeting in June 1963 was a sad anticlimax.

The underlying reason was not personalities but power. During this decade Britain's residual capability as a great power was eroded, and with it Britain's special value to the United States. The decline was apparent in Europe itself, where British air and ground contributions to NATO's Central Front had been of particular significance in the 1950s. But the Federal Republic of Germany (FRG) joined NATO in May 1955 and in April 1957 the Sandys Defence White Paper announced the end of conscription after 1960—a belated reversion to normal British peacetime policy. In 1964 for the first time West Germany's armed forces exceeded those of Britain at 430,000 to 425,000. Moreover, the British army (like the French) was still spread around the globe, whereas Germany's was completely assigned to NATO's Central Front. The disparity in that crucial theatre was therefore much greater—274,000 Germans to 53,000 British—and the FRG's troop contribution even surpassed that of the United States, whose 7th Army in Central Europe had been reduced from 275,000 to 237,000 in 1964.[28] Manpower figures are only a crude measure of military strength, but they do indicate that during Macmillan's premiership the FRG had replaced Britain as the European pillar of NATO.

This decline in military capability reflected fundamental economic weakness. In the late 1950s and the 1960s Britain was unable to keep up not only with the superpowers but with its European neighbours. In 1951 Britain had been the world's third economic power, measured in GNP. Ten years later it had been overtaken by the FRG, and France was close behind. By 1971 Japan was in third place, followed by West Germany and the French, while Britain's GNP was roughly half Japan's.[29]

The German economic 'miracle' and the later French modernization were reflected institutionally in the success of the EEC. Britain's disdain for the Community in the mid-1950s had been understandable. British economic strategy was to develop the sterling area, and few anticipated the EEC's success in reducing tariffs or predicted the extent and pace of the German-led Continental boom. By 1961 a penitent Macmillan government had opted for entry, having been assured by Kennedy 'that relations between the United States and the UK would be strengthened not weakened, if the UK moved towards membership'.[30]

[28] *The Military Balance, 1964–5* (London, 1964), 17–18, 21–4.
[29] *The Military Balance, 1972–3* (London, 1972), 73.
[30] McGeorge Bundy to President, 7 Apr. 1961, National Security Files 170 (John F. Kennedy Library, Boston, Mass.).

The intensity of subsequent US pressure on the negotiators showed how strongly the administration felt about this, but the de Gaulle vetoes of 1963 and 1967 meant that Britain was in limbo for a decade until Heath's successful negotiations after the General resigned in 1969. During that time Britain was increasingly bypassed in US–European relations, with much of America's diplomacy directed towards the EEC and, after the French withdrawal from the integrated military command of NATO in 1966–7, towards the FRG.

During this decade Britain also proved much less successful as a broker between the two superpowers. Macmillan had played a significant part in achieving the 1963 Partial Test Ban Treaty. The British were naturally involved in these discussions as a nuclear-testing power. But the nuclear issue of the later 1960s, leading up to the SALT I agreements of May 1972, was the question of controlling weapons systems. Here the superpowers were in a league of their own, and the British had little influence on the central arms control negotiations.

The other great superpower diplomatic issue of the 1960s was Vietnam. Again the British played only a minor role, despite Wilson's best endeavours. Under the 1954 accords, Britain and the Soviet Union were co-chairmen of the Geneva Conference on Indochina—another example of how Britain's previous status as a great power provided residual leverage. But Wilson's repeated efforts to bring the belligerents to the negotiating table, most notably during Kosygin's visit to London in February 1967, earned him only LBJ's growing distrust. 'I won't tell you how to run Malaysia and you don't tell us how to run Vietnam', the President responded sharply when Wilson tried to temper US policy after the bombing of North Vietnam commenced in February 1965.[31]

LBJ's reference to Malaysia is a reminder that the British were also embattled in south-east Asia during these years, and they proved even less able than the Americans to sustain their exposed position. Sukarno's challenge to the Malaysian federation tied down some 30,000 British troops in 1963–4—more than in any other conflict since the end of the war. Although Sukarno's regime collapsed in 1966, the sustained operation at a time of acute financial crisis, forced the Cabinet to reassess Britain's global role. When he came to power Wilson had declared that 'We are a world power, and a world influence, or we are nothing.'[32] But recurrent balance-of-payments crises and the drain on Britain's reserves necessitated retrenchment, reductions, and finally rapid retreat in the wake of the devaluation of November 1967. The Cabinet then decided to abandon the Persian Gulf and Singapore by the end of 1971 and to give up any capability for operation east of Suez. The Heath government modified that policy, but did not alter it fundamentally.

This precipitate relinquishment of Britain's world role came as a shock to the United States. In December 1964 Denis Healey, the Minister of Defence, just

[31] Harold Wilson, *The Labour Government, 1964–70: a Personal Record* (London, 1971), 80.
[32] *The Times*, 17 Nov. 1964, p. 6, reporting his Guildhall speech the previous day.

back from Washington, told the Cabinet that what the Americans wanted Britain to do 'was not to maintain huge bases but to keep a foothold in Hong Kong, Malaya, the Persian Gulf, to enable us to do things for the alliance which they can't do'. Healey added that 'they think that our forces are much more useful to the alliance outside Europe than in Germany'.[33] The abandonment of this major out-of-area role was therefore keenly opposed in Washington. When Foreign Secretary George Brown reported the Cabinet's post-devaluation decision to withdraw forces in Washington, Dean Rusk and the State Department were horrified. 'Be British, George, be British—how can you betray us?' pleaded one official.[34] The main US complaint was not about the Far East but the Gulf. It was there that the British position was deemed especially important.

By the early 1970s Britain had therefore lost much of its special importance for the United States. Germany had replaced Britain as the principal European pillar of NATO, the EEC was a major focus for America's alliance diplomacy, the United Kingdom had little influence on superpower relations, and Britain's economic decline had forced it to abandon its global commitments more rapidly than it intended or the Americans desired. During this period Britain had often seemed importunate rather than important—begging for IMF loans to shore up the pound, begging for entry into the EEC, begging still to be taken seriously on the international stage. But this was a period of unprecedented change, managed by men brought up on the idea of Britain as ruler of a quarter of the world. Britain was adjusting to the status of a primarily European power, albeit with continuing global interests.

Many predicted that Britain's belated entry into the European Community in 1973 would mark the end of the 'special relationship' but this did not happen. European institutions were essentially economic and political; Britain (and the EC as a whole) continued to rely on the United States for defence or at least deterrence in the Cold War. In the 1970s and 1980s, the Royal Navy remained the second largest in NATO, guarding the Channel and the Eastern Atlantic. Although by the mid-1980s the British Army of the Rhine and its RAF support (totalling 67,000 men) were substantially smaller than the American and West German contributions, they were still essential strategically and symbolically to NATO's Central Front.[35] The *specialités* remained significant, with the intelligence axis moving into the satellite age in the 1970s and the nuclear alliance updated by the Trident deal of 1980. The rapport between Ronald Reagan and Margaret Thatcher was a notable feature of the 1980s, but as before the consultative networks lower down were equally important. Close personal ties between the two naval establishments, cemented by Defense Secretary Caspar Weinberger, a

---

[33] Richard Crossman, *The Diaries of a Cabinet Minister* (London, 1975–7, 3 vols.), i. 95, entry for 11 Dec. 1964.   [34] Crossman, *Diaries*, ii. 646.

[35] Figures from *The Military Balance, 1984–5* (London, 1984), 35, 40.

noted anglophile, ensured crucial logistic support for the hard-pressed British forces during the Falklands War of 1982.

In the 1970s and 1980s, therefore, the continued sense of Soviet threat kept the alliance together. But the years 1989–91 marked the end of the Cold War. In quick succession, the Soviet bloc in Eastern Europe disintegrated, Germany was unified, and in 1991 the Soviet Union itself fell apart. The early 1990s saw a new surge of European integration—with the Maastricht Treaty of 1991, a further round of enlargement in 1995, and the achievement of monetary union in 1999 for eleven of the fourteen member states. Although John Major and especially Tony Blair were more sympathetic to the European Union than Thatcher, Britain under their leadership remained on the margins. Part of the reason was Europe's continued 'security deficit'. The brutal Bosnian war, which the Europeans tried to manage themselves, was not settled until the Clinton Administration intervened in the summer of 1995, showing that only American air power (and air transport) could make a decisive difference. Britain was well placed to work with the Americans because only its defence forces (and those of France) had maintained the capability to act outside the NATO area. British forces were a valuable part of the American-led coalition that won the First Gulf War of 1991 and were essential in its sequel, in 2003, when Britain was America's sole significant military ally. By this time the al-Qaeda suicide attacks on New York and Washington in September 2001 had brought to an end the post-Cold War confusion, as the Bush Administration identified its global 'war on terror' as the top priority for the Western world.

So security still mattered and that, in the view of successive British governments, meant reliance on the United States and therefore cultivation of the special relationship. The build-up to the 2003 Gulf War suggested that attitudes had not moved very far from the 1960s, with the French still making very public objections, against the familiar British refrain of 'Yes, but'. But British policy towards America cannot be explained purely as a power calculation; the relationship is closer today, on both sides, than one would expect if judging simply by Britain's diminished world role and this is because it also reflects ties of culture. Churchill may have sentimentalized those ties for political ends but, in essence, he was right that the relationship cannot be properly understood without them. Of central importance is a shared tradition of political and economic liberalism that America inherited from Britain and then transformed.[36]

American democracy built on the principles of English liberty established in the seventeenth and eighteenth centuries: freedom under the law, the sanctity of private property, the rights of the legislature against the executive. These were the standards against which the colonists measured British rule in the 1770s and on

---

[36] What follows is a revised version of David Reynolds, 'Rethinking Anglo-American Relations', *International Affairs*, 65 (1989), 100–4. See also Nigel J. Ashton, *Kennedy, Macmillan and the Cold War: The Irony of Interdependence* (London, 2002), esp. ch. 1.

which they justified the creation of a new nation. After the Revolution, Americans created a new Constitution, designed to avoid the centralizing tendencies of British Cabinet government and based on the sovereignty of the people not the legislature. As they went on in the nineteenth century to redefine 'the people' in ever-wider terms, their theories penetrated and unsettled British political debate about franchise reform. In mid-century, British and American campaigners against slavery, drink, and war drew on each other for support, ideas, and inspiration. Most important for us here, at the end of the century a liberal critique of British foreign policy was to lay the basis of a major tradition of American diplomacy in the twentieth century.

For Victorian Radicals such as Richard Cobden and John Bright, free trade was not merely an economic doctrine but the harbinger of peace and progress. 'Commerce', wrote Cobden in 1836, 'is the great panacea, which, like a beneficent medical discovery, will serve to innoculate with the healthy and saving taste for civilization all the nations of the world.'[37] William Ewart Gladstone integrated Cobdenite ideals in a larger theory of international relations, particularly during his Midlothian campaign of 1879–80 when he enunciated six 'right principles of foreign policy'. The fundamentals were international peace and 'the equality of nations' and these should be maintained by a 'Concert' of European states. But the goal was not peace at any price: it must be based on justice and the rule of law. Gladstone's principles were therefore flexible: where a government behaved with flagrant injustice, the equality of nations took second place. In 1882 he sent a British army to restore order in Egypt, telling the Commons, 'We should not fully discharge our duty if we did not endeavour to convert the present interior state of Egypt from anarchy and conflict to peace and order. We shall look...to the co-operation of the Powers of civilised Europe... But if every chance of obtaining co-operation is exhausted, the work will be undertaken by the single power of England.'[38] Internationally if possible; unilaterally if necessary—that was Gladstone's maxim when he deemed fundamental moral principles to be at stake. Of course, Gladstone's intervention in Egypt was in large measure to protect British financial interests but, to quote W. E. Forster, a colleague turned critic, the Prime Minister had a 'wonderful power of persuasion. He can persuade most people of most things, and above all he can persuade himself of almost anything.'[39]

The liberal tradition in foreign policy, laid down by Cobden, Bright, and Gladstone, was a recurrent theme of British politics right up to the First World War. But it struck a dissenting note, because the dominant voices in Liberal foreign policy were 'Liberal Imperialists' such as Lord Rosebery and Sir Edward Grey, who sought to consolidate Britain's empire, strengthen its defences against the German challenge, and build ententes with France and Russia. In August

---

[37] Richard Cobden, *England, Ireland, and America* (Edinburgh, 1836), 12.
[38] John Morley, *The Life of William Ewart Gladstone*, vol. iii (London, 1903), 82.
[39] Philip Magnus, *Gladstone: A Biography* (London, 1954), 315.

1914 the Gladstonians in the Cabinet, including Gladstone's biographer John Morley, failed to keep Britain out of the continental conflict. By 1916 old-style Liberalism had been almost overwhelmed by a total war in which conscription, censorship, and state control of the economy were the means of survival.

Meanwhile, Gladstonian principles were being refined across the Atlantic. The 'Grand Old Man' of British politics was Woodrow Wilson's teenage hero. He hung Gladstone's portrait over his desk and in 1880, soon after graduating from Princeton, penned a eulogy of the statesman 'whose works have been the works of progress; whose impulses have been the impulses of nobility'.[40] President Wilson's proposed League of Nations was an enlarged and institutionalized version of the Concert that had inspired Gladstonian Liberals. Is it implausible to detect in Wilson's 'Fourteen Points' of January 1917, including peace, freer trade, and reduced armaments, a conscious echo of Gladstone's 'six right principles' of 1879? The President, of course, was no altruistic internationalist: like Gladstone he had a keen, often casuistic sense of how ideals could reinforce national interest and saw his country as the instrument of God's Providence. In the words of Robert Lansing, Wilson's disenchanted Secretary of State: 'Even established facts were ignored if they did not fit in with this intuitive sense, this semi-divine power to select the right.'[41] Wilsonianism can be therefore seen as British Liberalism transformed by America's crusading sense of mission and energized by the country's vast strength. The creed apparently abandoned by the Old World was being used against it by the Messiah from the New.

Once the fighting stopped, Wilson lost his leverage over his Allies and the Treaty of Versailles was a far cry from the liberal war aims he had promulgated in 1917–18. At home the crusade went sour and the Messiah fell from grace. Yet although America abandoned the League, Wilsonianism was resurrected by the Democratic party in the 1930s and 1940s, as the United States moved from isolationism to global leadership in opposition and apposition to Britain. Franklin Roosevelt himself was a realistic Wilsonian, sensitive to the use and limits of power in international affairs yet articulating his goals in the language of Wilsonian values. The Four Freedoms, the Atlantic Charter, and the UN Declaration became benchmarks for a new international order. Similarly, the State Department's campaign to break down Britain's network of imperial preferences was justified in Cobdenite language of peace and prosperity. 'Nations which act as enemies in the marketplace cannot long be friends at the council table', insisted Assistant Secretary of State Will Clayton in 1945. Little wonder

[40] 'Mr Gladstone, a character sketch', in Arthur S. Link, ed., *The Papers of Woodrow Wilson*, vol. i (Princeton, 1966), 642, 627. See also Arthur S. Link, *The Higher Realism of Woodrow Wilson* (Nashville, Tenn., 1971), 30, and more generally Frank Ninkovich, *The Wilsonian Century: U.S. Foreign Policy since 1900* (Chicago, 1999).

[41] Quoted in Margaret MacMillan, *Peacemakers: The Paris Peace Conference of 1919 and its Attempt to End the War* (London, 2001), 18.

that Brendan Bracken, Churchill's confidant, observed in 1937 that Cordell Hull, the inspiration of State Department trade policy, was 'the only true begotten Cobdenite left on earth'.[42]

What made American pressure harder for the British to deal with was the fact that the liberal tradition still persisted as an important theme in British foreign policy. In the Suez crisis of 1956, for instance, the French had little compunction about conspiring with Israel and using force to defend national interests. But Anthony Eden, who had made his name in the 1930s as a champion of the League, needed to present himself as a defender of international morality. Hence the specious cover story, the need to hold back his invasion force until a pretext had been established, and his sensitivity to the chorus of international denunciation at the United Nations—the latest version of an international Concert, which he had helped to create. On the other hand, the liberal tradition could also be turned on the United States, as it was with a vengeance over South Vietnam during the 1960s and early 1970s. The Americans claimed to be helping a free people in its battle for self-determination. This forced them to adopt covert means to get their way, for instance, Kennedy conniving in the Saigon coup to topple the corrupt Diem government in 1963 or Nixon keeping secret from world opinion his massive bombing of Cambodia in 1969–70.

Yet, the liberal tradition, whether honoured in the breach or the observance, set the two countries off from the other major powers. At the end of the Second World War, British and American economists were the architects of the new 'Bretton Woods' international economic order—aimed at the reopening of multilateral commerce through the reduction of barriers to trade and the assistance of a Concert of financial powers. More generally, in a world threatened by 'totalitarian' values, first Nazism and then communism, the differences between British and American versions of liberalism seemed far less important than the similarities. This theme needs to be set against the palpable decline of British power after 1945. In December 1962, Dean Acheson, the former US Secretary of State, notoriously asserted that 'Britain has lost an empire and not yet found a role' and that the attempt to maintain a global role 'based on a "special relationship" with the United States . . . is about to be played out'. But, with the full approval of President Kennedy, White House aide McGeorge Bundy issued a statement for the press saying that 'US-UK relations are not based only on a power calculus, but also on deep community of purpose and long practice of cooperation . . . "Special relationship" may not be a perfect phrase, but sneers at Anglo-American reality would be equally foolish.'[43]

---

[42] Quotations from Robert A. Pollard, *Economic Security and the Origins of the Cold War, 1945–1950* (New York, 1985), 2; Bracken to Beaverbrook, 14 Jan. 1937, Beaverbrook papers, C56 (HLRO).

[43] Acheson speech, 5 Dec. 1962, in Ian S. MacDonald, ed., *Anglo-American Relations since the Second World War* (New York, 1974), 181–2; McGeorge Bundy to Robert J. Manning, 7 Dec. 1962, National Security Files, NSF 170A/34 (John F. Kennedy Library, Boston).

The persistence of this 'deep community of purpose' was no more evident than in the run-up to the Iraq war of 2003. George W. Bush was a born-again evangelical Christian who used the terrorist attacks on America in September 2001 to justify 'regime change' in Iraq. Blair offered support in part because of the 'Never Say No' imperative of the special relationship, persuading himself that, if America was going to war, Britain would exert more influence as an ally and an insider. The French President, Jacques Chirac, true to the Gaullist tradition, shouted 'Non' furiously from the sidelines. But Blair was also a true believer in Bush's crusade. Personally very religious, though in a more private way than the President, he was steeped in the values of Christian socialism. Moreover, he explicitly cited Gladstone as 'one of my political heroes' and developed a Gladstonian justification for humanitarian intervention in the internal affairs of nation states.[44] Over the Serbian ethnic cleansing of Kosovo in 1999, Blair was even keener to send troops than were the Americans. Chided for his selectivity of his targets, the Prime Minister said he would be happy to get rid of other repressive regimes such as that of Robert Mugabe in Zimbabwe or the Burmese junta. 'I don't because I can't, but when you can, you should.'[45]

Blair's policy over the Iraq War was therefore a mixture of conviction and calculation. The precise balance is hard to calibrate—Blair, like Gladstone and Wilson, seemed able to persuade himself of the rightness of anything he did[46]—but what matters here is simply that morality reinforced pragmatism. Blair and Bush viewed the world in essentially the same way; their values remained rooted in the historic tradition of Anglo-American liberalism and that often set them apart from the Continentals. Thirty years after withdrawing from east of Suez and joining the European Community, Britain still often behaves as if the Atlantic Ocean is narrower than the English Channel. The persistence of the 'special relationship' idea therefore cannot be understood solely in terms of power politics. It reminds us of the importance of cultural relations in international affairs—a theme that I take up in a more theoretical way in the final chapter of this book.

---

[44] Peter Riddell, *Hug Them Close: Blair, Clinton, Bush and the 'Special Relationship'* (London, 2003), 7, 113.

[45] Peter Stothard, *30 Days: A Month at the Heart of Blair's War* (London, 2003), 42.

[46] 'No Prime Minister since Gladstone...has been so influenced by his religion' writes biographer Anthony Seldon. 'Blair's religious belief informs his unshakeable confidence that he alone can resolve difficulties, especially in a crisis, even when the highest Christian authorities on earth differ from him... But there is a sense of him shoehorning his policies in to fit the principles retrospectively.' Antony Seldon, *Blair* (London, 2004), 515–16, 527–8, 531.

18

Culture, Discourse, and Policy

Reflections on the New International History

These essays seek to illuminate the wartime Anglo-American relationship and its place in the history of the 1940s. They also raise questions about the methodology of international history, some of which I now try to address. This concluding chapter reflects on the evolution of international history from its nineteenth-century roots in 'diplomatic history', looking particularly at how it has adapted to recent developments in the historical discipline as a whole such as the so-called linguistic and cultural 'turns'. I do so with reference to some of the material on the 1940s deployed in earlier chapters of this book.

'International history' is not one of the most celebrated branches of our profession. Looking in some of the recent textbooks on historical method, one will not find it even in the index.[1] 'Diplomatic history' is the label still generally employed,[2] and then mostly in rather dismissive terms, as a relic of old-fashioned political history practised through a close and often uncritical reading of government documents and usually predicated on a 'great man' theory of history. In 1936 G. M. Young didn't discern even a touch of greatness: in the words of his oft-quoted aphorism 'the greater part of what passes for diplomatic history is little more than the record of what one clerk said to another clerk'.[3] In *The Nature of History*, published in 1970, Arthur Marwick claimed that diplomatic

Earlier versions of this chapter were given as a paper to the International History Seminar at the Institute of Historical Research in London in October 2001 and as the annual Bindoff Lecture at Queen Mary College, London University, in February 2005. I am grateful to Susan Bayly, Ludmilla Jordanova, and Alexandra Shepard for comments on a draft. A shorter published version, without discussion of the linguistic turn, appeared in *Cultural and Social History*, 3 (2006).

[1] e.g. Joyce Appleby, Lynn Hunt, and Margaret Jacob, *Telling the Truth about History* (New York, 1994); Jeremy Black and Donald M. MacRaild, *Studying History* (2nd edn., London, 2000); Ludmilla Jordanova, *History in Practice* (London, 2000); Arthur Marwick, *The New Nature of History: Knowledge, Evidence, Language* (2nd edn., London, 2001).

[2] e.g. John Tosh, *The Pursuit of History* (3rd edn., London, 2000). Juliet Gardiner, ed., *What is History Today...?* (London, 1988), 131–42, included a chapter on diplomatic history but, in a more recent tour d'horizon of the profession, David Cannadine, ed., *What is History Now?* (London, 2002), it was one of the sub-disciplines omitted for reasons of space (p. vii).

[3] G. M. Young, *Victorian England: Portrait of an Age* (London, 1936), 103.

history had 'the reputation of being the most arid and sterile of all the sub-disciplines, with a particularly piddling expertise of its own'.[4]

To narrate the story of diplomatic history takes us on a journey from the centre to the periphery of our profession. Leopold von Ranke, the so-called 'father of historical science', was also the man who put diplomatic history on the map. His close analysis of the archives was animated by a conviction that political relations between states were the decisive factor in historical development—what later became known as the 'primacy of foreign policy'.[5] Ranke worked particularly on the Reformation era, but his insights had wider relevance. Diplomatic history took off in France after the Franco-Prussian war of 1870: understanding defeat was an overwhelming problem for the nation, to which scholars such as Hippolyte Taine and Albert Sorel responded in their different ways. The German question stayed at the centre of French politics and mentality for the next century, thanks to two world wars and the debate over European integration. Diplomatic history was given an even greater fillip after 1918 by the argument over the origins of the war: the Weimar government's publication of a large but selective collection of documents in an effort to overturn the 'war guilt' clause of the Treaty of Versailles forced the British and French to reply in kind. The result was a massive amount of new source material, spawning in turn an extensive secondary literature. Much the same happened in the 1960s and 1970s after the opening of the American and then British archives for the 1930s and 1940s. This produced an explosion of writing on appeasement, the Second World War, and the origins of the Cold War, of which the essays in this volume are a small part.

By the 1950s and 1960s, however, diplomatic history was under threat. One challenge came from the new discipline of 'international relations'—a branch of political science that developed most precociously in the United States. Indeed, IR has been called 'an American social science' because it was intended by pioneers such as Hans Morgenthau to help policy-makers understand and, even more, to manage the new superpower's role in an unfamiliar world. Also important were the porous nature of American government, with academics and consultants moving in and out of senior policy-making positions, and the constellation of wealthy foundations such as Rockefeller, Ford, and RAND, which provided institutional support. In the 1950s IR creamed off much of Cold War history, using it to generate theories of the international system and of interstate relations.[6] This was a threat to historians of US foreign relations, who

---

[4] Arthur Marwick, *The Nature of History* (London, 1970), 93.
[5] A phrase coined not by Ranke but probably by Wilhelm Dilthey. See Wolfgang J. Mommsen, 'Ranke and the Neo-Rankean School in Imperial Germany', in Georg G. Iggers and James M. Powell, eds., *Leopold von Ranke and the Shaping of the Historical Discipline* (Syracuse, NY, 1990), 130.
[6] Stanley Hoffmann, 'An American Social Science: International Relations', *Daedalus*, 106/3 (Spring 1977), 41–60.

engaged in turf and budget wars against IR colleagues within American universities. But IR also provided scholars of traditional diplomatic history with some convenient theoretical baggage in the form of 'realism'. Critical of the supposed 'utopianism' of Wilsonian diplomacy, Morgenthau and his colleagues highlighted the egoism of human nature and the lack of world government. They saw international politics largely as a realm of power politics in which states pursued rationally defined national interests. Despite wide varieties of emphasis between, say, classical realists like Morgenthau, more conscious of human nature, and neo-realists such as Kenneth Waltz, who stressed the structural context of international anarchy, the realist approach provided a philosophical underpinning to IR and, more loosely, an intellectual justification for the priorities of diplomatic history.[7] Some specific work by IR practitioners, such as Graham Allison on the way bureaucratic politics complicated simple rationalist theories of decision-making based on calculations of national interest, was readily taken up by diplomatic historians seeking a way through their paper trails in the archives.[8]

A different challenge to traditional diplomatic history came from the redefinitions of the historical discipline after the Second World War. In France, the *Annales* school offered a radical critique of traditional political history for being obsessed, to quote Fernand Braudel, with 'the crests of foam' on the deeper 'tides of history', the latter, he argued, being driven by climate and geography, by economic systems and social forces.[9] In Germany, proponents of a Rankean approach, such as Andreas Hillgruber and Klaus Hildebrand, were challenged in the 1960s by Hans-Ulrich Wehler and other social historians, who stressed the decisive role not of foreign policy but of domestic interest groups and social trends in shaping national history. In Britain and America social historians, demanded 'history from below'. E. P. Thompson's pioneering manifesto on that theme began with a diatribe about how history departments still 'languish under the Norman yoke' of elite political history and how 'the seed of William the Bastard occupies the Chairs'.[10] From different angles, the explosion of women's history, historical demography, and the history of the family also questioned the fixation of diplomatic history with a few elite males.

Challenge provoked response. For instance, Pierre Renouvin and Jean-Baptiste Duroselle, the deans of post-war French diplomatic history, divided their 1964 textbook *Introduction à l'Histoire des Relations Internationales* into two parts—the first looking in a Braudelian way at the 'underlying forces' (*les forces*

---

[7] For an overview see e.g. Jack Donnelly, *Realism and International Relations* (Cambridge, 2000).

[8] Graham Allison, *Essence of Decision: Explaining the Cuban Missile Crisis* (Boston, 1971); Graham Allison and Morton H. Halperin, 'Bureaucratic Politics: A Paradigm and some Policy Implications', *World Politics*, 24 supplement (1972), 40–89.

[9] Fernand Braudel, *The Mediterranean and the Mediterranean World in the Age of Philip II*, trans. Sian Reynolds (London, 1972), 21.

[10] E. P. Thompson, 'History from Below', *Times Literary Supplement*, 7 Apr. 1966, 279.

profondes), the second at 'the statesman' and policy-making.[11] Another response, popular in Britain, was the neologism 'international history'. This was intended to signify that such scholars were interested not just in the antics of a few diplomats but in much broader historical patterns of international relations—including finance, trade, and the military.[12] Across the Atlantic, American diplomatic historians were stung by the charge of parochialism and by the call to investigate non-American archives and even learn some foreign languages. This, argued Charles S. Maier, should be part of a shift from diplomatic decision-making to studies of the international system.[13]

The expansion of 'history' in the 1950s and 1960s therefore left its mark on diplomatic historians. But their work still privileged relations between states. The cultural turn of the 1980s and 1990s forced them into a more expansive definition of what should be studied and questioned traditional reliance on government archives as the principal source. 'Culture', of course, became such a capacious term as to lose all precision: that was part of its power. But the 'common ground of cultural historians', according to Peter Burke, is 'a concern with the symbolic and its interpretations'[14]—where symbols are understood to be material or behavioural as much as visual or intellectual. Much of this work was stimulated by the writings of anthropologists, notably Clifford Geertz. The 'turn' to culture has been so profound that many practitioners of political and economic history have redefined themselves as scholars of political or economic culture, while social historians, even more embattled, have often changed labels to 'cultural historians'. Some proponents of the so-called 'New Cultural History' pushed this further by insisting that cultural symbols did not simply represent reality but construct it—an approach exemplified in Benedict Anderson's now famous definition of a nation as a 'cultural artefact', an 'imagined political community'.[15]

This shift from 'representation' to 'construction' drew on the related 'linguistic turn' prompted by postmodern and post-structuralist philosophy. Postmodernism, like realism, was a house with many mansions, but its main point was to question the idea of any unmediated access to 'the past' and to insist that all we had were 'texts' built upon other texts. From this cycle of intertextuality

[11] Pierre Renouvin and Jean-Baptiste Duroselle, *Introduction à l'histoire des relations internationales* (Paris, 1964).

[12] Ernest R. May, 'The Decline of Diplomatic History', in George A. Billias and Gerald N. Grob, eds., *American History: Retrospect and Prospect* (New York, 1971), 430; Alexander de Conde, 'Essay and Reflection: On the Nature of International History', *International History Review*, 10 (1988), 282–301.

[13] Charles S. Maier, 'Marking Time: The Historiography of International Relations', in Michael Kammen, eds., *The Past Before Us: Historical Writing in the United States* (Ithaca, NY, 1980), 355–87.

[14] Peter Burke, *What is Cultural History?* (Cambridge, 2004), 3. See also Lynn Hunt, ed., *The New Cultural History* (Berkeley, 1989).

[15] Benedict Anderson, *Imagined Communities: Reflections on the Origin and Spread of Nationalism* [1983] (2nd edn., London, 1991), 4, 6.

there could be no escape. In the celebrated formula of Jacques Derrida, 'il y n'a pas de hors-texte'—there's nothing outside the text, no context, all the world's a text. In extreme forms, post-modernism undermined not merely 'grand narratives', such as a Marxist or Whig theory of historical evolution, but the possibility of historical 'knowledge' in any form.[16]

The cultural and linguistic turns posed particular problems for traditional historians of diplomatic decision-making, claiming to use archival evidence to 'reconstruct' in a Rankean manner what actually happened. The crisis has been particularly acute in the United States,[17] perhaps because disciplinary boundaries there are more open than in Europe at the undergraduate level yet more rigid at the professional level. Historians of American foreign relations, who had earlier felt threatened by the challenge from IR, now seemed marginalized by the cultural turn in American history departments. More positively, female historians of foreign relations—a larger minority in American academia than elsewhere—have taken the lead in applying 'culture' and particularly gender to diplomatic history. International events also had an effect. In the 1970s and 1980s many diplomatic historians (and Americans at large) had been preoccupied with the ideological struggle of the Cold War. Its abrupt end and messy outcomes (such as the new ethnic wars in the Balkans and fevered talk about an impending 'clash of civilizations') suddenly suggested that issues of culture really mattered.[18] Where American scholars have led, Europeans have followed. Recent volumes of essays on the methodology of international history from Germany and Britain demonstrate the pervasiveness of debate about the implications of the cultural and linguistic turns.[19]

Why this matters can be seen by a glance at one of the liveliest sub-fields of international history at the moment—intelligence. In the 1970s it became a cliché that intelligence was 'the missing dimension of most diplomatic history'. That laconic aside from a senior British diplomat, Sir Alexander Cadogan, became the title of a pioneering set of essays edited by Christopher Andrew and David Dilks

---

[16] For a useful overview see Elizabeth A. Clark, *History, Theory, Text: Historians and the Linguistic Turn* (Cambridge, Mass., 2004) and, more generally, Ernst Breisach, *On the Future of History: The Postmodernist Challenge and its Aftermath* (Chicago, 2003). For a sampling of the debate, edited by a dogmatic postmodernist, see Keith Jenkins, ed., *The Postmodern History Reader* (London, 1997).

[17] For a measure of how the debate opened up during the 1990s, compare the contents pages of the first and second editions of Michael J. Hogan and Thomas G. Paterson, eds., *Explaining the History of American Foreign Relations* (New York, 1991 and 2004).

[18] See Samuel P. Huntington, 'The Clash of Civilizations?', *Foreign Affairs*, 72/3 (Summer 1993), 22–49, and id., *The Clash of Civilizations and the Remaking of World Order* (New York, 1996). Note how the question mark disappeared from the title as a stimulating think-piece outgrew itself to become a dogmatic book.

[19] Wilfried Loth and Jürgen Osterhammel, eds., *Internationale Geschichte: Themen, Ergebnisse, Aussichten* (Munich, 2000); Jessica C. E. Gienow-Hecht and Frank Schumacher, eds., *Culture and International History* (Oxford, 2003); Patrick Finney, ed., *Palgrave Advances in International History* (London, 2005).

in 1984.[20] Sparked by the revelations of wartime practitioners, assisted by the belated opening of American and British archives, and reinforced by the creation of at least four new journals, intelligence history took off during the 1990s. The new concern was not so much human intelligence (humint)—spies have been a part of history writing for centuries—but signals intelligence (sigint) such as the Ultra and Magic intercepts from the wartime Axis and the Venona decrypts revealing the extent of Soviet penetration of British and American government.

Undoubtedly this new material has forced us to reconsider many aspects of diplomatic and strategic history.[21] Yet some of the work has been characterized by an old-fashioned positivism now decried by cultural historians and post-modernists alike. Perhaps because of the waves of documents that keep crashing into the archives, some scholars and students have been content to wallow in the 'information' without always paying as much attention to how it was understood by policy-makers. There were, for instance, plenty of straws in the wind suggesting the Japanese attack on Pearl Harbor: the root problem was that these were ignored because few American policy-makers believed that the Japanese were capable of mounting such a daring and devastating operation. Churchill's dismissal of the Japanese in August 1941 as 'the Wops of the Pacific'—on a par with the Italians in the Mediterranean—summed up the prevailing mood in London and Washington.[22] This is not to deny the quality of some of the best work in intelligence history, for instance, by Wesley Wark and Peter Jackson on British and French perceptions of the German threat in the 1930s, and by Anthony Best and Richard Aldrich on the West and Japan before and during the Second World War. In these monographs, intelligence is set within a broader framework of political and cultural perceptions.[23] But not all the literature is at that level, particularly in journals, and this demonstrates the need for a cultural approach to intelligence history and a more probing evaluation of archival texts.[24]

---

[20] David Dilks, ed., *The Diaries of Sir Alexander Cadogan, OM, 1938–1945* (London, 1971), 21; cf. Christopher Andrew and David Dilks, eds., *The Missing Dimension: Governments and Intelligence Communities in the Twentieth Century* (London, 1984).

[21] For a couple of examples, taken simply from the Second World War, see Ralph Bennett, *Behind the Battle: Intelligence in the War with Germany, 1939–1945* (2nd edn., London, 1999); Michael Smith and Ralph Erskine, eds., *Action This Day* (London, 2001).

[22] Quoted in David Reynolds, *The Creation of the Anglo-American Alliance, 1937–1941: A Study in Competitive Cooperation* (London, 1981), 249.

[23] Wesley Wark, *The Ultimate Enemy: British Intelligence and Nazi Germany, 1933–1939* (Oxford, 1986); Peter Jackson, *France and the Nazi Menace: Intelligence and Policy Making, 1933–1939* (Oxford, 2000); Anthony Best, *British Intelligence and the Japanese Challenge in Asia, 1914–41* (London, 2002); Richard J. Aldrich, *Intelligence and the War against Japan: Britain, America and the Politics of Secret Service* (Cambridge, 2000).

[24] This mirrors the complaint that intelligence itself is 'the most undertheorized area of international relations'. James Der Derian, *Antidiplomacy: Spies, Terror, Speed, and War* (Oxford, 1992), 19. Though see Michael G. Fry and Miles Hochstein, 'Epistemic Communities: Intelligence Studies and International Relations', *Intelligence and National Security*, 8 (1993), 14–28, and Andrew Rathmell, 'Towards Postmodern Intelligence', *Intelligence and National Security*, 17 (2002), 87–104.

How, then, have the linguistic and cultural turns affected international history? The former has had less effect, perhaps because of the nihilist implications of postmodernism. In the words of Ernst Breisach: 'The ban of all claims to authoritative truth was inconsistent with the claim made for the exclusive and universal validity of poststructuralist postmodern theory.' In other words, its critique of historical knowledge also undermines the truth status of its, and all other, prescriptions. Although defenders of postmodernism vehemently deny this charge of relativism, that is how most historical practitioners—myself included—have taken it, in its extreme forms.[25]

Nevertheless, it seems to me more loosely that the postmodern attention to language can be of considerable value for international historians. The point has been taken up by some scholars but mainly with reference to the way that diplomatic language has been 'engendered'; I shall come to this in a moment when discussing gender and cultural international history. There are, however, other points to be made about discourse. International historians are particularly interested in how policy is formed and the diplomatic archives constitute their main source. Those papers are voluminous—unlike many historians, particularly medievalists, we often feel we are being given a detailed and intimate insight into the minds of past leaders and that can be very seductive. Notoriously so in the case of the British Foreign Office, whose files are formed around incoming telegrams on which officials reflect (in the form of 'minutes') and then draft replies. The result is a mass of comment—often lengthy, particularly in the case of junior staff, sometimes erudite, and occasionally entertaining. It is a commonplace that the opening of such official archives can often encourage historians to see the past only through official eyes, to conclude that what was done was the only thing that could have been done. Although a more sympathetic view of appeasement was already emerging in the 1960s, the opening of the Whitehall archives under the new Thirty-Year Rule of 1967 led to a series of revisionist accounts of appeasement that largely endorsed the approach of Chamberlain, the Treasury, and the Chiefs of Staff—from which it has taken years to develop a critical distance.[26]

In such a text-based area of history as diplomatic history, scholars must therefore be extremely sensitive to language. Not merely with regard to evaluative terminology such as 'special relationship' and 'iron curtain', as I suggested in earlier chapters, but when looking at the key concepts used by diplomats. Examples include how and when they refer to 'interests' or 'values', the categories used to understand foreign leaders (FDR on Hitler as a 'nut'), or the way in which particular regions of the world are grouped or conceptualized (such as the

---

[25] Breisach, *On the Future of History*, 109–10; cf. Patrick Finney, 'Beyond the Postmodern Moment?', *Journal of Contemporary History*, 40 (2005), 156, 160.

[26] John Baxendale and Chris Pawling, *Narrating the Thirties. A Decade in the Making: 1930 to the Present* (London, 1996), 149–54; cf. D. C. Watt, 'Appeasement: The Rise of a Revisionist School?', *Political Quarterly*, 36 (1965), 191–213.

Orient or the Balkans). Some diplomatic terms, of course, gain currency far outside the policy-making circles, among politicians, the media and historians—such as 'world war', discussed in my opening chapter. A case study still awaiting proper analysis is the dramatic and durable shift in the use and evaluative force of the noun 'appeasement'. In November 1925, Austen Chamberlain, the Foreign Secretary, described the Locarno Treaty between Germany and its neighbours 'not as the end of the work of appeasement and reconciliation, but as its beginning'. In April 1938, his half-brother, Neville, told the Commons that 'if only we could find some peaceful solution of this Czechoslovak question, I should feel myself that the way was open again for a further effort for general appeasement'. In both these cases, 'appeasement' was used to describe the search for a peaceful settlement of international grievances; it was a descriptive term, with approbratory overtones. But as disillusion with Munich set in and especially after the Fall of France, which cast a wholly new light on British policy in the 1930s, 'appeasement' took on very different connotations. So much so that by 1946 Sir Orme Sargent, Permanent Under-Secretary at the Foreign Office, considered that the word had been 'debased to a term of abuse'.[27]

Another such linguistic turn, on the other side of the Atlantic, is the move from 'isolation' (referring to America's historic distancing from European entanglements) to 'isolationist' (a term of abuse against opponents of Roosevelt's and Truman's foreign policies). Most of these opponents advocated a different policy, such as 'hemisphere defence' rather than intervention in 1940–1, or concentration on communist China and the Korean War instead of the Truman Administration's Atlantic alliance in 1949–50, but 'isolationist' implied an unrealistic, head in the sand view of America's place in the world.[28] One might also reflect on the way in which early conceptualization of American Cold War policy as one of 'containment', particularly by George Kennan in the 1940s, has acted as not merely a prism but a prison for subsequent comment by policy-makers and historians. 'Containment' implied, as the US government wanted, that American objectives were essentially defensive—to 'contain' Soviet expansion—and also gave an erroneous impression of a single, coherent grand strategy.[29]

In looking at such shifts in diplomatic language, international historians might learn from intellectual historians. The German scholar Reinhart Koselleck has pioneered *Begriffsgeschichte*, the study of how and why key concepts have

---

[27] These quotations—and many others could be deployed—are all from Martin Gilbert, *The Roots of Appeasement* (New York, 1966), quoting pp. 115, 170, 220.

[28] Although the conceptual shift has not been properly chronicled, there is much relevant material in Wayne S. Cole, *Roosevelt and the Isolationists, 1932–1945* (Lincoln, Neb., 1983), and Justus D. Doenecke, *Not to the Swift: The Old Isolationists in the Cold War Era* (Cranbury, NJ, 1979).

[29] See the stimulating discussion by Sarah-Jane Corke, 'History, Historians and the Naming of Foreign Policy: A Postmodern Reflection on American Strategic Thinking during the Truman Administration', *Intelligence and National Security*, 16 (2001), 146–63.

changed over time, whose most famous product, published during the 1970s, was a multi-volume dictionary. Many of the 115 terms studied in these long essays are central to the work of international historians, such as 'war', 'peace', 'neutrality', and 'power'. Similar work has been done in other Continental countries and, promulgated and amended by anglophone exponents such as Melvin Richter and Terence Ball, it has been taken up in Britain and especially the United States.[30]

'Conceptual history' is, however, broad-brush stuff and its use of evidence can sometimes be imprecise. Approaching the same problem from a different angle, the British historian Quentin Skinner has charted how concepts such as 'the state' or 'liberty' have metamorphosed but he is particularly interested in 'what can be done with them in argument'. This is a more dynamic approach than that of many recent students of discourse. Stimulated by J. L. Austin's approach to language as 'speech acts'—'how to do things with words', in the title of his most influential book—Skinner has set out a detailed methodology for detecting and understanding how concepts were used normatively and descriptively to alter the terms of political debate. This 'rhetorical perspective' on intellectual history has considerable potential for international historians, who all operate in an area where concepts are deployed persuasively to effect changes of policy and action. Skinner's analysis of how seventeenth-century advocates of a commercial society manipulated words such as 'frugality' and 'providence' to suit their agenda, for instance, suggests methods that could be applied to terms such as 'appeasement' or 'isolationist'.[31]

In a loose, less dogmatic form, the linguistic turn therefore has some interesting implications. But international historians have tended to pay more attention to the cultural turn. One sign of this is the new interest in cultural diplomacy. We now have a large variety of studies of how the United States used music, literature, art, and other cultural products as weapons in the Cold War. This is no peripheral matter: David Caute has reminded us that the 'Cold War' was relatively 'cool' in purely military terms, when compared with much more brutal cultural conflicts such as the Crusades or the sixteenth-century wars of religion. By contrast, the ideological and cultural competition between the superpowers was ferocious and total.[32] Recent work on American Cold War cultural policy, for instance, shows how the promotion of 'freedom' within and beyond 'the free

---

[30] See Melvin Richter, *The History of Political and Social Concepts: A Critical Introduction* (New York, 1995), esp. ch. 1; cf. Otto Brunner, Werner Conze, Reinhart Koselleck, eds., *Geschichtliche Grundbegriffe: Historisches Lexikon zur politisch-sozialer Sprache in Deutschland* (8 vols., Stuttgart, 1972–97).

[31] See the methodological essays in Quentin Skinner, *Visions of Politics: 1, Regarding Method* (Cambridge, 2002), esp. chs 8–10, quoting pp. 176, 179, and more generally James Tully, ed., *Meaning and Context: Quentin Skinner and His Critics* (Cambridge, 1988).

[32] David Caute, *The Dancer Defects: The Struggle for Cultural Supremacy during the Cold War* (Oxford, 2003), 5–7.

world' was often done by distinctly illiberal methods—bribery, propaganda, and coercion. The ideology of 'freedom' also required that this be concealed from public gaze, for instance by covertly funding unions, journalists, scholars, and private groups. Thus, the Truman Administration allocated ten million dollars from its 'Exchange Stabilization Fund' to help defeat the communists in the crucial Italian elections of April 1948, but the money was channelled via 'unvouchered and private sources'.[33]

Scholars in this area, though rooted in the Frankfurt School's critique of 'mass culture' and 'cultural imperialism', now prefer to talk of cultural 'transfer' or 'transmission', to suggest a two-way relationship.[34] Yet even these labels have their own problems because much of this work is paradoxical in character. On the one hand it demonstrates the extent and intensity of US cultural diplomacy during the Cold War; on the other, it demonstrates that these programmes often did not succeed in their precise aims. Many of them promoted 'high culture' in music, art, and literature, yet it was American popular culture in the form of film, jazz, and jeans that had most appeal in Western Europe, particularly among the young. Furthermore, American forms and practices were frequently altered and adapted in cultural transmission. Reinhold Wagnleitner's book, *Coca-Colonization and the Cold War*, shows how young Austrians embraced American values in their own ways and for their own reasons in the late 1940s and early 1950s, to help move on their country from the social and political norms of the National Socialist era. In Wagnleitner's phrase, this was colonization as self-colonization. Jessica Gienow-Hecht's study of American cultural diplomacy in post-war West Germany reached parallel conclusions. She argues that Germans embraced Elvis and Disney but jealously guarded their own high culture (Goethe and Mozart) as part of national identity. American culture, in short, could not replace German *Kultur*: cultural transmission, she claims, was 'mission impossible'.[35]

Although these studies of cultural diplomacy have highlighted an important and neglected aspect of American foreign policy and have also encouraged similar work for other countries, they show the difficulties entailed in

---

[33] Scott Lucas, *Freedom's War: The US Crusade against the Soviet Union, 1954–1956* (Manchester, 1999), esp. pp. 3, 44.

[34] Jessica C. E. Gienow-Hecht, 'Cultural Transfer', in Hogan and Paterson, eds., *Explaining the History of American Foreign Relations* (2004 edn.), 257–78. For case studies see Lary May, ed., *Recasting America: Culture and Politics in the Age of the Cold War* (Chicago, 1989); Rob Kroes, Robert W. Rydell, and Doeko F.J. Bosscher, eds., *Cultural Transmissions and Receptions: American Mass Culture in Europe* (Amsterdam, 1993); and the special issue of *Intelligence and National Security*, 18/2 (2002) devoted to 'The Cultural Cold War in Western Europe, 1945–1960'.

[35] Reinhold Wagnleitner, *Coca-Colonization and the Cold War: The Cultural Mission of the United States in Austria after the Second World War* (Chapel Hill, NC, 1994), quoting p. 2; Jessica C. E. Gienow-Hecht, *Transmission Impossible: American Journalism as Cultural Diplomacy in Postwar Germany* (Baton Rouge, La., 1999), esp. pp. 10–11, 183–4. These works echo some of the themes in the study by Richard Kuisel, *Seducing the French: The Dilemma of Americanization* (Berkeley, 1993).

establishing direct relationships between diplomacy and cultural change. The dominant approach of what has been called 'culturalist international history'[36] is therefore to investigate the cultural context of foreign policy. Briefly I wish to explore three important areas in which the study of cultural attitudes has had an effect on international history: masculinity, memory, and alterity.

Gender only began to impinge on international history in the 1990s, through the work of American scholars such as Emily S. Rosenberg.[37] One obvious impediment was the limited number of female decision-makers at the very top. The first women leaders of modern democratic states emanated from outside the West during the 1960s, in the persons of Sirimavo Bandaranaike of Ceylon, Indira Gandhi of India, and Golda Meir of Israel.[38] No woman has yet attained the presidency of the United States; though in recent years there have been two female Secretaries of State—Madeleine Albright and Condoleeza Rice. There has only been one British female Prime Minister, and it is striking that Margaret Thatcher's foreign policy has been appraised largely by reference to ideology rather than gender.[39]

So the injunction 'cherchez la femme' does not get us far down the corridors of power. A more fruitful field has been the 'women's history of international relations', which has explored for instance the symbiosis of feminism and internationalism in the Atlantic world of the late nineteenth and early twentieth centuries. This includes women in 'feminized' areas of international contact, such as nursing and missionaries, but also the role of women in the politically influential movements for peace, disarmament, and social amelioration that developed during and after the First World War. This work contributes to our understanding of 'the construction of internationalism', as against nationalist self-consciousness, in twentieth-century history.[40] Other scholars have explored how women's rights became established from the 1970s in the burgeoning human rights agenda of international politics. Here the role of female non-governmental organizations has been of particular importance, for instance in finally persuading the United Nations in 1993 to expand its definition of 'war crimes' to include systematic rape.[41]

---

[36] e.g. Andrew J. Rotter, 'Culture', in Finney, ed., *Palgrave Advances in International History*, 270.

[37] See Emily S. Rosenberg, 'Gender', *Journal of American History*, 77 (1990), 116–24, and the essay by Kristin Hoganson, 'What's Gender got to do with it? Gender history as Foreign Relations History', in Hogan and Paterson, eds., *Explaining the History of American Foreign Relations* (2004 edition), 304–22.

[38] Sirimavo Bandaranaike (1960–5 and 1970–7); Indira Gandhi (1966–77 and 1980–4); Golda Meir (1969–74). Isabel Peron was President of Argentina in 1974–6. See Olga S. Opfell, *Women Prime Ministers and Presidents* (Jefferson, NC, 1993).

[39] Cf. Paul Sharp, *Thatcher's Diplomacy: The Revival of British Foreign Policy* (London, 1997).

[40] e.g. Leila J. Rupp, *Worlds of Women: The Making of an International Women's Movement* (Princeton, 1997).

[41] See the literature cited in Kenneth Cmiel, 'The Recent History of Human Rights', *American Historical Review*, 109 (2004), 118, 125.

Yet such work still leaves us on the margins: it does little, for instance, to explain why internationalism collapsed so completely in the 1930s or why human rights suddenly became a serious diplomatic issue in the late twentieth century. Many scholars have therefore followed a precept from international relations theory and moved from the 'woman' question to the 'man' question.[42] This, of course, parallels the approach of Joan W. Scott and others in the 1980s in redefining women's history as gender history and focusing on the ways in which male–female relations have been conceived and constructed.[43]

The American historian Frank Costigliola is an imaginative analyst of how diplomatic language may be engendered, seeking to 'discern how emotive meanings can constrain and actively shape rational analysis'. He has, for instance, detected a general pattern of post-war American officials, 'with varying and probably unknowable degrees of intentionality', employing language that depicted difficult allies, notably France in the 1940s and 1950s, as 'beings that were in some way diminished from the norm of a healthy heterosexual male: sick patients, hysterical women, naïve children, emasculated men.' In the 1930s, similarly, British diplomats sometimes characterized isolationist and erratic America in gender stereotypes. According to His Majesty's Ambassador in Washington in 1937, 'she resembles a young lady just launched into society and highly susceptible to a little deference from an older man'. Britain's self--conceived role was therefore to 'educate' America into its international responsibilities. By 1963 a senior British diplomat acknowledged that the new realities of transatlantic dependence entailed 'a rather feminine role for Great Britain in relation to the United States'. But he evoked another conno-tation of femininity by suggesting that this allowed his government to exercise 'latent power' behind the scenes in 'a rather traditionally British kind' of dip-lomacy, '*suaviter in modo, fortiter in re*'.[44] Here is another example of Britain's 'never say "no", say "yes, but"' conception of the special relationship, discussed in the previous chapter.

There has also been a series of studies of 'masculinity', focusing particularly on US imperialism at the end of the nineteenth century and on the conduct of the Vietnam War.[45] Robert Dean, for instance, has examined the determination of the Kennedy Administration not to seem 'weak' in the Cold War, seeking to

---

[42] The title of the introduction to the essays edited by Marysia Zalewski and Jane Parpart, *The 'Man' Question in International Relations* (Boulder, Colo., 1998).

[43] Joan W. Scott, 'Gender: A Useful Category of Historical Analysis', *American Historical Review*, 91 (1986), 1053–75—developed in book form as *Gender and the Politics of History* (New York, 1988).

[44] Frank Costigliola, 'The Nuclear Family: Tropes of Gender and Pathology in the Western Alliance', *Diplomatic History*, 21 (1997), 163–83, quoting pp. 165, 183; Sir Ronald Lindsay, dispatch, 22 Mar. 1937, FO 371/20651, A2378; Rohan Butler, memo, 24 May 1963, para. 21, FO 371/173334 (TNA).

[45] e.g. Kristin L. Hoganson, *Fighting for American Manhood: How Gender Politics Provoked the Spanish-American and Philippine-American Wars* (New Haven, Conn., 1998); Robert D. Dean, *Imperial Brotherhood: Gender and the Making of Cold War Foreign Policy* (Amherst, Mass., 2002).

relate it to the cult of manliness instilled in leading policy-makers by their upbringing, prep school education, and war service. Their macho manner, Dean argues, was not merely 'style', because 'gender is a fundamental element in the make-up of an individual worldview' and therefore 'must be understood not as an independent *cause* of policy decisions, but as a part of the very fabric of reasoning employed by officeholders'. Volker Depkat, however, has responded that 'to understand cultural constructions in such a broad fashion actually means that there is no aspect of past realities that is not gendered'—which may be true but is no longer very useful, because it 'explains everything and nothing'.[46] To put the point concretely: JFK may have felt the need to prove he had 'guts' and 'balls' but to find out why he did so in Vietnam rather than elsewhere we need an archivally based assessment of the options available to him in 1961, after he had failed to topple the Castro regime in Cuba, had accepted the neutralization of Laos, and shied away from a nuclear confrontation over the Berlin Wall. As he told an insider journalist after a bruising meeting with the Soviet leader in June, Nikita Khrushchev: 'If he thinks I'm inexperienced and have no guts, until we remove those ideas we won't get anywhere with him. So we have to act . . . and Vietnam looks like the place.' Even then, Kennedy did not intervene directly but gradually, introducing American military 'advisers' piecemeal—a further reminder of the limits of 'masculinity' as an all-purpose explanatory tool.[47]

Memory is another theme that has evoked much recent interest among international historians. This research, of course, is part of the fallout from the explosion of studies on the cultural memory of war as expressed in monuments, memorials, and art, following the pioneering work of Pierre Nora in the 1980s. In international history there have been several recent attempts to examine the relationships between so-called 'collective memory' and decision-making through historical analogies that arouse emotions and exert prescriptive force.[48] A classic example is the shorthand 'Yalta', employed by the Republican right in America in the late 1940s to blast Roosevelt and the Democrats for selling out Eastern Europe and China to communism. Equally potent, yet very different, was the use of 'Yalta' by Charles de Gaulle as a symbol of the superpowers dividing Europe and the world between them over the heads of the Europeans.[49]

---

[46] Robert Dean, 'Masculinity as Ideology: John F. Kennedy and the Domestic Politics of Foreign Policy', *Diplomatic History*, 22 (1998), 30; Volker Depkat, 'Cultural Approaches to International Relations', in Gienow-Hecht and Schumacher, eds., *Culture and International History*, 181.

[47] James Reston, quoted in David Halberstam, *The Best and the Brightest* (New York, pbk edn., 1972), 97; cf. Lawrence Freedman, *Kennedy's Wars: Berlin, Cuba, Laos and Vietnam* (Oxford, 2000), 317–19, 475.

[48] Cyril Buffet and Beatrice Heuser, eds., *Haunted by History: Myths in International Relations* (Oxford, 1998); Jan-Werner Müller, ed., *Memory and Power in Post-War Europe: Studies in the Presence of the Past* (Cambridge, 2002). See also the older work by Ernest R. May, '*Lessons' of the Past: The Use and Misuse of History in American Foreign Policy* (New York, 1973).

[49] Athan G. Theoharis, *The Yalta Myths: An Issue in U.S. Politics, 1945–1955* (Columbia, Mo., 1970); Buffet and Heuser, eds., *Haunted by History*, 80–91, 104–7, 169–73.

Two points should be noted briefly here. First, the term 'collective memory' has not gone unchallenged: some argue that it involves a misleading meta-phorical transfer from individual consciousness to public attitudes. Alternatives include the older and confusing word 'myth' or, more neutrally, 'collective beliefs'. Both these terms seem more effective than 'memory' in conveying the constructedness of such communal attitudes.[50] This is important, secondly, because the best of this work emphasizes that the relationship between memory and power is two-way: historical shorthands such as 'Yalta' or 'Munich' help establish a framework for decision-making but, conversely, 'policy goals have a decisive influence' on how such cultural frameworks are constructed.[51]

This interest in memory has stimulated exploration of the ways in which governments have tried to control historical research and writing, in order to justify current policies. This indicates another important way, apart from his-torical analogies, in which memory relates to power, namely as a form of legitimation. For instance, the question of German war guilt was central to the diplomacy of the Versailles treaty and the bitter wrangle over reparations in the 1920s. Hence the eagerness of the German government to publish and pro-mulgate its collection of diplomatic documents about the origins of the war; hence, too, the reluctant but vigorous response in kind by the British and French governments. Full-scale official histories of the two world wars were also com-missioned to shape public attitudes, and these projects are now attracting scholarly attention.[52] Perhaps the most striking example is C. E. W. Bean, Australia's official historian of the Great War, who was instrumental in estab-lishing a national image of 'the Digger'—the Australian new man, forged by life in the bush or in the egalitarian cities. Thanks to shrewd marketing by the Australian War Memorial in Canberra—a foundation that Bean helped estab-lish—his books sold far more widely than most official histories.[53]

Sometimes governments have been able to influence the discourse of history indirectly. A striking example, I have argued, is how Whitehall covertly spon-sored and supported Churchill's memoirs, *The Second World War*, in the late 1940s. The Cabinet Office saw his work as a semi-official overview of Britain's war effort that would reach a far wider readership than its Official Histories and would combat the spate of American memoirs that were already giving their

[50] e.g. Noa Gedi and Yigal Elam, 'Collective Memory: What is it?' *History and Memory*, 8/1 (1996), 30–47; Marwick, *The New Nature of History*, 147.

[51] Robert Gildea, 'Myth, Memory and Policy in France since 1945', in Müller, ed., *Memory and Power*, 59. Two leading historians of commemoration favour the term 'collective remembrance' for similar reasons. See Jay Winter and Emmanuel Sivan, 'Setting the Framework', in Winter and Sivan, eds., *War and Remembrance in the Twentieth Century* (Cambridge, 1999), 9.

[52] Keith Wilson, ed., *Forging the Collective Memory: Governments and International Historians through the Two World Wars* (Oxford, 1996); Jeffrey Gray, *The Last Word? Essays on Official History in the United States and the British Commonwealth* (Westport, Conn., 2003).

[53] Joan Beaumont, 'The Anzac Legend', in Beaumont, ed., *Australia's War, 1914–1918* (St Leonards, New South Wales, 1995), 149–80; Michael McKernan, *Here is Their Spirit: A History of the Australian War Memorial, 1917–1990* (St Lucia, Queensland, 1991), esp. 130, 134–8.

own, nationalist spin on how the war was won.[54] In the United States, a 1947 article by Henry Stimson, FDR's Secretary of War, was enormously important in establishing the orthodox defence of America's use of the atomic bomb against Japan. This essay, ghosted by the young McGeorge Bundy, was prompted by alarm in the American establishment about growing criticism of Hiroshima and Nagasaki as morally indefensible and strategically unnecessary. Buttressing his case, like Churchill, with many contemporary documents, Stimson claimed he had been informed that subduing the Japanese home islands 'might be expected to cost over a million casualties, to American forces alone', and this figure was recycled in numerous subsequent accounts. The rough prediction in June 1945 by senior military was no more than 50,000 deaths but Bundy did not have any statistics before him when he wrote the article. He later admitted to his biographer that 'one million' was simply a nice round figure that he and Stimson agreed to use.[55] The stories of Bean, Churchill, and Stimson are all examples of the need for what Patrick Finney, an avowedly postmodernist international historian, has called 'critical historiographical studies' to see how the paradigms of interpretation were gradually created.[56]

Memory, like masculinity, has therefore proved a fertile area for recent work in international history. My third and final example is the concept of Otherness, or 'alterity', as popularized by Edward Said in his polemical critique of European *Orientalism* (1978). Some international historians have used Said's concept to understand American policies in the Middle East since 1945. Others have detected a similar set of enduring and powerful European stereotypes about the Balkans and have used 'Balkanism' as a tool to understand Western policies in south-eastern Europe.[57] In some of this work, as Said's critics warned, there is a danger of reification—of making an intellectual tendency into a monolithic entity with dominant explanatory power. 'Otherness' has been harnessed to the new discipline of 'critical geopolitics' pioneered by Yves Lacoste in the 1970s in France and developed by the Dutch scholar Gertjan Dijkink to delineate the

---

[54] David Reynolds, 'Official History: How Churchill and the Cabinet Office Wrote *The Second World War*', *Historical Research*, 78/201 (Aug. 2005) 400–22; also more generally Reynolds, *In Command of History: Churchill Writing and Fighting the Second World War* (London, 2004).

[55] Henry L. Stimson, 'The Decision to Use the Atomic Bomb', *Harper's Magazine*, Feb. 1947, 97–107, quoting p. 102; Kai Bird, *The Color of Truth. McGeorge Bundy and William Bundy: Brothers in Arms* (New York, 1998), 89–93, 419. Official projections of casualty figures for the invasion of Japan is a hotly contested issue among historians, but see the useful discussion in J. Samuel Walker, 'Recent Literature on Truman's Atomic Bomb Decision: A Search for Middle Ground', *Diplomatic History*, 29 (2005), 311–34.

[56] Patrick Finney, 'International History, Theory and the Origins of the Second World War', *Rethinking History*, 1 (1997), 357–79, quoting p. 370.

[57] Andrew J. Rotter, 'Saidism without Said: Orientalism and U.S. Diplomatic History', *American Historical Review*, 105 (2000), 1205–17; Douglas Little, *American Orientalism: The United States and the Middle East since 1945* (Chapel Hill, NC, 2002); Patrick Finney, 'Raising Frankenstein: Great Britain, "Balkanism" and the Search for a Balkan Locarno in the 1920s', *European History Quarterly*, 33 (2003), 317–42.

'geopolitical visions' of policy-makers—their mental 'landscapes of security'. It has also been used to analyze the process of national self-definition, for instance by Linda Colley in her account of the construction of British identity (as anti-French and anti-Catholic).[58] Similarly, according to historian David Campbell, a sense of identity in America, one of the most heterogeneous of Western nations, has depended historically on the recurrent 'articulation of danger through foreign policy'—postulating an external threat in order to consolidate internal unity, with Cold War rhetoric just one phase in that process. For Campbell, the concept of 'threat' is culturally determined (not an objective matter of challenge and response as in realist accounts of foreign policy).[59]

Conceptions of the Other lend themselves to graphic representation. A vivid example is John Dower's study of the Pacific War, which demonstrated the prevalence of vicious racist stereotypes on both sides. The ubiquitous American and British image showed the Japanese as monkeys or apes; in Japan Roosevelt and Churchill were often literally demonized with horns and claws. Dower's work is celebrated and his images are often reproduced. Less often noted is another theme of his book—how these apparently formidable images dissolved so quickly during the American occupation of Japan after 1945. As possible explanations, Dower offered not just closer mutual acquaintance—the good liberal internationalist remedy—but also the flexibility of these images in evaluative terms (brutal apes were easily transformed into tame monkeys; horrific demons became strangers bearing gifts). In addition, he suggested that the monolithic character of the images aided this process of rapid and total mutation: the Other, bad or good, 'remained, essentially, homogeneous'.[60]

The plasticity of such national stereotypes has also been noted by historian David Kennedy. Insisting that 'alterity' is not 'enmity'—that a sense of the Other does not automatically mean hostility—he argues that America's sense of identity has *not* rested historically on the construction of an external menace. And he observes that the hostile, often racist imagery of Germans in 1917–18 came and went as quickly as the stereotyping of the Japanese in 1941–5. In Kennedy's view, unlike Campbell's, Americans did not *need* an enemy image to define their identity, but he goes on to argue that when they did have an enemy they portrayed it in ways that revealed their sense of themselves. The enemy image thus served not to *define* the nation but to *mobilize* it for the challenge of war, by depicting the adversary as a threat to shared and fundamental values.

[58] Gertran Dijkink, *National Identity and Geopolitical Visions: Maps of Pride and Pain* (London, 1996); Linda Colley, 'Britishness and Otherness: An Argument', *Journal of British Studies*, 31 (1992), 309–29.

[59] David Campbell, *Writing Security: United States Foreign Policy and the Politics of Identity* (Manchester, 1992); see also Ragnhild Fiebig-von Hase and Ursula Lehmkuhl, eds., *Enemy Images in American History* (Oxford, 1997).

[60] John W. Dower, *War without Mercy: Race and Power in the Pacific War* (London, 1986), pp. xi, 301–11, quoting p. 308.

This approach again shifts the locus of argument from the cultural to the political—images of the Other not so much a cause of war as a product of it.[61]

In the previous section, I sketched some of the varied responses of international historians to the cultural turn. Themes such as gender, memory, and alterity have been taken up with enthusiasm, resulting in work that extends our under-standing, indeed our definition, of international relations. And at the meth-odological level, scholars in the field such as Patrick Finney have prodded colleagues to take theory seriously.[62]

On the other hand, I feel that some of this new work is not actually very novel. My own intellectual development as a young historian in this field owed much to some of the dedicatees of this book—scholars such as Donald Cameron Watt, who insisted on studying policy-makers as people, with their rich and varied cultural and social backgrounds; Zara Steiner, who showed the need to under-stand the complex political and bureaucratic culture of a foreign ministry; Harry Hinsley, who opened up intelligence history as a story of both information and assumptions; and Christopher Thorne, who, before his premature death, traced the intricate cultural and racial dimensions of the Pacific War.[63]

There are also, I think, some real problems with this new 'culturalist' inter-national history. It borrows conceptually from other disciplines, but sometimes rather superficially—with little more than a ritual nod to Foucault, Geertz, or Said—and is possibly in danger of making 'culture' an explanatory *deus ex machina*. Anthropologists, meanwhile, have become more self-conscious about the term and its problems. This was partly in response to the charge of post-colonialists that they were treating non-Western societies—traditionally their main area of study—as subordinated or exoticized objects. More generally it reflected the philosophical reaction against structuralism, which tended to reify 'culture' and 'society' as forces that control individual behaviour.[64]

---

[61] David M. Kennedy, 'Culture Wars: The Sources and Use of Enmity in American History', in Fiebig-von Hase and Lehmkuhl, eds., *Enemy Images*, 339–56. For some broader criticisms of the use of 'the Other' in cultural history, see Peter Mandler, 'The Problem with Cultural History', *Cultural and Social History*, 1 (2004), 111–13.

[62] See Finney, 'International History, Theory and the Origins of the Second World War', and his more general article 'Still "Marking Time"? Text, Discourse and Truth in International History', *Review of International Studies*, 27 (2001), 291–308.

[63] For representative works see D. Cameron Watt, *Succeeding John Bull: America in Britain's Place, 1900–1975* (Cambridge, 1984); Zara Steiner, *The Foreign Office and Foreign Policy, 1898–1914* (Cambridge, 1969); F. H. Hinsley et al., *British Intelligence in the Second World War* (4 vols., London, 1979–90); Christopher Thorne, *Allies of a Kind: The United States, Britain and the War against Japan, 1941–1945* (London, 1978).

[64] Susan Wright, 'The Politicization of "Culture"', *Anthropology Today*, 14/1 (Feb. 1998), 7; cf. Sherry B. Ortner, 'Theory in Anthropology since the Sixties', *Comparative Studies in Society and History*, 26 (1984), 126–66. See also William H. Sewell, 'The Concept(s) of Culture', in Victoria E. Bonnell and Lynn Hunt, eds., *Beyond the Cultural Turn: New Directions in the Study of Society and Culture* (Berkeley, 1999), 35–61.

Post-structuralists have offered a more flexible definition of 'culture'—as a web of contested symbolic meanings rather than a system of patterned behaviour—but the problem remains. Are individuals determined by their culture? Are they, crudely, 'cultural dopes'?[65] To state this point more concretely with reference to some of the examples I have just given: how exactly do we connect the masculine self-images of policy-makers, their historical memories or their sense of national identity to the actual policies they choose, advocate, and execute? I have already suggested that this pushes us back into the realm of the political, to issues of decision-making, and to the narrative mode. But in our postmodern, post-structuralist era, that raises some serious philosophical problems about agency and causality.[66]

Explaining social actions requires, first of all, a concept of purposive human agency, which extreme postmodernism has sought to wash away, in Foucault's famous phrase, 'like a face drawn in sand at the edge of the sea'.[67] Few would now go that far but, in a larger sense, the circumscribing of individual human agency had been a goal for all the so-called *social* sciences. Rejecting the heroic voluntarism of great-men theories of historical change, they emphasized the structural forces of society, economy, or culture that defined and confined individual action. But anthropologists and sociologists have now reacted against structuralism, and the precise place of human agency is very much a matter of debate. Anthony Giddens, for instance, has coined the term 'structuration' to denote the reciprocity of structure and action—social practices shape individual behaviour yet those practices are created and modified by human activity—but that defines the problem rather than solving it. Across the social sciences, theorists are struggling to develop effective new theories of social action and these matter particularly to international historians, much of whose work has dealt with supposedly decisive actions by individuals.[68]

The problem of agency leads me into the related question of causality. It is striking how far the term 'cause' has slipped out of the working vocabulary of most historians and of philosophers of history since the 1960s when E. H. Carr could assert baldly that '[t]he study of history is a study of causes' and philosophers such as G. W. Hempel, Patrick Gardiner, and W. H. Dray jousted over whether causal explanation in history conformed to the 'covering law model'

---

[65] See the essay on 'Culture' in Nigel Rapport and Joanna Overing, *Social and Cultural Anthropology: The Key Concepts* (London, 2000), 96.

[66] Here I am developing points aired by, among others, Charles S. Maier, 'A Surfeit of Memory? Reflections on History, Melancholy, and Denial', *History and Memory*, 5/2 (1993), 141; Rotter, 'Saidism without Said', 1208, 1210–11. See also more generally Patricia O'Brien, 'Michel Foucault's History of Culture' and Aletta Biersack, 'Local Knowledge, Local History: Geertz and Beyond', in Hunt, ed., *The New Cultural History*, 25–46, 72–96.

[67] Michel Foucault, *The Order of Things: An Archaeology of the Human Sciences* (London, 1970), 387.

[68] Anthony Giddens, *Sociology* (4th edn., Cambridge, 2001), 668, 700; Ortner, 'Theory in Anthropology since the Sixties', 158–9.

supposedly dominant in natural science.[69] There are many possible reasons for the decline of causality, such as the increased complexity of evidence, on the one hand, and of types of history, on the other, which combine to challenge the credibility of simple causal chains.[70] This complexity is related to the recent shift in the locus of historical activity from explanation to representation, from causes to meanings, sometimes even from the dynamic to the static. John Tosh has argued that the tension between these two modes, what he calls the 'explanatory' and the 're-creative', is as old as the historical discipline itself. But the cultural turn has surely prompted a big shift from explaining change to understanding context or meaning.[71] And for a sub-discipline like international history, traditionally interested in why wars begin and end, a concept of causation—or something like it—is especially important. Yet I do not think recent work on historical methodology and the postmodernist challenge has really come to grips with this problem.[72]

In fact, these problems have attracted more attention of late from political scientists interested in international relations. The 1990s saw an intense bout of radical self-criticism among IR theorists because traditional structural realism had failed to predict or explain the end of the Cold War. Faced by relative Soviet decline, Gorbachev had responded not by aggression or retrenchment, as realist theory might suggest, but with a policy revolution abroad and at home, intended to end the Cold War and shift the Soviet Union towards social democracy. For their part, Reagan and Bush, far from trying to keep the Soviet Union weak, encouraged reforms intended to foster capitalism and democracy, thereby creating a potentially more efficient competitor to the United States.[73] One response to this failure of theory has been a turn away from structural realism and systemic constructs to a neoclassical realism that focuses again on human nature, on leaders, belief systems, and domestic change. Another trend is the emergence of 'constructivism' as a new school of thought, meaning here an insistence that national interests are not fixed but constructed by reference to social 'norms', derived either from domestic or international society. And the unanticipated outcomes of the Soviet crisis of the 1980s have also encouraged greater interest among IR theorists in cause and consequence, understood now in terms of multiple causal chains rather than a single, overriding causal condition. Several political scientists have turned in this vein to complex causal analyses of

[69] E. H. Carr, *What is History?* (Harmondsworth, 1964), 87; cf. William H. Dray, *Laws and Explanation in History* (London, 1957); Patrick Gardiner, *The Nature of Historical Explanation* (London, 1961). [70] See Jordanova, *History in Practice*, 108–11.

[71] Tosh, *Pursuit of History*, 192; see also Richard J. Evans, *In Defence of History*, (2nd edn., London, 2002), 159–60; Cannadine, ed., *What is History Now?*, pp. ix–xii.

[72] e.g. Mary Fulbrook, *Historical Theory* (London, 2002), and Breisach, *On the Future of History*—both of whom address the question of individual agency at some length but have very little to say on causation.

[73] See the discussion in John A. Vasquez, *The Power of Power Politics: From Classical Realism to Neotraditionalism* (Cambridge, 1998), ch. 13.

the origins of the First World War.[74] It is to such IR theorists that we must turn for recent theoretical discussion of agency and causality.

Some may respond that international historians should stop fussing about old-fashioned questions such as the causes of war. In other words, the 'real' subject of international history today is society not the state, cultural relations rather than power politics, discourse instead of action. A less hegemonic reply would be to affirm that there is room for a pluralism of approaches. To quote the American scholar Emily Rosenberg, international history is 'not a methodological prescription' but 'a vast empty plain with undetermined borders'.[75]

Up to a point I agree. My own work has tried to embrace the cultural dimension of Anglo-Americana, notably in *Rich Relations*, which studied the impact of three million GIs on wartime Britain both as a political problem and a socio-cultural phenomenon.[76] That work is reflected in the essays in Part IV. Yet I think it would be profoundly unfortunate if international historians lost their traditional concern with the formulation of policy and the making of decisions. Consider the intense and persistent argument about the origins and execution of *Endlösung*, the Nazis' so-called 'Final Solution' to the 'Jewish problem'. This fits into the larger debate between 'Intentionalists' and 'Structuralists' about the nature of the Third Reich—how far policy was decided at the top by Hitler and a few others, how far it reflected deeper structural pressures in German economy and society. While 'modernists' may be right that the Nazi extermination programme represented the gruesome application of modern economic methods to a perceived social problem, this does not take us very far along the explanatory chain. Nor do general cultural accounts of the development of Nazi racial ideology. What matters are critical moments of decision. For some years, attention centred on the Wannsee conference in January 1942; since the unearthing of documents from former communist archives, the focus has shifted into the summer and autumn of 1941, to what was said or implied at meetings between Hitler and Himmler. Historians are searching for individual agents and causal links in a way that may seem old-fashioned but is clearly of enormous historical importance and which arouses interest far beyond the confines of academia.[77]

---

[74] For these themes see generally Colin Elman and Miriam Fendius Elman, eds., *Bridges and Boundaries: Historians, Political Scientists, and the Study of International Relations* (Cambridge, Mass., 2001), 28–35; and Miriam Fendius Elman, 'International Relations Theories and Methods', in Finney, ed., *Palgrave Advances in International History*, 144–9. On constructivism, see Ted Hopf, 'The Promise of Constructivism in International Relations Theory', *International Security*, 23 (1998), 171–200; John M. Hobson, *The State and International Relations* (Cambridge, 2000), ch. 5.

[75] Emily S. Rosenberg, 'Walking the Borders', in Michael J. Hogan and Thomas G. Paterson, eds., *Explaining the History of American Foreign Relations* (1st edn., New York, 1991), 24–5.

[76] David Reynolds, *Rich Relations: The American Occupation of Britain, 1942–1945* (London, 1995).

[77] See generally Ian Kershaw, *The Nazi Dictatorship: Problems and Perspectives of Interpretation* (4th edn., London, 2000), chs. 4–6.

In other words, despite the welcome new interest in the cultural dimensions of international relations, questions about states, power, and policy still matter, especially at the interface between peace and war. These questions were, after all, the original stimuli for studying the history of international relations. Think of Taine and Sorel in France after the disaster of 1870, or the continuation of war by documentary means across Europe in the 1920s, or the clash of traditionalist and revisionist interpretations of the Cold War as America sank into the quagmire of Vietnam. 9/11 and the Iraq War have, I think, stimulated a similar interest in questions of war, peace, and decision-making on both sides of the Atlantic. For instance, six months after the attack on the Twin Towers, the President of the American Historical Association noted that the questions for historians 'keep changing as current events force us to re-evaluate our past' and went on to speculate that the 'next big thing' in the discipline might well be 'some kind of revival or refashioning of diplomatic and/or military history'. The writer was, in fact, Lynn Hunt, a pioneer of the New Cultural History.[78]

In this final chapter, I have sketched a number of ways in which international history has been enriched by the cultural and linguistic turns. Not only in opening up new areas of research but also in correcting a tendency towards documentary positivism. But I have argued that in our study of these documents we could gain more from the methods of intellectual historians than from the theories of extreme postmodernism. And I have urged that cultural concepts such as masculinity, memory, and alterity should not become explanatory panaceas: we still need to construct narratives of how these culturally shaped actors made and implemented policy in specific and contingent historical situations. I have also suggested that this project raises fundamental questions of agency and causality—concepts that, however problematic philosophically, are recognized as being central to all the social sciences.

This does not mean I am predicting a sudden 'diplomatic turn' to replace the cultural turn. But I am suggesting that there has been a recurrent diplomatic twitch in the saga of international history. And that is because, at its core, this sub-discipline tries to address socially important questions—literally matters of life and death—in a historical way, often near the cutting edge of contemporary events. Of course, the diplomatic twitch must take account of the cultural turn: analyses of America's 'war on terror', for instance, cannot ignore the prevalence of 'Orientalist' language about the 'threat' from Islam. But my hunch is that future generations will keep twitching back to issues of war and peace, policy and decision-making, long after our current culture wars have turned into history. And the 1940s, that momentous decade of World War and Cold War, will remain at the centre of their attention.

---

[78] Lynn Hunt, 'Where Have All the Theories Gone?', in *American Historical Association Perspectives*, 40 (March 2002), 5–7.

Permissions

For permission to quote copyright material I am grateful to

Joseph P. Alsop
Beaverbrook Foundation and the late A. J. P. Taylor
Birmingham University Library
Borthwick Institute, University of York
British Library of Political and Economic Science, London
Lord Citrine
Curtis Brown Ltd., London, on behalf of The Estate of Sir Winston
    S. Churchill, copyright © Winston S. Churchill
Houghton Library, Harvard University
Liddell Hart Centre for Military Archives, King's College, London
Sidgwick and Jackson Ltd., publishers
And copyright holders of previously published material, where indicated in the
    opening note of a chapter.

Index